Project Management

The Managerial Process

The McGraw-Hill/Irwin Series Operations and Decision Sciences

Project Management

The Managerial Process

Fifth Edition

Erik W. Larson
Oregon State University

Clifford F. Gray
Oregon State University

Boston   Burr Ridge, IL   Dubuque, IA   New York   San Francisco   St. Louis
Bangkok   Bogotá   Caracas   Kuala Lumpur   Lisbon   London   Madrid   Mexico City
Milan   Montreal   New Delhi   Santiago   Seoul   Singapore   Sydney   Taipei   Toronto

PROJECT MANAGEMENT: THE MANAGERIAL PROCESS
International Edition 2011

Exclusive rights by McGraw-Hill Education (Asia), for manufacture and export. This book cannot be re-exported from the country to which it is sold by McGraw-Hill. This International Edition is not to be sold or purchased in North America and contains content that is different from its North American version.

10 09 08 07 06 05 04
20 15 14 13 12 11
CTP   MPM

When ordering this title, use ISBN 978-007-128929-0 or MHID 007-128929-1

Printed in Singapore

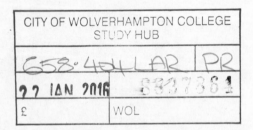

About the Authors

Erik W. Larson

ERIK W. LARSON is professor of project management at the College of Business, Oregon State University. He teaches executive, graduate, and undergraduate courses on project management, organizational behavior, and leadership. His research and consulting activities focus on project management. He has published numerous articles on matrix management, product development, and project partnering. He has been honored with teaching awards from both the Oregon State University MBA program and the University of Oregon Executive MBA program. He has been a member of the Portland, Oregon, chapter of the Project Management Institute since 1984. In 1995 he worked as a Fulbright scholar with faculty at the Krakow Academy of Economics on modernizing Polish business education. In 2005 he was a visiting professor at Chulalongkorn University in Bangkok, Thailand. He received a B.A. in psychology from Claremont McKenna College and a Ph.D. in management from State University of New York at Buffalo. He is a certified project management professional (PMP) and Scrum Master.

Clifford F. Gray

CLIFFORD F. GRAY is professor emeritus of management at the College of Business, Oregon State University. He continues to teach undergraduate and graduate project management courses overseas and in the United States; he has personally taught more than 100 executive development seminars and workshops. His research and consulting interests have been divided equally between operations management and project management; he has published numerous articles in these areas, plus a text on project management. He has also conducted research with colleagues in the International Project Management Association. Cliff has been a member of the Project Management Institute since 1976 and was one of the founders of the Portland, Oregon, chapter. He was a visiting professor at Kasetsart University in Bangkok, Thailand in 2005. He was the president of Project Management International, Inc. (a training and consulting firm specializing in project management) 1977–2005. He received his B.A. in economics and management from Millikin University, M.B.A. from Indiana University, and doctorate in operations management from the College of Business, University of Oregon. He is certified Scrum Master.

"Man's mind, once stretched by a new idea, never regains its original dimensions."

Oliver Wendell Holmes, Jr.

To my family who have always encircled me with love and encouragement—my parents (Samuel and Charlotte), my wife (Mary), my sons and their wives (Kevin and Dawn, Robert and Sally) and their children (Ryan, Carly, Connor and Lauren).

C.F.G.

"We must not cease from exploration and the end of all exploring will be to arrive where we begin and to know the place for the first time."

T. S. Eliot

To Ann whose love and support has brought out the best in me. And, to our girls Mary, Rachel, and Tor-Tor for the joy and pride they give me. Finally, to my muse, Neil, for the faith and inspiration he instills.

E.W.L

Preface

Since you are reading this text, you have made a decision that learning more about project management will have a positive impact for you. You are absolutely right! Project management has become an organization-wide core competency; nearly every manager, regardless of discipline is involved in managing one or more projects. This text is designed to provide project managers and prospective project managers with the knowledge and skills that are transferable across industries and countries.

Our motivation for writing this text was to provide students with a holistic, integrative view of project management. A holistic view focuses on how projects contribute to the strategic goals of the organization. The linkages for integration include the process of selecting projects that best support the strategy of a particular organization and that in turn can be supported by the technical and managerial processes made available by the organization to bring projects to completion. The goals for prospective project managers are to understand the role of a project in their organizations and to master the project management tools, techniques, and interpersonal skills necessary to orchestrate projects from start to finish.

The role of projects in organizations is receiving increasing attention. Projects are the major tool for implementing and achieving the strategic goals of the organization. In the face of intense, worldwide competition, many organizations have reorganized around a philosophy of innovation, renewal, and organizational learning to survive. This philosophy suggests an organization that is flexible and project driven. Project management has developed to the point where it is a professional discipline having its own body of knowledge and skills. Today it is nearly impossible to imagine anyone at any level in the organization who would not benefit from some degree of expertise in the process of managing projects.

Audience

This text is written for a wide audience. It covers concepts and skills that are used by managers to propose, plan, secure resources, budget, and lead project teams to successful completions of their projects. The text should prove useful to students and prospective project managers in helping them understand why organizations have developed a formal project management process to gain a competitive advantage. Readers will find the concepts and techniques discussed in enough detail to be immediately useful in new-project situations. Practicing project managers will find the text to be a valuable guide and reference when dealing with typical problems that arise in the course of a project. Managers will also find the text useful in understanding the role of projects in the missions of their organizations. Analysts will find the text useful in helping to explain the data needed for project implementation as well as the operations of inherited or purchased software. Members of the Project Management Institute will find the text is well structured to meet the needs of those wishing to prepare for PMP (Project Management Professional) or CAPM (Certified Associate in Project Management) certification exams. The text has in-depth coverage of the most critical topics found in PMI's *Project Management*

Body of Knowledge (PMBOK). People at all levels in the organization assigned to work on projects will find the text useful not only in providing them with a rationale for the use of project management tools and techniques but also because of the insights they will gain on how to enhance their contributions to project success.

Our emphasis is not only on how the management process works, but more importantly, on *why* it works. The concepts, principles, and techniques are universally applicable. That is, the text does not specialize by industry type or project scope. Instead, the text is written for the individual who will be required to manage a variety of projects in a variety of different organizational settings. In the case of some small projects, a few of the steps of the techniques can be omitted, but the conceptual framework applies to all organizations in which projects are important to survival. The approach can be used in pure project organizations such as construction, research organizations, and engineering consultancy firms. At the same time, this approach will benefit organizations that carry out many small projects while the daily effort of delivering products or services continues.

Content

In this latest edition of the book, we have responded to feedback received from both students and teachers, which is deeply appreciated. As a result of the this feedback, the following changes have been made to the fifth edition:

- Restructuring of text to include four supplemental chapters that cover topics beyond the project management core.
- Inclusion of a supplemental chapter on agile project management which has enjoyed success on new product and software development projects.
- Terms and concepts have been updated to be consistent with the fourth edition of the *Project Management Body of Knowledge* (2008).
- Revised Chapter 14 to include project retrospectives. Chapters 2, 4, 6, 7, and 12, have been updated.
- New student exercises and cases have been added to most chapters.
- Answers to selected exercises are now available in Appendix 1
- A third major computer exercise has been added to the Appendix 2;
- The "Snapshot from Practice" boxes feature a number of new examples of project management in action as well as new research highlights that continue to promote practical application of project management.

Overall the text addresses the major questions and issues the authors have encountered over their 60 combined years of teaching project management and consulting with practicing project managers in domestic and foreign environments. The following questions represent the issues and problems practicing project managers find consuming most of their effort: What is the strategic role of projects in contemporary organizations? How are projects prioritized? What organizational and managerial styles will improve chances of project success? How do project managers orchestrate the complex network of relationships involving vendors, subcontractors, project team members, senior management, functional managers, and customers that affect project success? What factors contribute to the development of a high-performance project team? What project management system can be set up to gain some measure of control? How do managers prepare for a new international project in a foreign culture? How does one pursue a career in project management?

Project managers must deal with all these concerns to be effective. All of these issues and problems represent linkages to an integrative project management view. The chapter content of the text has been placed within an overall framework that integrates these topics in a holistic manner. Cases and snapshots are included from the experiences of practicing managers. The future for project managers appears to be promising. Careers will be determined by success in managing projects.

Student Learning Aids

The text Web site (www.mhhe.com/larsongray5e) includes study outlines, online quizzes, PowerPoint slides, videos, Microsoft Project Video Tutorials and Web links.

Acknowledgments

We would like to thank Richard Bruce, Ottawa University for updating the Test Bank and Online Quizzes; Charlie Cook, University of West Alabama for revising the PowerPoint slides; Oliver F. Lehmann for providing access to PMBOK study questions; and Mink for accuracy checking the text and Instructor's Resource Manual content.

Next, it is important to note that the text includes contributions from numerous students, colleagues, friends, and managers gleaned from professional conversations. We want them to know we sincerely appreciate their counsel and suggestions. Almost every exercise, case, and example in the text is drawn from a real-world project. Special thanks to managers who graciously shared their current project as ideas for exercises, subjects for cases, and examples for the text. Shlomo Cohen, John A. Drexler, Jim Moran, John Sloan, Pat Taylor, and John Wold, whose work is printed, are gratefully acknowledged. Special gratitude is due Robert Breitbarth of Interact Management, who shared invaluable insights on prioritizing projects. University students and managers deserve special accolades for identifying problems with earlier drafts of the text and exercises.

We are indebted to the reviewers of past editions who shared our commitment to elevating the instruction of project management. The reviewers include Paul S. Allen, Rice University; Denis F. Cioffi, George Washington University; Joseph D. DeVoss, DeVry University; Edward J. Glantz, Pennsylvania State University; Michael Godfrey, University of Wisconsin–Oshkosh; Robert Key, University of Phoenix; Dennis Krumwiede, Idaho State University; Nicholas C. Petruzzi, University of Illinois–Urbana/Champaign; William R. Sherrard, San Diego State University; S. Narayan Bodapati, Southern Illinois University at Edwardsville; Warren J. Boe, University of Iowa; Burton Dean, San Jose State University; Kwasi Amoako-Gyampah, University of North Carolina–Greensboro; Owen P. Hall, Pepperdine University; Bruce C. Hartman, University of Arizona; Richard Irving, York University; Robert T. Jones, DePaul University; Richard L. Luebbe, Miami University of Ohio; William Moylan, Lawrence Technological College of Business; Edward Pascal, University of Ottawa; James H. Patterson, Indiana University; Art Rogers, City University; Christy Strbiak, U.S. Air Force

Academy; David A. Vaughan, City University; and Ronald W. Witzel, Keller Graduate School of Management. Nabil Bedewi, Georgetown University; Scott Bailey, Troy University; Michael Ensby, Clarkson University; Eldon Larsen, Marshall University; Steve Machon, DeVry University–Tinley Park; William Matthews, William Patterson University; Erin Sims, DeVry University–Pomona; Kenneth Solheim, DeVry University–Federal Way; and Oya Tukel, Cleveland State University.

In the fifth edition we continue to commit to improving the text content and improving instruction of project management. We are grateful to those reviewers who provided helpful critiques and insights on the fourth edition, which helped us prepare this revision. The reviewers for the fifth edition include. Gregory Anderson, Weber State University; Dana Bachman, Colorado Christian University; Alan Cannon, University of Texas, Arlington; Susan Cholette, San Francisco State; Michael Ensby, Clarkson University; Charles Franz, University of Missouri, Columbia; Raouf Ghattas, DeVry University; Robert Groff, Westwood College; Raffael Guidone, New York City College of Technology; George Kenyon, Lamar University; Elias Konwufine, Keiser University; Rafael Landaeta, Old Dominion University; Muhammad Obeidat, Southern Polytechnic State University; Linda Rose, Westwood College; Oya Tukel, Cleveland State University; and Mahmoud Watad, William Paterson University. We thank you for your many thoughtful suggestions and for making our book better. Of course we accept responsibility for the final version of the text.

In addition, we would like to thank our colleagues in the College of Business at Oregon State University for their support and help in completing this project. In particular, we recognize Ray Brooks, Jim Moran and Ping-Hung Hsieh for their helpful advice and suggestions. We also wish to thank the many students who helped us at different stages of this project, most notably Neil Young, Rebecca Keepers, Katherine Knox, Dat Nguyen, Lacey McNeely and Amanda Bosworth. Mary Gray deserves special credit for editing and working under tight deadlines on earlier editions. Special thanks go to Pinyarat Sirisomboonsuk for her help in preparing the last two editions.

Finally, we want to extend our thanks to all the people at McGraw-Hill/Irwin for their efforts and support. First, we would like to thank Dick Hercher for continuing to champion and provide editorial direction and guidance, and Gail Korosa, who took over management of the book's development fifth edition. And we would also like to thank Denise Showers, Carol Blelski, Mary Sander, Jeremy Cheshareck, Grey Bates, and Harvey Yep for managing the final production, design, supplement, and media phases of the fifth edition.

Erik W. Larson

Clifford F. Gray

Note to Student

You will find the content of this text highly practical, relevant, and current. The concepts discussed are relatively simple and intuitive. As you study each chapter we suggest you try to grasp not only how things work, but why things work. You are encouraged to use the text as a handbook as you move through the three levels of competency:

I know.

I can do.

I can adapt to new situations.

Project management is both people and technical oriented. Project management involves understanding the cause-effect relationships and interactions among the sociotechnical dimensions of projects. Improved competency in these dimensions will greatly enhance your competitive edge as a project manager.

The field of project management is growing in importance and at an exponential rate. It is nearly impossible to imagine a future management career that does not include management of projects. Résumés of managers will soon be primarily a description of the individual's participation in and contributions to projects.

Good luck on your journey through the text and on your future projects.

Brief Contents

Contents

Modern Project Management

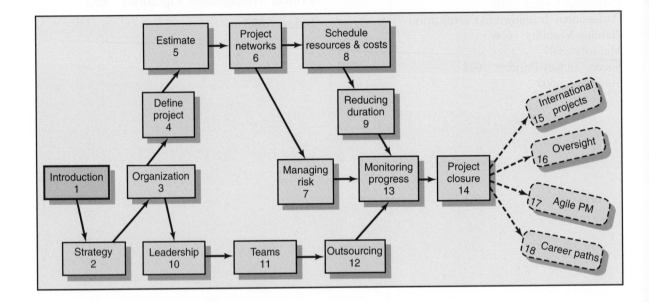

Modern Project Management
What Is a Project?
The Importance of Project Management
Project Management Today—An Integrative Approach
Summary
Text Overview

All of mankind's greatest accomplishments—from building the great pyramids to discovering a cure for polio to putting a man on the moon—began as a project.

This is a good time to be reading a book about project management. Business leaders and experts have proclaimed that project management is a strategic imperative. Project management provides people with a powerful set of tools that improves their ability to plan, implement, and manage activities to accomplish specific organizational objectives. But project management is more than just a set of tools; it is a results-oriented management style that places a premium on building collaborative relationships among a diverse cast of characters. Exciting opportunities await people skilled in project management.

The project approach has long been the style of doing business in the construction industry, U.S. Department of Defense contracts, and Hollywood as well as big consulting firms. Now project management has spread to all avenues of work. Today, project teams carry out everything from port expansions to hospital restructuring to upgrading information systems. They are creating next generation, fuel efficient vehicles, developing sustainable sources of energy, and exploring the farthest reaches of outer space. The impact of project management is most profound in the electronics industry, where the new folk heroes are young professionals whose Herculean efforts lead to the constant flow of new hardware and software products.

Project management is not limited to the private sector. Project management is also a vehicle for doing good deeds and solving social problems. Endeavors such as providing emergency aid to the Gulf Coast devastated by hurricane Katrina, devising a strategy for reducing crime and drug abuse within a city, or organizing a community effort to renovate a public playground would and do benefit from the application of modern project management skills and techniques.

Perhaps the best indicator of demand for project management can be seen in the rapid expansion of the Project Management Institute (PMI), a professional organization for project managers. PMI membership has grown from 93,000 in 2002 to more than 270,000 currently. See the PMI Snapshot from Practice for information regarding professional certification in project management.

It's nearly impossible to pick up a newspaper or business periodical and not find something about projects. This is no surprise! Approximately $2.5 trillion (about 25 percent of the U.S. gross national product) are spent on projects each year in the United States alone. Other countries are increasingly spending more on projects. Millions of people around the world consider project management the major task in their profession.

Project management is not without problems. The Standish Group has tracked the management of information technology (IT) projects since 1994. This firm's periodic landmark reports summarize the continued need for improved project management. For over a decade the Standish Reports of management of IT projects showed improvements. In 1994 approximately 16 percent of IT projects were completed on time, on budget; in 2004 the success rate moved up to 29 percent.

3

SNAPSHOT FROM PRACTICE   The Project Management Institute

The Project Management Institute (PMI) was founded in 1969 as an international society for project managers. Today PMI has members from more than 125 countries and more than 270,000 members. PMI professionals come from virtually every major industry, including aerospace, automotive, business management, construction, engineering, financial services, information technology, pharmaceuticals, health care, and telecommunications.

PMI provides certification as a ***Project Management Professional (PMP)***—someone who has documented sufficient project experience, agreed to follow the PMI code of professional conduct, and demonstrated mastery of the field of project management by passing a comprehensive examination. The number of people earning PMP status has grown dramatically in recent years. In 1996 there were fewer than 3,000 certified project management professionals. By the end of 2009 there were more than 350,000 PMPs!

Just as the CPA exam is a standard for accountants, passing the PMP exam may become the standard for project managers. Some companies are requiring that all their project managers be PMP certified. Moreover, many job postings are restricted to PMPs. Job seekers, in general, are finding that being PMP certified is an advantage in the marketplace.

PMI recently added a certification as a *Certified Associate in Project Management (CAPM)*. CAPM is designed for project team members and entry-level project managers, as well as qualified undergraduate and graduate students who want a credential to recognize their mastery of the project management body of knowledge. CAPM does not require the extensive project management experience associated with the PMP. For more details on PMP and CAPM, "google" PMI to find the current Web site for the Project Management Institute.

Failed projects also declined from 31 percent in 1994 to 18 percent in 2004. However, the CHAOS Summary 2009 report shows a small decrease in the numbers. This survey report shows only 32 percent of IT projects were delivered on time and within budget. However, 44 percent were "challenged," which means they were late, over budget, and/or missed meeting performance requirements. In addition, 24 percent failed, were cancelled, or never used. Jim Crear, Standish Group CIO, notes this is the highest failure rate in over a decade.

The need for elevating performance continues to challenge the project management profession. The waste on failed projects and cost overruns is estimated in the neighborhood of over $150 billion!

Most of the people who excel at managing projects never have the title of project manager. They include accountants, lawyers, administrators, scientists, contractors, public health officials, teachers, and community advocates whose success depends upon being able to lead and manage project work. For them project management is not a title but a critical job requirement. It is hard to think of a profession or a career path that would not benefit from being good at managing projects.

Not only is project management critical to most careers, the skill set is transferable across most businesses and professions. At its core, project management fundamentals are universal. The same project management methodology that is used to develop a new product can be adapted to create new services, organize events, refurbish aging operations, and so forth. In a world where it is estimated that each person is likely to experience three to four career changes, managing projects is a talent worthy of development.

The significance of project management can also be seen in the classroom. Twenty years ago major universities offered one or two classes in project management, primarily for engineers. Today, most universities offer multiple sections of project management classes, with the core group of engineers being supplemented by business students majoring in marketing, management information systems (MIS), and finance, as well as students from other disciplines such as oceanography, health sciences, computer sciences, and liberal arts. These students are finding that their exposure to project management is providing them with distinct advantages when it comes time to look for jobs. More and more employers are looking for graduates with project management skills. The logical starting point for developing these skills is understanding the uniqueness of a project and of project managers.

What Is a Project?

What do the following headlines have in common?

    Superbowl half-time show scores a touchdown
    Citywide WiFi system set to go live
    1000 acre Wind Farm turns on the juice
    Apple's new iPhone hits the market
    City receives stimulus funds to expand light rail system

All of these events represent projects.

Photo by: Paul Drinkwater/NBCU Photobank via AP Images

The Project Management Institute provides the following definition of a project:

A **project** is a temporary endeavor undertaken to create a unique product, service, or result.

Like most organizational effort, the major goal of a project is to satisfy a customer's need. Beyond this fundamental similarity, the characteristics of a project help differentiate it from other endeavors of the organization. The major characteristics of a project are as follows:

1. An established objective.
2. A defined life span with a beginning and an end.
3. Usually, the involvement of several departments and professionals.
4. Typically, doing something that has never been done before.
5. Specific time, cost, and performance requirements.

First, projects have a defined objective—whether it is constructing a 12-story apartment complex by January 1 or releasing version 2.0 of a specific software package as quickly as possible. This singular purpose is often lacking in daily organizational life in which workers perform repetitive operations each day.

Second, because there is a specified objective, projects have a defined endpoint, which is contrary to the ongoing duties and responsibilities of traditional jobs. In many cases, individuals move from one project to the next as opposed to staying in one job. After helping to install a security system, an IT engineer may be assigned to develop a database for a different client.

Third, unlike much organizational work that is segmented according to functional specialty, projects typically require the combined efforts of a variety of specialists. Instead of working in separate offices under separate managers, project participants, whether they be engineers, financial analysts, marketing professionals, or quality control specialists, work closely together under the guidance of a project manager to complete a project.

The fourth characteristic of a project is that it is nonroutine and has some unique elements. This is not an either/or issue but a matter of degree. Obviously, accomplishing something that has never been done before, such as building a hybrid (electric/gas) automobile or landing two mechanical rovers on Mars, requires solving previously unsolved problems and breakthrough technology. On the other hand, even basic construction projects that involve established sets of routines and procedures require some degree of customization that makes them unique.

Finally, specific time, cost, and performance requirements bind projects. Projects are evaluated according to accomplishment, cost, and time spent. These triple constraints impose a higher degree of accountability than you typically find in most jobs. These three also highlight one of the primary functions of project management, which is balancing the trade-offs between time, cost, and performance while ultimately satisfying the customer.

What a Project Is Not Projects should not be confused with everyday work. A project is not routine, repetitive work! Ordinary daily work typically requires doing the same or similar work over and over, while a project is done only once; a new product or service exists when the project is completed. Examine the list in Table 1.1 that compares routine, repetitive work and projects. Recognizing the difference is important because too often resources can be used up on daily operations which may not contribute to longer range organization strategies that require innovative new products.

Program versus Project In practice the terms project and program cause confusion. They are often used synonymously. *A* **program** *is a group of related projects designed to accomplish a common goal over an extended period of time.* Each project within a program has a project manager. The major differences lie in scale and time span.

Program management is the process of *managing* a group of ongoing, interdependent, related *projects* in a coordinated way to achieve strategic objectives. For

TABLE 1.1
Comparison of Routine Work with Projects

Routine, Repetitive Work	Projects
Taking class notes	Writing a term paper
Daily entering sales receipts into the accounting ledger	Setting up a sales kiosk for a professional accounting meeting
Responding to a supply-chain request	Developing a supply-chain information system
Practicing scales on the piano	Writing a new piano piece
Routine manufacture of an Apple iPod	Designing an iPod that is approximately 2×4 inches, interfaces with PC, and stores 10,000 songs
Attaching tags on a manufactured product	Wire-tag projects for GE and Wal-Mart

example, a pharmaceutical organization could have a program for curing cancer. The cancer program includes and coordinates *all* cancer projects that continue over an extended time horizon. Coordinating all cancer projects under the oversight of a cancer team provides benefits not available from managing them individually. This cancer team also oversees the selection and prioritizing of cancer projects that are included in their special "Cancer" portfolio. Although each project retains its own goals and scope, the project manager and team are also motivated by the higher program goal. Program goals are closely related to broad strategic organization goals.

The Project Life Cycle

Another way of illustrating the unique nature of project work is in terms of the **project life cycle.** Some project managers find it useful to use the project life cycle as the cornerstone for managing projects. The life cycle recognizes that projects have a limited life span and that there are predictable changes in level of effort and focus over the life of the project. There are a number of different life-cycle models in project management literature. Many are unique to a specific industry or type of project. For example, a new software development project may consist of five phases: definition, design, code, integration/test, and maintenance. A generic cycle is depicted in Figure 1.1.

The project life cycle typically passes sequentially through four stages: defining, planning, executing, and delivering. The starting point begins the moment the project is given the go-ahead. Project effort starts slowly, builds to a peak, and then declines to delivery of the project to the customer.

1. **Defining stage:** Specifications of the project are defined; project objectives are established; teams are formed; major responsibilities are assigned.
2. **Planning stage:** The level of effort increases, and plans are developed to determine what the project will entail, when it will be scheduled, whom it will benefit, what quality level should be maintained, and what the budget will be.

FIGURE 1.1
Project Life Cycle

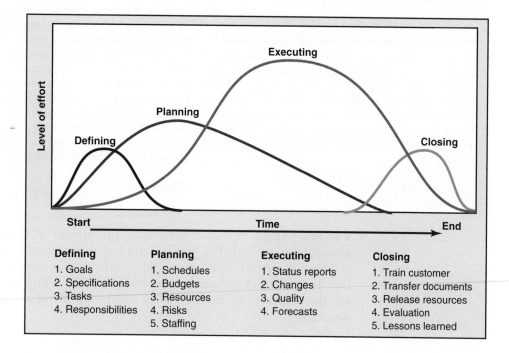

Defining	Planning	Executing	Closing
1. Goals	1. Schedules	1. Status reports	1. Train customer
2. Specifications	2. Budgets	2. Changes	2. Transfer documents
3. Tasks	3. Resources	3. Quality	3. Release resources
4. Responsibilities	4. Risks	4. Forecasts	4. Evaluation
	5. Staffing		5. Lessons learned

SNAPSHOT FROM PRACTICE | Project Management in Action: 2009

© The McGraw-Hill Companies, Inc./Jill Braaten, photographer.

Businesses thrive and survive based on their ability to manage projects that produce products and services that meet market needs. Below is a small sample of projects that are important to their company's future.

COMPANY: NINTENDO
Project: Next Generation Nintendo Wii Game Console
According to Internet rumors, the new console will be based on entirely new hardware that will pump out HD visuals, contain expanded storage, and run using digitally distributed content rather than physical discs. The new console will expand the capability of Wii's revolutionary handheld pointer device that detects movement in three dimensions. At stake is Nintendo's position in the $10 billion plus gaming industry.

—C. Faylor, 2008

COMPANY: OAKLAND A's BASEBALL TEAM
Project: Cisco Stadium
In November 2006, the future of the Oakland A's looked bright as the team announced plans to build a new ballpark in Fremont, CA. Upon announcing plans to build a ballpark, the Oakland A's sold the naming rights to the ballpark to Cisco Systems for $4 million/year over 30 years. The ballpark design mimicked classic ballparks of the past, while combining the most advanced technology in the world. Those plans have since been derailed as opposition increased from major retailers and homeowners near the stadium site. It now appears that the A's will have to develop a plan that may lead the team to building the ballpark in Oakland, near the coliseum, or possibly in San Jose, CA. The A's need the new stadium to turn around lagging attendance, which has been at or near the bottom among major league baseball clubs.

—BBoA, 2009

3. **Executing stage:** A major portion of the project work takes place—both physical and mental. The physical product is produced (a bridge, a report, a software program). Time, cost, and specification measures are used for control. Is the project on schedule, on budget, and meeting specifications? What are the forecasts of each of these measures? What revisions/changes are necessary?

COMPANY: GENERAL MOTORS
Project: Chevrolet Volt

The Chevrolet Volt is a plug-in hybrid electric vehicle to go on sale in 2011. Unlike most currently available hybrids, the actual propulsion of the Volt is accomplished exclusively by the electric motor, and the internal combustion engine is used as another charging method. What's at stake is the future of GM. With the company's recent emergence from bankruptcy protection, the chief of GM product development, Tom Stephens, pronounced, "We cannot afford to have anything but a hit . . . every launch . . . has to be a home-run."

—T. Krisher, 2009

COMPANY: KOREAN MIDLAND POWER CO
Project: World's Largest Tidal Turbine Farm

Korean Midland Power Co. has signed an agreement with Lunar Energy, Britain's leading tidal power company, to build a colossal 300 turbine field in the Wando Hoenggan WaterWay off the South Korean coast by 2015. The $800 million plus project is expected to provide 300MW of renewable energy, enough to power 200,000 homes. The project entails installing a series of 60 ft-high tidal turbines in deep ocean water. A 1MW pilot plant would be installed first to evaluate the environmental impact before the full-blown is allowed. If successful, the ecological impact is expected to be much less than conventional tidal barges which destroy bird habitats and hinder the passage of migratory fish such as salmon and eels.

—Lunar Energy, 2008

COMPANY: MOTOROLA
Project: Google Android Smart Phones

Motorola is set to release multiple Google Android smart phones at several different price points. According to chief executive Sanjay Jha, Android has over 3,000 third-party applications available and "significant developer interest" making it a "large enough eco-system" to become a successful platform. Motorola has seen its phone sales plummet in recent years. The company's global market share has declined to 6 percent after commanding 23 percent in 2006. The new phones are seen as a key to Motorola re-establishing itself in the booming smart phone business.

—S. Segan, 2009

COMPANY: WARNER BROTHERS
Project: *Harry Potter and the Deathly Hallows Part I* and *Part II*

The *Harry Potter* film franchise is the second highest grossing film franchise of all time, with the five films released to date only slightly behind the 22 *James Bond* films. The adaption of the final novel in the series, *Harry Potter and the Deathly Hallows*, will be split into two films, with Part I scheduled to be released in 2010 and Part II in 2011. The Harry Potter franchise is seen by movie insiders as critical to staving off the general decline in movie attendance due to economic woes and home entertainment systems.

—J. Kay, 2009

COMPANY: HUMAN GENOMIC SCIENCES
Project: Benlysta

The new drug, Benlysta, is the first treatment for lupus in decades to show potential far into the testing phase. Lupus is a chronic autoimmune disease in which the body attacks its own healthy tissue. Symptoms include fatigue, headaches, joint pain, light sensitivity, and rashes. Benlysta targets the specific protein that becomes overactive, causing the body to attack its own organs. At stake is relief for the millions of sufferers of lupus worldwide.

—C. Rothman, 2009

4. **Closing stage:** Closing includes three activities: delivering the project product to the customer, redeploying project resources, and post-project review. Delivery of the project might include customer training and transferring documents. Redeployment usually involves releasing project equipment/materials to other projects and finding new assignments for team members. Post-project reviews include not only assessing performance but also capturing lessons learned.

In practice, the project life cycle is used by some project groups to depict the timing of major tasks over the life of the project. For example, the design team might plan a major commitment of resources in the defining stage, while the quality team would expect their major effort to increase in the latter stages of the project life cycle. Because most organizations have a portfolio of projects going on concurrently, each at a different stage of each project's life cycle, careful planning and management at the organization and project levels are imperative.

The Project Manager

In a small sense project managers perform the same functions as other managers. That is, they plan, schedule, motivate, and control. However, what makes them unique is that they manage temporary, nonrepetitive activities, to complete a fixed life project. Unlike functional managers, who take over existing operations, project managers create a project team and organization where none existed before. They must decide what and how things should be done instead of simply managing set processes. They must meet the challenges of each phase of the project life cycle, and even oversee the dissolution of their operation when the project is completed.

Project managers must work with a diverse troupe of characters to complete projects. They are typically the direct link to the customer and must manage the tension between customer expectations and what is feasible and reasonable. Project managers provide direction, coordination, and integration to the project team, which is often made up of part-time participants loyal to their functional departments. They often must work with a cadre of outsiders—vendors, suppliers, subcontractors—who do not necessarily share their project allegience.

Project managers are ultimately responsible for performance (frequently with too little authority). They must ensure that appropriate trade-offs are made between the time, cost, and performance requirements of the project. At the same time, unlike their functional counterparts, project managers generally possess only rudimentary technical knowledge to make such decisions. Instead, they must orchestrate the completion of the project by inducing the right people, at the right time, to address the right issues and make the right decisions.

While project management is not for the timid, working on projects can be an extremely rewarding experience. Life on projects is rarely boring; each day is different from the last. Since most projects are directed at solving some tangible problem or pursuing some useful opportunity, project managers find their work personally meaningful and satisfying. They enjoy the act of creating something new and innovative. Project managers and team members can feel immense pride in their accomplishment, whether it is a new bridge, a new product, or needed service. Project managers are often stars in their organization and well compensated.

Good project managers are always in demand. Every industry is looking for effective people who can get the right things done on time. Clearly, project management is a challenging and exciting profession. This text is intended to provide the necessary knowledge, perspective, and tools to enable students to accept the challenge.

The Importance of Project Management

Project management is no longer a special-need management. It is rapidly becoming a standard way of doing business. See Snapshot from Practice: Project Management in Action: 2009. An increasing percentage of the typical firm's effort is being devoted to projects. The future promises an increase in the importance and the role of projects in contributing to the strategic direction of organizations. Several reasons why this is the case are briefly discussed below.

Compression of the Product Life Cycle

One of the most significant driving forces behind the demand for project management is the shortening of the product life cycle. For example, today in high-tech industries the product life cycle is averaging 1 to 3 years. Only 30 years ago, life cycles of 10 to 15 years were not uncommon. *Time to market* for new products with short life cycles has become increasingly important. A common rule of thumb in the world of high-tech product development is that a six-month project delay can result in a 33 percent loss in product revenue share. Speed, therefore, becomes a competitive advantage; more and more organizations are relying on cross-functional project teams to get new products and services to the market as quickly as possible.

Knowledge Explosion

The growth in new knowledge has increased the complexity of projects because projects encompass the latest advances. For example, building a road 30 years ago was a somewhat simple process. Today, each area has increased in complexity, including materials, specifications, codes, aesthetics, equipment, and required specialists. Similarly, in today's digital, electronic age it is becoming hard to find a new product that does not contain at least one microchip. Product complexity has increased the need to integrate divergent technologies. Project management has emerged as an important discipline for achieving this task.

Triple Bottom Line (planet, people, profit)

The threat of global warming has brought sustainable business practices to the forefront. Businesses can no longer simply focus on maximizing profit to the detriment of the environment and society. Efforts to reduce carbon imprint and utilize renewable resources are realized through effective project management. The impact of this movement towards sustainability can be seen in changes in the objectives and techniques used to complete projects. See Snapshot from Practice: Dell's Children Becomes World's First "Green" Hospital.

Corporate Downsizing

The last decade has seen a dramatic restructuring of organizational life. Downsizing (or rightsizing if you are still employed) and sticking to core competencies have become necessary for survival for many firms. Middle management is a mere skeleton of the past. In today's flatter and leaner organizations, where change is a constant, project management is replacing middle management as a way of ensuring that things get done. Corporate downsizing has also led to a change in the way organizations approach projects. Companies outsource significant segments of project work, and project managers have to manage not only their own people but also their counterparts in different organizations.

Increased Customer Focus

Increased competition has placed a premium on customer satisfaction. Customers no longer simply settle for generic products and services. They want customized products and services that cater to their specific needs. This mandate requires a much closer working relationship between the provider and the receiver. Account executives and sales representatives are assuming more of a project manager's role as they work with their organization to satisfy the unique needs and requests of clients.

Increased customer attention has also prompted the development of customized products and services. For example, 10 years ago buying a set of golf clubs was a relatively simple process: You picked out a set based on price and feel. Today, there are golf clubs for tall players and short players, clubs for players who tend to slice the ball and clubs for those who hook the ball, high-tech clubs with the latest metallurgic discovery guaranteed to add distance, and so forth. Project management is critical both to development of customized products and services and to sustaining lucrative relationships with customers.

SNAPSHOT FROM PRACTICE Dell Children's Becomes World's First "Green" Hospital*

Dateline 1/7/2009, Austin Texas: Dell Children's Medical Center becomes the first hospital in the world to receive platinum LEED (Leadership in Energy & Environmental Design) certification. Platinum certification is the highest award granted by the U.S. Green Building Council.

Dell Children's occupies nearly one-half million square feet on 32 acres that were once part of Austin's old Mueller Airport. Its environmentally sensitive design not only conserves water and electricity, but positively impacts the hospital's clinical environment by improving air quality, making natural sunlight readily available, and reducing a wide range of pollutants.

In order to receive LEED certification, buildings are rated in five key areas: sustainable site development, water savings, energy efficiency, materials selection, and environmental quality. Listed below are some of the accomplishments in each LEED category:

Sustainable Site

- 47,000 tons of Mueller Airport runway material was reused on site.
- About 40 percent fly ash instead of Portland cement in concrete yields a drop in carbon dioxide emissions equivalent to taking 450 cars off the road.
- 925 tons of construction waste was recycled on site.

Water Efficiency and Water Conservation

- Reclaimed water is used for irrigation; xeriscaped landscaping uses native plants, which require less water.
- Low-flow plumbing fixtures.

Energy Efficiency and Energy Conservation

- An on-site natural gas turbine supplies all electricity, which is 75 percent more efficient than coal-fired plants.
- Converted steam energy from a heating/cooling plant supplies all chilled water needs.

Indoor Environment Quality and Lighting

- Most interior spaces are within 32 feet of a window.
- Motion and natural light sensors shut off unneeded lights.

Conservation of Materials and Resources

- Use of local and regional materials saves fuel for shipping.
- Special paints and flooring emit low levels of volatile organic compounds (VOCs).

"Even before the first plans were drawn up, we set our sight on creating a world-class children's hospital, and becoming the first LEED Platinum hospital in the world was definitely part of that," said Robert Bonar, president and CEO, Dell Children's Medical Center of Central Texas. "Our motivation to pursue LEED Platinum was not just environmental. Being a 'green' hospital has profound, measurable effect on healing. What's good for the environment and good for our neighbors is also good for our patients."

* **Austin Business Journal**, 1-11-2009; www.dellchildrens.net/about_us/news/2009/01/08

Small Projects Represent Big Problems

The velocity of change required to remain competitive or simply keep up has created an organizational climate in which hundreds of projects are implemented concurrently. This climate has created a multiproject environment and a plethora of new problems. Sharing and prioritizing resources across a portfolio of projects is a major challenge for senior management. Many firms have no idea of the problems involved with inefficient management of small projects. Small projects typically carry the same or more risk as do large projects. Small projects are perceived as having little impact on the bottom line because they do not demand large amounts of scarce resources and/or money. Because so many small projects are going on concurrently and because the perception of the inefficiency impact is small, measuring inefficiency is usually nonexistent. Unfortunately, many small projects soon add up to large sums of money. Many customers and millions of dollars are lost each year on small projects in product and service organizations. Small projects can represent hidden costs not measured in the accounting system.

Organizations with many small projects going on concurrently face the most difficult project management problems. A key question becomes one of how to create an organizational environment that supports multiproject management. A process is needed to prioritize and develop a portfolio of small projects that supports the mission of the organization.

In summary, there are a variety of environmental forces interacting in today's business world that contribute to the increased demand for good project management across all industries and sectors. Project management appears to be ideally suited for a business environment requiring accountability, flexibility, innovation, speed, and continuous improvement.

Project Management Today—An Integrative Approach

Competing in a global market influenced by rapid change, innovation, and time to market means organizations manage more and more projects. Some means for coordinating and managing projects in this changing environment is needed. Centralization of project management processes and practices has been the practical outcome. For example, Dell, IBM, Hewlett-Packard, and Intel all have over 1,000 projects being implemented concurrently every day of the year across borders and differing cultures. *Questions: How do these organizations oversee the management of all these projects? How were these projects selected? How do they ensure performance measurement and accountability? How can project management continually improve?* Centralization entails integration of all project processes and practices to improve project management.

Integration is designed to improve project management in the whole organization over the long haul. The rationale for integration of project management was to provide senior management with:

- An overview of all project management activities;
- A big picture of how organizational resources are being used;
- An assessment of the risk their portfolio of projects represents;
- A rough metric for measuring the improvement of managing projects relative to others in the industry;
- Linkages of senior management with actual project execution management.

Full insight of all components of the organization is crucial for aligning internal business resources with the requirements of the changing environment. Integration enables management to have greater flexibility and better control of all project management activities.

Operationally, what does project management integration mean? It necessitates combining all of the major dimensions of project management under one umbrella. Each dimension is connected in one seamless, integrated domain. Integration means applying a set of knowledge, skills, tools, and techniques to a collection of projects in order to move the organization toward its strategic goals. This integration movement represents a major thrust of project driven organizations across all industries. See Figure 1.2, Integrated Management of Projects.

Integration of Projects with Organizational Strategy

Today, projects are the *modus operandi* for implementing strategy. Yet in some organizations, selection and management of projects often fail to support the strategic

FIGURE 1.2
Integrated
Management of
Projects

plan of the organization. Strategic plans are written by one group of managers, projects selected by another group, and projects implemented by another. These independent decisions by different groups of managers create a set of conditions leading to conflict, confusion, and frequently an unsatisfied customer. Under these conditions, resources of the organization are wasted in non-value-added activities/projects.

Since projects are the modus operandi, strategic alignment of projects is of major importance to conserving and effective use of organization resources. Selection criteria need to ensure each project is prioritized and contributes to strategic goals. Anything less is a waste of scarce organizational resources—people, capital, and equipment. Ensuring alignment requires a selection process that is systematic, open, consistent, and balanced. All of the projects selected become part of a project portfolio that balances the total risk for the organization. Management of the project portfolio ensures that only the most valuable projects are approved and managed across the entire organization.

Integration of Projects through Portfolio Management

The portfolio management domain encompasses project management oversight at the organization level through the project level. Management has the capability to zoom to a wide-angle view or zoom in to a very specific element of a specific project activity or process. Full insight of all components of the organization is crucial for aligning internal business resources with the requirements of the changing environment. Project portfolios are frequently managed by a project office that serves as a bridge between senior management and project managers and teams. The major functions of portfolio management are to

- Oversee project selection.
- Monitor aggregate resource levels and skills.
- Encourage use of best practices.
- Balance projects in the portfolio in order to represent a risk level appropriate to the organization.
- Improve communication among all stakeholders.
- Create a total organization perspective that goes beyond silo thinking.
- Improve the overall management of projects over time.

Portfolio management manages the integration of elements of organizational strategy with projects, along with their interdependencies. At the project level, the management of the portfolio is directed toward creation and use of best practices.

Integration of the Processes of Implementing Actual Projects

Senior management is often involved in selecting projects but seldom involved in implementing them. Implementing the project is the challenge.

There are two dimensions within the actual execution of projects (see Figure 1.3, The Technical and Sociocultural Dimensions of the Project Management Process). The first dimension is the technical side of the management process, which consists of the formal, disciplined, purely logical parts of the process. This technical dimension includes planning, scheduling, and controlling projects. Clear project scope statements are written to link the project and customer and to facilitate planning and control. Creation of the deliverables and work breakdown structures facilitates planning and monitoring the progress of the project. The work breakdown structure serves as a database that links all levels in the organization, major deliverables, and all work—right down to the tasks in a work package. Effects of project changes are documented and traceable. Thus, any change in one part of the project is traceable to the source by the integrated linkages of the system. This integrated information approach can provide all project managers and the customer with decision information appropriate to their level and needs. A successful project manager will be well trained in the technical side of managing projects.

The second and opposing dimension is the sociocultural side of project management. In contrast to the orderly world of project planning, this dimension involves the much messier, often contradictory and paradoxical world of implementation. It centers on creating a temporary social system within a larger organizational environment that combines the talents of a divergent set of professionals working to

FIGURE 1.3
The Technical and Sociocultural Dimensions of the Project Management Process

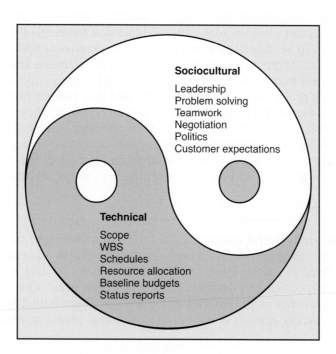

Sociocultural
Leadership
Problem solving
Teamwork
Negotiation
Politics
Customer expectations

Technical
Scope
WBS
Schedules
Resource allocation
Baseline budgets
Status reports

The phrase "works well with others" has long been a staple on grade school report cards; now, in the IT world, it's the No. 1 criterion for management candidates. In a nationwide survey conducted in 1999, 27 percent of chief information officers (CIOs) cited strong interpersonal skills as the single most important quality for reaching management levels. Advanced technical skills came in second, receiving 23 percent of the response.

The project was sponsored by RHI Consulting, which provides information technology professionals on a project basis. An independent research firm was hired to administer the survey. Over 1,400 CIOs responded to the questionnaire.

Survey respondents were also asked:

In 2005, how frequently will employees in your IT department work on project-based teams with members of other departments throughout the company?

Their responses:	
Very frequently	57%
Somewhat frequently	26%
Somewhat infrequently	10%
Very infrequently	6%
Never	1%

Greg Scileppi, RHI Consulting's executive director, recommends that IT professionals develop their interpersonal skills. "The predominance of project teams has created a corresponding need for strong communication and team-player abilities. Technical staff put these skills to test daily as they work with employees at all levels to create and implement IT solutions ranging from simple troubleshooting to corporate web initiatives and system wide upgrades."

* Joanita M. Nellenbach, "People Skills Top Technical Knowledge, CIOs Insist," *PMNetwork* (August 1999), pp. 7–8.

complete the project. See Research Highlight: Works Well with Others. Project managers must shape a project culture that stimulates teamwork and high levels of personal motivation as well as a capacity to quickly identify and resolve problems that threaten project work. This dimension also involves managing the interface between the project and external environment. Project managers have to assuage and shape expectations of customers, sustain the political support of top management, negotiate with their functional counterparts, monitor subcontractors, and so on. Overall, the manager must build a cooperative social network among a divergent set of allies with different standards, commitments, and perspectives.

Some suggest that the technical dimension represents the "science" of project management while the sociocultural dimension represents the "art" of managing a project. To be successful, a manager must be a master of both. Unfortunately, some project managers become preoccupied with the planning and technical dimension of project management. Often their first real exposure to project management is through project management software, and they become infatuated with network charts, Gantt diagrams, and performance variances; they attempt to manage a project from a distance. Conversely, there are other managers who manage projects by the "seat of their pants," relying heavily on team dynamics and organizational politics to complete a project. Good project managers balance their attention to both the technical and sociocultural aspects of project management.

Summary

There are powerful environmental forces contributing to the rapid expansion of project management approaches to business problems and opportunities. A project is defined as a nonroutine, one-time effort limited by time, resources, and performance specifications designed to meet customer needs. One of the distinguishing characteristics of project management is that it has both a beginning and an end and typically consists of four phases: defining, planning, executing, and closing.

Effective project management begins with selecting and prioritizing projects that support the firm's mission and strategy. Successful implementation requires both technical and social skills. Project managers have to plan and budget projects as well as orchestrate the contributions of others.

Text Overview

This text is written to provide the reader with a comprehensive, integrative understanding of the project management process. The text focuses both on the science of project management and the art of managing projects. Following this introductory chapter, Chapter 2 focuses on how organizations go about evaluating and selecting projects. Special attention is devoted to the importance of linking project selection to the mission and strategy of the firm. The organizational environment in which projects are implemented is the focus of Chapter 3. The discussion of matrix management and other organizational forms is augmented by a discussion of the role the culture of an organization plays in the implementation of projects.

The next six chapters focus on developing a plan for the project; after all, project success begins with a good plan. Chapter 4 deals with defining the scope of the project and developing a work breakdown structure (WBS). The challenge of formulating cost and time estimates is the subject of Chapter 5. Chapter 6 focuses on utilizing the information from the WBS to create a project plan in the form of a timed and sequenced network of activities.

Risks are a potential threat to project management, and Chapter 7 examines how organizations and managers identify and manage risks associated with project work. Resource allocation is added to the plan in Chapter 8 with special attention devoted to how resource limitations impact the project schedule. After a resource schedule is established, a project time-phased budget is developed. Finally, Chapter 9 examines strategies for reducing ("crashing") project time either prior to the initiation of the project or in response to problems or new demands placed on the project.

Chapters 10 through 12 focus on project implementation and the sociocultural side of project management, beginning with Chapter 10, which focuses on the role of the project manager as a leader and stresses the importance of managing project stakeholders within the organization. Chapter 11 focuses on the core project team; it combines the latest information on team dynamics with leadership skills/techniques for developing a high-performance project team. Chapter 12 continues the theme of managing project stakeholders by discussing how to outsource project work and negotiate with contractors, customers, and suppliers.

Chapter 13 focuses on the kinds of information managers use to monitor project progress, with special attention devoted to the key concept of earned value. The project life cycle is completed with Chapter 14, which covers closing out a project and the important assessment of performance and lessons learned. Four "supplemental" chapters are included to augment the project management core. Implementation of project management in multicultural, international environments is the subject of Chapter 15. Chapter 16 focuses the need for organizational oversight and how it impacts the management of projects. The emergence of agile project management, a more flexible approach to managing complex projects, is the subject of Chapter 17. Finally, Chapter 18 concludes with coverage of career issues in the field of project management.

Throughout this text you will be exposed to the major aspects of the project management system. However, a true understanding of project management comes not from knowing what a scope statement is, or the critical path, or partnering with contractors, but from comprehending how the different elements of the project management system interact to determine the fate of a project. If, by the end of this text, you come to appreciate and begin to master both the technical and sociocultural dimensions of project management, you should have a distinct competitive advantage over others aspiring to work in the field of project management.

Key Terms

Program, *6*
Project, *5*
Project life cycle, *6*

Project Management
Professional (PMP), *4*

Review Questions

1. Define a project. What are five characteristics that help differentiate projects from other functions carried out in the daily operations of the organization?
2. What are some of the key environmental forces that have changed the way projects are managed? What has been the effect of these forces on the management of projects?
3. Why is the implementation of projects important to strategic planning and the project manager?
4. The technical and sociocultural dimensions of project management are two sides to the same coin. Explain.
5. What is meant by an integrative approach to project management? Why is this approach important in today's environment?

Exercises

1. Review the front page of your local newspaper, and try to identify all the projects contained in the articles. How many were you able to find?
2. Individually identify what you consider to be the greatest achievements accomplished by mankind in the last five decades. Now share your list with three to five other students in the class, and come up with an expanded list. Review these accomplishments in terms of the definition of a project. What does your review suggest about the importance of project management?
3. Individually identify projects assigned in previous terms. Were both sociocultural and technical elements factors in the success or difficulties in the projects?
4. Check out the Project Management Institute's home page at *www.pmi.org*.

   a. Review general information about PMI as well as membership information.
   b. See if there is a PMI chapter in your state. If not, where is the closest one?
   c. Use the search function at the PMI home page to find information on Project Management Body of Knowledge (PMBOK). What are the major knowledge areas of PMBOK?
   d. Explore other links that PMI provides. What do these links tell you about the nature and future of project management?

Note: If you have any difficulty accessing any of the Web addresses listed here or elsewhere in the text, you can find up-to-date addresses on the home page of Dr. Erik Larson, coauthor of this text: *http://www.bus.oregonstate.edu/faculty/bio .htm?UserName=Larson*

References

Ball Parks of Baseball, "Cisco Field," *http://www.ballparksofbaseball.com/future/ CiscoField.htm* (accessed June 2, 2009).

Benko, C., and F. W. McFarlan, *Connecting the Dots* (Boston: HBS Press, 2003).

Cohen, D. J., and R. J. Graham, *The Project Manager's MBA* (San Francisco: Jossey-Bass, 2001).

Faylor, C., "Next Generation Wii Is Rumored to Hit the Market in 2011," *Shacknews.com* (Oct. 1, 2008).

Kay, J., "US Box Office Spellbound by Harry Potter and the Half-Blood Prince," *www.guardian.uk.co.filmblog* (accessed July 15, 2009).

Krisher, T., "GM Product Chief Says New Vehicles Must be Hits," *www. businessweek.com* (accessed July 20, 2009).

Larkowski, K., "Standish Group Report Shows Project Success Improves 50 Percent," *www.standishgroup.com,* 2004, Third Quarter.

Lunar Energy, "British Firm Announces World's Largest Tidal Power Development," *Lunarenergy.co.uk* (March 11, 2008).

Peters, T., *PM Network,* January 2004, Vol. 18, No. 1, p. 19.

Project Management Institute, *Leadership in Project Management Annual* (Newton Square, PA: PMI Publishing, 2006).

Project Management Institute, *A Guide to the Project Management Body of Knowledge (PMBOK),* (Newton Square, PA: PMI Publishing 2008).

Rothman, C., "Promising New Lupus Drug Stirs Hope for Millions," *The Star-Ledger* (July 21, 2009), *www.nj.com/news/ledger/jersey/index.ssf?/base* (accessed July 25, 2009).

Sagan, Sascha, "Motorola Hangs Smartphone Future on Android," *PCMag.com* (April 20, 2009).

The Standish Group, *CHAOS Summary 2009,* pp. 1–4.

Stewart, T. A., "The Corporate Jungle Spawns a New Species: The Project Manager," *Fortune* (September 1996), pp. 14–15.

Case

A Day in the Life

Rachel, the project manager of a large information systems project, arrives at her office early to get caught up with work before her co-workers and project team arrive. However, as she enters the office she meets Neil, one of her fellow project managers, who also wants to get an early start on the day. Neil has just completed a project overseas. They spend 10 minutes socializing and catching up on personal news.

It takes Rachel 10 minutes to get to her office and settle in. She then checks her voice mail and turns on her computer. She was at her client's site the day before until 7:30 P.M. and has not checked her e-mail or voice mail since 3:30 P.M. the previous day. There are 7 phone messages, 16 e-mails, and 4 notes left on her desk. She spends 15 minutes reviewing her schedule and "to do" lists for the day before responding to messages that require immediate attention.

Rachel spends the next 25 minutes going over project reports and preparing for the weekly status meeting. Her boss, who just arrived at the office, interrupts her. They spend 20 minutes discussing the project. He shares a rumor that a team member is using stimulants on the job. She tells him that she has not seen anything suspicious but will keep an eye on the team member.

The 9:00 A.M. project status meeting starts 15 minutes late because two of the team members have to finish a job for a client. Several people go to the cafeteria to get coffee and doughnuts while others discuss last night's baseball game. The team members arrive, and the remaining 45 minutes of the progress review meeting surface project issues that have to be addressed and assigned for action.

After the meeting Rachel goes down the hallway to meet with Victoria, another IS project manager. They spend 30 minutes reviewing project assignments since the two of them share personnel. Victoria's project is behind schedule and in need of help. They broker a deal that should get Victoria's project back on track.

She returns to her office and makes several phone calls and returns several e-mails before walking downstairs to visit with members of her project team. Her intent is to follow up on an issue that had surfaced in the status report meeting. However, her simple, "Hi guys, how are things going?" elicits a stream of disgruntled responses from the "troops." After listening patiently for over 20 minutes, she realizes that among other things several of the client's managers are beginning to request features that were not in the original project scope statement. She tells her people that she will get on this right away.

Returning to her office she tries to call her counterpart John at the client firm but is told that he is not expected back from lunch for another hour. At this time, Eddie drops by and says, "How about lunch?" Eddie works in the finance office and they spend the next half hour in the company cafeteria gossiping about internal politics. She is surprised to hear that Jonah Johnson, the director of systems projects, may join another firm. Jonah has always been a powerful ally.

She returns to her office, answers a few more e-mails, and finally gets through to John. They spend 30 minutes going over the problem. The conversation ends with John promising to do some investigating and to get back to her as soon as possible.

Rachel puts a "Do not disturb" sign on her door, and lies down in her office. She listens to the third and fourth movement of Ravel's string quartet in F on headphones.

Rachel then takes the elevator down to the third floor and talks to the purchasing agent assigned to her project. They spend the next 30 minutes exploring ways of getting necessary equipment to the project site earlier than planned. She finally authorizes express delivery.

When she returns to her office, her calendar reminds her that she is scheduled to participate in a conference call at 2:30. It takes 15 minutes for everyone to get online. During this time, Rachel catches up on some e-mail. The next hour is spent exchanging information about the technical requirements associated with a new version of a software package they are using on systems projects like hers.

Rachel decides to stretch her legs and goes on a walk down the hallway where she engages in brief conversations with various co-workers. She goes out of her way to thank Chandra for his thoughtful analysis at the status report meeting. She returns to find that John has left a message for her to call him back ASAP. She contacts John, who informs her that, according to his people, her firm's marketing rep had made certain promises about specific features her system would provide. He doesn't know how this communication breakdown occurred, but his people are pretty upset over the situation. Rachel thanks John for the information and immediately takes the stairs to where the marketing group resides.

She asks to see Mary, a senior marketing manager. She waits 10 minutes before being invited into her office. After a heated discussion, she leaves 40 minutes later with Mary agreeing to talk to her people about what was promised and what was not promised.

She goes downstairs to her people to give them an update on what is happening. They spend 30 minutes reviewing the impact the client's requests could have on the project schedule. She also shares with them the schedule changes she and Victoria had agreed to. After she says good night to her team, she heads upstairs to her boss's office and spends 20 minutes updating him on key events of the day. She returns to her office and spends 30 minutes reviewing e-mails and project documents. She logs on to the MS project schedule of her project and spends the next 30 minutes working with "what-if" scenarios. She reviews tomorrow's schedule and writes some personal reminders before starting off on her 30-minute commute home.

1. How effectively do you think Rachel spent her day?
2. What does the case tell you about what it is like to be a project manager?

Organization Strategy and Project Selection

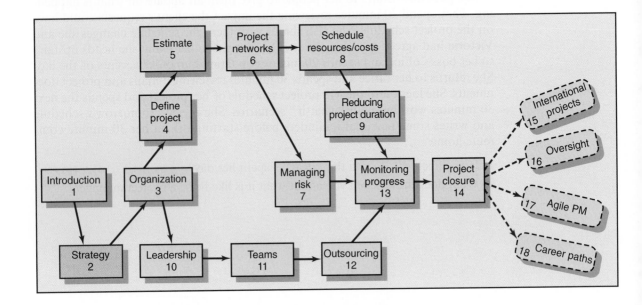

Strategy is implemented through projects. Every project should have a clear link to the organization's strategy.

Strategy is fundamentally deciding how the organization will compete. Organizations use projects to convert strategy into new products, services, and processes needed for success. For example, Intel's major strategy is one of differentiation. Its projects target innovation and time to market. Currently, Intel is directing its strategy toward specialty chips for products other than computers, such as autos, security, cell phones, air controls. Another goal is to reduce project cycle times. Intel, NEC, General Electric, and AT&T have reduced their cycle times by 20–50 percent. Projects and project management play the key role in supporting strategic goals. It is vital for project managers to think and act strategically.

Aligning projects with the strategic goals of the organization is crucial for project success. Today's economic climate is unprecedented by rapid changes in technology, global competition, and financial uncertainty. These conditions make strategy/project alignment even more essential for success. Every major project needs to have a strong linkage to the strategic plan. Ensuring a strong link between the strategic plan and projects is a difficult task that demands constant attention from top and middle management.

The larger and more diverse an organization, the more difficult it is to create and maintain this strong link. Ample evidence still suggests that many organizations have not developed a process that clearly aligns project selection to the strategic plan. The result is poor utilization of the organization's resources—people, money, equipment, and core competencies. Conversely, organizations that have a coherent link of projects to strategy have more cooperation across the organization, perform better on projects, and have fewer projects.

How can an organization ensure this link and alignment? The answer requires integration of projects with the strategic plan. Integration assumes the existence of a strategic plan and a process for prioritizing projects by their contribution to the plan. A crucial factor to ensure the success of integrating the plan with projects lies in the creation of a process that is open and transparent for all participants to review. This chapter presents an overview of the importance of strategic planning and the process for developing a strategic plan. Typical problems encountered when strategy and projects are not linked are noted. A generic methodology that ensures integration by creating very strong linkages of project selection and priority to the strategic plan is then discussed. The intended outcomes are clear organization focus, best use of scarce organization resources (people, equipment, capital), and improved communication across projects and departments.

Why Project Managers Need to Understand Strategy

Project management historically has been preoccupied solely with the planning and execution of projects. Strategy was considered to be under the purview of senior management. This is old-school thinking. New-school thinking recognizes that project management is at the apex of strategy and operations. Aaron Shenhar speaks to this issue when he states, ". . . it is time to expand the traditional role of the project manager from an operational to a more strategic perspective. In the modern evolving organization, project managers will be focused on business aspects, and their role will expand from getting the job done to achieving the business results and winning in the market place."

There are two main reasons why project managers need to understand their organization's mission and strategy. The first reason is so they can make appropriate decisions and adjustments. For example, how a project manager would respond to a suggestion to modify the design of a product to enhance performance will vary depending upon whether his company strives to be a product leader through innovation or to achieve operational excellence through low cost solutions. Similarly, how a project manager would respond to delays may vary depending upon strategic concerns. A project manager will authorize overtime if her firm places a premium on getting to the market first. Another project manager will accept the delay if speed is not essential.

J. P. Descamps has observed that project managers who do not understand the role their project plays in accomplishing the strategy of their organization tend to make the following serious mistakes:

- Focusing on problems or solutions that have low priority strategically
- Focusing on the immediate customer rather than the whole market place and value chain
- Overemphasizing technology as an end in and of itself, resulting in projects that wander off pursuing exotic technology that does not fit the strategy or customer need
- Trying to solve every customer issue with a product or service rather than focusing on the 20 percent with 80 percent of the value (Pareto's Law)
- Engaging in a never-ending search for perfection that no one except the project team really cares about

The second reason project managers need to understand their organization's strategy is so they can be effective project advocates. Project managers have to be able to demonstrate to senior management how their project contributes to their firm's mission. Protection and continued support come from being aligned with corporate objectives. Project managers also need to be able to explain to team members and other stakeholders why certain project objectives and priorities are critical. This is essential for getting buy-in on contentious trade-off decisions.

For these reasons project managers will find it valuable to have a keen understanding of strategic management and project selection processes, which are discussed next.

The Strategic Management Process: An Overview

Strategic management is the process of assessing "what we are" and deciding and implementing "what we intend to be and how we are going to get there." Strategy describes how an organization intends to compete with the resources available in the existing and perceived future environment.

SNAPSHOT FROM PRACTICE   Move Beyond Computers*

INTEL CEO Craig R. Barrett is planning his last hurrah only 15 months before his retirement as chairman of the board. His vision for INTEL is to move beyond computers: think INTEL everywhere. Barrett says, "Everything in the world is going digital." He wants INTEL chips to be the guts of every digital device on the planet—especially in the communications, consumer electronics, and entertainment industries. Think—cell phones, wireless home networks, video players, flat panel TVs—INTEL's expertise fits right in.

He is hitting the market today with a chip technology called WiMax "that can be used to deliver high speed Internet access throughout a small city (or 30 miles) for about $100,000, which is about one-tenth the cost of rolling out fiber optic lines today." (A competitor, WiFi, has a range of about 200 feet.) Cable and phone companies are very interested because of low entry costs.

Some critics believe Barrett's shotgun approach is too risky. He doesn't see it that way. Rather than following INTEL's past go-it-alone approach to new products, he wants INTEL to forge closer ties with customers by designing products they need rather than designing products no one asked for. He admits going into consumer markets will be a challenge and a half. He intends to provide financial support and cooperation for companies creating new products that will use INTEL chips. Barrett feels the risk of providing financial support for smaller companies creating new products is low, even if some go bust. If most of the new products take off, risk is minimized because their markets will lead to increasing demand for new, larger, and faster PCs where INTEL manufacturing dominates cost.

Courtesy Intel Corporation.

Implementing the new vision will not keep INTEL's manufacturing from remaining on the cutting edge. By 2005 five new factories will manufacture 12-inch wafers printed with 90-nanometer circuit lines, just 0.1 percent the width of a human hair. These plants are expected to slash chip costs in half.

The mission has been set: Create INTEL chips to meet the need of new digital products. Right or wrong, everyone in the organization knows the game plan and can focus their efforts in this new consumer-oriented direction. Projects related to digital products will be ranked high priority.

* Adapted from Cliff Edwards, "What Is CEO Craig Barrett Up To?" *Business Week,* March 8, 2004, pp. 56–64.

Two major dimensions of strategic management are responding to changes in the external environment and allocating scarce resources of the firm to improve its competitive position. Constant scanning of the external environment for changes is a major requirement for survival in a dynamic competitive environment. The second dimension is the internal responses to new action programs aimed at enhancing the competitive position of the firm. The nature of the responses depends on the type of business, environment volatility, competition, and the organizational culture.

Strategic management provides the theme and focus of the future direction of the organization. It supports consistency of action at every level of the organization. It encourages integration because effort and resources are committed to common goals and strategies. See Snapshot from Practice: Move Beyond Computers. It is a continuous, iterative process aimed at developing an integrated and coordinated long-term plan of action. Strategic management positions the organization to meet the needs and requirements of its customers for the long term. With the long-term position identified, objectives are set, and strategies are developed to achieve objectives and then translated into actions by implementing projects. Strategy can decide the survival of an organization. Most organizations are successful in *formulating* strategies for what course(s) they should pursue. However, the problem in many organizations is *implementing* strategies—that is, making them happen. Integration of strategy formulation and implementation often does not exist.

The components of strategic management are closely linked, and all are directed toward the future success of the organization. Strategic management requires strong links among mission, goals, objectives, strategy, and implementation. The mission gives the general purpose of the organization. Goals give global targets within the mission. Objectives give specific targets to goals. Objectives give rise to formulation of strategies to reach objectives. Finally, strategies require actions and tasks to be implemented. In most cases the actions to be taken represent projects. Figure 2.1 shows a schematic of the **strategic management process** and major activities required.

Four Activities of the Strategic Management Process

The typical sequence of activities of the strategic management process is outlined here; a description of each activity then follows:

1. Review and define the organizational mission.
2. Set long-range goals and objectives.
3. Analyze and formulate strategies to reach objectives.
4. Implement strategies through projects.

Review and Define the Organizational Mission

The mission identifies "what we want to become," or the raison d'être. Mission statements identify the scope of the organization in terms of its product or service. A written mission statement provides focus for decision making when shared by organizational managers and employees. Everyone in the organization should be keenly aware of the organization's mission. For example, at one large consulting firm, partners who fail to recite the mission statement on demand are required to buy lunch. The mission statement communicates and identifies the purpose of the organization to all stakeholders. Mission statements can be used for evaluating organization performance.

Traditional components found in mission statements are major products and services, target customers and markets, and geographical domain. In addition, statements frequently include organizational philosophy, key technologies, public image, and contribution to society. Including such factors in mission statements relates directly to business success.

Mission statements change infrequently. However, when the nature of the business changes or shifts, a revised mission statement may be required. For example, Steve Jobs of Apple Computer envisioned the use of computer technology beyond the PC desktop. His mission was to look at computer technology as the vehicle for work and entertainment. As a result he developed the iPod for selling music and masterminded the development of animated movies such as *Finding Nemo* through the Pixar organization. See the adjacent Apple Snapshot

FIGURE 2.1
Strategic
Management
Process

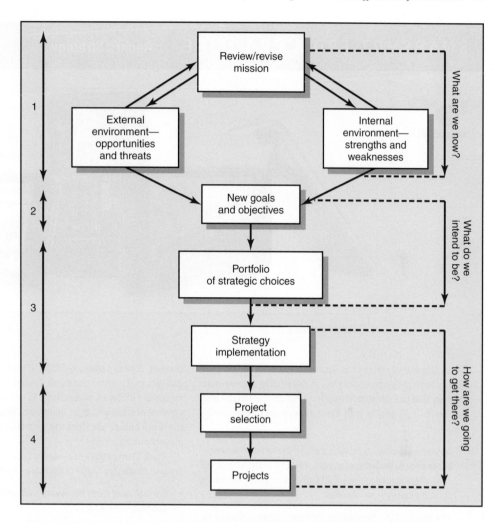

from Practice to find out more about how Apple's mission shapes new product development projects.

More specific mission statements tend to give better results because of a tighter focus. Mission statements decrease the chance of false directions by stakeholders. For example, compare the phrasing of the following mission statements:

Provide hospital design services.

Provide voice/data design services.

Provide information technology services.

Increase shareholder value.

Provide high-value products to our customer.

Clearly, the first two statements leave less chance for misinterpretation than the others. A rule-of-thumb test for a mission statement is, if the statement can be anybody's mission statement, it will not provide the guidance and focus intended. The mission sets the parameters for developing objectives.

SNAPSHOT FROM PRACTICE Apple's Strategy

© PRNewsFoto/Apple

Since Steve Jobs returned to Apple Computer as CEO in 1997, he has been strikingly successful in developing a turnaround strategy that has developed new markets and increased market share. It all begins with strict adherence to the mission statement:

> Apple is committed to bringing the best personal computing experience to students, educators, creative professionals and consumers around the world through its innovative hardware, software and Internet offerings.

The thrust of the turnaround strategy includes mass customization and targeting market segments. Apple's primary competitive advantage is that it controls both the hardware and software aspects of most of its products. The vision, coupled with this strong strategic advantage, allows Apple to offer innovation in hardware, software, and Internet offerings. From the vision statement many product strategies have been forthcoming. For example, Jobs first segmented Apple's market into consumer and professional. This segmentation reduces the number of products and sharply targets products to specific end users.

Several specific strategies have developed for the consumer market. For example, Jobs believes users should be able to connect their MP3 players, iPods, DVD players, CD players, digital cameras, PDAs, DV camcorders, and other gadgets to a central computer, known as the digital hub. Development of iTunes allows users to mix and burn CDs from the comfort and ease of their computer. Along with burning CDs, users are able to use iTunes to sync their music files with MP3 players such as iPod.

Apple's competitive advantages provide strong support for its product strategies. Some of the more obvious are listed here:

- Control over both hardware and software—avoids compatibility problems
- High quality and innovation image
- Common architecture fits most products and eases development time
- Free software
- Ease of use
- Loyal customer base

For over ten years the string of innovative products from Apple has been spectacular. No end is in sight. Each new product endeavor closely aligns with the mission statement and current strategies. Launching new products in new markets requires executing projects within tight time, cost, and scope constraints.

Set Long-Range Goals and Objectives

Objectives translate the organization mission into specific, concrete, measurable terms. Organizational objectives set targets for all levels of the organization. Objectives pinpoint the direction managers believe the organization should move toward. Objectives answer in detail *where* a firm is headed and *when* it is going to get there. Typically, objectives for the organization cover markets, products, innovation, productivity, quality, finance, profitability, employees, and consumers. In every case, objectives should be as operational as possible. That is, objectives should include a time frame, be measurable, be an identifiable state, and be realistic. Doran created the memory device shown in Exhibit 2.1, which is useful when writing objectives.

Each level below the organizational objectives should support the higher-level objectives in more detail; this is frequently called cascading of objectives. For example, if a firm making leather luggage sets an objective of achieving a 40 percent increase in sales through a research and development strategy, this charge is passed to the marketing, production, and R&D departments. The R&D department accepts the firm's strategy as their objective, and their strategy becomes the design and development of a new "pull-type luggage with hidden retractable wheels." At this point the objective becomes a project to be implemented—to develop the retractable wheel luggage for market within six months within a budget of $200,000. In summary, organizational objectives drive your projects.

Analyze and Formulate Strategies to Reach Objectives

Formulating strategy answers the question of *what* needs to be done to reach objectives. Strategy formulation includes determining and evaluating alternatives that support the organization's objectives and selecting the best alternative. The first step is a realistic evaluation of the past and current position of the enterprise. This step typically includes an analysis of "who are the customers" and "what are their needs as they (the *customers*) see them."

The next step is an assessment of the internal and external environments. What are the internal strengths and weaknesses of the enterprise? Examples of internal strengths or weaknesses could be core competencies, such as technology, product quality, management talent, low debt, and dealer networks. Managers can alter internal strengths and weaknesses. Opportunities and threats usually represent external forces for change such as technology, industry structure, and competition. Competitive benchmarking tools are sometimes used here to assess current and future directions. Opportunities and threats are the flip sides of each other. That is, a threat can be perceived as an opportunity, or vice versa. Examples of perceived external threats could be a slowing of the economy, a maturing life cycle, exchange rates, or government regulation. Typical opportunities are increasing demand, emerging markets, and demographics. Managers or individual firms have

EXHIBIT 2.1
Characteristics of Objectives

S	**Specific**	Be specific in targeting an objective
M	**Measurable**	Establish a measurable indicator(s) of progress
A	**Assignable**	Make the objective assignable to one person for completion
R	**Realistic**	State what can realistically be done with available resources
T	**Time related**	State when the objective can be achieved, that is, duration

limited opportunities to influence such external environmental factors; however, in recent years notable exceptions have been new technologies such as Apple using the iPod to create a market to sell music. The keys are to attempt to forecast fundamental industry changes and stay in a proactive mode rather than a reactive one. This assessment of the external and internal environments is known as the SWOT analysis (strengths, weaknesses, opportunities, and threats).

From this analysis, critical issues and a portfolio of strategic alternatives are identified. These alternatives are compared with the current portfolio and available resources; strategies are then selected that should support the basic mission and objectives of the organization. Critical analysis of the strategies includes asking questions: Does the strategy take advantage of our core competencies? Does the strategy exploit our competitive advantage? Does the strategy maximize meeting customers' needs? Does the strategy fit within our acceptable risk range?

Strategy formulation ends with cascading objectives or projects assigned to lower divisions, departments, or individuals. Formulating strategy might range around 20 percent of management's effort, while determining *how* strategy will be implemented might consume 80 percent.

Implement Strategies through Projects

Implementation answers the question of *how* strategies will be realized, given available resources. The conceptual framework for strategy implementation lacks the structure and discipline found in strategy formulation. Implementation requires action and completing tasks; the latter frequently means mission-critical projects. Therefore, implementation must include attention to several key areas.

First, completing tasks requires allocation of resources. Resources typically represent funds, people, management talents, technological skills, and equipment. Frequently, implementation of projects is treated as an "addendum" rather than an integral part of the strategic management process. However, multiple objectives place conflicting demands on organizational resources. Second, implementation requires a formal and informal organization that complements and supports strategy and projects. Authority, responsibility, and performance all depend on organization structure and culture. Third, planning and control systems must be in place to be certain project activities necessary to ensure strategies are effectively performed. Fourth, motivating project contributors will be a major factor for achieving project success. Finally, an area receiving more attention in recent years is prioritizing projects. Although the strategy implementation process is not as clear as strategy formulation, all managers realize that, without implementation, success is impossible.

Scenario Planning: A Supplement to Traditional Strategic Planning

Overview Given the *Flat, Hot, and Crowded* world described by author Thomas Friedman, the rate of change is accelerating. Forward strategic planning for a period of the next 5–10 years has been reduced to the next 2–4 years. Most planning today represents incremental, tactical planning. The emphasis is on fast **payback,** internal projects, small teams, daily or weekly status reporting. But how do we ensure we have given serious consideration to the potential environment 5–10 years out? That is, how might the future unfold: What is the risk of being too late to adapt? How do we plan for the future when we don't know what the future holds? The strategic planning team must address such questions.

With accelerating changes and uncertainty in the world about us, some organizations are forced to supplement strategic planning with the longer view called **scenario planning.** Scenario planning was popularized by Royal Dutch Shell during the petroleum shortage of 1973. Since then numerous organizations have adapted scenario planning: IBM, Microsoft, AT&T, Weyerhaeuser, US Steel, unions, and numerous governmental agencies. In the words of one executive, "Scenario planning is risk contingency planning, without really moving organizational resources."

Scenario Planning Process   Scenarios are stories of how we believe things could play out in the longer run. **Scenario planning** is a structured process of thinking about future possible environments that would have potential high impact to disrupt the way you do business, and then developing potential strategies to compete in these altered environments.

Assessing Your Core Business and Industry   How will the future unfold for your business? The first step of scenario planning is clarification and agreement on the core business of your organization and the environment in which it exists. What product or service does your organization provide society? How fast is your industry changing? What are the driving environmental forces that can cause your industry to change? How long would it take for your industry to make a major change to a new direction—e.g., technology breakthrough, new legislation, political movement or regulation? Reviewing the core business and drivers up front provides a foundation for thinking about scenarios that can alter the model your organization uses to provide its service or product.

Potential Scenarios and Impact   With agreement reached on the core business and characteristics of your operating environment, the next step is brainstorming potential global forces that could have a substantial impact and alter the way your organization does business. Typical global forces influencing scenarios are social, technological, environmental, economic, political (STEEP), and global institutions. For example, will the green movement to protect the environment influence the way you do business? Since nearly every country has some commission or agency exploring ways to reduce carbon emissions, many organizations are considering events, movements, and government regulations that could alter the way they operate. New governmental regulations are appearing daily. When might you have to respond by devoting resources to adjust to potential new regulations?

With perhaps over 100 potential events identified, the team narrows the list to a small number of events that could alter your current business model. The few remaining potential scenarios (say 2–4) are evaluated to determine what each scenario means for your organization and to assess how you may address the event if it occurs. For example, what options are available to you? Will the scenario destroy a large segment of your market? Will you need to eat costs to establish a new market? Of the few remaining scenarios, which have the highest chance of occurring? Highest impact? Offering opportunities? What are the underlying causes for each scenario?

Potential Strategies   Assuming the scenario occurs, what strategy(s) would you use to move the organization to respond to the change? How does the industry make major changes today—in 1–2 years, 3–5 years, 6–10 years? Given your core competencies, is your organization capable of changing to operate in this future environment? How would your competition react to this new scenario? What strategic options would work best for your organization?

Examples Assume you are a law firm specializing in carbon-free energy. A potential scenario is a new technology developed to store mass amounts of electricity for use when it is needed (imagine a large battery big enough to store enough electricity for a large city). What impact would this have on the wind and solar industries—consolidation, price wars? How will your business model change? Assume you are a Saudi Arabian or Russian oil company. One scenario is demand for oil dries up and drops to 5 percent of today's demand. Should these companies begin to slowly invest in projects to develop and become experts in alternative energy sources?

Another example: Around 1990 IBM changed focus from a hardware/software company to a service focus company. The impetus for the change was recognition that hardware and software products were moving toward "commodities," which typically lead to increased competition and low margins. Generically, the strategies could be categorized as fold up, continue as is, or prepare to make long-term investments that accommodate the risk of the scenario occurring. IBM moved resources to the service side of the business. Better to prepare contingency strategies that can be used as opportunities, rather than react too late.

Triggers Finally, scenario planning concludes with identifying early indicators for different scenarios and establishing "triggers" that tell you the event is quickly approaching and detailed strategic planning is needed. What upstream factors and driving forces cause the scenario to move forward (technology, political, economic, and social)? What must come true for the scenario event to materialize and cause you to take action?

Summary With the external operating environment changing at an ever-increasing rate, traditional strategic planning has been supplemented with scenario planning. Scenario planning has become the leading methodology for imagining how the future will develop and changing organizations accordingly. Scenario planning gets organization stakeholders thinking of the big picture and longer run survivability of the organization—as opposed to maximizing their individual silos. Scenario planning improves the organization's ability to foresee concealed weaknesses and inflexibilities and to adapt to uncertainty and change. It positions the organization to respond to changing forces in the environment by anticipating the kinds of projects that will need to be implemented. For example, since 1974 General Motors and Ford have been threatened with government compliance to increase gas mileage and reduce auto size. Both have tentative plans (projects) for autos that meet the compliance standards of 2009, but it takes time to implement.

The Need for an Effective Project Portfolio Management System

Implementation of projects without a strong **priority system** linked to strategy creates problems. Three of the most obvious problems are discussed below. A **project portfolio** system can go a long way to reduce, or even eliminate, the impact of these problems.

Problem 1: The Implementation Gap

In organizations with short product life cycles, it is interesting to note that frequently participation in strategic planning and implementation includes participants from all levels within the organization. However, in perhaps 80 percent of the remaining product and service organizations, top management pretty much formulates strategy and leaves strategy implementation to functional managers. Within these broad constraints, more detailed strategies and objectives are developed by the functional managers. The fact that these objectives and strategies are made *independently* at different levels by functional groups within the organization hierarchy causes manifold problems.

Some symptoms of organizations struggling with strategy disconnect and unclear priorities are presented here.

- Conflicts frequently occur among functional managers and cause lack of trust.
- Frequent meetings are called to establish or renegotiate priorities.
- People frequently shift from one project to another, depending on current priority. Employees are confused about which projects are important.
- People are working on multiple projects and feel inefficient.
- Resources are not adequate.

Because clear linkages do not exist, the organizational environment becomes dysfunctional, confused, and ripe for ineffective implementation of organization strategy and, thus, of projects. The **implementation gap** refers to the lack of understanding and consensus of organization strategy among top and middle-level managers.

A scenario the authors have seen repeated several times follows. Top management picks their top 20 projects for the next planning period, without priorities. Each functional department—marketing, finance, operations, engineering, information technology, and human resources—selects projects from the list. Unfortunately independent department priorities across projects are not homogenous. A project that rates first in the IT department can rate 10th in the finance department. Implementation of the projects represents conflicts of interest with animosities developing over organization resources.

If this condition exists, how is it possible to effectively implement strategy? The problem is serious. One study found that only about 25 percent of *Fortune 500* executives believe there is a strong linkage, consistency, and/or agreement between the strategies they formulate and implementation. In another study of Deloitte Consulting, Jeff MacIntyre reports, "Only 23 percent of nearly 150 global executives considered their project portfolios aligned with the core business." Middle managers considered organizational strategy to be under the purview of others or not in their realm of influence. It is the responsibility of senior management to set policies that show a distinct link between organizational strategy and objectives and projects that implement those strategies. The research of Fusco suggests the implementation gap and prioritizing projects are still overlooked by many organizations. He surveyed 280 project managers and found that 24 percent of their organizations did not even publish or circulate their objectives; in addition, 40 percent of the respondents reported that priorities among competing projects were not clear, while only 17 percent reported clear priorities.

Problem 2: Organization Politics

Politics exist in every organization and can have a significant influence on which projects receive funding and high priority. This is especially true when the criteria and process for selecting projects are ill-defined and not aligned with the mission of the firm. Project selection may be based not so much on facts and sound reasoning, but rather on the persuasiveness and power of people advocating projects.

The term **"sacred cow"** is often used to denote a project that a powerful, high-ranking official is advocating. Case in point, a marketing consultant confided that he was once hired by the marketing director of a large firm to conduct an independent, external market analysis for a new product the firm was interested in developing. His extensive research indicated that there was insufficient demand to warrant the financing of this new product. The marketing director chose to bury the report and made the consultant promise never to share this information with anyone. The director explained that this new product was the "pet idea" of the new CEO, who saw it as his legacy to the firm. He went on to describe the CEO's irrational obsession with the project and how he referred to it as his "new baby." Like a parent fiercely protecting his child, the marketing director believed that he would lose his job if such critical information ever became known.

Having a project sponsor can play a significant role in the selection and successful implementation of product innovation projects. Project sponsors are typically high-ranking managers who endorse and lend political support for the completion of a specific project. They are instrumental in winning approval of the project and in protecting the project during the critical development stage. Savvy project managers recognize the importance of having "friends in higher courts" who can advocate for their case and protect their interests.

The significance of corporate politics can be seen in the ill-fated ALTO computer project at Xerox during the mid-1970s. The project was a tremendous technological success; it developed the first workable mouse, the first laser printer, the first user-friendly software, and the first local area network. All of these developments were five years ahead of their nearest competitor. Over the next five years this opportunity to dominate the nascent personal computer market was squandered because of internal in-fighting at Xerox and the absence of a strong project sponsor.

Politics can play a role not only in project selection but also in the aspirations behind projects. Individuals can enhance their power within an organization by managing extraordinary and critical projects. Power and status naturally accrue to successful innovators and risk takers rather than to steady producers. Many ambitious managers pursue high-profile projects as a means for moving quickly up the corporate ladder. For example, Lee Iacocca's career was built on successfully leading the design and development of the highly successful Ford Mustang. Managers become heroes by leading projects that contribute significantly to an organization's mission or solve a pressing crisis.

Many would argue that politics and project management should not mix. A more proactive response is that projects and politics invariably mix and that effective project managers recognize that any significant project has political ramifications. Likewise, top management needs to develop a system for identifying and selecting projects that reduces the impact of internal politics and fosters the selection of the best projects for achieving the mission and strategy of the firm.

Problem 3: Resource Conflicts and Multitasking

Most project organizations exist in a multiproject environment. This environment creates the problems of project interdependency and the need to share resources. For example, what would be the impact on the labor resource pool of a construction company if it should win a contract it would like to bid on? Will existing labor be adequate to deal with the new project—given the completion date? Will current projects be delayed? Will subcontracting help? Which projects will have priority? Competition among project managers can be contentious. All project managers seek to have the best people for their projects. The problems of sharing resources and scheduling resources across projects grow exponentially as the number of projects rises. In multiproject environments the stakes are higher and the benefits or penalties for good or bad resource scheduling become even more significant than in most single projects.

Resource sharing also leads to multitasking. Multitasking involves starting and stopping work on one task to go and work on another project, and then returning to the work on the original task. People working on several tasks concurrently are far less efficient, especially where conceptual or physical shutdown and startup are significant. Multitasking adds to delays and costs. Changing priorities exacerbate the multitasking problems even more. Likewise, multitasking is more evident in organizations that have too many projects for the resources they command.

The number of small and large projects in a portfolio almost always exceeds the available resources (typically by a factor of three to four times the available resources). This capacity overload inevitably leads to confusion and inefficient use of scarce organizational resources. The presence of an implementation gap, of power politics, and of multitasking adds to the problem of which projects are allocated resources first. Employee morale and confidence suffer because it is difficult to make sense of an ambiguous system. A multiproject organization environment faces major problems without a priority system that is clearly linked to the strategic plan.

In essence, to this point we have suggested that many organizations have no meaningful process for addressing the problems we have described. The first and most important change that will go a long way in addressing these and other problems is the development and use of a meaningful project priority process for project selection.

How can the implementation gap be narrowed so that understanding and consensus of organizational strategies run through all levels of management? How can power politics be minimized? Can a process be developed in which projects are consistently prioritized to support organizational strategies? Can the prioritized projects be used to allocate scarce organizational resources—for example, people, equipment? Can the process encourage bottom-up initiation of projects that support clear organizational targets?

What is needed is a set of integrative criteria and a process for evaluating and selecting projects that support higher-level strategies and objectives. A single-project priority system that ranks projects by their contribution to the strategic plan would make life easier. Easily said, but difficult to accomplish in practice. Organizations that managed independent projects and allocated resources ad hoc have shifted focus to selecting the right portfolio of projects to achieve their strategic objectives. This is a quickening trend. The advantages of successful project portfolio systems are becoming well recognized in project-driven organizations. See Exhibit 2.2, which lists a few key benefits; the list could easily be extended.

A project portfolio system is discussed next with emphasis on selection criteria, which is where the power of the portfolio system is established.

EXHIBIT 2.2
Benefits of Project Portfolio Management

- Builds discipline into project selection process.
- Links project selection to strategic metrics.
- Prioritizes project proposals across a common set of criteria, rather than on politics or emotion.
- Allocates resources to projects that align with strategic direction.
- Balances risk across all projects.
- Justifies killing projects that do not support organization strategy.
- Improves communication and supports agreement on project goals.

A Portfolio Management System

Succinctly put, the aim of portfolio management is to ensure that projects are aligned with strategic goals and prioritized appropriately. As Foti points out, portfolio management asks "What is strategic to our organization?" Portfolio management provides information that allows people to make better business decisions. Since projects clamoring for funding and people usually outnumber available resources, it is important to follow a logical and defined process for selecting the projects to implement.

Design of a project portfolio system should include classification of a project, selection criteria depending upon classification, sources of proposals, evaluating proposals, and managing the portfolio of projects.

Classification of the Project

Many organizations find they have three different kinds of projects in their portfolio: *compliance* and emergency (must do), *operational,* and *strategic* projects. (See Figure 2.2.) Compliance projects are typically those needed to meet regulatory conditions required to operate in a region; hence, they are called "must do" projects. Emergency projects, such as rebuilding a soybean factory destroyed by fire, meet the must do criterion. Compliance and emergency projects usually have penalties if they are not implemented. Operational projects are those that are needed to support current operations. These projects are designed to improve efficiency of delivery systems, reduce product costs, and improve performance. Total quality management (TQM) projects are examples of operational projects. Finally, strategic projects are those that directly support the organization's long-run mission. They frequently are directed toward increasing revenue or market share. Examples of strategic projects are new products, research, and development. For a good, complete discussion on classification schemes found in practice, see Crawford, Hobbs, and Turne.

The strategic value of a proposed project must be determined before it can be placed in the project portfolio. Under rare circumstances, there are projects that "must" be selected. These compliance or emergency projects are those that must be implemented or the firm will fail or suffer dire penalties or consequences. For example, a manufacturing plant must install an electrostatic filter on top of a smokestack in six months or close down. EU courts are trying to force Microsoft to open their software architecture to allow competing software firms to be

FIGURE 2.2
Portfolio of Projects by Type

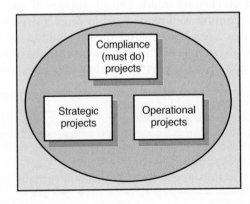

compatible and interact with Microsoft. This decision may become a compliance project for Microsoft. Any project placed in the "must" category ignores other selection criteria. A rule of thumb for placing a proposed project in this category is that 99 percent of the organization stakeholders would agree that the project must be implemented; there is no perceived choice but to implement the project. All other projects are selected using selection criteria linked to organization strategy.

Selection Criteria

Although there are many criteria for selecting projects, selection criteria are typically identified as *financial* and *nonfinancial*. A short description of each is given next, followed by a discussion of their use in practice.

Financial Criteria

Financial Models   For most managers financial criteria are the preferred method to evaluate projects. These models are appropriate when there is a high level of confidence associated with estimates of future cash flows. Two models and examples are demonstrated here—payback and **net present value** (NPV).

Project A has an initial investment of $700,000 and projected cash inflows of $225,000 for 5 years.

Project B has an initial investment of $400,000 and projected cash inflows of $110,000 for 5 years.

1. The payback model measures the time it will take to recover the project investment. Shorter paybacks are more desirable. Payback is the simplest and most widely used model. Payback emphasizes cash flows, a key factor in business. Some managers use the payback model to eliminate unusually risky projects (those with lengthy payback periods). The major limitations of payback are that it ignores the time value of money, assumes cash inflows for the investment period (and not beyond), and does not consider profitability. The payback formula is

Payback period (yrs) = Estimated Project Cost/Annual Savings

Exhibit 2.3 compares the payback for Project A and Project B. The payback for Project A is 3.1 years and for Project B is 3.6 years. Using the payback method both projects are acceptable since both return the initial investment in less than five years and have returns on the investment of 32.1 and 27.5 percent.

Exhibit 2.3 A presents the net present value model.

2. The net present value (NPV) model uses management's minimum desired rate-of-return (discount rate, for example, 20 percent) to compute the present value of all net cash inflows. If the result is positive (the project meets the minimum desired rate of return), it is eligible for further consideration. If the result is negative, the project is rejected. Thus, higher positive NPV's are desirable. Excel uses this formula

$$\text{Project NPV} = I_0 + \sum_{t=1}^{n} \frac{F_t}{(1 + k)^t} \quad \text{where}$$

I_0 = Initial investment (since it is an outflow, the number will be negative)
F_t = Net cash inflow for period t
k = Required rate of return

EXHIBIT 2.3 **Example Comparing Two Projects Using Payback and Net Present Value Method**

	A	B	C	D	E	F	G	H	I	J	K	L	M
1					Exhibit 2.3A								
2													
3				Example Comparing Two Projects Using the Payback Method									
4													
5				Project A		Project B				Formulas			
6													
7													
8		Investment		$700,000		$400,000				Project A: Payback = (D8/D9)			
9		Annual savings		$225,000		$110,000				Project B: Payback = (F8/F9)			
10													
11		Payback period*		3.1 years		3.6 years							
12													
13		Rate of return **		32.1%		27.5%				Project A: Rate of return = (D9/D8)			
14										Project B: Rate of return = (F9/F8)			
15	Project A: Accept. Less than 5 years and exceeds 15% desired rate.												
16													
17	Project B: Accept. Less than 5 years and exceeds 15% desired rate.												
18													
19	* Note: Payback does not use the time value of money.												
20	** Note: Rate of return is reciprocal of Payback.												
21													
22													

J3   ▾   *fx*

	A	B	C	D	E	F	G	H	I	J	K	L	M
1													
2					Exhibit 2.3B								
3													
4				Example Comparing Two Projects Using NPV									
5	Project A		Year 0	Year 1	Year 2	Year 3	Year 4	Year 5	Total		Formulas		
6	Required	15%											
7	Outflows		-$700,000						-$700,000				
8	Inflows			$225,000	$225,000	$225,000	$225,000	$225,000	$1,125,000				
9	Net inflows			$225,000	$225,000	$225,000	$225,000	$225,000	$425,000	Project A: =C7+NPV(B6,D9:H9)			
10	NPV	$54,235											
11													
12													
13	Project B												
14	Required	15%											
15	Outflows		-$400,000						-$400,000				
16	Inflows			$110,000	$110,000	$110,000	$110,000	$110,000	$550,000				
17	Net inflows			$110,000	$110,000	$110,000	$110,000	$110,000	$150,000	Project B: =C15+NPV(B14,D17:H17)			
18	NPV	-$31,263											
19													
20													
21													
22	NPV comparison: Accept Project A—NPV is positive.												
23	Reject Project B—NPV is negative.												

Exhibit 2.3B presents the NPV model using Microsoft Excel software. The NPV model accepts project A, which has a *positive* NPV of $54,235. Project B is rejected since the NPV is *negative* $31,263. Compare the NPV results with the payback results. The NPV model is more realistic because it considers the time value of money, cash flows, and profitability.

When using the NPV model, the discount rate (return on investment hurdle rate) can differ for different projects. For example, the expected ROI on strategic projects is frequently set higher than operational projects. Similarly, ROI's can differ for riskier versus safer projects. The criteria for setting the ROI hurdle rate should be clear and applied consistently.

Unfortunately, pure financial models fail to include many projects where financial return is impossible to measure and/or other factors are vital to the accept or reject decision. One research study by Foti showed that companies using predominantly financial models to prioritize projects yielded unbalanced portfolios and projects that aren't strategically oriented. Other studies make similar claims.

Nonfinancial Criteria

Financial return, while important, does not always reflect strategic importance. The sixties and seventies saw firms become overextended by diversifying too much. Now the prevailing thinking is that long-term survival is dependent upon developing and maintaining core competencies. Companies have to be disciplined in saying no to potentially profitable projects that are outside the realm of their core mission. This requires other criteria be considered beyond direct financial return. For example, a firm may support projects that do not have high profit margins for other strategic reasons including:

To capture larger market share

To make it difficult for competitors to enter the market

To develop an enabler product, which by its introduction will increase sales in more profitable products

To develop core technology that will be used in next-generation products

To reduce dependency on unreliable suppliers

To prevent government intervention and regulation

Less tangible criteria may also apply. Organizations may support projects to restore corporate image or enhance brand recognition. Many organizations are committed to corporate citizenship and support community development projects.

Since no single criterion can reflect strategic significance, portfolio management requires multi-criteria screening models. These models often weight individual criteria so those projects that contribute to the most important strategic objectives are given higher consideration.

Two Multi-Criteria Selection Models

Since no single criterion can reflect strategic significance, portfolio management requires multi-criteria screening models. Two models, the checklist and multi-weighted scoring models, are described next.

Checklist Models
The most frequently used method in selecting projects has been the checklist. This approach basically uses a list of questions to review potential projects and to determine their acceptance or rejection. Several of the typical questions found in practice are listed in Exhibit 2.4. One large, multiproject organization has 250 different questions!

A justification of checklist models is that they allow great flexibility in selecting among many different types of projects and are easily used across different divisions and locations. Although many projects are selected using some variation

EXHIBIT 2.4
Sample Selection Questions Used in Practice

Topic	Question
Strategy/alignment	What specific organization strategy does this project align with?
Driver	What business problem does the project solve?
Success metrics	How will we measure success?
Sponsorship	Who is the project sponsor?
Risk	What is the impact of not doing this project?
Risk	What is the project risk to our organization?
Risk	Where does the proposed project fit in our risk profile?
Benefits, value, ROI	What is the value of the project to this organization?
Benefits, value, ROI	When will the project show results?
Objectives	What are the project objectives?
Organization culture	Is our organization culture right for this type of project?
Resources	Will internal resources be available for this project?
Approach	Will we build or buy?
Schedule	How long will this project take?
Schedule	Is the time line realistic?
Training/resources	Will staff training be required?
Finance/portfolio	What is the estimated cost of the project?
Portfolio	Is this a new initiative or part of an existing initiative?
Portfolio	How does this project interact with current projects?
Technology	Is the technology available or new?

of the checklist approach, this approach has serious shortcomings. Major shortcomings of this approach are that it fails to answer the relative importance or value of a potential project to the organization and fails to allow for comparison with other potential projects. Each potential project will have a different set of positive and negative answers. How do you compare? Ranking and prioritizing projects by their importance is difficult, if not impossible. This approach also leaves the door open to the potential opportunity for power plays, politics, and other forms of manipulation. To overcome these serious shortcomings experts recommend the use of a multi-weighted scoring model to select projects, which is examined next.

Multi-Weighted Scoring Models   A weighted scoring model typically uses several weighted selection criteria to evaluate project proposals. Weighted scoring models will generally include qualitative and/or quantitative criteria. Each selection criterion is asssigned a weight. Scores are assigned to each criterion for the project, based on its importance to the project being evaluated. The weights and scores are multiplied to get a total weighted score for the project. Using these multiple screening criteria, projects can then be compared using the weighted score. Projects with higher weighted scores are considered better.

Selection criteria need to mirror the critical success factors of an organization. For example, 3M set a target that 25 percent of the company's sales would come from products fewer than four years old versus the old target of 20 percent. Their priority system for project selection strongly reflects this new target. On the other hand, failure to pick the right factors will render the screening process "useless" in short order. See Snapshot from Practice: Crisis IT.

Figure 2.3 represents a project scoring matrix using some of the factors found in practice. The screening criteria selected are shown across the top of the matrix

SNAPSHOT FROM PRACTICE   Crisis IT

In May 2007, Frontier Airlines Holdings hired Gerry Coady as chief information officer (CIO). Nearly a year later the airline filed for bankruptcy under Chapter 11. In an interview Coady describes how he managed IT projects during the bankruptcy and recession crisis of 2008–2009.

Fundamentally, Coady faced a situation of too many projects and too few resources. Coady used a strategy of focusing on reducing the number of projects in the portfolio. He put together a steering committee of senior management that reviewed several hundred projects. The end result was a reduction to less than 30 projects remaining in the portfolio.

© PRNewsFoto/Genesis, Inc.

How Can You Get to a Backlog of over 100 Projects?

"There are never enough resources to get everything done." Backlogs build over time. Sacred cow projects get included in the selection system. Projects proposed from people who have left the airline still reside in the project portfolio. Non-value-added projects somehow make their way into the project portfolio. Soon the queue gets longer. With everyone in IT working on too many projects concurrently, project completion and productivity are slow.

Which Projects Remain?

To cut the number of projects, the steering committee used a weighting scheme that reflected the airline's priorities, which were: fly safe, generate revenue, reduce costs, and customer service. The weighting scheme easily weeded out the fluff.

Coady noted that "by the time you get to the 20s the margin of differentiation gets narrower and narrower." Of the remaining projects, project sponsors had to have solid justification why their project is important. Reduction of the number of projects places emphasis on high value projects.

What Advice Does Coady Have for Crisis Management?

In times of crisis, it is easier to take bold steps to make changes. But you need to have a clear vision of what you should be focusing on with the resources available. Coady suggests, "It comes back to really having a good idea of what the initial business case for a project is and what resources it is consuming, both people and otherwise."

Source: Worthen, B., "Crisis IT," *The Wall Street Journal*, April 20, 2009, p-R6.

FIGURE 2.3
Project Screening Matrix

Criteria / Weight	Stay within core competencies	Strategic fit	Urgency	25% of sales from new products	Reduce defects to less than 1%	Improve customer loyalty	ROI of 18% plus	Weighted total
	2.0	3.0	2.0	2.5	1.0	1.0	3.0	
Project 1	1	8	2	6	0	6	5	66
Project 2	3	3	2	0	0	5	1	27
Project 3	9	5	2	0	2	2	5	56
Project 4	3	0	10	0	0	6	0	32
Project 5	1	10	5	10	0	8	9	102
Project 6	6	5	0	2	0	2	7	55
⋮								
Project n	5	5	7	0	10	10	8	83

(e.g., stay within core competencies . . . ROI of 18 percent plus). Management weights each criterion (a value of 0 to a high of, say, 3) by its relative importance to the organization's objectives and strategic plan. Project proposals are then submitted to a project **priority team** or project office.

Each project proposal is then evaluated by its relative contribution/value added to the selected criteria. Values of 0 to a high of 10 are assigned to each criterion for each project. This value represents the project's fit to the specific criterion. For example, project 1 appears to fit well with the strategy of the organization since it is given a value of 8. Conversely, project 1 does nothing to support reducing defects (its value is 0). Finally, this model applies the management weights to each criterion by importance using a value of 1 to 3. For example, ROI and strategic fit have a weight of 3, while urgency and core competencies have weights of 2. Applying the weight to each criterion, the priority team derives the weighted total points for each project. For example, project 5 has the highest value of 102 $[(2 \times 1) + (3 \times 10) + (2 \times 5) + (2.5 \times 10) + (1 \times 0) + (1 \times 8) + (3 \times 9) = 102]$ and project 2 has a low value of 27. If the resources available create a cutoff threshold of 50 points, the priority team would eliminate projects 2 and 4. (Note: Project 4 appears to have some urgency, but it is not classified as a "must" project. Therefore, it is screened with all other proposals.) Project 5 would receive first priority, project n second, and so on. In rare cases where resources are severely limited and project proposals are similar in weighted rank, it is prudent to pick the project placing less demand on resources. Weighted multiple criteria models similar to this one are rapidly becoming the dominant choice for prioritizing projects.

At this point in the discussion it is wise to stop and put things into perspective. While selection models like the one above may yield numerical solutions to project selection decisions, models should not make the final *decisions*—the people using the models should. No model, no matter how sophisticated, can capture the total reality it is meant to represent. Models are tools for guiding the evaluation process so that the decision-makers will consider relevant issues and reach a meeting of the minds as to which projects should be supported and not supported. This is a much more subjective process than calculations suggest.

Applying a Selection Model

Project Classification It is not necessary to have exactly the same criteria for the different types of projects discussed above (strategic and operations). However, experience shows most organizations use similar criteria across all types of projects, with perhaps one or two criteria specific to the type of project—e.g., strategic breakthrough versus operational.

Regardless of criteria differences among different types of projects, the most important criterion for selection is the project's fit to the organization strategy. Therefore, this criterion should be consistent across all types of projects and carry a high priority relative to other criteria. This uniformity across all priority models used can keep departments from suboptimizing the use of organization resources. Anyone generating a project proposal should classify their proposal by type, so the appropriate criteria can be used to evaluate their proposal.

Selecting a Model   In the past, financial criteria were used almost to the exclusion of other criteria. However, in the last two decades we have witnessed a dramatic shift to include multiple criteria in project selection. Concisely put, profitability alone is simply not an adequate measure of contribution; however, it is still an important criterion, especially for projects that enhance revenue and market share such as breakthrough R&D projects.

Today, senior management is interested in identifying the potential mix of projects that will yield the best use of human and capital resources to maximize return on investment in the long run. Factors such as researching new technology, public image, ethical position, protection of the environment, core competencies, and strategic fit might be important criteria for selecting projects. Weighted scoring criteria seem the best alternative to meet this need.

Weighted scoring models result in bringing projects to closer alignment with strategic goals. If the scoring model is published and available to everyone in the organization, some discipline and credibility are attached to the selection of projects. The number of wasteful projects using resources is reduced. Politics and "sacred cow" projects are exposed. Project goals are more easily identified and communicated using the selection criteria as corroboration. Finally, using a weighted scoring approach helps project managers understand how their project was selected, how their project contributes to organization goals, and how it compares with other projects. Project selection is one of the most important decisions guiding the future success of an organization.

Criteria for project selection are the area where the power of your portfolio starts to manifest itself. New projects are aligned with the strategic goals of the organization. With a clear method for selecting projects in place, project proposals can be solicited.

Sources and Solicitation of Project Proposals

As you would guess, projects should come from anyone who believes his or her project will add value to the organization. However, many organizations restrict proposals from specific levels or groups within the organization. This could be an opportunity lost. Good ideas are not limited to certain types or classes of organization stakeholders. Encourage and keep solicitations open to all sources—internal and external sponsors.

Figure 2.4A provides an example of a proposal form for an automatic vehicular tracking (Automatic Vehicle Location) public transportation project. Figure 2.4B presents a preliminary risk analysis for a 500-acre wind farm. Many organizations use risk analysis templates to gain a quick insight of a project's inherent risks. This information is useful in balancing the project portfolio and identifying major risks when executing the project. Project risk analysis is the subject of Chapter 7.

In some cases organizations will solicit ideas for projects when the knowledge requirements for the project are not available in the organization. Typically, the organization will issue an RFP (Request for Proposal) to contractors/vendors with adequate experience to implement the project. In one example, a hospital published an RFP that asked for a bid to design and build a new operating room that uses the latest technology. Several architecture firms submitted bids to the hospital. The bids for the project were evaluated internally against other potential projects. When the project was accepted as a go, other criteria were used to select the best qualified bidder. See Appendix 2.1 of this chapter for a complete description of requests for proposal (RFP).

FIGURE 2.4A

A Proposal Form for an Automatic Vehicular Tracking (AVL) Public Transportation Project.

Project Proposal Form

Date: Jan 22, 2xxx   Proposal # 11   Sponsor J. Moran

Project classification?

Strategic_____ Infrastructure __X__ Compliance_____

What business problem does the project solve?

Increase customer satisfaction through kiosk and Web site for bus, streetcar, and fast rail
Enhance driver and traveler safety   Hyperlink to: AVL.tri-met.org

How does this project align with our organization strategy?

Increase customer ridership through better passenger travel planning & scheduling decisions
Faster response to accidents

What are the major deliverables of the project?

GPS vehicle tracking system, Internet access, schedule screen

What is the impact of not doing this project?

Not meeting ridership goals

What are the three major risks for this project?

Cost overruns   Integration of fast rail, bus, and streetcar systems
Hacking system

How will we measure success?   Increased ridership
                                   Customer satisfaction
                                   Meeting budget and schedule

Yes ☒ No ☐ Will this project require internal resources?
Yes ☒ No ☐ Available?

What is the estimated cost of the project? $10 million

How long will this project take? __22__ Weeks

Oversight action: Accept ☒   Return ☐

Signature __XXXXXX__   Date: Oct. 7, 2xxx

Ranking Proposals and Selection of Projects

Culling through so many proposals to identify those that add the most value requires a structured process. Figure 2.5 shows a flow chart of a screening process beginning with the creation of an idea for a project. See template for evaluating contractors in Appendix 2.1.

Data and information are collected to assess the value of the proposed project to the organization and for future backup. If the sponsor decides to pursue the project on the basis of the collected data, it is forwarded to the project priority

FIGURE 2.4B

**Risk Analysis for a
500-Acre Wind Farm**

What are the three major risks for this project?				
1. *Federal incentives curtailed*				
2. *Land use injunction*				
3. *Energy price decrease*				
What is the probability of the above risks occuring?	0 to 1.0 none high	Risk 1 above		*.30*
		Risk 2 above		*.20*
		Risk 3 above		*.10*
What is the impact on project success if these risks do occur?	0 to 1.0 none high	Risk 1 above		*1.0*
		Risk 2 above		*.30*
		Risk 3 above		*.10*

RESOURCES AVAILABLE? ____X____ Yes _____ No

CURRENT PROJECT STATUS

Start date ___*2/22/xx*___ **Estimated finish date** ___*9/25/xx*___

STATUS: ☐ **Active** ☐ **On-hold**

UPDATE:

   Start in 3 weeks

PRIORITY TEAM ACTION: ☒ **ACCEPTED** ☐ **RETURNED**

☐ DISCOVERY—project not defined ☒ Duplicate to: *Dat Nguyen*

☐ OPERATIONAL—proposal not a project Project # | 676 |

☐ NEED MORE INFORMATION—to prioritize project ☐ COMPLETED project

team (or the project office). Note that the sponsor knows which criteria will be used to accept or reject the project. Given the selection criteria and current portfolio of projects, the priority team rejects or accepts the project. If the project is accepted, the priority team sets implementation in motion.

Figure 2.6 is a partial example of an evaluation form used by a large company to prioritize and select new projects. The form distinguishes between must and want objectives. If a project does not meet designated "must" objectives, it is not considered and removed from consideration. Organization (or division) objectives have been ranked and weighted by their relative importance—for example, "Improve external customer service" carries a relative weight of 83 when compared to other want objectives. The want objectives are directly linked to objectives found in the strategic plan.

FIGURE 2.5

Project Screening Process

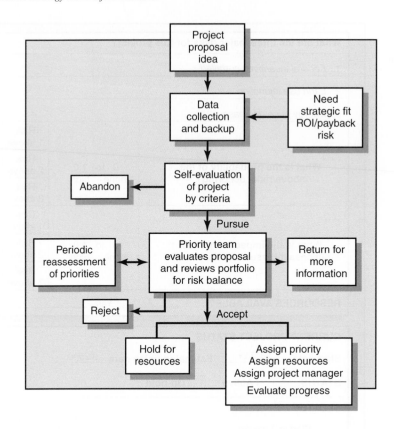

Impact definitions represent a further refinement to the screening system. They are developed to gauge the predicted impact a specific project would have on meeting a particular objective. A numeric scheme is created and anchored by defining criteria. To illustrate how this works, let's examine the $5 million in new sales objective. A "0" is assigned if the project will have no impact on sales or less than $100,000, a "1" is given if predicted sales are more than $100,000 but less than $500,000, a "2" if greater than $500,000. These impact assessments are combined with the relative importance of each objective to determine the predicted overall contribution of a project to strategic objectives. For example, project 26 creates an opportunity to fix field problems, has no effect on sales, and will have major impact on customer service. On these three objectives, project 26 would receive a score of 265 [99 + 0 + (2 × 83)]. Individual weighted scores are totaled for each project and are used to prioritize projects.

Responsibility for Prioritizing

Prioritizing can be an uncomfortable exercise for managers. But prioritizing projects is a major responsibility for senior management. Prioritizing means discipline, accountability, responsibility, constraints, reduced flexibility, and loss of power. Top management commitment means more than giving a blessing to the priority system; it means management will have to rank and weigh, in concrete terms, the objectives and strategies they believe to be most critical to the organization. This public declaration of commitment can be risky if the ranked objectives later prove to be poor choices, but setting the course for the organization is

FIGURE 2.6
Priority Analysis

Must objectives	Must meet if impacts	...26	27	28	29
		Project number			
All activities meet current legal, safety, and environmental standards	Yes-Meets objective No-Does not meet obj N/A-No impact	**n/a**			
All new products will have a complete market analysis	Yes-Meets objective No-Does not meet obj N/A-No impact	**yes**			
Want objectives	Relative Importance 1-100 / Single project impact definitions	Weighted score	Weighted score	Weighted score	Weighted score
Provides immediate response to field problems	**99** — 0 ≤ Does not address 1 = Opportunity to fix 2 ≥ Urgent problem	**99**			
Create $5 million in new sales by 20xx	**88** — 0 < $100,000 1 = $100,000–500,000 2 > $500,000	**0**			
Improve external customer service	**83** — 0 ≤ Minor impact 1 = Significant impact 2 ≥ Major impact	**166**			
Total weighted score					
Priority					

top management's job. The good news is, if management is truly trying to direct the organization to a strong future position, a good project priority system supports their efforts and develops a culture in which everyone is contributing to the goals of the organization.

Managing the Portfolio System

Managing the portfolio takes the selection system one step higher in that the merits of a particular project are assessed within the context of existing projects. At the same time it involves monitoring and adjusting selection criteria to reflect the strategic focus of the organization. This requires constant effort. The priority system can be managed by a small group of key employees in a small organization. Or, in larger organizations, the priority system can be managed by the project office or the enterprise management group.

Senior Management Input

Management of a portfolio system requires two major inputs from senior management. First, senior management must provide guidance in establishing selection criteria that strongly align with the current organization strategies. Second, senior management must annually decide how they wish to balance the available organizational resources (people and capital) among the different types of projects. A preliminary decision of balance must be made by top management (e.g., 20 percent compliance, 50 percent strategic, and 30 percent operational) before project selection takes place, although the balance may be changed when the projects submitted are reviewed. Given these inputs the priority team or project office can carry out its many responsibilities, which include supporting project sponsors and representing the interests of the total organization.

The Priority Team Responsibilities

The priority team, or project office, is responsible for publishing the priority of every project and ensuring the process is open and free of power politics. For example, most organizations using a priority team or project office use an electronic bulletin board to disperse the current portfolio of projects, the current status of each project, and current issues. This open communication discourages power plays. Over time the priority team evaluates the progress of the projects in the portfolio. If this whole process is managed well, it can have a profound impact on the success of an organization.

Constant scanning of the external environment to determine if organizational focus and/or selection criteria need to be changed is imperative! Periodic priority review and changes need to keep current with the changing environment and keep a unified vision of organization focus. Regardless of the criteria used for selection, each project should be evaluated by the same criteria. If projects are classified by must do, operation, and strategic, each project in its class should be evaluated by the same criteria. Enforcing the project priority system is crucial. Keeping the whole system open and aboveboard is important to maintaining the integrity of the system and keeping new, young executives from going around the system. For example, communicating which projects are approved, project ranks, current status of in-process projects, and any changes in priority criteria will discourage people from bypassing the system.

Balancing the Portfolio for Risks and Types of Projects

A major responsibility of the priority team is to balance projects by type, risk, and resource demand. This requires a total organization perspective. Hence, a proposed project that ranks high on most criteria may not be selected because the organization portfolio already includes too many projects with the same characteristics—e.g., project risk level, use of key resources, high cost, nonrevenue producing, long durations. Balancing the portfolio of projects is as important as project selection. Organizations need to evaluate each new project in terms of what it adds to the project mix. Short-term needs need to be balanced with long-term potential. Resource usage needs to be optimized across all projects, not just the most important project.

Two types of risk are associated with projects. First are risks associated with the total portfolio of projects, which should reflect the organization's risk profile. Second are specific project risks that can inhibit the execution of a project, such as

FIGURE 2.7
**Project Portfolio
Matrix**

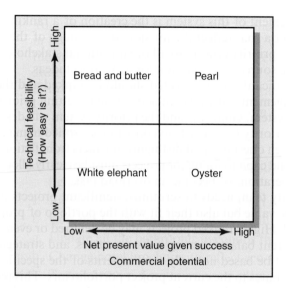

schedule, cost, and technical. In this chapter we look only to balancing the organizational risks inherent in the project portfolio, such as market risk, ability to execute, time to market, and technology advances. Project-specific risks will be covered in detail in Chapter 7.

David and Jim Matheson studied R&D organizations and developed a matrix that could be used for assessing a project portfolio (see Figure 2.7). The vertical axis the degree of difficulty. The horizontal axis reflects potential commercial value. The grid has four quadrants, each with different project dimensions.

Bread and butter projects typically involve evolutionary improvements to current products and services. Examples include software upgrades and manufacturing cost reduction efforts.

Pearls represent revolutionary commercial advances using proven technical advances. Examples include next-generation integrated circuit chip and subsurface imaging to locate oil and gas.

Oysters involve technological breakthroughs with high commercial payoffs. Examples include embryonic DNA treatments and new kinds of metal alloys.

White elephants are projects that at one time showed promise but are no longer viable. Examples include products for a saturated market or a potent energy source with toxic side effects.

The Mathesons report that organizations often have too many white elephants and too few pearls and oysters. To maintain strategic advantage they recommend that organizations capitalize on pearls, eliminate or reposition white elephants, and balance resources devoted to bread-and-butter and oyster projects to achieve alignment with overall strategy. Although their research centers on R&D organizations, their observations appear to hold true for all types of project organizations.

Summary

Multiple competing projects, limited skilled resources, dispersed virtual teams, time to market pressures, and limited capital serve as forces for the emergence of project portfolio management that provides the infrastructure for managing multiple projects and linking business strategy with project selection. The most

5.* You are the head of the project selection team at SIMSOX. Your team is considering three different projects. Based on past history, SIMSOX expects at least a rate of return of 20 percent. Your financial advisors predict inflation to remain at 3 percent into the foreseeable future.

Given the following information for each project, which one should be SIMSOX first priority? Should SIMSOX fund any of the other projects? If so, what should be the order of priority based on return on investment?

Project: **Dust Devils**

Year	Investment	Revenue Stream
0	$500,000	0
1		50,000
2		250,000
3		350,000

Project: **Ospry**

Year	Investment	Revenue Stream
0	$250,000	0
1		75,000
2		75,000
3		75,000
4		50,000

Project: **Voyagers**

Year	Investment	Revenue Stream
0	$75,000	0
1		15,000
2		25,000
3		50,000
4		50,000
5		150,000

6. You are the head of the project selection team at Broken Arrow records. Your team is considering three different recording projects. Based on past history, Broken Arrow expects at least a rate of return of 20 percent. Your financial advisors predict inflation to remain at 2 percent into the foreseeable future.

Given the following information for each project, which one should be Broken Arrow's first priority? Should Broken Arrow fund any of the other projects? If so, what should be the order of priority based on return on investment?

Recording Project: **Time Fades Away**

Year	Investment	Revenue Stream
0	$600,000	0
1		600,000
2		75,000
3		20,000
4		15,000
5		10,000

* The solution to this exercise can be found in Appendix One.

Recording Project: **On the Beach**

Year	Investment	Revenue Stream
0	$400,000	0
1		400,000
2		100,000
3		25,000
4		20,000
5		10,000

Recording Project: **Tonight's the Night**

Year	Investment	Revenue Stream
0	$200,000	0
1		200,000
2		125,000
3		75,000
4		20,000
5		10,000

7. The Custom Bike Company has set up a weighted scoring matrix for evaluation of potential projects. Below are three projects under consideration.

   a. Using the scoring matrix below, which project would you rate highest? Lowest?

   b. If the weight for "Strong Sponsor" is changed from 2.0 to 5.0, will the project selection change? What are the three highest weighted project scores with this new weight?

   c. Why is it important that the weights mirror critical strategic factors?

Project Screening Matrix

Criteria / Weight	Strong sponsor	Supports business strategy	Urgency	10% of sales from new products	Competition	Fill market gap	Weighted total
	2.0	5.0	4.0	3.0	1.0	3.0	
Project 1	9	5	2	0	2	5	
Project 2	3	7	2	0	5	1	
Project 3	6	8	2	3	6	8	
Project 4	1	0	5	10	6	9	
Project 5	3	10	10	1	8	0	

References

Adler, P. S., et al, "Getting the Most Out of Your Product Development Process," *Harvard Business Review,* vol. 74 (2), pp. 134–52.

Benko, C., and F. W. McFarlan, *Connecting the Dots: Aligning Projects With Objectives in Unpredictable Times* (Boston: Harvard Business School Press, 2003).

Bigelow, D., "Want to Ensure Quality? Think Project Portfolio Management," *PM Network,* vol. 16 (1) April 2002, pp. 16–17.

Boyer, C., "Make Profit Your Priority," *PM Network,* vol. 15 (10) October 2003, pp. 37–42.

Cohen, D., and R. Graham, *The Project Manager's MBA* (San Francisco: Jossey-Bass, 2001), pp. 58–59.

Crawford, L., B. Hobbs, and J. R. Turne, "Aligning Capability with Strategy: Categorizing of Projects to Do the Right Projects and Do Them Right," *Project Management Journal,* vol. 37 (2) June 2006, pp. 38–50.

Descamps, J. P., "Mastering the Dance of Change: Innovation as a Way of Life," *Prism,* Second Quarter, 1999, pp. 61–67.

Doran, G. T., "There's a Smart Way to Write Management Goals and Objectives," *Management Review,* November 1981, pp. 35–36.

Floyd, S. W., and B. Woolridge, "Managing Strategic Consensus: The Foundation of Effectiveness Implementation," *Academy of Management Executives,* vol. 6 (4) 1992, pp. 27–39.

Foti, R., "Louder Than Words," *PM Network,* December 2002, pp. 22–29.

Frank, L., "On Demand," *PM Network,* vol. 18 (4) April 2004, pp. 58–62.

Friedman, Thomas L., *Hot, Flat, and Crowded* (New York: Farrar, Straus, and Giroux, 2008).

Fusco, J. C., "Better Policies Provide the Key to Implementing Project Management," *Project Management Journal,* vol. 28 (3) 1997, pp. 38–41.

Helm, J., and K. Remington, "Effective Project Sponsorship: An Evaluation of the Executive Sponsor in Complex Infrastructure Projects by Senior Project Managers," *Project Management Journal,* vol. 36 (1) September 2005, pp. 51–61.

Hutchens, G., "Doing the Numbers," *PM Network,* vol. 16 (4) March 2002, p. 20.

Johnson, R. E., "Scrap Capital Project Evaluations," *Chief Financial Officer,* May 1998, p. 14.

Kaplan, R. S., and D. P. Norton, "The Balanced Scorecard—Measures That Drive Performance," *Harvard Business Review,* January–February 1992, pp. 73–79.

Kenny, J., "Effective Project Management for Strategic Innovation and Change in an Organizational Context," *Project Management Journal,* vol. 34 (1) 2003, pp. 45–53.

Kharbanda, O. P., and J. K. Pinto, *What Made Gertie Gallop: Learning from Project Failures* (New York: Van Nostrand Reinhold, 1996), pp. 106–11, 263–83.

Korte, R. F., and T. J. Chermack, "Changing Organizational Culture with Scenario Planning," *Futures,* vol. 39 (6) August 2007, pp. 645–56.

Leifer, R., C. M. McDermott, G. C. O'Connor, L. S. Peters, M. Price, and R. W. Veryzer, *Radical Innovation: How Mature Companies Can Outsmart Upstarts* (Boston: Harvard Business School Press, 2000).

MacIntyre, J., *PM Network,* vol. 20 (11) November 2006, pp. 32–35.

Matheson, D., and J. Matheson, *The Smart Organization* (Boston: Harvard Business School Press, 1998), pp. 203–09.

Milosevic, D. Z., and S. Srivannaboon, "A Theoretical Framework for Aligning Project Management with Business Strategy," *Project Management Journal,* vol. 37 (3) August 2006, pp. 98–110.

Morris, P. W., and A. Jamieson, "Moving from Corporate Strategy to Project Strategy," *Project Management Journal,* vol. 36 (4) December 2005, pp. 5–18.

Raskin, P., et al, *Great Transitions: The Promise and Lure of the Times Ahead,* retrieved 6-3-08. See *www.gtinitiative.org/documents/Great_Transitions.pdf*

Schwartz, Peter, and Doug Randall, "An Abrupt Climate Change Scenario and its Implications for United States National Security," Global Business Network, Inc., October 2003.

Shenhar, A., "Strategic Project Leadership: Focusing Your Project on Business Success," *Proceedings of the Project Management Institute Annual Seminars & Symposium,* San Antonio, Texas, October 3–10, 2002, CD.

Woodward, H., "Winning in a World of Limited Project Spending," *Proceedings of the Project Management Institute Global Congress North America,* Baltimore, Maryland, September 18–12, 2003, CD.

Case

Hector Gaming Company

Hector Gaming Company (HGC) is an educational gaming company specializing in young children's educational games. HGC has just completed their fourth year of operation. This year was a banner year for HGC. The company received a large influx of capital for growth by issuing stock privately through an investment banking firm. It appears the return on investment for this past year will be just over 25 percent with zero debt! The growth rate for the last two years has been approximately 80 percent each year. Parents and grandparents of young children have been buying HGC's products almost as fast as they are developed. Every member of the 56-person firm is enthusiastic and looking forward to helping the firm grow to be the largest and best educational gaming company in the world. The founder of the firm, Sally Peters, has been written up in *Young Entrepreneurs* as "the young entrepreneur to watch." She has been able to develop an organization culture in which all stakeholders are committed to innovation, continuous improvement, and organization learning.

Last year, 10 top managers of HGC worked with McKinley Consulting to develop the organization's strategic plan. This year the same 10 managers had a retreat in Aruba to formulate next year's strategic plan using the same process suggested by McKinley Consulting. Most executives seem to have a consensus of where the firm should go in the intermediate and long term. But there is little consensus on how this should be accomplished. Peters, now president of HGC, feels she may be losing control. The frequency of conflicts seems to be increasing. Some individuals are always requested for any new project created. When resource conflicts occur among projects, each project manager believes his or her project is most important. More projects are not meeting deadlines and are coming in over budget. Yesterday's management meeting revealed some top HGC talent have been working on an international business game for college students. This project does not fit the organization vision or market niche. At times it seems everyone is marching to his or her own drummer. Somehow more focus is needed to ensure everyone agrees on *how* strategy should be implemented, given the resources available to the organization.

Yesterday's meeting alarmed Peters. These emerging problems are coming at a bad time. Next week HGC is ramping up the size of the organization, number of new products per year, and marketing efforts. Fifteen new people will join HGC next month. Peters is concerned that policies be in place that will ensure the new people are used most productively. An additional potential problem looms on the horizon. Other gaming companies have noticed the success HGC is having in their niche market; one company tried to hire a key product development employee away from HGC. Peters wants HGC to be ready to meet any potential competition head on and to discourage any new entries into their market. Peters knows HGC is project driven; however, she is not as confident that she has a good handle on how such an organization should be managed—especially with such a fast growth rate and potential competition closer to becoming a reality. The magnitude of emerging problems demands quick attention and resolution.

Peters has hired you as a consultant. She has suggested the following format for your consulting contract. You are free to use another format if it will improve the effectiveness of the consulting engagement.

What is our major problem?

Identify some symptoms of the problem.

What is the major cause of the problem?

Provide a detailed action plan that attacks the problem. Be specific and provide examples that relate to HGC.

Case

Film Prioritization

The purpose of this case is to give you experience in using a project priority system that ranks proposed projects by their contribution to the organization's objectives and strategic plan.

COMPANY PROFILE

The company is the film division for a large entertainment conglomerate. The main office is located in Anaheim, California. In addition to the feature film division, the conglomerate includes theme parks, home videos, a television channel, interactive games, and theatrical productions. The company has been enjoying steady growth over the past 10 years. Last year total revenues increased by 12 percent to $21.2 billion. The company is engaged in negotiations to expand its theme park empire to mainland China and Poland. The film division generated $274 million in revenues, which was an increase of 7 percent over the past year. Profit margin was down 3 percent to 16 percent because of the poor response to three of the five major film releases for the year.

COMPANY MISSION

The mission for the firm:

Our overriding objective is to create shareholder value by continuing to be the world's premier entertainment company from a creative, strategic, and financial standpoint.

The film division supports this mission by producing four to six high-quality, family entertainment films for mass distribution each year. In recent years, the CEO of the company has advocated that the firm take a leadership position in championing environmental concerns.

COMPANY "MUST" OBJECTIVES

Every project must meet the must objectives as determined by executive management. It is important that selected film projects not violate such objectives of high strategic priority. There are three must objectives:

1. All projects meet current legal, safety, and environmental standards.
2. All film projects should receive a PG or lower advisory rating.
3. All projects should not have an adverse effect on current or planned operations within the larger company.

COMPANY "WANT" OBJECTIVES

Want objectives are assigned weights for their relative importance. Top management is responsible for formulating, ranking, and weighting objectives to ensure that projects support the company's strategy and mission. The following is a list of the company's want objectives:

1. Be nominated for and win an academy award for Best Picture of the Year.
2. Create at least one new animated character each year that can star in a cartoon or TV series.
3. Generate additional merchandise revenue (action figures, dolls, interactive games, music CDs).
4. Raise public consciousness about environmental issues and concerns.
5. Generate profit in excess of 18 percent.
6. Advance the state of the art in film animation, and preserve the firm's reputation.
7. Provide the basis for the development of a new ride at a company-owned theme park.

ASSIGNMENT

You are a member of the priority team in charge of evaluating and selecting film proposals. Use the provided evaluation form to formally evaluate and rank each proposal. Be prepared to report your rankings and justify your decisions.

Assume that all of the projects have passed the estimated hurdle rate of 14 percent ROI. In addition to the brief film synopsis, the proposals include the following financial projections of theater and video sales: 80 percent chance of ROI, 50 percent chance of ROI, and 20 percent chance of ROI.

For example, for proposal #1 (Dalai Lama) there is an 80 percent chance that it will earn at least 8 percent return on investment (ROI), a 50-50 chance the ROI will be 18 percent, and a 20 percent chance that the ROI will be 24 percent.

FILM PROPOSALS

PROJECT PROPOSAL 1: MY LIFE WITH DALAI LAMA

An animated, biographical account of the Dalai Lama's childhood in Tibet based on the popular children's book *Tales from Nepal*. The Lama's life is told through the eyes of "Guoda," a field snake, and other local animals who befriend the Dalai and help him understand the principles of Buddhism.

Probability	80%	50%	20%
ROI	8%	18%	24%

PROJECT PROPOSAL 2: HEIDI

A remake of the classic children's story with music written by award-winning composers Syskle and Obert. The big-budget film will feature top-name stars and breathtaking scenery of the Swiss Alps.

Probability	80%	50%	20%
ROI	2%	20%	30%

PROJECT PROPOSAL 3: THE YEAR OF THE ECHO

A low-budget documentary that celebrates the career of one of the most influential bands in rock-and-roll history. The film will be directed by new-wave director Elliot Cznerzy and will combine concert footage and behind-the-scenes interviews spanning the 25-year history of the rock band the Echos. In addition to great music, the film will focus on the death of one of the founding members from a heroin overdose and reveal the underworld of sex, lies, and drugs in the music industry.

Probability	80%	50%	20%
ROI	12%	14%	18%

PROJECT PROPOSAL 4: ESCAPE FROM RIO JAPUNI

An animated feature set in the Amazon rainforest. The story centers around Pablo, a young jaguar who attempts to convince warring jungle animals that they must unite and escape the devastation of local clear cutting.

Probability	80%	50%	20%
ROI	15%	20%	24%

PROJECT PROPOSAL 5: NADIA!

The story of Nadia Comaneci, the famous Romanian gymnast who won three gold medals at the 1976 Summer Olympic Games. The low-budget film will document her life as a small child in Romania and how she was chosen by Romanian authorities to join their elite, state-run, athletic program. The film will highlight how Nadia maintained her independent spirit and love for gymnastics despite a harsh, regimented training program.

Probability	80%	50%	20%
ROI	8%	15%	20%

PROJECT PROPOSAL 6: KEIKO—ONE WHALE OF A STORY

The story of Keiko, the famous killer whale, will be told by an imaginary offspring Seiko, who in the distant future is telling her children about their famous grandfather. The big-budget film will integrate actual footage of the whale within a realistic animated environment using state-of-the-art computer imagery. The story will reveal how Keiko responded to his treatment by humans.

Probability	80%	50%	20%
ROI	6%	18%	25%

Project Priority Evaluation Form

Must objectives	Must meet if impacts	1	2	3	4	5	6	7
Meets all safety and environmental standards	Y = yes N = no N/A = not applicable							
PG or G rating	Y = yes N = no N/A = not applicable							
No adverse effect on other operations	Y = yes N = no N/A = not applicable							

Want objectives	Relative Importance 1–100	Single project impact definitions	Weighted Score	Weighted Score	Weighted Score	Weighted Score	Weighted Score	Weighted Score	Weighted Score
Be nominated for Best Picture of the Year	60	0 = No potential 1 = Low potential 2 = High potential							
Create a new, major animated character	20	0 = No potential 1 = Low potential 2 = High potential							
Generate additional merchandise	10	0 = No potential 1 = Low potential 2 = High potential							
Raise environmental concerns	55	0 = No potential 1 = Low potential 2 = High potential							
Generate profit greater than 18%	70	0 < 18% 1 = 18–22% 2 > 22%							
Advance state of film animation	40	0 = No impact 1 = Some impact 2 = Great impact							
Provide basis for new theme ride	10	0 = No potential 1 = Low potential 2 = High potential							
		Total weighted score							
		Priority							

PROJECT 7: GRAND ISLAND

The true story of a group of junior-high biology students who discover that a fertilizer plant is dumping toxic wastes into a nearby river. The moderate-budget film depicts how students organize a grassroots campaign to fight local bureaucracy and ultimately force the fertilizer plant to restore the local ecosystem.

Probability	80%	50%	20%
ROI	9%	15%	20%

Appendix 2.1

Request for Proposal (RFP)

Once an organization selects a project, the customer or project manager is frequently responsible for developing a request for proposal (RFP) for the project or sections of the project.

The responsible project manager will require input data from all stakeholders connected to the activities covered in the RFP. The RFP will be announced to external contractors/vendors with adequate experience to implement the project. For example, government projects frequently advertise with a "request for proposal" to outside contractors for roads, buildings, airports, military hardware, space vehicles. Similarly, businesses use RFPs to solicit bids for building a clean room, developing a new manufacturing process, delivering software for insurance billing, conducting a market survey. In all of these examples, requirements and features must be in enough detail that contractors have a clear description of the final deliverable that will meet the customer's needs. In most cases the RFP also specifies an expected format for the contractor's bid proposal so the responses of different contractors can be fairly evaluated. Although we typically think of RFPs for external contractors, in some organizations RFPs are used internally; that is, the organization sends out an RFP to different divisions or departments.

The content of the RFP is extremely important. In practice, the most common error is to offer an RFP that lacks sufficient detail. This lack of detail typically results in conflict issues, misunderstandings, often legal claims between the contractor and owner, and, in addition, an unsatisfied customer. All RFPs are different, but the outline in Figure A2.1 is a good starting point for the development of a detailed RFP. Each step is briefly described next.

FIGURE A2.1
Request for Proposal

1. Summary of needs and request for action
2. Statement of work (SOW) detailing the scope and major deliverables
3. Deliverable specifications/requirements, features, and tasks
4. Responsibilities—vendor and customer
5. Project schedule
6. Costs and payment schedule
7. Type of contract
8. Experience and staffing
9. Evaluation criteria

1. Summary of needs and request for action. The background and a simple description of the final project deliverable are given first. For example, through simulated war games, the U.S. Navy has found their giant warships of the past are too vulnerable against today's technology (an example is the Silkworm antiship missiles). In addition, the Navy's mission has shifted to supporting ground forces and peacekeeping missions, which require getting closer to shore. As a result, the Navy is revamping ships for near-shore duty. The Navy will select three designs for further refinement from the responses to its RFP. In general, it is expected that the new ship will be capable of at least 55 knots, measure between 80 and 250 feet in length, and be fitted with radar absorbing panels to thwart guided missiles.

2. Statement of work (SOW) detailing the scope and major deliverables. For example, if the project involves a market research survey, the major deliverables could be design, data collection, data analysis, and providing recommendations by February 21, 2011, for a cost not to exceed $300,000.

3. Deliverable specifications/requirements, features, and tasks. This step should be very comprehensive so bid proposals from contractors can be validated and later used for control. Typical specifications cover physical features such as size, quantity, materials, speed, and color. For example, an IT project might specify requirements for hardware, software, and training in great detail. Tasks required to complete deliverables can be included if they are known.

4. Responsibilities—vendor and customer. Failing to spell out the responsibilities for both parties is notorious for leading to serious problems when the contractor implements the project. For example, who pays for what? (If the contractor is to be on site, will the contractor be required to pay for office space?) What are the limits and exclusions for the contractor? (For example, who will supply test equipment?) What communication plan will be used by the contractor and owner? If escalation of an issue becomes necessary, what process will be used? How will progress be evaluated? Well-defined responsibilities will avoid many unforeseen problems later.

5. Project schedule. This step is concerned with getting a "hard" schedule which can be used for control and evaluating progress. Owners are usually very demanding in meeting the project schedule. In today's business environment, time-to-market is a major "hot button" that influences market share, costs, and profits. The schedule should spell out what, who, and when.

6. Costs and payment schedule. The RFP needs to set out very clearly how, when, and the process for determining costs and conditions for progress payments.

7. Type of contract. Essentially there are two types of contracts—fixed-price and cost-plus. Fixed-price contracts agree on a price or lump sum in advance, and it remains as long as there are no changes to the scope provisions of the agreement. This type is preferred in projects that are well defined with predictable costs and minimal risks. The contractor must exercise care estimating cost because any underestimating of costs will cause the contractor's profit to be reduced. In cost-plus contracts the contractor is reimbursed for all or some of the expenses incurred during performance of the contract. This fee is negotiated in advance and usually involves a percent of total costs. "Time and materials" plus a profit factor are typical of cost-plus contracts. Both types of contracts can include incentive clauses for superior performance in time and cost, or in some cases, penalties—for example, missing the opening date of a new sports stadium.

8. Experience and staffing. The ability of the contractor to implement the project may depend on specific skills; this necessary experience should be specified, along with assurance such staff will be available for this project.

9. Evaluation criteria. The criteria for evaluating and awarding the project contract should be specified. For example, selection criteria frequently include methodology, price, schedule, and experience; in some cases these criteria are weighted. Use of the outline in Figure A2.1 will help to ensure key items in the proposal are not omitted. A well-prepared RFP will provide contractors with sufficient guidelines to prepare a proposal that clearly meets the project and customer's needs.

SELECTION OF CONTRACTOR FROM BID PROPOSALS

Interested contractors respond to project RFPs with a written bid proposal. It is likely that several contractors will submit bid proposals to the customer.

The final step in the RFP process is to select the contractor who best meets the requirements requested in the RFP. The selection criteria given in the RFP are used to evaluate which contractor is awarded the contract to implement the project. Losing contractors should be given an explanation of the key factors that led to the selection of the winning contractor/vendor; appreciation for their participation and effort should be acknowledged. See Figure A2.2, Contractor Evaluation Template, adapted from one used in practice.

FIGURE A2.2   **Contractor Evaluation Template**

Contractor Evaluation Template	Maximum Weight	Proposal 1	Proposal 2	Proposal 3	Proposal 4
Contractor qualifications	Weight = 10				
Technical skills available	Weight = 20				
Understanding of contract and conditions	Weight = 5				
Financial strength to implement project	Weight = 15				
Understanding of proposal specifications	Weight = 10				
Innovativeness and originality of proposal	Weight = 5				
Reputation for delivering on time and budget	Weight = 15				
Price	Weight = 20				
Total	**100**				

Organization:
Structure and Culture

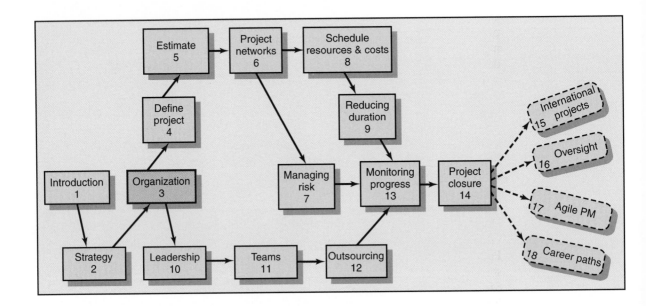

Matrix management works, but it sure is difficult at times. All matrix managers must keep up their health and take Stress-Tabs.

—A Project Manager

Once management approves a project then the question becomes, how will the project be implemented? This chapter examines three different project management structures used by firms to implement projects: functional organization, dedicated project teams, and matrix structure. Although not exhaustive, these structures and their variant forms represent the major approaches for organizing projects. The advantages and disadvantages of each of these structures are discussed as well as some of the critical factors that might lead a firm to choose one form over others.

Whether a firm chooses to complete projects within the traditional functional organization or through some form of matrix arrangement is only part of the story. Anyone who has worked for more than one organization realizes that there are often considerable differences in how projects are managed within certain firms with similar structures. Working in a matrix system at AT&T is different from working in a matrix environment at Hewlett-Packard. Many researchers attribute these differences to the organizational culture at AT&T and Hewlett-Packard. A simple explanation of *organizational culture* is that it reflects the "personality" of an organization. Just as each individual has a unique personality, so each organization has a unique culture. Toward the end of this chapter, we examine in more detail what organizational culture is and the impact that the culture of the parent organization has on organizing and managing projects.

Both the project management structure and the culture of the organization constitute major elements of the environment in which projects are implemented. It is important for project managers and participants to know the "lay of the land" so that they can avoid obstacles and take advantage of pathways to complete their projects.

Project Management Structures

A project management system provides a framework for launching and implementing project activities within a parent organization. A good system appropriately balances the needs of both the parent organization and the project by defining the interface between the project and parent organization in terms of authority, allocation of resources, and eventual integration of project outcomes into mainstream operations.

Many business organizations have struggled with creating a system for organizing projects while managing ongoing operations. One of the major reasons for this

FIGURE 3.1
Functional
Organizations

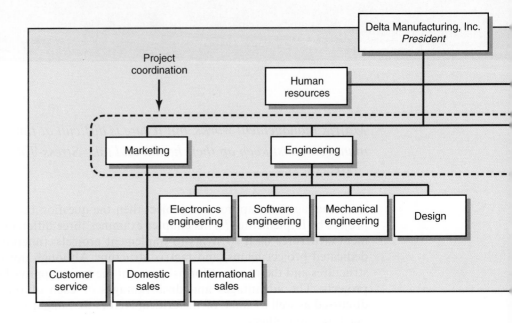

struggle is that projects contradict fundamental design principles associated with traditional organizations. Projects are unique, one-time efforts with a distinct beginning and end. Most organizations are designed to efficiently manage ongoing activities. Efficiency is achieved primarily by breaking down complex tasks into simplified, repetitive processes, as symbolized by assembly-line production methods. Projects are not routine and therefore can be like ducks out of water in these work environments. With this in mind, we will start the discussion of project management structures.

Organizing Projects within the Functional Organization

One approach to organizing projects is to simply manage them within the existing functional hierarchy of the organization. Once management decides to implement a project, the different segments of the project are delegated to the respective functional units with each unit responsible for completing its segment of the project (see Figure 3.1). Coordination is maintained through normal management channels. For example, a tool manufacturing firm decides to differentiate its product line by offering a series of tools specially designed for left-handed individuals. Top management decides to implement the project, and different segments of the project are distributed to appropriate areas. The industrial design department is responsible for modifying specifications to conform to the needs of left-handed users. The production department is responsible for devising the means for producing new tools according to these new design specifications. The marketing department is responsible for gauging demand and price as well as identifying distribution outlets. The overall project will be managed within the normal hierarchy, with the project being part of the working agenda of top management.

The functional organization is also commonly used when, given the nature of the project, one functional area plays a dominant role in completing the project

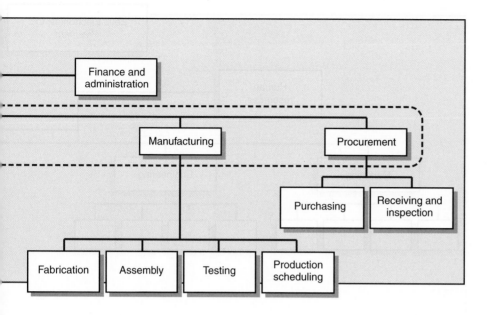

or has a dominant interest in the success of the project. Under these circumstances, a high-ranking manager in that area is given the responsibility of coordinating the project. For example, the transfer of equipment and personnel to a new office would be managed by a top-ranking manager in the firm's facilities department. Likewise, a project involving the upgrading of the management information system would be managed by the information systems department. In both cases, most of the project work would be done within the specified department and coordination with other departments would occur through normal channels.

There are advantages and disadvantages for using the existing functional organization to administer and complete projects. The major advantages are the following:

1. **No Change.** Projects are completed within the basic functional structure of the parent organization. There is no radical alteration in the design and operation of the parent organization.

2. **Flexibility.** There is maximum flexibility in the use of staff. Appropriate specialists in different functional units can temporarily be assigned to work on the project and then return to their normal work. With a broad base of technical personnel available within each functional department, people can be switched among different projects with relative ease.

3. **In-Depth Expertise.** If the scope of the project is narrow and the proper functional unit is assigned primary responsibility, then in-depth expertise can be brought to bear on the most crucial aspects of the project.

4. **Easy Post-Project Transition.** Normal career paths within a functional division are maintained. While specialists can make significant contributions to projects, their functional field is their professional home and the focus of their professional growth and advancement.

FIGURE 3.2
**Dedicated Project
Team**

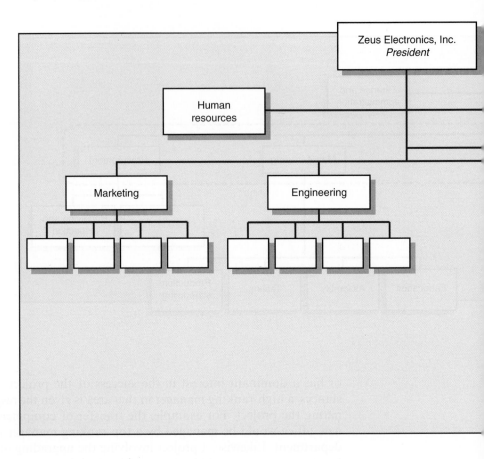

Just as there are advantages for organizing projects within the existing functional organization, there are also disadvantages. These disadvantages are particularly pronounced when the scope of the project is broad and one functional department does not take the dominant technological and managerial lead on the project:

1. **Lack of Focus.** Each functional unit has its own core routine work to do; sometimes project responsibilities get pushed aside to meet primary obligations. This difficulty is compounded when the project has different priorities for different units. For example, the marketing department may consider the project urgent while the operations people considered it only of secondary importance. Imagine the tension if the marketing people have to wait for the operations people to complete their segment of the project before they proceed.

2. **Poor Integration.** There may be poor integration across functional units. Functional specialists tend to be concerned only with their segment of the project and not with what is best for the total project.

3. **Slow.** It generally takes longer to complete projects through this functional arrangement. This is in part attributable to slow response time—project information and decisions have to be circulated through normal management channels. Furthermore, the lack of horizontal, direct communication among functional groups contributes to rework as specialists realize the implications of others' actions after the fact.

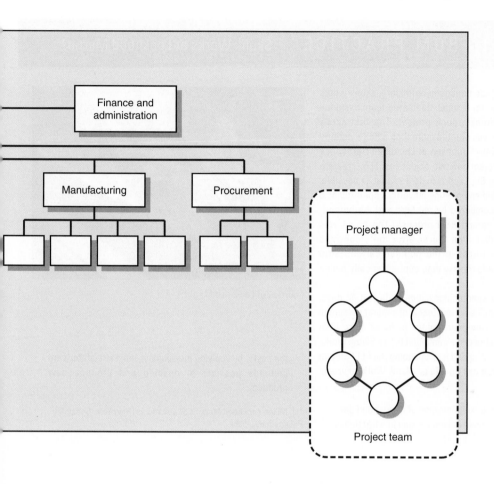

Finance and administration

Manufacturing

Procurement

Project manager

Project team

4. **Lack of Ownership.** The motivation of people assigned to the project can be weak. The project may be seen as an additional burden that is not directly linked to their professional development or advancement. Furthermore, because they are working on only a segment of the project, professionals do not identify with the project. Lack of ownership discourages strong commitment to project-related activities.

Organizing Projects as Dedicated Teams

At the other end of the structural spectrum is the creation of **dedicated project teams.** These teams operate as separate units from the rest of the parent organization. Usually a full-time project manager is designated to pull together a core group of specialists who work full time on the project. The project manager recruits necessary personnel from both within and outside the parent company. The subsequent team is physically separated from the parent organization and given marching orders to complete the project (see Figure 3.2).

The interface between the parent organization and the project teams will vary. In some cases, the parent organization maintains a tight rein through financial controls. In other cases, firms grant the project manager maximum freedom to get the project done as he sees fit. Lockheed Martin has used this approach to develop next-generation jet airplanes. See Snapshot from Practice: Skunk Works.

In project management folklore, skunk works is code for a small, dedicated team assigned to a breakthrough project. The first skunk works was created more than a half a century ago by Clarence L. "Kelly" Johnson at Lockheed Aerospace Corporation. Kelly's project had two objectives: 1) to create a jet fighter, the Shooting Star, and 2) to do it as fast as possible. Kelly and a small band of engineering mavericks operated as a dedicated team unencumbered by red tape and the bureaucratic delays of the normal R&D process. The name was coined by team member Irvin Culver after the moonshine brewery deep in the forest in the popular cartoon strip Lil'Abner. The homemade whisky was euphemistically called kickapoo joy juice.

The project was a spectacular success. In just 43 days, Johnson's team of 23 engineers and teams of support personnel put together the first American fighter to fly at more than 500 miles per hour. Lockheed has continued to use Skunk Works to develop a string of high speed jets, including the F117 Stealth Fighter. Lockheed Martin has an official Skunk Works division. Their charter is:

The Skunk Works is a concentration of a few good people solving problems far in advance—and at a fraction of

Courtesy of Lockheed Martin.

the cost—by applying the simplest, most straightforward methods possible to develop and produce new products.

* J. Miller, *Lockheed Martin's Skunk Works* (New York: Speciality Publications, 1996).

In the case of firms where projects are the dominant form of business, such as a construction firm or a consulting firm, the entire organization is designed to support project teams. Instead of one or two special projects, the organization consists of sets of quasi-independent teams working on specific projects. The main responsibility of traditional functional departments is to assist and support these project teams. For example, the marketing department is directed at generating new business that will lead to more projects, while the human resource department is responsible for managing a variety of personnel issues as well as recruiting and training new employees. This type of organization is referred to in the literature as a **Projectized Organization** and is graphically portrayed in Figure 3.3. It is important to note that not all projects are dedicated project teams; personnel can work part-time on several projects.

As in the case of functional organization, the dedicated project team approach has strengths and weaknesses. The following are recognized as strengths:

1. **Simple.** Other than taking away resources in the form of specialists assigned to the project, the functional organization remains intact with the project team operating independently.
2. **Fast.** Projects tend to get done more quickly when participants devote their full attention to the project and are not distracted by other obligations and duties. Furthermore, response time tends to be quicker under this arrangement because

FIGURE 3.3 **Projectized Organization Structure**

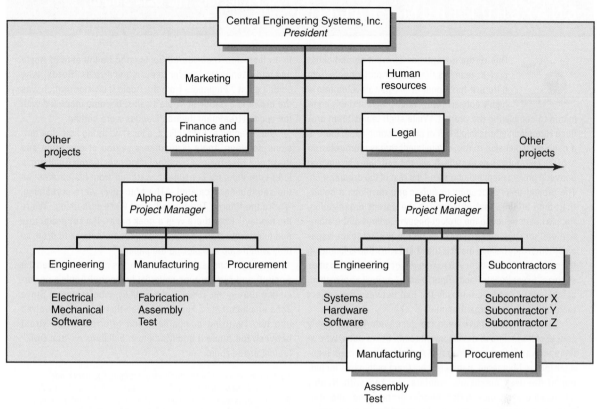

most decisions are made within the team and are not deferred up the hierarchy.

3. **Cohesive.** A high level of motivation and cohesiveness often emerges within the project team. Participants share a common goal and personal responsibility toward the project and the team.

4. **Cross-Functional Integration.** Specialists from different areas work closely together and, with proper guidance, become committed to optimizing the project, not their respective areas of expertise.

In many cases, the project team approach is the optimum approach for completing a project when you view it solely from the standpoint of what is best for completing the project. Its weaknesses become more evident when the needs of the parent organization are taken into account:

1. **Expensive.** Not only have you created a new management position (project manager), but resources are also assigned on a full-time basis. This can result in duplication of efforts across projects and a loss of economies of scale.

2. **Internal Strife.** Sometimes dedicated project teams take on an entity of their own and a disease known as projectitis develops. See Snapshot from Practice: Projectitis—The Dark Side. A strong we–they divisiveness emerges between the project team and the parent organization. This divisiveness can undermine not only the integration of the eventual outcomes of the project into mainstream

SNAPSHOT FROM PRACTICE   Projectitis: The Dark Side to Project Teams*

One of the advantages of creating dedicated project teams is that project participants from different functional areas can develop into a highly cohesive work team that is strongly committed to completing the project. While such teams often produce Herculean efforts in pursuit of project completion, there is a negative dimension to this commitment that is often referred to in the literature as **projectitis**. A we–they attitude can emerge between project team members and the rest of the organization. The project team succumbs to *hubris* and develops a holier-than-thou attitude that antagonizes the parent organization. People not assigned to the project become jealous of the attention and prestige being showered on the project team, especially when they believe that it is their hard work that is financing the endeavor. The tendency to assign project teams exotic titles such as "Silver Bullets" and "Tiger Teams," as well as give them special perks, tends to intensify the gap between the project team and the parent organization.

Such appears to have been the case with Apple's highly successful Macintosh development team. Steve Jobs, who at the time was both the chairman of Apple and the project manager for the Mac team, pampered his team with perks including at-the-desk massages, coolers stocked with freshly squeezed orange juice, a Bosendorfer grand piano, and first-class plane tickets. No other employees at Apple got to travel

first class. Jobs considered his team to be the elite of Apple and had a tendency to refer to everyone else as "Bozos" who "didn't get it." Engineers from the Apple II division, which was the bread and butter of Apple's sales, became incensed with the special treatment their colleagues were getting.

One evening at Ely McFly's, a local watering hole, the tensions between Apple II engineers seated at one table and those of a Mac team at another boiled over. Aaron Goldberg, a long-time industry consultant, watched from his barstool as the squabbling escalated. "The Mac guys were screaming, 'We're the future!' The Apple II guys were screaming, 'We're the money!' Then there was a geek brawl. Pocket protectors and pens were flying. I was waiting for a notebook to drop, so they would stop and pick up the papers."

Although comical from a distance, the discord between the Apple II and Mac groups severely hampered Apple's performance during the 1980s. John Sculley, who replaced Steve Jobs as chairman of Apple, observed that Apple had evolved into two "warring companies" and referred to the street between the Apple II and Macintosh buildings as "the DMZ" (demilitarized zone).

* J. Carlton, *Apple: The Inside Story of Intrigue, Egomania, and Business Blunders* (New York: Random House, 1997), pp. 13–14; J. Sculley, *Odyssey: Pepsi to Apple . . . A Journey of Adventure, Ideas, and the Future* (New York: Harper & Row, 1987), pp. 270–79.

operations but also the assimilation of project team members back into their functional units once the project is completed.

3. **Limited Technological Expertise.** Creating self-contained teams inhibits maximum technological expertise being brought to bear on problems. Technical expertise is limited somewhat to the talents and experience of the specialists assigned to the project. While nothing prevents specialists from consulting with others in the functional division, the we–they syndrome and the fact that such help is not formally sanctioned by the organization discourage this from happening.

4. **Difficult Post-Project Transition.** Assigning full-time personnel to a project creates the dilemma of what to do with personnel after the project is completed. If other project work is not available, then the transition back to their original functional departments may be difficult because of their prolonged absence and the need to catch up with recent developments in their functional area.

Organizing Projects within a Matrix Arrangement

One of the biggest management innovations to emerge in the past 30 years has been the matrix organization. **Matrix** management is a hybrid organizational form in which a horizontal project management structure is "overlaid" on the normal functional hierarchy. In a matrix system, there are usually two chains of command, one along functional lines and the other along project lines. Instead of delegating segments of a project to different units or creating an autonomous team, project participants report simultaneously to both functional and project managers.

Companies apply this matrix arrangement in a variety of different ways. Some organizations set up temporary matrix systems to deal with specific projects, while "matrix" may be a permanent fixture in other organizations. Let us first look at its general application and then proceed to a more detailed discussion of finer points. Consider Figure 3.4. There are three projects currently under way: A, B, and C. All three project managers (PM A-C) report to a director of project management, who supervises all projects. Each project has an administrative assistant, although the one for project C is only part time.

Project A involves the design and expansion of an existing production line to accommodate new metal alloys. To accomplish this objective, project A has assigned to it 3.5 people from manufacturing and 6 people from engineering. These individuals are assigned to the project on a part-time or full-time basis, depending on the project's needs during various phases of the project. Project B involves the development of a new product that requires the heavy representation of engineering, manufacturing, and marketing. Project C involves forecasting changing needs of an existing customer base. While these three projects, as well as others, are being completed, the functional divisions continue performing their basic, core activities.

The matrix structure is designed to optimally utilize resources by having individuals work on multiple projects as well as being capable of performing normal functional duties. At the same time, the matrix approach attempts to achieve greater integration by creating and legitimizing the authority of a project manager. In theory, the matrix approach provides a dual focus between functional/technical expertise and project requirements that is missing in either the project team or functional approach to project management. This focus can most easily be seen in the relative input of functional managers and project managers over key project decisions (see Table 3.1).

Different Matrix Forms

In practice there are really different kinds of matrix systems, depending on the relative authority of the project and functional managers. Here is a thumbnail sketch of the three kinds of matrices:

- **Weak matrix**—This form is very similar to a functional approach with the exception that there is a formally designated project manager responsible for coordinating project activities. Functional managers are responsible for

TABLE 3.1
Division of Project Manager and Functional Manager Responsibilities in a Matrix Structure

Project Manager	Negotiated Issues	Functional Manager
What has to be done?	Who will do the task?	How will it be done?
When should the task be done?	Where will the task be done?	
How much money is available to do the task?	Why will the task be done?	How will the project involvement impact normal functional activities?
How well has the total project been done?	Is the task satisfactorily completed?	How well has the functional input been integrated?

3. **Easier Post-Project Transition.** Because the project organization is overlaid on the functional divisions, specialists maintain ties with their functional group, so they have a homeport to return to once the project is completed.

4. **Flexible.** Matrix arrangements provide for flexible utilization of resources and expertise within the firm. In some cases functional units may provide individuals who are managed by the project manager. In other cases the contributions are monitored by the functional manager.

The strengths of the matrix structure are considerable. Unfortunately, so are the potential weaknesses. This is due in large part to the fact that a matrix structure is more complicated and the creation of multiple bosses represents a radical departure from the traditional hierarchical authority system.

Furthermore, one does not install a matrix structure overnight. Experts argue that it takes 3–5 years for a matrix system to fully mature. So many of the problems described below represent growing pains.

1. **Dysfunctional Conflict.** The matrix approach is predicated on tension between functional managers and project managers who bring critical expertise and perspectives to the project. Such tension is viewed as a necessary mechanism for achieving an appropriate balance between complex technical issues and unique project requirements. While the intent is noble, the effect is sometimes analogous to opening Pandora's box. Legitimate conflict can spill over to a more personal level, resulting from conflicting agendas and accountabilities. Worthy discussions can degenerate into heated arguments that engender animosity among the managers involved.

2. **Infighting.** Any situation in which equipment, resources, and people are being shared across projects and functional activities lends itself to conflict and competition for scarce resources. Infighting can occur among project managers, who are primarily interested in what is best for their project.

3. **Stressful.** Matrix management violates the management principle of unity of command. Project participants have at least two bosses—their functional head and one or more project managers. Working in a matrix environment can be extremely stressful. Imagine what it would be like to work in an environment in which you are being told to do three conflicting things by three different managers.

4. **Slow.** In theory, the presence of a project manager to coordinate the project should accelerate the completion of the project. In practice, decision making can get bogged down as agreements have to be forged across multiple functional groups. This is especially true for the balanced matrix.

When the three variant forms of the matrix approach are considered, we can see that advantages and disadvantages are not necessarily true for all three forms of matrix. The Strong matrix is likely to enhance project integration, diminish internal power struggles, and ultimately improve control of project activities and costs. On the downside, technical quality may suffer because functional areas have less control over their contributions. Finally, projectitis may emerge as the members develop a strong team identity.

The Weak matrix is likely to improve technical quality as well as provide a better system for managing conflict across projects because the functional manager assigns personnel to different projects. The problem is that functional control is often maintained at the expense of poor project integration. The Balanced matrix can achieve better balance between technical and project requirements, but it is a very delicate system to manage and is more likely to succumb to many of the problems associated with the matrix approach.

What Is the Right Project Management Structure?

There is growing empirical evidence that project success is directly linked to the amount of autonomy and authority project managers have over their projects. However, most of this research is based on what is best for managing specific projects. It is important to remember what was stated in the beginning of the chapter—that the best system balances the needs of the project with those of the parent organization. So what project structure should an organization use? This is a complicated question with no precise answers. A number of issues need to be considered at both the organization and project level.

Organization Considerations

At the organization level, the first question that needs to be asked is how important is project management to the success of the firm? What percentage of core work involves projects? If over 75 percent of work involves projects, then an organization should consider a fully projectized organization. If an organization has both standard products and projects, then a matrix arrangement would appear to be appropriate. If an organization has very few projects, then a less formal arrangement is probably all that is required. Dedicated teams could be created on an as-needed basis and the organization could outsource project work.

A second key question is resource availability. Remember, matrix evolved out of the necessity to share resources across multiple projects and functional domains while at the same time creating legitimate project leadership. For organizations that cannot afford to tie up critical personnel on individual projects, a matrix system would appear to be appropriate. An alternative would be to create a dedicated team but outsource project work when resources are not available internally.

Within the context of the first two questions, an organization needs to assess current practices and what changes are needed to more effectively manage projects. A strong project matrix is not installed overnight. The shift toward a greater emphasis on projects has a host of political implications that need to be worked through, requiring time and strong leadership. For example, we have observed many companies that make the transition from a functional organization to a matrix organization begin with a weak functional matrix. This is due in part to resistance by functional and department managers toward transferring authority to project managers. With time, these matrix structures eventually evolve into a project matrix. Many organizations have created Project Management Offices to support project management efforts. See Snapshot from Practice: POs: Project Offices.

Project Considerations

At the project level, the question is how much autonomy the project needs in order to be successfully completed. Hobbs and Ménard identify seven factors that should influence the choice of project management structure:

- Size of project.
- Strategic importance.

SNAPSHOT FROM PRACTICE POs: Project Offices

Project offices (POs) were originally developed as a response to the poor track record many companies had in completing projects on time, within budget, and according to plan. They were often established to help matrix systems mature into more effective project delivery platforms.

Today, POs come in many different shapes and forms. One interesting way of classifying POs was set forth by Casey and Peck, who describe certain POs in terms of being (1) a weather station, (2) a control tower, or (3) a resource pool. Each of these models performs a very different function for its organization.

- **Weather Station.** The primary function of the weather station PO is to track and monitor project performance. It is typically created to satisfy top management's need to stay on top of the portfolio of projects under way in the firm. Staff provides an independent forecast of project performance. The questions answered for specific projects include:

  - How are our projects progressing? Which ones are on track? Which ones are not?

  - How are we doing in terms of cost? Which projects are over or under budget?

  - What are the major problems confronting projects? Are contingency plans in place? What can the organization do to help the project?

- **Control Tower.** The primary function of the control tower PO is to improve project execution. It considers project management as a profession to be protected and advanced. Staff at the PO identify best practices and standards for project management excellence. They work as consultants and trainers to support project managers and their teams.

- **Resource Pool.** The goal of the resource pool PO is to provide the organization with a cadre of trained project managers and professionals. It operates like an academy for continually upgrading the skills of a firm's project professionals. In addition to training, this kind of PO also serves to elevate the stature of project management within the organization.

Source: W. Casey and W. Peck, "Choosing the Right PMO Setup," *PM Network,* vol. 15, no. 2(2001), pp. 40–47.

- Novelty and need for innovation.
- Need for integration (number of departments involved).
- Environmental complexity (number of external interfaces).
- Budget and time constraints.
- Stability of resource requirements.

The higher the levels of these seven factors, the more autonomy and authority the project manager and project team need to be successful. This translates into using either a dedicated project team or a project matrix structure. For example, these structures should be used for large projects that are strategically critical and are new to the company, thus requiring much innovation. These structures would also be appropriate for complex, multidisciplinary projects that require input from many departments, as well as for projects that require constant contact with customers to assess their expectations. Dedicated project teams should also be used for urgent projects in which the nature of the work requires people working steadily from beginning to end.

Many firms that are heavily involved in project management have created a flexible management system that organizes projects according to project requirements. For example, Chaparral Steel, a mini-mill that produces steel bars and beams from scrap metal, classifies projects into three categories: advanced development, platform, and incremental. Advanced development projects are high-risk endeavors involving the creation of a breakthrough product or process. Platform projects are medium-risk projects involving system upgrades that yield new products and processes. Incremental projects are low-risk, short-term projects that involve minor adjustments in existing products and processes. At any point in time,

Chaparral might have 40–50 projects underway, of which only one or two are advanced, three to five are platform projects, and the remainder are small, incremental projects. The incremental projects are almost all done within a weak matrix with the project manager coordinating the work of functional subgroups. A strong matrix is used to complete the platform projects, while dedicated project teams are typically created to complete the advanced development projects. More and more companies are using this "mix and match" approach to managing projects.

Organizational Culture

The decision for combining a discussion of project management structures and organizational cultures in this chapter can be traced to a conversation we, the authors, had with two project managers who work for a medium-sized information technology firm.

The managers were developing a new operating platform that would be critical to the future success of their company. When they tried to describe how this project was organized, one manager began to sketch out on a napkin a complicated structure involving 52 different teams, each with a project leader and a technical leader! In response to our further probing to understand how this system worked, the manager stopped short and proclaimed, "The key to making this structure work is the culture in our company. This approach would never work at company Y, where I worked before. But because of our culture here we are able to pull it off."

This comment, our observations of other firms, and research suggest there is a strong connection between project management structure, organizational culture, and project success. We have observed organizations successfully manage projects within the traditional functional organization because the culture encouraged cross-functional integration. Conversely we have seen matrix structures break down because the culture of the organization did not support the division of authority between project managers and functional managers. We have also observed companies relying on independent project teams because the dominant culture would not support the innovation and speed necessary for success.

What Is Organizational Culture?

Organizational culture refers to a system of shared norms, beliefs, values, and assumptions which binds people together, thereby creating shared meanings. This system is manifested by customs and habits that exemplify the values and beliefs of the organization. For example, egalitarianism may be expressed in the informal dress worn at a high-tech firm. Conversely, mandated uniforms at a department store reinforce respect for the hierarchy.

Culture reflects the personality of the organization and, similar to an individual's personality, can enable us to predict attitudes and behaviors of organizational members. Culture is also one of the defining aspects of an organization that sets it apart from other organizations even in the same industry.

Research suggests that there are 10 primary characteristics which, in aggregate, capture the essence of an organization's culture:

1. **Member identity**—the degree to which employees identify with the organization as a whole rather than with their type of job or field of professional expertise.
2. **Team emphasis**—the degree to which work activities are organized around groups rather than individuals.

3. **Management focus**—the degree to which management decisions take into account the effect of outcomes on people within the organization.
4. **Unit integration**—the degree to which units within the organization are encouraged to operate in a coordinated or interdependent manner.
5. **Control**—the degree to which rules, policies, and direct supervision are used to oversee and control employee behavior.
6. **Risk tolerance**—the degree to which employees are encouraged to be aggressive, innovative, and risk seeking.
7. **Reward criteria**—the degree to which rewards such as promotion and salary increases are allocated according to employee performance rather than seniority, favoritism, or other nonperformance factors.
8. **Conflict tolerance**—the degree to which employees are encouraged to air conflicts and criticisms openly.
9. **Means versus end orientation**—the degree to which management focuses on outcomes rather than on techniques and processes used to achieve those results.
10. **Open-systems focus**—the degree to which the organization monitors and responds to changes in the external environment.

As shown in Figure 3.5, each of these dimensions exists on a continuum. Assessing an organization according to these 10 dimensions provides a composite picture of the organization's culture. This picture becomes the basis for feelings of shared understanding that the members have about the organization, how things are done, and the way members are supposed to behave.

Culture performs several important functions in organizations. An organization's culture *provides a sense of identity* for its members. The more clearly an organization's shared perceptions and values are stated, the more strongly people can identify with their organization and feel a vital part of it. Identity generates

FIGURE 3.5
Key Dimensions Defining an Organization's Culture

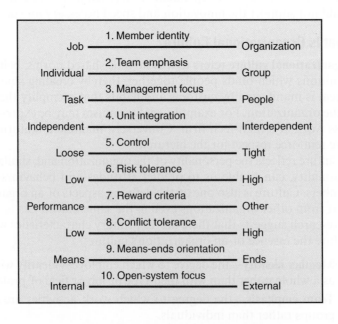

SNAPSHOT FROM PRACTICE   Software Development Teams at Microsoft*

Microsoft Corporation is the leading computer software company in the world. Microsoft's success stems in part from a corporate culture that supports teams of software developers to create and refine new products. No matter how big the project—even a complex one such as the development of the successful Windows 2000 operating system—the project is broken down into small parts that can be handled by teams of about 12 developers. The segment of the project each team is assigned is further subdivided so that each developer is assigned a specific part of the project to work on. Developers with greater experience are given more responsibilities than new members of the team, but the entire team knows that project success depends on the sum of their individual inputs.

Team members provide considerable support for each other. It is not uncommon to see two team members hunched over a computer screen trying to solve a problem. Team members can also be stern critics if a team member fails to perform at an acceptable level.

Developers are granted considerable autonomy in performing their work. At the same time, behavior at Microsoft is governed by a shared work culture that almost everyone follows. One set of informal rules governs the basic issue of working hours. Developers are free to adopt whatever work schedule suits them. If a developer has a sudden insight at midnight, it is not unusual for people to work until dawn. Likewise, if a developer's child is sick, the developer can stay

© AP Photo/Alyssa Hurst

home to take care of the child, and do makeup work at some other time. Along with these "rules" on flexible working hours, almost all developers abide by another norm: They put in the hours necessary to get the job done, even if it requires staying up all night to work on a particularly difficult part of a program.

* K. Rebello, "Inside Microsoft," *Business Weekly,* July 15, 1996, pp. 56–67; B. Filipczak "Beyond the Gates of Microsoft," *Training,* September 1992, pp. 37–44.

commitment to the organization and reasons for members to devote energy and loyalty to the organization.

A second important function is that culture *helps legitimize the management system* of the organization. Culture helps clarify authority relationships. It provides reasons why people are in a position of authority and why their authority should be respected.

Most importantly, organizational culture *clarifies and reinforces standards of behavior.* Culture helps define what is permissible and inappropriate behavior. These standards span a wide range of behavior from dress code and working hours to challenging the judgment of superiors and collaborating with other departments. Ultimately, culture *helps create social order* within an organization. Imagine what it would be like if members didn't share similar beliefs, values, and assumptions—chaos! The customs, norms, and ideals conveyed by the culture of an organization provide the stability and predictability in behavior that is essential for an effective organization. See Snapshot from Practice: Software Development Teams at Microsoft for an example of this.

Although our discussion of organizational culture may appear to suggest one culture dominates the entire organization, in reality this is rarely the case. "Strong" or "thick" are adjectives used to denote a culture in which the organization's core values and customs are widely shared within the entire organization. Conversely, a "thin" or "weak" culture is one that is not widely shared or practiced within a firm.

Even within a strong organizational culture, there are likely to be subcultures often aligned within specific departments or specialty areas. As noted earlier in our discussion of project management structures, it is not uncommon for norms, values, and customs to develop within a specific field or profession such as marketing, finance, or operations. People working in the marketing department may have a different set of norms and values than those working in finance.

Countercultures sometimes emerge within organizations that embody a different set of values, beliefs, and customs—often in direct contradiction with the culture espoused by top management. How pervasive these subcultures and countercultures are affect the strength of the culture of the organization and the extent to which culture influences members' actions and responses.

Identifying Cultural Characteristics

Deciphering an organization's culture is a highly interpretative, subjective process that requires assessment of both current and past history. The student of culture cannot simply rely on what people report about their culture. The physical environment in which people work, as well as how people act and respond to different events that occur, must be examined. Figure 3.6 contains a worksheet for diagnosing

FIGURE 3.6
Organizational
Culture Diagnosis
Worksheet

Power Corp.

I. Physical Characteristics:
Architecture, office layout, décor, attire

Corporate HQ is 20 story modern building—president on top floor. Offices are bigger in the top floors than lower floors. Formal business attire (white shirts, ties, power suits, . . .). Power appears to increase the higher up you are.

II. Public Documents:
Annual reports, internal newsletters, vision statements

At the heart of the Power Corp. way is our vision . . . to be the global energy company most admired for its people, partnership, and performance.

Integrity. We are honest with others and ourselves. We meet the highest ethical standards in all business dealings. We do what we say we will do.

III. Behavior:
Pace, language, meetings, issues discussed, decision-making style, communication patterns, rituals

Hierarchical decision-making, pace brisk but orderly, meetings start on time and end on time, subordinates choose their words very carefully when talking to superiors, people rarely work past 6:00 P.M., president takes top performing unit on a boat cruise each year . . .

IV. Folklore:
Stories, anecdotes, heroines, heroes, villains

Young project manager was fired after going over his boss's head to ask for additional funds.

Stephanie C. considered a hero for taking complete responsibility for a technical error.

Jack S. was labeled a traitor for joining chief competitor after working for Power Corp. for 15 years.

the culture of an organization. Although by no means exhaustive, the checklist often yields clues about the norms, customs, and values of an organization:

1. **Study the physical characteristics of an organization.** What does the external architecture look like? What image does it convey? Is it unique? Are the buildings and offices the same quality for all employees? Or are modern buildings and fancier offices reserved for senior executives or managers from a specific department? What are the customs concerning dress? What symbols does the organization use to signal authority and status within the organization? These physical characteristics can shed light on who has real power within the organization, the extent to which the organization is internally differentiated, and how formal the organization is in its business dealings.

2. **Read about the organization.** Examine annual reports, mission statements, press releases, and internal newsletters. What do they describe? What principles are espoused in these documents? Do the reports emphasize the people who work for the organization and what they do or the financial performance of the firm? Each emphasis reflects a different culture. The first demonstrates concern for the people who make up the company. The second may suggest a concern for results and the bottom line.

3. **Observe how people interact within the organization.** What is their pace—is it slow and methodical or urgent and spontaneous? What rituals exist within the organization? What values do they express? Meetings can often yield insightful information. Who are the people at the meetings? Who does the talking? To whom do they talk? How candid is the conversation? Do people speak for the organization or for the individual department? What is the focus of the meetings? How much time is spent on various issues? Issues that are discussed repeatedly and at length are clues about the values of the organization's culture.

4. **Interpret stories and folklore surrounding the organization.** Look for similarities among stories told by different people. The subjects highlighted in recurring stories often reflect what is important to an organization's culture. For example, many of the stories that are repeated at Versatec, a Xerox subsidiary that makes graphic plotters for computers, involve their flamboyant cofounder, Renn Zaphiropoulos. According to company folklore, one of the very first things Renn did when the company was formed was to assemble the top management team at his home. They then devoted the weekend to handmaking a beautiful teak conference table around which all future decisions would be made. This table came to symbolize the importance of teamwork and maintaining high standards of performance, two essential qualities of the culture at Versatec. Try to identify who the heroes and villains are in the folklore company. What do they suggest about the culture's ideals? Returning to the Versatec story, when the company was eventually purchased by Xerox many employees expressed concern that Versatec's informal, play hard/work hard culture would be overwhelmed by the bureaucracy at Xerox. Renn rallied the employees to superior levels of performance by arguing that if they exceeded Xerox's expectations they would be left alone. Autonomy has remained a fixture of Versatec's culture long after Renn's retirement.

It is also important to pay close attention to the basis for promotions and rewards. What do people see as the keys to getting ahead within the organization? What contributes to downfalls? These last two questions can yield important insights into the qualities and behaviors which the organization honors as well as the cultural taboos and behavioral land mines that can derail a career. For example, one project manager confided that a former colleague was sent to project management purgatory soon after publicly questioning the validity of a marketing report. From that point on, the project manager was extra careful to privately consult the marketing department whenever she had questions about their data.

With practice an observer can assess how strong the dominant culture of an organization is and the significance of subcultures and countercultures. Furthermore, learners can discern and identify where the culture of an organization stands on the 10 cultural dimensions presented earlier and, in essence, begin to build a cultural profile for a firm. Based on this profile, conclusions can be drawn about specific customs and norms that need to be adhered to as well as those behaviors and actions that violate the norms of a firm.

Implications of Organizational Culture for Organizing Projects

Project managers have to be able to operate in several, potentially diverse, organizational cultures. First, they have to interact with the culture of their parent organization as well as the subcultures of various departments (e.g., marketing, accounting). Second, they have to interact with the project's client or customer organizations. Finally, they have to interact in varying degrees with a host of other organizations connected to the project. These organizations include suppliers and vendors, subcontractors, consulting firms, government and regulatory agencies, and, in many cases, community groups. Many of these organizations are likely to have very different cultures. Project managers have to be able to read and speak the culture they are working in to develop strategies, plans, and responses that are likely to be understood and accepted. Still, the emphasis of this chapter is on the relationship between organizational culture and project management structure, and it is necessary to defer further discussion of these implications until Chapters 10–12, which focus on leadership, team building, and outsourcing.

Earlier we stated that we believe there are strong relationships among project management structure, organizational culture, and successful project management. To explore these relationships further, let us return to the dimensions that can be used to characterize the culture of an organization. When examining these dimensions we could hypothesize that certain aspects of the culture of an organization would support successful project management while other aspects would deter or interfere with effective management. Figure 3.7 attempts to identify which cultural characteristics create an environment conducive to completing most complex projects involving people from different disciplines.

Note that, in many cases, the ideal culture is not at either extreme. For example, a fertile project culture would likely be one in which management balances its focus on the needs of both the task and the people. An optimal culture would balance concern with output (ends) and processes to achieve those outcomes (means). In other cases, the ideal culture would be on one end of a dimension or the other. For example, because most projects require collaboration across disciplines, it would be desirable that the culture of the organization emphasize working in teams and identifying with the organization, not just the professional domain. Likewise it is important that the culture support a certain degree of risk taking and a tolerance for constructive conflict.

FIGURE 3.7
Cultural Dimensions of an Organization Supportive of Project Management

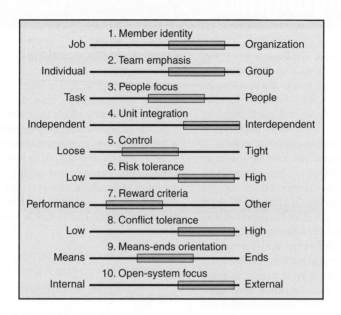

One organization that appears to fit this ideal profile is 3M. 3M has received acclaim for creating an entrepreneurial culture within a large corporate framework. The essence of its culture is captured in phrases that have been chanted often by 3Mers throughout its history: "Encourage experimental doodling." "Hire good people and leave them alone." "If you put fences around people, you get sheep. Give people the room they need." Freedom and autonomy to experiment are reflected in the "15 percent rule," which encourages technical people to spend up to 15 percent of their time on projects of their own choosing and initiative. This fertile culture has contributed to 3M's branching out into more than 60,000 products and 35 separate business units.

The metaphor we choose to describe the relationship between organizational culture and project management is that of a riverboat trip. Culture is the river and the project is the boat. Organizing and completing projects within an organization in which the culture is conducive to project management is like paddling downstream: much less effort is required. In many cases, the current can be so strong that steering is all that is required. Such is the case for projects that operate in a project-friendly environment where team-work and cross-functional cooperation are the norms, where there is a deep commitment to excellence, and where healthy conflict is voiced and dealt with quickly and effectively.

Conversely, trying to complete a project in a toxic culture is like paddling upstream: much more time, effort, and attention are needed to reach the destination. This would be the situation in cultures that discourage teamwork and cooperation, that have a low tolerance for conflict, and where getting ahead is based less on performance and more on cultivating favorable relationships with superiors. In such cases, the project manager and her people not only have to overcome the natural obstacles of the project but also have to overcome the prevailing negative forces inherent in the culture of the organization.

The implications of this metaphor are important. Greater project authority and time are necessary to complete projects that encounter a strong, negative cultural current. Conversely, less formal authority and fewer dedicated resources are

In *The Secret of Success: The Double Helix of Formal and Informal Structures in an R&D Laboratory* Polly Rizova revealed the results of a year-long investigation into the inner workings of a Fortune 500 R&D Lab. Through interviews with key participants and analysis of social networking data, Rizova assessed the efficacy of six high-tech development projects.

Four critical success factors emerged from her research. One element that is crucial to success is a heavy reliance on open and unrestricted patterns of communication, coupled with a low degree of formal reporting. In other words, team members freely interacted with each other regardless of title, experience, or discipline. A second key is having individuals on the project who are highly respected across the laboratory for their exceptional technical skills and experience. Similarly, it is also vital to have individuals involved in the project who are highly respected for their organizational expertise and experience. Having both "technical stars" and "organizational stars" on the project team were essential to success. The final factor is a strong and sustained support for the project from the company's corporate management. What's more, her analysis revealed interactive nature of the four conditions; namely that no one condition was likely to produce successful outcomes on its own, but only when put together in a way in which they reinforce each other. Here the culture of the laboratory was seen as the key catalyst.

Rizova describes a matrix system in which people work on multiple projects simultaneously but with a different wrinkle. Individuals occupy different positions and play different roles depending upon the project. For example, it is common for a senior engineer to be the manager of one project and a researcher on another that is led by his or her subordinate. In essence one must "boss" his or her own boss. At first glance this formal structure should create destructive tensions. However, Rizova argues that the organizational culture of the lab is the glue that keeps things running smoothly.

She described a culture in which the social norms of cooperation, respect, and civility are upheld and reproduced. It is a culture characterized by trust and a strong drive toward superior individual and organizational learning and achievement. The culture is captured in the comments of researchers:

> That is one of the nicest things around here. Your opinions are listened to. Superiors consider our advice. You will find that most of the projects here are a team effort.
> What I like most is the positive thinking and the "whatever it takes" attitude. Personality conflicts can be devastating. Here everyone helps you and supports you. There is no "I" in the word team.
> Very friendly environment . . . I met new people and learned a lot from them. They do not mind sharing their expertise.

* Polly S. Rizova, *The Secret of Success: The Double Helix of Formal and Informal Structures in an R&D Laboratory*. Stanford, CA: (Stanford University Press, 2007.)

needed to complete projects in which the cultural currents generate behavior and cooperation essential to project success.

The key issue is the degree of interdependency between the parent organization and the project team. In cases where the prevalent organizational culture supports the behaviors essential to project completion, a weaker, more flexible project management structure can be effective. For example, one of the major reasons Chaparral Steel is able to use a functional matrix to successfully complete incremental projects is that its culture contains strong norms for cooperation. See the Research Highlight: The Secret of Success for another example of how culture supports successful project management.

When the dominant organization culture inhibits collaboration and innovation, it is advisable to insulate the project team from the dominant culture. Here it becomes necessary to create a self-sufficient project team. If a dedicated project team is impossible because of resource constraints, then at least a project matrix should be used where the project manager has dominant control over the project. In both cases, the managerial strategy is to create a distinct team subculture in which a new set of norms, customs, and values evolve that will be conducive to project completion.

Under extreme circumstances this project culture could even represent a counterculture in that many of the norms and values are the antithesis of the dominant, parent culture. Such was the case when IBM decided to develop their personal computer quickly in 1980. They knew that the project could get bogged down by the overabundance of computer knowledge and bureaucracy in the company. They also realized that they would have to work closely with suppliers and make use of many non-IBM parts if they were to get to the market quickly. This was not the IBM way at the time, so IBM established the PC project team in a warehouse in Boca Raton, Florida, far from corporate headquarters and other corporate development facilities that existed within the organization.

Summary

This chapter examined two major characteristics of the parent organization that affect the implementation and completion of projects. The first is the formal structure of the organization and how it chooses to organize and manage projects. Although the individual project manager may have very little say as to how the firm chooses to manage projects, he or she must be able to recognize the options available as well as the inherent strengths and weaknesses of different approaches.

Three basic project management structures were described and assessed as to their weaknesses and strengths. Only under unique circumstances can a case be made for managing a project within the normal functional hierarchy. When thinking only in terms of what is best for the project, the creation of an independent project team is clearly favored. However, the most effective project management system appropriately balances the needs of the project with those of the parent organization. Matrix structures emerged out of the parent organization's need to share personnel and resources across multiple projects and operations while creating legitimate project focus. The matrix approach is a hybrid organizational form that combines elements of both the functional and project team forms in an attempt to realize the advantages of both.

The second major characteristic of the parent organization that was discussed in this chapter is the concept of organizational culture. Organizational culture is the pattern of beliefs and expectations shared by an organization's members. Culture includes the behavioral norms, customs, shared values, and the "rules of the game" for getting along and getting ahead within the organization. It is important for project managers to be "culture sensitive" so that they can develop appropriate strategies and responses and avoid violating key norms that would jeopardize their effectiveness within the organization.

The interaction between project management structure and organizational culture is a complicated one. We have suggested that in certain organizations, culture encourages the implementation of projects. In this environment the project management structure used plays a less decisive role in the success of the project. Conversely, for other organizations in which the culture stresses internal competition and differentiation, just the opposite may be true. The prevailing norms, customs, and attitudes inhibit effective project management, and the project management structure plays a more decisive role in the successful implementation of projects. At a minimum, under adverse cultural conditions, the project manager needs to have significant authority over the project team; under more extreme conditions firms should use dedicated project teams to complete critical projects. In both

Brown, S., and K. R. Eisenhardt, "Product Development: Past Research, Present Findings, and Future Directions," *Academy of Management Review,* 20 (2) 1995, pp. 343–78.

Cameron, K. S., and R. E. Quinn, *Diagnosing and Changing Organizational Culture: Based on the Competing Values Framework* (Upper Saddle River, NJ: Prentice Hall, 1999).

Carlton, J., *Apple: The Inside Story of Intrigue, Egomania, and Business Blunders* (New York: Random House, 1997), pp. 13–14.

Casey, W., and W. Peck, "Choosing the Right PMO Setup," *PM Network,* 15 (2) 2001, pp. 40–47.

Collins, J. C., and J. I. Porras, *Built to Last: The Successful Habits of Visionary Companies* (New York: HarperCollins, 1994), pp. 150–58.

Deal, T. E., and A. A. Kennedy, *Corporate Cultures: The Rites and Rituals of Corporate Life* (Reading, MA: Addison-Wesley, 1982).

De Laat, P. B., "Matrix Management of Projects and Power Struggles: A Case Study of an R&D Laboratory," *IEEE Engineering Management Review* Winter 1995.

Filipczak, B., "Beyond the Gates of Microsoft," *Training,* September 1992, pp. 37–44.

Gallagher, R. S., *The Soul of an Organization: Understanding the Values That Drive Successful Corporate Cultures* (Chicago: Dearborn Trade Publishing, 2002).

Graham, R. J., and R. L. Englund, *Creating an Environment for Successful Projects: The Quest to Manage Project Management* (San Francisco: Jossey-Bass, 1997).

Gray, C., S. Dworatschek, D. H. Gobeli, H. Knoepfel, and E. W. Larson, "International Comparison of Project Organization Structures: Use and Effectiveness," *International Journal of Project Management,* vol. 8, no. 1 February 1990, pp. 26–32.

Harrison, M. T., and J. M. Beyer, *The Culture of Organizations* (Englewood Cliffs, NJ: Prentice Hall, 1993).

Hobbs, B., and P. Ménard, "Organizational Choices for Project Management," in Paul Dinsmore (ed.), *The AMA Handbook of Project Management* (New York: AMACOM, 1993).

Hobday, M., "The Project-Based Organization: An Ideal Form for Managing Complex Products and Systems?" *Research Policy,* vol. 29, no. 17 2000.

Jassawalla, A. R., and H. C. Sashittal, "Cultures that Support Product-Innovation Processes," *Academy of Management Executive,* 15 (3) 2002, pp. 42–54.

Johnson, C. L., M. Smith, and L. K. Geary, *More Than My Share in All* (Washington, D.C.: Smithsonian Institute Publications, 1990).

Kerzner, H., *In Search of Excellence in Project Management* (New York: Von Nostrand Reinhold, 1997).

Kerzner, H., "Strategic Planning for the Project Office," *Project Management Journal,* 34 (2) 2003, pp. 13–25.

Larson, E. W. "Project Management Structures" in *The Wiley Handbook for Managing Projects,* P. Morris & J. Pinto (eds.) (New York: Wiley, 2004), pp. 48–66.

Larson, E. W., and D. H. Gobeli, "Organizing for Product Development Projects," *Journal of Product Innovation Management,* vol. 5 1988, pp. 180–90.

Larson, E. W., and D. H. Gobeli, "Matrix Management: Contradictions and Insights," *California Management Review,* vol. 29, no. 4 Summer 1987, p. 137.

Larsson, U. (ed.), *Cultures of Creativity: The Centennial Exhibition of the Nobel Prize* (Canton, MA: Science History Publications, 2001).

Laslo, Z., and A. I. Goldberg, "Matrix Structures and Performance: The Search for Optimal Adjustments to Organizational Objectives?" *IEEE Transactions in Engineering Management,* vol. 48, no. 12 2001.

Lawrence, P. R., and J. W. Lorsch, *Organization and Environment* (Homewood, IL: Irwin, 1969).

Majchrzak, A., and Q. Wang, "Breaking the Functional Mind-Set in Process Organizations," *Harvard Business Review* Sept.–Oct. 1996, pp. 93–99.

Miller, J., *Lockheed Martin's Skunk Works* (New York: Speciality Publications, 1996).

Olson, E. M., O. C. Walker, Jr., and R. W. Ruekert, "Organizing for Effective New Product Development: The Moderating Role of Product Innovativeness," *Journal of Marketing,* vol. 59 (January), 1995, pp. 48–62.

O'Reilly, C. A., J. Chatman, and D. F. Caldwell, "People and Organizational Culture: A Profile Comparison Approach to Assessing Person-Organization Fit," *Academy of Management Journal,* vol. 34, no. 3 September 1991, pp. 487–516.

Pettegrew, A. M., "On Studying Organizational Culture," *Administrative Science Quarterly,* vol. 24, no. 4 1979, pp. 570–81.

Powell, M., and J. Young, "The Project Management Support Office" in *The Wiley Handbook for Managing Projects,* P. Morris and J. Pinto (eds.) (New York: Wiley, 2004) pp. 937–69.

Rebello, K., "Inside Microsoft," *Business Weekly,* July 15, 1996, pp. 56–67.

Rizova, P., *The Secret of Success: The Double Helix of Formal and Informal Structures in an R&D Laboratory* (Stanford, CA: Stanford University Press, 2007).

Schein, E., *Organizational Culture and Leadership: A Dynamic View* (San Francisco, CA: Jossey-Bass, 1985).

Sculley, J., *Odyssey: Pepsi to Apple . . . A Journey of Adventure, Ideas, and the Future* (New York: Harper & Row, 1987), pp. 270–79.

Shenhar, A. J., "From Theory to Practice: Toward a Typology of Project Management Styles," *IEEE Transactions in Engineering Management,* 41 (1) 1998, pp. 33–48.

Shenhar, A. J., D. Dvir, T. Lechler, and M. Poli, "One Size Does Not Fit All—True for Projects, True for Frameworks," *Frontiers of Project Management Research and Application,* Proceedings of PMI Research Conference, Seattle, 2002, pp. 99–106.

Smith, P. G., and D. G. Reinertsen, *Developing Products in Half the Time* (New York: Van Nostrand Reinhold, 1995).

Stuckenbruck, L. C., *Implementation of Project Management* (Upper Darby, PA: Project Management Institute, 1981).

Youker, R., "Organizational Alternatives for Project Management," *Project Management Quarterly,* vol. 8 March 1977, pp. 24–33.

Case

Moss and McAdams Accounting Firm

Bruce Palmer had worked for Moss and McAdams (M&M) for six years and was just promoted to account manager. His first assignment was to lead an audit of Johnsonville Trucks. He was quite pleased with the five accountants who had been assigned to his team, especially Zeke Olds. Olds was an Army vet who returned to school to get a double major in accounting and computer sciences. He was on top of the latest developments in financial information systems and had a reputation for coming up with innovative solutions to problems.

M&M was a well-established regional accounting firm with 160 employees located across six offices in Minnesota and Wisconsin. The main office, where Palmer worked, was in Green Bay, Wisconsin. In fact, one of the founding members, Seth Moss, played briefly for the hometown NFL Packers during the late 1950s. M&M's primary services were corporate audits and tax preparation. Over the last two years the partners decided to move more aggressively into the consulting business. M&M projected that consulting would represent 40 percent of their growth over the next five years.

M&M operated within a matrix structure. As new clients were recruited, a manager was assigned to the account. A manager might be assigned to several accounts, depending on the size and scope of the work. This was especially true in the case of tax preparation projects, where it was not uncommon for a manager to be assigned to 8 to 12 clients. Likewise, senior and staff accountants were assigned to multiple account teams. Ruby Sands was the office manager responsible for assigning personnel to different accounts at the Green Bay office. She did her best to assign staff to multiple projects under the same manager. This wasn't always possible, and sometimes accountants had to work on projects led by different managers.

M&M, like most accounting firms, had a tiered promotion system. New CPAs entered as junior or staff accountants. Within two years, their performance was reviewed and they were either asked to leave or promoted to senior accountant. Sometime during their fifth or sixth year, a decision was made to promote them to account manager. Finally, after 10 to 12 years with the firm, the manager was considered for promotion to partner. This was a very competitive position. During the last five years, only 20 percent of account managers at M&M had been promoted to partner. However, once a partner, they were virtually guaranteed the position for life and enjoyed significant increases in salary, benefits, and prestige. M&M had a reputation for being a results-driven organization; partner promotions were based on meeting deadlines, retaining clients, and generating revenue. The promotion team based its decision on the relative performance of the account manager in comparison to his or her cohorts.

One week into the Johnsonville audit, Palmer received a call from Sands to visit her office. There he was introduced to Ken Crosby, who recently joined M&M after working nine years for a Big 5 accounting firm. Crosby was recruited to manage special consulting projects. Sands reported that Crosby had just secured a major consulting project with Springfield Metals. This was a major coup for the firm: M&M had competed against two Big 5 accounting firms for the project. Sands went on to explain that she was working with Crosby to put together his team. Crosby insisted that Zeke Olds be assigned to his team. Sands told him that this would be impossible because Olds was already assigned to work on the Johnsonville audit. Crosby persisted, arguing that Olds's expertise was essential to the Springfield project. Sands decided to work out a compromise and have Olds split time across both projects.

At this time Crosby turned to Palmer and said, "I believe in keeping things simple. Why don't we agree that Olds works for me in the mornings and you in the afternoons. I'm sure we can work out any problems that come up. After all, we both work for the same firm."

SIX WEEKS LATER

Palmer could scream whenever he remembered Crosby's words, "After all, we both work for the same firm." The first sign of trouble came during the first week of the new arrangement when Crosby called, begging to have Olds work all of Thursday on his project. They were conducting an extensive client visit, and Olds was critical to the assessment. After Palmer reluctantly agreed, Crosby said he owed him one. The next week when Palmer called Crosby to request that he return the favor, Crosby flatly refused and said any other time but not this week. Palmer tried again a week later and got the same response.

At first Olds showed up promptly at 1:00 P.M. at Palmer's office to work on the audit. Soon it became a habit to show up 30 to 60 minutes late. There was always a good reason. He was in a meeting in Springfield and couldn't just leave, or an urgent task took longer than planned. One time it was because Crosby took his entire team out to lunch at the new Thai restaurant—Olds was over an hour late because of slow service. In the beginning Olds would usually make up the time by working after hours, but Palmer could tell from conversations he overheard that this was creating tension at home.

What probably bothered Palmer the most were the e-mails and telephone calls Olds received from Crosby and his team members during the afternoons when he was supposed to be working for Palmer. A couple of times Palmer could have sworn that Olds was working on Crosby's project in his (Palmer's) office.

Palmer met with Crosby to talk about the problem and voice his complaints. Crosby acted surprised and even a little bit hurt. He promised things would change, but the pattern continued.

Palmer was becoming paranoid about Crosby. He knew that Crosby played golf with Olds on the weekends and could just imagine him badmouthing the Johnsonville project and pointing out how boring auditing work was. The sad fact was that there probably was some truth to what he was saying. The Johnsonville project was getting bogged down, and the team was slipping behind schedule. One of the contributing factors was Olds's performance. His work was not up to its usual standards. Palmer approached Olds about this, and Olds became defensive. Olds later apologized and confided that he found it difficult switching his thinking from consulting to auditing and then back to consulting. He promised to do better, and there was a slight improvement in his performance.

The last straw came when Olds asked to leave work early on Friday so that he could take his wife and kids to a Milwaukee Brewers baseball game. It turned out Springfield Metals had given Crosby their corporate tickets, and he decided to treat his team with box seats right behind the Brewers dugout. Palmer hated to do it, but he had to refuse the request. He felt guilty when he overheard Olds explaining to his son on the telephone why they couldn't go to the game.

Palmer finally decided to pick up the phone and request an urgent meeting with Sands to resolve the problem. He got up enough nerve and put in the call only to be told that Sands wouldn't be back in the office until next week. As he put the receiver down, he thought maybe things would get better.

TWO WEEKS LATER

Sands showed up unexpectedly at Palmer's office and said they needed to talk about Olds. Palmer was delighted, thinking that now he could tell her what had been going on. But before he had a chance to speak, Sands told him that Olds had come to see her yesterday. She told him that Olds confessed that he was having a hard time working on both Crosby's and Palmer's projects. He was having difficulty concentrating on the auditing work in the afternoon because he was thinking about some of the consulting issues that had emerged during the morning. He was putting in extra hours to try to meet both of the projects' deadlines, and this was creating problems at home. The bottom line was that he was stressed out and couldn't deal with the situation. He asked that he be assigned full-time to Crosby's project. Sands went on to say that Olds didn't blame Palmer, in fact he had a lot of nice things to say about him. He just enjoyed the consulting work more and found it more challenging. Sands concluded by saying, "We talked some more and ultimately I agreed with him. I hate to do this to you, Bruce, but Olds is a valuable employee, and I think this is the best decision for the firm."

1. If you were Palmer at the end of the case, how would you respond?
2. What, if anything, could Palmer have done to avoid losing Olds?
3. What advantages and disadvantages of a matrix type organization are apparent from this case?
4. What could the management at M&M do to more effectively manage situations like this?

Case

ORION Systems (A)*

The office erupted into cheers when it was announced over the PA system that ORION had just been awarded the government contract to build the next generation of high-speed, light-rail trains. Everyone came over to shake Mike Rosas's hand and congratulate him. It was well known that Rosas would be the project manager for this important project, which would be code named Jaguar. Once the celebration subsided, Rosas gazed out the window and thought about what he had just gotten himself into.

The Jaguar project would be a high-profile project that would affect procurement of future contracts with the government. Increased competition had raised performance expectations regarding completion time, quality, reliability, and cost. He knew that major changes in how ORION organized and managed projects would be necessary to meet the expectations of the Jaguar project.

* Prepared by Shlomo Cohen.

PROJECT MANAGEMENT AT ORION

ORION was a division of a large aerospace company with 7,000 employees. ORION evolved from a project organization into a matrix structure to conserve costs and better utilize limited resources. At any point in time, ORION could be working on three to five large projects such as the Jaguar project and 30 to 50 smaller projects. Project managers negotiated personnel assignments with the VP of operations, who ultimately decided project assignments. It was not uncommon for an engineer to be working on two to three projects during a week.

Figure C3.1 portrays how new-product development projects were organized at ORION. Project management was limited only to the design and development of the new product. Once the final design and prototype were completed, they were turned over to manufacturing for production and delivery to the customer. A four-person management team oversaw the completion of the project and their responsibilities are briefly described here:

- *Project manager*—responsible for all aspects of design and development of the product.
- *Planning and control manager*—responsible for building an overall project network, scheduling, managing the budget, controlling and evaluating the design and development program, and preparing status reports.
- *Electronics system engineer*—responsible for providing technical expertise on electronic systems issues.
- *Mechanics system engineer*—responsible for providing technical expertise on mechanical system issues.

The core work was completed by 12 to 20 design teams. Each team had a leader, who was responsible for designing, developing, building, and testing a specific

FIGURE C3.1
Organization of Product Development Projects at ORION

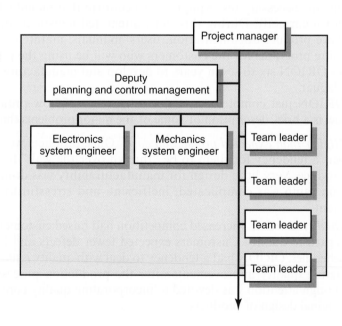

FIGURE C3.2
Traditional Master
Plan at ORION

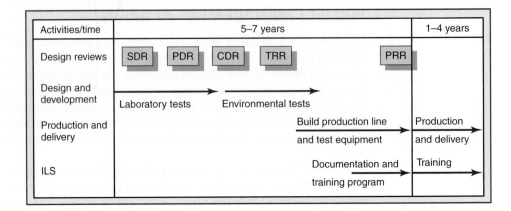

subsystem of the product. The size of individual teams varied from 5 to 15 engineers, depending on the scope of their work. These engineers split time across multiple projects.

Design engineers ran the show at ORION, and manufacturing, marketing, and other groups were expected to follow their lead. The special status of the design engineers was reinforced by the fact that they were actually paid on higher pay curves than the manufacturing engineers.

The overall product development and manufacturing process is captured in the master plan chart (Figure C3.2). New-product design and development evolves around five major reviews: system design review (SDR), preliminary design review (PDR), critical design review (CDR), test readiness review (TRR), and production readiness review (PRR).

Design and development work begins within the laboratory and progresses to field tests of specific subsystems and ultimately final product prototypes. Once completed, the design and prototype are turned over to manufacturing, which begins building the production line for the new product. Manufacturing also develops the necessary test equipment to confirm that manufactured components perform correctly. During this time, integrated logistical support (ILS) teams prepare product documentation, users' manuals, maintenance programs, and training programs for the customers who will be using the product. It typically takes ORION six to seven years to develop and manufacture a product such as the Jaguar.

ORION just completed a major assessment of how projects are managed. Below is a brief description of some of the major problems that were identified:

- *Higher than expected production costs.* Once products were developed, there was a tendency for them to be "thrown over the wall" to manufacturing to produce. Very little design for manufacturability was done, and the production ramp was complicated, inefficient, and stressful to the people in the plant.
- *Quality concerns.* Increased competition had raised customer expectations with regard to quality. Customers expected fewer defects and longer replacement schedules. ORION had a tendency to deal with quality issues after the fact, initiating quality improvements after the production process was set up. Not enough attention was devoted to incorporating quality considerations into the original design of products.

- *Problems with customer support.* User manuals and technical documentation sometimes failed to address all of a customer's concerns, and the follow-up training was not always adequately prepared. These problems contributed to increased costs in customer service and a decline in customer satisfaction.

- *Lack of strong project ownership.* While everyone accepted that a matrix arrangement was the only way to accommodate all the projects at ORION, the shifting back and forth of personnel across multiple projects took its toll on the progress of individual projects. Members often failed to identify with individual projects and develop the sense of excitement that contributed to superior performance. The shuffling of personnel slowed down progress because additional time had to be devoted to bringing returning members up to speed on current developments.

- *Scope creep.* ORION was renowned for its engineering prowess. However, there was a tendency for design engineers to get so absorbed with the science of the project that they lost focus on the practical considerations. This led to costly delays and sometimes design modifications that were inconsistent with customer requirements.

Rosas was aware of these and other concerns as he sat down with his staff to figure out the best way to organize the new Jaguar project.

1. What recommendations would you make to Rosas about organizing the Jaguar project, and why?
2. How would you change the organizational chart and master plan to reflect these changes?

Case

ORION Systems (B)

ROSAS'S PLAN

Rosas and his staff worked hard over the past week to develop a plan to establish a new standard for completing projects at ORION. The Jaguar project management team will be expanded to seven managers, who will be responsible for overseeing the completion of the project from design to delivery to the customer. A brief description of the responsibilities for the three new positions follows (see Figure C3.3):

- *Production manager*—responsible for raising production issues during the design phase; responsible for building and managing the production line.

- *ILS (integrated logistical support) manager*—responsible for all activities that require project/customer support after delivery including customer training, documentation, and equipment testing.

- *QA (quality assurance) manager*—responsible for implementing a quality program that will enhance the reliability, availability, and maintainability of the product.

These seven managers (the three just described plus the four discussed in Part A) will coordinate the completion of the project and see that their respective

FIGURE C3.3
Proposed Project Organization for the Jaguar Project

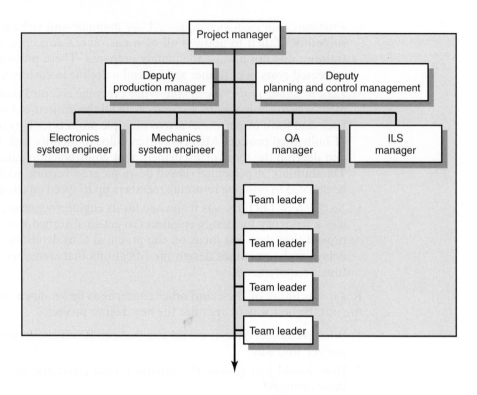

disciplines are factored into all major decisions. Rosas, as project manager, will work toward achieving consensus, but he will have the authority to intervene and make decisions if necessary.

The core work will be completed by 35 teams. Each team will have a "leader," who will be responsible for designing, developing, building, and testing a specific subsystem of the project. They will also be responsible for the quality and productivity of the subsystems and for doing the work on time and within budget.

Individual teams will consist of 5 to 12 members, and Rosas insists that at least half of each team be assigned to work full time on the project. This will help ensure continuity and enhance commitment to the project.

The second key feature to the plan is the development of the overall master plan for the project. This involves abandoning the traditional sequential approach to product development and adopting a concurrent engineering approach to the project (see Figure C3.4).

Once the system design is reviewed and approved, different teams will begin working within the laboratory to design, develop, and test specific subsystems and components. Soon after this has begun the ILS team will start gathering information and preparing product documentation. Once the PDR is completed, the production teams will begin designing the necessary production lines. The CDR will include not only resolution of major technical questions but also a plan for manufacturing. Once the CDR is completed, project teams will begin field tests under a variety of different environmental conditions according to government specifications. Subsequent design refinements will be closely coordinated with manufacturing and ILS teams so that, ideally, ORION will be ready to begin producing the Jaguar upon completion of the PRR.

FIGURE C3.4
Jaguar Master Plan

Rosas believes that the phasing of the production and documentation work alongside the core development work will accelerate project completion, reduce production costs, and contribute to customer satisfaction.

1. What are the major changes between this plan and the way ORION has managed projects in the past?
2. How well do you believe these changes deal with the problems identified in Part A?
3. Who is likely to support this plan? Who is not likely to support this plan?

Defining the Project

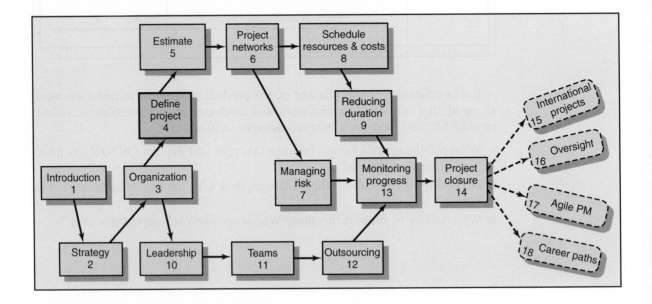

Defining the Project

Step 1: Defining the Project Scope

Step 2: Establishing Project Priorities

Step 3: Creating the Work Breakdown Structure

Step 4: Integrating the WBS with the Organization

Step 5: Coding the WBS for the Information System

Responsibility Matrices

Project Communication Plan

Summary

Select a dream
Use your dream to set a goal
Create a plan
Consider resources
Enhance skills and abilities
Spend time wisely
Start! Get organized and go

. . . it is one of those acro-whatevers,
said Pooh. *

Project managers in charge of a single small project can plan and schedule the project tasks without much formal planning and information. However, when the project manager must manage several small projects or a large complex project, a threshold is quickly reached in which the project manager can no longer cope with the detail.

This chapter describes a disciplined, structured method for selectively collecting information to use through all phases of the project life cycle, to meet the needs of all stakeholders (e.g., customer, project manager), and to measure performance against the strategic plan of the organization. The method suggested is a selective outline of the project called the *work breakdown structure*. The early stages of developing the outline serve to ensure that all tasks are identified and that participants of the project have an understanding of what is to be done. Once the outline and its detail are defined, an integrated information system can be developed to schedule work and allocate budgets. This baseline information is later used for control. With the work of the project defined through the *work breakdown structure,* the chapter concludes with the process of creating a communication plan used to help coordinate project activities and follow progress.

The five generic steps described herein provide a structured approach for collecting the project information necessary for developing a work breakdown structure. These steps and the development of project networks found in the next chapters all take place concurrently, and several iterations are typically required to develop dates and budgets that can be used to manage the project. The old saying "We can control only what we have planned" is true; therefore, defining the project is the first step.

* Roger E. Allen and Stephen D. Allen, *Winnie-the-Pooh on Success* (New York: Penguin, 1997), p. 10.

Step 1: Defining the Project Scope

Defining the project scope sets the stage for developing a project plan. Project scope is a definition of the end result or mission of your project—a product or service for your client/customer. The primary purpose is to define as clearly as possible the deliverable(s) for the end user and to focus project plans. As fundamental and essential as scope definition appears, it is frequently overlooked by project leaders of well-managed, large corporations.

Research clearly shows that a poorly defined scope or mission is the most frequently mentioned barrier to project success. In a study involving more than 1,400 project managers in the United States and Canada, Gobeli and Larson found that approximately 50 percent of the planning problems relate to unclear definition of scope and goals. This and other studies suggest a strong correlation between project success and clear scope definition. The scope document directs focus on the project purpose throughout the life of the project for the customer and project participants.

The scope should be developed under the direction of the project manager and customer. The project manager is responsible for seeing that there is agreement with the owner on project objectives, deliverables at each stage of the project, technical requirements, and so forth. For example, a deliverable in the early stage might be specifications; for the second stage, three prototypes for production; for the third, a sufficient quantity to introduce to market; and finally, marketing promotion and training.

Your project scope definition is a document that will be published and used by the project owner and project participants for planning and measuring project success. *Scope* describes what you expect to deliver to your customer when the project is complete. Your project scope should define the results to be achieved in specific, tangible, and measurable terms.

Employing a Project Scope Checklist

Clearly, project scope is the keystone interlocking all elements of a project plan. To ensure that scope definition is complete, you may wish to use the following checklist:

Project Scope Checklist

---
1. Project objective
2. Deliverables
3. Milestones
4. Technical requirements
5. Limits and exclusions
6. Reviews with customer

---

1. **Project objective.** The first step of project scope definition is to define the overall objective to meet your customer's need(s). For example, as a result of extensive market research a computer software company decides to develop a program that automatically translates verbal sentences in English to Russian. The project should be completed within three years at a cost not to exceed

$1.5 million. Another example is to design and produce a completely portable, hazardous waste, thermal treatment system in 13 months at a cost not to exceed $13 million. The project objective answers the questions of what, when, and how much.

2. **Deliverables.** The next step is to define major deliverables—the expected outputs over the life of the project. For example, deliverables in the early design phase of a project might be a list of specifications. In the second phase deliverables could be software coding and a technical manual. The next phase could be to test prototypes. The final phase could be final tests and approved software.

3. **Milestones.** A milestone is a significant event in a project that occurs at a point in time. The milestone schedule shows only major segments of work; it represents first, rough-cut estimates of time, cost, and resources for the project. The milestone schedule is built using the deliverables as a platform to identify major segments of work and an end date—for example, testing complete and finished by July 1 of the same year. Milestones should be natural, important control points in the project. Milestones should be easy for all project participants to recognize.

4. **Technical requirements.** More frequently than not, a product or service will have technical requirements to ensure proper performance. For example, a technical requirement for a personal computer might be the ability to accept 120-volt alternating current or 240-volt direct current without any adapters or user switches. Another well-known example is the ability of 911 emergency systems to identify the caller's phone number and location of the phone. Examples from information systems projects include speed and capacity of database systems and connectivity with alternative systems. For understanding the importance of key requirements, see Snapshot from Practice: Big Bertha.

5. **Limits and exclusions.** The limits of scope should be defined. Failure to do so can lead to false expectations and to expending resources and time on the wrong problem. Examples of limits are: local air transportation to and from base camps will be outsourced; system maintenance and repair will be done only up to one month after final inspection; client will be billed for additional training beyond that prescribed in the contract. Exclusions further define the boundary of the project by stating what is not included. Examples include: data will be collected by the client, not the contractor; a house will be built, but no landscaping or security devices added; software will be installed, but no training given.

6. **Reviews with customer.** Completion of the scope checklist ends with a review with your customer—internal or external. The main concern here is the understanding and agreement of expectations. Is the customer getting what he or she desires in deliverables? Does the project definition identify key accomplishments, budgets, timing, and performance requirements? Are questions of limits and exclusions covered? Clear communication in all these issues is imperative to avoid claims or misunderstanding.

Scope definition should be as brief as possible but complete; one or two pages are typical for small projects. See Snapshot from Practice: Scope Statement on page 105.

SNAPSHOT FROM PRACTICE | Big Bertha II versus the USGA's COR Requirement*

© Time & Life Pictures/Getty Images

In 1991 Callaway Golf Equipment introduced their Big Bertha driver and revolutionized the golf equipment business. Big Bertha—named after the World War I German long-distance cannon—was much larger than conventional woods and lacked a hosel (the socket in the head of the club into which the shaft is inserted) so that the weight could be better distributed throughout the head. This innovative design gave the clubhead a larger sweet spot, which allowed a player to strike the golf ball off-center and not suffer much loss in distance or accuracy. Callaway has maintained its preeminent position in the golf industry by utilizing space-age technology to extend the accuracy and distance of golf equipment.

In 2000 Callaway introduced the Big Bertha ERC II forged titanium driver. The driver was technologically superior to any driver on the market. However, there was one big problem. The new version of Bertha did not conform to the coefficient of restitution (COR) requirement established by the United States Golf Association (USGA). As a result it was barred from use by golfers in North America who intended to play by USGA's Rules of Golf.

The USGA believed that the rapid technological advances in golf equipment made by Callaway Golf and other golf manufacturers were threatening the integrity of the game. Players were hitting balls so much farther and straighter that golf courses around the world were being redesigned to make them longer and more difficult.

So in 1998 the USGA established performance thresholds for all new golf equipment. In order to prevent manufacturers from developing more powerful clubs, the USGA limited the COR of new golf equipment to 0.83. The COR was calculated by firing a golf ball at a driver out of a cannon-like machine at 109 miles per hour. The speed that the ball returned to the cannon could not exceed 83 percent of its initial speed (90.47 mph). The USGA called the ratio of incoming to outgoing velocity the coefficient of restitution (COR). The intent of the USGA COR threshold was to limit the distance that golf balls could be hit since studies indicated that 0.01 increase in COR resulted in two extra yards of carry. The Big Bertha ERC II's COR was 0.86.

After numerous efforts to get USGA to change its technical requirements, Callaway's engineers went back to the drawing board and in 2002 introduced Great Big Bertha II, which conformed to USGA's 0.83 COR restriction.

* John E. Gamble. "Callaway Golf Company: Sustaining Advantage in a Changing Industry," in A. A. Thompson, J. E. Gamble, and A. J. Strickland, *Strategy: Winning in the Marketplace,* Boston: McGraw-Hill/Irwin, 2004, pp. C204–C228.

SNAPSHOT FROM PRACTICE   Scope Statement

PROJECT OBJECTIVE

To construct a high-quality, custom home within five months at cost not to exceed $350,000.

DELIVERABLES

- A 2,200-square-foot, 2½-bath, 3-bedroom, finished home.
- A finished garage, insulated and sheetrocked.
- Kitchen appliances to include range, oven, microwave, and dishwasher.
- High-efficiency gas furnace with programmable thermostat.

MILESTONES

1. Permits approved—March 5
2. Foundation poured—March 14
3. Drywall in. Framing, sheathing, plumbing, electrical, and mechanical inspections passed—May 25
4. Final inspection—June 7

TECHNICAL REQUIREMENTS

1. Home must meet local building codes.
2. All windows and doors must pass NFRC class 40 energy ratings.
3. Exterior wall insulation must meet an "R" factor of 21.
4. Ceiling insulation must meet an "R" factor of 38.
5. Floor insulation must meet an "R" factor of 25.
6. Garage will accommodate two large-size cars and one 20-foot Winnebago.
7. Structure must pass seismic stability codes.

LIMITS AND EXCLUSIONS

1. The home will be built to the specifications and design of the original blueprints provided by the customer.
2. Owner responsible for landscaping.
3. Refrigerator is not included among kitchen appliances.
4. Air conditioning is not included but prewiring is included.
5. Contractor reserves the right to contract out services.
6. Contractor responsible for subcontracted work.
7. Site work limited to Monday through Friday, 8:00 A.M. to 6:00 P.M.

CUSTOMER REVIEW

John and Joan Smith

The checklist on page 102–103 is generic. Different industries and companies will develop unique checklists and templates to fit their needs and specific kinds of projects. Many companies engaged in contracted work refer to **scope statements** as *statements of work* (SOW). Other organizations use the term *project charter.* However, the term **project charter** has emerged to have a special meaning in the world of project management. A project charter refers to a document that authorizes the project manager to initiate and lead the project. This document is issued by upper management and provides the project manager with written authority to use organizational resources for project activities. Often the charter will include a brief scope description as well as such items as risk limits, customer needs, spending limits, and even team composition.

Many projects suffer from **scope creep,** which is the tendency for the project scope to expand over time—usually by changing requirements, specifications, and priorities. Scope creep can be reduced by carefully writing your scope statement. A scope statement that is too broad is an invitation for scope creep. Scope creep can have a positive or negative effect on the project, but in most cases scope creep means added costs and possible project delays. Changes in requirements, specifications, and priorities frequently result in cost overruns and delays. Examples are abundant—Denver airport baggage handling system; Boston's new freeway system ("The Big Dig"); China's fast train in Shanghai; and the list goes on. On software development projects, scope creep is manifested in bloated products in which added functionality undermines ease of use.

Finally, the matrix is useful midway in the project for approaching a problem that must be solved.

One caveat must be mentioned; during the course of a project, priorities may change. The customer may suddenly need the project completed one month sooner, or new directives from top management may emphasize cost saving initiatives. The project manager needs to be vigilant in order to anticipate and confirm changes in priorities and make appropriate adjustments.

Step 3: Creating the Work Breakdown Structure

Major Groupings Found in a WBS

Once the scope and deliverables have been identified, the work of the project can be successively subdivided into smaller and smaller work elements. The outcome of this hierarchical process is called the **work breakdown structure (WBS).** The WBS is a map of the project. Use of WBS helps to assure project managers that all products and work elements are identified, to integrate the project with the current organization, and to establish a basis for control. Basically, the WBS is an outline of the project with different levels of detail.

Figure 4.3 shows the major groupings commonly used in the field to develop a hierarchical WBS. The WBS begins with the project as the final deliverable.

FIGURE 4.3
Hierarchical Breakdown of the WBS

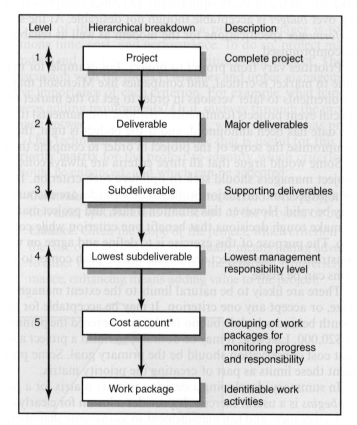

Level	Hierarchical breakdown	Description
1	Project	Complete project
2	Deliverable	Major deliverables
3	Subdeliverable	Supporting deliverables
4	Lowest subdeliverable	Lowest management responsibility level
5	Cost account*	Grouping of work packages for monitoring progress and responsibility
	Work package	Identifiable work activities

* This breakdown groups work packages by type of work within a deliverable and allows assignment of responsibility to an organizational unit. This extra step facilitates a system for monitoring project progress (discussed in Chapter 13).

Major project work deliverables/systems are identified first; then the subdeliverables necessary to accomplish the larger deliverables are defined. The process is repeated until the subdeliverable detail is small enough to be manageable and where one person can be responsible. This subdeliverable is further divided into work packages. Because the lowest subdeliverable usually includes several work packages, the work packages are grouped by type of work—for example, hardware, programming, testing. These groupings within a subdeliverable are called cost accounts. This grouping facilitates a system for monitoring project progress by work, cost, and responsibility.

How WBS Helps the Project Manager

The WBS defines all the elements of the project in a hierarchical framework and establishes their relationships to the project end item(s). Think of the project as a large work package that is successively broken down into smaller work packages; the total project is the summation of all the smaller work packages. This hierarchical structure facilitates evaluation of cost, time, and technical performance at all levels in the organization over the life of the project. The WBS also provides management with information appropriate to each level. For example, top management deals primarily with major deliverables, while first-line supervisors deal with smaller subdeliverables and work packages.

Each item in the WBS needs a time and cost estimate. With this information it is possible to plan, schedule, and budget your project. The WBS also serves as a framework for tracking cost and work performance.

As the WBS is developed, organizational units and individuals are assigned responsibility for executing work packages. This integrates the work and the organization. In practice, this process is sometimes called the organization breakdown structure (OBS), which will be further discussed later in the chapter.

Use of the WBS provides the opportunity to "roll up" (sum) the budget and actual costs of the smaller work packages into larger work elements so that performance can be measured by organizational units and work accomplishment.

The WBS can also be used to define communication channels and assist in understanding and coordinating many parts of the project. The structure shows the work and organizational units responsible and suggests where written communication should be directed. Problems can be quickly addressed and coordinated because the structure integrates work and responsibility.

WBS Development

Figure 4.4 on page 112 shows a simplified WBS for development of a new personal computer project. At the top of the chart (level 1) is the project end item—a deliverable product or service. Note how the levels of the structure can represent information for different levels of management. For example, level 1 information represents the total project objective and is useful to top management; levels 2, 3, and 4 are suitable for middle management; and level 5 is for first-line managers.

Level 2 shows a partial list of deliverables necessary to develop the personal computer. One deliverable is the disk storage unit (shaded), which is made up of three subdeliverables—external USB, optical, and hard disks. Finally, the hard disk requires four subdeliverables—motor, circuit board, chassis frame, and read/write head. These subdeliverables represent the lowest manageable elements

SNAPSHOT FROM PRACTICE   London 2012 Olympic Games

On July 27, 2012, the London Olympic Games will start. Olympic Delivery Authority (ODA), the Olympics' project client, makes it clear: "Not starting on that day is not an option. The deadline is 100 percent fixed!" This is the mandate for both the general contractors and the information services (IS) teams. Each must meet the schedule while contributing to the overall objectives of the Olympic team.

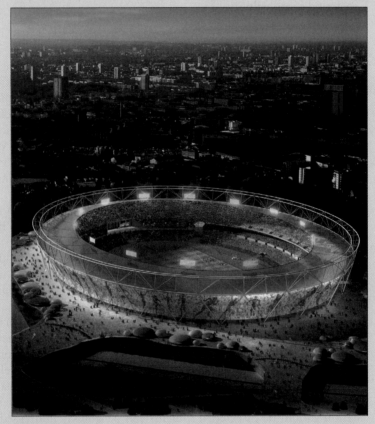

© PA Photos/Landov

2012 Olympic Project Team Objectives:

- To stage the 2012 Olympic and Paralympic games: 27 July–12 August, 2012;
- To deliver an Olympic park and related venues;

- To maximize economic, social, health, and environmental benefits for London and for the UK;
- To provide sustained improvement in UK sports pre and post games;

of the project. Each subdeliverable requires work packages that will be completed by an assigned organizational unit. Each deliverable will be successively divided in this manner. It is not necessary to divide all elements of the WBS to the same level.

The lowest level of the WBS is called a **work package.** Work packages are short-duration tasks that have a definite start and stop point, consume resources, and represent cost. Each work package is a control point. A work package manager is

- To ensure the venues are used for something useful post games.

  Below is the initial timeline for the 2012 Olympic event:

  2006: Set foundations
  2007: Strategic planning
  2008: Review all past Olympics
  2010: Operational planning
  2011: Test events
  2012: Operational readiness
  2013: Close down

Source: ComputerWeekly.com

Physical facilities and information services are two of the major areas that need massive coordination and represent a sizable part of the total budget.

London 2012 will be the sixth Olympic Games that Atos Origin will design, build and operate the IS infrastructure. Michele Hyron, their chief integrator responsible for the event's information systems, will be overseeing one of the biggest information technology projects ever. She is a seasoned Olympics project manager who has served as IS operations manager in previous Olympic Games in Athens and Beijing. By examining the processes and lessons learned in the earlier games, she hopes past mistakes can be avoided. For example, from the Beijing games four lessons learned were better training of support staff, freezing design four months before games, isolating IT from the Internet, and better planning.

Hyron carries over about 40 to 50 percent of systems planning from one Olympics to the next, and then adjusts to local conditions. Hyron has designed and is building fully redundant systems for 2012 that will be used for two years of testing of over 1,000 scenarios to study how the systems and technical personnel respond. Test scenarios might include a security breach, a fire in a living facility, staff contracting food poisoning, and events delayed.

Physical facilities and logistics are equally as important as IS infrastructure. The Olympic Delivery Authority (ODA) selected EDAW Consortium to design a master plan for the Olympic Park's infrastructure, including utilities, waterways, landscape, platforms for the site, roads, and bridges.

A 500-acre Olympic Park in Stratford, east London, will be the epicenter of the Games. The Olympic Stadium will house the 80,000-seat coliseum as well as the aquatics center that has two pools and a diving pool. A Channel Tunnel Rail Link (CTRL) will carry a high-speed shuttle service between central London and the Olympic Park in just seven minutes. This link will also connect with service to continental Europe. Transportation to the Olympics will be supported with improved underground services. Planners expect to have a train arriving at the Olympic Park every 15 seconds. There will be 20 km of new roads and more than 30 new bridges to connect the Olympic Park with nearby communities. Prime Minister Gordon Brown estimates that nearly 30,000 workers will build the Olympic Park and Olympic Village.

From the outset, cost estimating has been a challenge. When London announced its bid for the 2012 Games, the estimated cost for the games was £4 billion. By 2007 the estimated costs climbed to £9.325 billion. In mid-2009, 500 industry professionals estimate the costs will rise to £11.6 billion. Some estimates have run as high as £12.6 billion.

The National Audit Office study identified two major problems with the Olympic Games project: no one single individual is in charge and there is no proper budget. In addition, the committee offered the following suggestions: (a) clarify key deliverables and expected costs, (b) establish a baseline for budget control, and (c) manage both contingency and project funds more rigorously.

The Olympics Games are often called "the greatest show on earth." For the project managers of the 2012 Olympics, there are many challenges and opportunities to be addressed before the Games are over.

responsible for seeing that the package is completed on time, within budget, and according to technical specifications. Practice suggests a work package should not exceed 10 workdays or one reporting period. If a work package has a duration exceeding 10 days, check or monitoring points should be established within the duration, say, every three to five days, so progress and problems can be identified before too much time has passed. Each work package of the WBS should be as independent of other packages of the project as possible. No work package is described in more than one subdeliverable of the WBS.

FIGURE 4.4 **Work Breakdown Structure**

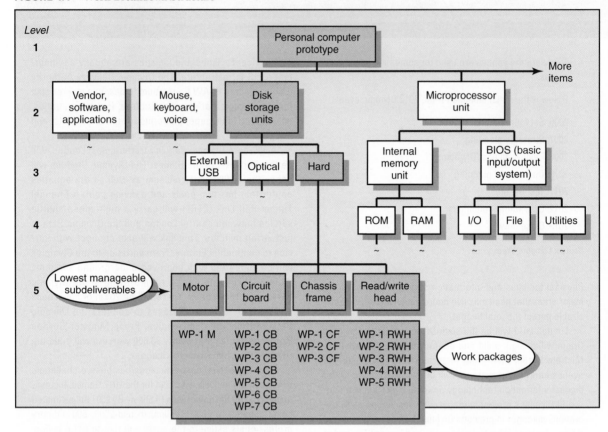

There is an important difference from start to finish between the last work breakdown subdeliverable and a work package. Typically, a work breakdown subdeliverable includes the outcomes of more than one work package from perhaps two or three departments. Therefore, the subdeliverable does not have a duration of its own and does not consume resources or cost money directly. (In a sense, of course, a duration for a particular work breakdown element can be derived from identifying which work package must start first [earliest] and which package will be the latest to finish; the difference from start to finish becomes the duration for the subdeliverable.) The higher elements are used to identify deliverables at different phases in the project and to develop status reports during the execution stage of the project life cycle. Thus, the work package is the basic unit used for planning, scheduling, and controlling the project.

To review, each work package in the WBS

1. Defines work (what).
2. Identifies time to complete a work package (how long).
3. Identifies a time-phased budget to complete a work package (cost).
4. Identifies resources needed to complete a work package (how much).

5. Identifies a single person responsible for units of work (who).
6. Identifies monitoring points for measuring progress (how well).

Creating a WBS from scratch can be a daunting task. Project managers should take advantage of relevant examples from previous projects to begin the process.

WBSs are products of group efforts. If the project is small, the entire project team may be involved breaking down the project into its components. For large, complex projects, the people responsible for the major deliverables are likely to meet to establish the first two levels of deliverables. In turn, further detail would be delegated to the people responsible for the specific work. Collectively this information would be gathered and integrated into a formal WBS by a project support person. The final version would be reviewed by the inner echelon of the project team. Relevant stakeholders (most notably customers) would be consulted to confirm agreement and revise when appropriate.

Project teams developing their first WBS frequently forget that the structure should be end-item, output oriented. First attempts often result in a WBS that follows the organization structure—design, marketing, production, finance. If a WBS follows the organization structure, the focus will be on the organization function and processes rather than the project output or deliverables. In addition, a WBS with a process focus will become an accounting tool that records costs by function rather than a tool for "output" management. Every effort should be made to develop a WBS that is output oriented in order to concentrate on concrete deliverables. See Snapshot from Practice: Creating a WBS for more advice on creating a WBS. This process is discussed next.

Step 4: Integrating the WBS with the Organization

The WBS is used to link the organizational units responsible for performing the work. In practice, the outcome of this process is the **organization breakdown structure (OBS).** The OBS depicts how the firm has organized to discharge work responsibility. The purposes of the OBS are to provide a framework to summarize organization unit work performance, identify organization units responsible for work packages, and tie the organizational unit to cost control accounts. Recall, cost accounts group similar work packages (usually under the purview of a department). The OBS defines the organization subdeliverables in a hierarchical pattern in successively smaller and smaller units. Frequently, the traditional organization structure can be used. Even if the project is completely performed by a team, it is necessary to break down the team structure for assigning responsibility for budgets, time, and technical performance.

As in the WBS, the OBS assigns the lowest organizational unit the responsibility for work packages within a cost account. Herein lies one major strength of using WBS and OBS; they can be *integrated* as shown in Figure 4.5. The intersection of work packages and the organizational unit creates a project control point **(cost account)** that integrates work and responsibility. The intersection of the WBS and OBS represents the set of work packages necessary to complete the subdeliverable located immediately above and the organizational unit on the left responsible for accomplishing the packages at the intersection. Later we will use the intersection as a cost account for management control of projects. For example, the circuit

SNAPSHOT FROM PRACTICE   Creating a WBS

 Figure 4.4 represents the classic WBS in which the project is broken down to the lowest manageable deliverable and subsequent work packages. Many situations do not require this level of detail. This begs the questions of how far you should break down the work.

There is no set answer to this question. However, here are some tips given by project managers:

Break down the work until you can do an estimate that is accurate enough for your purposes. If you are doing a ballpark estimate to see if the project is worthy of serious consideration, you probably do not need to break it down beyond major deliverables. On the other hand, if you are pricing a project to submit a competitive bid, then you are likely to go down to the work package level.

The WBS should conform to how you are going to schedule work. For example, if assignments are made in terms of days, then tasks should be limited as best as possible to one day or more to complete. Conversely, if hours are the smallest unit for scheduling, then work can be broken down to one-hour increments.

Final activities should have clearly defined start/end events. Avoid open-ended tasks like "research" or "market analysis." Take it down to the next level in which deliverables/outcomes are more clearly defined. Instead of ending with market analysis include items such as identify market share, list user requirements, or write a problem statement.

If accountability and control are important, then break the work down so that one individual is clearly responsible

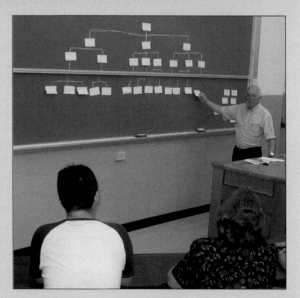

for the work. For example, instead of stopping at product design, take it to the next level and identify specific components of the design (i.e., electrical schematics, power source, etc.) that different individuals will be responsible for creating.

The bottom line is that the WBS should provide the level of detail needed to manage the specific project successfully.

board element requires completion of work packages whose primary responsibility will include the design, production, test, and software departments. Control can be checked from two directions—outcomes and responsibility. In the execution phase of the project, progress can be tracked vertically on deliverables (client's interest) and tracked horizontally by organization responsibility (management's interest).

Step 5: Coding the WBS for the Information System

Gaining the maximum usefulness of a breakdown structure depends on a coding system. The codes are used to define levels and elements in the WBS, organization elements, work packages, and budget and cost information. The codes allow reports to be consolidated at any level in the structure. The most commonly used scheme in practice is numeric indention. An example for the

FIGURE 4.5 Integration of WBS and OBS

new computer project and the "Disk storage units" in Figure 4.5 is presented here:

```
1.0   Computer project
      1.1   Disk storage units
            1.1.1   External USB
            1.1.2   Optical
            1.1.3   Hard
                    1.1.3.1   Motor
                              1.1.3.1.1   Sourcing work package
                                          .

                                          .

                    1.1.3.4   Read/write head
                              1.1.3.4.1   Cost account
                              1.1.3.4.2   Cost account
                                          1.1.3.4.2.1            WP
                                          1.1.3.4.2.2            WP
                                          1.1.3.4.2.3            WP
                              1.1.3.4.3   Cost account
                                          .

                                          .

                                          .

                                          etc.
```

Note the project identification is 1.0. Each successive indention represents a lower element or work package. Ultimately the numeric scheme reaches down to the work package level, and all tasks and elements in the structure have an identification code. The "cost account" is the focal point because all budgets, work assignments, time, cost, and technical performance come together at this point.

This coding system can be extended to cover large projects. Additional schemes can be added for special reports. For example, adding a "−3" after the code could indicate a site location, an elevation, or a special account such as labor. Some letters can be used as special identifiers such as "M" for materials or "E" for engineers. You are not limited to only 10 subdivisions (0–9); you can extend each subdivision to large numbers—for example, .1–.99 or .1–.9999. If the project is small, you can use whole numbers. The following example is from a large, complex project:

$$3R-237A-P2-33.6$$

where 3R identifies the facility, 237A represents elevation and the area, P2 represents pipe two inches wide, and 33.6 represents the work package number. In practice most organizations are creative in combining letters and numbers to minimize the length of WBS codes.

Responsibility Matrices

In many cases, the size and scope of the project do not warrant an elaborate WBS or OBS. One tool that is widely used by project managers and task force leaders of small projects is the **responsibility matrix** (RM). The RM (sometimes

FIGURE 4.6   **Responsibility Matrix for a Market Research Project**

Task	Project Team				
	Richard	Dan	Dave	Linda	Elizabeth
Identify target customers	R	S		S	
Develop draft questionnaire	R	S	S		
Pilot-test questionnaire		R		S	
Finalize questionnaire	R	S	S	S	
Print questionnaire					R
Prepare mailing labels					R
Mail questionnaires					R
Receive and monitor returned questionnaires				R	S
Input response data			R		
Analyze results		R	S	S	
Prepare draft of report	S	R	S	S	
Prepare final report	R		S		

R = Responsible
S = Supports/assists

called a linear responsibility chart) summarizes the tasks to be accomplished and who is responsible for what on a project. In its simplest form an RM consists of a chart listing all the project activities and the participants responsible for each activity. For example, Figure 4.6 illustrates an RM for a market research study. In this matrix the R is used to identify the committee member who is responsible for coordinating the efforts of other team members assigned to the task and making sure that the task is completed. The S is used to identify members of the five-person team who will support and/or assist the individual responsible. Simple RMs like this one are useful not only for organizing and assigning responsibilities for small projects but also for subprojects of large, more complex projects.

More complex RMs not only identify individual responsibilities but also clarify critical interfaces between units and individuals that require coordination. For example, Figure 4.7 is an RM for a larger, more complex project to develop a new piece of automated equipment. Notice that within each cell a numeric coding scheme is used to define the nature of involvement on that specific task. Such an RM extends the WBS/OBS and provides a clear and concise method for depicting responsibility, authority, and communication channels.

Responsibility matrices provide a means for all participants in a project to view their responsibilities and agree on their assignments. They also help clarify the extent or type of authority exercised by each participant in performing an activity in which two or more parties have overlapping involvement. By using an RM and by defining authority, responsibility, and communications within its framework, the relationship between different organizational units and the work content of the project is made clear.

FIGURE 4.7 Responsibility Matrix for the Conveyor Belt Project

Deliverables	Design	Development	Documentation	Assembly	Testing	Purchasing	Quality Assur.	Manufacturing
Architectural designs	1	2			2		3	3
Hardware specifications	2	1				2	3	
Kernel specifications	1	3						3
Utilities specifications	2	1			3			
Hardware design	1			3		3		3
Disk drivers	3	1	2					
Memory management	1	3			3			
Operating system documentation	2	2	1					3
Prototypes	5		4	1	3	3	3	4
Integrated acceptance test	5	2	2		1		5	5

Organization

1 Responsible
2 Support
3 Consult
4 Notification
5 Approval

Project Communication Plan

Once the project deliverables and work are clearly identified, following up with an internal communication plan is vital. Stories abound of poor communication as a major contributor to project failure. Having a robust communications plan can go a long way toward mitigating project problems and can ensure that customers, team members, and other stakeholders have the information to do their jobs.

The communication plan is usually created by the project manager and/or the project team in the early stage of project planning.

Communication is a key component in coordinating and tracking project schedules, issues, and action items. The plan maps out the flow of information to different stakeholders and becomes an integral part of the overall project plan. The purpose of a project communication plan is to express what, who, how, and when information will be transmitted to project stakeholders so schedules, issues, and action items can be tracked.

Project communication plans address the following core questions:

- What information needs to be collected and when?
- Who will receive the information?
- What methods will be used to gather and store information?
- What are the limits, if any, on who has access to certain kinds of information?
- When will the information be communicated?
- How will it be communicated?

Developing a communication plan that answers these questions usually entails the following basic steps:

1. **Stakeholder analysis.** Identify the target groups. Typical groups could be the customer, sponsor, project team, project office, or anyone who needs project information to make decisions and/or contribute to project progress.

2. **Information needs.** What information is pertinent to stakeholders who contribute to the project's progress? For example, top management needs to know how the project is progressing, whether it is encountering critical problems, and the extent to which project goals are being realized. This information is required so that they can make strategic decisions and manage the portfolio of projects. Project team members need to see schedules, task lists, specifications, and the like, so they know what needs to be done next. External groups need to know any changes in the schedule and performance requirements of the components they are providing. Frequent information needs found in communication plans are:

Project status reports	Deliverable issues
Changes in scope	Team status meetings
Gating decisions	Accepted request changes
Action items	Milestone reports

3. **Sources of information.** When the information needs are identified, the next step is to determine the sources of information. That is, where does the information reside? How will it be collected? For example, information relating to the milestone report, team meetings, and project status meetings would be found in the minutes and reports of various groups.

4. **Dissemination modes.** In today's world, traditional status report meetings are being supplemented by e-mail, teleconferencing, Lotus Notes, SharePoint, and a variety of database sharing programs to circulate information. In particular, many companies are using the Web to create a "virtual project office" to store project information. Project management software feeds information directly to the Web site so that different people have immediate access to relevant project information. In some cases, appropriate information is routed automatically to key stakeholders. Backup paper hardcopy to specific stakeholders is still critical for many project changes and action items.

5. **Responsibility and timing.** Determine who will send out the information. For example, a common practice is to have secretaries of meetings forward the minutes or specific information to the appropriate stakeholders. In some cases the responsibility lies with the project manager or project office. Timing and frequency of distribution appropriate to the information need to be established.

The advantage of establishing a communication plan is that instead of responding to information requests, you are controlling the flow of information. This reduces confusion and unnecessary interruptions, and it can provide project managers greater autonomy. Why? By reporting on a regular basis how things are going and what is happening, you allow senior management to feel more comfortable about letting the team complete the project without interference. See Figure 4.8 for a sample Shale Oil Research Project Communication Plan.

FIGURE 4.8 **Shale Oil Research Project Communication Plan**

What Information	Target Audience	When?	Method of Communication	Provider
Milestone report	Senior management and project manager	Bimonthly	E-mail and hardcopy	Project office
Project status reports & agendas	Staff and customer	Weekly	E-mail and hardcopy	Project manager
Team status reports	Project manager and project office	Weekly	E-mail	Team recorder
Issues report	Staff and customer	Weekly	E-mail	Team recorder
Escalation reports	Staff and customer	When needed	Meeting and hardcopy	Project manager
Outsourcing performance	Staff and customer	Bimonthly	Meeting	Project manager
Accepted change requests	Project office, senior mgmt., customer, staff, and project mgr.	Anytime	E-mail and hardcopy	Design department
Oversight gate decisions	Senior management and project manager	As required	E-mail meeting report	Oversight group or project office

The importance of establishing up-front a plan for communicating important project information cannot be overstated. Many of the problems that plague a project can be traced back to insufficient time devoted to establishing a well-grounded internal communication plan.

Summary

The project scope definition, priorities, and breakdown structure are the keys to nearly every aspect of managing the project. The scope definition provides focus and emphasis on the end item(s) of the project. Establishing project priorities allows managers to make appropriate trade-off decisions. The structure helps ensure all tasks of the project are identified and provides two views of the project—one on deliverables and one on organization responsibility. The WBS avoids having the project driven by organization function or by a finance system. The structure forces attention to realistic requirements of personnel, hardware, and budgets. Use of the structure provides a powerful framework for project control that identifies deviations from plan, identifies responsibility, and spots areas for improved performance. No well-developed project plan or control system is possible without a disciplined, structured approach. The WBS, OBS, and cost account codes provide this discipline. The WBS will serve as the database for developing the project network which establishes the timing of work, people, equipment, and costs.

In small projects responsibility matrices may be used to clarify individual responsibility.

Clearly defining your project is the first and most important step in planning. The absence of a clearly defined project plan consistently shows up as the major reason for project failures. Whether you use a WBS or responsibility matrix will depend primarily on the size and nature of your project. Whatever method you use, definition of your project should be adequate to allow for good control as the project is being implemented. Follow-up with a clear communication plan for coordinating and tracking project progress will help keep important stakeholders informed and avoid some potential problems.

Key Terms

Cost account, *113*
Milestone, *103*
Organization
  breakdown
  structure (OBS), *113*

Priority matrix, *106*
Project charter, *105*
Responsibility
  matrix, *116*
Scope creep, *105*

Scope statement, *105*
Work breakdown
  structure (WBS), *108*
Work package, *110*

Review Questions

1. What are the six elements of a typical scope statement?
2. What questions does a project objective answer? What would be an example of a good project objective?
3. What does it mean if the priorities of a project include: Time-constrain, Scope-accept, and Cost-enhance?
4. What kinds of information are included in a work package?
5. When would it be appropriate to create a responsibility matrix rather than a full-blown WBS?
6. How does a communication plan benefit management of projects?

Exercises

1. You are in charge of organizing a dinner-dance concert for a local charity. You have reserved a hall that will seat 30 couples and have hired a jazz combo.

   a. Develop a scope statement for this project that contains examples of all the elements. Assume that the event will occur in 4 weeks and provide your best guess estimate of the dates for milestones.

   b. What would the priorities likely be for this project?

2. In small groups, identify real life examples of a project that would fit each of the following priority scenarios:

   a. Time-constrain, Scope-enhance, Cost-accept

   b. Time-accept, Scope-constrain, Cost-accept

   c. Time-constrain, Scope-accept, Cost-enhance

3. Develop a WBS for a project in which you are going to build a bicycle. Try to identify all of the major components and provide three levels of detail.

4. You are the father or mother of a family of four (kids ages 13 and 15) planning a weekend camping trip. Develop a responsibility matrix for the work that needs to be done prior to starting your trip.

5. Develop a WBS for a local stage play. Be sure to identify the deliverables and organizational units (people) responsible. How would you code your system? Give an example of the work packages in one of your cost accounts. Develop a corresponding OBS which identifies who is responsible for what.

6. Use an example of a project you are familiar with or are interested in. Identify the deliverables and organizational units (people) responsible. How would you code your system? Give an example of the work packages in one of your cost accounts.

7. Develop a communication plan for an airport security project. The project entails installing the hardware and software system that (1) scans a passenger's eyes, (2) fingerprints the passenger, and (3) transmits the information to a central location for evaluation.

8. Go to an Internet search engine (e.g., Google) and type in "project communication plan." Check three or four that have ".gov" as their source. How are they similar or dissimilar? What would be your conclusion concerning the importance of an internal communication plan?

9. Your roommate is about to submit a scope statement for a spring concert sponsored by the entertainment council at Western Evergreen State University (WESU). WESU is a residential university with over 22,000 students. This will be the first time in six years since WESU sponsored a spring concert. The entertainment council has budgeted $40,000 for the project. The event is to occur on June 5th. Since your roommate knows you are taking a class on project management she has asked you to review her scope statement and make suggestions for improvement. She considers the concert a resume-building experience and wants to be as professional as possible. Below is a draft of her scope statement. What suggestions would you make and why?

WESU Spring Music Concert

Project Objective

To organize and deliver a 6-hour music concert

Deliverables

- Concert security
- Contact local newspapers and radio stations

- Separate beer garden
- Six hours of musical entertainment
- Design a commemorative concert t-shirt
- Local sponsors
- Food venues
- Event insurance
- Safe environment

Milestones

1. Secure all permissions and approvals
2. Sign big-name artist
3. Contact secondary artists
4. Secure vendor contracts
5. Advertising campaign
6. Plan set-up
7. Concert
8. Clean-up

Technical Requirements

1. Professional sound stage and system
2. At least five performing acts
3. Restroom facilities
4. Parking
5. Compliance with WESU and city requirements/ordinances

Limits and Exclusions

- Seating capacity for 8,000 students.
- Performers are responsible for travel arrangement to and from WESU.
- Performers must provide own liability insurance.
- Performers and security personnel will be provided lunch and dinner on the day of the concert.
- Vendors contribute 25 percent of sales to concert fund.
- Concert must be over at 12:15 A.M.

Customer Review: WESU

References

Ashley, D. B., et al., "Determinants of Construction Project Success," *Project Management Journal,* 18 (2) June 1987, p. 72.

Chilmeran, A. H., "Keeping Costs on Track," *PM Network,* 19 (2) 2004, pp. 45–51.

Gobeli, D. H., and E. W. Larson, "Project Management Problems," *Engineering Management Journal,* 2, 1990, pp. 31–36.

Ingebretsen, M., "Taming the Beast," *PM Network,* July 2003, pp. 30–35.

Katz, D. M., "Case Study: Beware 'Scope Creep' on ERP Projects," *CFO.com,* March 27, 2001.

Kerzner, H., *Project Management: A Systems Approach to Planning,* 8th ed. (New York: Van Nostrand Reinhold, 2003).

Lewis, J. P., *Project Planning, Scheduling and Controlling,* 3rd ed. (Burr Ridge, IL: McGraw-Hill, 2000).

Luby, R. E., D. Peel, and W. Swahl, "Component-Based Work Breakdown Structure," *Project Management Journal,* 26 (2) December 1995, pp. 38–44.

Murch, R., *Project Management: Best Practices for IT Professionals* (Upper Darby, NJ: Prentice Hall, 2001).

Pinto, J. K., and D. P. Slevin, "Critical Success Factors Across the Project Life Cycle," *Project Management Journal,* 19 (3) June 1988, p. 72.

Pitagorsky, G., "Realistic Project Planning Promotes Success," *Engineer's Digest,* 29 (1) 2001.

PMI Standards Committee, *Guide to the Project Management Body of Knowledge* (Newton Square, PA: Project Management Institute, 2000).

Posner, B. Z., "What It Takes to Be a Good Project Manager," *Project Management Journal,* 18 (1) March 1987, p. 52.

Raz, T., and S. Globerson, "Effective Sizing and Content Definition of Work Packages," *Project Management Journal,* 29 (4) 1998, pp. 17–23.

Tate, K., and K. Hendrix, "Chartering IT Projects," *Proceedings, 30th Annual, Project Management Institute* (Philadelphia, PA. 1999), CD.

Zimmerman, E., "Preventing Scope Creep," *Manage,* February 2000.

Case

Manchester United Soccer Club

Nicolette Larson was loading the dishwasher with her husband, Kevin, and telling him about the first meeting of the Manchester United Tournament Organizing Committee. Nicolette, a self-confessed "soccer mom," had been elected tournament director and was responsible for organizing the club's first summer tournament.

Manchester United Soccer Club (MUSC) located in Manchester, New Hampshire, was formed in 1992 as a way of bringing recreational players to a higher level of competition and preparing them for the State Olympic Development Program and/or high school teams. The club currently has 24 boys and girls (ranging in age from under 9 to 16) on teams affiliated with the Hampshire Soccer Association and the Granite State Girls Soccer League. The club's board of directors decided in the fall to sponsor a summer invitational soccer tournament to generate revenue. Given the boom in youth soccer, hosting summer tournaments has become a popular method for raising funds. MUSC teams regularly compete in three to four tournaments each summer at different locales in New England. These tournaments have been reported to generate between $50,000 and $70,000 for the host club.

MUSC needs additional revenue to refurbish and expand the number of soccer fields at the Rock Rimmon soccer complex. Funds would also be used to augment the club's scholarship program, which provides financial aid to players who cannot afford the $450 annual club dues.

Nicolette gave her husband a blow-by-blow account of what transpired during the first tournament committee meeting that night. She started the meeting by having everyone introduce themselves and by proclaiming how excited she was that the club was going to sponsor its own tournament. She then suggested that the committee brainstorm what needed to be done to pull off the event; she would record their ideas on a flipchart.

What emerged was a free-for-all of ideas and suggestions. One member immediately stressed the importance of having qualified referees and spent several minutes describing in detail how his son's team was robbed in a poorly officiated championship game. This was followed by other stories of injustice on the soccer field. Another member suggested that they needed to quickly contact the local colleges to see if they could use their fields. The committee spent more than 30 minutes talking about how they should screen teams and how much they should charge as an entry fee. An argument broke out over whether they should reward the winning teams in each age bracket with medals or trophies. Many members felt that medals were too cheap, while others thought the trophies would be too expensive. Someone suggested that they seek local corporate sponsors to help fund the tournament. The proposed sale of tournament T-shirts and sweatshirts was followed by a general critique of the different shirts parents had acquired at different tournaments. One member advocated that they recruit an artist he knew to develop a unique silk-screen design for the tournament. The meeting adjourned 30 minutes late with only half of the members remaining until the end. Nicolette drove home with seven sheets of ideas and a headache.

As Kevin poured a glass of water for the two aspirin Nicolette was about to take, he tried to comfort her by saying that organizing this tournament would be a big project not unlike the projects he works on at his engineering and design firm. He offered to sit down with her the next night and help her plan the project. He suggested that the first thing they needed to do was to develop a WBS for the project.

1. Make a list of the major deliverables for the project and use them to develop a draft of the work breakdown structure for the tournament that contains at least three levels of detail. What are the major deliverables associated with hosting an event such as a soccer tournament?
2. How would developing a WBS alleviate some of the problems that occurred during the first meeting and help Nicolette organize and plan the project?
3. Where can Nicolette find additional information to help her develop a WBS for the tournament?
4. How could Nicolette and her task force use the WBS to generate cost estimates for the tournament? Why would this be useful information?

Estimating Project Times and Costs

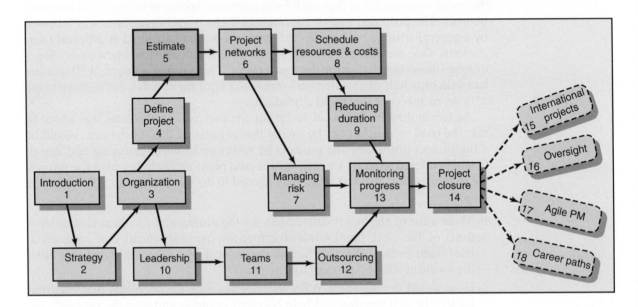

Estimating Project Times and Costs
Factors Influencing the Quality of Estimates
Estimating Guidelines for Times, Costs, and Resources
Top-Down versus Bottom-Up Estimating
Methods for Estimating Project Times and Costs
Level of Detail
Types of Costs
Refining Estimates
Creating a Database for Estimating
Summary
Appendix 5.1: Learning Curves for Estimating

Project estimation is indeed a yardstick for project cost control. And if the yardstick is faulty, you start on the "wrong foot." . . . we exhort you not to underestimate the estimate.*

Given the urgency to start work on the project, managers sometimes minimize or avoid the effort to follow through on estimating project time and cost. This attitude is a huge mistake and costly. There are important reasons to make the effort and incur the cost of estimating for your project. Exhibit 5.1 summarizes some key reasons.

Estimating is the process of forecasting or approximating the time and cost of completing project deliverables. Estimating processes are frequently classified as top-down and bottom-up. Top-down estimates are usually done by senior management. Management will often derive estimates from analogy, group consensus, or mathematical relationships. Bottom-up estimates are typically performed by the people who are doing the work. Their estimates are based on estimates of elements found in the work breakdown structure.

All project stakeholders prefer accurate cost and time estimates, but they also understand the inherent uncertainty in all projects. Inaccurate estimates lead to false expectations and consumer dissatisfaction. Accuracy is improved with greater effort, but is it worth the time and cost—estimating costs money! Project estimating becomes a trade-off, balancing the benefits of better accuracy against the costs for securing increased accuracy.

EXHIBIT 5.1
Why Estimating Time and Cost Are Important

- Estimates are needed to support good decisions.
- Estimates are needed to schedule work.
- Estimates are needed to determine how long the project should take and its cost.
- Estimates are needed to determine whether the project is worth doing.
- Estimates are needed to develop cash flow needs.
- Estimates are needed to determine how well the project is progressing.
- Estimates are needed to develop time-phased budgets and establish the project baseline.

* O. P. Kharbanda and J. K. Pinto. *What Made Gertie Gallop: Learning from Project Failures* (New York: Von Nostrand Reinhold, 1996), p 73.

Cost, time, and budget estimates are the lifeline for control; they serve as the standard for comparison of actual and plan throughout the life of the project. Project status reports depend on reliable estimates as the major input for measuring variances and taking corrective action. Ideally, the project manager, and in most cases the customer, would prefer to have a database of detailed schedule and cost estimates for every work package in the project. Regrettably, such detailed data gathering is not always possible or practical and other methods are used to develop project estimates.

Factors Influencing the Quality of Estimates

A typical statement in the field is the desire to "have a 95 percent probability of meeting time and cost estimates." *Past experience* is a good starting point for developing time and cost estimates. But past experience estimates must almost always be refined by other considerations to reach the 95 percent probability level. Factors related to the uniqueness of the project will have a strong influence on the accuracy of estimates. Project, people, and external factors all need to be considered to improve quality of estimates for project times and costs.

Planning Horizon

The quality of the estimate depends on the *planning horizon;* estimates of current events are close to 100 percent accurate but are reduced for more distant events. The accuracy of time and cost estimates should improve as you move from the conceptual phase to the point where individual work packages are defined.

Project Duration

Time to implement new *technology* has a habit of expanding in an increasing, nonlinear fashion. Sometimes poorly written scope specifications for new technology result in errors in estimating times and costs. Long-duration projects increase the uncertainty in estimates.

People

The *people* factor can also introduce errors in estimating times and cost. For example, accuracy of estimates depends on the skills of the people making the estimates. A close match of people skills to the task will influence productivity and learning time. Similarly, whether members of the project team have worked together before on similar projects will influence the time it takes to coalesce into an effective team. Sometimes factors such as staff turnover can influence estimates. It should be noted that adding new people to a project increases time spent communicating. Typically, people have only five to six productive hours available for each working day; the other hours are taken up with indirect work, such as meetings, paperwork, answering e-mail.

Project Structure and Organization

Which *project structure* is chosen to manage the project will influence time and cost estimates. One of the major advantages of a dedicated project team discussed earlier is the speed gained from concentrated focus and localized project decisions. This speed comes at an additional cost of tying up personnel full time. Conversely, projects operating in a matrix environment may reduce costs by more efficiently sharing personnel across projects but may take longer to complete since attention is divided and coordination demands are higher.

Padding Estimates

In some cases people are inclined to *pad estimates*. For example, if you are asked how long it takes you to drive to the airport, you might give an average time of 30 minutes, assuming a 50/50 chance of getting there in 30 minutes. If you are asked the fastest you could possibly get there, you might reduce the driving time to 20 minutes. Finally, if you are asked how long the drive would take if you absolutely had to be there to meet with the president, it is likely you would increase the estimate to say 50 minutes to ensure not being late. In work situations where you are asked for time and cost estimates, most of us are inclined to add a little padding to increase the probability and reduce the risk of being late. If everyone at all levels of the project adds a little padding to reduce risk, the project duration and cost are seriously overstated. This phenomenon causes some managers or owners to call for a 10–15 percent cut in time and/or cost for the project. Of course the next time the game is played, the person estimating cost and/or time will pad the estimate to 20 percent or more. Clearly such games defeat chances for realistic estimates, which is what is needed to be competitive.

Organization Culture

Organization culture can significantly influence project estimates. In some organizations padding estimates is tolerated and even privately encouraged. Other organizations place a premium on accuracy and strongly discourage estimating gamesmanship. Organizations vary in the importance they attach to estimates. The prevailing belief in some organizations is that detailed estimating takes too much time and is not worth the effort or that it's impossible to predict the future. Other organizations subscribe to the belief that accurate estimates are the bedrock of effective project management. Organization culture shapes every dimension of project management; estimating is not immune to this influence.

Other Factors

Finally, *nonproject factors* can impact time and cost estimates. For example, equipment down-time can alter time estimates. National holidays, vacations, and legal limits can influence project estimates. Project priority can influence resource assignment and impact time and cost.

Project estimating is a complex process. The quality of time and cost estimates can be improved when these variables are considered in making the estimates. Estimates of time and cost together allow the manager to develop a time-phased budget, which is imperative for project control. Before discussing macro and micro estimating methods for times and costs, a review of estimating guidelines will remind us of some of the important "rules of the game" that can improve estimating.

Estimating Guidelines for Times, Costs, and Resources

Managers recognize time, cost, and resource estimates must be accurate if project planning, scheduling, and controlling are to be effective. However, there is substantial evidence suggesting poor estimates are a major contributor to projects that have failed. Therefore, every effort should be made to see that initial estimates are as accurate as possible since the choice of no estimates leaves a great deal to luck and is not palatable to serious project managers. Even though a project has never been done before, a manager can follow seven guidelines to develop useful work package estimates.

1. **Responsibility.** At the work package level, estimates should be made by the person(s) most familiar with the task. Draw on their expertise! Except for super-technical tasks, those responsible for getting the job done on schedule and within budget are usually first-line supervisors or technicians who are experienced and familiar with the type of work involved. These people will not have some preconceived, imposed duration for a deliverable in mind. They will give an estimate based on experience and best judgment. A secondary benefit of using those responsible is the hope they will "buy in" to seeing that the estimate materializes when they implement the work package. If those involved are not consulted, it will be difficult to hold them responsible for failure to achieve the estimated time. Finally, drawing on the expertise of team members who will be responsible helps to build communication channels early.

2. **Use several people to estimate.** It is well known that a cost or time estimate usually has a better chance of being reasonable and realistic when several people with relevant experience and/or knowledge of the task are used. True, people bring different biases based on their experience. But discussion of the individual differences in their estimate leads to consensus and tends to eliminate extreme estimate errors. This approach is similar to the Delphi estimating method, which can also be used.

3. **Normal conditions.** When task time, cost, and resource estimates are determined, they are based on certain assumptions. *Estimates should be based on normal conditions, efficient methods, and a normal level of resources.* Normal conditions are sometimes difficult to discern, but it is necessary to have a consensus in the organization as to what normal conditions mean in this project. If the normal workday is eight hours, the time estimate should be based on an eight-hour day. Similarly, if the normal workday is two shifts, the time estimate should be based on a two-shift workday. Any time estimate should reflect efficient methods for the resources normally available. The time estimate should represent the normal level of resources—people or equipment. For example, if three programmers are available for coding or two road graders are available for road construction, time and cost estimates should be based on these normal levels of resources unless it is anticipated the project will change what is currently viewed as "normal." In addition, possible conflicts in demand for resources on parallel or concurrent activities should not be considered at this stage. The need for adding resources will be examined when resource scheduling is discussed in a later chapter.

4. **Time units.** Specific time units to use should be selected early in the development phase of the project network. *All task time estimates need consistent time units.* Estimates of time must consider whether normal time is represented by calendar days, workdays, workweeks, person days, single shift, hours, minutes, etc. In practice the use of workdays is the dominant choice for expressing task duration. However, in projects such as a heart transplant operation, minutes probably would be more appropriate as a time unit. One such project that used minutes as the time unit was the movement of patients from an old hospital to an elegant new one across town. Since there were several life-endangering moves, minutes were used to ensure patient safety so proper emergency life-support systems would be available if needed. The point is, network analysis requires a standard unit of time. When computer programs allow more than one option, some notation should be

made of any variance from the standard unit of time. If the standard unit of time is a five-day workweek and the estimated activity duration is in calendar days, it must be converted to the normal workweek.

5. **Independence.** Estimators should treat each task as independent of other tasks that might be integrated by the WBS. Use of first-line managers usually results in considering tasks independently; this is good. Top managers are prone to aggregate many tasks into one time estimate and then deductively make the individual task time estimates add to the total. If tasks are in a chain and performed by the same group or department, it is best not to ask for all the time estimates in the sequence at once to avoid the tendency for a planner or a supervisor to look at the whole path and try to adjust individual task times in the sequence to meet an arbitrary imposed schedule or some rough "guesstimate" of the total time for the whole path or segment of the project. This tendency does not reflect the uncertainties of individual activities and generally results in optimistic task time estimates. In summary, each task time estimate should be considered independently of other activities.

6. **Contingencies.** *Work package estimates should not include allowances for contingencies.* The estimate should assume normal or average conditions even though every work package will not materialize as planned. For this reason top management needs to create an extra fund for contingencies that can be used to cover unforeseen events.

7. **Adding risk assessment to the estimate helps to avoid surprises to stakeholders.** It is obvious some tasks carry more time and cost risks than others. For example, a new technology usually carries more time and cost risks than a proven process. Simply identifying the degree of risk lets stakeholders consider alternative methods and alter process decisions. A simple breakdown by optimistic, most likely, and pessimistic for task time could provide valuable information regarding time and cost. See Chapter 7 for further discussion of project risk.

Where applicable, these guidelines will greatly help to avoid many of the pitfalls found so often in practice.

Top-Down versus Bottom-Up Estimating

Since estimating efforts cost money, the time and detail devoted to estimating is an important decision. Yet, when estimating is considered, you as a project manager may hear statements such as these:

> *Rough order of magnitude is good enough. Spending time on detailed estimating wastes money.*
>
> *Time is everything; our survival depends on getting there first! Time and cost accuracy is not an issue.*
>
> *The project is internal. We don't need to worry about cost.*
>
> *The project is so small, we don't need to bother with estimates. Just do it.*
>
> *We were burned once. I want a detailed estimate of every task by the people responsible.*

However, there are sound reasons for using top-down or bottom-up estimates. Table 5.1 depicts conditions that suggest when one approach is preferred over another.

TABLE 5.1
Conditions for
Preferring Top-Down
or Bottom-Up Time
and Cost Estimates

Condition	Top-Down Estimates	Bottom-Up Estimates
Strategic decision making	X	
Cost and time important		X
High uncertainty	X	
Internal, small project	X	
Fixed-price contract		X
Customer wants details		X
Unstable scope	X	

Top-down estimates usually are derived from someone who uses experience and/or information to determine the project duration and total cost. These estimates are sometimes made by top managers who have very little knowledge of the processes used to complete the project. For example, a mayor of a major city making a speech noted that a new law building would be constructed at a cost of $23 million and would be ready for occupancy in two and one-half years. Although the mayor probably asked for an estimate from someone, the estimate could have come from a luncheon meeting with a local contractor who wrote an estimate (guesstimate) on a napkin. This is an extreme example, but in a relative sense this scenario is frequently played out in practice. See Snapshot from Practice: Council Fumes, for another example of this. But the question is, *do these estimates represent low-cost, efficient methods?* Do the top-down estimates of project time and cost become a self-fulfilling prophecy in terms of setting time and cost parameters?

If possible and practical, you want to push the estimating process down to the work package level for bottom-up estimates that establish low-cost, efficient methods. This process can take place after the project has been defined in detail. Good sense suggests project estimates should come from the people most knowledgeable about the estimate needed. The use of several people with relevant experience with the task can improve the time and cost estimate. The **bottom-up** approach at the work package level can serve as a check on cost elements in the WBS by rolling up the work packages and associated cost accounts to major deliverables. Similarly, resource requirements can be checked. Later, the time, resource, and cost estimates from the work packages can be consolidated into time-phased networks, resource schedules, and budgets that are used for control.

The bottom-up approach also provides the customer with an opportunity to compare the low-cost, efficient method approach with any imposed restrictions. For example, if the project completion duration is imposed at two years and your bottom-up analysis tells you the project will take two and one-half years, the client can now consider the trade-off of the low-cost method versus compressing the project to two years—or in rare cases canceling the project. Similar trade-offs can be compared for different levels of resources or increases in technical performance. The assumption is any movement away from the low-cost, efficient method will increase costs—e.g., overtime. The preferred approach in defining the project is to make rough top-down estimates, develop the WBS/OBS, make bottom-up estimates, develop schedules and budgets, and reconcile differences between top-down and bottom-up estimates. Hopefully, these steps will be done *before* final negotiation with either an internal or external customer. In conclusion, the ideal approach is for the project manager to allow enough time for both the top-down

SNAPSHOT FROM PRACTICE   Council Fumes as Tram Tale Unfolds*

Portland, Oregon's, Willamette riverfront development has exploded with seven condominium towers and a new health sciences center under construction. The health science complex is to be linked with Oregon Health Sciences University (OHSU), which is high on a nearby hill, with an aerial cable tram.

The aerial tram linking the waterfront district to OHSU is to support the university expansion, to increase biotechnology research, and to become Portland's icon equivalent to Seattle's Space Needle. All of the hype turned south when news from a hearing suggested that the real budget for the tram construction, originally estimated at $15 million, is going to be about $55–$60 million, nearly triple the original estimate. The estimate could even go higher. Commissioners want to find out why city staff knowingly relied on flawed estimates. Mike Lindberg, president of the nonprofit Aerial Transportation Inc., acknowledged "the $15 million number was not a good number. It was simply a guesstimate."

* *The Oregonian,* January 13, 2006, by Frank Ryan, pages A1 and A14, and April 2, 2006, page A1.

Commissioner Erik Sten said, "Those numbers were presented as much more firm than they appear to have been. . . . It appears the actual design wasn't costed out. That's pretty shoddy."

and bottom-up estimates to be worked out so a complete plan based on reliable estimates can be offered to the customer. In this way false expectations are minimized for all stakeholders and negotiation is reduced.

Methods for Estimating Project Times and Costs

Top-Down Approaches for Estimating Project Times and Costs

At the strategic level top-down estimating methods are used to evaluate the project proposal. Sometimes much of the information needed to derive accurate time and cost estimates is not available in the initial phase of the project—for example, design is not finalized. In these situations top-down estimates are used until the tasks in the WBS are clearly defined.

Consensus Methods

This method simply uses the pooled experience of senior and/or middle managers to estimate the total project duration and cost. This typically involves a meeting where experts discuss, argue, and ultimately reach a decision as to their best guess estimate. Firms seeking greater rigor will use the Delphi Method to make these macro estimates. See Snapshot from Practice: The Delphi Method.

It is important to recognize that these first top-down estimates are only a rough cut and typically occur in the "conceptual" stage of the project. The

SNAPSHOT FROM PRACTICE The Delphi Method

Originally developed by the RAND Corporation in 1969 for technological forecasting, the **Delphi Method** is a group decision process about the likelihood that certain events will occur. The Delphi Method makes use of a panel of experts familiar with the kind of project in question. The notion is that well-informed individuals, calling on their insights and experience, are better equipped to estimate project costs/times than theoretical approaches or statistical methods. Their responses to estimate questionnaires are anonymous, and they are provided with a summary of opinions.

Experts are then encouraged to reconsider, and if appropriate, to change their previous estimate in light of the replies of other experts. After two or three rounds it is believed that the group will converge toward the "best" response through this consensus process. The midpoint of responses is statistically categorized by the median score. In each succeeding round of questionnaires, the range of responses by the panelists will presumably decrease and the median will move toward what is deemed to be the "correct" estimate.

One distinct advantage of the Delphi Method is that the experts never need to be brought together physically. The process also does not require complete agreement by all panelists, since the majority opinion is represented by the median. Since the responses are anonymous, the pitfalls of ego, domineering personalities, and the "bandwagon or halo effect" in responses are all avoided. On the other hand, future developments are not always predicted correctly by iterative consensus nor by experts, but at times by creative, "off the wall" thinking.

top-down estimates are helpful in initial development of a complete plan. However, such estimates are sometimes significantly off the mark because little detailed information is gathered. At this level individual work items are not identified. Or, in a few cases, the top-down estimates are not realistic because top management "wants the project." Nevertheless, the initial top-down estimates are helpful in determining whether the project warrants more formal planning, which would include more detailed estimates. Be careful that macro estimates made by senior managers are not dictated to lower level managers who might feel compelled to accept the estimates even if they believe resources are inadequate.

Although your authors prefer to avoid the top-down approach if possible, we have witnessed surprising accuracy in estimating project duration and cost in isolated cases. Some examples are building a manufacturing plant, building a distribution warehouse, developing air control for skyscraper buildings, and road construction. However, we have also witnessed some horrendous miscalculations, usually in areas where the technology is new and unproven. Top-down methods can be useful if experience and judgment have been accurate in the past.

Ratio Methods

Top-down methods (sometimes called parametric) usually use ratios, or surrogates, to estimate project times or costs. Top-down approaches are often used in the concept or "need" phase of a project to get an initial duration and cost estimate for the project. For example, contractors frequently use number of square feet to estimate the cost and time to build a house; that is, a house of 2,700 square feet might cost $160 per square foot (2,700 feet × $160 per foot equals $432,000). Likewise, knowing the square feet and dollars per square foot, experience suggests it should take approximately 100 days to complete. Two other common examples of top-down cost estimates are the cost for a new plant estimated by capacity size, or a software product estimated by features and complexity.

Apportion Methods

This method is an extension to the ratio method. **Apportionment** is used when projects closely follow past projects in features and costs. Given good historical data, estimates can be made quickly with little effort and reasonable accuracy. This method is very common in projects that are relatively standard but have some small variation or customization.

Anyone who has borrowed money from a bank to build a house has been exposed to this process. Given an estimated total cost for the house, banks and the FHA (Federal Housing Authority) authorize pay to the contractor by completion of specific segments of the house. For example, foundation might represent 3 percent of the total loan, framing 25 percent, electric, plumbing and heating 15 percent, etc. Payments are made as these items are completed. An analogous process is used by some companies that apportion costs to deliverables in the WBS—given average cost percentages from past projects. Figure 5.1 presents an example similar to one found in practice. Assuming the total project cost is estimated, using a top-down estimate, to be $500,000, the costs are apportioned as a percentage of the total cost. For example, the costs apportioned to the "Document" deliverable are 5 percent of the total, or $25,000. The subdeliverables "Doc-1 and Doc-2" are allocated 2 and 3 percent of the total—$10,000 and $15,000, respectively.

Function Point Methods for Software and System Projects

In the software industry, software development projects are frequently estimated using weighted macro variables called **"function points"** or major parameters such as number of inputs, number of outputs, number of inquiries, number of data files, and number of interfaces. These weighted variables are adjusted for a complexity factor and added. The total adjusted count provides the basis for estimating the labor effort and cost for a project (usually using a regression formula derived from data of past projects). This latter method assumes adequate historical data by type of software project for the industry—for example, MIS systems. In the

FIGURE 5.1 **Apportion Method of Allocating Project Costs Using the Work Breakdown Structure**

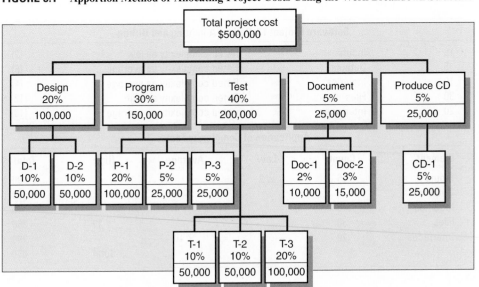

TABLE 5.2
Simplified Basic Function Point Count Process for a Prospective Project or Deliverable

	Complexity Weighting			
Element	Low	Average	High	Total
Number of *inputs*	_____ × 2 +	_____ × 3 +	_____ × 4	= _____
Number of *outputs*	_____ × 3 +	_____ × 6 +	_____ × 9	= _____
Number of *inquiries*	_____ × 2 +	_____ × 4 +	_____ × 6	= _____
Number of *files*	_____ × 5 +	_____ × 8 +	_____ × 12	= _____
Number of *interfaces*	_____ × 5 +	_____ × 10 +	_____ × 15	= _____

U.S. software industry, one-person month represents on average five function points. A person working one month can generate on average (across all types of software projects) about five function points. Of course each organization needs to develop its own average for its specific type of work. Such historical data provide a basis for estimating the project duration. Variations of this top-down approach are used by companies such as IBM, Bank of America, Sears Roebuck, HP, AT&T, Ford Motors, GE, DuPont and many others. See Table 5.2 and Table 5.3 for a simplified example of function point count methodology.

From historical data the organization developed the weighting scheme for complexity found in Table 5.2. Function points are derived from multiplying the number of kinds of elements by weighted complexity.

Table 5.3 shows the data collected for a specific task or deliverable: Patient Admitting and Billing—the number of inputs, outputs, inquiries, files, and interfaces along with the expected complexity rating. Finally, the application of the element count is applied and the function point count total is 660. Given this count and the fact that one-person month has historically been equal to 5 function points, the job will require 132 person months (660/5 = 132). Assuming you have 10 programmers who can work on this task, the duration would be

TABLE 5.3
Example: Function Point Count Method

Software Project 13: Patient Admitting and Billing			
15	Inputs	Rated complexity as low	(2)
5	Outputs	Rated complexity as average	(6)
10	Inquiries	Rated complexity as average	(4)
30	Files	Rated complexity as high	(12)
20	Interfaces	Rated complexity as average	(10)

Application of Complexity Factor					
Element	Count	Low	Average	High	Total
Inputs	15	× 2			= 30
Outputs	5		× 6		= 30
Inquiries	10		× 4		= 40
Files	30			× 12	= 360
Interfaces	20		× 10		= 200
				Total	660

approximately 13 months. The cost is easily derived by multiplying the labor rate per month times 132 person months. For example, if the monthly programmer rate is $4,000, then the estimated cost would be $528,000 (132 × 4,000). Although function point metrics are useful, their accuracy depends on adequate historical data, currency of data, and relevancy of the project/deliverable to past averages.

Learning Curves

Some projects require that the same task, group of tasks, or product be repeated several times. Managers know intuitively that the time to perform a task improves with repetition. This phenomenon is especially true of tasks that are labor intensive. In these circumstances the pattern of improvement phenomenon can be used to predict the reduction in time to perform the task. From empirical evidence across *all* industries, the pattern of this improvement has been quantified in the **learning curve** (also known as improvement curve, experience curve, and industrial progress curve), which is described by the following relationship:

Each time the output quantity doubles, the unit labor hours are reduced at a constant rate.

In practice the improvement ratio may vary from 60 percent, representing very large improvement, to 100 percent, representing no improvement at all. Generally, as the difficulty of the work decreases the expected improvement also decreases and the improvement ratio that is used becomes greater. One significant factor to consider is the proportion of labor in the task in relation to machine-paced work. Obviously, a lower percentage of improvement can occur only in operations with high labor content. Appendix 5.1 at the end of the chapter provides a detailed example of how the improvement phenomenon can be used to estimate time and cost for repetitive tasks.

The main disadvantage of top-down approaches to estimating is simply that the time and cost for a specific task are not considered. Grouping many tasks into a common basket encourages errors of omission and the use of imposed times and costs.

Micro estimating methods are usually more accurate than macro methods.

Bottom-Up Approaches for Estimating Project Times and Costs

Template Methods

If the project is similar to past projects, the costs from past projects can be used as a starting point for the new project. Differences in the new project can be noted and past times and costs adjusted to reflect these differences. For example, a ship repair drydock firm has a set of standard repair projects (i.e., templates for overhaul, electrical, mechanical) that are used as starting points for estimating the cost and duration of any new project. Differences from the appropriate standardized project are noted (for times, costs, and resources) and changes are made. This approach enables the firm to develop a potential schedule, estimate costs, and develop a budget in a very short time span. Development of such templates in a database can quickly reduce estimate errors.

Parametric Procedures Applied to Specific Tasks

Just as parametric techniques such as cost per square foot can be the source of top-down estimates, the same technique can be applied to specific tasks. For example, as part of an MS Office conversion project, 36 different computer workstations needed to be converted. Based on past conversion projects, the project manager determined that on average one person could convert three workstations per day. Therefore the task of converting the 36 workstations would take three technicians four days [(36/3)/3]. Similarly, to estimate the wallpapering allowance on a house remodel, the contractor figured a cost of $5 per square yard of wallpaper and $2 per yard to install it, for a total cost of $7. By measuring the length and height of all the walls she was able to calculate the total area in square yards and multiply it by $7.

Range Estimating

When do you use range estimating? **Range estimating** works best when work packages have significant uncertainty associated with the time or cost to complete. If the work package is routine and carries little uncertainty, using a person most familiar with the work package is usually the best approach. They know from experience or know where to find the information to estimate work package durations and costs. However, when work packages have significant uncertainty associated with the time or cost to complete, it is a prudent policy to require three time estimates—low, average, and high (borrowed off of PERT methodology that uses probability distributions). The low to high give a range within which the average estimate will fall. Determining the low and high estimates for the activity is influenced by factors such as complexity, technology, newness, familiarity.

How do you get the estimates? Since range estimating works best for work packages that have significant uncertainty, having a group determine the low, average, and high cost or duration gives best results. Group estimating tends to refine extremes by bringing more evaluative judgments to the estimate and potential risks. The judgment of others in a group helps to moderate extreme perceived risks associated with a time or cost estimate. Involving others in making activity estimates gains buy in and credibility to the estimate.

Figure 5.2 presents an abridged estimating template using three time estimates for work packages developed by a cross functional group(s) of project stakeholders. The group estimates show the low, average, and high for each work package. The Risk Level column is the group's independent assessment of the degree of confidence that the actual time will be very close to the estimate. In a sense this number represents the group's evaluation of many factors (e.g., complexity, technology) that might impact the average time estimate. In our example, the group feels work packages 104, 108, 110, 111, and 114 have a high chance that the average time may vary from expected. Likewise, the group's confidence feels the risk of work packages 102, 105 and 112 not materializing as expected is low.

How do you use the estimate? Group range estimating gives the project manager and owner an opportunity to assess the confidence associated with project times (and/or costs). The approach helps to reduce surprises as the project progresses. The range estimating method also provides a basis for assessing risk, managing resources, and determining the project contingency fund. (See Chapter 7 for a discussion of contingency funds.) Range estimating is popular in software and new product projects where up-front requirements are fuzzy and not well known. Group range estimating is often used with phase estimating, which is discussed next.

FIGURE 5.2
Range Estimating Template

	A	B	C	D	E	F	G	H
1	Project number: 18				Project Manager: Dawn O'Connor			
2	Project description: New Organic Wine Launch				Date: 2/17/2xxx			
3			Organic Wine Launch Project					
4			Range Estimates					
5								
6	WBS	Description	Low	Average	High	Range	Risk	
7	ID		Estimate	Estimate	Estimate		Level	
8			Days	Days	Days	Days		
9								
10	102	Approval	1	1	3	2	low	
11	103	Design packaging	4	7	12	8	medium	
12	104	ID potential customers	14	21	35	21	high	
13	105	Design bottle logo	5	7	10	5	low	
14	106	Contract kiosk space	8	10	15	7	medium	
15	107	Construct kiosk	4	4	8	4	medium	
16	108	Design fair brochure	6	7	12	6	high	
17	109	Trade journal advertising	10	12	15	5	medium	
18	110	Production test	10	14	20	10	high	
19	111	Produce to inventory	5	5	10	5	high	
20	112	Business card scanner hookup	1	2	3	2	low	
21	113	Video hook up	2	2	4	2	medium	
22	114	Event rehearsal	2	2	5	3	high	

A Hybrid: Phase Estimating

This approach begins with a top-down estimate for the project and then refines estimates for phases of the project as it is implemented. Some projects by their nature cannot be rigorously defined because of the uncertainty of design or the final product. Although rare, such projects do exist. These projects are often found in aerospace projects, IT projects, new technology projects, and construction projects where design is incomplete. In these projects, phase or life-cycle estimating is frequently used.

Phase estimating is used when an unusual amount of uncertainty surrounds a project and it is impractical to estimate times and costs for the entire project. Phase estimating uses a two-estimate system over the life of the project. A detailed estimate is developed for the immediate phase and a macro estimate is made for the remaining phases of the project. Figure 5.3 depicts the phases of a project and the progression of estimates over its life.

For example, when the project need is determined, a macro estimate of the project cost and duration is made so analysis and decisions can be made. Simultaneously a detailed estimate is made for deriving project specifications and a macro

FIGURE 5.3
Phase Estimating over Project Life Cycle

SNAPSHOT FROM PRACTICE   Estimate Accuracy

The smaller the element of a work package, the more accurate the overall estimate is likely to be. The extent of this improvement varies by type of project. The table below is developed to reflect this observation. For example, information technology projects that determine their time and cost estimates in the conceptual stage can expect their "actuals" to err up to 200 percent over cost and duration and, perhaps, as much as 30 percent under estimates. Conversely, estimates for buildings, roads, etc., made after the work packages are clearly defined, have a smaller error in actual costs and times of 15 percent over estimate and 5 percent less than estimate. Although these estimates vary by project, they can serve as ballpark numbers for project stakeholders selecting how project time and cost estimates will be derived.

Time and Cost Estimate Accuracy by Type of Project

	Bricks and Mortar	Information Technology
Conceptual stage	+60% to −30%	+200% to −30%
Deliverables defined	+30% to −15%	+100% to −15%
Work packages defined	+15% to −5%	+50% to −5%

estimate for the remainder of the project. As the project progresses and specifications are solidified, a detailed estimate for design is made and a macro estimate for the remainder of the project is computed. Clearly, as the project progresses through its life cycle and more information is available, the reliability of the estimates should be improving.

Phase estimating is preferred by those working on projects where the final product is not known and the uncertainty is very large—for example, the integration of wireless phones and computers. The commitment to cost and schedule is only necessary over the next phase of the project and commitment to unrealistic future schedules and costs based on poor information is avoided. This progressive macro/micro method provides a stronger basis for using schedule and cost estimates to manage progress during the next phase.

Unfortunately your customer—internal or external—will want an accurate estimate of schedule and cost the moment the decision is made to implement the project. Additionally, the customer who is paying for the project often perceives phase estimating as a blank check because costs and schedules are not firm over most of the project life cycle. Even though the reasons for phase estimating are sound and legitimate, most customers have to be sold on its legitimacy. A major advantage for the customer is the opportunity to change features, re-evaluate, or even cancel the project in each new phase. In conclusion, phase estimating is very useful in projects that possess huge uncertainties concerning the final nature (shape, size, features) of the project.

See Figure 5.4 for a summary of the differences between top-down and bottom-up estimates.

Obtaining accurate estimates is a challenge. Committed organizations accept the challenge of coming up with meaningful estimates and invest heavily in developing their capacity to do so. Accurate estimates reduce uncertainty and support a discipline for effectively managing projects.

FIGURE 5.4
Top-Down and
Bottom-Up Estimates

Top-Down Estimates	Bottom-Up Estimates
Intended Use	**Intended Use**
Feasibility/conceptual phase	Budgeting
Rough time/cost estimate	Scheduling
Fund requirements	Resource requirements
Resource capacity planning	Fund timing
Preparation Cost	**Preparation Cost**
1/10 to 3/10 of a percent of total project cost	3/10 of a percent to 1.0 percent of total project cost
Accuracy	**Accuracy**
Minus 20%, to plus 60%	Minus 10%, to plus 30%
Method	**Method**
Consensus	Template
Ratio	Parametric
Apportion	WBS packages
Function point	Range estimates
Learning curves	

Level of Detail

Level of detail is different for different levels of management. At any level the detail should be no more than is necessary and sufficient. Top management interests usually center on the total project and major milestone events that mark major accomplishments—e.g., "Build Oil Platform in the North Sea" or "Complete Prototype." Middle management might center on one segment of the project or one milestone. First-line managers' interests may be limited to one task or work package. One of the beauties of WBS is the ability to aggregate network information so each level of management can have the kind of information necessary to make decisions.

Getting the level of detail in the WBS to match management needs for effective implementation is crucial, but the delicate balance is difficult to find. See Snapshot from Practice: Level of Detail. The level of detail in the WBS varies with the complexity of the project; the need for control; the project size, cost, duration; and other factors. If the structure reflects excessive detail, there is a tendency to break the work effort into department assignments. This tendency can become a barrier to success, since the emphasis will be on departmental outcomes rather than on deliverable outcomes. Excessive detail also means more unproductive paperwork. Note that if the level of the WBS is increased by one, the number of cost accounts may increase geometrically. On the other hand, if the level of detail is not adequate, an organization unit may find the structure falls short of meeting its needs. Fortunately, the WBS has built-in flexibility. Participating organization units may expand their portion of the structure to meet their special needs. For example, the engineering department may wish to further break their work on a deliverable into smaller packages by electrical, civil, and mechanical. Similarly, the marketing department may wish to break their new product promotion into TV, radio, periodicals, and newspapers.

SNAPSHOT FROM PRACTICE   Level of Detail—Rule of Thumb

Practicing project managers advocate keeping the level of detail to a minimum. But there are limits to this suggestion. One of the most frequent errors of new project managers is to forget that the task time estimate will be used to control schedule and cost performance. A frequent rule of thumb used by practicing project managers says that a task duration should not exceed 5 workdays or at the most 10 workdays, if workdays are the time units used for the project. Such a rule probably will result in a more detailed network, but the additional detail pays off in controlling schedule and cost as the project progresses.

Suppose the task is "build prototype computer-controlled conveyor belt," the time estimate is 40 workdays, and the budget $300,000. It may be better to divide the task into seven or eight smaller tasks for control purposes. If one of the smaller tasks gets behind because of problems or a poor time estimate, it will be possible to take corrective action quickly and avoid delaying successive tasks and the project. If the single

task of 40 workdays is used, it is possible that no corrective action would be taken until day 40, since many people have a tendency to "wait and see" or avoid admitting they are behind or passing on bad news; the result may mean far more than 5 days behind schedule.

The 5- to 10-day rule of thumb applies to cost and performance goals. If using the rule of thumb suggested above results in too many network tasks, an alternative is available, but it has conditions. The activity time can be extended beyond the 5- to 10-day rule only *IF* control monitoring checkpoints for segments of the task can be established so clear measures of progress can be identified by a specific percent complete.

This information is invaluable to the control process of measuring schedule and cost performance—for example, payments for contract work are paid on "percent complete" basis. Defining a task with clear definable start and end points and intermediate points enhances the chances of early detection of problems, corrective action, and on-time project completion.

Types of Costs

Assuming work packages are defined, detailed cost estimates can be made. Here are typical kinds of costs found in a project:

1. Direct costs
   a. Labor
   b. Materials
   c. Equipment
   d. Other
2. Direct project overhead costs
3. General and administrative (G&A) overhead costs

The total project cost estimate is broken down in this fashion to sharpen the control process and improve decision making.

Direct Costs

These costs are clearly chargeable to a specific work package. **Direct costs** can be influenced by the project manager, project team, and individuals implementing the work package. These costs represent real cash outflows and must be paid as the project progresses; therefore, direct costs are usually separated from overhead costs. Lower-level project rollups frequently include only direct costs.

Direct Project Overhead Costs

Direct overhead rates more closely pinpoint which resources of the organization are being used in the project. Direct project **overhead costs** can be tied to project deliverables or work packages. Examples include the salary of the project manager and temporary rental space for the project team. Although overhead is not an

FIGURE 5.5
Contract Bid
Summary Costs

Direct costs	$80,000
Direct overhead	$20,000
Total direct costs	$100,000
G&A overhead (20%)	$20,000
Total costs	$120,000
Profit (20%)	$24,000
Total bid	$144,000

immediate out-of-pocket expense, it is *real* and must be covered in the long run if the firm is to remain viable. These rates are usually a ratio of the dollar value of the resources used—e.g., direct labor, materials, equipment. For example, a direct labor burden rate of 20 percent would add a direct overhead charge of 20 percent to the direct labor cost estimate. A direct charge rate of 50 percent for materials would carry an additional 50 percent charge to the material cost estimate. Selective direct overhead charges provide a more accurate project (job or work package) cost, rather than using a blanket overhead rate for the whole project.

General and Administrative (G&A) Overhead Costs

These represent organization costs that are not directly linked to a specific project. These costs are carried for the duration of the project. Examples include organization costs across all products and projects such as advertising, accounting, and senior management above the project level. Allocation of G&A costs varies from organization to organization. However, G&A costs are usually allocated as a percent of total direct cost, or a percent of the total of a specific direct cost such as labor, materials, or equipment.

Given the totals of direct and overhead costs for individual work packages, it is possible to cumulate the costs for any deliverable or for the entire project. A percentage can be added for profit if you are a contractor. A breakdown of costs for a proposed contract bid is presented in Figure 5.5.

Perceptions of costs and budgets vary depending on their users. The project manager must be very aware of these differences when setting up the project budget and when communicating these differences to others. Figure 5.6 depicts these

FIGURE 5.6
Three Views of Cost

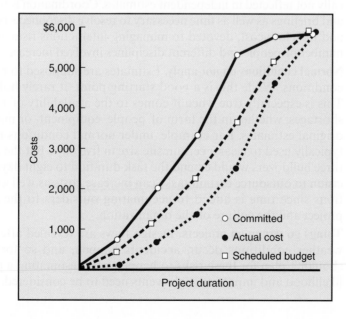

different perceptions. The project manager can commit costs months before the resource is used. This information is useful to the financial officer of the organization in forecasting future cash outflows. The project manager is interested in when the budgeted cost is expected to occur, and when the budgeted cost actually is charged (earned); the respective timings of these two cost figures are used to measure project schedule and cost variances.

Refining Estimates

As described earlier in Chapter 4, detailed work package estimates are aggregated and "rolled up" by deliverable to estimate the total direct cost of the project. Similarly, estimated durations are entered into the project network to establish the project schedule and determine the overall duration of the project. Experience tells us that for many projects the total estimates do not materialize and the actual costs and schedule of some projects significantly exceed original work package–based estimates. See Snapshot from Practice: How Do You Estimate the Cost of a Nuclear Power Plant? for a dramatic example of this. In order to compensate for the problem of actual cost and schedule exceeding estimates, some project managers adjust total costs by some multiplier (i.e., total estimated costs × 1.20).

The practice of adjusting original estimates by 20 or even 100 percent begs the question of why, after investing so much time and energy on detailed estimates, could the numbers be so far off? There are a number of reasons for this, most of which can be traced to the estimating process and the inherent uncertainty of predicting the future. Some of these reasons are discussed below.

- **Interaction costs are hidden in estimates.** According to the guidelines, each task estimate is supposed to be done independently. However, tasks are rarely completed in a vacuum. Work on one task is dependent upon prior tasks, and the hand-offs between tasks require time and attention. For example, people working on prototype development need to interact with design engineers after the design is completed, whether to simply ask clarifying questions or to make adjustments in the original design. Similarly, the time necessary to coordinate activities is typically not reflected in independent estimates. Coordination is reflected in meetings and briefings as well as time necessary to resolve disconnects between tasks. Time, and therefore cost, devoted to managing interactions rises exponentially as the number of people and different disciplines involved increases on a project.

- **Normal conditions do not apply.** Estimates are supposed to be based on normal conditions. While this is a good starting point, it rarely holds true in real life. This is especially true when it comes to the availability of resources. Resource shortages, whether in the form of people, equipment, or materials, can extend original estimates. For example, under normal conditions four bulldozers are typically used to clear a certain site size in five days, but the availability of only three bulldozers would extend the task duration to eight days. Similarly, the decision to outsource certain tasks can increase costs as well as extend task durations since time is added to acclimating outsiders to the particulars of the project and the culture of the organization.

- **Things go wrong on projects.** Design flaws are revealed after the fact, extreme weather conditions occur, accidents happen, and so forth. Although you shouldn't plan for these risks to happen when estimating a particular task, the likelihood and impact of such events need to be considered.

How Do You Estimate the Cost of a Nuclear Power Plant?

O. P. Kharbanda in his book (co-authored with Jeffrey Pinto) *What Made Gertie Gallop: Learning from Project Failures* makes the important point that estimating is as much an art as a skill. For example, early in his career (1960s), he was involved with the fabrication of a nuclear reactor in India at a time when the local facilities were not geared for such sophisticated jobs. Having had no experience in building complex equipment with (almost) unheard of tolerances and precision, it was virtually impossible to create a reasonable advance estimate of the cost. The estimators did the best they could, then added a little more than normal margin before quoting a price to the client.

Soon after, O. P. happened to attend a week-long international nuclear power conference that included stalwarts in this field from all over the world. About midweek, he was fortunate to come face-to-face with the chief engineer of the company that had supplied the first reactor to India, identical in design to the one his company had recently bid on. This was the chance of a lifetime to finally get the inside information on accurate cost estimating. In fact, the expert confessed that his company lost "their shirt" on the Indian reactor. Then in reply to the innocent question, "How do you estimate a nuclear reactor?" the expert answered with cool confidence, "Do your normal cautious estimating, add more than normal margin and then after a short pause, double it!" O. P. confessed that in their ignorance, they had skipped the last vital step, but this short, casual conversation proved most valuable. "We were forewarned, we took it seriously, and got forearmed. It saved us several millions of dollars."

- **Changes in project scope and plans.** As one gets further and further into the project, a manager obtains a better understanding of what needs to be done to accomplish the project. This may lead to major changes in project plans and costs. Likewise, if the project is a commercial project, changes often have to be made midstream to respond to new demands by the customer and/or competition. Unstable project scopes are a major source of cost overruns. While every effort should be made up front to nail down the project scope, it is becoming increasingly difficult to do so in our rapidly changing world.

The reality is that for many projects not all of the information needed to make accurate estimates is available, and it is impossible to predict the future. The dilemma is that without solid estimates, the credibility of the project plan is eroded. Deadlines become meaningless, budgets become rubbery, and accountability becomes problematic.

Challenges similar to those described above will influence the final time and cost estimates. Even with the best estimating efforts, it may be necessary to revise estimates based on relevant information *prior* to establishing a baseline schedule and budget.

Effective organizations adjust estimates of specific tasks once risks, resources, and particulars of the situation have been more clearly defined. They recognize that the rolled up estimates generated from a detailed estimate based on the WBS are just the starting point. As they delve further into the project-planning process, they make appropriate revisions both in the time and cost of specific activities. They factor the final assignment of resources into the project budget and schedule. For example, when they realize that only three instead of four bulldozers are available to clear a site, they adjust both the time and cost of that activity. They adjust estimates to account for specific actions to mitigate potential risks on the project. For example, to reduce the chances of design code errors, they would add the cost of independent testers to the schedule and budget. Finally, organizations adjust estimates to take into account abnormal conditions. For example, if soil samples reveal excessive ground water, then they adjust foundation costs and times.

There will always be some mistakes, omissions, and adjustments that will require additional changes in estimates. Fortunately every project should have a change management system in place to accommodate these situations and any impact on the project baseline. Change management and contingency funds will be discussed later in Chapter 7.

Creating a Database for Estimating

The best way to improve estimates is to collect and archive data on past project estimates and actuals. Saving historical data—estimates and actuals—provides a knowledge base for improving project time and cost estimating. Creating an estimating database is a "best practice" among leading project management organizations.

Some organizations have large estimating departments of professional estimators—e.g., Boeing, Kodak, IBM—that have developed large **time and cost databases.** Others collect these data through the project office. This database approach allows the project estimator to select a specific work package item from the database for inclusion. The estimator then makes any necessary adjustments concerning the materials, labor, and equipment. Of course any items not found in the database can be added to the project—and ultimately to the database if desired. Again, the quality of the database estimates depends on the experience of the estimators, but over time the data quality should improve. Such structured databases serve as feedback for estimators and as benchmarks for cost and time for each project. In addition, comparison of estimate and actual for different projects can suggest the degree of risk inherent in estimates. See Figure 5.7 for the structure of a database similar to those found in practice.

FIGURE 5.7
Estimating Database Templates

Summary

Quality time and cost estimates are the bedrock of project control. Past experience is the best starting point for these estimates. The quality of estimates is influenced by other factors such as people, technology, and downtimes. The key for getting estimates that represent realistic average times and costs is to have an organization culture that allows errors in estimates without incriminations. If times represent average time, we should expect that 50 percent will be less than the estimate and 50 percent will exceed the estimate. The use of teams that are highly motivated can help in keeping task times and costs near the average. For this reason, it is crucial to get the team to buy into time and cost estimates.

Using top-down estimates is good for initial and strategic decision making or in situations where the costs associated with developing better estimates have little benefit. However, in most cases the bottom-up approach to estimating is preferred and more reliable because it assesses each work package, rather than the whole project, section, or deliverable of a project. Estimating time and costs for each work package facilitates development of the project schedule and a time-phased budget, which are needed to control the project as it is implemented. Using the estimating guidelines will help eliminate many common mistakes made by those unacquainted with estimating times and costs for project control. Establishing a time and cost estimating database fits well with the learning organization philosophy.

The level of time and cost detail should follow the old saying of "no more than is necessary and sufficient." Managers must remember to differentiate between committed outlays, actual costs, and scheduled costs. It is well known that up-front efforts in clearly defining project objectives, scope, and specifications vastly improve time and cost estimate accuracy.

Finally, how estimates are gathered and how they are used can affect their usefulness for planning and control. The team climate, organization culture, and organization structure can strongly influence the importance attached to time and cost estimates and how they are used in managing projects.

Key Terms

Apportionment, *135*
Bottom-up
 estimates, *132*
Delphi Method, *134*
Direct costs, *142*
Function points, *135*

Learning curves, *137*
Overhead costs, *142*
Padding estimates, *129*
Phase estimating, *139*
Range estimating, *138*
Ratio methods, *134*

Template method, *137*
Time and cost
 databases, *146*
Top-down estimates, *132*

**Review
Questions**

1. Why are accurate estimates critical to effective project management?
2. How does the culture of an organization influence the quality of estimates?
3. What are the differences between bottom-up and top-down estimating approaches? Under what conditions would you prefer one over the other?
4. What are the major types of costs? Which costs are controllable by the project manager?

Exercises

1. Mrs. Tolstoy and her husband, Serge, are planning their dream house. The lot for the house sits high on a hill with a beautiful view of the Appalachian Mountains. The plans show the size of the house to be 2,900 square feet. The average price for a lot and house similar to this one has been $120 per square foot. Fortunately, Serge is a retired plumber and feels he can save money

by installing the plumbing himself. Mrs. Tolstoy feels she can take care of the interior decorating.

The following average cost information is available from a local bank that makes loans to local contractors and disperses progress payments to contractors when specific tasks are verified as complete.

24%	Excavation and framing complete
8%	Roof and fireplace complete
3%	Wiring roughed in
6%	Plumbing roughed in
5%	Siding on
17%	Windows, insulation, walks, plaster, and garage complete
9%	Furnace installed
4%	Plumbing fixtures installed
10%	Exterior paint, light fixtures installed, finish hardware installed
6%	Carpet and trim installed
4%	Interior decorating
4%	Floors laid and finished

a. What is the estimated cost for the Tolstoy's house if they use contractors to complete all of the house?

b. Estimate what the cost of the house would be if the Tolstoys use their talents to do some of the work themselves.

2. Below is a project WBS with cost apportioned by percents. If the total project cost is estimated to be $600,000, what are the estimated costs for the following deliverables?
a. Design?
b. Programming?
c. In-house testing?

What weaknesses are inherent in this estimating approach?

EXERCISE 5.3
WBS Figure

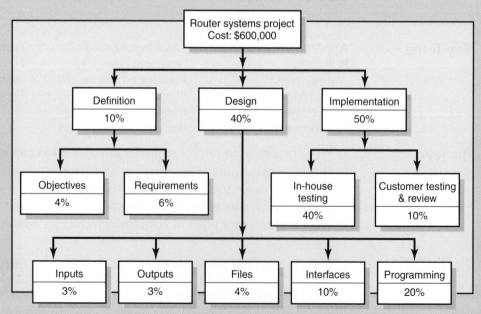

3. Firewall Project XT. Using the "complexity weighting" scheme shown in Exercise 5.3 and the function point complexity weighted table shown below,

estimate the total function point count. Assume historical data suggest five function points equal one person a month and six people can work on the project.

Complexity Weight Table		
Number of inputs	10	Rated complexity low
Number of outputs	20	Rated complexity average
Number of inquires	10	Rated complexity average
Number of files	30	Rated complexity high
Number of interfaces	50	Rated complexity high

   a. What is the estimated project duration?

   b. If 20 people are available for the project, what is the estimated project duration?

   c. If the project must be completed in six months, how many people will be needed for the project?

References

Dalkey, N. C., D. L. Rourke, R. Lewis, and D. Snyder, *Studies in the Quality of Life: Delphi and Decision Making* (Lexington, MA: Lexington Books, 1972).

Gray, N. S., "Secrets to Creating the Elusive 'Accurate Estimate,'" *PM Network,* 15 (8) August 2001, p. 56.

Jeffery, R., G. C. Low, and M. Barnes, "A Comparison of Function Point Counting Techniques," *IEEE Transactions on Software Engineering,* 19 (5) 1993, pp. 529–32.

Jones, C., *Applied Software Measurement* (New York: McGraw-Hill, 1991).

Jones, C., *Estimating Software Costs* (New York: McGraw-Hill, 1998).

Kharbanda, O. P., and J. K. Pinto, *What Made Gertie Gallop: Learning from Project Failures* (New York: Von Nostrand Reinhold, 1996).

Magne, E., K. Emhjellenm, and P. Osmundsen, "Cost Estimation Overruns in the North Sea," *Project Management Journal* 34 (1) 2003, pp. 23–29.

McLeod, G., and D. Smith, *Managing Information Technology Projects* (Cambridge, MA: Course Technology, 1996).

Milosevic, D. Z., *Project Management ToolBox* (Upper Saddle River, NJ: John Wiley, 2003), p. 229.

Pressman, R. S., *Software Engineering: A Practitioner's Approach,* 4th ed. (New York: McGraw-Hill, 1997).

Symons, C. R., "Function Point Analysis: Difficulties and Improvements," *IEEE Transactions on Software Engineering,* 14 (1) 1988, pp. 2–11.

Case

Sharp Printing, AG

Three years ago the Sharp Printing (SP) strategic management group set a goal of having a color laser printer available for the consumer and small business market for less than $200. A few months later the senior management met off-site to discuss the new product. The results of this meeting were a set of general technical specifications along with major deliverables, a product launch date, and a cost estimate based on prior experience.

Shortly afterward, a meeting was arranged for middle management explaining the project goals, major responsibilities, the project start date, and importance of meeting the product launch date within the cost estimate. Members of all departments involved attended the meeting. Excitement was high. Although everyone saw the risks as high, the promised rewards for the company and the personnel were emblazoned in their minds. A few participants questioned the legitimacy of the project duration and cost estimates. A couple of R&D people were worried about the technology required to produce the high-quality product for less than $200. But given the excitement of the moment, everyone agreed the project was worth doing and doable. The color laser printer project was to have the highest project priority in the company.

Lauren was selected to be the project manager. She had 15 years of experience in printer design and manufacture, which included successful management of several projects related to printers for commercial markets. Since she was one of those uncomfortable with the project cost and time estimates, she felt getting good bottom-up time and cost estimates for the deliverables was her first concern. She quickly had a meeting with the significant stakeholders to create a WBS identifying the work packages and organizational unit responsible for implementing the work packages. Lauren stressed she wanted time and cost estimates from those who would do the work or were the most knowledgeable, if possible. Getting estimates from more than one source was encouraged. Estimates were due in two weeks.

The compiled estimates were placed in the WBS/OBS. The corresponding cost estimate seemed to be in error. The cost estimate was $1,250,000 over the senior management estimate; this represents about a 20 percent overrun! The time estimate from the developed project network was only four months over the top management time estimate. Another meeting was scheduled with the significant stakeholders to check the estimates and to brainstorm for alternative solutions; the cost and time estimates appeared to be reasonable. Some of the suggestions for the brainstorming session are listed below.

- Change scope.
- Outsource technology design.
- Use the priority matrix (found in Chapter 4) to get top management to clarify their priorities.
- Partner with another organization or build a research consortium to share costs and to share the newly developed technology and production methods.
- Cancel the project.
- Commission a break-even study for the laser printer.

Very little in the way of concrete savings was identified, although there was consensus that time could be compressed to the market launch date, but at additional costs.

Lauren met with the marketing (Connor), production (Kim), and design (Gage) managers who yielded some ideas for cutting costs, but nothing significant enough to have a large impact. Gage remarked, "I wouldn't want to be the one to deliver the message to top management that their cost estimate is $1,250,000 off! Good luck, Lauren."

1. At this point, what would you do if you were the project manager?
2. Was top management acting correctly in developing an estimate?
3. What estimating techniques should be used for a mission critical project such as this?

Appendix 5.1

Learning Curves for Estimating

A forecast estimate of the time required to perform a work package or task is a basic necessity for scheduling the project. In some cases, the manager simply uses judgment and past experience to estimate work package time, or may use historical records of similar tasks.

Most managers and workers intuitively know that improvement in the amount of time required to perform a task or group of tasks occurs with repetition. A worker can perform a task better/quicker the second time and each succeeding time she/he performs it (without any technological change). It is this pattern of improvement that is important to the project manager and project scheduler.

This improvement from repetition generally results in a reduction of labor hours for the accomplishment of tasks and results in lower project costs. From empirical evidence across *all* industries, the pattern of this improvement has been quantified in the *learning curve* (also known as improvement curve, experience curve, and industrial progress curve), which is described by the following relationship:

> *Each time the output quantity doubles, the unit labor hours are reduced at a constant rate.*

For example, assume that a manufacturer has a new contract for 16 prototype units and a total of 800 labor hours were required for the first unit. Past experience has indicated that on similar types of units the improvement rate was 80 percent. This relationship of improvement in labor hours is shown below:

Unit		Labor Hours
1		800
2	800 × .80 =	640
4	640 × .80 =	512
8	512 × .80 =	410
16	410 × .80 =	328

By using Table A5.1 unit values, similar labor hours per unit can be determined. Looking across the 16 unit level and down the 80 percent column, we find a ratio of .4096. By multiplying this ratio times the labor hours for the first unit, we obtained the per unit value:

$$.4096 \times 800 = 328 \text{ hours or } 327.68$$

TABLE A5.1
Learning Curves
Unit Values

Units	60%	65%	70%	75%	80%	85%	90%	95%
1	1.0000	1.0000	1.0000	1.0000	1.0000	1.0000	1.0000	1.0000
2	.6000	.6500	.7000	.7500	.8000	.8500	.9000	.9500
3	.4450	.5052	.5682	.6338	.7021	.7729	.8462	.9219
4	.3600	.4225	.4900	.5625	.6400	.7225	.8100	.9025
5	.3054	.3678	.4368	.5127	.5956	.6857	.7830	.8877
6	.2670	.3284	.3977	.4754	.5617	.6570	.7616	.8758
7	.2383	.2984	.3674	.4459	.5345	.6337	.7439	.8659
8	.2160	.2746	.3430	.4219	.5120	.6141	.7290	.8574
9	.1980	.2552	.3228	.4017	.4930	.5974	.7161	.8499
10	.1832	.2391	.3058	.3846	.4765	.5828	.7047	.8433
12	.1602	.2135	.2784	.3565	.4493	.5584	.6854	.8320
14	.1430	.1940	.2572	.3344	.4276	.5386	.6696	.8226
16	.1296	.1785	.2401	.3164	.4096	.5220	.6561	.8145
18	.1188	.1659	.2260	.3013	.3944	.5078	.6445	.8074
20	.1099	.1554	.2141	.2884	.3812	.4954	.6342	.8012
22	.1025	.1465	.2038	.2772	.3697	.4844	.6251	.7955
24	.0961	.1387	.1949	.2674	.3595	.4747	.6169	.7904
25	.0933	.1353	.1908	.2629	.3548	.4701	.6131	.7880
30	.0815	.1208	.1737	.2437	.3346	.4505	.5963	.7775
35	.0728	.1097	.1605	.2286	.3184	.4345	.5825	.7687
40	.0660	.1010	.1498	.2163	.3050	.4211	.5708	.7611
45	.0605	.0939	.1410	.2060	.2936	.4096	.5607	.7545
50	.0560	.0879	.1336	.1972	.2838	.3996	.5518	.7486
60	.0489	.0785	.1216	.1828	.2676	.3829	.5367	.7386
70	.0437	.0713	.1123	.1715	.2547	.3693	.5243	.7302
80	.0396	.0657	.1049	.1622	.2440	.3579	.5137	.7231
90	.0363	.0610	.0987	.1545	.2349	.3482	.5046	.7168
100	.0336	.0572	.0935	.1479	.2271	.3397	.4966	.7112
120	.0294	.0510	.0851	.1371	.2141	.3255	.4830	.7017
140	.0262	.0464	.0786	.1287	.2038	.3139	.4718	.6937
160	.0237	.0427	.0734	.1217	.1952	.3042	.4623	.6869
180	.0218	.0397	.0691	.1159	.1879	.2959	.4541	.6809
200	.0201	.0371	.0655	.1109	.1816	.2887	.4469	.6757
250	.0171	.0323	.0584	.1011	.1691	.2740	.4320	.6646
300	.0149	.0289	.0531	.0937	.1594	.2625	.4202	.5557
350	.0133	.0262	.0491	.0879	.1517	.2532	.4105	.6482
400	.0121	.0241	.0458	.0832	.1453	.2454	.4022	.6419
450	.0111	.0224	.0431	.0792	.1399	.2387	.3951	.6363
500	.0103	.0210	.0408	.0758	.1352	.2329	.3888	.6314
600	.0090	.0188	.0372	.0703	.1275	.2232	.3782	.6229
700	.0080	.0171	.0344	.0659	.1214	.2152	.3694	.6158
800	.0073	.0157	.0321	.0624	.1163	.2086	.3620	.6098
900	.0067	.0146	.0302	.0594	.1119	.2029	.3556	.6045
1,000	.0062	.0137	.0286	.0569	.1082	.1980	.3499	.5998
1,200	.0054	.0122	.0260	.0527	.1020	.1897	.3404	.5918
1,400	.0048	.0111	.0240	.0495	.0971	.1830	.3325	.5850
1,600	.0044	.0102	.0225	.0468	.0930	.1773	.3258	.5793
1,800	.0040	.0095	.0211	.0446	.0895	.1725	.3200	.5743
2,000	.0037	.0089	.0200	.0427	.0866	.1683	.3149	.5698
2,500	.0031	.0077	.0178	.0389	.0606	.1597	.3044	.5605
3,000	.0027	.0069	.0162	.0360	.0760	.1530	.2961	.5530

That is, the 16th unit should require close to 328 labor hours, assuming an 80 percent improvement ratio.

Obviously, a project manager may need more than a single unit value for estimating the time for some work packages. The cumulative values in Table A5.2 provide factors for computing the cumulative total labor hours of all units. In the previous example, for the first 16 units, the total labor hours required would be

$$800 \times 8.920 = 7,136 \text{ hours}$$

By dividing the total cumulative hours (7,136) by the units, the average unit labor hours can be obtained:

$$7,136 \text{ labor hours/16 units} = 446 \text{ average labor hours per unit}$$

Note how the labor hours for the 16th unit (328) differs from the average for all 16 units (446). The project manager, knowing the average labor costs and processing costs, could estimate the total prototype costs. (The mathematical derivation of factors found in Tables A5.1 and A5.2 can be found in Jelen, F. C. and J. H. Black, *Cost and Optimization Engineering,* 2nd ed. (New York: McGraw-Hill, 1983.)

FOLLOW-ON CONTRACT EXAMPLE

Assume the project manager gets a follow-on order of 74 units; how should she estimate labor hours and cost? Going to the cumulative Table A5.2 we find at the 80 percent ratio and 90 total units intersection—a 30.35 ratio.

$800 \times 30.35 =$	24,280 labor hours for 90 units
Less previous 16 units =	7,136
Total follow-on order =	17,144 labor hours
17,144/74 equals 232 average labor hours per unit	

Labor hours for the 90th unit can be obtained from Table A5.1: $.2349 \times 800 = 187.9$ labor hours. (For ratios between given values, simply estimate.)

Exercise A5.1

Norwegian Satellite Development Company
Cost Estimates
for
World Satellite Telephone Exchange Project

NSDC has a contract to produce eight satellites to support a worldwide telephone system (for Alaska Telecom, Inc.) that allows individuals to use a single, portable telephone in any location on earth to call in and out. NSDC will develop and produce the eight units. NSDC has estimated that the R&D costs will be NOK (Norwegian Krone) 12,000,000. Material costs are expected to be NOK 6,000,000. They have estimated the design and production of the first satellite will require 100,000 labor hours and an 80 percent improvement curve is expected.

TABLE A5.2
Learning Curves
Cumulative Values

Units	60%	65%	70%	75%	80%	85%	90%	95%
1	1.000	1.000	1.000	1.000	1.000	1.000	1.000	1.000
2	1.600	1.650	1.700	1.750	1.800	1.850	1.900	1.950
3	2.045	2.155	2.268	2.384	2.502	2.623	2.746	2.872
4	2.405	2.578	2.758	2.946	3.142	3.345	3.556	3.774
5	2.710	2.946	3.195	3.459	3.738	4.031	4.339	4.662
6	2.977	3.274	3.593	3.934	4.299	4.688	5.101	5.538
7	3.216	3.572	3.960	4.380	4.834	5.322	5.845	6.404
8	3.432	3.847	4.303	4.802	5.346	5.936	6.574	7.261
9	3.630	4.102	4.626	5.204	5.839	6.533	7.290	8.111
10	3.813	4.341	4.931	5.589	6.315	7.116	7.994	8.955
12	4.144	4.780	5.501	6.315	7.227	8.244	9.374	10.62
14	4.438	5.177	6.026	6.994	8.092	9.331	10.72	12.27
16	4.704	5.541	6.514	7.635	8.920	10.38	12.04	13.91
18	4.946	5.879	6.972	8.245	9.716	11.41	13.33	15.52
20	5.171	6.195	7.407	8.828	10.48	12.40	14.64	17.13
22	5.379	6.492	7.819	9.388	11.23	13.38	15.86	18.72
24	5.574	6.773	8.213	9.928	11.95	14.33	17.10	20.31
25	5.668	6.909	8.404	10.19	12.31	14.80	17.71	21.10
30	6.097	7.540	9.305	11.45	14.02	17.09	20.73	25.00
35	6.478	8.109	10.13	12.72	15.64	19.29	23.67	28.86
40	6.821	8.631	10.90	13.72	17.19	21.43	26.54	32.68
45	7.134	9.114	11.62	14.77	18.68	23.50	29.37	36.47
50	7.422	9.565	12.31	15.78	20.12	25.51	32.14	40.22
60	7.941	10.39	13.57	17.67	22.87	29.41	37.57	47.65
70	8.401	11.13	14.74	19.43	25.47	33.17	42.87	54.99
80	8.814	11.82	15.82	21.09	27.96	36.80	48.05	62.25
90	9.191	12.45	16.83	22.67	30.35	40.32	53.14	69.45
100	9.539	13.03	17.79	24.18	32.65	43.75	58.14	76.59
120	10.16	14.16	19.57	27.02	37.05	50.39	67.93	90.71
140	10.72	15.08	21.20	29.67	41.22	56.78	77.46	104.7
160	11.21	15.97	22.72	32.17	45.20	62.95	86.80	118.5
180	11.67	16.79	24.14	34.54	49.03	68.95	95.96	132.1
200	12.09	17.55	25.48	36.80	52.72	74.79	105.0	145.7
250	13.01	19.28	28.56	42.08	61.47	88.83	126.9	179.2
300	13.81	20.81	31.34	46.94	69.66	102.2	148.2	212.2
350	14.51	22.18	33.89	51.48	77.43	115.1	169.0	244.8
400	15.14	23.44	36.26	55.75	84.85	127.6	189.3	277.0
450	15.72	24.60	38.48	59.80	91.97	139.7	209.2	309.0
500	16.26	25.68	40.58	63.68	98.85	151.5	228.8	340.6
600	17.21	27.67	44.47	70.97	112.0	174.2	267.1	403.3
700	18.06	29.45	48.04	77.77	124.4	196.1	304.5	465.3
800	18.82	31.09	51.36	84.18	136.3	217.3	341.0	526.5
900	19.51	32.60	54.46	90.26	147.7	237.9	376.9	587.2
1,000	20.15	34.01	57.40	96.07	158.7	257.9	412.2	647.4
1,200	21.30	36.59	62.85	107.0	179.7	296.6	481.2	766.6
1,400	22.32	38.92	67.85	117.2	199.6	333.9	548.4	884.2
1,600	23.23	41.04	72.49	126.8	218.6	369.9	614.2	1001.
1,800	24.06	43.00	76.85	135.9	236.8	404.9	678.8	1116.
2,000	24.83	44.84	80.96	144.7	254.4	438.9	742.3	1230.
2,500	26.53	48.97	90.39	165.0	296.1	520.8	897.0	1513.
3,000	27.99	52.62	98.90	183.7	335.2	598.9	1047.	1791.

Skilled labor cost is NOK 300 per hour. Desired profit for all projects is 25 percent of total costs.

A. How many labor hours should the eighth satellite require?
B. How many labor hours for the whole project of eight satellites?
C. What price would you ask for the project? Why?
D. Midway through the project your design and production people realize that a 75 percent improvement curve is more appropriate. What impact does this have on the project?
E. Near the end of the project Deutsch Telefon AG has requested a cost estimate for four satellites identical to those you have already produced. What price will you quote them? Justify your price.

Developing a Project Plan

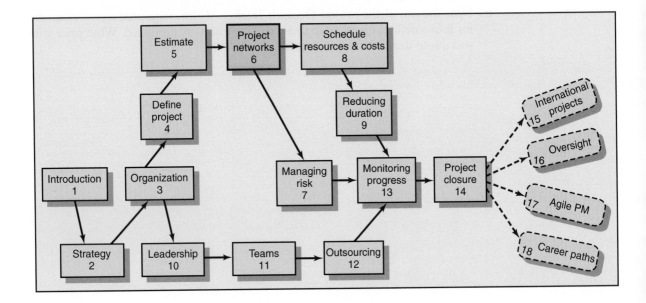

I keep six honest serving-men (they taught me all I knew); their names are What and Why and When and How and Where and Who.

Rudyard Kipling

Developing the Project Network

The project network is the tool used for planning, scheduling, and monitoring project progress. The network is developed from the information collected for the WBS and is a graphic flow chart of the project job plan. The network depicts the project activities that must be completed, the logical sequences, the interdependencies of the activities to be completed, and in most cases the times for the activities to start and finish along with the longest path(s) through the network—the *critical path*. The network is the framework for the project information system that will be used by the project managers to make decisions concerning project time, cost, and performance.

Developing the project networks takes time for someone or some group to develop; therefore, they cost money! Are networks really worth the struggle? The answer is definitely yes, except in cases where the project is considered trivial or very short in duration. The network is easily understood by others because the network presents a graphic display of the flow and sequence of work through the project. Once the network is developed, it is very easy to modify or change when unexpected events occur as the project progresses. For example, if materials for an activity are delayed, the impact can be quickly assessed and the whole project revised in only a few minutes with the computer. These revisions can be communicated to all project participants quickly (for example, via e-mail or project Web site).

The project network provides other invaluable information and insights. It provides the basis for scheduling labor and equipment. It enhances communication that melds all managers and groups together in meeting the time, cost, and performance objectives of the project. It provides an estimate of project duration rather than picking a project completion date from a hat or someone's preferred date. The network gives the times when activities can start and finish and when they can be delayed. It provides the basis for budgeting the cash flow of the project. It identifies which activities are "critical" and, therefore, should not be delayed if the project is to be completed as planned. It highlights which activities to consider if the project needs to be compressed to meet a deadline.

There are other reasons project networks are worth their weight in gold. Basically, project networks minimize surprises by getting the plan out early and allowing corrective feedback. A commonly heard statement from practitioners is that the project network represents three-quarters of the planning process. Perhaps this is an exaggeration, but it signals the perceived importance of the network to project managers in the field.

From Work Package to Network

Project networks are developed from the WBS. The project network is a visual flow diagram of the sequence, interrelationships, and dependencies of all the activities that must be accomplished to complete the project. *An **activity** is an element in the project that consumes time—for example, work or waiting.* Work packages from the WBS are used to build the activities found in the project network. An activity can include one or more work packages. The activities are placed in a sequence that provides for orderly completion of the project. Networks are built using nodes (boxes) and arrows (lines). The node depicts an activity, and the arrow shows dependency and project flow.

Integrating the work packages and the network represents a point where the management process often fails in practice. The primary explanations for this failure are that (1) different groups (people) are used to define work packages and activities and (2) the WBS is poorly constructed and not deliverable/output oriented. Integration of the WBS and project network is crucial to effective project management. The project manager must be careful to guarantee continuity by having some of the same people who defined the WBS and work packages develop the network activities.

Networks provide the project schedule by identifying dependencies, sequencing, and timing of activities, which the WBS is not designed to do. The primary inputs for developing a project network plan are work packages. Remember, a work package is defined independently of other work packages, has definite start and finish points, requires specific resources, includes technical specifications, and has cost estimates for the package. However, dependency, sequencing, and timing of each of these factors are not included in the work package. A network activity can include one or more work packages.

Figure 6.1 shows a segment of the WBS example from Chapter 4 and how the information is used to develop a project network. The lowest level deliverable in Figure 6.1 is "circuit board." The cost accounts (design, production, test, software) denote project work, organization unit responsible, and time-phased budgets for the work packages. Each cost account represents one or more work packages. For example, the design cost account has two work packages (D-1-1 and D-1-2)—specifications and documentation. The software and production accounts also have two work packages. Developing a network requires sequencing tasks from all work packages that have measurable work.

Figure 6.1 traces how work packages are used to develop a project network. You can trace the use of work packages by the coding scheme. For example,

FIGURE 6.1
WBS/Work Packages to Network

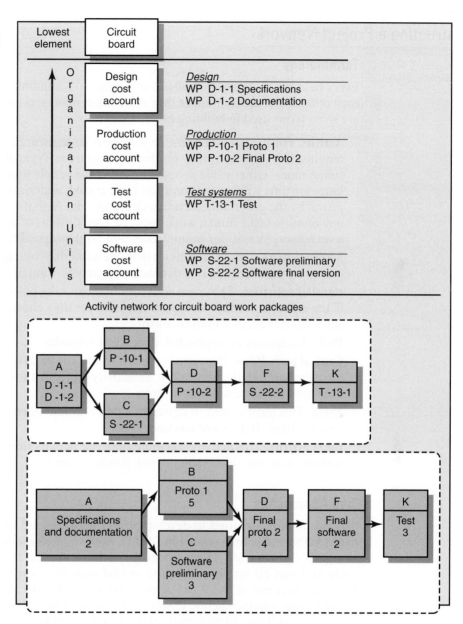

activity A uses work packages D-1-1 and D-1-2 (specifications and documentation), while activity C uses work package S-22-1. This methodology of selecting work packages to describe activities is used to develop the project network, which sequences and times project activities. Care must be taken to include all work packages. *The manager derives activity time estimates from the task times in the work package.* For example, activity B (proto 1) requires five weeks to complete; activity K (test) requires three weeks to complete. After computing the activity **early and late times,** the manager can schedule resources and time-phase budgets (with dates).

Constructing a Project Network

Terminology

Every field has its jargon that allows colleagues to communicate comfortably with each other about the techniques they use. Project managers are no exception. Here are some terms used in building project networks.

Activity. For project managers, an *activity* is an element of the project that requires time. It may or may not require resources. Typically an activity consumes time—either while people work or while people wait. Examples of the latter are time waiting for contracts to be signed, materials to arrive, drug approval by the government, budget clearance, etc. Activities usually represent one or more tasks from a work package. Descriptions of activities should use a verb/noun format: for example, develop product specifications.

Merge activity. This is an activity that has more than one activity immediately preceding it (more than one dependency arrow flowing to it).

Parallel activities. These are activities that can take place at the same time, if the manager wishes. However, the manager may choose to have parallel activities *not* occur simultaneously.

Path. A sequence of connected, dependent activities.

Critical path. When this term is used, it means the path(s) with the longest duration through the network; if an activity on the path is delayed, the project is delayed the same amount of time.

Event. This term is used to represent a point in time when an activity is started or completed. It does not consume time.

Burst activity. This activity has more than one activity immediately following it (more than one dependency arrow flowing from it).

Two Approaches

The two approaches used to develop project networks are known as **activity-on-node (AON)** and **activity-on-arrow (AOA).** *Both methods use two building blocks—the arrow and the node.* Their names derive from the fact that the former uses a node to depict an activity, while the second uses an arrow to depict an activity. From the first use of these two approaches in the late 1950s, practitioners have offered many enhancements; however, the basic models have withstood the test of time and still prevail with only minor variations in form.

In practice, the activity-on-node (AON) method has come to dominate most projects. Hence, this text will deal primarily with AON. However, for those who find their organization using the activity-on-arrow (AOA) approach, the chapter includes an appendix demonstrating AOA methods (Appendix 6.1). There are good reasons for students of project management to be proficient in both methods. Different departments and organizations have their "favorite" approaches and are frequently loyal to software that is already purchased and being used. New employees or outsiders are seldom in a position to govern choice of method. If subcontractors are used, it is unreasonable to ask them to change their whole project management system to conform to the approach you are using. The point is, a project manager should feel comfortable moving among projects that use either AON or AOA.

Basic Rules to Follow in Developing Project Networks

The following eight rules apply in general when developing a project network:

1. Networks flow typically from left to right.
2. An activity cannot begin until all preceding connected activities have been completed.
3. Arrows on networks indicate precedence and flow. Arrows can cross over each other.
4. Each activity should have a unique identification number.
5. An activity identification number must be larger than that of any activities that precede it.
6. Looping is not allowed (in other words, recycling through a set of activities cannot take place).
7. Conditional statements are not allowed (that is, this type of statement should not appear: If successful, do something; if not, do nothing).
8. Experience suggests that when there are multiple starts, a common start node can be used to indicate a clear project beginning on the network. Similarly, a single project end node can be used to indicate a clear ending.

Read the Snapshot from Practice: The Yellow Sticky Approach (page 165) to see how these rules are used to create project networks.

Activity-on-Node (AON) Fundamentals

The wide availability of personal computers and graphics programs has served as an impetus for use of the activity-on-node (AON) method (sometimes called the *precedence diagram method*). Figure 6.2 shows a few typical uses of building blocks for the AON network construction. An **activity** is represented by a *node* (box). The node can take many forms, but in recent years the node represented as a rectangle (box) has dominated. The dependencies among activities are depicted by *arrows* between the rectangles (boxes) on the AON network. The arrows indicate how the activities are related and the sequence in which things must be accomplished. The length and slope of the arrow are arbitrary and set for convenience of drawing the network. The letters in the boxes serve here to identify the activities while you learn the fundamentals of network construction and analysis. In practice, activities have identification numbers and descriptions.

There are three basic relationships that must be established for activities included in a project network. The relationships can be found by answering the following three questions for each activity:

1. Which activities must be completed immediately *before* this activity? These activities are called *predecessor* activities.
2. Which activities must immediately *follow* this activity? These activities are called *successor* activities.
3. Which activities can occur *while* this activity is taking place? This is known as a *concurrent* or *parallel* relationship.

Sometimes a manager can use only questions 1 and 3 to establish relationships. This information allows the network analyst to construct a graphic flow chart of the sequence and logical interdependencies of project activities.

FIGURE 6.2
Activity-on-Node
Network
Fundamentals

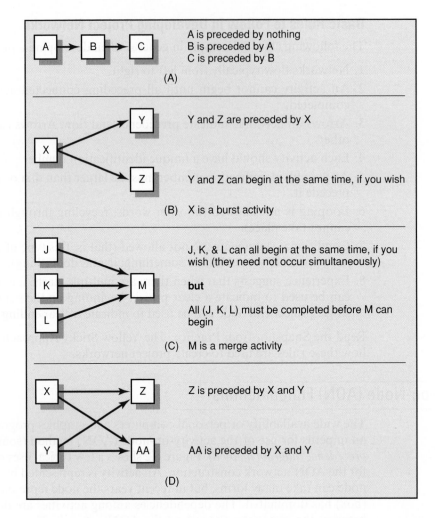

Figure 6.2A is analogous to a list of things to do where you complete the task at the top of the list first and then move to the second task, etc. This figure tells the project manager that activity A must be completed before activity B can begin, and activity B must be completed before activity C can begin.

Figure 6.2B tells us that activities Y and Z cannot begin until activity X is completed. This figure also indicates that activities Y and Z can occur concurrently or simultaneously if the project manager wishes; however, it is not a necessary condition. For example, pouring a concrete driveway (activity Y) can take place while landscape planting (activity Z) is being accomplished, but land clearing (activity X) must be completed before activities Y and Z can start. Activities Y and Z are considered *parallel* activities. Parallel paths allow concurrent effort, which may shorten time to do a series of activities. Activity X is sometimes referred to as a *burst* activity because more than one arrow bursts from the node. The number of arrows indicates how many activities immediately follow activity X.

Figure 6.2C shows us activities J, K, and L can occur simultaneously if desired, and activity M cannot begin until activities J, K, and L are all completed. Activities J, K, and L are parallel activities. Activity M is called a *merge* activity because more than one activity must be completed before M can begin. Activity M could also be called a milestone—a significant accomplishment.

TABLE 6.1
Network Information

KOLL BUSINESS CENTER County Engineers Design Department		
Activity	**Description**	**Preceding Activity**
A	Application approval	None
B	Construction plans	A
C	Traffic study	A
D	Service availability check	A
E	Staff report	B, C
F	Commission approval	B, C, D
G	Wait for construction	F
H	Occupancy	E, G

In Figure 6.2D, activities X and Y are parallel activities that can take place at the same time; activities Z and AA are also parallel activities. But activities Z and AA cannot begin until activities X and Y are both completed.

Given these fundamentals of AON, we can practice developing a simple network. Remember, the arrows can cross over each other (e.g., Figure 6.2D), be bent, or be any length or slope. Neatness is not a criterion for a valid, useful network—only accurate inclusion of all project activities, their dependencies, and time estimates. Information for a simplified project network is given in Table 6.1. This project represents a new business center that is to be developed and the work and services the county engineering design department must provide as it coordinates with other groups—such as the business center owners and contractors.

Figure 6.3 shows the first steps in constructing the AON project network from the information in Table 6.1. We see that activity A (application approval) has nothing preceding it; therefore, it is the first node to be drawn. Next, we note that activities B, C, and D (construction plans, traffic study, and service availability check) are all preceded by activity A. We draw three arrows and connect them to activities B, C, and D. This segment shows the project manager that activity A

FIGURE 6.3
Koll Business Center—Partial Network

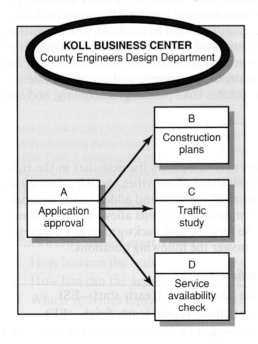

TABLE 6.2
Network Information

	KOLL BUSINESS CENTER County Engineers Design Department		
Activity	**Description**	**Preceding Activity**	**Activity Time**
A	Application approval	None	5
B	Construction plans	A	15
C	Traffic study	A	10
D	Service availability check	A	5
E	Staff report	B, C	15
F	Commission approval	B, C, D	10
G	Wait for construction	F	170
H	Occupancy	E, G	35

The terms in parentheses represent the acronyms used in most texts and computer programs and by project managers. The forward and backward pass process is presented next.

Forward Pass—Earliest Times

The forward pass starts with the first project activity(ies) and traces each path (chain of sequential activities) through the network to the last project activity(ies). As you trace along the path, you *add* the activity times. The longest path denotes the project completion time for the plan and is called the critical path (CP). Table 6.2 lists the activity times in workdays for the Koll Business Center example we used for drawing a network.

Figure 6.5 shows the network with the activity time estimate found in the node (see "DUR" for duration in the legend). For example, activity A has an activity duration of 5 workdays, and activity G has a duration of 170 workdays. The forward pass begins with the project start time, which is usually time zero. (Note: Calendar times can be computed for the project later in the planning phase.) In our Koll Business Center example, the early start time for the first activity (activity A) is zero. This time is found in the upper left corner of the activity A node in Figure 6.6. The early finish for activity A is 5 (ES + DUR = EF or 0 + 5 = 5). Next, we see that activity A is the predecessor for activities B, C, and D. Therefore, the earliest these activities can begin is the instant in time when activity A is completed; this time is 5 workdays. You can now see in Figure 6.6 that activities B, C, and D can all start the moment activity A is complete and, therefore, have an early start (ES) of 5. Using the formula ES + DUR = EF, the early finish (EF) times for activities B, C, and D are 20, 15, and 10. What is the ES for activity E, then, which is a merge activity? Is it 15 or 20? The answer is 20 because all activities immediately preceding activity E (B and C) must be completed before activity E can begin. Because activity B will take the longest to complete, it controls the ES of activity E. The same process is used for determining the ES for activity F. It is preceded by activities B, C, and D. The controlling early finish (EF) time is activity B, which has the longer early finish (20 versus 15 and 10) of the immediate predecessors (activities B, C, and D) of activity F. Stated differently, the forward pass assumes every activity will start the instant in time when the last of its predecessors is finished.

FIGURE 6.5   **Activity-on-Node Network**

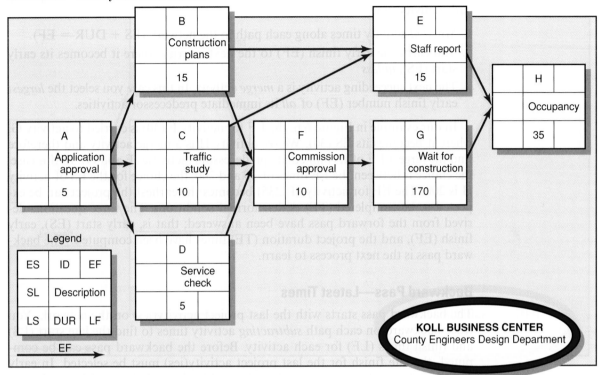

FIGURE 6.6   **Activity-on-Node Network Forward Pass**

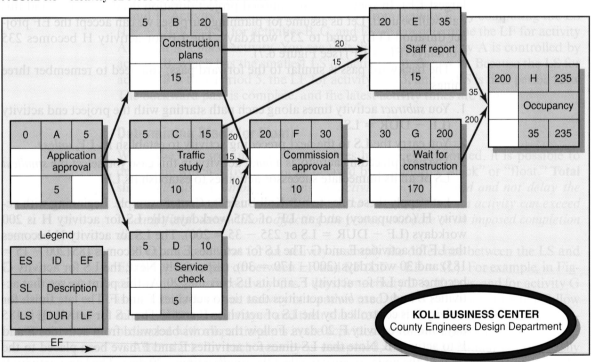

FIGURE 6.8 **Activity-on-Node Network with Slack**

or LS − ES = 0). *The critical path is the network path(s) that has (have) the least slack in common.* This awkward arrangement of words is necessary because a problem arises when the project finish activity has an LF that differs from the EF found in the forward pass—for example, an imposed duration date. If this is the case, the slack on the critical path will *not* be zero; it will be the difference between the project EF and the imposed LF of the last project activity. For example, if the EF for the project is 235 days, but the imposed LF or target date is set at 220 days, all activities on the critical path would have a slack of minus 15 days. Of course, this would result in a late start of −15 days for the first project activity—a good trick if the project is to start now. Negative slack occurs in practice when the critical path is delayed.

In Figure 6.8 the critical path is marked with dashed arrows and nodes—activities A, B, F, G, and H. Delay of any of these activities will delay the total project by the same number of days. Critical activities typically represent about 10 percent of the activities of the project. Therefore, project managers pay close attention to the critical path activities to be sure they are not delayed. See Snapshot from Practice: The Critical Path.

We use the term **sensitivity** to reflect the likelihood the original critical path(s) will change once the project is initiated. Sensitivity is a function of the number of critical or near-critical paths. A network schedule that has only one critical path and noncritical activities that enjoy significant slack would be labeled insensitive. Conversely, a sensitive network would be one or more than critical paths and/or noncritical activities with very little slack. Under these circumstances the original critical path is much more likely to change once work gets under way on the project.

SNAPSHOT FROM PRACTICE   The Critical Path

The critical path method (CPM) has long been considered the "Holy Grail" of project management. Here are comments made by veteran project managers when asked about the significance of the critical path in managing projects:

- I try to make it a point whenever possible to put my best people on critical activities or on those activities that stand the greatest chance of becoming critical.

- I pay extra attention when doing risk assessment to identifying those risks that can impact the critical path, either directly or indirectly, by making a noncritical activity so late that it becomes critical. When I've got money to spend to reduce risks, it usually gets spent on critical tasks.

- I don't have time to monitor all the activities on a big project, but I make it a point to keep in touch with the people who are working on critical activities. When I have the time, they are the ones I visit to find out firsthand how things are going. It's amazing how much more I can find out from talking to the rank and file who are doing the work and by reading the facial expressions of people—much more than I can gain from a number-driven status report.

- When I get calls from other managers asking to "borrow" people or equipment, I'm much more generous when it involves resources from working on noncritical activities. For example, if another project manager needs an electrical engineer who is assigned to a task with five days of slack, I'm willing to share that engineer with another project manager for two to three days.

- The most obvious reason the critical path is important is because these are the activities that impact completion time. If I suddenly get a call from above saying they need my project done two weeks earlier than planned, the critical path is where I schedule the overtime and add extra resources to get the project done more quickly. In the same way, if the project schedule begins to slip, it's the critical activities I focus on to get back on schedule.

How sensitive is the Koll Business Center schedule? Not very, since there is only one critical path and each of the three noncritical activities have significant slack when compared to the estimated duration.

Project managers assess the sensitivity of their network schedules to determine how much attention they should devote to managing the critical path.

Free Slack (Float)

Free slack (FS) is unique. *It is the amount of time an activity can be delayed without delaying any immediately following (successor) activity. Or, free slack is the amount of time an activity can exceed its early finish date without affecting the early start date of any successor(s).* Free slack can never be negative. Only activities that occur at the end of a chain of activities, where you have a merge activity, can have free slack. Since the Koll Business Center project does not work well to demonstrate free slack, see Figure 6.9.

In Figure 6.9 activity 6 has free slack of 15, while activities 2 and 3 do not. In this case, activity 6 is the last activity in the upper path, and it merges to activity 7. Hence, to delay activity 6 up to 15 time units does not delay any following activities and requires no coordination with managers of other activities. Conversely, if either activity 2 or 3 is delayed, the managers of following activities need to be notified that the slack has been used so they can adjust their start schedules. For example, if activity 2 is delayed 5 time units, the activity 2 manager should notify those in charge of the following activities (3 and 6) their slack has been reduced to 10 time units. Free slack for activity 6 is also reduced to 10 units.

Free slack occurs at the last activity in a chain of activities. In many situations the "chain" can have only one link. Activity 4 in Figure 6.9 is an example.

FIGURE 6.9 **Free Slack Example**

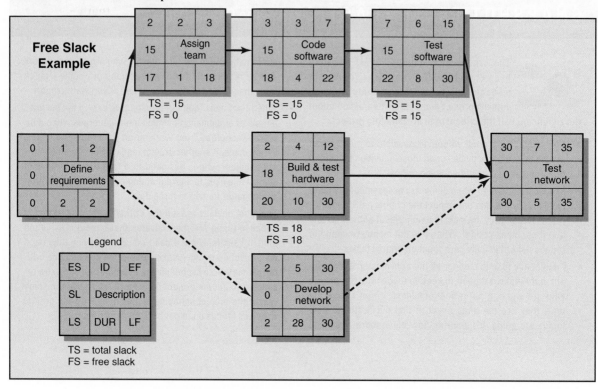

It has free slack of 18 time units. Note that it needs no coordination with other activities—unless a delay exceeds the slack of 18 time units.

For a more typical example, imagine a chain of 20 activities. Except for the last activity in the chain, delaying any of the other 19 activities requires notifying the managers of the remaining activities in the chain that you will be late. Again, note that total slack is for the whole path. Thus, if all the slack is used on the second activity in the 20-activity chain, the remaining activities in the chain will have zero slack. The slack is not available for use by the other managers affected; it is gone!

Using the Forward and Backward Pass Information

Returning to the Koll Business Center project network in Figure 6.8, what does a slack of 10 workdays for activity D (Service check, refer to Figure 6.8) mean for the project manager? In this specific case it means activity D can be delayed 10 days. In a larger sense the project manager soon learns that slack is important because it allows flexibility in scheduling scarce project resources—personnel and equipment—that are used on more than one parallel activity or another project.

Knowing the four activity times of ES, LS, EF, and LF is invaluable for the planning, scheduling, and controlling phases of the project. The ES and LF tell the project manager the time interval in which the activity should be completed. For example, activity E (Staff report) must be completed within the time interval 20 and 200 workdays; the activity can start as early as day 20 or finish as late as day 200. Conversely, activity F (Commission approval), must start on day 20, or the project will be delayed.

When the critical path is known, it is possible to tightly manage the resources of the activities on the critical path so no mistakes are made that will result in delays. In addition, if for some reason the project must be expedited to meet an earlier date, it is possible to select those activities, or combination of activities, that will cost the least to shorten the project. Similarly, if the critical path is delayed and the time must be made up by shortening some activity or activities on the critical path to make up any negative slack, it is possible to identify the activities on the critical path that cost the least to shorten. If there are other paths with very little slack, it may be necessary to shorten activities on those paths also.

Level of Detail for Activities

Time-phasing work and budgets of the project mandate careful definition of the activities that make up the project network. Typically an activity represents one or more tasks from a work package. How many tasks you include in each activity sets the level of detail. In some cases it is possible to end up with too much information to manage, and this can result in increased overhead costs. Managers of small projects have been able to minimize the level of detail by eliminating some of the preliminary steps to drawing networks. Larger firms also recognize the cost of information overload and are working to cut down the level of detail in networks and in most other dimensions of the project.

Practical Considerations

Network Logic Errors

Project network techniques have certain logic rules that must be followed. One rule is that conditional statements such as "if test successful build proto, if failure redesign" are not permitted. The network is not a decision tree; it is a project plan that we assume will materialize. If conditional statements were allowed, the forward and backward pass would make little sense. Although in reality a plan seldom materializes as we expect in every detail, it is a reasonable initial assumption. You shall see that once a network plan is developed, it is an easy step to make revisions to accommodate changes.

Another rule that defeats the project network and computation process is *looping*. Looping is an attempt by the planner to return to an earlier activity. Recall that the activity identification numbers should always be higher for the activities following an activity in question; this rule helps to avoid the illogical precedence relationships among the activities. An activity should only occur once; if it is to occur again, the activity should have a new name and identification number and should be placed in the right sequence on the network. Figure 6.10 shows an illogical loop. If this loop were allowed to exist, this path would perpetually repeat itself. Many computer programs catch this type of logic error.

FIGURE 6.10
Illogical Loop

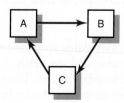

Activity Numbering

Each activity needs a unique identification code—usually a number. In practice very elegant schemes exist. Most schemes number activities in ascending order, that is, each succeeding activity has a larger number so that the flow of the project activities is toward project completion. It is customary to leave gaps between numbers (1, 5, 10, 15 . . .). Gaps are desirable so you can add missing or new activities later. Because it is nearly impossible to draw a project network perfectly, numbering networks is frequently not done until after the network is complete.

In practice you will find computer programs that accept numeric, alphabetic, or a combination of activity designations. Combination designations are often used to identify cost, work skill, departments, and locations. As a general rule, activity numbering systems should be ascending and as simple as possible. The intent is to make it as easy as you can for project participants to follow work through the network and locate specific activities.

Use of Computers to Develop Networks

All of the tools and techniques discussed in this chapter can be used with computer software currently available. Two examples are shown in Figures 6.11 and 6.12. Figure 6.10 presents a generic AON computer output for the Air Control project. The critical path is identified by the unshaded nodes (activities 1, 4, 6, 7, and 8). The activity description is shown on the top line of the activity node. The activity identification and duration are found on the right side of the node. The early start and early finish are on the left side of the node. The project starts on January 1 and is planned to finish February 14.

Figure 6.12 presents an early start **Gantt chart.** Bar charts are popular because they present an easy-to-understand, clear picture on a time-scaled horizon. They are used during planning, resource scheduling, and status reporting. The format is a two-dimensional representation of the project schedule, with activities down the rows and time across the horizontal axis. In this computer output the shaded bars represent the activity durations. The extended lines from the bars represent slack. For example, "software development" has a duration of 18 time units (shaded area of the bar) and 20 days slack (represented by the extended line). The bar also indicates the activity has an early start of January 3, would end January 20, but can finish as late as February 9 because it has 20 days of slack. When calendar dates are used on the time axis, Gantt charts provide a clear overview of the project schedule and can be often found posted on the walls of project offices. Unfortunately, when projects have many dependency relationships, the dependency lines soon become overwhelming and defeat the simplicity of the Gantt chart.

Project management software can be a tremendous help in the hands of those who understand and are familiar with the tools and techniques discussed in this text. However, there is nothing more dangerous than someone using the software with little or no knowledge of how the software derives its output. Mistakes in input are very common and require someone skilled in the concepts, tools, and information system to recognize that errors exist so false actions are avoided.

Calendar Dates

Ultimately you will want to assign calendar dates to your project activities. If a computer program is not used, dates are assigned manually. Lay out a calendar of workdays (exclude nonworkdays), and number them. Then relate the calendar workdays to the workdays on your project network. Most computer programs will

FIGURE 6.11 Air Control Project—Network Diagram

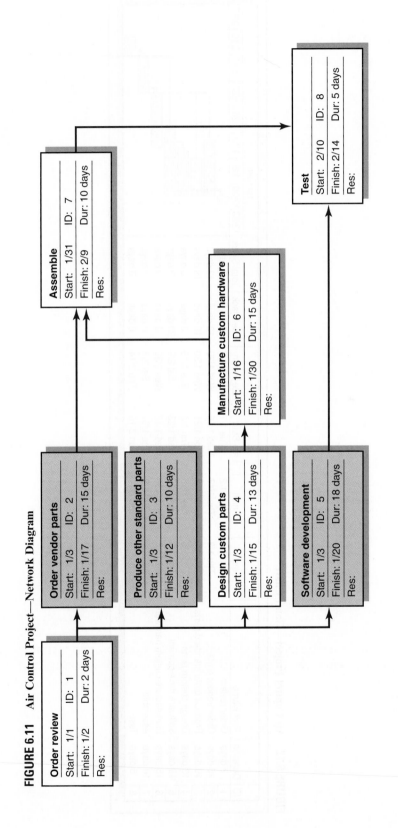

Order review		
Start: 1/1	ID: 1	
Finish: 1/2	Dur: 2 days	
Res:		

Order vendor parts		
Start: 1/3	ID: 2	
Finish: 1/17	Dur: 15 days	
Res:		

Produce other standard parts		
Start: 1/3	ID: 3	
Finish: 1/12	Dur: 10 days	
Res:		

Design custom parts		
Start: 1/3	ID: 4	
Finish: 1/15	Dur: 13 days	
Res:		

Software development		
Start: 1/3	ID: 5	
Finish: 1/20	Dur: 18 days	
Res:		

Assemble		
Start: 1/31	ID: 7	
Finish: 2/9	Dur: 10 days	
Res:		

Manufacture custom hardware		
Start: 1/16	ID: 6	
Finish: 1/30	Dur: 15 days	
Res:		

Test		
Start: 2/10	ID: 8	
Finish: 2/14	Dur: 5 days	
Res:		

FIGURE 6.12 Air Control Project—Gantt Chart

ID	Duration	Task Name	Start	Finish	Late Start	Late Finish	Free Slack	Total Slack
1	2 days	Order review	Tue 1/1	Wed 1/2	Tue 1/1	Wed 1/2	0 days	0 days
2	15 days	Order vendor parts	Thu 1/3	Thu 1/17	Wed 1/16	Wed 1/30	13 days	13 days
3	10 days	Produce other standard parts	Thu 1/3	Sat 1/12	Mon 1/21	Wed 1/30	18 days	18 days
4	13 days	Design custom parts	Thu 1/3	Tue 1/15	Thu 1/3	Tue 1/15	0 days	0 days
5	18 days	Software development	Thu 1/3	Sun 1/20	Wed 1/23	Sat 2/9	20 days	20 days
6	15 days	Manufacture custom hardware	Wed 1/16	Wed 1/30	Wed 1/16	Wed 1/30	0 days	0 days
7	10 days	Assemble	Thu 1/31	Sat 2/9	Thu 1/31	Sat 2/9	0 days	0 days
8	5 days	Test	Sun 2/10	Thu 2/14	Sun 2/10	Thu 2/14	0 days	0 days

assign calendar dates automatically after you identify start dates, time units, nonworkdays, and other information.

Multiple Starts and Multiple Projects

Some computer programs require a common start and finish event in the form of a node—usually a circle or rectangle—for a project network. Even if this is not a requirement, it is a good idea because it avoids "dangler" paths. Dangler paths give the impression that the project does not have a clear beginning or ending. If a project has more than one activity that can begin when the project is to start, each path is a dangler path. The same is true if a project network ends with more than one activity; these unconnected paths are also called danglers. Danglers can be avoided by tying dangler activities to a common project start or finish node.

When several projects are tied together in an organization, using a common start and end node helps to identify the total planning period of all projects. Use of pseudo or dummy wait activities from the common start node allows different start dates for each project.

Extended Network Techniques to Come Closer to Reality

The method for showing relationships among activities in the last section is called the finish-to-start relationship because it assumes all immediate preceding connected activities must be completed before the next activity can begin. In an effort to come closer to the realities of projects, some useful extensions have been added. The use of *laddering* was the first obvious extension practitioners found very useful.

Laddering

The assumption that all immediate preceding activities must be 100 percent complete is too restrictive for some situations found in practice. This restriction occurs most frequently when one activity overlaps the start of another and has a long duration. Under the standard finish-to-start relationship, when an activity has a long duration and will delay the start of an activity immediately following it, the activity can be broken into segments and the network drawn using a *laddering* approach so the following activity can begin sooner and not delay the work. This segmenting of the larger activity gives the appearance of steps on a ladder on the network, thus the name. The classic example used in many texts and articles is laying pipe, because it is easy to visualize. The trench must be dug, pipe laid, and the trench refilled. If the pipeline is one mile long, it is not necessary to dig one mile of trench before the laying of pipe can begin or to lay one mile of pipe before refill can begin. Figure 6.13 shows how these overlapping activities might appear in an AON network using the standard finish-to-start approach.

FIGURE 6.13
Example of Laddering Using Finish-to-Start Relationship

Use of Lags

The use of *lags* has been developed to offer greater flexibility in network construction. *A lag is the minimum amount of time a dependent activity must be delayed to begin or end.* The use of lags in project networks occurs for two primary reasons:

1. When activities of long duration delay the start or finish of successor activities, the network designer normally breaks the activity into smaller activities to avoid the long delay of the successor activity. Use of lags can avoid such delays and reduce network detail.
2. Lags can be used to constrain the start and finish of an activity.

The most commonly used relationship extensions are start-to-start, finish-to-finish, and combinations of these two. These relationship patterns are discussed in this section.

Finish-to-Start Relationship

The finish-to-start relationship represents the typical, generic network style used in the early part of the chapter. However, there are situations in which the next activity in a sequence must be delayed even when the preceding activity is complete. For example, removing concrete forms cannot begin until the poured cement has cured for two time units. Figure 6.14 shows this **lag relationship** for AON networks. Finish-to-start lags are frequently used when ordering materials. For example, it may take 1 day to place orders but take 19 days to receive the goods. The use of finish-to-start allows the activity duration to be only 1 day and the lag 19 days. This approach ensures the activity cost is tied to placing the order only rather than charging the activity for 20 days of work. This same finish-to-start lag relationship is useful to depict transportation, legal, and mail lags.

The use of finish-to-start lags should be carefully checked to ensure their validity. Conservative project managers or those responsible for completion of activities have been known to use lags as a means of building in a "slush" factor to reduce the risk of being late. A simple rule to follow is that the use of finish-to-start lags must be justified and approved by someone responsible for a large section of the project. The legitimacy of lags is not usually difficult to discern. The legitimate use of the additional relationship shown can greatly enhance the network by more closely representing the realities of the project.

Start-to-Start Relationship

An alternative to segmenting the activities as we did earlier is to use a start-to-start relationship. Typical start-to-start relationships are shown in Figure 6.15. Figure 6.15A shows the start-to-start relationship with zero lag, while Figure 6.15B shows the same relationship with a lag of five time units. It is important to note that the relationship may be used with or without a lag. If time is assigned, it is usually shown on the dependency arrow of an AON network.

In Figure 6.15B, activity Q cannot begin until five time units after activity P begins. This type of relationship typically depicts a situation in which you can perform a portion of one activity and begin a following activity before completing

FIGURE 6.14
Finish-to-Start Relationship

FIGURE 6.15
Start-to-Start
Relationship

the first. This relationship can be used on the pipe-laying project. Figure 6.16 shows the project using an AON network. The start-to-start relationship reduces network detail and project delays by using lag relationships.

It is possible to find compression opportunities by changing finish-to-start relations to start-to-start relationships. A review of finish-to-start critical activities may point out opportunities that can be revised to be parallel by using start-to-start relationships. For example, in place of a finish-to-start activity "design house, then build foundation," a start-to-start relationship could be used in which the foundation can be started, say, five days (lag) after design has started—assuming the design of the foundation is the first part of the total design activity. This start-to-start relationship with a small lag allows a sequential activity to be worked on in parallel and to compress the duration of the critical path. This same concept is frequently found in projects in which concurrent engineering is used to speed completion of a project. **Concurrent engineering,** which is highlighted in the Snapshot from Practice: Concurrent Engineering, basically breaks activities into smaller segments so that work can be done in parallel and the project expedited. Start-to-start relationships can depict the concurrent engineering conditions and reduce network detail. Of course, the same result can be accomplished by breaking an activity into small packages that can be implemented in parallel, but this latter approach increases the network and tracking detail significantly.

FIGURE 6.16
Use of Lags to
Reduce Detail

Concurrent Engineering*

In the old days, when a new product development project was initiated by a firm, it would start its sequential journey in the research and development department. Concepts and ideas would be worked out and the results passed to the engineering department, which sometimes reworked the whole product. This result would be passed to manufacturing, where it might be reworked once more in order to ensure the product could be manufactured using existing machinery and operations. Quality improvements were initiated after the fact once defects and improvement opportunities were discovered during production. This sequential approach to product development required a great deal of time, and it was not uncommon for the final product to be totally unrecognizable when compared to original specifications.

Given the emphasis on speed to the market, companies have abandoned the sequential approach to product development and have adopted a more holistic approach titled concurrent engineering. In a nutshell, *concurrent engineering* entails the active involvement of all the relevant specialty areas throughout the design and development process. The traditional chainlike sequence of finish-to-start relationships is replaced by a series of start-to-start lag relationships as soon as meaningful work can be initiated for the next phase. Figure 6.17 summarizes the dramatic gains in time to market achieved by this approach.

FIGURE 6.17 **New Product Development Process**

For example, this approach was used by Chrysler Corporation to design its new line of SC cars including the popular *Neon* sedan. From the very beginning specialists from marketing, engineering, design, manufacturing, quality assurance, and other relevant departments were involved in every stage of the project. Not only did the project meet all of its objectives, it was completed six months ahead of schedule.

* O. Suris, "Competitors Blinded by Chrysler's Neon," *The Wall Street Journal,* January 10, 1994.

FIGURE 6.18
Finish-to-Finish
Relationship

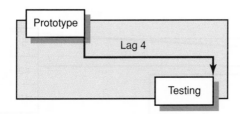

Finish-to-Finish Relationship

This relationship is found in Figure 6.18. The finish of one activity depends on the finish of another activity. For example, testing cannot be completed any earlier than four days after the prototype is complete. Note that this is not a finish-to-start relationship because the testing of subcomponents can begin before the prototype is completed, but four days of "system" testing is required after the prototype is finished.

Start-to-Finish Relationship

This relationship represents situations in which the finish of an activity depends on the start of another activity. For example, system documentation cannot end until three days after testing has started (see Figure 6.19). Here all the relevant information to complete the system documentation is produced after the first three days of testing.

Combinations of Lag Relationships

More than one lag relationship can be attached to an activity. These relationships are usually start-to-start and finish-to-finish combinations tied to two activities. For example, debug cannot begin until two time units after coding has started. Coding must be finished four days before debug can be finished (see Figure 6.20).

An Example Using Lag Relationships—The Forward and Backward Pass

The forward and backward pass procedures are the same as explained earlier in the chapter for finish-to-start relationships (without lags). The modifying technique lies in the need to check each new relationship to see if it alters the start or finish time of another activity.

FIGURE 6.19
Start-to-Finish
Relationship

FIGURE 6.20
Combination
Relationships

FIGURE 6.21 **Network Using Lags**

An example of the outcome of the forward and backward pass is shown in Figure 6.21. Order hardware depends upon the design of the system (start-to-start). Three days into the design of the system (activity A), it is possible to order the required hardware (activity B). It takes four days after the order is placed (activity B) for the hardware to arrive so it can begin to be installed (activity C). After two days of installing the software system (activity D), the testing of the system can begin (activity E). System testing (activity E) can be completed two days after the software is installed (activity D). Preparing system documentation (activity F) can begin once the design is completed (activity A), but it cannot be completed until two days after testing the system (activity E). This final relationship is an example of a finish-to-finish lag.

Note how an activity can have a critical finish and/or start. Activities E and F have critical finishes (zero slack), but their activity starts have 4 and 12 days of slack. It is only the finish of activities E and F that are critical. Conversely, activity A has zero slack to start but has five days of slack to finish. The critical path follows activity start and finish constraints that occur due to the use of the additional relationships available and the imposed lags. You can identify the critical path in Figure 6.21 by following the dashed line on the network.

If a lag relationship exists, each activity must be checked to see if the start or finish is constrained. For example, in the forward pass the EF of activity E (test system) (18) is controlled by the finish of activity D (install software) and the lag of two time units (16 + lag 2 = 18). Finally, in the backward pass, the LS of activity A (design system) is controlled by activity B (order hardware) and the lag relationship to activity A (3 − 3 = 0).

SNAPSHOT FROM PRACTICE   Hammock Activities

Hammock activities are frequently used to identify the use of fixed resources or costs over a segment of the project. Typical examples of hammock activities are inspection services, consultants, or construction management services. A hammock activity derives its duration from the time span between other activities. For example, a special color copy machine is needed for a segment of a tradeshow publication project. A hammock activity can be used to indicate the need for this resource and to apply costs over this segment of the project. This hammock is linked from the start of the first activity in the segment that uses the color copy machine to the end of the last activity that uses it. The hammock duration is simply the difference between the EF for the last activity and the ES of the first activity. The duration is computed after the forward pass and hence has no influence on other activity times. Figure 6.22 provides an example of a hammock activity used in a network. The duration for the hammock activity is derived from the early start of activity B and the early finish of activity F; that is, the difference between 13 and 5, or 8 time units. The hammock duration will change if any ES or EF in the chain-sequence changes. Hammock activities are very useful in assigning and controlling indirect project costs.

FIGURE 6.22   **Hammock Activity Example**

Another major use of hammock activities is to aggregate sections of a project. This is similar to developing a subnetwork, but the precedence is still preserved. This approach is some- times used to present a "macro network" for upper management levels. Using a hammock activity to group activities can facilitate getting the right level of detail for specific sections of a project.

Hammock Activities

Another of the extended techniques uses a **hammock activity.** This type of activity derives its name because it spans over a segment of a project. The hammock activity duration is determined *after* the network plan is drawn. The Snapshot from Practice: Hammock Activities describes how the hammock activity is used.

Drawing AON Networks

2. Draw a project network from the following information. What activity(s) is a burst activity? What activity(s) is a merge activity?

ID	Description	Predecessor
A	Survey site	None
B	Install drainage	A
C	Install power lines	A
D	Excavate site	B, C
E	Pour foundation	D

3.* Draw a project network from the following information. What activity(s) is a burst activity? What activity(s) is a merge activity?

ID	Description	Predecessor
A	Identify topic	None
B	Research topic	A
C	Draft paper	B
D	Edit paper	C
E	Create graphics	C
F	References	C
G	Final draft	D, E, F

4. Draw a project network from the following information. What activity(s) is a burst activity? What activity(s) is a merge activity?

ID	Description	Predecessor
A	Contract signed	None
B	Survey designed	A
C	Target market identified	B
D	Data collection	B, C
E	Develop presentation	B
F	Analyze results	D
G	Demographics	C
H	Presentation	E, F, G

5. Draw a project network from the following information. What activity(s) is a burst activity? What activity(s) is a merge activity?

ID	Description	Predecessor
A	Order review	None
B	Order standard parts	A
C	Produce standard parts	A
D	Design custom parts	A
E	Software development	A
F	Manufacture custom parts	C, D
G	Assemble	B, F
H	Test	E, G

* The solution to this exercise can be found in Appendix One.

AON Network Times

6. From the following information, develop an AON project network. Complete the forward and backward pass, compute activity slack, and identify the critical path. How many days will the project take?

ID	Description	Predecessor	Time
A	Survey site	None	2
B	Install drainage	A	5
C	Install power lines	A	3
D	Excavate site	B, C	4
E	Pour foundation	D	3

7. The project information for the custom order project of the Air Control Company is presented here. Draw a project network for this project. Compute the early and late activity times and the slack times. Identify the critical path.

ID	Activity	Predecessor	Time
A	Order review	None	2
B	Order standard parts	A	15
C	Produce standard parts	A	10
D	Design custom parts	A	13
E	Software development	A	18
F	Manufacture custom hardware	C, D	15
G	Assemble	B, F	10
H	Test	E, G	5

8. You have signed a contract to build a garage for the Simpsons. You will receive a $500 bonus for completing the project within 15 working days. The contract also contains a penalty clause in which you will lose $100 for each day the project takes longer than 15 working days.

Draw a project network given the information below. Complete the forward and backward pass, compute the activity slack, and identify the critical path. Do you expect to receive a bonus or a penalty on this project?

ID	Description	Predecessor	Time (days)
A	Pour foundation	None	3
B	Erect frame	A	4
C	Roof	B	4
D	Windows	B	1
E	Doors	B	1
F	Electrical	B	3
G	Rough-in frame	C, D, E, F	2
H	Door opener	E, F	1
I	Paint	G, H	2
J	Cleanup	I	1

9. You are creating a customer database for the Modesto Nuts minor league baseball team. Draw a project network given the information below. Complete the forward and backward pass, compute activity slack, and identify the critical path.

   How long will this project take? How sensitive is the network schedule? Calculate the free slack and total slack for all noncritical activities.

ID	Description	Predecessor	Time (days)
A	Systems design	None	2
B	Subsystem A design	A	1
C	Subsystem B design	A	1
D	Subsystem C design	A	1
E	Program A	B	2
F	Program B	C	2
G	Program C	D	2
H	Subsystem A test	E	1
I	Subsystem B test	F	1
J	Subsystem C test	G	1
K	Integration	H, I, J	2
L	Integration test	K	1

10. J. Wold, project manager of Print Software, Inc., wants you to prepare a project network; compute the early, late, and slack activity times; determine the planned project duration; and identify the critical path. His assistant has collected the following information for the Color Printer Drivers Software Project:

ID	Description	Predecessor	Time
A	External specifications	None	8
B	Review design features	A	2
C	Document new features	A	3
D	Write software	A	60
E	Program and test	B	60
F	Edit and publish notes	C	2
G	Review manual	D	2
H	Alpha site	E, F	20
I	Print manual	G	10
J	Beta site	H, I	10
K	Manufacture	J	12
L	Release and ship	K	3

11.* A large eastern city is requesting federal funding for a park-and-ride project. One of the requirements in the request application is a network plan for the design phase of the project. Catherine Walker, the chief engineer, wants you to develop a project network plan to meet this requirement. She has gathered

---

* The solution to this exercise can be found in Appendix One.

the activity time estimates and their dependencies shown here. Show your project network with the activity early, late, and slack times. Mark the critical path.

ID	Description	Predecessor	Time
A	Survey	None	5
B	Soils report	A	20
C	Traffic design	A	30
D	Lot layout	A	5
E	Approve design	B, C, D	80
F	Illumination	E	15
G	Drainage	E	30
H	Landscape	E	25
I	Signing	E	20
J	Bid proposal	F, G, H, I	10

12. You are creating a customer database for Winston-Salem Warthogs minor league baseball team. Draw a project network given the information below. Complete the forward and backward pass, compute activity slack, and identify the critical path.

   How long will this project take? How sensitive is the network schedule? Calculate the free slack and total slack for all noncritical activities.

ID	Description	Predecessor	Time (days)
A	Systems design	None	2
B	Subsystem A design	A	1
C	Subsystem B design	A	2
D	Subsystem C design	A	1
E	Program A	B	2
F	Program B	C	10
G	Program C	D	2
H	Subsystem A test	E	1
I	Subsystem B test	F	1
J	Subsystem C test	G	1
K	Integration	H, I, J	2
L	Integration test	K	1

13.* You are completing a group term paper. Given the project network that follows, complete the forward and backward pass, compute activity slack, and

* The solution to this exercise can be found in Appendix One.

identify the critical path. Use this information to create a Gantt chart for the project. Be sure to show slack for noncritical activities.

14. You are conducting a market research project for FUN Inc. Given the project network that follows, complete the forward and backward pass, compute activity slack, and identify the critical path. Use this information to create a Gantt chart for the project. Be sure to show slack for noncritical activities.

Computer Exercises

15. The planning department of an electronics firm has set up the activities for developing and production of a new MP3 Player. Given the information below, develop a project network using Microsoft Project. Assume a five-day workweek and the project starts on January 4, 2010.

Activity ID	Description	Activity Predecessor	Activity Time (weeks)
1	Staff	None	2
2	Develop market program	1	3
3	Select channels of distribution	1	8
4	Patent	1	12
5	Pilot production	1	4
6	Test market	5	4
7	Ad promotion	2	4
8	Set up for production	4, 6	16

The project team has requested that you create a network for the project, and determine if the project can be completed in 45 weeks.

16. Using Microsoft Project, set up the network and determine the critical path for Phase 1 of the project. The project workweek will be 5 days (M—F).

Whistler Ski Resort Project

Given the coming 2010 Winter Olympics in Vancouver and Whistler, BC, Canada, and the fact that the number of skiing visitors to Whistler has been increasing at an exciting rate, the Whistler Ski Association has been considering construction of another ski lodge and ski complex. The results of an economic feasibility study just completed by members of the staff show that a winter resort complex near the base of Whistler Mountain could be a very profitable venture. The area is accessible by car, bus, train, and air. The board of directors has voted to build the ten-million dollar complex recommended in the study. Unfortunately, due to the short summer season, the complex will have to be built in stages. The first stage (year 1) will contain a day lodge, chair lift, rope tow, generator house (for electricity), and a parking lot designed to accommodate 400 cars and 30 buses. The second and third stages will include a hotel, ice rink, pool, shops, two additional chair lifts, and other attractions. The board has decided that stage one should begin no later than April 1 and be completed by October 1, in time for the next skiing season. You have been assigned the task of project manager, and it is your job to coordinate the ordering of materials and construction activities to ensure the project's completion by the required date.

After looking into the possible sources of materials, you are confronted with the following time estimates. Materials for the chair lift and rope tow will take 30 days and 12 days, respectively, to arrive once the order is submitted. Lumber for the day lodge, generator hut, and foundations will take 9 days to arrive. The electrical and plumbing materials for the day lodge will take 12 days to arrive. The generator will take 12 days to arrive. Before actual construction can begin on the various facilities, a road to the site must be built; this will take 6 days. As soon as the road is in, clearing can begin concurrently on the sites of the day lodge, generator house, chair lift, and rope tow. It is estimated that the clearing task at each site will take 6 days, 3 days, 36 days, and 6 days, respectively. The clearing of the main ski slopes can begin after the area for the chair lift has been cleared; this will take 84 days.

The foundation for the day lodge will take 12 days to complete. Construction of the main framework will take an additional 18 days. After the framework is completed, electrical wiring and plumbing can be installed concurrently. These should take 24 and 30 days, respectively. Finally, the finishing construction on the day lodge can begin; this will take 36 days.

Installation of the chair lift towers (67 days) can begin once the site is cleared, lumber delivered, and the foundation completed (6 days). Also, when the chair lift site has been cleared, construction of a permanent road to the upper towers can be started; this will take 24 days. While the towers are being installed, the electric motor to drive the chair lift can be installed; the motor can be installed in 24 days. Once the towers are completed and the motor installed, it will take 3 days to install the cable and an additional 12 days to install the chairs.

Installation of the towers for the rope tow can begin once the site is cleared and the foundation is built and poured; it takes 4 days to build the foundation, pour the concrete and let it cure, and 20 days to install the towers for the rope tow. While the towers are being erected, installation of the electric motor to drive the rope tow can begin; this activity will take 24 days. After the towers and motor are installed, the rope tow can be strung in 1 day. The parking lot can be cleared once the rope tow is finished; this task will take 18 days.

The foundation for the generator house can begin at the same time as the foundation for the lodge; this will take 6 days. The main framework for the generator house can begin once the foundation is completed; framing will take 12 days. After the house is framed, the diesel generator can be installed in 18 days. Finishing construction on the generator house can now begin and will take 12 more days.

Assignment:

1. Identify the critical path on your network.
2. Can the project be completed by October 1?

Optical Disk Preinstallation Project

17. The optical disk project team has started gathering the information necessary to develop the project network—predecessor activities and activity times in weeks. The results of their meeting are found in the following table.

Activity	Description	Duration	Predecessor
1	Define scope	6	None
2	Define customer problems	3	1
3	Define data records and relationships	5	1
4	Mass storage requirements	5	2, 3
5	Consultant needs analysis	10	2, 3
6	Prepare installation network	3	4, 5
7	Estimate costs and budget	2	4, 5
8	Design section "point" system	1	4, 5
9	Write request proposal	5	4, 5
10	Compile vendor list	3	4, 5
11	Prepare mgmt. control system	5	6, 7
12	Prepare comparison report	5	9, 10
13	Compare system "philosophies"	3	8, 12

continued

Activity	Description	Duration	Predecessor
14	Compare total installation	2	8, 12
15	Compare cost of support	3	8, 12
16	Compare customer satisfaction level	10	8, 12
17	Assign philosophies points	1	13
18	Assign installation cost	1	14
19	Assign support cost	1	15
20	Assign customer satisfaction points	1	16
21	Select best system	1	11, 17, 18, 19, 20
22	Order system	1	21

The project team has requested that you create a network for the project, and determine if the project can be completed in 45 weeks.

Lag Exercises

18. From the following information, draw the project network. Compute the early, late, and slack times for each activity. Identify the critical path. (Hint: Draw the finish-to-start relationships first.)

ID	Duration	Finish-to-Start Predecessor	Finish-to-Start Lag	Additional Lag Relationships	Lag
A	5	None	0	None	0
B	10	A	0	None	0
C	15	A	0	Start-finish C to D	20
D	5	B	5	Start-start D to E	5
				Finish-finish D to E	25
E	20	B	0	Finish-finish E to F	0
F	15	D	0	None	0
G	10	C	10	Finish-finish G to F	10
H	20	F	0	None	0

19. Given the following information, draw the project network. Compute the early, late, and slack times for the project network. Which activities on the critical path have only the start or finish of the activity on the critical path?

ID	Duration	Finish-to-Start Predecessor	Finish-to-Start Lag	Additional Lag Relationships	Lag
A	2	None	0	None	0
B	4	A	0	None	0
C	6	A	0	Finish-finish C to F	7
D	8	A	0	None	0
E	18	B	0	Finish-finish E to G	9
		C	10		
F	2	D	0	None	
G	5	F	0	Start-start G to H	10
H	5	None	0	None	0
I	14	E	0	Finish-finish I to J	5
J	15	G, H	0	None	0

20.* Given the information in the following lag exercises, compute the early, late, and slack times for the project network. Which activities on the critical path have only the start or finish of the activity on the critical path?

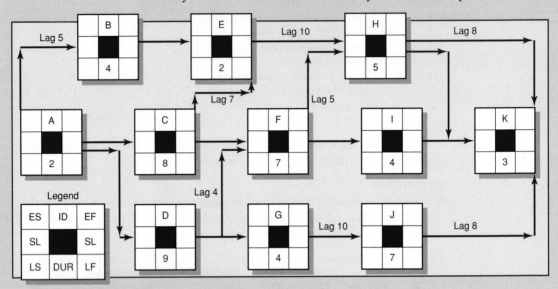

21. Given the network below, compute the early, late, and slack time for each activity.

The ES for Activity C is _____   The slack for the start of Activity G is _____   The slack for the finish of Activity H is _____
The LS for Activity E is _____   The slack for the start of Activity B is _____   The slack for the finish of Activity F is _____
The LS for Activity G is _____   The slack for the start of Activity E is _____   The slack for the finish of Activity G is _____

* The solution to this exercise can be found in Appendix One.

CyClon Project

22. The CyClon project team has started gathering information necessary to develop a project network-predecessor activities and activity time in days. The results of their meeting are found in the following table:

Activity	Description	Duration	Predecessor
1	*CyClon Project*		
2	Design	10	
3	Procure prototype parts	10	2
4	Fabricate parts	8	2
5	Assemble prototype	4	3, 4
6	Laboratory test	7	5
7	Field test	10	6
8	Adjust design	6	7
9	Order stock components	10	8
10	Order custom components	15	8
11	Assemble test production unit	10	9, 10
12	Test unit	5	11
13	Document results	3	12

Part A. Create a network based on the above information. How long will the project take? What is the critical path?

Part B. Upon further review the team recognizes that they missed three finish-to-start lags. Procure prototype parts will involve only 2 days of work but it will take 8 days for the parts to be delivered. Likewise, Order stock components will take 2 days of work and 8 days for delivery and Order custom components 2 days of work and 13 days for delivery.

Reconfigure the CyClon schedule by entering the three finish-to-start lags. What impact did these lags have on the original schedule? On the amount of work required to complete the project?

Part C. Management is still not happy with the schedule and wants the project completed as soon as possible. Unfortunately, they are not willing to approve additional resources. One team member pointed out that the network contained only finish-to-start relationships and that it might be possible to reduce project duration by creating start-to-start lags. After much deliberation the team concluded that the following relationships could be converted into start-to-start lags:

- Procure prototype parts could start 6 days after the start of Design.
- Fabricate parts could start 9 days after the start of Design.
- Laboratory test could begin 1 day after the start of Assemble prototype.
- Field test could start 5 days after the start of Laboratory test.
- Adjust design could begin 7 days after the start of Field test.
- Order stock and Order custom components could begin 5 days after Adjust design.
- Test unit could begin 9 days after the start of Assemble test production unit.
- Document results could start 3 days after the start of Test unit.

Reconfigure the CyClon schedule by entering all nine start-to-start lags. What impact did these lags have on the original schedule (Part A)? How long will the project take? Is there a change in the critical path? Is there a change in the sensitivity of the network? Why would management like this solution?

Case

Advantage Energy Technology Data Center Migration*

Brian Smith, network administrator at Advanced Energy Technology (AET), has been given the responsibility of implementing the migration of a large data center to a new office location. Careful planning is needed because AET operates in the highly competitive petroleum industry. AET is one of five national software companies that provide an accounting and business management package for oil jobbers and gasoline distributors. A few years ago, AET jumped into the "application service provider" world. Their large data center provides clients with remote access to AET's complete suite of application software systems. Traditionally, one of AET's primary competitive advantages has been the company's trademark IT reliability. Due to the complexity of this project, Brian will have to use a parallel method of implementation. Although this will increase project costs, a parallel approach is essential if reliability is not to be compromised.

Currently, AET's data center is located on the second floor of a renovated old bank building in downtown Corvallis, Oregon. The company is moving to a new, one-level building located in the recently developed industrial complex at the Corvallis International Airport. On February 1, Brian is formally assigned the task by the Vice-President of Operations, Dan Whitmore, with the following guidelines:

- From start to finish, it is anticipated the entire project will take three to four months to complete.
- It is essential that AET's 235 clients suffer no downtime.

Whitmore advises Brian to come back to the Executive Committee on February 15, with a presentation on the scope of the project that includes costs, "first-cut" timeline, and proposed project team members.

Brian had some preliminary discussions with some of AET's managers and directors from each of the functional departments and then arranged for a full-day scope meeting on February 4 with a few of the managers and technical representatives from operations, systems, facilities, and applications. The scope team determined the following:

- Three to four months is a feasible project timeline and first-cut cost estimate is $80,000–$90,000 (this includes the infrastructure upgrade of the new site).
- Critical to the "no-downtime" requirement is the need to completely rely on AET's remote disaster recovery "hot" site for full functionality.
- Brian will serve as project manager of a team consisting of one team member each from facilities, operations/systems, operations/telecommunications, systems & applications, and customer service.

Brian's Executive Committee report was positively received and, after a few modifications and recommendations, he was formally charged with responsibility for the project. Brian recruited his team and scheduled their first team meeting (March 1) as the initial task of his project planning process.

---

* Prepared by James Moran, a project management instructor at the College of Business, Oregon State University.

Once the initial meeting is conducted Brian can hire the contractors to renovate the new data center. During this time Brian will figure out how to design the network. Brian estimates that screening and hiring a contractor will take about one week and that the network design will take about two weeks. The new center requires a new ventilation system. The manufacturer's requirements include an ambient temperature of 67 degrees to keep all of the data servers running at optimal speeds. The ventilation system has a lead time of three weeks. Brian will also need to order new racks to hold the servers, switches, and other network devices. The racks have a two-week delivery time.

The data center supervisor requested that Brian replace all of the old power supplies and data cables. Brian will need to order these as well. Because Brian has a great relationship with the vendor, they guarantee that it will take only one week lead time for the power supplies and the data cables. Once the new ventilation system and racks arrive, Brian can begin installing them. It will take one week to install the ventilation system and three weeks to install the racks. The renovation of the new data center can begin as soon as the contractors have been hired. The contractors tell Brian that construction will take 20 days. Once the construction begins and before Brian installs the ventilation system and racks, the city inspector must approve the construction of the raised floor.

The city inspector will take two days to approve the infrastructure. After the city inspection and after the new power supplies and cables have arrived, Brian can install the power supplies and run the cables. Brian estimates that it will take five days to install the power supplies and one week to run all of the data cables. Before Brian can assign an actual date for taking the network off line and switching to the hot remote site, he must get approval from each of the functional units ("Switchover Approval"). Meetings with each of the functional units will require one week. During this time he can initiate a power check to ensure that each of the racks has sufficient voltage. This will require only one day.

Upon completion of the power check, he can take one week to install his test servers. The test servers will test all of the primary network functions and act as a safeguard before the network is taken off line. The batteries must be charged, ventilation installed, and test servers up and running before management can be assured that the new infrastructure is safe, which will take two days. Then they will sign off the Primary Systems check, taking one day of intense meetings. They will also set an official date for the network move.

Brian is happy that everything has gone well thus far and is convinced that the move will go just as smoothly. Now that an official date is set, the network will be shut down for a day. Brian must move all of the network components to the new data center. Brian will do the move over the weekend—two days—when user traffic is at low point.

ASSIGNMENT

1. Generate a priority matrix for AET's system move.
2. Develop a WBS for Brian's project. Include duration (days) and predecessors.
3. Using a project planning tool, generate a network diagram for this project.
   (Note: Base your plan on the following guidelines: eight-hour days, seven-day weeks, no holiday breaks, March 1, 2010, is the project start date.)

Case

Greendale Stadium Case

The G&E Company is preparing a bid to build the new 47,000 seat Greendale baseball stadium. The construction must start July 1, 2011, and be completed in time for the start of the 2014 season. A penalty clause of $100,000 per day of delay beyond May 20, 2014, is written into the contract.

Ben Keith, the president of the company, expressed optimism at obtaining the contract and revealed that the company could net as much as $2 million on the project. He also said if they are successful, the prospects for future projects are quite good since there is a projected renaissance in building classic ball parks with modern luxury boxes.

ASSIGNMENT

Given the information provided in Table 6.3, construct a network schedule for the stadium project and answer the following questions:

1. Will the project be able to be completed by the May 20 deadline? How long will it take?
2. What is the critical path for the project?
3. Based on the schedule would you recommend that G&E pursue this contact? Why? Include a one-page Gantt chart for the stadium schedule.

TABLE 6.3
Greendale Stadium Case

ID	Activity	Duration	Predecessor(s)
1	**Baseball Stadium**		
2	Clear stadium site	70 days	—
3	Demolish building	30 days	2
4	Set up construction site	70 days	3
5	Drive support piling	120 days	2
6	Pour lower concrete bowl	120 days	5
7	Pour main concourse	120 days	3,6
8	Install playing field	90 days	3,6
9	Construct upper steel bowl	120 days	3,6
10	Install seats	140 days	7,9
11	Build luxury boxes	90 days	7,9
12	Install jumbotron	30 days	7,9
13	Stadium infrastructure	120 days	7,9
14	Construct steel canopy	75 days	10
15	Light installation	30 days	14
16	Build roof supports	90 days	6
17	Construct roof	180 days	16
18	Install roof tracks	90 days	16
19	Install roof	90 days	17,18
20	Inspection	20 days	8,11,13,15,19

CASE APPENDIX: TECHNICAL DETAILS OF THE GREENDALE BASEBALL STADIUM

The baseball stadium is an outdoor structure with a retractable roof. The project begins with clearing the site, an activity that lasts 70 days. Once the site is clear, work can start simultaneously on the structure itself and demolishing an adjacent building site. This demolition is necessary to create a construction stage for storing materials and equipment. It will take 30 days to demolish the buildings and another 70 days to set up the construction site.

The work on the stadium begins by driving 160 support pilings, which will take 120 days. Next comes the pouring of the lower concrete bowl (120 days). Once this is done and the construction site has been set up, then the pouring of the main concourse (120 days), the installation of the playing field (90 days), and the construction of the upper steel bowl can occur (120 days).

Once the concourse and upper bowl are completed, work can start simultaneously on building the luxury boxes (90 days), installing the seats (140 days), installing the jumbotron (30 days), and installing stadium infrastructure (120 days) which includes: bathrooms, lockers, restaurants, etc. Once the seats are installed then the steel canopy can be constructed (75 days) followed by the installation of the lights (30 days).

The retractable roof represents the most significant technical challenge to the project. Building the roof track supports (90 days) can begin after the lower concrete bowl is constructed. At this time the dimensions of the roof can be finalized and the construction of the roof at a separate site can begin (180 days). After the roof supports are completed then the roof tracks can be installed (90 days). Once the tracks and the roof are completed then the roof can be installed and made operational (90 days). Once all activities are completed it will take 20 days to inspect the stadium.

For purposes of this case assume the following:

1. The following holidays are observed: January 1, Memorial Day (last Monday in May), July 4th, Labor Day (first Monday in September), Thanksgiving Day (4th Thursday in November), December 25 and 26.
2. If a holiday falls on a Saturday then Friday will be given as an extra day off, and if it falls on a Sunday then Monday will be given as a day off.
3. The construction crew work Monday through Friday.

Appendix 6.1

Activity-on-Arrow Method

DESCRIPTION

The activity-on-arrow (AOA) approach also uses the arrow and node as network building blocks. However, in this approach *the arrow represents an individual project activity that requires time.* The length and slope of the arrow have no significance. *The node represents an event; it is usually presented as a small circle.* Events represent points in time but do not consume time. Each activity on the network

FIGURE A6.3
Partial Koll Business Center AOA Network

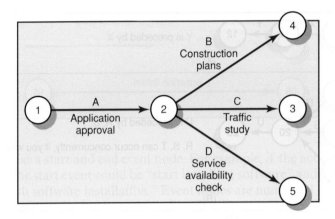

inserted to ensure each activity has its unique identification number. A dummy activity is depicted by a dashed arrow and its duration is zero. The dummy activity could be inserted before or after either activity B or C as shown in Figure A6.4 (see parts A through D). In Figure A6.4E we placed it after activity C with its own identification of X or 3–4.

Activity F in Figure A6.4E denotes another network problem in which activity dependencies exist but it is not convenient to connect the activities. In this case, the dummy activity can be used to maintain the logic of the network dependencies. Activity F is preceded by activities B, C, and D. Dummy activity Y (4–5) is necessary because activity B precedes both E and F. The dummy activity maintains the intended logic and sequence. Dummy activity 3–5 can be removed because it is redundant; that is, its removal does not change the intended relationships—the end event 4 precedes activity F. Typically, the first pass in drawing your network will include many dummy activities. After several passes forward and backward through the network, you will find ways to remove some of the dummy activities that are there solely to maintain logic. However, when two or more parallel activities have the same beginning and ending event nodes, dummy activities cannot be avoided. Figure A6.5 has a completed network for the Koll design project.

In this simple project network no activity networks cross over each other, a situation which is very rare. Remember the length and slope of the arrows is arbitrary. The activity durations are included and found below the arrows, near the middle. You should work through the AOA network exercises before moving to the next section. Your familiarity with the activity/event approach will help your initial understanding of the forward and backward pass on an AOA network.

Forward Pass—Earliest Times

The forward pass in AOA uses the same concepts found in the AON procedure. The major difference lies in recognition and use of events to set early and late start and finish times for activities. Figure A6.6 shows the Koll design project with all the activity durations and early start and finish times. Also near each event is a box that will allow us to record event times and slack. In the field this box is sometimes called a "T-box" because the shape within the box forms the letter T. There are many variations of the T-box found in the field, but they all use the basic T format.

The forward pass starts with the first activity(ies) and traces each path through the network. As in AON, you *add* (cumulate) the activity times along the path. When you come to a merge event, you select the largest early finish (EF) of all the activities merging to that event. Let's work through Figure A6.6. Event 1 is the project start

FIGURE A6.4
Partial AOA Koll
Business Center
Network

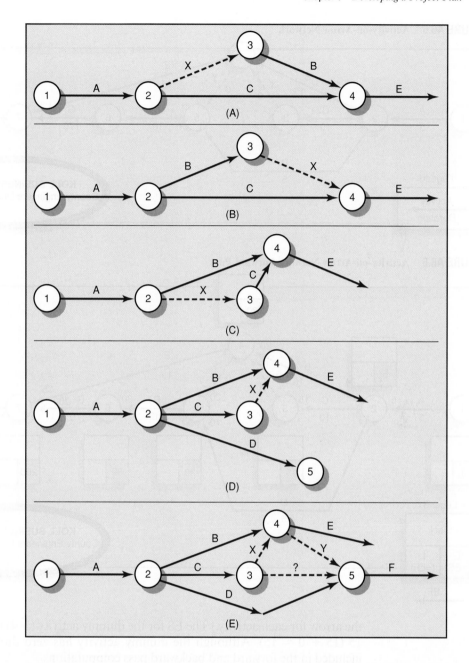

event; therefore, the earliest that event can occur is time zero. This early event time for event 1 is placed in the lower left side of the event box. The early event time is also the ES for any activity bursting from an event. Therefore, the zero in the box for event 1 is also the early start for activity A. The early finish for activity A is 5 workdays (ES + DUR = EF or 0 + 5 = 5). The EF for the activity is placed at the head of the arrow. The earliest event 2 can occur is the instant activity A is complete, which is 5 workdays; therefore, this time is placed in the lower left T-box of event 2. Again, note that the early event time is also the ES for any activity using the event as a start event. Hence, the ES for activities B, C, and D is 5 workdays. The EF for activity B is 20 (ES + DUR = EF), for activity C is 15, and for activity D is 10. (See the head of

FIGURE A6.5 **Activity-on-Arrow Network**

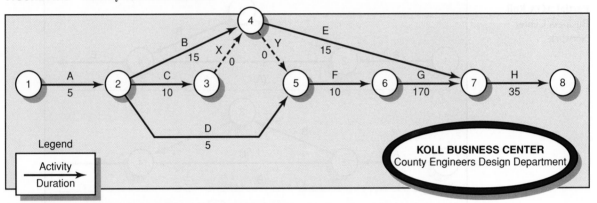

FIGURE A6.6 **Activity-on-Arrow Network Forward Pass**

the arrow for each activity.) The ES for the dummy activity (3–4) is 15, and its EF is 15 (15 + 0 = 15). Although the dummy activity has zero duration, it must be included in the forward and backward pass computations.

At this point you must determine the early event times for events 4 and 5. Both are merge events that require selection among activities merging into these events. Event 4 has B and X, the dummy activity (3–4). The largest EF for these two activities (20 and 15) is 20, which controls the early event time for event 4. Similarly, event 5 is controlled by activities D and Y. Because activity Y has the largest early finish (20 versus 10 workdays for activity D), it establishes the early event time for event 5 and activity F. Times are cumulated until merge event 7. The EFs for activities E and G are 35 and 200 workdays, respectively. Thus, event 7 and activity H have early times of 200 workdays. The early finish for the project is 235 workdays. Assuming we accept this planned duration of 235 days for the project, the LF for event 8 becomes 235 days, and you are ready to compute the backward pass.

Backward Pass—Latest Times

The backward pass procedure is similar to that used in the AON procedure. You start with the last project event node(s) and *subtract* activity times along each path (LF − DUR = LS) until you reach a burst event. When this happens, you pick the *smallest* LS of all the activities bursting from the event; this number denotes the latest that event can occur and not delay the project. Let's trace the backward pass for part of the Koll design project.

Figure A6.7 displays the late times for the events and activities. The late start for activity H is 200 days (LF − DUR = LS or 235 − 35 = 200). This time is found at the tail of the arrow. Because event 7 is not a burst event, the late start for activity H becomes the late time for event 7. This procedure continues until you reach event 4, which is a burst event. The LS for activity E is 185 and for activity Y is 20. The smallest time is 20 days and is the late time for event 4. The next burst event is event 2. Here the LS for activities B, C, and D are 5, 10, and 15 days, respectively. Activity B controls the late event time for event 2, which is 5 workdays. The late event time is also the LF for any activity using the event as an end event. For example, the late time for event 7 is 200 workdays; thus, activities E and G can finish no later than day 200, or the project will be delayed.

With the backward pass complete, the slack and critical path can be identified. Figure A6.8 presents the completed network. The event slack is entered above the T in the event box. Activity slack is the difference between LS and ES or LF and EF. For example, the slack for activity E is 165 days—LS − ES (185 − 20 = 165) or LF − EF (200 − 35 = 165). What are the slack values for activities B, C, and D? The answers are zero workdays (5 − 5 = 0 or 20 − 20 = 0), 5 workdays (10 − 5 = 5 or 20 − 15 = 5), and 10 workdays (15 − 5 = 10 or 20 − 10 = 10), respectively. The critical path is A, B, Y, F, G, H.

Compare the networks found in Figure A6.8 and in chapter text Figure 6.8 to see the differences between the AOA and AON methods. As in the AON method,

FIGURE A6.7   Activity-on-Arrow Network Backward Pass

FIGURE A6.8 Activity-on-Arrow Network Backward Pass, Forward Pass, and Slack

if the early and late time for the end project event are the same (L = E or LF = EF), the slack on the critical path will be zero. If the times are not the same, the slack on the critical path will equal the difference (L − E or LF − EF).

Computer-Generated Networks

Figure A6.9 presents a generic AOA computer output for the custom order project. AOA networks identify activities by the beginning and ending nodes—for example, the software development activity is identified as activity 2–6. Its duration is 18 time units; ES = 2; EF = 20; LS = 22; and LF = 40 time units. The critical

FIGURE A6.9 Air Control, Inc. Custom Order Project—AOA Network Diagram path is 1-2-3-4-5-6-7. Compare the AOA computer output in Figure A6.9 with the AON computer output in chapter Figure 6.11. Bar charts are identical to those developed for AON networks; see chapter Figure 6.12.

CHOICE OF METHOD—AON OR AOA

Your choice of method depends on the importance of various advantages and disadvantages of each method. Table A6.2 will assist you in making your choice.

TABLE A6.2
Comparison of AON and AOA Methods

AON Method
Advantages
1. No dummy activities are used.
2. Events are not used.
3. AON is easy to draw if dependencies are not intense.
4. Activity emphasis is easily understood by first-level managers.
5. The CPM approach uses deterministic times to construct networks.
Disadvantages
1. Path tracing by activity number is difficult. If the network is not available, computer outputs must list the predecessor and successor activities for each activity.
2. Network drawing and understanding are more difficult when dependencies are numerous.
AOA Method
Advantages
1. Path tracing is simplified by activity/event numbering scheme.
2. AOA is easier to draw if dependencies are intense.
3. Key events or milestones can easily be flagged.
Disadvantages
1. Use of dummy activities increases data requirements.
2. Emphasis on events can detract from activities. Activity delays cause events and projects to be late.

SUMMARY

In AOA networks, dummy activities meet two needs. First, when two parallel activities have the same start and end nodes, a dummy must be inserted to give each activity a unique identification number (see activity X in Figure A6.8). Next, dummy activities can be used to clarify dependency relationships (see activity Y in Figure A6.8). Dummy activities are very useful when activity dependencies are far apart on the network. In AOA networks the early event time is the ES for any activity emanating from the event. Conversely, the late event time is the LF for any activity merging to the event. The major advantage of the AOA method is the avoidance of having to list all the predecessor and successor activities for each activity in the network so activity sequence and dependency can be traced when a network is not available or shows incomplete information. Computer output is reduced manyfold.

REVIEW QUESTIONS

1. How do the building blocks of AON and AOA differ?
2. What are the purposes of dummy or pseudo activities?
3. How do activities differ from events?

Managing Risk

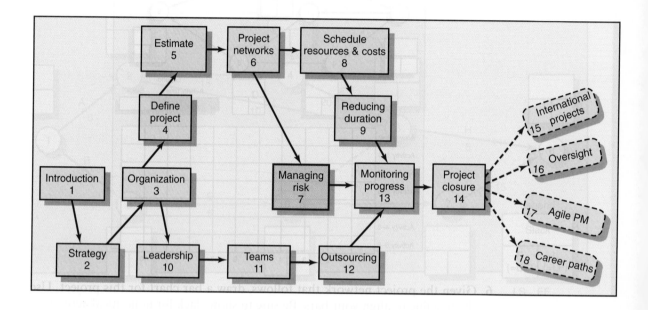

Managing Risk

Risk Management Process

Step 1: Risk Identification

Step 2: Risk Assessment

Step 3: Risk Response Development

Opportunity Management

Contingency Planning

Contingency Funding and Time Buffers

Step 4: Risk Response Control

Change Control Management

Summary

Appendix 7.1: PERT and PERT Simulation

You've got to go out on a limb sometimes because that's where the fruit is.

Will Rogers

Every project manager understands risks are inherent in projects. No amount of planning can overcome *risk,* or the inability to control chance events. In the context of projects, **risk** is an uncertain event or condition that, if it occurs, has a positive or negative effect on project objectives. A risk has a cause and, if it occurs, a consequence. For example, a cause may be a flu virus or change in scope requirements. The event is that team members get stricken with the flu or the product has to be redesigned. If either of these uncertain events occurs, it will impact the cost, schedule, and quality of the project.

Some potential risk events can be identified before the project starts—such as equipment malfunction or change in technical requirements. Risks can be anticipated consequences, like schedule slippages or cost overruns. Risks can be beyond imagination like the 2008 financial meltdown.

While risks can have positive consequences such as unexpected price reduction in materials, the focus of this chapter is on what can go wrong and the risk management process.

Risk management attempts to recognize and manage potential and unforeseen trouble spots that may occur when the project is implemented. Risk management identifies as many risk events as possible (what can go wrong), minimizes their impact (what can be done about the event before the project begins), manages responses to those events that do materialize (contingency plans), and provides contingency funds to cover risk events that actually materialize.

For a humorous, but ultimately embarrassing example of poor risk management see Snapshot from Practice: Giant Popsicle Gone Wrong.

Risk Management Process

Figure 7.1 presents a graphic model of the risk management challenge. The chances of a risk event occurring (e.g., an error in time estimates, cost estimates, or design technology) are greatest in the concept, planning, and start-up phases of the project. The cost impact of a risk event in the project is less if the event occurs earlier rather than later. The early stages of the project represent the period when the opportunity for minimizing the impact or working around a potential risk exists. Conversely, as the project passes the halfway implementation mark, the cost of a risk event occurring increases rapidly. For example, the risk event of a design flaw occurring after a prototype has been made has a greater cost or time impact than if the event occurred in the start-up phase of the project. Clearly, identifying project risk events and deciding a response

SNAPSHOT FROM PRACTICE   Giant Popsicle Gone Wrong*

An attempt to erect the world's largest Popsicle in New York City ended with a scene straight out of a disaster film, but much stickier.

The 25-foot-tall, $17\frac{1}{2}$-ton treat of frozen juice melted faster than expected, flooding Union Square in downtown Manhattan with kiwi-strawberry–flavored fluid.

Bicyclists wiped out in the stream of goo. Pedestrians slipped. Traffic was, well, frozen. Firefighters closed off several streets and used hoses to wash away the thick, sweet slime.

The Snapple Company, a leading maker of soft beverages, had been trying to promote a new line of frozen treats by setting a record for the world's largest Popsicle, but called off the stunt before the frozen giant was pulled fully upright by a construction crane.

Authorities said they were worried the $2\frac{1}{2}$-story popsicle would collapse.

Organizers were not sure why it melted so quickly. "We planned for it. We just didn't expect for it to happen so fast,"

© Zuma Press, Inc.

said Snapple spokeswoman Lauren Radcliffe. She said the company would offer to pay the city for the clean-up costs.

* Associated Press, June 23, 2005.

before the project begins is a more prudent approach than not attempting to manage risk.

The cost of mismanaged risk control early on in the project is magnified by the ill-fated 1999 NASA Mars Climate Orbiter. Investigations revealed that Lockheed Martin botched the design of critical navigation software. While flight computers on the ground did calculations based on pounds of thrust per second, the

FIGURE 7.1
Risk Event Graph

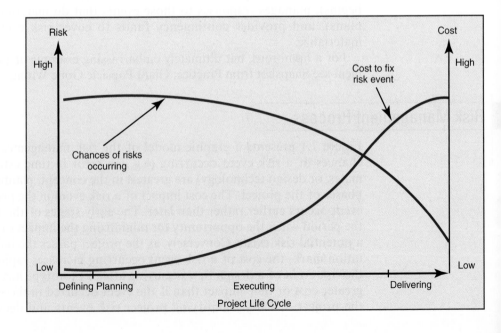

FIGURE 7.2
The Risk
Management Process

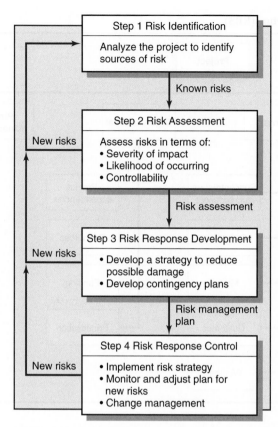

spacecraft's computer software used metric units called newtons. A check to see if the values were compatible was never done.

"Our check and balances processes did not catch an error like this that should have been caught," said Ed Weiler, NASA's associate administrator for space science. "That is the bottom line. Processes that were in place were not followed." (*Orlando Sentinel,* 1999.) After the nine-month journey to the Red Planet the $125 million probe approached Mars at too low an altitude and burned up in the planet's atmosphere.

Risk management is a proactive approach rather than reactive. It is a preventive process designed to ensure that surprises are reduced and that negative consequences associated with undesirable events are minimized. It also prepares the project manager to take action when a time, cost, and/or technical advantage is possible. Successful management of project risk gives the project manager better control over the future and can significantly improve chances of reaching project objectives on time, within budget, and meeting required technical (functional) performance.

The sources of project risks are unlimited. There are sources external to the organization, such as inflation, market acceptance, exchange rates, and government regulations. In practice, these risk events are often referred to as "threats" to differentiate them from those that are not within the project manager's or team's responsibility area. (Later we will see budgets for such risk events are placed in a "management reserve" contingency budget.) Since such external risks are usually considered before the decision to go ahead with the project, they will be excluded from the discussion of project risks. However, external risks are extremely important and must be addressed.

The major components of the risk management process are depicted in Figure 7.2. Each step will be examined in more detail in the remainder of the chapter.

Step 1: Risk Identification

The risk management process begins by trying to generate a list of all the possible risks that could affect the project. Typically the project manager pulls together, during the planning phase, a risk management team consisting of core team members and other relevant stakeholders. The team uses brainstorming and other problem identifying techniques to identify potential problems. Participants are encouraged to keep an open mind and generate as many probable risks as possible.

FIGURE 7.3 The Risk Breakdown Structure (RBS)

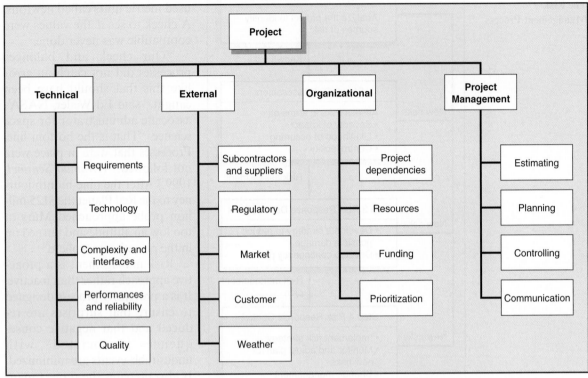

More than one project has been bushwhacked by an event that members thought was preposterous in the beginning. Later during the assessment phase, participants will have a chance to analyze and filter out unreasonable risks.

One common mistake that is made early in the risk identification process is to focus on objectives and not on the events that could produce consequences. For example, team members may identify failing to meet schedule as a major risk. What they need to focus on are the events that could cause this to happen (i.e., poor estimates, adverse weather, shipping delays, etc.). Only by focusing on actual events can potential solutions be found.

Organizations use **risk breakdown structures** (RBSs) in conjunction with work breakdown structures (WBSs) to help management teams identify and eventually analyze risks. Figure 7.3 provides a generic example of an RBS. The focus at the beginning should be on risks that can affect the whole project as opposed to a specific section of the project or network.

After the macro risks have been identified, specific areas can be checked. An effective tool for identifying specific risks is the work breakdown structure. Use of the RBS reduces the chance a risk event will be missed. On large projects multiple risk teams are organized around specific deliverables and submit their risk management reports to the project manager.

A risk profile is another useful tool. A **risk profile** is a list of questions that address traditional areas of uncertainty on a project. These questions have been developed and refined from previous, similar projects. Figure 7.4 provides a partial example of a risk profile.

FIGURE 7.4
Partial Risk
Profile for Product
Development Project

Technical Requirements	**Quality**
Are the requirements stable?	Are quality considerations built into the design?
Design	
Does the design depend on unrealistic or optimistic assumptions?	**Management**
	Do people know who has authority for what?
Testing	
Will testing equipment be available when needed?	**Work Environment**
	Do people work cooperatively across functional boundaries?
Development	
Is the development process supported by a compatible set of procedures, methods, and tools?	**Staffing**
	Is staff inexperienced or understaffed?
	Customer
Schedule	Does the customer understand what it will take to complete the project?
Is the schedule dependent upon the completion of other projects?	
	Contractors
Budget	Are there any ambiguities in contractor task definitions?
How reliable are the cost estimates?	

Good risk profiles, like RBSs, are tailored to the type of project in question. For example, building an information system is different from building a new car. They are organization specific. Risk profiles recognize the unique strengths and weaknesses of the firm. Finally, risk profiles address both technical and management risks. For example, the profile shown in Figure 7.4 asks questions about design *(Does the design depend upon unrealistic assumptions?)* and work environment *(Do people cooperate across functional boundaries?)*.

Risk profiles are generated and maintained usually by personnel from the project office. They are updated and refined during the postproject audit (see Chapter 14). These profiles, when kept up to date, can be a powerful resource in the risk management process. The collective experience of the firm's past projects resides in their questions.

Historical records can complement or be used when formal risk profiles are not available. Project teams can investigate what happened on similar projects in the past to identify potential risks. For example, a project manager can check the on-time performance of selected vendors to gauge the threat of shipping delays. IT project managers can access "best practices" papers detailing other companies' experiences converting software systems. Inquiries should not be limited to recorded data. Savvy project managers tap the wisdom of others by seeking the advice of veteran project managers.

The risk identification process should not be limited to just the core team. Input from customers, sponsors, subcontractors, vendors, and other stakeholders should be solicited. Relevant stakeholders can be formally interviewed or included on the risk management team. Not only do these players have a valuable perspective, but by involving them in the risk management process they also become more committed to project success.

One of the keys to success in risk identification is attitude. While a "can do" attitude is essential during implementation, project managers have to encourage critical thinking when it comes to risk identification. The goal is to find potential problems before they happen.

The RBS and risk profiles are useful tools for making sure no stones are left unturned. At the same time, when done well the number of risks identified can be overwhelming and a bit discouraging. Initial optimism can be replaced with griping and cries of "what have we gotten ourselves into?" It is important that project managers set the right tone and complete the risk management process so members regain confidence in themselves and the project.

Step 2: Risk Assessment

Step 1 produces a list of potential risks. Not all of these risks deserve attention. Some are trivial and can be ignored, while others pose serious threats to the welfare of the project. Managers have to develop methods for sifting through the list of risks, eliminating inconsequential or redundant ones and stratifying worthy ones in terms of importance and need for attention.

Scenario analysis is the easiest and most commonly used technique for analyzing risks. Team members assess the significance of each risk event in terms of:

• Probability of the event.
• Impact of the event.

Simply stated, risks need to be evaluated in terms of the likelihood the event is going to occur and the impact or consequences of its occurrence. The risk of a project manager being struck by lightning at a work site would have major negative impact on the project, but the likelihood is so low it is not worthy of consideration. Conversely, people do change jobs, so an event like the loss of key project personnel would have not only an adverse impact but also a high likelihood of occurring in some organizations. If so, then it would be wise for that organization to be proactive and mitigate this risk by developing incentive schemes for retaining specialists and/or engaging in cross-training to reduce the impact of turnover.

The quality and credibility of the risk analysis process requires that different levels of risk probabilities and impacts be defined. These definitions vary and should be tailored to the specific nature and needs of the project. For example, a relatively simple scale ranging from "very unlikely" to "almost certainly" may suffice for one project, whereas another project may use more precise numerical probabilities (e.g., 0.1, 0.3, 0.5, . . .).

Impact scales can be a bit more problematic since adverse risks affect project objectives differently. For example, a component failure may cause only a slight delay in project schedule but a major increase in project cost. If controlling cost is a high priority, then the impact would be severe. If, on the other hand, time is more critical than cost, then the impact would be minor.

Because impact ultimately needs to be assessed in terms of project priorities, different kinds of impact scales are used. Some scales may simply use rank-order descriptors, such as "low," "moderate," "high," and "very high," whereas others use numeric weights (e.g., 1–10). Some may focus on the project in general while others focus on specific project objectives. The risk management team needs to establish up front what distinguishes a 1 from a 3 or "moderate" impact from "severe" impact. Figure 7.5 provides an example of how impact scales could be defined given the project objectives of cost, time, scope, and quality.

FIGURE 7.5 **Defined Conditions for Impact Scales of a Risk on Major Project Objectives (Examples for negative impacts only)**

Project Objective	Relative or Numerical Scale				
	1 Very Low	2 Low	3 Moderate	4 High	5 Very High
Cost	Insignificant cost increase	< 10% cost increase	10–20% cost increase	20–40% cost increase	> 40% cost increase
Time	Insignificant time increase	< 5% time increase	5–10% time increase	10–20% time increase	> 20% time increase
Scope	Scope decrease barely noticeable	Minor areas of scope affected	Major areas of scope affected	Scope reduction unacceptable to sponsor	Project end item is effectively useless
Quality	Quality degradation barely noticeable	Only very demanding applications are affected	Quality reduction requires sponsor approval	Quality reduction unacceptable to sponsor	Project end item is effectively useless

Documentation of scenario analyses can be seen in various risk assessment forms used by companies. Figure 7.6 is a partial example of a risk assessment form used on an IS project involving the upgrade from Windows Vista to Windows 7.

Notice that in addition to evaluating the severity and probablity of risk events the team also assesses when the event might occur and its detection difficulty. Detection difficulty is a measure of how easy it would be to detect that the event was going to occur in time to take mitigating action, that is, how much warning would we have? So in the Windows 7 conversion example, the detection scale would range from 5 = no warning to 1 = lots of time to react.

Often organizations find it useful to categorize the severity of different risks into some form of risk assessment matrix. The matrix is typically structured around the impact and likelihood of the risk event. For example, the risk matrix

FIGURE 7.6
Risk Assessment Form

Risk Event	Likelihood	Impact	Detection Difficulty	When
Interface problems	4	4	4	Conversion
System freezing	2	5	5	Start-up
User backlash	4	3	3	Postinstallation
Hardware malfunctioning	1	5	5	Installation

FIGURE 7.7
Risk Severity Matrix

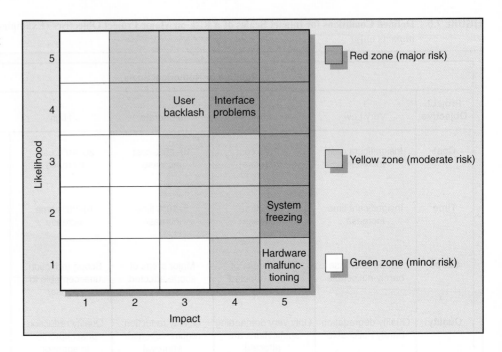

presented in Figure 7.7 consists of a 5 × 5 array of elements with each element representing a different set of impact and likelihood values.

The matrix is divided into red, yellow, and green zones representing major, moderate, and minor risks, respectively. The red zone is centered on the top right corner of the matrix (high impact/high likelihood), while the green zone is centered on the bottom left corner (low impact/low likelihood). The moderate risk, yellow zone extends down the middle of the matrix. Since impact is generally considered more important than likelihood (a 10 percent chance of losing $1,000,000 is usually considered a more severe risk than a 90 percent chance of losing $1,000), the red zone (major risk) extends farther down the high impact column.

Using the Windows 7 project again as an example, interface problems and system freezing would be placed in the red zone (major risk), while user backlash and hardware malfunctioning would be placed in the yellow zone (moderate risk).

The **risk severity matrix** provides a basis for prioritizing which risks to address. Red zone risks receive first priority followed by yellow zone risks. Green zone risks are typically considered inconsequential and ignored unless their status changes.

Failure Mode and Effects Analysis (FMEA) extends the risk severity matrix by including ease of detection in the equation:

$$\text{Impact} \times \text{Probability} \times \text{Detection} = \text{Risk Value}$$

Each of the three dimensions is rated according to a five-point scale. For example, detection is defined as the ability of the project team to discern that the risk event is imminent. A score of 1 would be given if even a chimpanzee could spot the risk coming. The highest detection score of 5 would be given to events that could only be discovered after it is too late (i.e., system freezing). Similar anchored scales would be applied for severity of impact and the probability of the event occurring. The weighting of the risks is then based on their overall score. For example, a risk with an impact in the "1" zone with a very low probability and an easy detection score might score a 1 ($1 \times 1 \times 1 = 1$). Conversely, a high-impact risk with a high probability and impossible to detect would score 125 ($5 \times 5 \times 5 = 125$). This broad range of numerical scores allows for easy stratification of risk according to overall significance.

No assessment scheme is absolutely foolproof. For example, the weakness of the FMEA approach is that a risk event rated Impact = 1, Probability = 5, and Detection = 5 would receive the same weighted score as an event rated Impact = 5, Probability = 5, and Detection = 1! This underscores the importance of *not* treating risk assessment as simply an exercise in mathematics. There is no substitute for thoughtful discussion of key risk events.

Probability Analysis

There are many statistical techniques available to the project manager that can assist in assessing project risk. Decision trees have been used to assess alternative courses of action using expected values. Statistical variations of net present value (NPV) have been used to assess cash flow risks in projects. Correlations between past projects' cash flow and S-curves (cumulative project cost curve—baseline— over the life of the project) have been used to assess cash flow risks.

PERT (program evaluation and review technique) and PERT simulation can be used to review activity and project risk. PERT and related techniques take a more macro perspective by looking at overall cost and schedule risks. Here the focus is not on individual events but on the likelihood the project will be completed on time and within budget. These methods are useful in assessing the overall risk of the project and the need for such things as contingency funds, resources, and time. The use of PERT simulation is increasing because it uses the same data required for PERT, and software to perform the simulation is readily available.

Basically PERT simulation assumes a statistical distribution (range between optimistic and pessimistic) for each activity duration; it then simulates the network (perhaps over 1,000 simulations) using a random number generator. The outcome is the relative probability, called a criticality index, of an activity becoming critical under the many different, possible activity durations for each activity. PERT simulation also provides a list of potential critical paths and their respective probabilities of occurring. Having this information available can greatly facilitate identifying and assessing schedule risk. (See Appendix 7.1 at the end of this chapter for a more detailed description and discussion.)

Step 3: Risk Response Development

When a risk event is identified and assessed, a decision must be made concerning which response is appropriate for the specific event. Responses to risk can be classified as mitigating, avoiding, transferring, sharing, or retaining.

Mitigating Risk

Reducing risk is usually the first alternative considered. There are basically two strategies for mitigating risk: (1) reduce the likelihood that the event will occur and/ or (2) reduce the impact that the adverse event would have on the project. Most risk teams focus first on reducing the likelihood of risk events since, if successful, this may eliminate the need to consider the potentially costly second strategy.

SNAPSHOT FROM PRACTICE   WAP or JAVA?*

Ellipsus Systems, AB, located in Vaxjo, Sweden, is a software design company whose products link corporate computer systems to mobile phones. Critical to the company's success is making the right technology decisions, especially around the standards and protocols its software uses. As wireless and mobile devices continue to take hold, there are two major emerging technical standards. One standard is WAP (Wireless Application Protocol). The second standard, Java, is based on Internet programming standards created by Sun Microsystems.

Rikard Kjellberg, one of Ellipsus's founders, was facing a conundrum: which standard to use? In one, Java was dominant; in the other, WAP was dominant. WAP was first to market. It generated huge excitement, and as Nokia prepared to launch the first wireless phone in late 1999, engineers across Europe left secure jobs to form WAP start-ups. At the same time some negative perceptions were developing about systems based on the WAP standard. Due to the slow response time, a Swedish newspaper ran a story titled "WAP is Crap." Java, on the other hand, had yet to establish itself with no commercial handsets available at the time.

Kjellberg's solution was to have projects in his company's portfolio based on both standards. Ellipsus built early prototypes of both systems and took them to a trade show, with both systems sitting side by side. "We knew within an hour which way to go," says Douglas Davies, the COO. Ellipsus began securing million dollar contracts to supply its Java-based system to leading U.S. operators.

* David Pringle, "How the U.S. Took the Wireless Lead Away from Europe," *The Wall Street Journal Europe,* 20 February 2002 http://www.network365.com/news.jsp?id=145 (accessed 10, November 2003).

contractor capable of absorbing the risk? Clearly identifying and documenting responsibility for absorbing risk is imperative.

Another more obvious way to transfer risk is insurance. However, in most cases this is impractical because defining the project risk event and conditions to an insurance broker who is unfamiliar with the project is difficult and usually expensive. Of course, low-probability and high-consequence risk events such as acts of God are more easily defined and insured. Performance bonds, warranties, and guarantees are other financial instruments used to transfer risk.

On large, international construction projects like petrochemical plants and oil refineries, host countries are insisting on contracts that enforce Build-Own-Operate-Transfer (BOOT) provisions. Here the prime project organization is expected not only to build the facility, but also to take over ownership until its operation capacity has been proven and all the debugging has occurred before final transfer of ownership to the client. In such cases, the host country has transferred financial risk of ownership until the project has been completed and capabilities proven.

Retaining Risk

In some cases a conscious decision is made to accept the risk of an event occurring. Some risks are so large it is not feasible to consider transferring or reducing the event (e.g., an earthquake or flood). The project owner assumes the risk because the chance of such an event occurring is slim. In other cases risks identified in the budget reserve can simply be absorbed if they materialize. The risk is retained by developing a contingency plan to implement if the risk materializes. In a few cases a risk event can be ignored and a cost overrun accepted should the risk event occur.

The more effort given to risk response before the project begins, the better the chances are for minimizing project surprises. Knowing that the response to a risk event will be retained, transferred, or mitigated greatly reduces stress and uncertainty. Again, control is possible with this structured approach.

Contingency Planning

A **contingency plan** is an alternative plan that will be used if a possible foreseen risk event becomes a reality. The contingency plan represents actions that will reduce or mitigate the negative impact of the risk event. A key distinction between a risk response and a contingency plan is that a response is part of the actual implementation plan and action is taken before the risk can materialize, while a contingency plan is not part of the initial implementation plan and only goes into effect after the risk is recognized.

Like all plans, the contingency plan answers the questions of what, where, when, and how much action will take place. The absence of a contingency plan, when a risk event occurs, can cause a manager to delay or postpone the decision to implement a remedy. This postponement can lead to panic, and acceptance of the first remedy suggested. Such after-the-event decision making under pressure can be potentially dangerous and costly. Contingency planning evaluates alternative remedies for possible foreseen events before the risk event occurs and selects the best plan among alternatives. This early contingency planning facilitates a smooth transition to the remedy or work-around plan. The availability of a contingency plan can significantly increase the chances for project success.

Conditions for activating the implementation of the contingency plan should be decided and clearly documented. The plan should include a cost estimate and identify the source of funding. All parties affected should agree to the contingency plan and have authority to make commitments. Because implementation of a contingency plan embodies disruption in the sequence of work, all contingency plans should be communicated to team members so that surprise and resistance are minimized.

Here is an example: A high-tech niche computer company intends to introduce a new "platform" product at a very specific target date. The project's 47 teams all agree delays will not be acceptable. Their contingency plans for two large component suppliers demonstrate how seriously risk management is viewed. One supplier's plant sits on the San Andreas Fault, which is prone to earthquakes. The contingency plan has an alternative supplier, who is constantly updated, producing a replica of the component in another plant. Another key supplier in Toronto, Canada, presents a delivery risk on their due date because of potential bad weather. This contingency plan calls for a chartered plane (already contracted to be on standby) if overland transportation presents a delay problem. To outsiders these plans must seem a bit extreme, but in high-tech industries where time to market is king, risks of identified events are taken seriously.

Risk response matrices such as the one shown in Figure 7.8 are useful for summarizing how the project team plans to manage risks that have been identified. Again, the Windows 7 project is used to illustrate this kind of matrix. The first step is to identify whether to reduce, share, transfer, or accept the risk. The team decided to reduce the chances of the system freezing by experimenting with a prototype of the system. Prototype experimentation not only allows them to identify and fix conversion "bugs" before the actual installation, but it also yields information that could be useful in enhancing acceptance by end-users. The project team is then able to identify and document changes between the old and new system that will be incorporated in the training the users receive. The risk of equipment malfunctioning is transferred by choosing a reliable supplier with a strong warranty program.

The next step is to identify contingency plans in case the risk still occurs. For example, if interface problems prove insurmountable, then the team would attempt a work-around until vendor experts arrived to help solve the problem. If

FIGURE 7.8 **Risk Response Matrix**

Risk Event	Response	Contingency Plan	Trigger	Who Is Responsible
Interface problems	Mitigate: Test prototype	Work around until help comes	Not solved within 24 hours	Nils
System freezing	Mitigate: Test prototype	Reinstall OS	Still frozen after one hour	Emmylou
User backlash	Mitigate: Prototype demonstration	Increase staff support	Call from top management	Eddie
Equipment malfunctions	Mitigate: Select reliable vendor Transfer: Warranty	Order replacement	Equipment fails	Jim

the system freezes after installation, the team will first try to reinstall the software. If user dissatisfaction is high, then the IS department will provide more staff support. If the team is unable to get reliable equipment from the original supplier, then it will order a different brand from a second dealer. The team also needs to discuss and agree what would "trigger" implementation of the contingency plan. In the case of the system freezing, the trigger is not being able to unfreeze the system within one hour or, in the case of user backlash, an angry call from top management. Finally, the individual responsible for monitoring the potential risk and initiating the contingency plan needs to be assigned. Smart project managers establish protocols for contingency responses before they are needed. For an example of the importance of establishing protocols see the Risk Management at the Top of the World Snapshot from Practice on page 225.

Some of the most common methods for handling risk are discussed here.

Technical Risks

Technical risks are problematic; they can often be the kind that cause the project to be shut down. What if the system or process does not work? Contingency or backup plans are made for those possibilities that are foreseen. For example, Carrier Transicold was involved in developing a new Phoenix refrigeration unit for truck-trailer applications. This new unit was to use rounded panels made of bonded metals, which at the time was new technology for Transicold. Furthermore, one of its competitors had tried unsuccessfully to incorporate similar bonded metals in their products. The project team was eager to make the new technology work, but it wasn't until the very end of the project that they were able to get the new adhesives to bond adequately to complete the project. Throughout the project, the team maintained a welded-panel fabrication approach just in case they were unsuccessful. If this contingency approach had been needed, it would have increased production costs, but the project still would have been completed on time.

In addition to backup strategies, project managers need to develop methods to quickly assess whether technical uncertainties can be resolved. The use of sophisticated CAD programs has greatly helped resolve design problems. At the same time, Smith and Reinertsen, in their book *Developing Products in Half the Time,* argue that there is no substitute for making something and seeing how it works, feels, or looks. They suggest that one should first identify the high-risk technical areas, then build models or design experiments to resolve the risk as quickly as possible. By isolating and testing the key technical questions early on in a project,

SNAPSHOT FROM PRACTICE

Risk Management at the Top of the World*

Into Thin Air, Jon Krakauer's gripping account of an ill-fated attempt to climb Mount Everest in which six climbers died, provides testimony to the risks of extreme mountain climbing. Thirteen days after the tragedy, David Breashears successfully led a film crew to the summit. Their footage can be seen in the spectacular IMAX film, *Everest.*

Accounts of Mount Everest expeditions provide insights into project risk management. First, most climbers spend more than three weeks acclimating their bodies to high-altitude conditions. Native Sherpas are used extensively to carry supplies and set up each of the four base camps that will be used during the final stages of the climb. To reduce the impact of hypoxia, lightheadedness, and disorientation caused by shortage of oxygen, most climbers use oxygen masks and bottles during the final ascent. If lucky enough not to be one of the first expeditions of the season, the path to the summit should be staked out and roped by previous climbers. Climbing guides receive last-minute weather reports by radio to confirm whether the weather conditions warrant the risk. Finally, for added insurance, most climbers join their Sherpas in an elaborate *puja* ritual intended to summon the divine support of the gods before beginning their ascent.

All of these efforts pale next to the sheer physical and mental rigors of making the final climb from base camp IV to the summit. This is what climbers refer to as the "death zone" because beyond 26,000 feet the mind and body begin to quickly deteriorate despite supplemental oxygen. Under fair conditions it takes around 18 hours to make the round-trip to the top and back to the base camp. Climbers leave as early as 1:00 A.M. in order to make it back before night falls and total exhaustion sets in.

The greatest danger in climbing Mount Everest is not reaching the summit but making it back to the base camp. One out of every five climbers who make it to the summit dies during their descent. The key is establishing a contingency plan in case the climbers encounter hard going or the weather changes. Guides establish a predetermined turnaround time (i.e., 2:00 P.M.) to ensure a safe return no matter how close the

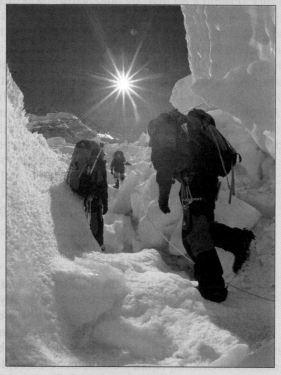

© Bobby Model/National Geographic Stock

climbers are to the summit. Accepting the time takes tremendous discipline. One who was caught up by time was solo climber Goran Krupp. He turned back 1,000 feet from the top after bicycling 8,000 miles from Stockholm to Katmandu!

Many lives have been lost by failing to adhere to the turnback time and pushing forward to the summit. As one climber put it, "With enough determination, any bloody idiot can get up the hill. The trick is to get back down alive."

* Jon Krakauer, *Into Thin Air* (New York: Doubleday, 1997), p. 190; Broughton Coburn, *Everest: Mountain without Mercy* (New York: National Geographic Society, 1997).

project feasibility can be quickly determined and necessary adjustments made such as reworking the process or in some cases closing down the project.

Schedule Risks

Often organizations will defer the threat of a project coming in late until it surfaces. Here contingency funds are set aside to expedite or "crash" the project to get it back on track. Crashing, or reducing project duration, is accomplished by shortening (compressing) one or more activities on the critical path. This comes percentage of the baseline, say, 5 percent, and calling it the contingency reserve is not a sound approach. Also, adding up all the identified contingency allotments and throwing them into one pot is not conducive to sound control of the reserve fund.

In practice, the contingency reserve fund is typically divided into budget and management reserve funds for control purposes. Budget reserves are set up to cover identified risks; these reserves are those allocated to specific segments or deliverables of the project. Management reserves are set up to cover unidentified risks and are allocated to risks associated with the total project. The risks are separated because their use requires approval from different levels of project authority. Because all risks are probabilistic, the reserves are not included in the baseline for each work package or activity; they are only activated when a risk occurs. If an identified risk does not occur and its chance of occurring is past, the fund allocated to the risk should be deducted from the budget reserve. (This removes the temptation to use budget reserves for other issues or problems.) Of course if the risk does occur, funds are removed from the reserve and added to the cost baseline.

It is important that contingency allowances be independent of the original time and cost estimates. These allowances need to be clearly distinguished to avoid time and budget game playing.

Budget Reserves

These reserves are identified for specific work packages or segments of a project found in the baseline budget or work breakdown structure. For example, a reserve amount might be added to "computer coding" to cover the risk of "testing" showing a coding problem. The reserve amount is determined by costing out the accepted contingency or recovery plan. The budget reserve should be communicated to the project team. This openness suggests trust and encourages good cost performance. However, distributing budget reserves should be the responsibility of both the project manager and the team members responsible for implementing the specific segment of the project. If the risk does not materialize, the funds are removed from the budget reserve. Thus, budget reserves decrease as the project progresses.

Management Reserves

These reserve funds are needed to cover major unforeseen risks and, hence, are applied to the total project. For example, a major scope change may appear necessary midway in the project. Because this change was not anticipated or identified, it is covered from the management reserve. Management reserves are established *after* budget reserves are identified and funds established. These reserves are independent of budget reserves and are controlled by the project manager and the "owner" of the project. The "owner" can be internal (top management) or external to the project organization. Most management reserves are set using historical data and judgments concerning the uniqueness and complexity of the project.

Placing technical contingencies in the management reserve is a special case. Identifying possible technical (functional) risks is often associated with a new, untried, innovative process or product. Because there is a chance the innovation may not work out, a fallback plan is necessary. This type of risk is beyond the control of the project manager. Hence, technical reserves are held in the management reserve and controlled by the owner or top management. The owner and project manager decide when the contingency plan will be implemented and the reserve funds used. It is assumed there is a high probability these funds will never be used.

TABLE 7.1
Contingency Fund Estimate (Thousands of Dollars)

Activity	Budget Baseline	Budget Reserve	Project Budget
Design	$500	$15	$515
Code	900	80	980
Test	20	2	22
Subtotal	$1,420	$97	$1,517
Management reserve	—	—	50
Total	$1,420	$97	$1,567

Table 7.1 shows the development of a contingency fund estimate for a hypothetical project. Note how budget and management reserves are kept separate; control is easily tracked using this format.

Time Buffers

Just as contingency funds are established to absorb unplanned costs, managers use time buffers to cushion against potential delays in the project. And like contingency funds, the amount of time is dependent upon the inherent uncertainty of the project. The more uncertain the project the more time should be reserved for the schedule. The strategy is to assign extra time at critical moments in the project. For example, buffers are added to

A. activities with severe risks.

B. merge activities that are prone to delays due to one or more preceding activities being late.

C. noncritical activities to reduce the likelihood that they will create another critical path.

D. activities that require scarce resources to ensure that the resources are available when needed.

In the face of overall schedule uncertainty, buffers are sometimes added to the end of the project. For example, a 300-working-day project may have a 30-day project buffer. While the extra 30 days would not appear on the schedule, it is available if needed. Like management reserves, this buffer typically requires the authorization of top management. A more systematic approach to buffer management is discussed in the Chapter 8 Appendix on critical chain project management.

Step 4: Risk Response Control

Typically the results of the first three steps of the risk management process are summarized in a formal document often called the risk register. A **risk register** details all identified risks, including descriptions, category, and probability of occurring, impact, responses, contingency plans, owners, and current status. The register is the backbone for the last step in the risk management process: risk control. Risk control involves executing the risk response strategy, monitoring triggering events, initiating contingency plans, and watching for new risks. Establishing a change management system to deal with events that require formal changes in the scope, budget, and/or schedule of the project is an essential element of risk control.

Project managers need to monitor risks just like they track project progress. Risk assessment and updating needs to be part of every status meeting and progress report system. The project team needs to be on constant alert for new, unforeseen risks. Management needs to be sensitive that others may not be forthright in acknowledging new risks and problems. Admitting that there might be a bug in the design code or that different components are not compatible reflects poorly on individual performance. If the prevailing organizational culture is one where mistakes are punished severely, then it is only human nature to protect oneself. Similarly, if bad news is greeted harshly and there is a propensity to "kill the messenger," then participants will be reluctant to speak freely. The tendency to suppress bad news is compounded when individual responsibility is vague and the project team is under extreme pressure from top management to get the project done quickly.

Project managers need to establish an environment in which participants feel comfortable raising concerns and admitting mistakes. The norm should be that mistakes are acceptable, hiding mistakes is intolerable. Problems should be embraced not denied. Participants should be encouraged to identify problems and new risks. Here a positive attitude by the project manager toward risks is a key.

On large, complex projects it may be prudent to repeat the risk identification/assessment exercise with fresh information. Risk profiles should be reviewed to test to see if the original responses held true. Relevant stakeholders should be brought into the discussion and the risk register needs to be updated. While this may not be practical on an ongoing basis, project managers should touch base with them on a regular basis or hold special stakeholder meetings to review the status of risks on the project.

A second key for controlling the cost of risks is documenting responsibility. This can be problematic in projects involving multiple organizations and contractors. Responsibility for risk is frequently passed on to others with the statement, "That is not my worry." This mentality is dangerous. Each identified risk should be assigned (or shared) by mutual agreement of the owner, project manager, and the contractor or person having line responsibility for the work package or segment of the project. It is best to have the line person responsible approve the use of budget reserve funds and monitor their rate of usage. If management reserve funds are required, the line person should play an active role in estimating additional costs and funds needed to complete the project. Having line personnel participate in the process focuses attention on the management reserve, control of its rate of usage, and early warning of potential risk events. If risk management is not formalized, responsibility and responses to risk will be ignored—*it is not my area.*

The bottom line is that project managers and team members need to be vigilant in monitoring potential risks and identify new land mines that could derail a project. Risk assessment has to be part of the working agenda of status meetings and when new risks emerge they need to be analyzed and incorporated into the risk management process.

Change Control Management

A major element of the risk control process is change management. Every detail of a project plan will not materialize as expected. Coping with and controlling project changes present a formidable challenge for most project managers. Changes come from many sources such as the project customer, owner, project manager,

FIGURE 7.9
Change Control
Process

team members, and occurrence of risk events. Most changes easily fall into three categories:

1. Scope changes in the form of design or additions represent big changes; for example, customer requests for a new feature or a redesign that will improve the product.
2. Implementation of contingency plans, when risk events occur, represent changes in baseline costs and schedules.
3. Improvement changes suggested by project team members represent another category.

Because change is inevitable, a well-defined change review and control process should be set up early in the project planning cycle.

Change management systems involve reporting, controlling, and recording changes to the project baseline. (Note: Some organizations consider change control systems part of configuration management.) In practice most change management systems are designed to accomplish the following:

1. Identify proposed changes.
2. List expected effects of proposed change(s) on schedule and budget.
3. Review, evaluate, and approve or disapprove changes formally.
4. Negotiate and resolve conflicts of change, conditions, and cost.
5. Communicate changes to parties affected.
6. Assign responsibility for implementing change.
7. Adjust master schedule and budget.
8. Track all changes that are to be implemented.

As part of the project communication plan, stakeholders define up front the communication and decision-making process that will be used to evaluate and accept changes. The process can be captured in a flow diagram like the one presented in Figure 7.9. On small projects this process may simply entail approval of a small group of stakeholders. On larger projects more elaborate decision-making processes are established, with different processes being used for different kinds of change. For example, changes in performance requirements may require multiple sign-offs, including the project sponsor and client, while switching suppliers may be authorized by the project manager. Regardless of the nature of the project, the goal is to establish the process for introducing necessary changes in the project in a timely and effective manner.

Of particular importance is assessing the impact of the change on the project. Often solutions to immediate problems have adverse consequences on other aspects of a project. For example, in overcoming a problem with the exhaust system for a hybrid automobile, the design engineers contributed to the prototype exceeding weight parameters. It is important that the implications of changes are assessed by people with appropriate expertise and perspective. On construction projects this is often the responsibility of the architecture firm, while "software architects" perform a similar function on software development efforts.

Organizations use change request forms and logs to track proposed changes. An example of a simplified change request form is depicted in Figure 7.10. Typically change request forms include a description of the change, the impact of not approving the change, the impact of the change on project scope/schedule/cost, and defined signature paths for review as well as a tracking log number.

FIGURE 7.10
Sample Change Request

Project name   *Irish/Chinese culture exchange*   Project sponsor   *Irish embassy*

Request number   *12*   Date   *June 6, 2xxx*

Originator   *Jennifer McDonald*   Change requested by   *Chinese culture office*

Description of requested change

1. *Request river dancers to replace small Irish dance group.*
2. *Request one combination dance with river dancers and China ballet group.*

Reason for change

River dancers will enhance stature of event. The group is well known and loved by Chinese people.

Areas of impact of proposed change—describe each on separate sheet

[X] Scope   [X] Cost   [ ] Other _____

[ ] Schedule   [ ] Risk

Disposition	Priority	Funding Source
[ ] Approve	[ ] Emergency	[ ] Mgmt. reserve
[X] Approve as amended	[X] Urgent	[ ] Budget reserve
[ ] Disapprove	[ ] Low	[X] Customer
[ ] Deferred		[ ] Other

Sign-off Approvals

Project manager   *William O'Mally*   Date   *June 12, 2xxx*

Project sponsor   *Kenneth Thompson*   Date   *June 13, 2xxx*

Project customer   *Hong Lee*   Date   *June 18, 2xxx*

Other   _____   Date   _____

An abridged version of a change request log for a construction project is presented in Figure 7.11. These logs are used to monitor change requests. They typically summarize the status of all outstanding change requests and include such useful information as source and date of the change, document codes for related information, cost estimates, and the current status of the request.

Every approved change must be identified and integrated into the plan of record through changes in the project WBS and baseline schedule. The plan of record is the current official plan for the project in terms of scope, budget, and schedule. The plan of record serves as a change management benchmark for future change requests as well as the baseline for evaluating project progress.

If the change control system is not integrated with the WBS and baseline, project plans and control will soon self-destruct. Thus, one of the keys to a successful

FIGURE 7.11   Change Request Log

			Dates				
Owner Requested Change Status Report—Open Items							**OSU—Weatherford**
Rc#	**Description**	**Reference Document**	**Date Rec'd**	**Date Submit**	**Amount**	**Status**	**Comments**
51	Sewer work offset				−188,129	OPEN	FUNDING FROM OTHER SOURCE
52	Stainless Plates at restroom Shower Valves	ASI 56	1/5/2008	3/30/2008	9,308	APPROVED	
53	Waterproofing Options	ASI 77	1/13/2008		169,386	OPEN	
54	Change Electrical floor box spec change	RFI 113	12/5/2008	3/29/2008	2,544	SUBMIT	
55	VE Option for Style and rail doors	Door samples	1/14/2008		−20,000	ROM	
56	Pressure Wash C tower	Owner request	3/15/2008	3/30/2008	14,861	SUBMIT	
57	Fire Lite glass in stairs	Owner request			8,000	QUOTE	ROM BASED ON FIRELITE NT
58	Cyber Café added tele/OFOI equipment	ASI 65	1/30/2008	3/29/2008	4,628	APPROVED	
59	Additional Dampers in C wing	ASI 68	2/4/2008	3/29/2008	1,085	SUBMIT	
60	Revise Corridor ceilings	ASI 72	2/13/2008	3/31/2008	−3,755	SUBMIT	

OPEN—Requires estimate   SUBMIT—RC letter submitted   ASI—Architect's supplemental instructions
ROM—Rough order magnitude   APPROVED—RC letter approved   RFI—Request for information
QUOTE—Subcontractor quotes   REVISE—RC letter to be reviewed

change control process is document, document, document! The benefits derived from change control systems are the following:

1. Inconsequential changes are discouraged by the formal process.
2. Costs of changes are maintained in a log.
3. Integrity of the WBS and performance measures is maintained.
4. Allocation and use of budget and management reserve funds are tracked.
5. Responsibility for implementation is clarified.
6. Effect of changes is visible to all parties involved.
7. Implementation of change is monitored.
8. Scope changes will be quickly reflected in baseline and performance measures.

Clearly, change control is important and requires that someone or some group be responsible for approving changes, keeping the process updated, and communicating changes to the project team and relevant stakeholders. Project control depends heavily on keeping the change control process current. This historical record can be used for satisfying customer inquiries, identifying problems in post-project audits, and estimating future project costs.

Summary

To put the processes discussed in this chapter in proper perspective one should recognize that the essence of project management is risk management. Every technique in this book is really a risk management technique. Each in its own way tries to prevent something bad from happening. Project selection systems try to reduce the likelihood that projects will not contribute to the mission of the firm. Project scope statements, among other things, are designed to avoid costly misunderstandings and reduce scope creep. Risk breakdown structures reduce the likelihood that some vital part of the project will be omitted or that the budget estimates are unrealistic. Teambuilding reduces the likelihood of dysfunctional conflict and breakdowns in coordination. All of the techniques try to increase stakeholder satisfaction and increase the chances of project success.

From this perspective managers engage in risk management activities to compensate for the uncertainty inherent in project management and that things never go according to plan. Risk management is proactive not reactive. It reduces the number of surprises and leads to a better understanding of the most likely outcomes of negative events.

Although many managers believe that in the final analysis, risk assessment and contingency depend on subjective judgment, some standard method for identifying, assessing, and responding to risks should be included in all projects. The very process of identifying project risks forces some discipline at all levels of project management and improves project performance.

Contingency plans increase the chance that the project can be completed on time and within budget. Contingency plans can be simple "work-arounds" or elaborate detailed plans. Responsibility for risks should be clearly identified and documented. It is desirable and prudent to keep a reserve as a hedge against project risks. Budget reserves are linked to the WBS and should be communicated to the project team. Control of management reserves should remain with the owner, project manager, and line person responsible. Use of contingency reserves should be closely monitored, controlled, and reviewed throughout the project life cycle.

Experience clearly indicates that using a formal, structured process to handle possible foreseen and unforeseen project risk events minimizes surprises, costs, delays, stress, and misunderstandings. Risk management is an iterative process that occurs throughout the lifespan of the project. When risk events occur or changes are necessary, using an effective change control process to quickly approve and record changes will facilitate measuring performance against schedule and cost. Ultimately successful risk management requires a culture in which threats are embraced not denied and problems are identified not hidden.

Key Terms

Avoiding risk, *220*
Budget reserve, *228*
Change management system, *231*
Contingency plan, *223*
Management reserve, *228*

Mitigating risk, *219*
Opportunity, *227*
Retaining Risk, *222*
Risk, *211*
Risk breakdown structure (RBS), *214*
Risk register, *229*

Risk profile, *214*
Risk severity matrix, *218*
Scenario analysis, *216*
Time buffer, *229*
Transferring risk, *221*

Review Questions

1. Project risks can/cannot be eliminated if the project is carefully planned. Explain.
2. The chances of risk events occurring and their respective costs increasing change over the project life cycle. What is the significance of this phenomenon to a project manager?
3. What is the difference between avoiding a risk and accepting a risk?
4. What is the difference between mitigating a risk and contingency planning?
5. Explain the difference between budget reserves and management reserves.
6. How are the work breakdown structure and change control connected?
7. What are the likely outcomes if a change control process is not used? Why?
8. What are the major differences between managing negative risks versus positive risks (opportunities)?

Exercises

1. Gather a small team of students. Think of a project most students would understand; the kinds of tasks involved should also be familiar. Identify and assess major and minor risks inherent to the project. Decide on a response type. Develop a contingency plan for two to four identified risks. Estimate costs. Assign contingency reserves. How much reserve would your team estimate for the whole project? Justify your choices and estimates.
2. You have been assigned to a project risk team of five members. Because this is the first time your organization has formally set up a risk team for a project, it is hoped that your team will develop a process that can be used on all future projects. Your first team meeting is next Monday morning. Each team member has been asked to prepare for the meeting by developing, in as much detail as possible, an outline that describes how you believe the team should proceed in handling project risks. Each team member will hand out their proposed outline at the beginning of the meeting. Your outline should include but not be limited to the following information:
   a. Team objectives.
   b. Process for handling risk events.
   c. Team activities.
   d. Team outputs.
3. The Manchester United Soccer Tournament project team (review the Manchester United case at the end of Chapter 4) has identified the following potential risks to their project:
   a. Referees failing to show up at designated games.
   b. Fighting between teams.
   c. Pivotal error committed by a referee that determines the outcome of a game.
   d. Abusive behavior along the sidelines by parents.
   e. Inadequate parking.
   f. Not enough teams sign up for different age brackets.
   g. Serious injury.
   How would you recommend that they respond (i.e., avoid, accept, . . .) to these risks and why?
4. Search the World Wide Web (WWW) using the key words: "best practices, project management." What did you find? How might this information be useful to a project manager?

References

Atkinson, W., "Beyond the Basics," *PM Network,* May 2003, pp. 38–43.

Baker, B., and R. Menon, "Politics and Project Performance: The Fourth Dimension of Project Management," *PM Network,* 9 (11) November 1995, pp. 16–21.

Carr, M. J., S. L. Konda, I. Monarch, F. C. Ulrich, and C. F. Walker, "Taxonomy-Based Risk Identification," *Technical Report CMU/SEI-93-TR 6, Software Engineering Institute,* Carnegie Mellon University, Pittsburgh, 1993.

Ford, E. C., J. Duncan, A. G. Bedeian, P. M. Ginter, M. D. Rousculp, and A. M. Adams, "Mitigating Risks, Visible Hands, Inevitable Disasters, and Soft Variables: Management Research that Matters to Managers," *Academy of Management Executive,* 19 (4) November 2005, pp. 24–38.

Graves, R., "Qualitative Risk Assessment," *PM Network,* 14 (10) October 2000, pp. 61–66.

Gray, C. F., and R. Reinman, "PERT Simulation: A Dynamic Approach to the PERT Technique," *Journal of Systems Management,* March 1969, pp. 18–23.

Hamburger, D. H., "The Project Manager: Risk Taker and Contingency Planner," *Project Management Journal,* 21 (4) 1990, pp. 11–16.

Hulett, D. T., "Project Schedule Risk Assessment," *Project Management Journal,* 26 (1) 1995, pp. 21–31.

Ingebretson, M., "In No Uncertain Terms," *PM Network,* 2002, pp. 28–32.

Levine, H. A., "Risk Management for Dummies: Managing Schedule, Cost and Technical Risk, and Contingency," *PM Network,* 9 (10) October 1995, pp. 31–33.

"Math Mistake Proved Fatal to Mars Orbiter," *The Orlando Sentinel,* November 23, 1999.

Pavlik, A., "Project Troubleshooting: Tiger Teams for Reactive Risk Management," *Project Management Journal,* 35 (4) December 2004, pp. 5–14.

Pinto, J. K., *Project Management: Achieving Competitive Advantage* (Upper Saddle River, NJ: Pearson, 2007).

Pritchard, C. L., "Advanced Risk—How Big Is Your Crystal Ball?" Proceedings of the 31st Annual Project Management Institute 2000 Seminars and Symposium, (Houston, TX, 2000) CD, pp. 933–36.

Project Management Body of Knowledge (Newton Square, PA: Project Management Institute, 2008), pp. 273–312.

Schuler, J. R., "Decision Analysis in Projects: Monte Carlo Simulation," *PM Network,* 7 (1) January 1994, pp. 30–36.

Smith, P. G., and G. M. Merritt, *Proactive Risk Management: Controlling Uncertainty in Product Development* (New York: Productivity Press, 2002).

Smith, P. G., and D. G. Reinertsen, *Developing Products in Half the Time* (New York: Van Nostrand Reinhold, 1995).

Case

Alaska Fly-Fishing Expedition*

You are sitting around the fire at a lodge in Dillingham, Alaska, discussing a fishing expedition you are planning with your colleagues at Great Alaska Adventures (GAA). Earlier in the day you received a fax from the president of BlueNote, Inc. The president wants to reward her top management team by taking them on an all-expense-paid fly-fishing adventure in Alaska. She would like GAA to organize and lead the expedition.

You have just finished a preliminary scope statement for the project (see below). You are now brainstorming potential risks associated with the project.

1. Brainstorm potential risks associated with this project. Try to come up with at least five different risks.
2. Use a risk assessment form similar to Figure 7.6 to analyze identified risks.
3. Develop a risk response matrix similar to Figure 7.8 to outline how you would deal with each of the risks.

PROJECT SCOPE STATEMENT

PROJECT OBJECTIVE

To organize and lead a five-day fly-fishing expedition down the Tikchik River system in Alaska from June 21 to 25 at a cost not to exceed $27,000.

DELIVERABLES

- Provide air transportation from Dillingham, Alaska, to Camp I and from Camp II back to Dillingham.
- Provide river transportation consisting of two eight-man drift boats with outboard motors.
- Provide three meals a day for the five days spent on the river.
- Provide four hours fly-fishing instruction.
- Provide overnight accommodations at the Dillingham lodge plus three four-man tents with cots, bedding, and lanterns.
- Provide four experienced river guides who are also fly fishermen.
- Provide fishing licenses for all guests.

MILESTONES

1. Contract signed January 22.
2. Guests arrive in Dillingham June 20.
3. Depart by plane to Base Camp I June 21.
4. Depart by plane from Base Camp II to Dillingham June 25.

TECHNICAL REQUIREMENTS

1. Fly in air transportation to and from base camps.
2. Boat transportation within the Tikchik River system.
3. Digital cellular communication devices.
4. Camps and fishing conform to state of Alaska requirements.

* This case was prepared with the assistance of Stuart Morigeau.

LIMITS AND EXCLUSIONS

1. Guests are responsible for travel arrangements to and from Dillingham, Alaska.
2. Guests are responsible for their own fly-fishing equipment and clothing.
3. Local air transportation to and from base camps will be outsourced.
4. Tour guides are not responsible for the number of King Salmon caught by guests.

CUSTOMER REVIEW

The president of BlueNote, Inc.

Case

Silver Fiddle Construction

You are the president of Silver Fiddle Construction (SFC), which specializes in building high-quality, customized homes in the Grand Junction, Colorado, area. You have just been hired by the Czopeks to build their dream home. You operate as a general contractor and employ only a part-time bookkeeper. You subcontract work to local trade professionals. Housing construction in Grand Junction is booming. You are tentatively scheduled to complete 11 houses this year. You have promised the Czopeks that the final costs will range from $450,000 to $500,000 and that it will take five months to complete the house once groundbreaking has begun. The Czopeks are willing to have the project delayed in order to save costs.

You have just finished a preliminary scope statement for the project (see below). You are now brainstorming potential risks associated with the project.

1. Identify potential risks associated with this project. Try to come up with at least five different risks.
2. Use a risk assessment form similar to Figure 7.6 to analyze identified risks.
3. Develop a risk response matrix similar to Figure 7.8 to outline how you would deal with each of the risks.

PROJECT SCOPE STATEMENT

PROJECT OBJECTIVE

To construct a high-quality, custom home within five months at a cost not to exceed $500,000.

DELIVERABLES

- A 2,500-square-foot, 2½-bath, 3-bedroom, finished home.
- A finished garage, insulated and sheetrocked.
- Kitchen appliances to include range, oven, microwave, and dishwasher.
- High-efficiency gas furnace with programmable thermostat.

MILESTONES

1. Permits approved July 5.
2. Foundation poured July 12.

3. "Dry in"—framing, sheathing, plumbing, electrical, and mechanical inspections—passed September 25.
4. Final inspection November 7.

TECHNICAL REQUIREMENTS

1. Home must meet local building codes.
2. All windows and doors must pass NFRC class 40 energy ratings.
3. Exterior wall insulation must meet an "R" factor of 21.
4. Ceiling insulation must meet an "R" factor of 38.
5. Floor insulation must meet an "R" factor of 25.
6. Garage will accommodate two cars and one 28-foot-long Winnebago.
7. Structure must pass seismic stability codes.

LIMITS AND EXCLUSIONS

1. The home will be built to the specifications and design of the original blueprints provided by the customer.
2. Owner is responsible for landscaping.
3. Refrigerator is not included among kitchen appliances.
4. Air conditioning is not included, but house is prewired for it.
5. SFC reserves the right to contract out services.

CUSTOMER REVIEW

"Bolo" and Izabella Czopek.

Case

Peak LAN Project

Peak Systems is a small, information systems consulting firm located in Meridian, Louisiana. Peak has just been hired to design and install a local area network (LAN) for the city of Meridian's social welfare agency. You are the manager for the project, which includes one Peak professional and two interns from a local university. You have just finished a preliminary scope statement for the project (see below). You are now brainstorming potential risks associated with the project.

1. Identify potential risks associated with this project. Try to come up with at least five different risks.
2. Use a risk assessment form similar to Figure 7.6 to analyze identified risks.
3. Develop a risk response matrix similar to Figure 7.8 to outline how you would deal with each of the risks.

PROJECT SCOPE STATEMENT

PROJECT OBJECTIVE

To design and install a local area network (LAN) within one month with a budget not to exceed $90,000 for the Meridian Social Service Agency.

DELIVERABLES

- Twenty workstations and twenty laptop computers.
- Server with dual-core processors.
- Two color laser printers.
- Windows 2008 R2 server and workstation operating system (Vista/Windows 7).
- Four hours of introduction training for client's personnel.
- Sixteen hours of training for client network administrator.
- Fully operational LAN system.

MILESTONES

1. Hardware January 22.
2. Setting users' priority and authorization January 26.
3. In-house whole network test completed February 1.
4. Client site test completed February 2.
5. Training completed February 16.

TECHNICAL REQUIREMENTS

1. Workstations with 17-inch flat panel monitors, dual-core processors, 2 GB RAM, 8X DVD+RW, wireless card, Ethernet card, 80 GB hard drive.
2. Laptops with 12-inch display monitor, dual-core processors, 2GB RAM, 8X DVD+RW, wireless card, Ethernet card, 60 GB hard drive and weigh less than 4½ lbs.
3. Wireless network interface cards and Ethernet connections.
4. System must support Windows Vista/Windows 7 platforms.
5. System must provide secure external access for field workers.

LIMITS AND EXCLUSIONS

1. System maintenance and repair only up to one month after final inspection.
2. Warranties transferred to client.
3. Only responsible for installing software designated by the client two weeks before the start of the project.
4. Client will be billed for additional training beyond that prescribed in the contract.

CUSTOMER REVIEW

Director of the city of Meridian's Social Service Agency.

Case

XSU Spring Concert

You are a member of the X State University (XSU) student body entertainment committee. Your committee has agreed to sponsor a spring concert. The motive behind this concert is to offer a safe alternative to Hasta Weekend. Hasta Weekend is a spring event in which students from XSU rent houseboats and engage in heavy partying. Traditionally this occurs during the last weekend in May. Unfortunately, the partying has a long history of getting out of hand, sometimes leading to fatal accidents. After one such tragedy last spring, your committee wants to offer an alternative experience for those who are eager to celebrate the change in weather and the pending end of the school year.

You have just finished a preliminary scope statement for the project (see below). You are now brainstorming potential risks associated with the project.

1. Identify potential risks associated with this project. Try to come up with at least five different risks.
2. Use a risk assessment form similar to Figure 7.6 to analyze identified risks.
3. Develop a risk response matrix similar to Figure 7.8 to outline how you would deal with each of the risks.

PROJECT SCOPE STATEMENT

PROJECT OBJECTIVE

To organize and deliver an eight-hour concert at Wahoo Stadium at a cost not to exceed $50,000 on the last Saturday in May.

DELIVERABLES

- Local advertising.
- Concert security.
- Separate Beer Garden.
- Eight hours of music and entertainment.
- Food venues.
- Souvenir concert t-shirts.
- Secure all licenses and approvals.
- Secure sponsors.

MILESTONES

1. Secure all permissions and approvals by January 15.
2. Sign big-name artist by February 15.
3. Complete artist roster by April 1.
4. Secure vendor contracts by April 15.
5. Setup completed on May 27.
6. Concert on May 28.
7. Cleanup completed by May 31.

TECHNICAL REQUIREMENTS

1. Professional sound stage and system.
2. At least one big-name artist.
3. At least seven performing acts.
4. Restroom facilities for 10,000 people.
5. Parking available for 1,000 cars.
6. Compliance with XSU and city requirements/ordinances.

TABLE A7.1
Activity Times and Variances

Activity	a	m	b	t_e	$[(b-a)/6]^2$
1–2	17	29	47	30	25
2–3	6	12	24	13	9
2–4	16	19	28	20	4
3–5	13	16	19	16	1
4–5	2	5	14	6	4
5–6	2	5	8	5	1

FIGURE A7.2
Hypothetical Network

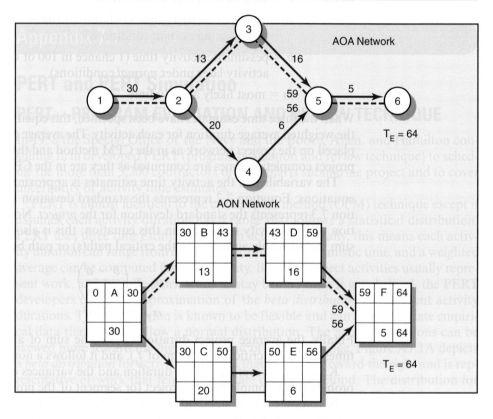

The expected project duration (T_E) is 64 time units; the critical path is 1-2-3-5-6. With this information, the probability of completing the project by a specific date can easily be computed using standard statistical methods. For example, what is the probability the project will be completed before a scheduled time (T_S) of 67? The normal curve for the project would appear as shown in Figure A7.3.

Using the formula for the Z value, the probability can be computed as follows:

$$Z = \frac{T_S - T_E}{\sqrt{\Sigma \sigma_{t_e}^2}}$$

$$= \frac{67 - 64}{\sqrt{25 + 9 + 1 + 1}}$$

$$= \frac{+3}{\sqrt{36}}$$

$$= +0.50$$

$$P = 0.69$$

FIGURE A7.3
Possible Project
Durations

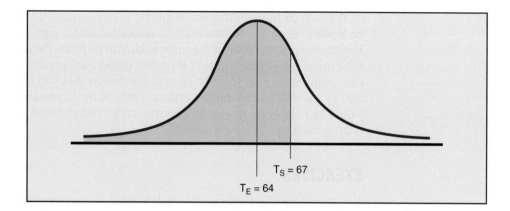

$T_S = 67$

$T_E = 64$

Reading from Table A7.2, a Z value of $+0.5$ gives a probability of 0.69, which is interpreted to mean there is a 69 percent chance of completing the project on or before 67 time units.

Conversely, the probability of completing the project by time period 60 is computed as follows:

$$Z = \frac{60 - 64}{\sqrt{25 + 9 + 1 + 1}}$$

$$= \frac{-4}{\sqrt{36}}$$

$$= -0.67$$

$$P \approx 0.26$$

From Table A7.2, a Z value of -0.67 gives an approximate probability of 0.26, which is interpreted to mean there is about a 26 percent chance of completing the project on or before 60 time units. Note that this same type of calculation can be made for any path or segment of a path in the network.

TABLE A7.2
Z Values and
Probabilities

Z Value	Probability	Z Value	Probability
−3.0	.001	+0.0	.500
−2.8	.003	+0.2	.579
−2.6	.005	+0.4	.655
−2.4	.008	+0.6	.726
−2.2	.014	+0.8	.788
−2.0	.023	+1.0	.841
−1.8	.036	+1.2	.885
−1.6	.055	+1.4	.919
−1.4	.081	+1.6	.945
−1.2	.115	+1.8	.964
−1.0	.159	+2.0	.977
−0.8	.212	+2.2	.986
−0.6	.274	+2.4	.992
−0.4	.345	+2.6	.995
−0.2	.421	+2.8	.997

When such probabilities are available to management, trade-off decisions can be made to accept or reduce the risk associated with a particular project duration. For example, if the project manager wishes to improve the chances of completing the project by 64 time units, at least two choices are available. First, management can spend money up front to change conditions that will reduce the duration of one or more activities on the critical path. A more prudent, second alternative would be to allocate money to a contingency fund and wait to see how the project is progressing as it is implemented.

EXERCISES

1. Given the project information below, what is the probability of completing the National Holiday Toy project in 93 time units?

Act. ID	Description	Predecessor	Optm. (a)	Most likely (m)	Pess. (b)	Act time t_e	Variance $[(b - a)/6]^2$	Critical
1	Design package	None	6	12	24			
2	Design product	1	16	19	28			
3	Build package	1	4	7	10			
4	Secure patent	2	21	30	39			
5	Build product	2	17	29	47			
6	Paint	3, 4, 5	4	7	10			
7	Test market	6	13	16	19			

2. The Global Tea and Organic Juice companies have merged.

The following information has been collected for the "Consolidation Project."

Activity	Description	Predecessor	a opt	m ml	b pess
1	Codify accounts	None	16	19	28
2	File articles of unification	None	30	30	30
3	Unify price and credit policy	None	60	72	90
4	Unify personnel policies	None	18	27	30
5	Unify data processing	1	17	29	47
6	Train accounting staff	1	4	7	10
7	Pilot run data processing	5	12	15	18
8	Calculate P & L and balance sheet	6, 7	6	12	24
9	Transfer real property	2	18	27	30
10	Train salesforce	3	20	35	50
11	Negotiate with unions	4	40	55	100
12	Determine capital needs	8	11	20	29
13	Explain personnel policies	11	14	23	26
14	Secure line of credit	9, 12	13	16	19
15	End	10, 12, 14	0	0	0

1. Compute the expected time for each activity.
2. Compute the variance for each activity.

3. Compute the expected project duration.

4. What is the probability of completing the project by day 112? Within 116 days?

5. What is the probability of completing "Negotiate with Unions" by day 90?

3. The expected times and variances for the project activities are given below. What is the probability of completing the project in 25 periods?

ID	Description	Predecessor	t_e	Variance $[(b - a)/6]^2$
1	Pilot production	None	6	3
2	Select channels of distrib.	None	7	4
3	Develop mktg. program	None	4	2
4	Test market	1	4	2
5	Patent	1	10	5
6	Full production	4	16	10
7	Ad promotion	3	3	2
8	Release	2,5,6,7	2	1

Case

International Capital, Inc.—Part A

International Capital, Inc. (IC), is a small investment banking firm that specializes in securing funds for small- to medium-sized firms. IC is able to use a standardized project format for each engagement. Only activity times and unusual circumstances change the standard network. Beth Brown has been assigned to this client as project manager partner and has compiled the network information and activity times for the latest client as follows:

Activity	Description	Immediate Predecessor
A	Start story draft using template	—
B	Research client firm	—
C	Create "due diligence" rough draft	A, B
D	Coordinate needs proposal with client	C
E	Estimate future demand and cash flows	C
F	Draft future plans for client company	E
G	Create and approve legal documents	C
H	Integrate all drafts into first-draft proposal	D, F, G
I	Line up potential sources of capital	G, F
J	Check, approve, and print final legal proposal	H
K	Sign contracts and transfer funds	I, J

	Time in Workdays		
Activity	Optimistic	Most Likely	Pessimistic
A	4	7	10
B	2	4	8
C	2	5	8
D	16	19	28
E	6	9	24
F	1	7	13
G	4	10	28
H	2	5	14
I	5	8	17
J	2	5	8
K	17	29	45

MANAGERIAL REPORT

Brown and other broker partners have a policy of passing their plan through a project review committee of colleagues. This committee traditionally checks that all details are covered, times are realistic, and resources are available. Brown wishes you to develop a report that presents a planned schedule and expected project completion time in workdays. Include a project network in your report. The average duration for a sourcing capital project is 70 workdays. IC partners have agreed it is good business to set up projects with a 95 percent chance of attaining the plan. How does this project stack up with the average project? What would the average have to be to ensure a 95 percent chance of completing the project in 70 workdays?

Case

Advantage Energy Technology Data Center Migration—Part B

In Chapter 6, Brian Smith, network administrator at Advanced Energy Technology (AET), was given the responsibility of implementing the migration of a large data center to a new office location.

Careful planning was needed because AET operates in the highly competitive petroleum industry. AET is one of five national software companies that provide an accounting and business management package for oil jobbers and gasoline distributors. A few years ago, AET jumped into the "application service provider" world. Their large data center provides clients with remote access to AET's complete suite of application software systems. Traditionally, one of AET's primary competitive advantages has been the company's trademark IT reliability. Due to the complexity of this project, the Executive Committee insisted that preliminary analysis of the anticipated completion date be conducted.

Brian compiled the following information, in preparation for some PERT analysis:

		Time in Workdays			
Task Name	Optimistic Dur.	Most Likely Dur.	Pessimistic Dur.	Immediate Predecessor	Critical Path
1 **AET DATA CENTER MIGRATION**	54	68	92		
2 Team meeting	0.5	1	1.5		✓
3 Hire contractors	6	7	8	2	
4 Network design	12	14	16	2	
5 **Ventilation system**	—	—	—	—	
6 Order ventilation system	18	21	30	2	
7 Install ventilation system	5	7	9	6	
8 **New racks**	—	—	—	—	
9 Order new racks	13	14	21	2	✓
10 Install racks	17	21	25	9	✓
11 **Power supplies and cables**	—	—	—	—	
12 Order power supplies & cables	6	7	8	2	
13 Install power supplies	5	5	11	12, 16	
14 Install cables	6	8	10	12, 16	✓
15 Renovation of data center	19	20	27	3, 4	
16 City inspection	1	2	3	3, 7, 10	✓
17 **Switchover Meetings**	—	—	—	—	
18 Facilities	7	8	9	14	
19 Operations/systems	5	7	9	14	
20 Operations/telecommunications	6	7	8	14	
21 Systems & applications	7	7	13	14	
22 Customer service	5	6	13	14	✓
23 Power check	0.5	1	1.5	13, 14, 15	✓
24 Install test servers	5	7	9	2, 3, 18, 19, 20, 21	✓
25 Management safety check	1	2	3	7, 23, 24	✓
26 Primary systems check	1.5	2	2.5	25	✓
27 Set date for move	1	1	1	26	✓
28 Complete move	1	2	3	27	✓

1. Based on these estimates and the resultant expected project duration of 69 days, the executive committee wants to know what is the probability of completing the project before a scheduled time (T_S) of 68 days?

2. The significance of this project has the executive committee very concerned. The committee has decided that more analysis of the duration of each activity is needed. Prior to conducting that effort, they asked Brian to calculate what the expected project duration would have to be to ensure a 93 percent chance of completion within 68 days.

ADVANTAGE ENERGY TECHNOLOGY (AET)— ACCOUNTS PAYABLE SYSTEM

The AET sales department has been concerned about a new start-up company that is about to release an accounts payable system. Their investigation indicates that this new package will provide features which will seriously compete with AET's current Accounts Payable system and some cases, exceed what AET offers.

Tom Wright, senior applications developer at AET, has been given the responsibility of analyzing, designing, developing, and delivering a new accounts payable system (A/P) for AET customers.

Complicating the issue is the concern of the sales department about AET's recent inability to meet promised delivery dates. They have convinced CEO (Larry Martain) that a significant marketing effort will have to be expended to convince the clients they should wait for the AET product rather than jump to a package provided by a new entry to the petroleum software business. Companion to this effort is the importance of the performance of the software development group.

Consequently, Tom has decided to take the following action: tighten up the estimating effort by his developers; incorporate some new estimating procedures; and use some PERT techniques to generate probabilities associated with his delivery dates.

Tom's planning team made a first-cut at the set of activities and associated durations:

	Task Name	Time in Workdays			Immediate Predecessor	Critical Path
		Optimistic Dur.	Most Likely Dur.	Pessimistic Dur.		
1	**ACCOUNTS PAYABLE SYSTEM**					
2	Planning meeting	1	1	2		✓
3	Team assignments	3	4	5	2	✓
4	**Program specification**					
5	Customer requirements	8	10	12	3	✓
6	Feasibility study	3	5	7	5	
7	Systems analysis	6	8	10	5	✓
8	Prelim budget & schedule	1	2	3	7	✓
9	Functional specification	3	5	7	7	✓
10	Prelim design	10	12	14	9	✓
11	Configuration & perf needs	3	4	5	10	✓
12	Hardware requirements	4	6	8	11	✓
13	System specification	5	7	9	10	
14	Detailed design	12	14	16	12, 13	✓
15	Program specification	8	10	12	14	✓
16	Programming—first phase	27	32	37	15	✓
17	Documentation	14	16	18	10	
18	**Prototype**					
19	Development	5	7	9	16	✓
20	User testing & feedback	12	14	16	19	✓
21	Programming—second phase	10	12	14	16	
22	Beta testing	18	20	22	21	
23	Final documentation pkg	9	10	11	17, 20	✓
24	Training pkg	4	5	6	21SS, 23	✓
25	Product release	3	5	7	22, 23, 24	✓

SS = Start to Start lag

3. Based on these estimates and the critical path, the project duration is estimated at 149 days. But, an AET salesperson in the Southeast Region has discovered that the competing A/P package (with significant improvements) is scheduled for delivery in approximately 145 days. The sales force is very anxious to beat

that delivery time. The executive committee asks Tom for an estimated probability of reducing his expected project duration by two days.

4. The executive committee is advised by Tom that after all the estimating was completed, he determined that one of his two critical systems analysts might have to move out of the area for critical family reasons. Tom is still very confident that with some staff rearrangements, assistance from a subcontractor, and some "hands on" activities on his part he can still meet the original delivery date, based on 149 days.

This news is very disconcerting to the committee and the sales staff. At this point, the committee decides that based on the most recent delivery performance of AET, a modified, comfortable delivery date should be communicated to AET clients—one that Tom and his staff are very likely to meet. Consequently, Tom is asked to calculate what the expected project duration would have to be to ensure a 98 percent chance of completion within 160 days—that is a "published, drop dead date" that can be communicated to the clients.

Scheduling Resources and Costs

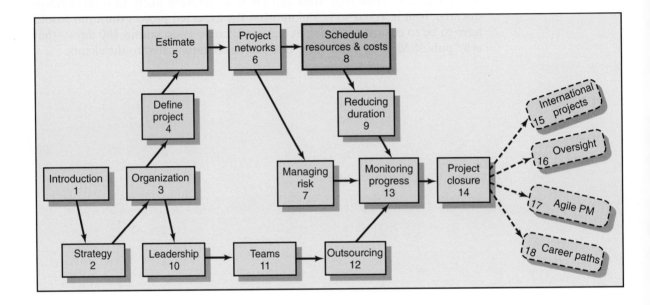

Project network times are not a schedule until resources have been assigned.
Cost estimates are not a budget until they have been time-phased.

We have consistently stressed that up-front planning results in big payoffs. For those who have diligently worked through the earlier planning processes chapters, you are nearly ready to launch your project. This chapter completes the final two planning tasks that become the master plan for your project—resource and cost scheduling. (See Figure 8.1.) This process uses the resource schedule to assign **time-phased** costs that provide the project budget *baseline*. Given this time-phased baseline, comparisons can be made with actual and planned schedule and costs. This chapter first discusses the process for developing the project resource schedule. This resource schedule will be used to assign the time-phased budgeted values to create a project budget baseline.

There are always more project proposals than there are available resources. The priority system needs to select projects that best contribute to the organization's objectives, within the constraints of the resources available. If all projects and their respective resources are computer scheduled, the feasibility and impact of adding a new project to those in process can be quickly assessed. With this information the project priority team will add a new project only if resources are available to be formally committed to that specific project. This chapter examines methods of scheduling resources so the team can make realistic judgments of resource availability and project durations. The project manager uses the same schedule for implementing the project. If changes occur during project implementation, the computer schedule is easily updated and the effects easily assessed.

Overview of the Resource Scheduling Problem

After staff and other resources were assigned to her project, a project manager listed the following questions that still needed to be addressed:

- Will the assigned labor and/or equipment be adequate and available to deal with my project?
- Will outside contractors have to be used?

FIGURE 8.1
Project Planning Process

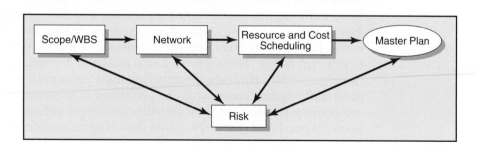

- Do unforeseen resource dependencies exist? Is there a new critical path?
- How much flexibility do we have in using resources?
- Is the original deadline realistic?

Clearly, this project manager has a good understanding of the problems she is facing. Any project scheduling system should facilitate finding quick, easy answers to these questions.

The planned network and activity project duration times found in previous chapters fail to deal with resource usage and availability. The time estimates for the work packages and network times were made independently with the implicit assumption that resources would be available. This may or may not be the case.

If resources are adequate but the demand varies widely over the life of the project, it may be desirable to even out resource demand by delaying noncritical activities (using slack) to lower peak demand and, thus, increase resource utilization. This process is called **resource smoothing.**

On the other hand, if resources are not adequate to meet peak demands, the late start of some activities must be delayed, and the duration of the project may be increased. This process is called *resource-constrained scheduling.* One research study of more than 50 projects by Woodworth and Willie found that planned project network durations were increased 38 percent when resources were scheduled.

The consequences of failing to schedule limited resources are costly and project delays usually manifest themselves midway in the project when quick corrective action is difficult. An additional consequence of failing to schedule resources is ignoring the peaks and valleys of resource usage over the duration of the project. Because project resources are usually overcommitted and because resources seldom line up by availability and need, procedures are needed to deal with these problems. This chapter addresses methods available to project managers for dealing with resource utilization and availability through resource leveling and resource-constrained scheduling.

Up to now the start and sequence of activities has been based solely on technical or logical considerations. For example, a project network for framing a house might show three activities in a sequence: (1) pour foundation, (2) build frame, and (3) cover roof. A network for a new software project could place the activities in the network, as a sequence of (1) design, (2) code, and (3) test. In other words, you cannot logically perform activity 2 until 1 is completed, and so on. The project network depicts technical constraints. (See Figure 8.2A). The network assumes the personnel and equipment are available to perform the required work. This is often not the case!

The absence or shortage of resources can drastically alter technical constraints. A project network planner may assume adequate resources and show activities occurring in parallel. However, parallel activities hold potential for resource conflicts. For example, assume you are planning a wedding reception that includes four activities—(1) plan, (2) hire band, (3) decorate hall, and (4) purchase refreshments. Each activity takes one day. Activities 2, 3, and 4 could be done in parallel by different people. There is no technical reason or dependency of one on another (see Figure 8.2B). However, if one person must perform all activities, the resource constraint requires the activities be performed in sequence or series. Clearly the consequence is a delay of these activities and a very different set of network relationships (see Figure 8.2C). Note that the resource dependency takes priority over

FIGURE 8.2
Constraint Examples

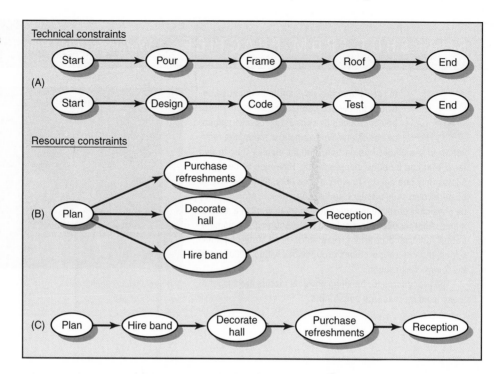

the technological dependency but *does not violate the technological dependency;*
that is, hire, decorate, and purchase may now have to take place in sequence rather
than concurrently, but they must all be completed before the reception can take
place.

The interrelationships and interactions among time and resource constraints
are complex for even small project networks. Some effort to examine these interactions before the project begins frequently uncovers surprising problems. Project
managers who do not consider resource availability in moderately complex projects usually learn of the problem when it is too late to correct. A deficit of resources can significantly alter project dependency relationships, completion
dates, and project costs. Project managers must be careful to schedule resources
to ensure availability in the right quantities and at the right time. Fortunately,
there are computer software programs that can identify resource problems during
the early project planning phase when corrective changes can be considered.
These programs only require activity resource needs and availability information
to schedule resources.

See the Snapshot from Practice: Working in Tight Places for a third constraint
that impinges on project schedules.

Types of Resource Constraints

Resources are people, equipment, and material that can be drawn on to accomplish something. In projects the availability or unavailability of resources will often influence the way projects are managed.

1. People. This is the most obvious and important project resource. Human resources are usually classified by the skills they bring to the project—for example,

SNAPSHOT FROM PRACTICE   Working in Tight Places

In rare situations, physical factors cause activities that would normally occur in parallel to be constrained by contractual or environmental conditions. For example, in theory the renovation of a sailboat compartment might involve four to five tasks that can be done independently. However, since space allows only one person to work at one time, all tasks have to be performed sequentially. Likewise, on a mining project it may be physically possible for only two miners to work in a shaft at a time. Another example would be the erection of a communication tower and nearby groundwork. For safety considerations, the contract prohibits groundwork within 2,000 feet of the tower construction.

The procedures for handling physical factors are similar to those used for resource constraints.

© Digital Vision/PunchStock

programmer, mechanical engineer, welder, inspector, marketing director, supervisor. In rare cases some skills are interchangeable, but usually with a loss of productivity. The many differing skills of human resources add to the complexity of scheduling projects.

2. Materials. Project materials cover a large spectrum: for example, chemicals for a scientific project, concrete for a road project, survey data for a marketing project.

Material availability and shortages have been blamed for the delay of many projects. When it is known that a lack of availability of materials is important and probable, materials should be included in the project network plan and schedule. For example, delivery and placement of an oil rig tower in a Siberian oil field has a very small time window during one summer month. Any delivery delay means a one-year, costly delay. Another example in which material was the major resource scheduled was the resurfacing and replacement of some structures on the Golden Gate Bridge in San Francisco. Work on the project was limited to the hours between midnight and 5:00 A.M. with a penalty of $1,000 per minute for any work taking place after 5:00 A.M. Scheduling the arrival of replacement structures was an extremely important part of managing the five-hour work-time window of the project. Scheduling materials has also become important in developing products where time-to-market can result in loss of market share.

3. Equipment. Equipment is usually presented by type, size, and quantity. In some cases equipment can be interchanged to improve schedules, but this is not typical. Equipment is often overlooked as a constraint. The most common oversight is to assume the resource pool is more than adequate for the project. For example, if a project needs one earthmoving tractor six months from now and the organization owns four, it is common to assume the resource will not delay the pending project. However, when the earthmoving tractor is due on-site in six months, all four machines in the pool might be occupied on other projects. In multiproject environments it is prudent to use a common resource pool for all projects. This approach forces a check of resource availability across all projects and reserves the equipment for specific project needs in the future. Recognition of equipment constraints before the project begins can avoid high crashing or delay costs.

Classification of a Scheduling Problem

Most of the scheduling methods available today require the project manager to classify the project as either *time constrained* or *resource constrained.* Project managers need to consult their priority matrix (see Figure 4.2) to determine which case fits their project. One simple test to determine if the project is time or resource constrained is to ask, "If the critical path is delayed, will resources be added to get back on schedule?" If the answer is yes, assume the project is time constrained; if no, assume the project is resource constrained.

A **time-constrained project** is one that must be completed by an imposed date. If required, resources can be added to ensure the project is completed by a specific date. Although time is the critical factor, resource usage should be no more than is necessary and sufficient.

A **resource-constrained project** is one that assumes the level of resources available cannot be exceeded. If the resources are inadequate, it will be acceptable to delay the project, but as little as possible.

In scheduling terms, time constrained means time (project duration) is fixed and resources are flexible, while resource constrained means resources are fixed and time is flexible. Methods for scheduling these projects are presented in the next section.

Resource Allocation Methods

Assumptions

Ease of demonstrating the allocation methods available requires some limiting assumptions to keep attention on the heart of the problem. The rest of the chapter depends entirely on the assumptions noted here. First, splitting activities will not be allowed. This means once an activity is placed in the schedule, assume it will be worked on continuously until it is finished; hence, an activity cannot be started, stopped for a period of time, and then finished. Second, the level of resources used for an activity cannot be changed. These limiting assumptions do not exist in practice, but simplify learning. It is easy for new project managers to deal with the reality of splitting activities and changing the level of resources when they meet them on the job.

Time-Constrained Projects: Smoothing Resource Demand

Scheduling time-constrained projects focuses on resource *utilization.* When demand for a specific resource type is erratic, it is difficult to manage, and utilization may be very poor. Practitioners have attacked the utilization problem using resource leveling techniques that balance demand for a resource.

Basically, all **leveling** techniques delay noncritical activities by using positive slack to reduce peak demand and fill in the valleys for the resources. An example will demonstrate the basic procedure for a time-constrained project. See Figure 8.3.

For the purpose of demonstration, the Botanical Garden project uses only one resource (backhoes); all backhoes are interchangeable. The top bar chart shows the activities on a time scale. The dependencies are shown with the vertical connecting arrows. The horizontal arrows following activities represent activity slack (for example, irrigation requires six days to complete and has six days slack). The number of backhoes needed for each task is shown in the shaded activity

FIGURE 8.3   **Botanical Garden**

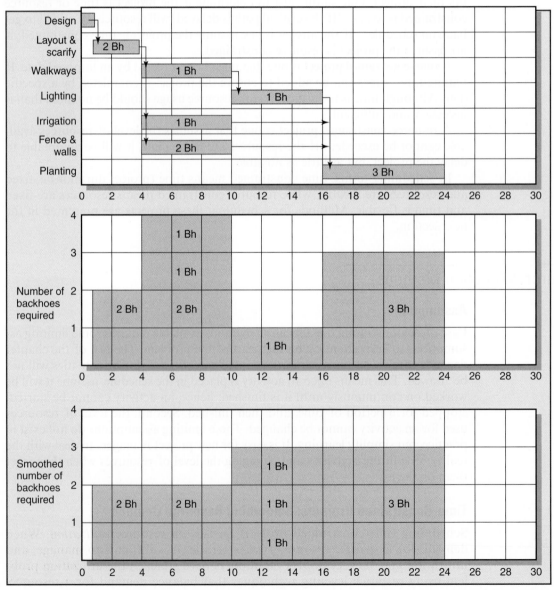

duration block (rectangle). After the land has been scarified and the plan laid out, work can begin on the walkways, irrigation, and fencing and retaining walls simultaneously. The middle chart shows the resource profile for the backhoes. For periods 4 through 10, four backhoes are needed.

Because this project is declared time constrained, the goal will be to reduce the peak requirement for the resource and thereby increase the utilization of the resource. A quick examination of the ES (early start) resource load chart suggests only two activities have slack that can be used to reduce the peak—fence and walls provide the best choice for smoothing the resource needs. Another choice could be irrigation, but it would result in an up and down resource profile. The choice will probably center on the activity that is perceived as having the least risk of being late. The smoothed resource loading chart shows the results of delaying the fence and walls activity. Note the differences in the resource profiles. The important point is the resources needed over the life of the project have been reduced from four to three (25 percent). In addition the profile has been smoothed, which should be easier to manage.

The Botanical Garden project schedule reached the three goals of smoothing:

- The peak of demand for the resource was reduced.
- Resources over the life of the project have been reduced.
- The fluctuations in resource demand were minimized.

The latter improves the utilization of resources. Backhoes are not easily moved from location to location. There are costs associated with changing the level of resources needed. The same analogy applies to the movement of people back and forth among projects. It is well known that people are more efficient if they can focus their effort on one project rather than multitasking their time among, say, three projects.

The downside of leveling is a loss of flexibility that occurs from reducing slack. The risk of activities delaying the project also increases because slack reduction can create more critical activities and/or near-critical activities. Pushing leveling too far for a perfectly level resource profile is risky. Every activity then becomes critical.

The Botanical Garden example gives a sense of the time-constrained problem and the smoothing approach. However, in practice the magnitude of the problem is very complex for even small projects. Manual solutions are not practical. Fortunately, the software packages available today have very good routines for leveling project resources. Typically, they use activities that have the most slack to level project resources. The rationale is those activities with the most slack pose the least risk. Although this is generally true, other risk factors such as reduction of flexibility to use reassigned resources on other activities or the nature of the activity (easy, complex) are not addressed using such a simple rationale. It is easy to experiment with many alternatives to find the one that best fits your project and minimizes risk of delaying the project.

Resource-Constrained Projects

When the number of people and/or equipment is not adequate to meet peak demand requirements and it is impossible to obtain more, the project manager faces a resource-constrained problem. Something has to give. The trick is to prioritize and allocate resources to minimize project delay without exceeding the resource limit or altering the technical network relationships.

The resource scheduling problem is a large combinatorial one. This means even a modest-size project network with only a few resource types might have several thousand feasible solutions. A few researchers have demonstrated *optimum* mathematical solutions to the resource allocation problem but only for small networks and very few resource types. The massive data requirements for larger problems make pure mathematical solutions (e.g., linear programming) impractical. An alternative approach to the problem has been the use of **heuristics** (rules of thumb) to solve large combinatorial problems. These practical decision or priority rules have been in place for many years.

Heuristics do not always yield an optimal schedule, but they are very capable of yielding a "good" schedule for very complex networks with many types of resources. The efficiency of different rules and combinations of rules has been well documented. However, because each project is unique, it is wise to test several sets of heuristics on a network to determine the priority allocation rules that minimize project delay. The computer software available today makes it very easy for the project manager to create a good resource schedule for the project. A simple example of the heuristic approach is illustrated here.

Heuristics allocate resources to activities to minimize project delay; that is, heuristics prioritize which activities are allocated resources and which activities are delayed when resources are not adequate.

The parallel method is the most widely used approach to apply heuristics, which have been found to consistently minimize project delay over a large variety of projects. The parallel method is an iterative process that starts from the beginning of project time and, when resources needed exceed the resources available, retains activities first by the priority rules:

1. Minimum slack.
2. Smallest duration.
3. Lowest activity identification number.

Those not able to be scheduled without delaying others are pushed out farther in time. However, do not attempt to move activities that have already started. When considering activities not to delay, consider the resources each activity uses. In any period when two or more activities require the same resource, the priority rules are applied. For example, if in period 5 three activities are eligible to start (i.e., have the same ES) and require the same resource, the first activity placed in the schedule would be the activity with the least slack (rule 1). However, if all activities have the same slack, the next rule would be invoked (rule 2), and the activity with the smallest duration would be placed in the schedule first. In very rare cases, when all eligible activities have the same slack and the same duration, the tie is broken by the lowest activity identification number (rule 3), since each activity has a unique ID number.

When a resource limit has been reached, the early start (ES) for succeeding activities not yet in the schedule will be delayed (and all successor activities not having free slack) and their slack reduced. In subsequent periods the procedure is repeated until the project is scheduled. The procedure is demonstrated next; see Figure 8.4. The shaded areas in the resource loading chart represent the "scheduling interval" of the *time-constrained* schedule (ES through LF). You can schedule the resource any place *within* the interval and not delay the project. Scheduling the activity beyond the LF will delay the project.

The Parallel Method:

Period	Action

——————————— See Figure 8.4 ———————————

Period	Action
0–1	Only activity 1 is eligible. It requires 2 programmers. Load activity 1 into schedule.
1–2	No activities are eligible to be scheduled.
2–3	Activities 2, 3, and 4 are eligible to be scheduled. Activity 3 has the least slack (0)—apply rule 1. Load Activity 3 into schedule. Activity 2 is next with slack of 2; however, activity 2 requires 2 programmers and only 1 is available. Delay activity 2. Update: ES = 3, slack = 1. The next eligible activity is activity 4, since it only requires 1 programmer. Load activity 4 into schedule.

——————————— See Figure 8.5 ———————————

Period	Action
3–4	Activity 2 is eligible but exceeds limit of 3 programmers in pool. Delay activity 2. Update: ES = 4, slack = 0.
4–5	Activity 2 is eligible but exceeds limit of 3 programmers in pool. Delay activity 2. Update: ES = 5, LF = 11, slack = −1. Delay activity 7. Update: ES = 11, LF = 13, slack = −1.
5–6	Activity 2 is eligible but exceeds limit of 3 programmers in pool. Delay activity 2. Update: ES = 6, LF = 12, slack = −2. Delay activity 7. Update: ES = 12, LF = 14, slack = −2.
6–7	Activities 2, 5, and 6 are eligible with slack of −2, 2, and 0, respectively. Load activity 2 into schedule (rule 1). Because activity 6 has 0 slack, it is the next eligible activity. Load activity 6 into schedule (rule 1). The programmer limit of 3 is reached. Delay activity 5. Update: ES = 7, slack = 1.
7–8	Limit is reached. No programmers available. Delay activity 5. Update: ES = 8, slack = 0.
8–9	Limit is reached. No programmers available. Delay activity 5. Update: ES = 9, LF = 11, slack = −1.
9–10	Limit is reached. No programmers available. Delay activity 5. Update: ES = 10, LF = 12, slack = −2.
10–11	Activity 5 is eligible. Load activity 5 into schedule. (Note: Activity 6 does not have slack because there are no programmers available—3 maximum.)
11–12	No eligible activities.
12–13	Activity 7 is eligible. Load activity 7 into schedule.

The programmers are limited to three. Follow the actions described in Figures 8.4 and 8.5. Note how the limit of three programmers starts to delay the project.

Observe how it is necessary to update each period to reflect changes in activity early start and slack times so the heuristics can reflect changing priorities. When using the parallel scheduling method, the network in Figure 8.5 on page 263 reflects the new schedule date of 14 time units, rather than the time-constrained

FIGURE 8.4   **Resource-Constrained Schedule through Period 2–3**

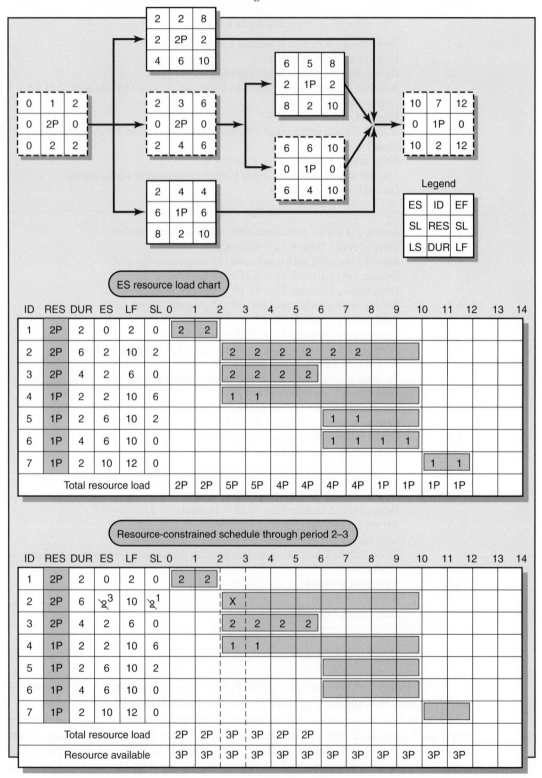

FIGURE 8.5   **Resource-Constrained Schedule through Period 5–6**

FIGURE 8.7 EMR Project before Resources Added

ID	Task Name	Start	Finish	Late Start	Late Finish	Free Slack	Total Slack
1	**EMR project**	**Tue 1/1**	**Thu 2/14**	**Tue 1/1**	**Thu 2/14**	**0 days**	**0 days**
2	Architectural decisions	Tue 1/1	Sat 1/5	Tue 1/1	Sat 1/5	0 days	0 days
3	Internal specs	Sun 1/6	Thu 1/17	Sat 1/19	Wed 1/30	0 days	13 days
4	External specs	Sun 1/6	Sat 1/12	Thu 1/24	Wed 1/30	5 days	18 days
5	Feature specs	Sun 1/6	Tue 1/15	Sun 1/6	Tue 1/15	0 days	0 days
6	Voice recognition SW	Fri 1/18	Sun 1/27	Thu 1/31	Sat 2/9	13 days	13 days
7	Case	Fri 1/18	Mon 1/21	Wed 2/6	Sat 2/9	19 days	19 days
8	Screen	Fri 1/18	Sat 1/19	Fri 2/8	Sat 2/9	21 days	21 days
9	Database	Wed 1/16	Sat 2/9	Wed 1/16	Sat 2/9	0 days	0 days
10	Microphone-soundcard	Wed 1/16	Sun 1/20	Tue 2/5	Sat 2/9	20 days	20 days
11	Digital devices	Wed 1/16	Tue 1/22	Sun 2/3	Sat 2/9	18 days	18 days
12	Computer I/O	Wed 1/16	Sun 1/20	Tue 2/5	Sat 2/9	20 days	20 days
13	Review design	Sun 2/10	Thu 2/14	Sun 2/10	Thu 2/14	0 days	0 days

FIGURE 8.8A   **EMR Project—Time-Constrained Resource Usage View, January 15–23**

Resource Name	Work	Jan 15						Jan 21		
		T	W	T	F	S	S	M	T	W
Design engineers	**3,024 hrs**	72h	136h	136h	168h	168h	144h	104h	88h	64h
Architectural decisions	200 hrs									
Internal specs	480 hrs	40h	40h	40h						
External specs	224 hrs									
Feature specs	320 hrs	32h								
Voice recognition SW	320 hrs				32h	32h	32h	32h	32h	32h
Case	64 hrs				16h	16h	16h	16h		
Screen	48 hrs				24h	24h				
Database	800 hrs		32h	32h	32h	32h	32h	32h	32h	32h
Microphone-soundcard	80 hrs		16h	16h	16h	16h	16h			
Digital devices	168 hrs		24h	24h	24h	24h	24h	24h	24h	
Computer I/O	120 hrs		24h	24h	24h	24h	24h			
Review design	200 hrs									

FIGURE 8.8B
**Resource Loading
Chart for
EMR Project,
January 15–23**

Peak Units	900%	1,700%	1,700%	2,100%	2,100%	1,800%	1,300%	1,100%	800%

Design Engineers   Overallocated: ▭   Allocated: ▭

loading chart for design engineers. Notice that the peak is 21 engineers and the limit of 8 engineers is shown by the gray shaded area.

To resolve this problem we use the "leveling" tool within the software and first try to solve the problem by leveling only within slack. This solution would preserve the original finish date. However, as expected, this does not solve all of the allocation problems. The next option is to allow the software to apply scheduling heuristics and level outside of slack. The new schedule is contained in the revised, resource-limited network chart presented in Figure 8.9. The resource-limited project network indicates the project duration has now been extended to 2/26, or 57 workdays (versus 45 days time limited). The critical path is now 2, 3, 9, 13.

Figure 8.10 presents the project bar chart and the results of leveling the project schedule to reflect the availability of only eight design engineers. The application of the heuristics can be seen in the scheduling of the internal, external, and feature

FIGURE 8.9 EMR Project Network View Schedule after Resources Leveled

EMR project
Start: 1/1   ID: 1
Finish: 2/26   Dur: 57 days
Comp: 0%

Architectural decisions
Start: 1/1   ID: 2
Finish: 1/5   Dur: 5 days
Res: Design Engineers [500%]

Internal specs
Start: 1/16   ID: 3
Finish: 1/27   Dur: 12 days
Res: Design Engineers [500%]

External specs
Start: 1/6   ID: 4
Finish: 1/12   Dur: 7 days
Res: Design Engineers [400%]

Feature specs
Start: 1/6   ID: 5
Finish: 1/15   Dur: 10 days
Res: Design Engineers [400%]

Voice recognition SW
Start: 2/2   ID: 6
Finish: 2/11   Dur: 10 days
Res: Design Engineers [400%]

Case
Start: 2/12   ID: 7
Finish: 2/15   Dur: 4 days
Res: Design Engineers [200%]

Screen
Start: 2/16   ID: 8
Finish: 2/17   Dur: 2 days
Res: Design Engineers [300%]

Database
Start: 1/28   ID: 9
Finish: 2/21   Dur: 25 days
Res: Design Engineers [400%]

Microphone-soundcard
Start: 1/16   ID: 10
Finish: 1/20   Dur: 5 days
Res: Design Engineers [200%]

Digital devices
Start: 1/26   ID: 11
Finish: 2/1   Dur: 7 days
Res: Design Engineers [300%]

Computer I/O
Start: 1/21   ID: 12
Finish: 1/25   Dur: 5 days
Res: Design Engineers [300%]

Review design
Start: 2/22   ID: 13
Finish: 2/26   Dur: 5 days
Res: Design Engineers [500%]

FIGURE 8.10 EMR Project Resources Leveled

ID	Task Name	Start	Finish	Late Start	Late Finish	Free Slack	Total Slack
1	**EMR project**	**Tue 1/1**	**Thu 2/26**	**Tue 1/1**	**Tue 2/26**	**0 days**	**0 days**
2	Architectural decisions	Tue 1/1	Sat 1/5	Tue 1/1	Sat 1/5	0 days	0 days
3	Internal specs	Wed 1/16	Sun 1/27	Sun 1/20	Thu 1/31	0 days	4 days
4	External specs	Sun 1/6	Sat 1/12	Fri 1/25	Thu 1/31	15 days	19 days
5	Feature specs	Sun 1/6	Tue 1/15	Sun 1/6	Tue 1/15	0 days	0 days
6	Voice recognition SW	Sat 2/2	Mon 2/11	Tue 2/12	Thu 2/21	10 days	10 days
7	Case	Tue 2/12	Fri 2/15	Mon 2/18	Thu 2/21	6 days	6 days
8	Screen	Sat 2/16	Sun 2/17	Wed 2/20	Thu 2/21	4 days	4 days
9	Database	Mon 1/28	Thu 2/21	Mon 1/28	Thu 2/21	0 days	0 days
10	Microphone-soundcard	Wed 1/16	Sun 1/20	Sun 2/17	Thu 2/21	32 days	32 days
11	Digital devices	Sat 1/26	Fri 2/1	Fri 2/15	Thu 2/21	20 days	20 days
12	Computer I/O	Mon 1/21	Fri 1/25	Sun 2/17	Thu 2/21	27 days	27 days
13	Review design	Fri 2/22	Tue 2/26	Fri 2/22	Tue 2/26	0 days	0 days

Legend:
Task
Critical task
Slack
Summary

269

specification activities. All three activities were originally scheduled to start imme-diately after activity 1, architectural decisions.

This is impossible, since the three activities collectively require 14 engineers. The software chooses to schedule activity 5 first because this activity is on the original critical path and has zero slack (heuristic rule # 1). Next, and concur-rently, activity 4 is chosen over activity 3 because activity 4 has a shorter dura-tion (heuristic rule # 2); internal specs, activity 3, is delayed due to the limitation of 8 design engineers. Notice that the original critical path no longer applies because of the resource dependencies created by having only eight design engineers. See Figure 8.9 for the original planned critical path.

Compare the bar chart in Figure 8.10 with the time-limited bar chart in Fig-ure 8.7. For example, note the different start dates for activity 8 (screen). In the time-limited plan (Figure 8.7), the start date for activity 8 is 1/18, while the start date in the resource limited schedule (Figure 8.10) is 2/16, almost a month later!

While resource bar graphs are commonly used to illustrate overallocation prob-lems, we prefer to view resource usage tables like the one presented in Figure 8.8A. This table tells you when you have an overallocation problem and identifies activi-ties that are causing the overallocation.

The Impacts of Resource-Constrained Scheduling

Like leveling schedules, the limited resource schedule usually reduces slack, re-duces flexibility by using slack to ensure delay is minimized, and increases the number of critical and near-critical activities. Scheduling complexity is increased because resource constraints are added to technical constraints; start times may now have two constraints. The traditional critical path concept of sequential ac-tivities from the start to the end of the project is no longer meaningful. The re-source constraints can break the sequence and leave the network with a set of disjointed critical activities. Conversely, parallel activities can become sequential. Activities with slack on a time-constrained network can change from critical to noncritical.

Splitting Activities

Splitting tasks is a scheduling technique used to get a better project schedule and/or to increase resource utilization. A planner splits the continuous work included in an activity by interrupting the work and sending the resource to another activity for a period of time and then having the resource resume work on the original activity. Splitting can be a useful tool if the work involved does not include large start-up or shutdown costs—for example, moving equipment from one activity location to an-other. The most common error is to interrupt "people work," where there are high conceptual start-up and shutdown costs. For example, having a bridge designer take time off to work on the design problem of another project may cause this individual to lose four days shifting conceptual gears in and out of two activities. The cost may be hidden, but it is real. Figure 8.11 depicts the nature of the splitting problem. The original activity has been split into three separate activities: A, B, and C. The shut-down and start-up times lengthen the time for the original activity.

Some have argued that the propensity to deal with resource shortages by splitting is a major reason why projects fail to meet schedule. We agree.

SNAPSHOT FROM PRACTICE   Assessing Resource Allocation

One of the strengths of today's project management software is the ability to identify and provide options for resolving resource allocation problems. A project manager who uses MS Project to plan projects shared with us the following checklist for dealing with resource conflicts after preliminary assignment of resources has been made.

1. Assess whether you have overallocation problems (see *Red* in the resource sheet view.)

2. Identify where and when conflicts occur by examining the resource usage view.

3. Resolve the problem by

   a. Replacing overallocated resources with appropriate resources that are available. Then ask if this solves the problem.

   If not:

   b. Use the leveling tool and choose the level within slack option.

   i Does this solve the problem? (Are resources still overallocated?)

   ii Check the sensitivity of the network and ask if this is acceptable.

   If not:

   c. Consider splitting tasks.

   i Make sure to readjust task durations to take into account additional start-up and shutdown time.

4. If 3 does not work then either:

   a. Use level tool default option and ask if you can live with the new completion date.

   If not:

   b. Negotiate for additional resources to complete the project. If not possible

   c. Consider reducing project scope to meet deadline.

While this checklist makes specific references to MS Project, the same steps can be used with most project management software.

Planners should avoid the use of splitting as much as possible, except in situations where splitting costs are known to be small or when there is no alternative for resolving the resource problem. Computer software offers the splitting option for each activity; use it sparingly. See Snapshot from Practice: Assessing Resource Allocation.

FIGURE 8.11
Splitting Activities

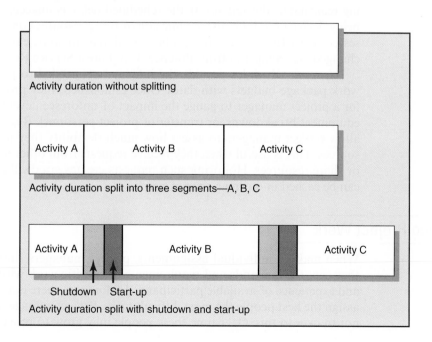

SNAPSHOT FROM PRACTICE U.S. Forest Service Resource Shortage

A major segment of work in managing U.S. Forest Service (USFS) forests is selling mature timber to logging companies that harvest the timber under contract conditions monitored by the Service. The proceeds are returned to the federal government. The budget allocated to each forest depends on the two-year plan submitted to the U.S. Department of Agriculture.

Olympic Forest headquarters in Olympia, Washington, was developing a two-year plan as a basis for funding. All of the districts in the forest submitted their timber sale projects (numbering more than 50) to headquarters, where they were compiled and aggregated into a project plan for the whole forest. The first computer run was reviewed by a small group of senior managers to determine if the plan was reasonable and "doable." Management was pleased and relieved to note all projects appeared to be doable in the two-year time frame until a question was raised concerning the computer printout. "Why

are all the columns in these projects labeled 'RESOURCE' blank?" The response from an engineer was, "We don't use that part of the program."

The discussion that ensued recognized the importance of resources in completing the two-year plan and ended with a request to "try the program with resources included." The new output was startling. The two-year program turned into a three-and-a-half-year plan because of the shortage of specific labor skills such as road engineer and environmental impact specialist. Analysis showed that adding only three skilled people would allow the two-year plan to be completed on time. In addition, further analysis showed hiring only a few more skilled people, beyond the three, would allow an extra year of projects to also be compressed into the two-year plan. This would result in additional revenue of more than $3 million. The Department of Agriculture quickly approved the requested extra dollars for additional staff to generate the extra revenue.

Benefits of Scheduling Resources

It is important to remember that, if resources are truly limited and activity time estimates are accurate, the resource-constrained schedule *will* materialize as the project is implemented—*not* the time-constrained schedule! Therefore, failure to schedule limited resources can lead to serious problems for a project manager. The benefit of creating this schedule *before* the project begins leaves time for considering reasonable alternatives. If the scheduled delay is unacceptable or the risk of being delayed too high, the assumption of being resource constrained can be reassessed. Cost-time trade-offs can be considered. In some cases priorities may be changed. See Snapshot from Practice: U.S. Forest Service Resource Shortage.

Resource schedules provide the information needed to prepare time-phased work package budgets with dates. Once established, they provide a quick means for a project manager to gauge the impact of unforeseen events such as turnover, equipment breakdowns, or transfer of project personnel. Resource schedules also allow project managers to assess how much flexibility they have over certain resources. This is useful when they receive requests from other managers to borrow or share resources. Honoring such requests creates goodwill and an "IOU" that can be cashed in during a time of need.

Assigning Project Work

When making individual assignments, project managers should match, as best they can, the demands and requirements of specific work with the qualifications and experience of available participants. In doing so, there is a natural tendency to assign the best people the most difficult tasks. Project managers need to be careful not to overdo this. Over time these people may grow to resent the fact that they

Eric Schmidt, after a successful career at Sun Microsystems, took over struggling Novell, Inc., and helped turn it around within two years. One of the keys to his success is his ability to manage the technical wizards who develop the sophisticated systems, hardware, and software that are the backbone of electronically driven companies. He uses the term "geek" (and he can, since he is one, with a Ph.D. in computer science) to describe this group of technologists who rule the cyberworld.

Schmidt has some interesting ideas about assigning geeks to projects. He believes that putting geeks together in project teams with other geeks creates productive peer pressure. Geeks care a great deal about how other geeks perceive them. They are good at judging the quality of technical work and are quick to praise as well as criticize each other's work. Some geeks can be unbearably arrogant, but Schmidt claims that having them work together on projects is the best way to control them—by letting them control each other.

At the same time, Schmidt argues that too many geeks spoil the soup. By this he means that, when there are too many geeks on a development team, there is a tendency for intense technical navel gazing. Members lose sight of deadlines, and delays are inevitable. To combat this tendency, he recommends using geeks only in small groups. He urges breaking up large projects into smaller, more manageable projects so that small teams of geeks can be assigned to them. This keeps the project on time and makes the teams responsible to each other.

* Mitchel Russ, "How to Manage Geeks," *Fast Company* (June 1999), pp. 175–80.

are always given the toughest assignments. At the same time, less experienced participants may resent the fact that they are never given the opportunity to expand their skill/knowledge base. Project managers need to balance task performance with the need to develop the talents of people assigned to the project.

Project managers not only need to decide who does what but who works with whom. A number of factors need to be considered in deciding who should work together. First, to minimize unnecessary tension, managers should pick people with compatible work habits and personalities but who complement each other (i.e., one person's weakness is the other person's strength). For example, one person may be brilliant at solving complex problems but sloppy at documenting his or her progress. It would be wise to pair this person with an individual who is good at paying attention to details. Experience is another factor. Veterans should be teamed up with new hires—not only so they can share their experience but also to help socialize the newcomers to the customs and norms of the organization. Finally, future needs should be considered. If managers have some people who have never worked together before but who have to later on in the project, they may be wise to take advantage of opportunities to have these people work together early on so that they can become familiar with each other. Finally, see the Snapshot in Practice: Managing Geeks for some interesting thoughts about how Novell, Inc., puts together teams.

Multiproject Resource Schedules

For clarity we have discussed key resource allocation issues within the context of a single project. In reality resource allocation generally occurs in a multiproject environment where the demands of one project have to be reconciled with the needs of other projects. Organizations must develop and manage systems for efficiently allocating and scheduling resources across several projects with different priorities, resource requirements, sets of activities, and risks. The system must be dynamic and capable of accommodating new projects as well as reallocating resources once project work is completed. While the same resource issues and principles that apply to a single project also apply to this multiproject environment, application and solutions are more complex, given the interdependency among projects.

The following lists three of the more common problems encountered in managing multiproject resource schedules. Note that these are macro manifestations of single-project problems that are now magnified in a multiproject environment:

1. **Overall schedule slippage.** Because projects often share resources, delays in one project can have a ripple effect and delay other projects. For example, work on one software development project can grind to a halt because the coders scheduled for the next critical task are late in completing their work on another development project.

2. **Inefficient resource utilization.** Because projects have different schedules and requirements, there are peaks and valleys in overall resource demands. For example, a firm may have a staff of 10 electricians to meet peak demands when, under normal conditions, only 5 electricians are required.

3. **Resource bottlenecks.** Delays and schedules are extended as a result of shortages of critical resources that are required by multiple projects. For example, at one Lattice Semiconductor facility, project schedules were delayed because of competition over access to test equipment necessary to debug programs. Likewise, several projects at a U.S. forest area were extended because there was only one silviculturist on the staff.

To deal with these problems, more and more companies create project offices or departments to oversee the scheduling of resources across multiple projects. One approach to multiple project resource scheduling is to use a first come–first served rule. A project queue system is created in which projects currently underway take precedence over new projects. New project schedules are based on the projected availability of resources. This queuing tends to lead to more reliable completion estimates and is preferred on contracted projects that have stiff penalties for being late. The disadvantages of this deceptively simple approach are that it does not optimally utilize resources or take into account the priority of the project. See the Snapshot from Practice: Multiple Project Resource Scheduling.

Many companies utilize more elaborate processes for scheduling resources to increase the capacity of the organization to initiate projects. Most of these methods approach the problem by treating individual projects as part of one big project and adapting the scheduling heuristics previously introduced to this "megaproject." Project schedulers monitor resource usage and provide updated schedules based on progress and resource availability across all projects. One major improvement in project management software in recent years is the ability to prioritize resource allocation to specific projects. Projects can be prioritized in ascending order (e.g., 1, 2, 3, 4, . . .), and these priorities will override scheduling heuristics so that resources go to the project highest on the priority list. (Note: This improvement fits perfectly with organizations that use project priority models similar to those described in Chapter 2.) Centralized project scheduling also makes it easier to identify resource bottlenecks that stifle progress on projects. Once identified, the impact of the bottlenecks can be documented and used to justify acquiring additional equipment, recruiting critical personnel, or delaying the project.

Finally, many companies are using outsourcing as a means for dealing with their resource allocation problems. In some cases, a company will reduce the number of projects they have to manage internally to only core projects and outsource

SNAPSHOT FROM PRACTICE Multiple Project Resource Scheduling

The case for a central source to oversee project resource scheduling is well known by practitioners. Here is a synopsis of a conversation with one middle manager.

Interviewer: Congratulations on acceptance of your multi-project scheduling proposal. Everyone tells me you were very convincing.

Middle Manager: Thanks. Gaining acceptance was easy this time. The board quickly recognized we have no choice if we are to keep ahead of competition by placing our resources on the right projects.

Interviewer: Have you presented this to the board before?

Middle Manager: Yes, but not this company. I presented the same spiel to the firm I worked for two years ago. For their annual review meeting I was charged to present a proposal suggesting the need and benefits of central capacity resource planning for managing the projects of the firm.

I tried to build a case for bringing projects under one umbrella to standardize practices and to forecast and assign key people to mission critical projects. I explained how benefits such as resource demands will be aligned with mission critical projects, proactive resource planning, and a tool for catching resource bottlenecks and resolving conflicts.

Almost everyone agreed the idea was a good one. I felt good about the presentation and felt confident something was going to happen. But the idea never really got off the ground; it just faded into the sunset.

With hindsight, managers really did not trust colleagues in other departments, so they only gave half-hearted support to central resource planning. Managers wanted to protect their turf and ensure that they would not have to give up power. The culture there was simply too inflexible for the world we live in today. They are still struggling with constant conflicts among projects.

I'm glad I made the switch to this firm. The culture here is much more team-oriented. Management is committed to improving performance.

noncritical projects to contractors and consulting firms. In other cases, specific segments of projects are outsourced to overcome resource deficiencies and scheduling problems. Companies may hire temporary workers to expedite certain activities that are falling behind schedule or contract project work during peak periods when there are insufficient internal resources to meet the demands of all projects. The ability to more efficiently manage the ebbs and flows of project work is one of the major driving forces behind outsourcing today.

Using the Resource Schedule to Develop a Project Cost Baseline

Once resource assignments have been finalized we are able to develop a baseline budget schedule for the project. Using your project schedule, you can *time-phase* work packages and assign them to their respective scheduled activities to develop a budget schedule over the life of your project. Understanding the reason for time-phasing your budget is very important. Without a time-phased budget good project schedule and cost control are impossible.

Why a Time-Phased Budget Baseline Is Needed

The need for a time-phased budget baseline is demonstrated in the following scenario. The development of a new product is to be completed in 10 weeks at an estimated cost of $400,000 per week for a total cost of $4 million. Management wants a status report at the end of five weeks. The following information has been collected:

- Planned costs for the first five weeks are $2,000,000.
- Actual costs for the first five weeks are $2,400,000.

How are we doing? It would be easy to draw the conclusion there is a $400,000 cost overrun. But we really have no way of knowing. The $400,000 may represent money spent to move the project ahead of schedule. Assume another set of data at the end of five weeks:

- Planned costs for the first five weeks are $2,000,000.
- Actual costs for the first five weeks are $1,700,000.

Is the project costing $300,000 less than we expected? Perhaps. But the $300,000 may represent the fact that the project is behind schedule and work has not started. Could it be the project is behind schedule and over cost? We cannot tell from these data. The many systems found in the real world that use only planned funds (a constant burn rate) and actual costs can provide false and misleading information. There is no way to be certain how much of the physical work has been accomplished. *These systems do not measure how much work was accomplished for the money spent! Hence, without time-phasing cost to match your project schedule, it is impossible to have reliable information for control purposes.*

Creating a Time-Phased Budget

By using information from your WBS and resource schedule, you can create a time-phased cost baseline. Remember from the WBS for the PC Project in Chapters 4 and 5 we integrated the WBS and OBS organization breakdown structure so the work packages could be tracked by deliverable and organization responsible. See Figure 8.12 for an example of the PC Prototype Project arranged by deliverable and organization unit responsible. For each intersection point of the WBS/OBS matrix, you see work package budgets and the total cost. The total cost at each intersection is called a cost or control account. For example, at the intersection of the Read/write head deliverable and the Production department we see there are three work packages with a total budget of $200,000. The sum of all cost accounts in a column should represent the total costs for the deliverable. Conversely, the sum of the cost accounts in a row should represent the costs or budget for the organizational unit responsible to accomplish the work. You can continue to "roll up" costs on the WBS/OBS to total project costs. This WBS provides the information you can use to time phase work packages and assign them to their respective scheduled activities over the life of the project.

Recall, from the development of your work breakdown structure for each work package, the following information needed to be developed:

1. Define work (what).
2. Identify time to complete a work package (how long).
3. Identify a time-phased budget to complete a work package (cost).
4. Identify resources needed to complete a work package (how much).
5. Identify a single person responsible for units of work (who).
6. Identify monitoring points for measuring progress (how well).

Number three, time-phasing the work package, is critical for the final step of creating your budget baseline. The process of time-phasing work packages, which is illustrated next, is demonstated in Figure 8.13. The work package has a duration of three weeks. Assuming labor, materials, and equipment are tracked separately, the work package costs for labor are distributed over the three weeks as they are expected to occur—$40,000, $30,000, and $50,000 for each week, respectively. When

FIGURE 8.12   **Direct Labor Budget Rollup ($000)**

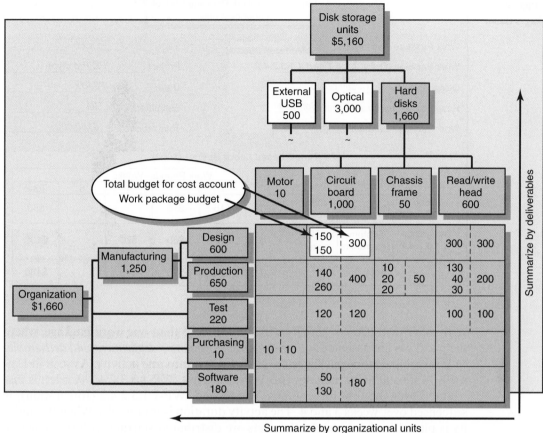

the three-week work package is placed in the network schedule, the costs are distributed to the time-phased budget for the same three scheduled weeks. Fortunately, most single WPs become an activity and the process of distributing costs is relatively simple. That is, the relationship is one-for-one. Such budget timing is directly from the work package to the activity.

FIGURE 8.13
Time-Phased Work
Package Budget
(labor cost only)

Time-Phased Work Package Budget
Labor cost only

Work Package Description ___Test___   Page ___1___ of ___1___

Work Package ID ___1.1.3.2.3___   Project ___PC Prototype___

Deliverable ___Circuit board___   Date ___3/24/xx___

Responsible organization unit ___Test___   Estimator ___CEG___

Work Package Duration ___3___ weeks   Total labor cost ___$120,000___

Time-Phased Labor Budget ($000)

Work Package	Resource	Labor rate	Work Periods--Weeks					Total
			1	2	3	4	5	
Code 1.1.3.2.3	Quality testers	$xxxx/ week	$40	$30	$50			$120

FIGURE 8.14
Two Time-Phased Work Packages (labor cost only)

Time-Phased Work Package Budget
Labor cost only

Work Package Description ___Software___   Page ___1___ of ___1___

Work Package ID *1.1.3.2.4.1 and 1.1.3.2.4.2*   Project ___PC Prototype___

Deliverable ___Circuit board___   Date ___3/24/xx___

Responsible organization unit ___Software___   Estimator ___LGG___

Work Package Duration ___4___ weeks   Total labor cost ___$180,000___

Time-Phased Labor Budget ($000)

Work Package	Resource	Labor rate	Work Periods--Weeks					
			1	2	3	4	5	Total
Code *1.1.3.2.4.1*	Program'rs	$2,000/ week	$20	$15	$15			$50
Integration *1.1.3.2.4.2*	System/ program'rs	$2,500/ week			$60	$70		$130
Total			$20	$15	$75	$70		$180

In a few instances an activity will include more than one work package, where the packages are assigned to *one responsible person or department and deliverable*. In this case the work packages are consolidated into one activity. As seen in Figure 8.14, this activity includes two WPs. The first, WP-1.1.3.2.4.1 (Code), is distributed over the first three weeks. The second, WP-1.1.3.2.4.2 (Integration), is sequenced over weeks 3 and 4. The actvity duration is four weeks. When the activity is placed in the schedule, the costs are distributed starting with the schedule start—$20,000, $15,000, $75,000, and $70,000, respectively.

These time-phased budgets for work packages are lifted from your WBS and are placed in your project schedule as they are expected to occur over the life of the project. The outcome of these budget allocations is the project *cost* baseline (also called **planned value**—PV), which is used to determine cost and schedule variances as the project is implemented.

Figure 8.15 shows the Patient Entry Project network schedule, which is used to place the time-phased work packages' budgets in the baseline. Figure 8.16 presents the project time-phased budget for the Patient Entry Project and the cumulative graph of the project budget baseline. In this figure you can see how the time-phased work package costs were placed into the network and how the cumulative project budget graph for a project is developed. Notice that costs do not have to be distributed linearly, but the costs should be placed as you expect them to occur.

You have now developed complete time and cost plans for your project. These project baselines will be used to compare planned schedule and costs using an integrative system called *earned value*. The application and use of project baselines to measure performance are discussed in detail in Chapter 13. With your project budget baseline established, you are also able to generate cash flow statements for your project like the one presented in Figure 8.17. Such statements prepare the firm to cover costs over the lifespan of the project. Finally, with resource assignments finalized you are able to generate resource usage schedules for your project (see Figure 8.18). These schedules map out the full deployment of personnel and equipment and can be used to generate individual work schedules.

FIGURE 8.15   Patient Entry Project Network

FIGURE 8.16
Patient Entry Time-Phased Work Packages Assigned

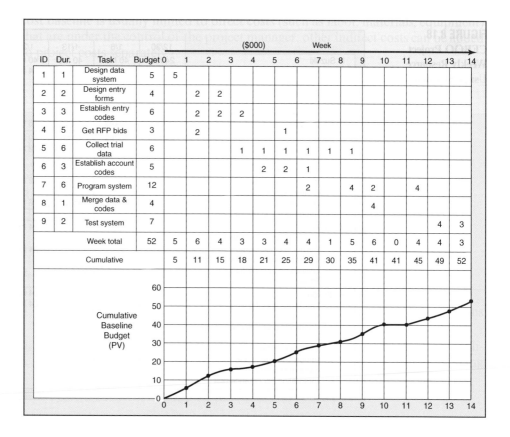

Exercises

1. Given the network plan that follows, compute the early, late, and slack times. What is the project duration? Using any approach you wish (e.g., trial and error), develop a loading chart for resources, Electrical Engineers (EE), and resource, Mechanical Engineers (ME). Assume only one of each resource exists. Given your resource schedule, compute the early, late, and slack times for your project. Which activities are now critical? What is the project duration now? Could something like this happen in real projects?

2. Given the network plan that follows, compute the early, late, and slack times. What is the project duration? Using any approach you wish (e.g., trial and error), develop a loading chart for resources Carpenters (C) and Electricians (E). Assume only one Carpenter is available and two Electricians are available.

Given your resource schedule, compute the early, late, and slack times for your project. Which activities are now critical? What is the project duration now?

3. Compute the early, late, and slack times for the activities in the network that follows, assuming a time-constrained network. Which activities are critical? What is the time-constrained project duration?

Note: Recall, in the schedule resource load chart the *time-constrained* scheduling interval (ES through LF) has been shaded. Any resource scheduled beyond the shaded area will delay the project.

Assume you have only three resources and you are using a computer that uses software that schedules projects by the parallel method and following heuristics. Schedule only one period at a time!

Minimum slack

Smallest duration

Lowest identification number

Keep a log of each activity change and update you make each period—e.g., period 0–1, 1–2, 2–3, etc. (Use a format similar to the one on page 261.) The log should include any changes or updates in ES and slack times each period, activities scheduled, and activities delayed. (Hint: Remember to maintain the technical dependencies of the network.) Use the resource load chart to assist you in scheduling (see pages 262–263—Figures 8.4 and 8.5).

List the order in which you scheduled the activities of the project. Which activities of your schedule are now critical?

Recompute your slack for each activity given your new schedule. What is the slack for activity 1? 4? 5?

4.*You have prepared the following schedule for a project in which the key resources is a tractor. There are three tractors available to the project. Activities A and D require one tractor to complete while activities B, C, E and F require 2 tractors.

   Develop a resource-constrained schedule in the loading chart that follows. Use the parallel method and heuristics given. Be sure to update each period as the computer would do. Record the early start (ES), late finish (LF) and slack (SL) for the new schedule.

5. Develop a resource schedule in the loading chart that follows. Use the parallel method and heuristics given. Be sure to update each period as the computer would do. Note: activities 2, 3, 5, and 6 use two of the resource skills. Three of the resource skills are available. How has slack changed for each activity? Has the risk of being late changed? How?

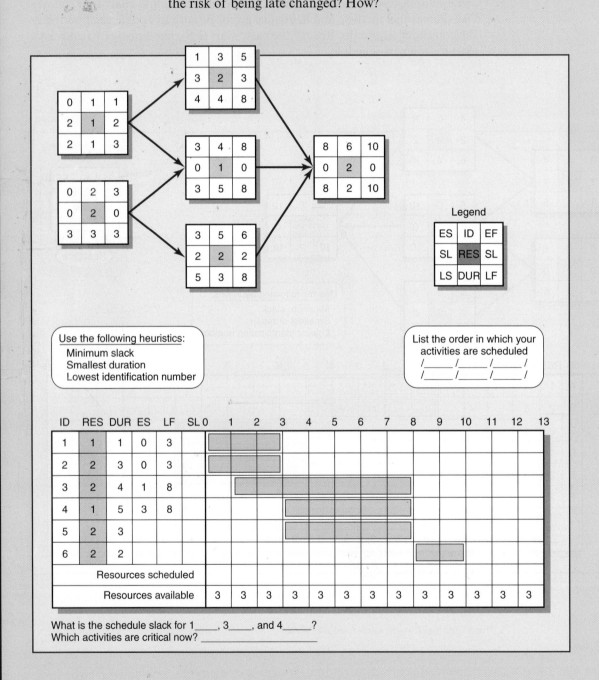

What is the schedule slack for 1_____, 3_____, and 4_____?
Which activities are critical now? _____

6. You have prepared the following schedule for a project in which the key resource is a backhoe. This schedule is contingent on having 3 backhoes. You receive a call from your partner, Brooker, who desperately needs 1 of your

backhoes. You tell Brooker you would be willing to let him have the backhoe if you are still able to complete your project in 11 months.

Develop a resource schedule in the loading chart that follows to see if it is possible to complete the project in 11 months with only 2 backhoes. Be sure to record the order in which you schedule the activities using scheduling heuristics. Activities 5 and 6 require 2 backhoes, while activities 1, 2, 3, and 4 require 1 backhoe. No splitting of activities is possible. Can you say yes to Brooker's request?

7. You are one of three carpenters assigned to complete a short construction project. Right before the start of the project, one of your fellow carpenters was hospitalized and will not be available to work on the project.

Develop a resource-constrained schedule in the loading chart that follows to see how long the project will take with only 2 carpenters. Be sure to record the order in which you schedule the activities using the scheduling heuristics.

Activities A, B, C, D, E, G, and H require 2 carpenters to complete. Activity F requires only 1 carpenter. No splitting of activities is possible.

You will receive a bonus if the project is completed within 15 days. Should you start planning how you will spend your bonus?

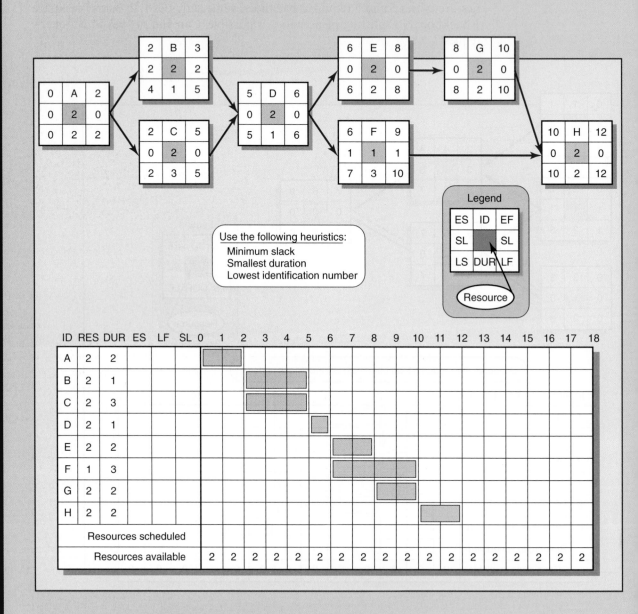

Use the following heuristics:
  Minimum slack
  Smallest duration
  Lowest identification number

*The solution to this exercise can be found in Appendix 1.

8. Given the time-phased work packages, complete the baseline budget form for the project.

Time-phased budget ($ 000)												
					Week							
Task	Budget	0	1	2	3	4	5	6	7	8	9	10
Activity 1	4	4											
Activity 2	6		1	3	2								
Activity 3	10		2	4	2	2							
Activity 4	8						2	3	3				
Activity 5	3										2	1	
Total	31												
Cumulative													

9. Given the time-phased work packages and network, complete the baseline budget form for the project.

Market Survey Project

WBS Work Package Cost by Week

WP Design	4	5	2			
WP Survey	2	2	4	4	4	5
WP Report	3	3	2			

Project Network

Time-Phased Budget

Task	Budget						Week						
		0	1	2	3	4	5	6	7	8	9	10	11	12
Design	11	4	5	2										
Survey	21													
Report	8													
Total	40													
Cumulative														

12. The National Oceanic Research Institute is planning a research study on global warming in Antarctica. The 16-month network schedule is presented below. It is followed by budgets for each activity. Create a time-phased budget for the research project in the form provided.

Global Warming Antarctic Research Project
Activity Time Phased Work Packages by Month ($000)

	Task	Duration	Budget	0	1	2	3	4	5	6
A	Preliminary plan	3	3	1	1	1				
B	Detail plan	2	2	1	1					
C	Hire staff	2	4	4						
D	Select equipment	1	5	5						
E	Train	1	3	3						
F	Purchase clothing	3	9	3	0	6				
G	Plane transportation	2	60	5	55					
H	Get custom equipment	5	36	5	5	10	10	6		
I	Additional equipment	3	20	10	5	5				
J	Test equipment	1	6	6						
K	Ship all supplies	5	15	3	3	0	0	9		
L	Travel	1	9	9						
	Total budget		172							

References

Arrow, K. J., and L. Hurowicz, *Studies in Resource Allocation Process* (New York: Cambridge University Press, 1997).

Brucker, P., A. Drexl, R. Mohring, L. Newmann, and E. Pesch, "Resource-constrained Project Scheduling: Notation, Classification, Models and Methods," *European Journal of Operational Research,* Vol. 112, 1999, pp. 3–42.

Burgess, A. R., and J. B. Kellebrew, "Variations in Activity Level on Cyclical Arrow Diagrams," *Journal of Industrial Engineering,* Vol. 13, March–April 1962, pp. 76–83.

Charnes, A., and W. W. Cooper, "A Network Interpretation and Direct Sub Dual Algorithm for Critical Path Scheduling," *Journal of Industrial Engineering,* July–August 1962.

Demeulemeester, E. L., and W. S. Herroelen, *Project Scheduling: A Research Handbook* (Norwell, Mass: Kluwer Academic Publishers, 2002).

Fendly, L. G., "Towards the Development of a Complete Multi Project Scheduling System," *Journal of Industrial Engineering,* Vol. 19, 1968, pp. 505–15.

Reinersten, D., "Is It Always a Bad Idea to Add Resources to a Late Project?" *Electric Design,* October 30, 2000, pp. 17–18.

Talbot, B. F., and J. H. Patterson, "Optimal Methods for Scheduling Under Resource Constraints," *Project Management Journal,* December 1979.

Wiest, J. D., "A Heuristic Model for Scheduling Large Projects with Unlimited Resources," *Management Science,* Vol. 18, February 1967, pp. 359–77.

Woodworth, B. M., and C. J. Willie, "A Heuristic Algorithm for Resource Leveling in Multiproject, Multiresource Scheduling," *Decision Sciences,* Vol. 6, July 1975, pp. 525–40.

Woodworth, B. M., and S. Shanahan, "Identifying the Critical Sequence in a Resource Constrained Project," *International Journal of Project Management,* Vol. 6, 1988, pp. 89–96.

Case

Power Train, Ltd.

We have smashing systems for reporting, tracking, and controlling costs on design projects. Our planning of projects is better than any I have seen at other companies. Our scheduling seemed to serve us well when we were small and we had only a few projects. Now that we have many more projects and schedule using multiproject software, there are too many occasions when the right people are not assigned to the projects deemed important to our success. This situation is costing us big money, headaches, and stress!

Claude Jones, VP, Design and Operations

HISTORY

Power Train, Ltd. (PT), was founded in 1970 by Daniel Gage, a skilled mechanical engineer and machinist. Prior to founding PT he worked for three years as design engineer for a company that designed and built transmissions for military tanks and trucks. It was a natural transition for Dan to start a company designing and building power trains for farm tractor companies. Today, Dan is no longer active in the management of PT but is still revered as its founder. He and his family still own 25 percent of the company, which went public in 1998. PT has been growing at a 6 percent clip for the last five years but expects industry growth to level off as supply exceeds demand.

Today, PT continues its proud tradition of designing and building the best-quality power trains for manufacturers of farm tractors and equipment. The company employs 178 design engineers and has about 1,800 production and support staff. Contract design projects for tractor manufacturers represent a major portion of PT's revenue. At any given time, about 45 to 60 design projects are going on concurrently. A small portion of their design work is for military vehicles. PT only accepts military contracts that involve very advanced, new technology and are cost plus.

A new phenomenon has attracted management of PT to look into a larger market. Last year a large Swedish truck manufacturer approached PT to consider designing power trains for its trucks. As the industry consolidates, the opportunities for PT should increase because these large firms are moving to more outsourcing to cut infrastructure costs and stay very flexible. Only last week a PT design engineer spoke to a German truck manufacturing manager at a conference. The German manager was already exploring outsourcing of drive trains to Porsche and was very pleased to be reminded of PT's expertise in the area. A meeting is set up for next month.

CLAUDE JONES

Claude Jones joined PT in 1999 as a new MBA from the University of Edinburgh. He worked as a mechanical engineer for U.K. Hydraulics for five years prior to returning to school for the MBA. "I just wanted to be part of the management team and where the action is." Jones moved quickly through the ranks. Today he is the vice president of design and operations. Sitting at his desk, Jones is pondering the conflicts and confusion that seem to be increasing in scheduling people to projects. He gets a real rush at the thought of designing power trains for large trucks; however, given their current project scheduling problems, a large increase in business would only compound their problems. Somehow these conflicts in scheduling have to be resolved before any serious thought can be given to expanding into design of power transmissions for truck manufacturers.

Jones is thinking of the problems PT had in the last year. The MF project is the first to come to mind. The project was not terribly complex and did not require their best design engineers. Unfortunately, the scheduling software assigned one of the most creative and expensive engineers to the MF project. A similar situation, but reversed, happened on the Deer project. This project involved a big customer and new hydrostatic technology for small tractors. In this project the scheduling software assigned engineers who were not familiar with small tractor transmissions. Somehow, thinks Jones, the right people need to be scheduled to the right projects. Upon reflection, this problem with scheduling has been increasing since PT went to multiproject scheduling. Maybe a project office is needed to keep on top of these problems.

A meeting with the information technology team and software vendors was positive but not very helpful because these people are not really into detailed scheduling problems. The vendors provided all sorts of evidence suggesting the heuristics used—least slack, shortest duration, and identification number—are absolutely efficient in scheduling people and minimizing project delays. One project software vendor, Lauren, kept saying their software would allow PT to customize the scheduling of projects and people to almost any variation selected. Lauren repeated over and over, "If the standard heuristics do not meet your requirements, create your own heuristics that do." Lauren even volunteered to assist in setting up the system. But she is not willing to spend time on the problem until PT can describe to her exactly what criteria will be used (and their sequence) to select and schedule people to projects.

WHAT NEXT?

Potential expansion into the truck power train business is not feasible until the confusion in project scheduling is solved or reduced significantly. Jones is ready to tackle this problem, but he is not sure where to start.

Appendix 8.1

The Critical-Chain Approach

In practice, project managers carefully manage slack on sensitive resource-limited projects. If possible, they will add slack at the end of the project by committing to a completion date that goes beyond the scheduled date. For example, the plans say the project should be completed on April 1, although the official completion date is May 1. Other managers take a more aggressive approach to managing slack within the schedule. They use an early start schedule and prohibit use of slack on any activity or work package to be used unless authorized by the project manager. Progress by percent complete and by remaining time are carefully monitored. Activities that are beating estimated completion times are reported so that succeeding activities can start ahead of schedule. This ensures that the time gained is used to start a succeeding activity earlier and time is not wasted. The overall intent is to create and save slack as a time buffer to complete the project early or to cover delay problems that may creep up on critical activities or paths.

Eliyahu Goldratt, who championed the "theory of constraints" in his popular book *The Goal,* advocates an alternative approach to managing slack. He has coined the term "critical-chain" to recognize that the project network may be constrained by both resource and technical dependencies. Each type of constraint can create task dependencies, and in the case of resource constraints, new task dependencies can be created! Remember how resource constraints shifted the critical path? If not, visit Figure 8.5 again. The critical chain refers to the longest string of dependencies that exist on the project. Chain is used instead of path, since the latter tends to be associated with just technical dependencies not resource dependencies. Goldratt uses the critical chain concept to develop strategies for accelerating the completion of projects. These strategies are based on his observations about time estimates of individual activities.

TIME ESTIMATES

Goldratt argues that there is a natural tendency for people to add safety (just-in-case) time to their estimations. It is believed that those who estimate activity times provide an estimate that has about an 80 to 90 percent chance of being completed on or before the estimated time. Hence, the median time (50/50 chance) is overestimated by approximately 30 to 40 percent. For example, a programmer may estimate that there is a 50/50 chance that he can complete an activity in six days. However, to ensure success and to protect against potential problems, he adds three days of safety time and reports that it will take nine days to complete the task. In this case the median (50/50) time is overestimated by approximately 50 percent. He now has a 50/50 chance of completing the project three days ahead of the schedule. If this hidden contingency is pervasive across a project, then most activities in theory should be completed ahead of schedule.

Not only do workers add safety, but project managers like to add safety to ensure that they will be able to bring the project in ahead of schedule. They will add a month to a nine-month project to cover any delays or risks that might spring up. This situation raises an interesting paradox:

Why, if there is a tendency to overestimate activity durations, and add safety to the end of a project, do so many projects come in behind schedule?

Critical-Chain Project Management (CCPM) offers several explanations:

- *Parkinson's law:* Work fills the time available. Why hustle to complete a task today when it isn't due until tomorrow? Not only will the pace of work be dictated by deadline, but workers will take advantage of perceived free time to catch up on other things. This is especially true in matrix environments where workers will use this time to clear work backlog on other projects and duties.

- *Self-protection:* Participants fail to report early finishes out of fear that management will adjust their future standards and demand more next time. For example, if a team member estimates that a task will take seven days and delivers it in five, the next time he is asked for an estimate, the project manager may want to trim the estimate based on past performance. Peer pressure may also be a factor here: to avoid being labeled a "rate buster," members may not report early finishes.

- *Dropped baton:* Goldratt uses the metaphor of project as relay race to illustrate the impact of poor coordination. Just as a runner's time is lost if the next runner is not ready to receive the baton, so is the time gained from completing a task early lost if the next group of people are not ready to receive the project work. Poor communication and inflexible resource schedules prevent progress from occurring.

- *Excessive multitasking:* The norm in most organizations is to have project personnel work on several projects, activities, or assignments at the same time. This leads to costly interruptions and excessive task splitting. As pointed out on p. 270, this adds time to each activity. When looked at in isolation the time loss may seem minimal, but when taken as a whole the transition costs can be staggering.

- *Resource bottlenecks:* In multiproject organizations projects are frequently delayed because test equipment or other necessary resources are tied up on other project work.

- *Student syndrome (procrastination):* Goldratt asserts that just as students delay writing a term paper until the last minute, workers delay starting tasks when they perceive that they have more than enough time to complete the task. The problem with delaying the start of a task is that obstacles are often not detected until the task is under way. By postponing the start of the task, the opportunity to cope with these obstacles and complete the task on time is compromised.

CRITICAL-CHAIN IN ACTION

CCPM's solution to reducing project time overruns is to insist on people using the "true 50/50" activity time estimates (rather than estimates which have an 80 to 90 percent chance of being completed before the estimated time); the 50/50 estimates result in a project duration about one-half the low risk of 80 to 90 percent estimates. This requires a corporate culture which values accurate estimates and refrains from blaming people for not meeting deadlines. According to CCPM, using 50/50 estimates will discourage Parkinson's law, the student syndrome, and self-protection from coming into play because there is less "free time" available. Productivity will be increased as individuals try to meet tighter deadlines. Similarly, the compressed time schedule reduces the likelihood of the dropped baton effect.

CCPM recommends inserting time buffers into the schedule to act as "shock absorbers" to protect the project completion date against task durations taking longer than the 50/50 estimate. The rationale is that by using 50/50 estimates you are in essence taking out all of the "safety" in individual tasks. CCPM also recommends using portions of this collective safety strategically by inserting time buffers where potential problems are likely to occur. There are three kinds of buffers in CCPM:

- *Project buffer:* First, since all activities along the critical chain have inherent *uncertainty* that is difficult to predict, project duration is uncertain. Therefore, a project time buffer is added to the expected *project duration*. CCPM recommends using roughly 50 percent of the aggregate safety. For example, if the modified schedule reduces the project duration by 20 days from 50 to 30, then a 10-day project buffer would be used.
- *Feeder buffers:* Buffers are added to the network where noncritical paths merge with the critical chain. These buffers protect the critical chain from being delayed.
- *Resource buffers:* Time buffers are inserted where scarce resources are needed for an activity. Resource time buffers come in at least two forms. One form is a time buffer attached to a critical resource to ensure that the resource is on call and available when needed. This preserves the relay race. The second form of time buffer is added to activities preceding the work of a scarce resource. This kind of buffer protects against resource bottlenecks by increasing the likelihood that the preceding activity will be completed when the resource is available.

All buffers reduce the risk of the project duration being late and increase the chance of early project completion.

CRITICAL-CHAIN VERSUS TRADITIONAL SCHEDULING APPROACH

To illustrate how CCPM affects scheduling let's compare it with the traditional approach to project scheduling. We will first resolve resource problems the way described in Chapter 8 and then the CCPM method. Figure A8.1A shows the *planned* Air Control project network without any concern for resources. That is, activities are assumed to be independent and resources will be made available and/or are interchangeable. Figure A8.1B depicts the bar chart for the project. The dark blue bars represent the durations of critical activities; the light blue bars represent the durations of noncritical activities; the bars represent slack. Note that the duration is 45 days and the critical path is represented by activities 1, 4, 6, 7, and 8.

FIGURE A8.1A **Air Control Project: Time Plan without Resources**

FIGURE A8.1B
Air Control Project:
Time Plan without
Resources

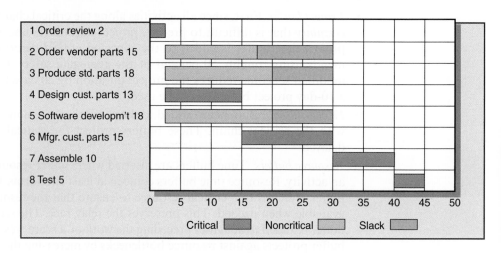

Parallel activities hold potential for resource conflicts. This is the case in this project. Ryan is the resource for activities 3 and 6. If you insert Ryan in the bar chart in Figure A8.1B for activities 3 and 6, you can see activity 3 overlaps activity 6 by five days—an impossible situation. Because Ryan cannot work two activities simultaneously and no other person can take his place, a resource dependency exists. The result is that two activities (3 and 6) that were assumed to be independent now become dependent. Something has to give! Figure A8.2A shows the Air Control project network with the resources included. A pseudo-dashed arrow has been added to the network to indicate the resource dependency. The bar chart in Figure A8.2B reflects the revised schedule resolving the overallocation of Ryan. Given the new schedule, slack for some activities has changed. More importantly, the critical path has changed. It is now 1, 3, 6, 7, 8. The resource schedule shows the new project duration to be 50 days rather than 45 days.

Now let's apply the CCPM approach to the Air Control project. Figure A8.3 details many of the changes. First, notice that task estimates now represent

FIGURE A8.2A   Air Control Project: Schedule with Resources Limited

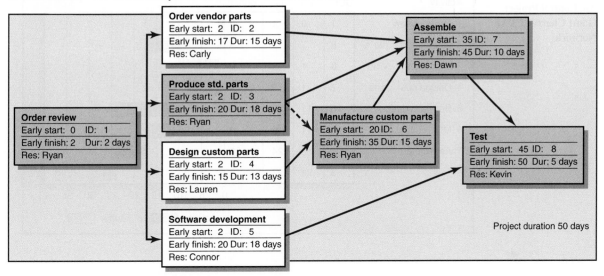

FIGURE A8.2B
Air Control Project:
Schedule with
Resources Limited

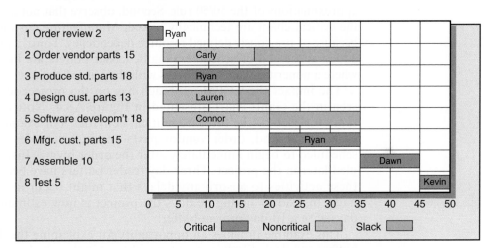

FIGURE A8.3   Air Control Project: CCPM Network

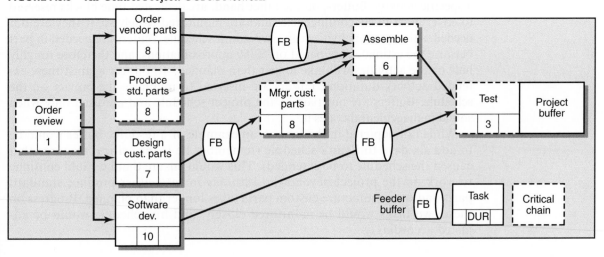

FIGURE A8.4
**Air Control Project
Gantt Chart: CCPM
Network**

Activity	DUR	LS	LF	Buffer
1. Order review	1	0	1	0
2. Order vendor parts	8	7	15	3
3. Produce std. parts	8	1	9	0
4. Design cust. parts	7	1	8	3
5. Software dev.	10	11	21	3
6. Mfgr. cust. parts	8	11	19	0
7. Assemble	6	18	24	0
8. Test	3	24	27	12

approximations of the 50/50 rule. Second, observe that not all of the activities on the critical chain are technically linked. Manufacture custom parts is included because of previously defined resource dependency. Third, a project time buffer is added at the end of schedule. Finally, feeder buffers are inserted at each point where a noncritical activity merges with the critical chain.

The impact the CCPM approach has on the project schedule can best be seen in the Gantt chart presented in Figure A8.4. Notice first the late start times for each of the three noncritical activities. For example, under the critical path method, order vendor parts and software development would be scheduled to begin immediately after the order review. Instead they are scheduled later in the project. Three-day feeder buffers have been added to each of these activities to absorb any delays that might occur in these activities. Finally, instead of taking 50 days the project is now estimated to take only 27 days with a 10-day project buffer!

This example provides an opportunity for explaining the differences between buffers and slack. Slack is spare time inherent in the schedule of noncritical activities and can be determined by differences between the early start and late start of a specific activity. Buffers, on the other hand, are dedicated time blocks reserved to cover most likely contingencies and are monitored closely so, if they are not needed, subsequent activities can proceed on schedule. Buffers are needed in part because the estimates are based on 50/50 approximations, and therefore roughly half of the activities will take longer than planned. To protect against these extended activity durations, buffers are inserted to minimize the impact on the schedule. Buffers are not part of the project schedule and are used only when sound management dictates it.

While not depicted in the figures, an example of a resource buffer would be to add six days to Ryan's schedule (remember he is the critical resource that caused the schedule to be extended). This would ensure that he could continue to work on the project beyond the 18th day in case either produce standard parts and/or manufacture custom parts takes longer than planned. Progress on these two tasks would be monitored closely, and his schedule would be adjusted accordingly.

FIGURE A8.5
Project Control—
Buffer Management

CCPM AND SPLITTING TASKS

Buffers do not address the insidious effects of pervasive task splitting, especially in a multiproject environment where workers are juggling different project assignments. CCPM has three recommendations that will help to reduce the impact of splitting activities:

1. Reduce the number of projects so people are not assigned to as many projects concurrently.
2. Control start dates of projects to accommodate resource shortages. Don't start projects until sufficient resources are available to work full time on the project.
3. Contract (lock in) for resources *before* the project begins.

MONITORING PROJECT PERFORMANCE

The CCPM method uses buffers to monitor project time performance. Remember that as shown in Figure A8.3 a project buffer is used to insulate the project against delays along the critical chain. For monitoring purposes, this buffer is typically divided into three zones—OK, Watch and Plan, and Act, respectively (see Figure A8.5). As the buffer begins to decrease and moves into the second zone, alarms are set off to seek corrective action. To be truly effective, buffer management requires comparing buffer usage with actual progress on the project. For example, if the project is 75 percent complete and you have only used 50 percent of the project buffer, then the project is in pretty good shape. Conversely, if the project is only 25 percent complete and 50 percent of the buffer has already been used, you are in trouble and corrective action is needed. A method for estimating percentage complete is described in Chapter 13.

THE CCPM METHOD TODAY

CCPM has generated considerable debate within the project management community. While sound in theory, support at this time is limited but growing. For example, Harris Semiconductor was able to build a new automated wafer fabrication facility within 13 months using CCPM methods when the industry standard for such a facility is 26–36 months. The Israeli aircraft industry has used CCPM techniques to reduce average maintenance work on aircraft from two months to two weeks. The U.S. Air Force and Navy as well as Boeing, Lucent Technologies, Intel, GM, and 3M are applying critical-chain principles to their multi-project environments.

CCPM is not without critics. First, CCPM does not address the biggest cause of project delays, which is an ill-defined and unstable project scope. Second, some critics challenge Goldratt's assumptions about human behavior. They question the tendency of experts to pad estimates and that employees act deliberately against the organization for their own interest and benefit. They also object to the insinuation that trained professionals would exhibit the student syndrome habits. Third, evidence of success is almost exclusively anecdotal and based on single case studies. The lack of systematic evidence raises questions about generalizability of application. CCPM may prove to work best for only certain kinds of projects.

One of the keys to implementing CCPM is the culture of the organization. If the organization honors noble efforts that fail to meet estimates as it does efforts that do meet estimates, then greater acceptance will occur. Conversely, if management treats honest failure differently from success, then resistance will be high. Organizations adopting the CCPM approach have to invest significant energy to obtaining "buy-in" on the part of all participants to its core principles and allaying the fears that this system may generate.

APPENDIX SUMMARY

Regardless of where one stands in the debate, the CCPM approach deserves credit for bringing resource dependency to the forefront, highlighting the modern ills of multitasking, and forcing us to rethink conventional methods of project scheduling.

APPENDIX REVIEW QUESTIONS

1. Explain how time is wasted in management of projects.
2. Distinguish between project and feeder buffers.
3. Buffers are not the same as slack. Explain.

APPENDIX EXERCISES

1. Check out the Goldratt Institute's homepage at *http://www.goldratt.com* for current information on the application of critical-chain techniques to project management.
2. Apply critical-chain scheduling principles to the Print Software, Inc., project presented in Chapter 6 on page •••. Revise the estimated time durations by 50 percent except round up the odd time durations (i.e., 3 becomes 4). Draw a CCPM network diagram similar to the one contained in Figure A8.3 for the Print Software project as well as a Gantt chart similar to Figure A8.4. How would these diagrams differ from the ones generated using the traditional scheduling technique?

 Case

The CCPM Dilemma

Pinyarat worked in the IT department of a diversified IT firm. She was describing the firm's early encounters with critical chain scheduling to a friend in another IT firm.

Three years ago management decided to add 10 percent time to all activity estimates because almost all projects were coming in late. One thought was people were simply working too hard and needed some relief. This approach did not work! Projects still came in late. Next, management decided to take away the extra time for activities and add 10 percent for project estimates to ensure project durations would be met. Again, nothing improved and projects continued to come in late. Recently, the firm hired a consultant who promoted critical chain scheduling, which was implemented for all projects in her division. Almost all failed to perform.

Pinyarat explained, "The estimates were basically impossible. The activity durations got squeezed down to less than the 50 percent guideline. We were late on nearly every task. In addition, I was not allowed to put in a big enough project buffer, which only added to projects being late. One colleague who was working on six projects gave up and quit; he said he was killing himself and saw no hope of things getting better. My projects are not the only ones having big problems. Some people had no idea why anyone would use CCPM scheduling. To quote one of my best programmers: 'They ask for an estimate and then they cut it 50 percent or more. What kind of game is this? Apparently they don't trust us."

A week later, to Pinyarat's surprise, she was called to the IT manager's office. Pinyarat imagined numerous bad scenarios of how the meeting would go—even to the remote possibility of being fired! The manager wanted the division to straighten out their project management practices and stop this business of nearly all IT projects being late. There are rumors of cleaning house or outsourcing IT work.

The manager believed Pinyarat, who passed the PMP exam, had the best chance of turning things around. He said, "Pinyarat, I'm nearing the desperate level; top management is reaching the end of the rope with our division. We need to turn this around for both our sakes. Give me a plan that I can sponsor within the week."

Pinyarat explained to her friend a few of her ideas—like squeezing estimates too far. But she said she would take any ideas she can get from anyone.

Give Pinyarat a report that identifies the key problems and a plan of action she can present to her sponsor. Limit your report to 800 words or less.

APPENDIX REFERENCES

Goldratt, *Critical Chain* (Great Barrington, MA: North River Press, 1997).

Herroelen, W., R. Leus, and E. Demeulemeester, "Critical Chain Project Scheduling: Do Not Oversimplify," *Project Management Journal,* Vol. 33 (4), 2002, pp. 48–60.

Leach, L. P., "Critical Chain Project Management," *Proceedings of 29th Annual Project Management Institute, 1998, Seminars and Symposium* (Newtown, PA: Project Management Institute, 1998), pp. 1239–44.

Levine, H. A., "Shared Contingency: Exploring the Critical Chain," *PM Network,* October 1999, pp. 35–38.

Newbold, R. C., *Project Management in the Fast Lane: Applying the Theory of Constraints* (Boca Raton, FL: St. Lucie Press, 1998).

Noreen, E., D. Smith, and J. Mackey, *The Theory of Constraints and Its Implication for Management Accounting* (Great Barrington, MA: North River Press, 1995).

Raz, T., R. Barnes, and D. Dvir, "A Critical Look at Critical Chain Project Management," *Project Management Journal,* December 2003, pp. 24–32.

Sood, S., "Taming Uncertainty: Critical-Chain Buffer Management Helps Minimize Risk in the Project Equation," *PM Network,* March 2003, pp. 57–59.

Zalmanson, E., "Readers Feedback," *PM Network,* Vol. 15 (1), 2001, p. 4.

Reducing Project Duration

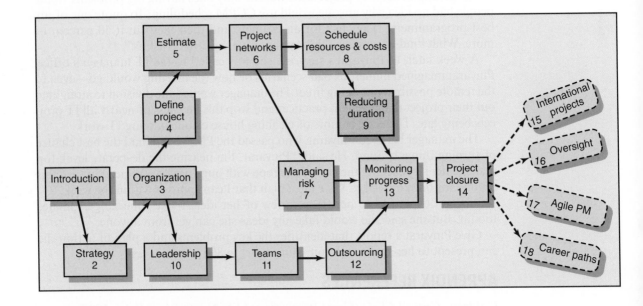

Reducing Project Duration

Rationale for Reducing Project Duration

Options for Accelerating Project Completion

Project Cost–Duration Graph

Constructing a Project Cost–Duration Graph

Practical Considerations

What if Cost, Not Time, Is the Issue?

Summary

In skating over thin ice our safety is in our speed.

—*Ralph Waldo Emerson*

Imagine the following scenarios:

—After finalizing your project schedule, you realize the estimated completion date is two months beyond what your boss publicly promised an important customer.

—Five months into the project, you realize that you are already three weeks behind the drop-dead date for the project.

—Four months into a project top management changes its priorities and now tells you that money is not an issue. Complete the project ASAP!

What do you do?

This chapter addresses strategies for reducing project duration either prior to setting the baseline for the project or in the midst of project execution. Choice of options is based on the constraints surrounding the project. Here the project priority matrix introduced in Chapter 4 comes into play. For example, there are many more options available for reducing project time if you are not resource constrained than if you cannot spend more than your original budget. We will begin first by examining the reasons for reducing project duration followed by a discussion of different options for accelerating project completion. The chapter will conclude with the classic time-cost framework for selecting which activities to "crash." Crash is a term that has emerged in the Project Management lexicon for shortening the duration of an activity or project beyond when it can be normally done.

Rationale for Reducing Project Duration

There are many good reasons for attempting to reduce the duration of a project. One of the more important reasons today is time to market. Intense global competition and rapid technological advances have made speed a competitive advantage. To succeed, companies have to spot new opportunities, launch project teams, and bring new products or services to the marketplace in a flash. Perhaps in no industry does speed matter as much as in the electronics industry. For example, a rule of thumb for moderate- to high-technology firms is that a six-month delay in bringing a product to market can result in a loss of market share of about 35 percent. In these cases, high-technology firms typically assume that the time savings and avoidance of lost profits are worth any additional costs to reduce time without any formal analysis. See the Snapshot from Practice: Cell-Phone Wars for more on this.

Business survival depends not only upon rapid innovation but also adaptability. Global recession and energy crises have stunned the business world, and those

SNAPSHOT FROM PRACTICE   Cell-Phone Wars*

Courtesy of Apple Inc.

Speed has been critical in business ever since the California Gold Rush. The cell-phone industry is a good example of an intensely competitive business that places a premium on speed and innovation. On July, 2008 Apple released iPhone 3G with a faster interface and a sleek design. Then on November 21, 2008, Research in Motion (RIM) released their new Blackberry phone—Storm. Gone were the buttons; the Blackberry Storm had a fully incorporated touch screen to compete with the iPhone. Soon thereafter, Google entered the fray with its ambitious G-1 phone that has both a touch screen and a flip out keyboard as well as a tracking ball for surfing the Web. "It's like having a popular nightclub. You have to keep opening new ones. To stay cool, you have to speed up," says Michael Greeson, president of market researcher Diffusion Group, Inc.

In order to survive, RIM, Nokia, and other cell-phone manufacturers have become masters at project management. They have been able to cut the market release time of new phones from 12–18 months to 6–9 months. What is at stake is over 500 million in forecasted sales of new cell phones each year.

* Steve Hamm, "Is Your Company Fast Enough?" *BusinessWeek*, March 27, 2006, pp. 68–76.

companies that survive will be those that can quickly adapt to new challenges. This requires speedy project management! For example, the fate of U.S. auto industry depends in part on how quickly they shift their efforts to develop fuel efficient, alternative forms of transportation.

Another common reason for reducing project time occurs when unforeseen delays—for example, adverse weather, design flaws, and equipment breakdown— cause substantial delays midway in the project. Getting back on schedule usually requires compressing the time on some of the remaining critical activities. The additional costs of getting back on schedule need to be compared with the consequences of being late. This is especially true when time is a top priority.

Incentive contracts can make reduction of project time rewarding—usually for both the project contractor and owner. For example, a contractor finished a bridge across a lake 18 months early and received more than $6 million for the early completion. The availability of the bridge to the surrounding community 18 months early to reduce traffic gridlock made the incentive cost to the community seem small to users. In another example, in a continuous improvement arrangement, the joint effort of the owner and contractor resulted in early completion of a river lock and a 50/50 split of the savings to the owner and contractor. See Snapshot from Practice: Northridge Earthquake for a situation in which a contractor went to great lengths to complete a project as quickly as possible.

"Imposed deadlines" is another reason for accelerating project completion. For example, a politician makes a public statement that a new law building will be available in two years. Or the president of a software company remarks in a speech that new advanced software will be available in one year. Such statements too often become imposed project duration dates—without any consideration of the problems or cost of meeting such a date. The project duration time is set while the project is in its "concept" phase before or without any detailed scheduling of all the activities in the project. This phenomenon occurs very frequently in practice! Unfortunately, this practice almost always leads to a higher cost project than one that is planned using low-cost and detailed planning. In addition, quality is sometimes compromised to meet deadlines. More important, these increased costs of imposed duration dates are seldom recognized or noted by project participants.

Sometimes very high overhead costs are recognized before the project begins. In these cases it is prudent to examine the direct costs of shortening the critical path versus the overhead cost savings. Usually there are opportunities to shorten a few critical activities at less than the daily overhead rate. Under specific conditions (which are not rare), huge savings are possible with little risk.

Finally there are times when it is important to reassign key equipment and/or people to new projects. Under these circumstances, the cost of compressing the project can be compared with the opportunity costs of not releasing key equipment or people.

Options for Accelerating Project Completion

Managers have several effective methods for crashing specific project activities when resources are not constrained. Several of these are summarized below.

SNAPSHOT FROM PRACTICE

Responding to the Northridge Earthquake*

On January 17, 1994, a 6.8-magnitude earthquake struck the Los Angeles basin, near suburban Northridge, causing 60 deaths, thousands of injuries, and billions of dollars in property damage. Nowhere was the destructive power of nature more evident than in the collapsed sections of the freeway system that disrupted the daily commute of an estimated 1 million Los Angelenos. The Northridge earthquake posed one of the greatest challenges to the California Department of Transportation (CalTrans) in its nearly 100-year history. To expedite the recovery process, Governor Pete Wilson signed an emergency declaration allowing CalTrans to streamline contracting procedures and offer attractive incentives for completing work ahead of schedule. For each day that the schedule was beaten, a sizable bonus was to be awarded. Conversely, for each day over the deadline, the contractor would be penalized the same amount. The amount ($50,000 to $200,000) varied depending on the importance of the work.

The incentive scheme proved to be a powerful motivator for the freeway reconstruction contractors. C. C. Myers, Inc., of Rancho Cordova, California, won the contract for the reconstruction of the Interstate 10 bridges. Myers pulled out all stops to finish the project in a blistering 66 days—a whopping 74 days ahead of schedule—and earning a $14.8 million bonus! Myers took every opportunity to save time and streamline operations. They greatly expanded the workforce. For example, 134 ironworkers were employed instead of the normal 15. Special lighting equipment was set up so that work could be performed around the clock. Likewise, the sites were prepared and special materials were used so that work could continue despite inclement weather that would normally shut down construction. The work was scheduled much like an assembly line so that critical activities were followed by the next critical activity. A generous incentive scheme was devised to reward teamwork and reach milestones early.

© David Butow/Corbis SABA

Carpenters and iron-workers competed as teams against each other to see who could finish first.

Although C. C. Myers received a substantial bonus for finishing early, they spent a lot of money on overtime, bonuses, special equipment, and other premiums to keep the job rolling along. CalTrans supported Myers's efforts. With reconstruction work going on 24 hours a day, including jackhammering and pile-driving, CalTrans temporarily housed many families in local motels. CalTrans even erected a temporary plastic soundwall to help reduce the construction noise traveling to a nearby apartment complex. The double-layer curtain, 450 feet long and 20 feet high, was designed to reduce construction noise by 10 decibels.

Despite the difficulties and expense incurred by around-the-clock freeway building, most of Los Angeles cheered CalTrans's quake recovery efforts. The Governor's Office of Planning and Research issued a report concluding that for every day the Santa Monica Freeway was closed, it cost the local economy more than $1 million.

* Jerry B. Baxter, "Responding to the Northridge Earthquake," *PM Network* (November 1994), pp. 13–22.

Options When Resources Are Not Constrained

Adding Resources

The most common method for shortening project time is to assign additional staff and equipment to activities. There are limits, however, as to how much speed can be gained by adding staff. Doubling the size of the workforce will not necessarily reduce completion time by half. The relationship would be correct only when tasks can be partitioned so minimal communication is needed between workers, as in harvesting a crop by hand or repaving a highway. Most projects are not set up that way; additional workers increase the communication

SNAPSHOT FROM PRACTICE

Outsourcing in Bio-Tech Picks Up Speed*

In the face of increasing time-to-market pressures, many bio-tech firms are turning to outsourcing to expedite the drug development process. Panos Kalaritis, vice president of operations for Irix Pharmaceuticals, says that outsourcing process development can accelerate a drug's evolution by allowing a pharmaceutical company to continue research while a contractor works on process optimization. Susan Dexter of Lonza Biologics identified different types of outsourcing contracts including agreements for product development, clinical trial supplies, in-market or commercial supplies, and technology transfer. Often, she said, a given project can encompass more than one of the above stages over a period of several years.

Using a contractor, said Paul Henricks, business manager for Patheon Inc., gives the client company access to specialized knowledge and infrastructure as well as flexible resources and capacity. The sponsoring company can also manage risks by sharing responsibilities through outsourcing.

"Communication is key to a successful outsourcing relationship," said Dan Gold, vice president of process development for Covance, which was formerly Corning Bio. "Contractors and sponsors should both assign project managers, and the two must work together to maintain, track, and document project completion. There must be a concerted effort on the part of both parties to work as partners to complete the project."

* Mathew Lerner, "Outsourcing in Bio-Technology Picks Up Speed," *Chemical Market Reporter,* Vol. 251, No. 14 (2002), p. 17.

requirements to coordinate their efforts. For example, doubling a team by adding two workers requires six times as much pairwise intercommunication than is required in the original two-person team. Not only is more time needed to coordinate and manage a larger team; there is the additional delay of training the new people and getting them up to speed on the project. The end result is captured in Brooks's law: Adding manpower to a late software project makes it later.

Frederick Brooks formulated this principle based on his experience as a project manager for IBM's System/360 software project during the early 1960s. While subsequent research confirmed Brooks's prediction, it also discovered that adding more people to a late project does not always cause the project to be later. The key is whether the new staff is added early so there is sufficient time to make up for lost ground once the new members have been fully assimilated.

Outsourcing Project Work

A common method for shortening the project time is to subcontract an activity. The subcontractor may have access to superior technology or expertise that will accelerate the completion of the activity. For example, contracting for a backhoe can accomplish in two hours what it can take a team of laborers two days to do. Likewise, by hiring a consulting firm that specializes in ADSI programming, a firm may be able to cut in half the time it would take for less experienced, internal programmers to do the work. Subcontracting also frees up resources that can be assigned to a critical activity and will ideally result in a shorter project duration. See Snapshot from Practice: Outsourcing Bio-Tech. Outsourcing will be addressed more fully in Chapter 12.

Scheduling Overtime

The easiest way to add more labor to a project is not to add more people, but to schedule overtime. If a team works 50 hours a week instead of 40, it might accomplish 20 percent more. By scheduling overtime you avoid the additional costs of coordination and communication encountered when new people are added. If people involved are salaried workers, there may be no real additional cost for the extra work. Another advantage is that there are fewer distractions when people work outside normal hours.

Overtime has disadvantages. First, hourly workers are typically paid time and a half for overtime and double time for weekends and holidays. Sustained overtime work by salaried employees may incur intangible costs such as divorce, burnout, and turnover. The latter is a key organizational concern when there is a shortage of workers. Furthermore, it is an oversimplification to assume that, over an extended period of time, a person is as productive during his or her eleventh hour at work as during his or her third hour of work. There are natural limits to what is humanly possible, and extended overtime may actually lead to an overall decline in productivity when fatigue sets in.

Overtime and working longer hours is the preferred choice for accelerating project completion, especially when the project team is salaried. The key is to use overtime judiciously. Remember a project is a marathon not a sprint! You do not want to run out of energy before the finish line.

Establish a Core Project Team

As discussed in Chapter 3, one of the advantages of creating a dedicated core team to complete a project is speed. Assigning professionals full time to a project avoids the hidden cost of multitasking in which people are forced to juggle the demands of multiple projects. Professionals are allowed to devote their undivided attention to a specific project. This singular focus creates a shared goal that can bind a diverse set of professionals into a highly cohesive team capable of accelerating project completion. Factors that contribute to the emergence of high-performing project teams will be discussed in detail in Chapter 11.

Do It Twice—Fast and Correctly

If you are in a hurry, try building a "quick and dirty" short-term solution, then go back and do it the right way. For example, the Rose Garden stadium in Portland, Oregon, was supposed to be completely finished in time for the start of the 1995–1996 National Basketball Association (NBA) season. Delays made this impossible, so the construction crew set up temporary bleachers to accommodate the opening-night crowd. The additional costs of doing it twice are often more than compensated for by the benefits of satisfying the deadline.

Options When Resources Are Constrained

A project manager has fewer options for accelerating project completion when additional resources are either not available or the budget is severely constrained. This is especially true once the schedule has been established. Below are some of these options, which are also available when resources are not constrained.

Fast-Tracking

Sometimes it is possible to rearrange the logic of the project network so that critical activities are done in parallel (concurrently) rather than sequentially. This alternative is a good one if the project situation is right. When this alternative is given serious attention, it is amazing to observe how creative project team members can be in finding ways to restructure sequential activities in parallel. As noted in Chapter 6, one of the most common methods for restructuring activities is to change a finish-to-start relationship to a start-to-start relationship. For example, instead of waiting for the final design to be approved, manufacturing engineers can begin building the production line as soon as key specifications have been established. Changing activities from sequential to parallel usually requires closer coordination among those responsible for the activities affected but can produce tremendous time savings.

Critical-Chain

Critical-chain project management (CCPM) is designed to accelerate project completion. As discussed in Chapter 8, the jury is still out in terms of its applicability. Still CCPM principles appear sound and worthy of experimentation if speed is essential. At the same time, it would be difficult to apply CCPM midstream in a project. CCPM requires considerable training and a shift in habits and perspectives that take time to adopt. Although there have been reports of immediate gains, especially in terms of completion times, a long-term management commitment is probably necessary to reap full benefits. See the Snapshot from Practice: The Fastest House in the World for an extreme example of CCPM application.

Reducing Project Scope

Probably the most common response for meeting unattainable deadlines is to reduce or scale back the scope of the project. This invariably leads to a reduction in the functionality of the project. For example, the new car will average only 25 mpg instead of 30, or the software product will have fewer features than originally planned. While scaling back the scope of the project can lead to big savings in both time and money, it may come at a cost of reducing the value of the project. If the car gets lower gas mileage, will it stand up to competitive models? Will customers still want the software minus the features?

The key to reducing a project scope without reducing value is to reassess the true specifications of the project. Often requirements are added under best-case, blue-sky scenarios and represent desirables, but not essentials. Here it is important to talk to the customer and/or project sponsors and explain the situation—you can get it your way but not until February. This may force them to accept an extension or to add money to expedite the project. If not, then a healthy discussion of what the essential requirements are and what items can be compromised in order to meet the deadline needs to take place. More intense reexamination of requirements may actually improve the value of the project by getting it done more quickly and for a lower cost.

Calculating the savings of reduced project scope begins with the work breakdown structure. Reducing functionality means certain tasks, deliverables, or requirements can be reduced or even eliminated. These tasks need to be found and the schedule adjusted. Focus should be on changes in activities on the critical path.

Compromise Quality

Reducing quality is always an option, but it is rarely acceptable or used. If quality is sacrificed, it may be possible to reduce the time of an activity on the critical path.

In practice the methods most commonly used to crash projects are scheduling overtime, outsourcing, and adding resources. Each of these maintains the essence of the original plan. Options that depart from the original project plan include do it twice and fast-tracking. Rethinking of project scope, customer needs, and timing become major considerations for these techniques.

SNAPSHOT FROM PRACTICE   The Fastest House in the World*

AP/Wide World.

December 17, 2002—After revving up their power tools and lining up volunteers, Shelby County Habitat for Humanity broke the world record for the fastest house ever built, clocking in at 3 hours, 26 minutes, and 34 seconds. Former record holder New Zealand's Habitat Affiliate Mannakau held the record for three years at 3 hours, 44 minutes, and 59 seconds. The Alabama project beat the New Zealand record by 18 minutes.

"This was different than any construction project that I've ever been a part of," said Project Manager Chad Calhoun. "The minute-by-minute schedule, the planning of each precise movement, the organization of all the teams and materials, could not have gone more smoothly on build day. All the long hours of planning definitely paid off."

In preparation for the build, Habitat volunteers put the foundation in place and constructed prefabricated wall panels. Once the whistle blew at 11:00 A.M. on December 17th, the exterior wall panels were raised into place, followed by the interior panel, which took only 16 minutes. Special color coded teams of workers connected the wiring and plumbing, put in insulation, installed appliances, laid carpet and tile, installed light fixtures, painted the house inside, applied vinyl siding outside, and attached assembled front and back porches.

At the same time, the roof was constructed on the ground next to the house. Once the roof was completed—approximately 1½ hours later—a Steel City crane lifted the 14,000–pound roof assembly into place. Crews attached the roof while others completed the interior work. There was even time to lay sod, plant shrubbery, and decorate a Christmas tree in the front yard—all within the official build time of 3 hours, 26 minutes, and 34 seconds.

The recipient of this wonderful holiday gift was Bonnie Lilly, a single mother and nursing technician who had applied to Habitat for Humanity three times before she was selected to receive the three-bedroom, two-bath home. "It's amazing," Lilly said. "Who am I to have this happen for me? A world record, hundreds of people coming together to build my house—I still can't believe it."

Habitat for Humanity is an international charitable organization that builds simple, affordable houses and sells them on a no-interest, no-profit basis to needy families.

* "The house that love built, really FAST—and just in time for Christmas kicker: Habitat for Humanity breaks world record set by New Zealand," Erin Drummond, www.csre.com. "Shelby County, Ala. Builds fastest Habitat House in three and a half hours," www.habitat .org/newsroom/2002archive.

Project Cost–Duration Graph

Nothing on the horizon suggests that the need to shorten project time will change. In fact, if anything the pressure to get projects done quicker and sooner is likely to increase in importance. The challenge for the project manager is to use a quick, logical method to compare the benefits of reducing project time with the cost. When sound, logical methods are absent, it is difficult to isolate those activities that will have the greatest impact on reducing project time at least cost. This section describes a procedure for identifying the costs of reducing project time so that comparisons can be made with the benefits of getting the project completed sooner. The method requires gathering direct and indirect costs for specific project durations. Critical activities are searched to find the lowest direct-cost activities that will shorten the project duration. Total cost for specific project durations are computed and then compared with the benefits of reducing project time—before the project begins or while it is in progress.

Explanation of Project Costs

The general nature of project costs is illustrated in Figure 9.1, **Project Cost–Duration Graph.** The total cost for each duration is the sum of the indirect and direct costs. Indirect costs continue for the life of the project. Hence, any reduction in project duration means a reduction in indirect costs. Direct costs on the graph grow at an increasing rate as the project duration is reduced from its original planned duration. With the information from a graph such as this for a project, managers can quickly judge any alternative such as meeting a time-to-market deadline. Further discussion of indirect and direct costs is necessary before demonstrating a procedure for developing the information for a graph similar to the one depicted in Figure 9.1.

Project Indirect Costs

Indirect costs generally represent overhead costs such as supervision, administration, consultants, and interest. Indirect costs cannot be associated with any particular

FIGURE 9.1
Project Cost–
Duration Graph

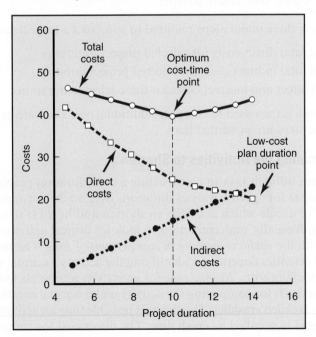

work package or activity, hence the term. Indirect costs vary directly with time. That is, any reduction in time should result in a reduction of indirect costs. For example, if the daily costs of supervision, administration, and consultants are $2,000, any reduction in project duration would represent a savings of $2,000 per day. If indirect costs are a significant percentage of total project costs, reductions in project time can represent very real savings (assuming the indirect resources can be utilized elsewhere).

Project Direct Costs

Direct costs commonly represent labor, materials, equipment, and sometimes subcontractors. Direct costs are assigned directly to a work package and activity, hence the term. The ideal assumption is that direct costs for an activity time represent normal costs, which typically mean low-cost, efficient methods for a normal time. When project durations are imposed, direct costs may no longer represent low-cost, efficient methods. Costs for the imposed duration date will be higher than for a project duration developed from ideal normal times for activities. Because direct costs are assumed to be developed from normal methods and time, any reduction in activity time should add to the costs of the activity. The sum of the costs of all the work packages or activities represents the total direct costs for the project.

The major plight faced in creating the information for a graph similar to Figure 9.1 is computing the direct cost of shortening individual critical activities and then finding the total direct cost for each project duration as project time is compressed; the process requires selecting those critical activities that cost the least to shorten. (Note: The graph implies that there is always an optimum cost-time point. This is only true if shortening a schedule has incremental indirect cost savings exceeding the incremental direct cost incurred. However, in practice there are almost always several activities in which the direct costs of shortening are less than the indirect costs.)

Constructing a Project Cost–Duration Graph

There are three major steps required to construct a project cost–duration graph:

1. Find total direct costs for selected project durations.
2. Find total indirect costs for selected project durations.
3. Sum direct and indirect costs for these selected durations.

The graph is then used to compare additional cost alternatives for benefits. Details of these steps are presented here.

Determining the Activities to Shorten

The most difficult task in constructing a cost–duration graph is finding the total direct costs for specific project durations over a relevant range. The central concern is to decide which activities to shorten and how far to carry the shortening process. Basically, managers need to look for critical activities that can be shortened with the *smallest increase in cost per unit of time.* The rationale for selecting critical activities depends on identifying the activity's normal and crash times and corresponding costs. *Normal time* for an activity represents low-cost, realistic, efficient methods for completing the activity under normal conditions. Shortening an activity is called **crashing.** The shortest possible time an activity can realistically be completed in is called its **crash time.** The direct cost for completing an activity in

FIGURE 9.2
Activity Graph

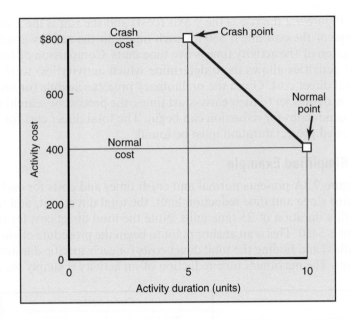

its crash time is called *crash cost*. Both normal and crash times and costs are collected from personnel most familiar with completing the activity. Figure 9.2 depicts a hypothetical cost–duration graph for an activity.

The normal time for the activity is 10 time units, and the corresponding cost is $400. The crash time for the activity is five time units and $800. The intersection of the normal time and cost represents the original low-cost, early-start schedule. The **crash point** represents the maximum time an activity can be compressed. The heavy line connecting the normal and crash points represents the slope, which assumes the cost of reducing the time of the activity is constant *per unit of time*. The assumptions underlying the use of this graph are as follows:

1. The cost-time relationship is linear.
2. Normal time assumes low-cost, efficient methods to complete the activity.
3. Crash time represents a limit—the greatest time reduction possible under realistic conditions.
4. Slope represents cost per unit of time.
5. All accelerations must occur within the normal and crash times.

Knowing the slope of activities allows managers to compare which critical activities to shorten. The less steep the cost slope of an activity, the less it costs to shorten one time period; a steeper slope means it will cost more to shorten one time unit. The cost per unit of time or slope for any activity is computed by the following equation:

$$\text{Cost slope} = \frac{\text{Rise}}{\text{Run}} = \frac{\text{Crash cost} - \text{Normal cost}}{\text{Normal time} - \text{Crash time}}$$

$$= \frac{\text{CC} - \text{NC}}{\text{NT} - \text{CT}} = \frac{\$800 - \$400}{10 - 5}$$

$$= \frac{\$400}{5} = \$80 \text{ per unit of time}$$

In Figure 9.2 the rise is the y axis (cost) and the run is the x axis (duration). The slope of the cost line is $80 for each time unit the activity is reduced; the limit reduction of the activity time is five time units. Comparison of the slopes of all critical activities allows us to determine which activity(ies) to shorten to minimize total direct cost. Given the preliminary project schedule (or one in progress) with all activities set to their early-start times, the process of searching critical activities as candidates for reduction can begin. The total direct cost for each specific compressed project duration must be found.

A Simplified Example

Figure 9.3A presents normal and crash times and costs for each activity, the computed slope and time reduction limit, the total direct cost, and the project network with a duration of 25 time units. Note the total direct cost for the 25-period duration is $450. This is an anchor point to begin the procedure of shortening the critical path(s) and finding the total direct costs for each specific duration less than 25 time units. The maximum time reduction of an activity is simply the difference between

FIGURE 9.3
Cost–Duration
Trade-off Example

Activity ID	Slope	Maximum crash time	Normal Time	Normal Cost	Crash Time	Crash Cost
A	$20	1	3	$50	2	$70
B	40	2	6	80	4	160
C	30	1	10	60	9	90
D	25	4	11	50	7	150
E	30	2	8	100	6	160
F	30	1	5	40	4	70
G	0	0	6	70	6	70

Total direct cost $450

Legend
ACT
DUR

Time 25

Initial total direct cost $ 450

(A)

Time 24

Total direct cost $ 470

Activities changed
A
$20

(B)

the normal and crash times for an activity. For example, activity D can be reduced from a normal time of 11 time units to a crash time of 7 time units, or a maximum of 4 time units. The positive slope for activity D is computed as follows:

$$\text{Slope} = \frac{\text{Crash cost} - \text{Normal cost}}{\text{Normal time} - \text{Crash time}} = \frac{\$150 - \$50}{11 - 7}$$

$$= \frac{\$100}{4} = \$25 \text{ per period reduced}$$

The network shows the critical path to be activities A, D, F, G. Because it is impossible to shorten activity G, activity A is circled because it is the least-cost candidate; that is, its slope ($20) is less than the slopes for activities D and F ($25 and $30). Reducing activity A one time unit cuts the project duration to 24 time units but increases the total direct costs to $470 ($450 + $20 = $470). Figure 9.3B reflects these changes. The duration of activity A has been reduced to two time units; the "x" indicates the activity cannot be reduced any further. Activity D is circled because it costs the least ($25) to shorten the project to 23 time units. Compare the cost of activity F. The total direct cost for a project duration of 23 time units is $495 (see Figure 9.4A).

FIGURE 9.4
Cost–Duration Trade-off Example (continued)

FIGURE 9.5 **Summary Costs by Duration**

Project duration	Direct costs	+	Indirect costs	=	Total costs
25	450		400		$850
24	470		350		820
23	495		300		795
22	525		250		775
21	610		200		810

FIGURE 9.6 **Project Cost–Duration Graph**

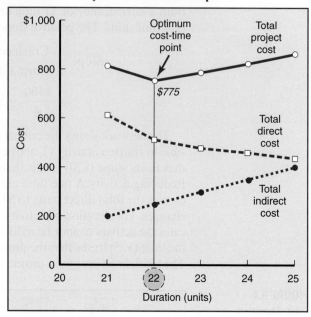

Observe that the project network in Figure 9.4A now has two critical paths—A, C, F, G and A, D, F, G. Reducing the project to 22 time units will require that activity F be reduced; thus, it is circled. This change is reflected in Figure 9.4B. The total direct cost for 22 time units is $525. This reduction has created a third critical path—A, B, E, G; all activities are critical. The least-cost method for reducing the project duration to 21 time units is the combination of the circled activities C, D, E which cost $30, $25, $30, respectively, and increase total direct costs to $610. The results of these changes are depicted in Figure 9.4C. Although some activities can still be reduced (those without the "x" next to the activity time), no activity or combination of activities will result in a reduction in the project duration.

With the total direct costs for the array of specific project durations found, the next step is to collect the indirect costs for these same durations. These costs are typically a rate per day and are easily obtained from the accounting department. Figure 9.5 presents the total direct costs, total indirect costs, and total project costs. These same costs are plotted in Figure 9.6. This graph shows that the optimum cost-time duration is 22 time units and $775. Assuming the project will actually materialize as planned, any movement away from this time duration will increase project costs. The movement from 25 to 22 time units occurs because, in this range, the absolute slopes of the indirect costs are greater than the direct cost slopes.

Practical Considerations

Using the Project Cost–Duration Graph

This graph, as presented in Figures 9.1 and 9.6, is valuable to compare any proposed alternative or change with the optimum cost and time. More importantly, the creation of such a graph keeps the importance of indirect costs in the forefront of decision making. Indirect costs are frequently forgotten in the field when the pressure for action is intense. Finally, such a graph can be used before the project begins or while the project is in progress. Creating the graph in the preproject planning phase without an imposed duration is the first choice because normal time is more meaningful. Creating the graph in the project planning phase with an imposed duration is less desirable because normal time is made to fit the imposed date and is probably not low cost. Creating the graph after the project has started is the least desirable because some alternatives may be ruled out of the decision process. Managers may choose not to use the formal procedure demonstrated. However, regardless of the method used, the principles and concepts inherent in the formal procedure are highly applicable in practice and should be considered in any cost–duration trade-off decision.

Crash Times

Collecting crash times for even a moderate-size project can be difficult. The meaning of crash time is difficult to communicate. What is meant when you define crash time as "the shortest time you can realistically complete an activity"? Crash time is open to different interpretations and judgments. Some estimators feel very uncomfortable providing crash times. Regardless of the comfort level, the accuracy of crash times and costs is frequently rough at best, when compared with normal time and cost.

Linearity Assumption

Because the accuracy of compressed activity times and costs is questionable, the concern of some theorists—that the relationship between cost and time is not linear but curvilinear—is seldom a concern for practicing managers. Reasonable, quick comparisons can be made using the linear assumption. The simple approach is adequate for most projects. There are rare situations in which activities cannot be crashed by single time units. Instead, crashing is "all or nothing." For example, activity A will take 10 days (for say $1,000) or it will take 7 days (for say $1,500), but no options exist in which activity A will take 8 or 9 days to complete. In a few rare cases of very large, complex, long-duration projects, the use of present value techniques may be useful; such techniques are beyond the scope of this text.

Choice of Activities to Crash Revisited

The cost–time crashing method relies on choosing the cheapest method for reducing the duration of the project. There are other factors that should be assessed beyond simply cost. First, the inherent risks involved in crashing particular activities need to be considered. Some activities are riskier to crash than others. For example, accelerating the completion of a software design code may not be wise if it increases the likelihood of errors surfacing downstream. Conversely, crashing a more expensive activity may be wise if fewer inherent risks are involved.

Second, the timing of activities needs to be considered. Crashing an early activity may be prudent if there is concern that subsequent activities are likely to be delayed, and absorb the time gained. Then the manager would still have the option of crashing final activities to get back on schedule.

SNAPSHOT FROM PRACTICE   I'll Bet You . . .

The focus of this chapter has been on how project managers crash activities by typically assigning additional manpower and equipment to cut significant time off of scheduled tasks. Project managers often encounter situations in which they need to motivate individuals to accelerate the completion of a specific, critical task. Imagine the following scenario.

Brue Young just received a priority assignment from corporate headquarters. The preliminary engineering sketches that were due tomorrow need to be e-mailed to the West Coast by 4:00 PM today so that the model shop can begin construction of a prototype to present to top management. He approaches Danny Whitten, the draftsman responsible for the task, whose initial response is, "That's impossible!" While he agrees that it would be very difficult he does not believe that it is as impossible as Danny suggests or that Danny truly believes that. What should he do?

He tells Danny that he knows this is going to be a rush job, but he is confident that he can do it. When Danny balks, he responds, "I tell you what, I'll make a bet with you. If you are able to finish the design by 4:00, I'll make sure you get two of the company's tickets to tomorrow night's Celtics–Knicks basketball game." Danny accepts the challenge, works feverishly to complete the assignment, and is able to take his daughter to her first professional basketball game.

Conversations with project managers reveal that many use bets like this one to motivate extraordinary performance. These bets range from tickets to sporting and entertainment events to gift certificates at high-class restaurants to a well-deserved afternoon off. For bets to work they need to adhere to the principles of expectancy theory of motivation. Boiled down to simple terms, expectancy theory rests on three key questions:

1. Can I do it (Is it possible to meet the challenge)?
2. Will I get it (Can I demonstrate that I met the challenge and can I trust the project manager will deliver his/her end of the bargain)?
3. Is it worth it (Is the payoff of sufficient personal value to warrant the risk and extra effort)?

If in the mind of the participant the answer to any of these three questions is no, then the person is unlikely to accept the challenge. However, when the answers are affirmative, then the individual is likely to accept the bet and be motivated to meet the challenge.

Bets can be effective motivational tools and add an element of excitement and fun to project work. But, the following practical advice should be heeded:

1. The bet has greater significance if it also benefits family members or significant others. Being able to take a son or daughter to a professional basketball game allows that individual to "score points" at home through work. These bets also recognize and reward the support project members receive from their families and reinforces the importance of their work to loved ones.

2. Bets should be used sparingly; otherwise everything can become negotiable. They should be used only under special circumstances that require extraordinary effort.

3. Individual bets should involve clearly recognizable individual effort, otherwise others may become jealous and discord may occur within a group. As long as others see it as requiring truly remarkable, "beyond the call of duty" effort, they will consider it fair and warranted.

Third, crashing frequently results in overallocation of resources. The resources required to accelerate a cheaper activity may suddenly not be available. Resource availability, not cost, may dictate which activities are crashed.

Finally, the impact crashing would have on the morale and motivation of the project team needs to be assessed. If the least-cost method repeatedly signals a subgroup to accelerate progress, fatigue and resentment may set in. Conversely, if overtime pay is involved, other team members may resent not having access to this benefit. This situation can lead to tension within the entire project team. Good project managers gauge the response that crashing activities will have on the entire project team. See Snapshot from Practice: I'll Bet You . . . for a novel approach to motivating employees to work faster.

Time Reduction Decisions and Sensitivity

Should the project owner or project manager go for the optimum cost-time? The answer is, "It depends." Risk must be considered. Recall from our example that the optimum project time point represented a reduced project cost and was less than the original normal project time (review Figure 9.6). The project direct-cost line near the normal point is usually relatively flat. Because indirect costs for the project are usually greater in the same range, the optimum cost-time point is less than the normal time point. Logic of the cost-time procedure suggests managers should reduce the project duration to the lowest total cost point and duration.

How far to reduce the project time from the normal time toward the optimum depends on the *sensitivity* of the project network. A network is sensitive if it has several critical or near-critical paths. In our example project movement toward the optimum time requires spending money to reduce critical activities, resulting in slack reduction and/or more critical paths and activities. Slack reduction in a project with several near-critical paths increases the risk of being late. The practical outcome can be a higher total project cost if some near-critical activities are de-layed and become critical; the money spent reducing activities on the original criti-cal path would be wasted. Sensitive networks require careful analysis. The bottom line is that compression of projects with several near-critical paths reduces schedul-ing flexibility and increases the risk of delaying the project. The outcome of such analysis will probably suggest only a partial movement from the normal time to-ward the optimum time.

There is a positive situation where moving toward the optimum time can result in very real, large savings—this occurs when the network is *insensitive.* A project network is insensitive if it has a dominant critical path, that is, no near-critical paths. In this project circumstance, movement from the normal time point to-ward the optimum time will *not* create new or near-critical activities. The bottom line here is that the reduction of the slack of noncritical activities increases the risk of their becoming critical only slightly when compared with the effect in a sensitive network. Insensitive networks hold the greatest potential for real, some-times large, savings in total project costs with a minimum risk of noncritical ac-tivities becoming critical.

Insensitive networks are not a rarity in practice; they occur in perhaps 25 per-cent of all projects. For example, a light rail project team observed from their net-work a dominant critical path and relatively high indirect costs. It soon became clear that by spending some dollars on a few critical activities, very large savings of indirect costs could be realized. Savings of several million dollars were spent extending the rail line and adding another station. The logic found in this example is just as applicable to small projects as large ones. Insensitive networks with high indirect costs can produce large savings.

Ultimately, deciding if and which activities to crash is a judgment call requiring careful consideration of the options available, the costs and risks involved, and the importance of meeting a deadline.

What if Cost, Not Time, Is the Issue?

In today's fast-paced world, there appears to be a greater emphasis on getting things done quickly. Still, organizations are always looking for ways to get things done cheaply. This is especially true for fixed-bid projects, where profit margin is derived from the difference between the bid and actual cost of the project. Every dollar saved is a dollar in your pocket. Sometimes, in order to secure a contract, bids are tight, which puts added pressure on cost containment. In other cases, there are financial incentives tied to cost containment.

Even in situations where cost is transferred to customers there is pressure to re-duce cost. Cost overruns make for unhappy customers and can damage future business opportunities. Budgets can be fixed or cut, and when contingency funds are exhausted, then cost overruns have to be made up with remaining activities.

As discussed earlier, shortening project duration may come at the expense of overtime, adding additional personnel, and using more expensive equipment and/or materials. Conversely, sometimes cost savings can be generated by extending the duration of a project. This may allow for a smaller workforce, less-skilled (ex-pensive) labor, and even cheaper equipment and materials to be used. Below are some of the more commonly used options for cutting costs.

Reduce Project Scope

Just as scaling back the scope of the project can gain time, delivering less than what was originally planned also produces significant savings. Again, calculating the savings of a reduced project scope begins with the work breakdown structure. However, since time is not the issue, you do not need to focus on critical activities. For example, on over-budget movie projects it is not uncommon to replace loca-tion shots with stock footage to cut costs.

Have Owner Take on More Responsibility

One way of reducing project costs is identifying tasks that customers can do themselves. Homeowners frequently use this method to reduce costs on home improvement projects. For example, to reduce the cost of a bathroom remodel, a homeowner may agree to paint the room instead of paying the contractor to do it. On IS projects, a customer may agree to take on some of the responsibil-ity for testing equipment or providing in-house training. Naturally, this ar-rangement is best negotiated before the project begins. Customers are less receptive to this idea if you suddenly spring it on them. An advantage of this method is that, while costs are lowered, the original scope is retained. Clearly this option is limited to areas in which the customer has expertise and the capa-bility to pick up the tasks.

Outsourcing Project Activities or Even the Entire Project

When estimates exceed budget, it not only makes sense to re-examine the scope but also search for cheaper ways to complete the project. Perhaps instead of re-lying on internal resources, it would be more cost effective to outsource seg-ments or even the entire project, opening up work to external price competition. Specialized subcontractors often enjoy unique advantages, such as material dis-counts for large quantities, as well as equipment that not only gets the work done more quickly but also less expensively. They may have lower overhead and labor costs. For example, to reduce costs of software projects, many American firms outsource work to firms operating in India where the salary of a software engineer is one-third that of an American software engineer. However, outsourc-ing means you have less control over the project and will need to have clearly definable deliverables.

Brainstorming Cost Savings Options

Just as project team members can be a rich source of ideas for accelerating project activities, they can offer tangible ways for reducing project costs. For example, one project manager reported that his team was able to come up with over $75,000 worth of cost saving suggestions without jeopardizing the scope of the project. Project managers should not underestimate the value of simply asking if there is a cheaper, better way.

Summary

The need for reducing the project duration occurs for many reasons such as imposed duration dates, time-to-market considerations, incentive contracts, key resource needs, high overhead costs, or simply unforeseen delays. These situations are very common in practice and are known as cost-time trade-off decisions. This chapter presented a logical, formal process for assessing the implications of situations that involve shortening the project duration. Crashing the project duration increases the *risk* of being late. How far to reduce the project duration from the normal time toward the optimum depends on the *sensitivity* of the project network. A sensitive network is one that has several critical or near-critical paths. Great care should be taken when shortening sensitive networks to avoid increasing project risks. Conversely, insensitive networks represent opportunities for potentially large project cost savings by eliminating some overhead costs with little downside risk.

Alternative strategies for reducing project time were discussed within the context of whether or not the project is resource limited. Project acceleration typically comes at a cost of either spending money for more resources or compromising the scope of the project. If the latter is the case, then it is essential that all relevant stakeholders be consulted so that everyone accepts the changes that have to be made. One other key point is the difference in implementing time-reducing activities in the midst of project execution versus incorporating them into the project plan. You typically have far fewer options once the project is underway than before it begins. This is especially true if you want to take advantage of the new scheduling methodologies such as fast-tracking and critical-chain. Time spent up front considering alternatives and developing contingency plans will lead to time savings in the end.

Key Terms

Crashing, *314*	Direct costs, *314*	Outsourcing, *309*
Crash point, *315*	Fast-tracking, *310*	Project cost–duration
Crash time, *314*	Indirect costs, *313*	graph, *313*

Review Questions

1. What are five common reasons for crashing a project?
2. What are the advantages and disadvantages of reducing project scope to accelerate a project? What can be done to reduce the disadvantages?
3. Why is scheduling overtime a popular choice for getting projects back on schedule? What are the potential problems for relying on this option?
4. Identify four indirect costs you might find on a moderately complex project. Why are these costs classified as indirect?
5. How can a cost–duration graph be used by the project manager? Explain.
6. Reducing the project duration increases the risk of being late. Explain.
7. It is possible to shorten the critical path and save money. Explain how.

Exercises

1. Draw a project network from the following information.

Activity	Predecessor	Duration
A	None	2
B	A	4
C	A	3
D	A	2
E	B	3
F	C	6
G	C, D	5
H	E, F	6
I	G	5
J	H, I	5

Activities B and H can be shortened to a minimum of 2 weeks. Which activity would you shorten to reduce the project duration by 2 weeks? Why?

2.* Use the information contained below to compress one time unit per move using the least cost method. Reduce the schedule until you reach the crash point of the network. For each move identify what activity(s) was crashed the adjusted total cost.

Act.	Crash Cost (Slope)	Maximum Crash Time	Normal Time	Normal Cost
A	0	0	1	100
B	100	2	3	150
C	50	1	4	200
D	60	1	3	200
E	70	2	4	200
F	90	1	3	150

3. Assume the network and data that follow. Compute the total direct cost for each project duration. If the indirect costs for each project duration are $400 (19 time units), $350 (18), $300 (17), and $250 (16), compute the total project cost for each duration. Plot the total direct, indirect, and project costs for each of these durations on a cost-time graph. What is the optimum cost-time schedule for the project? What is this cost?

---

* The solution to this exercise can be found in Appendix One.

Act.	Crash Cost (Slope)	Maximum Crash Time	Normal Time	Normal Cost
A	20	1	3	50
B	60	2	5	60
C	40	1	3	70
D	0	0	10	50
E	50	3	6	100
F	100	3	7	90
G	70	1	5	50
				$470

4. Given the data and information that follow, compute the total direct cost for each project duration. If the indirect costs for each project duration are $90 (15 time units), $70 (14), $50 (13), $40 (12), and $30 (11), compute the total project cost for each duration. What is the optimum cost-time schedule for the project? What is this cost?

Act.	Crash Cost (Slope)	Maximum Crash Time	Normal Time	Normal Cost
A	20	1	5	50
B	60	2	3	60
C	0	0	4	70
D	10	1	2	50
E	60	3	5	100
F	100	1	2	90
G	30	1	5	50
H	40	0	2	60
I	200	1	3	200
				$730

5. If the indirect costs for each duration are $1,200 for 16 weeks, $1,130 for 15 weeks, $1,000 for 14 weeks, $900 for 13 weeks, $860 for 12 weeks, $820 for 11 weeks, and $790 for 10 weeks, compute the total costs for each duration. Plot these costs on a graph. What is the optimum cost-time schedule?

Act.	Crash Cost (Slope)	Maximum Crash Time	Normal Time	Normal Cost
A	10	1	4	30
B	70	2	7	60
C	0	0	1	80
D	20	2	4	40
E	50	3	5	110
F	200	3	5	90
G	30	1	2	60
H	40	1	2	70
I	0	0	2	140
				$680

Time unit = 1 week

Project duration _16_

Total direct cost $ ____

6. If the indirect costs for each duration are $300 for 27 weeks, $240 for 26 weeks, $180 for 25 weeks, $120 for 24 weeks, $60 for 23 weeks, and $50 for 22 weeks, compute the direct, indirect and total costs for each duration. What is the optimum cost-time schedule? The customer offers you $10 for every week you shorten the project from your original network. Would you take it? If so for how many weeks?

Act.	Crash Cost (Slope)	Maximum Crash Time	Normal Time	Normal Cost
A	80	2	10	40
B	30	3	8	10
C	40	1	5	80
D	50	2	11	50
E	100	4	15	100
F	30	1	6	20
				$300

Time unit = 1 week

7. Use the information contained below to compress one time unit per move using the least cost method. Reduce the schedule until you reach the crash point of the network. For each move identify what activity(s) was crashed, the adjusted total cost, and explain your choice if you have to choose between activities that cost the same.

Note: Crash point of the network is the point in which the duration cannot be reduced any further.

Activity ID	Slope	Maximum Crash Time	Normal Time	Normal Cost	Crash Time	Crash Cost
A	—	0	4	$50	0	—
B	$40	3	5	70	2	$190
C	40	1	5	80	4	120
D	40	2	4	40	2	120
E	40	2	5	60	3	140
F	40	1	5	50	4	90
G	30	1	4	70	3	100
H	30	1	4	80	3	110
I	—	0	3	50	0	—

Total direct normal costs—$550

8.* Use the information contained below to compress one time unit per move using the least cost method. Reduce the schedule until you reach the crash point of the network. For each move identify what activity(s) was crashed, the adjusted total cost, and explain your choice if you have to choose between activities that cost the same.

If the indirect cost for each duration are $1,500 for 17 weeks, $1,450 for 16 weeks, $1,400 for 15 weeks, $1,350 for 14 weeks, $1,300 for 13 weeks, $1,250

---

* The solution to this exercise can be found in Appendix One.

for 12 weeks, $1,200 for 11 weeks, and $1,150 for 10 weeks, what is the optimum cost-time schedule for the project? What is the cost?

Act.	Crash Cost (Slope)	Maximum Crash Time	Normal Time	Normal Cost
A	0	0	3	150
B	100	2	4	200
C	60	1	3	250
D	40	1	4	200
E	0	0	2	250
F	30	2	3	200
G	20	1	2	250
H	60	2	4	300
I	200	1	2	200

References

Abdel-Hamid, T., and S. Madnick, *Software Project Dynamics: An Integrated Approach* (Englewood Cliffs, NJ: Prentice Hall, 1991).

Baker, B. M., "Cost/Time Trade-off Analysis for the Critical Path Method," *Journal of the Operational Research Society,* 48 (12) 1997, pp. 1241–44.

Brooks, F. P., Jr., *The Mythical Man-Month: Essays on Software Engineering Anniversary Edition* (Reading, MA: Addison-Wesley Longman, Inc., 1994), pp. 15–26.

DeMarco, T., *Slack: Getting Past Burnout, Busywork, and the Myth of Total Efficiency* (New York: Broadway, 2002).

Ibbs, C. W., S. A. Lee, and M. I. Li, "Fast-Tracking's Impact on Project Change," *Project Management Journal,* 29 (4) 1998, pp. 35–42.

Khang, D. B., and M. Yin, "Time, Cost, and Quality Tradeoff in Project Management," *International Journal of Project Management,* 17 (4) 1999, pp. 249–56.

Perrow, L. A., *Finding Time: How Corporations, Individuals, and Families Can Benefit From New Work Practices* (Ithaca, NY: Cornell University Press, 1997).

Roemer, T. R., R. Ahmadi, and R. Wang, "Time-Cost Trade-offs in Overlapped Product Development," *Operations Research,* 48 (6) 2000, pp. 858–65.

Smith, P. G., and D. G. Reinersten, *Developing Products in Half the Time* (New York: Van Nostrand Reinhold, 1995).

Verzuh, E., *The Fast Forward MBA in Project Management* (New York: John Wiley, 1999).

Vroom, V. H., *Work and Motivation* (New York: John Wiley & Sons, 1964).

Case

International Capital, Inc.—Part B

Given the project network derived in Part A of the case from Chapter 7, Brown also wants to be prepared to answer any questions concerning compressing the project duration. This question will almost always be entertained by the accounting department, review committee, and the client. To be ready for the compression question, Brown has prepared the following data in case it is necessary to crash the project. (Use your weighted average times (t_e) computed in Part A of the International Capital case found in Chapter 7.)

Activity	Normal Cost	Maximum Crash Time	Crash Cost/Day
A	$ 3,000	3	$ 500
B	5,000	2	1000
C	6,000	0	—
D	20,000	3	3,000
E	10,000	2	1,000
F	7,000	1	1,000
G	20,000	2	3,000
H	8,000	1	2,000
I	5,000	1	2,000
J	7,000	1	1,000
K	12,000	6	1,000
Total normal costs = $103,000			

Using the data provided, determine the activity crashing decisions and best-time cost project duration. Given the information you have developed, what suggestions would you give Brown to ensure she is well prepared for the project review committee? Assume the overhead costs for this project are $700 per workday. Will this alter your suggestions?

Case

Whitbread World Sailboat Race

Each year countries enter their sailing vessels in the nine-month Round the World Whitbread Sailboat Race. In recent years, about 14 countries entered sailboats in the race. Each year's sailboat entries represent the latest technologies and human skills each country can muster.

Bjorn Ericksen has been selected as a project manager because of his past experience as a master helmsman and because of his recent fame as the "best designer of racing sailboats in the world." Bjorn is pleased and proud to have the opportunity to design, build, test, and train the crew for next year's Whitbread entry for his country. Bjorn has picked Karin Knutsen (as chief design engineer) and Trygve Wallvik (as master helmsman) to be team leaders responsible for getting next year's entry ready for the traditional parade of all entries on the Thames River in the United Kingdom, which signals the start of the race.

As Bjorn begins to think of a project plan, he sees two parallel paths running through the project—design and construction and crew training. Last year's boat will be used for training until the new entry can have the crew on board to learn maintenance tasks. Bjorn calls Karin and Trygve together to develop a project plan. All three agree the major goal is to have a winning boat and crew ready to compete in next year's competition at a cost of $3.2 million. A check of Bjorn's calendar indicates he has 45 weeks before next year's vessel must leave port for the United Kingdom to start the race.

THE KICKOFF MEETING

Bjorn asks Karin to begin by describing the major activities and the sequence required to design, construct, and test the boat. Karin starts by noting that design of the hull, deck, mast, and accessories should only take six weeks—given the design prints from past race entries and a few prints from other countries' entries. After the design is complete, the hull can be constructed, the mast ordered, sails ordered, and accessories ordered. The hull will require 12 weeks to complete. The mast can be ordered and will require a lead time of eight weeks; the seven sails can be ordered and will take six weeks to get; accessories can be ordered and will take 15 weeks to receive. As soon as the hull is finished, the ballast tanks can be installed, requiring two weeks. Then the deck can be built, which will require five weeks. Concurrently, the hull can be treated with special sealant and friction-resistance coating, taking three weeks. When the deck is completed and mast and accessories received, the mast and sails can be installed, requiring two weeks; the accessories can be installed, which will take six weeks. When all of these activities have been completed, the ship can be sea-tested, which should take five weeks. Karin believes she can have firm cost estimates for the boat in about two weeks.

Trygve believes he can start selecting the 12-man or woman crew and securing their housing immediately. He believes it will take six weeks to get a committed crew on-site and three weeks to secure housing for the crew members. Trygve reminds Bjorn that last year's vessel must be ready to use for training the moment the crew is on-site until the new vessel is ready for testing. Keeping the old vessel operating will cost $4,000 per week as long as it is used. Once the crew is on-site and housed, they can develop and implement a routine sailing and maintenance training program, which will take 15 weeks (using the old vessel). Also, once the crew is selected and on-site, crew equipment can be selected, taking only two weeks. Then crew equipment can be ordered; it will take five weeks to arrive. When the crew equipment and maintenance training program are complete, crew maintenance on the new vessel can begin; this should take 10 weeks. But crew maintenance on the new vessel cannot begin until the deck is complete and the mast, sails, and accessories have arrived. Once crew maintenance on the new vessel begins, the new vessel will cost $6,000 per week until sea training is complete. After the new ship maintenance is complete and while the boat is being tested, initial sailing training can be implemented; training should take seven weeks. Finally, after the boat is tested and initial training is complete, regular sea training can be implemented—weather permitting; regular sea training requires eight weeks. Trygve believes he can put the cost estimates together in a week, given last year's expenses.

Bjorn is pleased with the expertise displayed by his team leaders. But he believes they need to have someone develop one of those critical path networks to see if they can safely meet the start deadline for the race. Karin and Trygve agree. Karin suggests the cost estimates should also include crash costs for any activities that can be compressed and the resultant costs for crashing. Karin also suggests the team complete the following priority matrix for project decision making:

FIGURE C9.1
Project Priority
Matrix: Whitbread
Project

	Time	Performance	Cost
Constrain			
Enhance			
Accept			

TWO WEEKS LATER

Karin and Trygve submit the following cost estimates for each activity and corresponding crash costs to Bjorn (costs are in thousands of dollars):

Activity		Normal Time	Normal Cost	Crash Time	Crash Cost	Slope
A	Design	6	$ 40	4	$ 160	60
B	Build hull	12	1,000	10	1,400	200
C	Install ballast tanks	2	100	2	100	—
D	Order mast	8	100	7	140	40
E	Order sails	6	40	6	40	—
F	Order accessories	15	600	13	800	100
G	Build deck	5	200	5	200	—
H	Coat hull	3	40	3	40	—
I	Install accessories	6	300	5	400	100
J	Install mast and sails	2	40	1	80	40
K	Test	5	60	4	100	40
L	Sea trials	8	200	7	450	250
M	Select crew	6	10	5	20	10
N	Secure housing	3	30	3	30	—
O	Select crew equipment	2	10	2	10	—
P	Order crew equipment	5	30	5	30	—
Q	Routine sail/maintenance	15	40	12	130	30
R	Crew maintenance training	10	100	9	340	240
S	Initial sail training	7	50	5	350	150
	Total direct cost		$2,990			

Bjorn reviews the materials and wonders if the project will come in within the budget of $3.2 million and in 45 weeks. Advise the Whitbread team of their situation.

Case

Nightingale Project—A

You are the assistant project manager to Rassy Brown, who is in charge of the Nightingale project. Nightingale was the code name given to the development of a handheld electronic medical reference guide. Nightingale would be designed for emergency medical technicians and paramedics who need a quick reference guide to use in emergency situations.

Rassy and her project team were developing a project plan aimed at producing 30 working models in time for MedCON, the biggest medical equipment trade show each year. Meeting the MedCON October 25 deadline was critical to success. All the major medical equipment manufacturers demonstrated and took orders for new products at MedCON. Rassy had also heard rumors that competitors were considering developing a similar product, and she knew that being first to market would have a significant sales advantage. Besides, top management made funding contingent upon developing a workable plan for meeting the MedCON deadline.

The project team spent the morning working on the schedule for Nightingale. They started with the WBS and developed the information for a network, adding activities when needed. Then the team added the time estimates they had collected for each activity. Following is the preliminary information for activities with duration time and predecessors:

Activity	Description	Duration	Predecessor
1	Architectural decisions	10	None
2	Internal specifications	20	1
3	External specifications	18	1
4	Feature specifications	15	1
5	Voice recognition	15	2,3
6	Case	4	2,3
7	Screen	2	2,3
8	Speaker output jacks	2	2,3
9	Tape mechanism	2	2,3
10	Database	40	4
11	Microphone/soundcard	5	4
12	Pager	4	4
13	Barcode reader	3	4
14	Alarm clock	4	4
15	Computer I/O	5	4
16	Review design	10	5,6,7,8,9,10,11,12,13,14,15
17	Price components	5	5,6,7,8,9,10,11,12,13,14,15
18	Integration	15	16,17
19	Document design	35	16
20	Procure prototype components	20	18
21	Assemble prototypes	10	20
22	Lab test prototypes	20	21
23	Field test prototypes	20	19,22
24	Adjust design	20	23
25	Order stock parts	15	24
26	Order custom parts	2	24
27	Assemble first production unit	10	25, FS—8 time units 26, FS—13 time units
28	Test unit	10	27
29	Produce 30 units	15	28
30	Train sales representatives	10	29

Use any project network computer program available to you to develop the schedule for activities (see Case Appendix for further instructions)—noting late and early times, the critical path, and estimated completion for the project.

Prepare a short memo that addresses the following questions:

1. Will the project as planned meet the October 25th deadline?
2. What activities lie on the critical path?
3. How sensitive is this network?

Case

Nightingale Project—B

Rassy and the team were concerned with the results of your analysis. They spent the afternoon brainstorming alternative ways for shortening the project duration. They rejected outsourcing activities because most of the work was developmental in nature and could only be done in-house. They considered altering the scope of the project by eliminating some of the proposed product features. After much debate, they felt they could not compromise any of the core features and be successful in the marketplace. They then turned their attention to accelerating the completion of activities through overtime and adding additional technical manpower. Rassy had built into her proposal a discretionary fund of $200,000. She was willing to invest up to half of this fund to accelerate the project, but wanted to hold onto at least $100,000 to deal with unexpected problems. After a lengthy discussion, her team concluded that the following activities could be reduced at the specified cost:

- Development of voice recognition system could be reduced from 15 days to 10 days at a cost of $15,000.
- Creation of database could be reduced from 40 days to 35 days at a cost of $35,000.
- Document design could be reduced from 35 days to 30 days at a cost of $25,000.
- External specifications could be reduced from 18 days to 12 days at a cost of $20,000.
- Procure prototype components could be reduced from 20 days to 15 days at a cost of $30,000.
- Order stock parts could be reduced from 15 days to 10 days at a cost of $20,000.

Ken Clark, a development engineer, pointed out that the network contained only finish-to-start relationships and that it might be possible to reduce project duration by creating start-to-start lags. For example, he said that his people would not have to wait for all of the field tests to be completed to begin making final adjustments in the design. They could start making adjustments after the first 15 days of testing. The project team spent the remainder of the day analyzing how they could introduce lags into the network to hopefully shorten the project. They concluded that the following finish-to-start relationships could be converted into lags:

- Document design could begin 5 days after the start of the review design.
- Adjust design could begin 15 days after the start of field test prototypes.

- Order stock parts could begin 5 days after the start of adjust design.
- Order custom parts could begin 5 days after the start of adjust design.
- Training sales representatives could begin 5 days after the start of test unit and completed 5 days after the production of 30 units.

As the meeting adjourns, Rassy turns to you and tells you to assess the options presented and try to develop a schedule that will meet the October 25th deadline. You are to prepare a report to be presented to the project team that answers the following questions:

1. Is it possible to meet the deadline?
2. If so, how would you recommend changing the original schedule (Part A) and why? Assess the relative impact of crashing activities versus introducing lags to shorten project duration.
3. What would the new schedule look like?
4. What other factors should be considered before finalizing the schedule?

CASE APPENDIX: TECHNICAL DETAILS

Create your project schedule and assess your options based on the following information:

1. The project will begin the first working day in January, 2010.
2. The following holidays are observed: January 1, Memorial Day (last Monday in May), July 4, Labor Day (first Monday in September), Thanksgiving Day (fourth Thursday in November), December 25 and 26.
3. If a holiday falls on a Saturday, then Friday will be given as an extra day off; if it falls on a Sunday, then Monday will be given as a day off.
4. The project team works Monday through Friday.
5. If you choose to reduce the duration of any one of the activities mentioned, then it must be for the specified time and cost (i.e., you cannot choose to reduce database to 37 days at a reduced cost; you can only reduce it to 35 days at a cost of $35,000).
6. You can only spend up to $100,000 to reduce project activities; lags do not contain any additional costs.

Case

The "Now" Wedding—Part A*

On December 31 of last year, Lauren burst into the family living room and announced that she and Connor (her college boyfriend) were going to be married. After recovering from the shock, her mother hugged her and asked, "When?" The following conversation resulted:

Lauren: January 21.
  Mom: What?

---

* This case was adapted from a case originally written by Professor D. Clay Whybark, University of North Carolina, Chapel Hill, N.C.

Dad: The Now Wedding will be the social hit of the year. Wait a minute. Why so soon?

Lauren: Because on January 30 Connor, who is in the National Guard, will be shipping out overseas. We want a week for a honeymoon.

Mom: But Honey, we can't possibly finish all the things that need to be done by then. Remember all the details that were involved in your sister's wedding? Even if we start tomorrow, it takes a day to reserve the church and reception hall, and they need at least 14 days' notice. That has to be done before we can start decorating, which takes 3 days. An extra $200 on Sunday would probably cut that 14 day notice to 7 days, though.

Dad: Oh, boy!

Lauren: I want Jane Summers to be my maid of honor.

Dad: But she's in the Peace Corps in Guatemala, isn't she? It would take her 10 days to get ready and drive up here.

Lauren: But we could fly her up in 2 days and it would only cost $1,000.

Dad: Oh, boy!

Mom: And catering! It takes 2 days to choose the cake and decorations, and Jack's Catering wants at least 5 days' notice. Besides, we'd have to have those things before we could start decorating.

Lauren: Can I wear your wedding dress, Mom?

Mother: Well, we'd have to replace some lace, but you could wear it, yes. We could order the lace from New York when we order the material for the bridesmaids' dresses. It takes 8 days to order and receive the material. The pattern needs to be chosen first, and that would take 3 days.

Dad: We could get the material here in 5 days if we paid an extra $20 to airfreight it. Oh, boy!

Lauren: I want Mrs. Jacks to work on the dresses.

Mom: But she charges $48 a day.

Dad: Oh, boy!

Mom: If we did all the sewing we could finish the dresses in 11 days. If Mrs. Jacks helped we could cut that down to 6 days at a cost of $48 for each day less than 11 days. She is very good too.

Lauren: I don't want anyone but her.

Mom: It would take another 2 days to do the final fitting and 2 more days to clean and press the dresses. They would have to be ready by rehearsal night. We must have rehearsal the night before the wedding.

Dad: Everything should be ready rehearsal night.

Mom: We've forgotten something. The invitations!

Dad: We should order the invitations from Bob's Printing Shop, and that usually takes 7 days. I'll bet he would do it in 6 days if we slipped him an extra $20!

Mom: It would take us 2 days to choose the invitation style before we could order them and we want the envelopes printed with our return address.

Lauren: Oh! That will be elegant.

Mom: The invitations should go out at least 10 days before the wedding. If we let them go any later, some of the relatives would get theirs too late to come and that would make them mad. I'll bet that if we didn't get them out until 8 days before the wedding, Aunt Ethel couldn't make it and she would reduce her wedding gift by $200.

Dad: Oh, boy!!

Mom:	We'll have to take them to the Post Office to mail them and that takes a day. Addressing would take 3 days unless we hired some part-time girls and we can't start until the printer is finished. If we hired the girls we could probably save 2 days by spending $40 for each day saved.
Lauren:	We need to get gifts for the bridesmaids. I could spend a day and do that.
Mom:	Before we can even start to write out those invitations we need a guest list. Heavens, that will take 4 days to get in order and only I can understand our address file.
Lauren:	Oh, Mom, I'm so excited. We can start each of the relatives on a different job.
Mom:	Honey, I don't see how we can do it. Why, I've got to choose the invitations and patterns and reserve the church and . . .
Dad:	Why don't you just take $3,000 and elope. Your sister's wedding cost me $2,400 and she didn't have to fly people up from Guatemala, hire extra girls and Mrs. Jacks, use airfreight, or anything like that.

1. Using a yellow sticky approach (see p. 153), develop a project network for the "Now" Wedding.
2. Create a schedule for the wedding using MS Project. Can you reach the deadline of January 21 for the "Now" Wedding? If you cannot, what would it cost to make the January 21 deadline and which activities would you change?

Case

The "Now" Wedding—Part B

Several complications arose during the course of trying to meet the deadline of January 20 for the "Now" Wedding rehearsal. Since Lauren was adamant on having the wedding on January 21 (as was Connor for obvious reasons), the implications of each of these complications had to be assessed.

1. On January 1 the chairman of the Vestry Committee of the church was left unimpressed by the added donation and said he wouldn't reduce the notice period from 14 to 7 days.
2. Mother comes down with the three-day flu as she starts work on the guest list January 2.
3. Bob's Printing Shop press was down for one day on January 5 in order to replace faulty brushes in the electric motor.
4. The lace and dress material are lost in transit. Notice of the loss is received on January 10.

Can the wedding still take place on January 21? If not to what options are available?

Leadership: Being an Effective Project Manager

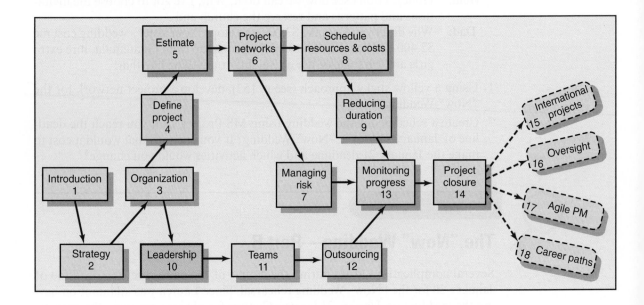

Leadership: Being an Effective Project Manager

Managing versus Leading a Project

Managing Project Stakeholders

Influence as Exchange

Social Network Building

Ethics and Project Management

Building Trust: The Key to Exercising Influence

Qualities of an Effective Project Manager

Summary

I couldn't wait to be the manager of my own project and run the project the way I thought it should be done. Boy, did I have a lot to learn!

—*first-time project manager*

This chapter is based on the premise that one of the keys to being an effective project manager is building cooperative relationships among different groups of people to complete projects. Project success does not just depend on the performance of the project team. Success or failure often depends on the contributions of top management, functional managers, customers, suppliers, contractors, and others.

The chapter begins with a brief discussion of the differences between leading and managing a project. The importance of managing project stakeholders is then introduced. Managers require a broad influence base to be effective in this area. Different sources of influence are discussed and are used to describe how project managers build social capital. This management style necessitates constant interacting with different groups of people whom project managers depend on. Special attention is devoted to managing the critical relationship with top management and the importance of leading by example. The importance of gaining cooperation in ways that build and sustain the trust of others is emphasized. The chapter concludes by identifying personal attributes associated with being an effective project manager. Subsequent chapters will expand on these ideas in a discussion of managing the project team and working with people outside the organization.

Managing versus Leading a Project

In a perfect world, the project manager would simply implement the project plan and the project would be completed. The project manager would work with others to formulate a schedule, organize a project team, keep track of progress, and announce what needs to be done next, and then everyone would charge along. Of course no one lives in a perfect world, and rarely does everything go according to plan. Project participants get testy; they fail to complement each other; other departments are unable to fulfill their commitments; technical glitches arise; work takes longer than expected. The project manager's job is to get the project back on track. A manager expedites certain activities; figures out ways to solve technical problems; serves as peacemaker when tensions rise; and makes appropriate trade-offs among time, cost, and scope of the project.

However, project managers do more than put out fires and keep the project on track. They also innovate and adapt to ever-changing circumstances. They often have to deviate from what was planned and introduce significant changes in the project scope and schedule to respond to unforeseen threats or opportunities. For example, customers' needs may change, requiring significant design changes midway through the project. Competitors may release new products that dictate crashing project deadlines. Working relationships among project participants may break down, requiring a reformulation of the project team. Ultimately, what was planned or expected in the beginning may be very different from what was accomplished by the end of the project.

Project managers are responsible for integrating assigned resources to complete the project according to plan. At the same time they need to initiate changes in plans and schedules as persistent problems make plans unworkable. In other words, managers want to keep the project going while making necessary adjustments along the way. According to Kotter these two different activities represent the distinction between management and leadership. Management is about coping with complexity, while leadership is about coping with change.

Good management brings about order and stability by formulating plans and objectives, designing structures and procedures, monitoring results against plans, and taking corrective action when necessary. Leadership involves recognizing and articulating the need to significantly alter the direction and operation of the project, aligning people to the new direction, and motivating them to work together to overcome hurdles produced by the change and to realize new objectives.

Strong leadership, while usually desirable, is not always necessary to successfully complete a project. Well-defined projects that encounter no significant surprises require little leadership, as might be the case in constructing a conventional apartment building in which the project manager simply administrates the project plan. Conversely, the higher the degree of uncertainty encountered on a project— whether in terms of changes in project scope, technological stalemates, breakdowns in coordination between people, and so forth—the more leadership is required. For example, strong leadership would be needed for a software development project in which the parameters are always changing to meet developments in the industry.

It takes a special person to perform both roles well. Some individuals are great visionaries who are good at exciting people about change. Too often though, these same people lack the discipline or patience to deal with the day-to-day drudgeries of managing. Likewise, there are other individuals who are very well organized and methodical but lack the ability to inspire others.

Strong leaders can compensate for their managerial weaknesses by having trusted assistants who oversee and manage the details of the project. Conversely, a weak leader can complement his or her strengths by having assistants who are good at sensing the need to change and rallying project participants. Still, one of the things that makes good project managers so valuable to an organization is that they have the ability to both manage and lead a project. In doing so they recognize the need to manage project interfaces and build a social network that allows them to find out what needs to be done and obtain the cooperation necessary to achieve it.

Managing Project Stakeholders

First-time project managers are eager to implement their own ideas and manage their people to successfully complete their project. What they soon find out is that project success depends on the cooperation of a wide range of individuals, many of whom do not directly report to them. For example, during the course of a system integration project, a project manager was surprised by how much time she was spending negotiating and working with vendors, consultants, technical specialists, and other functional managers:

> Instead of working with my people to complete the project, I found myself being constantly pulled and tugged by demands of different groups of people who were not directly involved in the project but had a vested interest in the outcome.

Too often when new project managers do find time to work directly on the project, they adopt a hands-on approach to managing the project. They choose this style not because they are power-hungry egomaniacs but because they are eager to achieve results. They become quickly frustrated by how slowly things operate, the number of people that have to be brought on board, and the difficulty of gaining cooperation. Unfortunately, as this frustration builds, the natural temptation is to exert more pressure and get more heavily involved in the project. These project managers quickly earn the reputation of "micro managing" and begin to lose sight of the real role they play on guiding a project.

Some new managers never break out of this vicious cycle. Others soon realize that authority does not equal influence and that being an effective project manager involves managing a much more complex and expansive set of interfaces than they had previously anticipated. They encounter a web of relationships that requires a much broader spectrum of influence than they felt was necessary or even possible.

For example, a significant project, whether it involves renovating a bridge, creating a new product, or installing a new information system, will likely involve in one way or another working with a number of different groups of stakeholders. First, there is the core group of specialists assigned to complete the project. This group is likely to be supplemented at different times by professionals who work on specific segments of the project. Second, there are the groups of people within the performing organization who are either directly or indirectly involved with the project. The most notable is top management, to whom the project manager is accountable. There are also other managers who provide resources and/or may be responsible for specific segments of the project, and administrative support services such as human resources, finance, etc. Depending on the nature of the project, there are a number of different groups outside the organization that influence the success of the project; the most important is the customer for which the project is designed (see Figure 10.1).

Each of these groups of stakeholders brings different expertise, standards, priorities, and agendas to the project. **Stakeholders** are people and organizations that are actively involved in the project, or whose interests may be positively or negatively affected by the project. The sheer breadth and complexity of stakeholder relationships distinguish project management from regular management. To be effective, a project manager must understand how stakeholders can affect the project and develop methods for managing the dependency. The nature of these dependencies is identified here:

- The **project team** manages and completes project work. Most participants want to do a good job, but they are also concerned with their other obligations and how their involvement on the project will contribute to their personal goals and aspirations.

FIGURE 10.1
Network of
Stakeholders

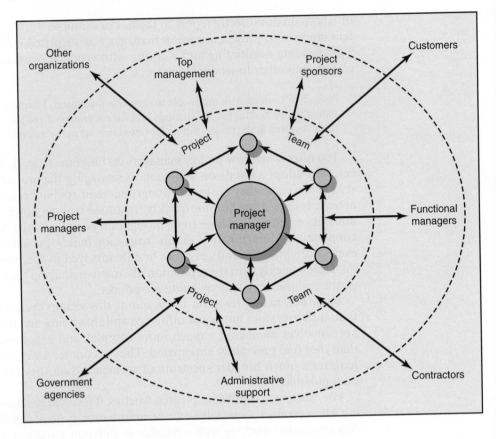

- **Project managers** naturally compete with each other for resources and the support of top management. At the same time they often have to share resources and exchange information.
- **Administrative support** groups, such as human resources, information systems, purchasing agents, and maintenance, provide valuable support services. At the same time they impose constraints and requirements on the project such as the documentation of expenditures and the timely and accurate delivery of information.
- **Functional managers,** depending on how the project is organized, can play a minor or major role toward project success. In matrix arrangements, they may be responsible for assigning project personnel, resolving technical dilemmas, and overseeing the completion of significant segments of the project work. Even in dedicated project teams, the technical input from functional managers may be useful, and acceptance of completed project work may be critical to in-house projects. Functional managers want to cooperate up to a point, but only up to a certain point. They are also concerned with preserving their status within the organization and minimizing the disruptions the project may have on their own operations.
- **Top management** approves funding of the project and establishes priorities within the organization. They define success and adjudicate rewards for

accomplishments. Significant adjustments in budget, scope, and schedule typically need their approval. They have a natural vested interest in the success of the project, but at the same time have to be responsive to what is best for the entire organization.

- **Project sponsors** champion the project and use their influence to gain approval of the project. Their reputation is tied to the success of the project, and they need to be kept informed of any major developments. They defend the project when it comes under attack and are a key project ally.

- **Contractors** may do all the actual work, in some cases, with the project team merely coordinating their contributions. In other cases, they are responsible for ancillary segments of the project scope. Poor work and schedule slips can affect work of the core project team. While contractors' reputations rest with doing good work, they must balance their contributions with their own profit margins and their commitments to other clients.

- **Government agencies** place constraints on project work. Permits need to be secured. Construction work has to be built to code. New drugs have to pass a rigorous battery of U.S. Food and Drug Administration tests. Other products have to meet safety standards, for example, Occupational Safety and Health Administration standards.

- **Other organizations,** depending on the nature of the project, may directly or indirectly affect the project. For example, suppliers provide necessary resources for completion of the project work. Delays, shortages, and poor quality can bring a project to a standstill. Public interest groups may apply pressure on government agencies. Customers often hire consultants and auditors to protect their interests on a project.

- **Customers** define the scope of the project, and ultimate project success rests in their satisfaction. Project managers need to be responsive to changing customer needs and requirements and to meeting their expectations. Customers are primarily concerned with getting a *good deal* and, as will be elaborated in Chapter 11, this naturally breeds tension with the project team.

These relationships are interdependent in that a project manager's ability to work effectively with one group will affect her ability to manage other groups. For example, functional managers are likely to be less cooperative if they perceive that top management's commitment to the project is waning. Conversely, the ability of the project manager to buffer the team from excessive interference from a client is likely to increase her standing with the project team.

The project management structure being used will influence the number and degree of external dependencies that will need to be managed. One advantage of creating a dedicated project team is that it reduces dependencies, especially within the organization, because most of the resources are assigned to the project. Conversely, a functional matrix structure increases dependencies, with the result that the project manager is much more reliant upon functional colleagues for work and staff.

The old-fashioned view of managing projects emphasized directing and controlling subordinates; the new perspective emphasizes managing project stakeholders and anticipating change as the most important jobs. Project managers need to be able to assuage concerns of customers, sustain support for the project

SNAPSHOT FROM PRACTICE   The Project Manager as Conductor

Metaphors convey meaning beyond words. For example, a meeting can be described as being difficult or "like wading through molasses." A popular metaphor for the role of a project manager is that of *conductor*. The conductor of an orchestra integrates the divergent sounds of different instruments to perform a given composition and make beautiful music. Similarly, the project manager integrates the talents and contributions of different specialists to complete the project. Both have to be good at understanding how the different players contribute to the performance of the whole. Both are almost entirely dependent upon the expertise and know-how of the players. The conductor does not have command of all the musical instruments. Likewise, the project manager usually possesses only a small proportion of the technical knowledge to make decisions. As

such, the conductor and project manager both facilitate the performance of others rather than actually perform.

Conductors use their arms, baton, and other nonverbal gestures to influence the pace, intensity, and involvement of different musicians. Likewise, project managers orchestrate the completion of the project by managing the involvement and attention of project members. Project managers balance time and process and induce participants to make the right decisions at the right time just as the conductor induces the wind instruments to perform at the right moment in a movement. Each controls the rhythm and intensity of work by managing the tempo and involvement of the players. Finally, each has a vision that transcends the music score or project plan. To be successful they must both earn the confidence, respect, and trust of their players.

at higher levels of the organization, quickly identify problems that threaten project work, while at the same time defend the integrity of the project and the interests of the project participants.

Within this web of relationships, the project manager must find out what needs to be done to achieve the goals of the project and build a cooperative network to accomplish it. Project managers must do so without the requisite authority to expect or demand cooperation. Doing so requires sound communication skills, political savvy, and a broad influence base. See the Snapshot from Practice: The Project Manager as Conductor for more on what makes project managers special.

Influence as Exchange

To successfully manage a project, a manager must adroitly build a cooperative network among divergent allies. Networks are mutually beneficial alliances that are generally governed by the **law of reciprocity**. The basic principle is that "one good deed deserves another, and likewise, one bad deed deserves another." The primary way to gain cooperation is to provide resources and services for others in exchange for future resources and services. This is the age-old maxim: "Quid pro quo (something for something)." Or in today's vernacular: "You scratch my back, I'll scratch yours."

Cohen and Bradford described the exchange view of influence as "currencies." If you want to do business in a given country, you have to be prepared to use the appropriate currency, and the exchange rates can change over time as conditions change. In the same way, what is valued by a marketing manager may be different from what is valued by a veteran project engineer, and you are likely to need to use different influence currency to obtain the cooperation of each individual. Although this analogy is a bit of an oversimplification, the key premise holds true that in the long run, "debit" and "credit" accounts must be balanced for

TABLE 10.1
Commonly Traded Organizational Currencies

Source: Adapted from A. R. Cohen and David L. Bradford, *Influence without Authority* (New York: John Wiley & Sons, 1990). Reprinted by permission of John Wiley & Sons, Inc.

Task-related currencies	
Resources	Lending or giving money, budget increases, personnel, etc.
Assistance	Helping with existing projects or undertaking unwanted tasks.
Cooperation	Giving task support, providing quicker response time, or aiding implementation.
Information	Providing organizational as well as technical knowledge.
Position-related currencies	
Advancement	Giving a task or assignment that can result in promotion.
Recognition	Acknowledging effort, accomplishments, or abilities.
Visibility	Providing a chance to be known by higher-ups or significant others in the organization.
Network/contacts	Providing opportunities for linking with others.
Inspiration-related currencies	
Vision	Being involved in a task that has larger significance for the unit, organization, customer, or society.
Excellence	Having a chance to do important things really well.
Ethical correctness	Doing what is "right" by a higher standard than efficiency.
Relationship-related currencies	
Acceptance	Providing closeness and friendship.
Personal support	Giving personal and emotional backing.
Understanding	Listening to others' concerns and issues.
Personal-related currencies	
Challenge/learning	Sharing tasks that increase skills and abilities.
Ownership/involvement	Letting others have ownership and influence.
Gratitude	Expressing appreciation.

cooperative relationships to work. Table 10.1 presents the commonly traded organizational currencies identified by Cohen and Bradford; they are then discussed in more detail in the following sections.

Task-Related Currencies

This form of influence comes directly from the project manager's ability to contribute to others' accomplishing their work. Probably the most significant form of this currency is the ability to respond to subordinates' requests for additional manpower, money, or time to complete a segment of a project. This kind of currency is also evident in sharing resources with another project manager who is in need. At a more personal level, it may simply mean providing direct assistance to a colleague in solving a technical problem.

Providing a good word for a colleague's proposal or recommendation is another form of this currency. Because most work of significance is likely to generate some form of opposition, the person who is trying to gain approval for a plan or proposal can be greatly aided by having a "friend in court."

Another form of this currency includes extraordinary effort. For example, fulfilling an emergency request to complete a design document in two days instead of the normal four days is likely to engender gratitude. Finally, sharing valuable information that would be useful to other managers is another form of this currency.

Position-Related Currencies

This form of influence stems from the manager's ability to enhance others' positions within their organization. A project manager can do this by giving someone a challenging assignment that can aid their advancement by developing their skills and abilities. Being given a chance to prove yourself naturally generates a strong sense of gratitude. Sharing the glory and bringing to the attention of higher-ups the efforts and accomplishments of others generate goodwill.

Project managers confide that a useful strategy for gaining the cooperation of professionals in other departments/organizations is figuring out how to make these people look good to their bosses. For example, a project manager worked with a subcontractor whose organization was heavily committed to total quality management (TQM). The project manager made it a point in top-level briefing meetings to point out how quality improvement processes initiated by the contractor contributed to cost control and problem prevention.

Another variation of recognition is enhancing the reputation of others within the firm. "Good press" can pave the way for lots of opportunities, while "bad press" can quickly shut a person off and make it difficult to perform. This currency is also evident in helping to preserve someone's reputation by coming to the defense of someone unjustly blamed for project setbacks.

Finally, one of the strongest forms of this currency is sharing contacts with other people. Helping individuals expand their own networks by introducing them to key people naturally engenders gratitude. For example, suggesting to a functional manager that he should contact Sally X if he wants to find out what is really going on in that department or to get a request expedited is likely to engender a sense of indebtedness.

Inspiration-Related Currencies

Perhaps the most powerful form of influence is based on inspiration. Most sources of inspiration derive from people's burning desire to make a difference and add meaning to their lives. Creating an exciting, bold vision for a project can elicit extraordinary commitment. For example, many of the technological breakthroughs associated with the introduction of the original Macintosh computer were attributed to the feeling that the project members had a chance to change the way people approached computers. A variant form of vision is providing an opportunity to do something really well. Being able to take pride in your work often drives many people.

Often the very nature of the project provides a source of inspiration. Discovering a cure for a devastating disease, introducing a new social program that will help those in need, or simply building a bridge that will reduce a major traffic bottleneck can provide opportunities for people to feel good about what they are doing and that they are making a difference. Inspiration operates as a magnet—pulling people as opposed to pushing people toward doing something.

Relationship-Related Currencies

These currencies have more to do with strengthening the relationship with someone than directly accomplishing the project tasks. The essence of this form of influence is forming a relationship that transcends normal professional boundaries and extends into the realm of friendship. Such relationships develop by giving personal and emotional backing. Picking people up when they are feeling down, boosting their confidence, and providing encouragement naturally breed goodwill. Sharing a sense of humor and making difficult times fun is another form of this currency. Similarly, engaging in non-work-related activities such as sports and family outings is another way relationships are naturally enhanced.

Perhaps the most basic form of this currency is simply listening to other people. Psychologists suggest that most people have a strong desire to be understood and that relationships break down because the parties stop listening to each other. Sharing personal secrets/ambitions and being a wise confidant also creates a special bond between individuals.

Personal-Related Currencies

This last form of currency deals with individual needs and an overriding sense of self-esteem. Some argue that self-esteem is a primary psychological need; the extent to which we can help others feel a sense of importance and personal worth will naturally generate goodwill. A project manager can enhance a colleague's sense of worth by sharing tasks that increase skills and abilities, delegating authority over work so that others experience ownership, and allowing individuals to feel comfortable stretching their abilities. This form of currency can also be seen in sincere expressions of gratitude for the contributions of others. Care, though, must be exercised in expressing gratitude since it is easily devalued when overused. That is, the first *thank you* is likely to be more valued than the twentieth.

The bottom line is that a project manager will be influential only insofar as she can offer something that others value. Furthermore, given the diverse cast of people a project manager depends on, it is important that she be able to acquire and exercise different influence currencies. The ability to do so will be constrained in part by the nature of the project and how it is organized. For example, a project manager who is in charge of a dedicated team has considerably more to offer team members than a manager who is given the responsibility of coordinating the activities of different professionals across different departments and organizations. In such cases, that manager will probably have to rely more heavily on personal and relational bases of influence to gain the cooperation of others.

Social Network Building

Mapping Dependencies

The first step to building a **social network** is identifying those on whom the project depends for success. The project manager and his or her key assistants need to ask the following questions:

- Whose cooperation will we need?
- Whose agreement or approval will we need?
- Whose opposition would keep us from accomplishing the project?

Many project managers find it helpful to draw a map of these dependencies. For example, Figure 10.2 contains the dependencies identified by a project manager responsible for installing a new financial software system in her company.

It is always better to overestimate rather than underestimate dependencies. All too often, otherwise talented and successful project managers have been derailed because they were blindsided by someone whose position or power they had not

FIGURE 10.2
Dependencies for
Financial Software
Installation Project

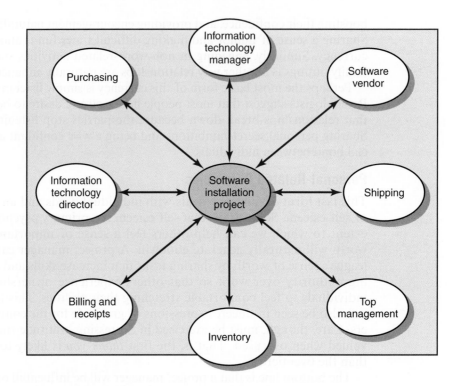

anticipated. After identifying whom you will depend on, you are ready to "step into their shoes" and see the project from their perspective:

- What differences exist between myself and the people on whom I depend (goals, values, pressures, working styles, risks)?
- How do these different people view the project (supporters, indifferents, antagonists)?
- What is the current status of the relationship I have with the people I depend on?
- What sources of influence do I have relative to those on whom I depend?

Once you start this analysis you can begin to appreciate what others value and what currencies you might have to offer as a basis on which to build a working relationship. You begin to realize where potential problems lie—relationships in which you have a current debit or no convertible currency. Furthermore, diagnosing another's point of view as well as the basis for their positions will help you anticipate their reactions and feelings about your decisions and actions. This information is vital for selecting the appropriate influence strategy and tactics and conducting win/win negotiations.

For example, after mapping her dependency network, the project manager who was in charge of installing the software system realized that she was likely to have serious problems with the manager of the receipts department, who would be one of the primary users of the software. She had no previous history of working with this individual but had heard through the grapevine that the manager was upset with the choice of software and that he considered this project to be another unnecessary disruption of his department's operation. Prior to project initiation the project manager arranged to have lunch with the manager, where she sat patiently and listened to his concerns. She invested additional time and attention to educate him and his staff about the benefits of the new software. She tried to minimize the disruptions the transition would cause in his department. She altered the implementation schedule to accommodate his preferences as to when the actual software would be installed and the subsequent training would occur. In turn, the receipts manager and his people were much more accepting of the change, and the transition to the new software went more smoothly than anticipated.

Management by Wandering Around (MBWA)

The preceding example illustrates the next step in building a supportive social network. Once you have established who the key players are that will determine success, then you initiate contact and begin to build a relationship with those players. Building this relationship requires a management style employees at Hewlett-Packard refer to as **"management by wandering around" (MBWA)** to reflect that managers spend the majority of their time outside their offices. MBWA is somewhat of a misnomer in that there is a purpose/pattern behind the "wandering." Through face-to-face interactions, project managers are able to stay in touch with what is really going on in the project and build cooperation essential to project success.

Effective project managers initiate contact with key players to keep abreast of developments, anticipate potential problems, provide encouragement, and reinforce the objectives and vision of the project. They are able to intervene to resolve conflicts and prevent stalemates from occurring. In essence, they "manage" the project. By staying in touch with various aspects of the project they become the focal point for information on the project. Participants turn to them to obtain the most current and comprehensive information about the project which reinforces their central role as project manager.

We have also observed less-effective project managers who eschew MBWA and attempt to manage projects from their offices and computer terminals. Such managers proudly announce an open-door policy and encourage others to see them when a problem or an issue comes up. To them no news is good news. This allows their contacts to be determined by the relative aggressiveness of others. Those who take the initiative and seek out the project manager get too high a proportion of the project manager's attention. Those people less readily available (physically removed) or more passive get ignored. This behavior contributes to the adage, "Only the squeaky wheel gets greased," which breeds resentment within the project team.

Effective project managers also find the time to regularly interact with more distal stakeholders. They keep in touch with suppliers, vendors, top management, and other functional managers. In doing so they maintain familiarity with different parties, sustain friendships, discover opportunities to do favors, and understand the motives and needs of others. They remind people of commitments and champion the cause of their project. They also shape people's expectations (see Snapshot from Practice: Managing Expectations). Through frequent communication they alleviate people's concerns about the project, dispel rumors, warn people of potential problems, and lay the groundwork for dealing with setbacks in a more effective manner.

Unless project managers take the initiative to build a network of supportive relationships, they are likely to see a manager (or other stakeholder) only when there is bad news or when they need a favor (e.g., they don't have the data they promised or the project has slipped behind schedule). Without prior, frequent,

SNAPSHOT FROM PRACTICE   Managing Expectations*

 Dorothy Kirk, a project management consultant and program manager with Financial Solutions Group of Mynd, offers several keen insights about the art of managing stakeholder expectations:

. . . expectations are hardy. All they need to take root is the absence of evidence to the contrary. Once rooted, the unspoken word encourages growth. They can develop and thrive without being grounded in reality. For this reason, project managers do daily battle with unrealistic expectations.

She goes on to offer several tips for managing expectations:

- The way you present information can either clarify or muddy expectations. For example, if you estimate that a task will take 317 hours, you are setting high expectations by your precision. The stakeholder is likely to be unhappy if it takes 323 hours. The stakeholder will not be unhappy with 323 hours if you quoted an estimate of 300–325 hours.

- Recognize that it is only human nature to interpret a situation in one's best interest. For example, if you tell someone it will be done by January, you are inclined to interpret it to your advantage and assume you have to the end of January, while the other person believes it will be done January 1st.

- Seize every opportunity to realign expectations with reality. Too often we avoid opportunities to adjust expectations because we hold onto a false hope that things will somehow work out.

- Do not ask for stakeholder suggestions for improvement if you do not intend to do something with their input. Asking for their input raises expectations.

- State the obvious. What is obvious to you may be obscure to others.

- Don't avoid delivering bad news. Communicate openly and in person. Expect some anger and frustration. Do not get defensive in return. Be prepared to explain the impact of the problems. For example, never say the project is going to be late without being able to give a new date. Explain what you are doing to see that this does not continue to happen.

All stakeholders have expectations about the schedule, cost, and project benefits. Project managers need to listen for, understand, and manage these expectations.

* D. Kirk, "Managing Expectations," *PM Network,* August 2000, pp. 59–62.

easy give-and-take interactions around nondecisive issues, the encounter prompted by the problem is likely to provoke excess tension. The parties are more likely to act defensively, interrupt each other, and lose sight of the common problem.

Experienced project managers recognize the need to build relationships before they need them. They initiate contact with the key stakeholders at times when there are no outstanding issues or problems and therefore no anxieties and suspicions. On these social occasions, they engage in small talk and responsive banter. They respond to others' requests for aid, provide supportive counsel, and exchange information. In doing so they establish credit in that relationship, which will allow them to deal with more serious problems down the road. When one person views another as pleasant, credible, and helpful based on past contact, he or she is much more likely to be responsive to requests for help and less confrontational when problems arise.

Managing Upward Relations

Research consistently points out that project success is strongly affected by the degree to which a project has the support of top management. Such support is reflected in an appropriate budget, responsiveness to unexpected needs, and a clear signal to others in the organization of the importance of cooperation.

Visible top management support is not only critical for securing the support of other managers within an organization, but it also is a key factor in the project manager's ability to motivate the project team. Nothing establishes a manager's right to lead more than her ability to defend. To win the loyalty of team members, project managers have to be effective advocates for their projects. They have to be able to get top management to rescind unreasonable demands, provide additional resources, and recognize the accomplishments of team members. This is more easily said than done.

Working relationships with upper management is a common source of consternation. Laments like the following are often made by project managers about upper management:

> They don't know how much it sets us back losing Neil to another project.
>
> I would like to see them get this project done with the budget they gave us.
>
> I just wish they would make up their minds as to what is really important.

While it may seem counterintuitive for a subordinate to "manage" a superior, smart project managers devote considerable time and attention to influencing and garnering the support of top management. Project managers have to accept profound differences in perspective and become skilled at the art of persuading superiors.

Many of the tensions that arise between upper management and project managers are a result of differences in perspective. Project managers become naturally absorbed with what is best for their project. To them the most important thing in the world is their project. Top management should have a different set of priorities. They are concerned with what is best for the entire organization. It is only natural for these two interests to conflict at times. For example, a project manager may lobby intensively for additional personnel only to be turned down because top management believes that the other departments cannot afford a reduction in staff. Although frequent communication can minimize differences, the project manager has to accept the fact that top management is inevitably going to see the world differently.

Once project managers accept that disagreements with superiors are more a question of perspective than substance, they can focus more of their energy on the art of persuading upper management. But before they can persuade superiors, they must first prove loyalty. Loyalty in this context simply means that most of the time project managers have to show that they consistently follow through on requests and adhere to the parameters established by top management without a great deal of grumbling or fuss. Once managers have proven loyalty to upper management, senior management is much more receptive to their challenges and requests.

FIGURE 10.3

The Significance of a Project Sponsor

Project managers have to cultivate strong ties with upper managers who are sponsoring the project. As noted earlier, these are high-ranking officials who championed approval and funding of the project; as such, their reputations are aligned with the project. Sponsors are also the ones who defend the project when it is under attack in upper circles of management. They shelter the project from excessive interference (see Figure 10.3). Project managers should *always* keep such people informed of any problems that may cause embarrassment or disappointment. For example, if costs are beginning to outrun the budget or a technical glitch is threatening to delay the completion of the project, managers make sure that the sponsors are the first to know.

Timing is everything. Asking for additional budget the day after disappointing third-quarter earnings are reported is going to be much more difficult than making a similar request four weeks later. Good project managers pick the optimum time to appeal to top management. They enlist their project sponsors to lobby their

Ancona and Caldwell studied the performance of 45 new-product teams in five high-technology companies and produced some startling results. The most significant was that internal team dynamics were not related to performance. That is, high-performance teams were not distinguished by clearer goals, smoother workflow among members, or greater ability to satisfy the individual goals of team members. What related to team performance were level and intensity of external interactions between the project team and the rest of the organization. Ancona and Caldwell identified four key patterns of activity which contribute to creating a high-performance team:

1. *Ambassador* activities are aimed at representing the team to others and protecting the team from interference. The project manager typically takes on this responsibility, which involves buffering the team from political pressures and building support for the project within the hierarchy of the company.

2. *Task coordinator* activities are aimed at coordinating the team's efforts with other units and organizations. Unlike the ambassador role, which is focused upward, these are more lateral activities and involve negotiating and interacting with interested parties within the organization.

3. *Scouts* act as a scout on an expedition; that is, they go out from the team to bring back information about what is going on elsewhere in the organization. This is a much less focused task than task coordinator.

4. *Guard* activities differ from the other activities in that they are intended to keep information and resources inside the team, preventing drainage out of the group. A key guard activity is keeping necessary information secret until it is appropriate to share it.

Ancona and Caldwell found that the importance of these activities varies during the product development life cycle if the project team is to be successful. For example, scouting activities are more critical during the creation phase, when the product idea is being formulated and the team is being developed. Ambassador activities are especially critical during the development phase, when product specifications have been agreed upon and the major task is developing a prototype.

Ancona and Caldwell caution that their findings do not mean that teamwork and the internal operations of a project team are not important to project success. Effective team dynamics are necessary to successfully integrate information from outside sources and coordinate activities across groups. Their research supports the adage that problems and opportunities often lie at the borders of projects, and that one of the primary jobs of a project manager is to manage the interface between his or her team and the rest of the organization.

* D. G. Ancona and D. Caldwell, "Improving the Performance of New-Product Teams," *Research Technology Management,* Vol. 33, No. 2 (March–April 1990), pp. 25–29.

cause. They also realize there are limits to top management's accommodations. Here, the Lone Ranger analogy is appropriate—you have only so many silver bullets, so use them wisely.

Project managers need to adapt their communication pattern to that of the senior group. For example, one project manager recognized that top management had a tendency to use sports metaphors to describe business situations, so she framed a recent slip in schedule by admitting that "we lost five yards, but we still have two plays to make a first down." Smart project managers learn the language of top management and use it to their advantage.

Finally, a few project managers admit ignoring chains of command. If they are confident that top management will reject an important request and that what they want to do will benefit the project, they do it without asking permission. While acknowledging that this is very risky, they claim that bosses typically won't argue with success.

Leading by Example

A highly visible, interactive management style is not only essential to building and sustaining cooperative relationships, it also allows project managers to utilize their most powerful leadership tool—their own behavior. Often, when faced with

SNAPSHOT FROM PRACTICE   Leading at the Edge*

In 1914, the intrepid explorer Ernest Shackleton embarked on the *Endurance* with his team of seamen and scientists, intent upon crossing the unexplored Antarctic continent. What happened in the two years between their departure and their ultimate incredible rescue has rarely been matched in the annals of survival: a ship crushed by expanding ice pack . . . a crew stranded on the floes of the frozen Weddell Sea . . . two perilous treks in open boats across a raging Southern Ocean . . . a team marooned on the wild, forlorn Elephant Island, stretched to the limits of human endurance.

This adventure provided the basis for the book *Leading at the Edge: Leadership Lessons from the Extraordinary Saga of Shackleton's Antarctic Expedition* written by Dennis Perkins. Perkins provides numerous incidents of how Shackleton's personal example influenced the behavior of his beleaguered crew. For example, from the beginning of the Trans-Atlantic expedition to its end Shackleton consistently encouraged behavior that emphasized caring and respect:

> After the destruction of the *Endurance* Shackleton heated hot milk for the crew and went from tent to tent with the "life giving" drink. After the sail to the island of South Georgia, when the exhausted crew had landed, Shackleton took the first watch, which he kept for three hours instead of the usual one.

Crew members emulated the caring behaviors that Shackleton modeled. A good example of this occurred during one of the most dramatic moments in the *Endurance* saga. The food supply had dwindled to perilously low levels. Less than a week's supply remained, and the tiny ration of seal steak usually served at breakfast was eliminated. The waste meat generally used to feed the dogs was inspected for edible scraps.

Under these wretched conditions, and after a wet sleepless night, an argument broke out among some of the team members. Caught in the middle, one crew member (Greenstreet) spilled his tiny ration of powdered milk and shouted at the biologist (Clark). Alfred Lansing described what happened next:

> Greenstreet paused to get his breath, and in that instant his anger was spent and he suddenly fell silent. Everyone else in the tent became quiet, too, and looked at Greenstreet,

© Topham/The Image Works

> shaggy-haired, bearded, and filthy with blubber soot, holding his empty mug in his hand and looking helplessly down into the snow that had thirstily soaked up his precious milk. The loss was so tragic he seemed almost on the point of weeping. Without speaking, Clark reached out and poured some milk into Greenstreet's mug. Then Worsely, then Macklin, and Rickerson and Kerr, Orde-Lees, and finally Blackborrow. They finished in silence.

* Adapted from Dennis N. T. Perkins, *Leading at the Edge: Leadership Lessons from the Extraordinary Saga of Shackleton's Antarctica Expedition* (New York: AMACOM Press, 2000), pp. 94–95; and Alfred Lansing, *Endurance: Shackleton's Incredible Voyage* (New York: Carroll & Graf, 1998), p. 127.

uncertainty, people look to others for cues as to how to respond and demonstrate a propensity to mimic the behavior of superiors. A project manager's behavior symbolizes how other people should work on the project. Through her behavior a project manager can influence how others act and respond to a variety of issues related to the project. (See Snapshot from Practice: Leading at the Edge for a dramatic example of this.)

FIGURE 10.4
Leading by Example

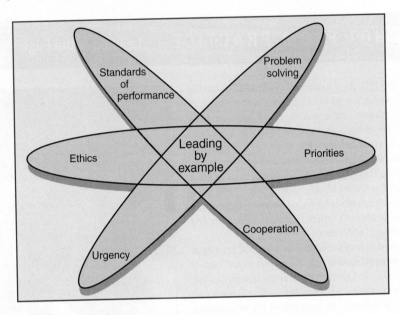

To be effective, project managers must "walk the talk" (see Figure 10.4). Six aspects of leading by example are discussed next.

Priorities

Actions speak louder than words. Subordinates and others discern project managers' priorities by how they spend their time. If a project manager claims that this project is critical and then is perceived as devoting more time to other projects, then all his verbal reassurances are likely to fall on deaf ears. Conversely, a project manager who takes the time to observe a critical test instead of simply waiting for a report affirms the importance of the testers and their work. Likewise, the types of questions project managers pose communicate priorities. By repeatedly asking how specific issues relate to satisfying the customer, a project manager can reinforce the importance of customer satisfaction.

Urgency

Through their actions project managers can convey a sense of urgency, which can permeate project activities. This urgency in part can be conveyed through stringent deadlines, frequent status report meetings, and aggressive solutions for expediting the project. The project manager uses these tools like a metronome to pick up the beat of the project. At the same time, such devices will be ineffective if there is not also a corresponding change in the project manager's behavior. If they want others to work faster and solve problems quicker, then they need to work faster. They need to hasten the pace of their own behavior. They should accelerate the frequency of their interactions, talk and walk more quickly, get to work sooner, and leave work later. By simply increasing the pace of their daily interaction patterns, project managers can reinforce a sense of urgency in others.

Problem Solving

How project managers respond to problems sets the tone for how others tackle problems. If bad news is greeted by verbal attacks, then others will be reluctant to be forthcoming. If the project manager is more concerned with finding out who is to blame instead of how to prevent problems from happening again, then others will tend to cover their tracks and cast the blame elsewhere. If, on the other hand, project managers focus more on how they can turn a problem into an opportunity or what can be learned from a mistake, then others are more likely to adopt a more proactive approach to problem solving.

Cooperation

How project managers act toward outsiders influences how team members interact with outsiders. If a project manager makes disparaging remarks about the "idiots" in the marketing department, then this oftentimes becomes the shared view of the entire team. If project managers set the norm of treating outsiders with respect and being responsive to their needs, then others will more likely follow suit.

Standards of Performance

Veteran project managers recognize that if they want participants to exceed project expectations then they have to exceed others' expectations of a good project manager. They establish a high standard for project performance through the quality of their daily interactions. They respond quickly to the needs of others, carefully prepare and run crisp meetings, stay on top of all the critical issues, facilitate effective problem solving, and stand firm on important matters.

Ethics

How others respond to ethical dilemmas that arise in the course of a project will be influenced by how the project manager has responded to similar dilemmas. In many cases, team members base their actions on how they think the project manager would respond. If project managers deliberately distort or withhold vital information from customers or top management, then they are signaling to others that this kind of behavior is acceptable. Project management invariably creates a variety of ethical dilemmas; this would be an appropriate time to delve into this topic in more detail.

Ethics and Project Management

Questions of ethics have already arisen in previous chapters that discussed padding of cost and time estimations, exaggerating pay-offs of project proposals, and so forth. Ethical dilemmas involve situations where it is difficult to determine whether conduct is right or wrong. Is it acceptable to falsely assure customers that everything is on track when, in reality, you are only doing so to prevent them from panicking and making matters worse?

In a survey of project managers, 81 percent reported that they encounter ethical issues in their work. These dilemmas range from being pressured to alter status reports, backdate signatures, or shade documentation to mask the reality of project progress to falsifying cost accounts, compromising safety standards to accelerate progress, and approving shoddy work.

Project management is complicated work, and, as such, ethics invariably involve gray areas of judgment and interpretation. For example, it is difficult to distinguish deliberate falsification of estimates from genuine mistakes or the willful exaggeration of project payoffs from genuine optimism. It becomes problematic to

SNAPSHOT FROM PRACTICE   The Collapse of Arthur Andersen*

© AP Photo/Stephen J. Carrera

"Think straight and talk straight" was the principle on which Arthur E. Andersen built his accounting firm in the early 1900s. It was a phrase his mother taught him and became the firm's motto. The commitment to integrity and a systematic, planned approach to work were instrumental in Arthur Andersen becoming one of the largest and best-known accounting firms in the world.

> Working for Arthur Andersen was not for everyone. It could be a tough culture. It was much too hierarchical and top down for the more free spirited. Many people left after less than two years, believing the rewards did not warrant the demands that were made on them. Others learned to play by the rules and some even thrived. To remain in the firm, staff members were expected to work hard, respect authority of rank, and maintain a high level of conformity. In return they were rewarded with support, promotion, and the possibility of making partner. Those individuals who made a career with the firm grew old together, professionally and personally, and most had never worked anywhere else. To these survivors, Andersen was their second family, and they developed strong loyalties to the firm and its culture. (p. 133)

On October 23, 2001, David Duncan told his Enron project team that they needed to start complying with Andersen's new policy on handling audit documents. The policy had been instituted to make sure that the firm's extraneous paperwork could not be used in court cases. Although the document retention policy required that papers supporting the firm's opinions and audit be retained, it allowed a broad category of secondary documents to be destroyed. The team reacted with stunned silence to Duncan's directive. Then everyone got up and began racing to do what they had been told to do. No one asked Duncan to explain further. None asked whether what they were doing was wrong. No one questioned whether what he or she were doing might be illegal. Andersen's Houston staff just reacted, following orders without question.

On November 9, 2001, the day after the Securities Exchange Commission (SEC) issued a subpoena to Andersen, the shredding stopped. More than one ton of documents had been destroyed and 30,000 e-mails and Enron-related computer files erased. According to Andersen's legal defense team, the shredding was business as usual. The lawyers claimed that the shredding was standard practice for eliminating unnecessary files. To the SEC, it appeared to be the start of a deep cover-up operation. Subsequently one of the most respected accounting firms in the world closed its doors.

* Susan E. Squires, Cynthia J. Smith, Lorna McDougall, and William R. Yeak, *Inside Arthur Andersen: Shifting Values, Unexpected Consequences* (Upper Saddle River, NJ: Prentice Hall, 2004).

determine whether unfulfilled promises were deliberate deception or an appropriate response to changing circumstances.

To provide greater clarity to business ethics, many companies and professional groups publish a code of conduct. Cynics see these documents as simply window dressing, while advocates argue that they are important, albeit limited, first steps. In practice, personal ethics do not lie in formal statutes but at the intersection of one's work, family, education, profession, religious beliefs, and daily interactions. Most project managers report that they rely on their own private sense of right and wrong—what one project manager called his "internal compass." One common rule of thumb for testing whether a response is ethical is to ask, "Imagine that whatever you did was going to be reported on the front page of your local newspaper. How would you like that? Would you be comfortable?"

Unfortunately, scandals at Enron, Worldcom, and Arthur Andersen have demonstrated the willingness of highly trained professionals to abdicate personal responsibility for illegal actions and to obey the directives of superiors (see Snapshot from Practice: The Collapse of Arthur Andersen). Top management and the culture of an organization play a decisive role in shaping members' beliefs of what is right and wrong. Many organizations encourage ethical transgressions by creating a "win at all cost" mentality. The pressures to succeed obscure consideration of whether the ends justify the means. Other organizations place a premium on "fair play" and command a market position by virtue of being trustworthy and reliable.

Many project managers claim that ethical behavior is its own reward. By following your own internal compass your behavior expresses your personal values. Others suggest that ethical behavior is doubly rewarding. You not only are able to fall asleep at night but you also develop a sound and admirable reputation. As will be explored in the next section, such a reputation is essential to establishing the trust necessary to exercise influence effectively.

Building Trust: The Key to Exercising Influence

We all know people who have influence but whom we do not trust; these individuals are often referred to as "political animals" or "jungle fighters." While these individuals are often very successful in the short run, the prevalent sense of mistrust prohibits long-term efficacy. Successful project managers not only need to be influential, they also need to exercise influence in a manner that builds and sustains the trust of others.

The significance of trust can be discerned by its absence. Imagine how different a working relationship is when you distrust the other party as opposed to trusting them. When people distrust each other, they often spend inordinate amounts of time and energy attempting to discern hidden agendas and the true meaning of communications and then securing guarantees to promises. They are much more cautious with each other and hesitant to cooperate. Here is what one line manager had to say about how he reacted to a project manager he did not trust:

> Whenever Jim approached me about something, I found myself trying to read between the lines to figure what was really going on. When he made a request, my initial reaction was "no" until he proved it.

- **Hands-off/Hands-on.** Project managers have to intervene, resolve stalemates, solve technical problems, and insist on different approaches. At the same time they have to recognize when it is appropriate to sit on the sidelines and let other people figure out what to do.
- **Flexible but firm.** Project managers have to be adaptable and responsive to events and outcomes that occur on the project. At the same time they have to hold the line at times and tough it out when everyone else wants to give up.
- **Team versus organizational loyalties.** Project managers need to forge a unified project team whose members stimulate one another to extraordinary performance. But at the same time they have to counter the excesses of cohesion and the team's resistance to outside ideas. They have to cultivate loyalties to both the team and the parent organization.

Managing these and other contradictions requires finesse and balance. Finesse involves the skillful movement back and forth between opposing behavioral patterns. For example, most of the time project managers actively involve others, move by increment, and seek consensus. There are other times when project managers must act as autocrats and take decisive, unilateral action. Balance involves recognizing the danger of extremes and that too much of a good thing invariably becomes harmful. For example, many managers have a tendency to always delegate the most stressful, difficult assignments to their best team members. This habit often breeds resentment among those chosen ("why am I always the one who gets the tough work?") and never allows the weaker members to develop their talents further.

There is no one management style or formula for being an effective project manager. The world of project management is too complicated for formulas. Successful project managers have a knack for adapting styles to specific circumstances of the situation.

So, what should one look for in an effective project manager? Many authors have addressed this question and have generated list after list of skills and attributes associated with being an effective manager. When reviewing these lists, one sometimes gets the impression that to be a successful project manager requires someone with superhuman powers. While we agree that not everyone has the right stuff to be an effective project manager, there are some core traits and skills that can be developed to successfully perform the job. Eight of these traits are noted below.

1. **Systems thinker.** Project managers must be able to take a holistic rather than a reductionist approach to projects. Instead of breaking up a project into individual pieces (planning, budget) and managing it by understanding each part, a systems perspective focuses on trying to understand how relevant project factors collectively interact to produce project outcomes. The key to success then becomes managing the interaction between different parts and not the parts themselves.

2. **Personal integrity.** Before you can lead and manage others, you have to be able to lead and manage yourself. Begin by establishing a firm sense of who you are, what you stand for, and how you should behave. This inner strength provides the buoyancy to endure the ups and downs of the project life cycle and the credibility essential to sustaining the trust of others.

3. **Proactive.** Good project managers take action before it is needed to prevent small concerns from escalating into major problems. They spend the majority of their time working within their sphere of influence to solve problems and not dwelling on things they have little control over. Project managers can't be whiners.

Emotional intelligence (EQ) describes the ability or skill to perceive, assess, and manage the emotions of one's self and others. Although the notion of EQ emerged in the 1920s, it was not until Daniel Goleman published his book *Emotional Intelligence* that the concept captured the attention of business people and public alike.

Goleman divided EQ into the following five emotional competences:

- **Self-awareness**—knowing your emotions, recognizing feelings as they occur, and understanding the link between your emotions and your behavior. Self-awareness is reflected in confidence, realistic assessment of personal strengths/weaknesses, and ability to make fun of oneself.

- **Self-regulation**—being able to control disruptive impulses and moods and respond appropriately to situations. Self-regulation is reflected in trustworthiness and openness to change.

- **Self-motivation**—being able to gather up your feelings and pursue goals with energy, passion, and persistence. The hallmarks of self-motivation include a strong desire to achieve and internal optimism.

- **Empathy**—being able to recognize the feelings of others and tuning into their verbal and nonverbal cues. Empathy is reflected in the ability to sustain relationships and in cross-cultural sensitivity.

- **Social skills**—being able to build social networks and rapport with different kinds of people. Social skills include being able to lead change, resolve conflicts, and build effective teams.

Not much imagination is needed to see how EQ would contribute to being an effective project manager.

In Goleman's view, these competences build on each other in a hierarchy. At the bottom of his hierarchy is self-awareness. Some level of self-awareness is needed to move to self-regulation. Ultimately, social skills requires all four of the other competences in order to begin to be proficient at leading others. Experts believe that most people can learn to significantly increase their EQ. Numerous training programs and materials have emerged to help individuals realize their EQ potential.

* T. Bradberry, and J. Graves, *The Emotional Intelligence Quick Book: How to Put Your EQ to Work* (New York: Simon & Schuster, 2005); J. Cabanis-Brewin, "The Human Task of a Project Leader: Daniel Goleman on the Value of High EQ," *PM Network*, November 1999, pp. 38–42.

4. **High emotional intelligence (EQ).** Project management is not for the meek. Project managers have to have command of their emotions and be able to respond constructively to others when things get a bit out of control. See the Research Highlight: Emotional Intelligence to read more about this quality.

5. **General business perspective.** Because the primary role of a project manager is to integrate the contributions of different business and technical disciplines, it is important that a manager have a general grasp of business fundamentals and how the different functional disciplines interact to contribute to a successful business.

6. **Effective time management.** Time is a manager's scarcest resource. Project managers have to be able to budget their time wisely and quickly adjust their priorities. They need to balance their interactions so no one feels ignored.

7. **Skillful politician.** Project managers have to be able to deal effectively with a wide range of people and win their support and endorsement of their project. They need to be able to sell the virtues of their project without compromising the truth.

8. **Optimist.** Project managers have to display a can-do attitude. They have to be able to find rays of sunlight in a dismal day and keep people's attention positive. A good sense of humor and a playful attitude are often a project manager's greatest strength.

So how does one develop these traits? Workshops, self-study, and courses can upgrade one's general business perspective and capacity for systems thinking. Training programs can improve emotional intelligence and political skills. People can also be taught stress and time management techniques. However, we know of no workshop or magic potion that can transform a pessimist into an optimist or provide a sense of purpose when there is not one. These qualities get at the very soul or being of a person. Optimism, integrity, and even being proactive are not easily developed if there is not already a predisposition to display them.

Summary

To be successful, project managers must build a cooperative network among a diverse set of allies. They begin by identifying who the key stakeholders on a project are, followed by a diagnosis of the nature of the relationships, and the basis for exercising influence. Effective project managers are skilled at acquiring and exercising a wide range of influence. They use this influence and a highly interactive management style to monitor project performance and initiate appropriate changes in project plans and direction. They do so in a manner that generates trust, which is ultimately based on others' perceptions of their character and competence.

Project managers are encouraged to keep in mind the following suggestions:

- *Build relationships before you need them.* Identify key players and what you can do to help them before you need their assistance. It is always easier to receive a favor after you have granted one. This requires the project manager to see the project in systems terms and to appreciate how it affects other activities and agendas inside and outside the organization. From this perspective they can identify opportunities to do good deeds and garner the support of others.
- *Trust is sustained through frequent face-to-face contact.* Trust withers through neglect. This is particularly true under conditions of rapid change and uncertainty that naturally engender doubt, suspicion, and even momentary bouts of paranoia. Project managers must maintain frequent contact with key stakeholders to keep abreast of developments, assuage concerns, engage in reality testing, and focus attention on the project. Frequent face-to-face interactions affirm mutual respect and trust in each other.

Ultimately, exercising influence in an effective and ethical manner begins and ends with how you view the other parties. Do you view them as potential partners or obstacles to your goals? If obstacles, then you wield your influence to manipulate and gain compliance and cooperation. If partners, you exercise influence to gain their commitment and support. People who view social network building as building partnerships see every interaction with two goals: resolving the immediate problem/concern and improving the working relationship so that next time it will be even more effective. Experienced project managers realize that "what goes around comes around" and try at all cost to avoid antagonizing players for quick success.

Key Terms

Emotional intelligence (EQ), *361*
Inspiration-related currencies, *346*
Law of reciprocity, *344*
Leading by example, *352*
Management by wandering around (MBWA), *349*

Personal-related currencies, *347*
Position-related currencies, *346*
Proactive, *360*
Relationship-related currencies, *346*

Social network building, *347*
Stakeholder, *341*
Systems thinking, *360*
Task-related currencies, *345*

Review Questions

1. What is the difference between leading and managing a project?

2. Why is a conductor of an orchestra an appropriate metaphor for being a project manager? What aspects of project managing are not reflected by this metaphor? Can you think of other metaphors that would be appropriate?

3. What does the exchange model of influence suggest you do to build cooperative relationships to complete a project?

4. What differences would you expect to see between the kinds of influence currencies that a project manager in a functional matrix would use and the influence a project manager of a dedicated project team would use?

5. Why is it important to build a relationship before you need it?

6. Why is it critical to keep the project sponsor informed?

7. Why is trust a function of both character and competence?

8. Which of the eight traits/skills associated with being an effective project manager is the most important? The least important? Why?

Exercises

1. Do an Internet search for the Keirsey Temperament Sorter Questionnaire and find a site that appears to have a reputable self-assessment questionnaire. Respond to the questionnaire to identify your temperament type. Read supportive documents associated with your type. What does this material suggest are the kinds of projects that would best suit you? What does it suggest your strengths and weaknesses are as a project manager? How can you compensate for your weaknesses?

2. Access the Project Management Institute Web site and review the standards contained in PMI Member Ethical Standards section. How useful is the information for helping someone decide what behavior is appropriate and inappropriate?

3. You are organizing an AIDS benefit concert in your hometown that will feature local heavy metal rock groups and guest speakers. Draw a dependency map identifying the major groups of people that are likely to affect the success of this project. Who do you think will be most cooperative? Who do you think will be the least cooperative? Why?

4. You are the project manager responsible for the overall construction of a new international airport. Draw a dependency map identifying the major groups of people that are likely to affect the success of this project. Who do you think will be most cooperative? Who do you think will be the least cooperative? Why?

5. Identify an important relationship (co-worker, boss, friend) in which you are having trouble gaining cooperation. Assess this relationship in terms of the influence currency model. What kinds of influence currency have you been exchanging in this relationship? Is the "bank account" for this relationship in the "red" or the "black"? What kinds of influence would be appropriate for building a stronger relationship with that person?

6. Each of the following six mini-case scenarios involve ethical dilemmas associated with project management. How would you respond to each situation, and why?

Jack Nietzche

You returned from a project staffing meeting in which future project assignments were finalized. Despite your best efforts, you were unable to persuade the director of project management to promote one of your best assistants, Jack Nietzche, to a project manager position. You feel a bit guilty because you dangled the prospect of this promotion to motivate Jack. Jack responded by putting in extra hours to ensure that his segments of the project were completed on time. You wonder how Jack will react to this disappointment. More importantly, you wonder how his reaction might affect your project. You have five days remaining to meet a critical deadline for a very important customer. While it won't be easy, you believed you would be able to complete the project on time. Now you're not so sure. Jack is halfway through completing the documentation phase, which is the last critical activity. Jack can be pretty emotional at times, and you are worried that he will blow up once he finds he didn't get the promotion. As you return to your office, you wonder what you should do. Should you tell Jack that he isn't going to be promoted? What should you say if he asks about whether the new assignments were made?

Seaburst Construction Project

You are the project manager for the Seaburst construction project. So far the project is progressing ahead of schedule and below budget. You attribute this in part to the good working relationship you have with the carpenters, plumbers, electricians, and machine operators who work for your organization. More than once you have asked them to give 110 percent, and they have responded.

One Sunday afternoon you decide to drive by the site and show it to your son. As you point out various parts of the project to your son, you discover that several pieces of valuable equipment are missing from the storage shed. When you start work again on Monday you are about to discuss this matter with a supervisor when you realize that all the missing equipment is back in the shed. What should you do? Why?

The Project Status Report Meeting

You are driving to a project status report meeting with your client. You encountered a significant technical problem on the project that has put your project behind schedule. This is not good news because completion time is the number one priority for the project. You are confident that your team can solve the problem if they are free to give their undivided attention to it and that with hard work you can get back on schedule. You also believe if you tell the client about the problem, she will demand a meeting with your team to discuss the implications of the problem. You can also expect her to send some of her personnel to oversee the solution to the problem. These interruptions will likely further delay the project. What should you tell your client about the current status of the project?

Gold Star LAN project

You work for a large consulting firm and were assigned to the Gold Star LAN project. Work on the project is nearly completed and your clients at Gold Star appear to be pleased with your performance. During the course of the project, changes in the original scope had to be made to accommodate specific needs of managers at Gold Star. The costs of these changes were documented as well as overhead and submitted to the centralized accounting department. They processed the information and submitted a change order bill for your signature. You are surprised to see the bill is 10 percent higher than what you submitted. You contact Jim Messina in the accounting office and ask if a mistake has been made. He curtly replies that no mistake was made and that management adjusted the bill. He recommends that you sign the document. You talk to another project manager about this and she tells you off the record that overcharging clients on change orders is common practice in your firm. Would you sign the document? Why? Why not?

Cape Town Bio-Tech

You are responsible for installing the new Double E production line. Your team has collected estimates and used the WBS to generate a project schedule. You have confidence in the schedule and the work your team has done. You report to top management that you believe that the project will take 110 days and be completed by March 5. The news is greeted positively. In fact, the project sponsor confides that orders do not have to be shipped until April 1. You leave the meeting wondering whether you should share this information with the project team or not.

Ryman Pharmaceuticals

You are a test engineer on the Bridge project at Ryman Pharmaceuticals in Nashville, Tennessee. You have just completed conductivity tests of a new electrochemical compound. The results exceeded expectations. This new compound should revolutionize the industry. You are wondering whether to call your stockbroker and ask her to buy $20,000 worth of Ryman stock before everyone else finds out about the results. What would you do and why?

References

Abrashoff, D. M., *It's Your Ship* (New York: Business Plus, 2002).

Ancona, D. G., and D. Caldwell, "Improving the Performance of New-Product Teams," *Research Technology Management,* 33 (2) March-April 1990, pp. 25–29.

Anand, V., B. E. Ashforth, and M. Joshi, "Business as Usual: The Acceptance and Perpetuation of Corruption in Organizations," *Academy of Management Executive,* 19(4) 2005, pp. 9–23.

Badaracco, J. L. Jr., and A. P. Webb, "Business Ethics: A View from the Trenches," *California Management Review,* 37 (2) Winter 1995, pp. 8–28.

Baker, B., "Leadership and the Project Manager," *PM Network,* December 2002, p. 20.

Baker, W. E., *Network Smart: How to Build Relationships for Personal and Organizational Success* (New York: McGraw-Hill, 1994).

Bennis, W., *On Becoming a Leader* (Reading, MA: Addison-Wesley, 1989).

Bradberry, T., and J. Graves, *The Emotional Intelligence Quick Book: How to Put Your EQ to Work* (New York: Simon & Schuster, 2005).

Cabanis, J., "A Question of Ethics: The Issues Project Managers Face and How They Resolve Them," *PM Network,* December 1996, pp. 19–24.

Cabanis-Brewin, J., "The Human Task of a Project Leader: Daniel Goleman on the Value of High EQ," *PM Network,* November 1999, pp. 38–42.

Cohen, A. R., and D. L. Bradford, *Influence Without Authority* (New York: John Wiley & Sons, 1990).

Covey, S. R., *The Seven Habits of Highly Effective People* (New York: Simon & Schuster, 1989).

Dinsmore, P. C., "Will the Real Stakeholders Please Stand Up?" *PM Network,* December 1995, pp. 9–10.

Gabarro, S. J., *The Dynamics of Taking Charge* (Boston: Harvard Business School Press, 1987).

Hill, L. A., *Becoming a Manager: Mastery of a New Identity* (Boston: Harvard Business School Press, 1992).

Kaplan, R. E., "Trade Routes: The Manager's Network of Relationships," *Organizational Dynamics,* 12 (4) Spring 1984, pp. 37–52.

Kirk, D., "Managing Expectations," *PM Network,* August 2000, pp. 59–62.

Kotter, J. P., "What Leaders Really Do," *Harvard Business Review,* 68 (3) May–June 1990, pp. 103–11.

Kouzes, J. M., and B. Z. Posner, *The Leadership Challenge* (San Francisco: Jossey-Bass, 1987).

Kouzes, J. M., and B. Z. Posner, *Credibility: How Leaders Gain and Lose It. Why People Demand It* (San Francisco: Jossey-Bass, 1993).

Larson, E. W., and J. B. King, "The Systemic Distortion of Information: An Ongoing Management Challenge," *Organizational Dynamics,* 24 (3) Winter 1996, pp. 49–62.

Lewis, M. W., M. A. Welsh, G. E. Dehler, and S. G. Green, "Product Development Tensions: Exploring Contrasting Styles of Project Management," *Academy of Management Journal,* 45 (3) 2002, pp. 546–64.

Peters, L. H., "A Good Man in a Storm: An Interview with Tom West," *Academy of Management Executive,* 16 (4) 2002, pp. 53–63.

Peters, L. H., "Soulful Ramblings: An Interview with Tracy Kidder," *Academy of Management Executive,* 16 (4) 2002, pp. 45–52.

Peters, T., *Thriving on Chaos: Handbook for a Management Revolution* (New York: Alfred A. Knopf, 1988).

Pinto, J. K., and S. K. Mantel, "The Causes of Project Failure," *IEEE Transactions in Engineering Management,* 37 (4) 1990, pp. 269–76.

Pinto, J. K., and D. P. Sleven, "Critical Success Factors in Successful Project Implementation," *IEEE Transactions in Engineering Management,* 34 (1) 1987, pp. 22–27.

Posner, B. Z., "What It Takes to Be an Effective Project Manager," *Project Management Journal,* March 1987, pp. 51–55.

Project Management Institute, *Leadership in Project Management Annual* (Newton Square, PA: PMI Publishing, 2006).

Robb, D. J., "Ethics in Project Management: Issues, Practice, and Motive," *PM Network,* December 1996, pp. 13–18.

Sayles, L. R., *Leadership: Managing in Real Organizations* (New York: McGraw-Hill, 1989), pp. 70–78.

Sayles, L. R., *The Working Leader* (New York: Free Press, 1993).

Senge, P. M., *The Fifth Discipline* (New York: Doubleday, 1990).

Shenhar, A. J., and B. Nofziner, "A New Model for Training Project Managers," *Proceedings of the 28th Annual Project Management Institute Symposium,* 1997, pp. 301–6.

Shtub, A., J. F. Bard, and S. Globerson, *Project Management: Engineering, Technology, and Implementation* (Englewood Cliffs, NJ: Prentice Hall, 1994).

Case

Western Oceanography Institute

It was already 72 degrees when Astrid Young pulled into the parking lot at the Western Oceanography Institute (WOI). The radio announcer was reminding listeners to leave out extra water for their pets because the temperature was going to be in the high 90s for the third straight day. Young made a mental note to call her husband, Jon, when she got to her office and make sure that he left plenty of water outside for their cat, Figaro. Young was three-quarters of the way through the Microsoft NT conversion project. Yesterday had been a disaster, and she was determined to get back on top of things.

ASTRID YOUNG

Astrid Young was a 27-year-old graduate of Western State University (WSU) with a B.S. degree in management information systems. After graduation she worked for five years at Evergreen Systems in Seattle, Washington. While at WSU she worked part time for an oceanography professor, Ahmet Green, creating a customized database for a research project he was conducting. Green was recently appointed director of WOI, and Young was confident that this prior experience was instrumental in her getting the job as information services (IS) director at the Institute. Although she took a significant pay cut, she jumped at the opportunity to return to her alma mater. Her job at Evergreen Systems had been very demanding. The long hours and extensive traveling had created tension in her marriage. She was looking forward to a normal job with reasonable hours. Besides, Jon would be busy pursuing his MBA at Western State. While at Evergreen, Young worked on Y2000 projects and installed NT servers. She was confident that she had the requisite technical expertise to excel at her new job.

Western Oceanography Institute was an independently funded research facility aligned with Western State University. Approximately 60 full- and part-time staff worked at the Institute. They worked on research grants funded by the National Science Foundation (NSF) and the United Nations (UN), as well as research financed by private industry. There were typically 7 to 8 major research projects under way at any one time as well as 20 to 25 smaller projects. One-third of the Institute's scientists had part-time teaching assignments at WSU and used the Institute to conduct their own basic research.

FIRST FOUR MONTHS AT WOI

Young worked at the Institute for four months prior to initiating the NT conversion project. She made a point of introducing herself to the various groups of people upon her arrival at the Institute. Still, her contact with the staff had been limited. She spent most of her time becoming familiar with WOI's information system, training her staff, responding to unexpected problems, and planning the conversion project. Young suffered from food allergies and refrained from informal staff lunches at nearby restaurants. She stopped regularly attending the biweekly staff meetings in order to devote more time to her work. She now only attended the meetings when there was a specific agenda item regarding her operation.

Last month the system was corrupted by a virus introduced over the Internet. She devoted an entire weekend to restoring the system to operation. A recurring headache was one of the servers code-named "Poncho" that would occasionally shut down for no apparent reason. Instead of replacing it, she decided to nurse Poncho along until it was replaced by the new NT system. Her work was frequently interrupted by frantic calls from staff researchers who needed immediate help on a variety of computer-related problems. She was shocked at how computer illiterate some of the researchers were and how she had to guide them through some of the basics of e-mail management and database configuration. She did find time to help Assistant Professor Amanda Johnson on a project. Johnson was the only researcher to respond to Young's e-mail announcing that the IS staff was available to help on projects. Young created a virtual project office on the Internet so that Johnson could collaborate with colleagues from institutes in Italy and Thailand on a UN research grant. She looked forward to the day when she could spend more time on fun projects like that.

Young had a part-time team of five student assistants from the computer science department. At first she was not sure how freely she could delegate work to the students, and she closely supervised their work. She quickly realized that they were all very bright, competent workers who were anxious to leverage this work experience into a lucrative career upon graduation. She admitted that she sometimes had a hard time relating to students who were preoccupied with fraternity bashes and X-games. She lost her temper only once, and that was at Samantha Eggert for failing to set up an adequate virus screening system that would have prevented the Internet corruption that occurred. She kept a close eye on Eggert's work after that, but in time, Eggert proved her worth. Young saw a lot of herself in Eggert's work habits.

THE MICROSOFT NT CONVERSION PROJECT

Young laid the groundwork for the NT conversion project in her recruitment interview with the director by arguing that conversion was a critical skill she would bring to the position. Once hired she was able to sell the director and his immediate staff on the project, but not without some resistance. Some associate directors questioned whether it was necessary to go through another conversion so soon after the Windows 95 conversion 16 months ago. Some of the researchers lobbied that the money would be better spent on installing a centralized air-conditioning system at WOI. Ultimately, the director signed off on the project after Young assured him that the conversion would be relatively painless and the Institute would then have a state-of-the-art information system.

The conversion was scheduled to take eight weeks to complete and consisted of four major phases: server setup, network installation, data migration, and workstation conversion. The project would be completed during the summer so that the student assistants could work full time on the project. Young and her student team would first need to purchase and set up seven new NT servers. They would then create a new local area network (LAN). Next they would migrate data to the new Oracle NT database. Finally, they would convert the existing 65 client computers into NT workstations capable of functioning on the new system. Young had been actively involved in four similar conversions when working at Evergreen Systems and was confident that she and her team could complete the project with a minimum of technical problems. She also believed that this conversion would not be traumatic to the staff at the Institute because the NT interface was very similar to the Windows 95 interface.

Young knew that in order for the project to be considered successful, there needed to be minimum disruption of daily staff functions. She held a staff briefing meeting to outline the scope of the project and the impact it would have on the Institute's operations. She was disappointed by the light attendance at the meeting. One problem was the irregular hours staff worked at WOI. Several of the researchers were night owls who preferred to work late into the night. Other staff traveled frequently. She ended up holding two other briefing meetings, including one in the evening. Still the attendance was less than desired.

The staff's major concerns were the amount of downtime that would occur and whether the software and databases they were currently using would work on the new system. Young assured them that most of the downtime would occur on the weekends and would be posted well in advance. The only disruption would be two hours necessary to convert their existing computer into a workstation. Young invested extra energy in researching the compatibility issue and sent an e-mail to everyone listing the software that was known to not work in the NT system. The only software problems involved specially written DOS v2.1 or older programs that would not function in the new NT operating environment. In one case, she assigned a student to rewrite and enhance the present program for a researcher. In the other case, she was able to persuade the staff member to use a newer, better program.

Young sent a second e-mail asking staff members to clean up their hard drives and get rid of old, obsolete files because the new NT software would take up considerably more space than the Windows 95 operating system. In some cases, she replaced existing hard drives with bigger drives so that this would not be a problem. She circulated a workstation conversion schedule by e-mail so that staff could pick a preferred time for when their computer would be down and when her assistants could upgrade the computer into a workstation. Seventy percent of the staff responded to the e-mail request, and she and her staff contacted the remaining staff by telephone to schedule the conversion.

The first six weeks of the project went relatively smoothly. The NT servers arrived on time and were installed and configured on schedule. The completion of the network was delayed three days when the fire marshal showed up earlier than planned to inspect the electrical wiring. Young had never met the marshal before and was surprised at how nit-picking he was. They failed the inspection, and it took three days to reschedule and pass inspection. Word about failing the fire inspection circulated the hallways at the Institute. One joker put a Smokey the Bear sign on the IS office door. Young later found out that as a result of a recent fire in town, the fire marshals had been instructed to be extra vigilant in their inspections.

Data migration to the new Oracle database took a little longer than planned because the new version was not as compatible with the old version as advertised. Still, this only added three days to the project. The project was entering the fourth and final phase—conversion of client computers into NT workstations. This phase involved her staff deleting the old operating system and installing new operating software in each computer at the Institute. Young had scheduled two hours per machine and had organized a daily workload of 10 computers so that adequate backup could be made just in case something went wrong.

Young chose to convert the director's office first and told Green that everything was going according to plan. Soon the project began to experience nagging problems. First, some of the staff forgot when they were scheduled to be converted. The team had to wait for them to abandon what they were doing so they could convert the computer. Second, the drivers on some of the computers were not compatible, and the team had to devote extra time downloading new drivers off the Internet. Third, a few of the staff failed to create adequate hard drive space to accommodate the new NT software. In most cases, the team worked with the staff member to delete or compress unnecessary files. One time the staff member could not be found, and Young had to decide which files to delete. This wasn't a problem since the hard drive contained computer games and ancient Word Perfect files. To compound matters, midway through the third day, one of the student assistants, Steve Stills, was diagnosed with a moderate case of carpal tunnel and was told to take two weeks off from computer work.

After three days only 22 computers had been converted to NT stations. Young ended the day by sending an e-mail to the remaining users apologizing for the delays and posting a revised schedule for their system configuration.

THE CALL

Young and her staff were working diligently on converting computers into NT workstations when she received an urgent call from the director's secretary requesting that she drop everything and come downstairs to the staff meeting. The secretary's voice appeared tense, and Young wondered what was up. As she gathered her things, the student assistant, Eggert, cleared her throat and confided that there may be problems with some of the Institute's Web sites. She discovered yesterday that some of the links in the Web pages created using Netscape weren't working in the Microsoft environment. Young demanded to know why she wasn't told about this sooner. Eggerts confessed that she thought she had fixed the problem last night. Young told her that they would talk about this when she got back and left.

Young entered the meeting room and immediately recognized that there were more than the usual faces in attendance. The director welcomed her by saying, "We're glad you could find the time to visit with us. My staff meeting has just erupted into a series of complaints about your NT conversion project. As it turns out Dr. Phillips over here can't access his documents because his Word Perfect file mysteriously disappeared. Dr. Simon's geothermal assessment program, which he has used for the past seven years, doesn't seem to work anymore. Now it appears that the Web site we use to coordinate our research with the Oslo Institute is a mess. Everyone is complaining about how the revised installation schedule is going to disrupt work. I want to know why I wasn't informed about these problems. These guys want to lynch me for approving your project!"

1. How would you respond to the director?
2. What mistakes did Young make that contributed to the problems at the end of the case?
3. How could she have managed the conversion project better?

Case

Tom Bray

Tom Bray was mulling over today's work schedule as he looked across the bay at the storm that was rolling in. It was the second official day of the Pegasus project and now the real work was about to begin.

Pegasus was a two-month renovation project for AtlantiCorp, a major financial institution headquartered in Boston, Massachusetts. Tom's group was responsible for installing the furniture and equipment in the newly renovated accounts receivable department on the third floor. The Pegasus project was a dedicated project team formed out of AtlantiCorp facilities department with Tom as the project lead.

Tom was excited because this was his first *major league* project and he was looking forward to practicing a new management style—MBWA, aka management by wandering around. He had been exposed to MBWA in a business class in college, but it wasn't until he attended an AtlantiCorp leadership training seminar that he decided to change how he managed people. The trainer was devout MBWA champion ("You can't manage people from a computer!"). Furthermore, the testimonies from his peers reinforced the difference that MBWA can make when it comes to working on projects.

Tom had joined the facilities group at AtlantiCorp five years earlier after working for EDS for six years. He quickly demonstrated technical competences and good work habits. He was encouraged to take all the internal project management workshops offered by AtlantiCorp. On his last two projects he served as assistant project manager responsible for procurement and contract management.

He had read books about the soft side of project management and MBWA made sense—after all, people not tools get projects done. His boss had told him he needed to refine his people skills and work on developing rapport with team members. MBWA seemed like a perfect solution.

Tom reviewed the list of team member names; some of the foreign names were real tongue twisters. For example, one of his better workers was from Thailand and her name was Pinyarat Sirisomboonsuk. He practiced saying "Pin-ya-răt See-rē-som-boon-sook." He got up, tucked in his shirt, and walked out of his office and down to the floor where his team was busy unloading equipment.

Tom said "Hi" to the first few workers he met until he encountered Jack and three other workers. Jack was busy pulling hardware out of a box while his teammates were standing around talking. Tom blurted, "Come on guys, we've got work to do." They quickly separated and began unloading boxes.

The rest of the visit seemed to go well. He helped Shari unload a heavy box and managed to get an appreciative grin from Pinyarat when he almost correctly pronounced her name. Satisfied, Tom went back up to his office thinking that MBWA wouldn't be that tough to do.

After responding to e-mail and calling some vendors, Tom ventured back out to see how things were going downstairs. When he got there, the floor was weirdly quiet. People were busy doing their work and his attempts at generating conversation elicited stiff responses. He left thinking that maybe MBWA is going to be tougher than he thought.

1. What do you think is going on at the end of this case?
2. What should Tom do next and why?
3. What can be learned from this case?

Case

Cerberus Corporation*

Cerberus is a successful producer of specialty chemicals. It operates nine large campus sites in the United States, with a number of different business units on each site. These business units operate independently, with direct reporting to

---

* Courtesy of John Sloan, Oregon State University.

corporate headquarters. Site functions such as safety, environmental, and facilities management report to a host organization—typically the business unit that is the largest user of their services.

SUSAN STEELE

Susan Steele has worked in the Facilities group at the Cerberus Richmond site for the last two years. The Facilities manager, Tom Stern, reports to the General Manager of the largest business unit on site, the highly profitable Adhesives and Sealants Division. Susan started with Cerberus when she graduated with her business degree from Awsum University. She was excited about her new assignment—leading a project for the first time. She remembered Tom saying, "We've got office furniture dating back to the 80s. There are those ugly green-top desks that look like they came from military surplus! I'm especially concerned about computer workstation ergonomics—it's a major issue that we absolutely must fix! I want you to lead a project to transition our office furniture to the new corporate standard."

Susan assembled her project team: Jeff, the site safety/ergonomics engineer; Gretchen, the space planner; Cindy, the move coordinator; and Kari, the accounting liaison for Facilities. At their first meeting, everyone agreed that ergonomics was the most urgent concern. All five business units responded to a workstation survey that identified injury-causing ergonomics. The team was developing a plan to replace old desks with new, ergo-adjustable furniture by the end of the year. Susan asked Kari about the budget, and Kari responded, "Facilities should not pay for this. We want the individual business units to pay so that the costs will show where they are incurred."

Gretchen spoke up: "You know, we've got lots of department moves going on constantly. Everybody is always jockeying for space and location as their business needs change. Besides the ergonomics, could we say that only corporate standard furniture gets moved? That would force changing some of the stuff that's just plain ugly." Everyone agreed that this was a great idea.

Susan presented the project plan to Tom and got a green light to proceed.

JON WOOD

Jon Wood is a planning manager, with 22 years experience at Cerberus. His business unit, Photographic Chemicals Division (PCD), is losing money. Digital photography is continuing to reduce the size of the market, and PCD is having trouble matching the competition's relentless price-cutting. Jon recently transferred to Richmond from corporate headquarters, where he ran the economic forecasting group. He is considered a new broom, and he is determined to sweep clean.

One of Jon's early actions was to negotiate with his general manager for a department move. Money was tight, and the site facilities function charged an arm and a leg for moves (covering all their fixed overhead, the operations people groused). However, Jon felt it was important to move from Building 4, where they were next to Production, to Building 6, where they could be close to Marketing, Forecasting, and Accounting. His General Manager agreed, and there was lots of excitement in his team about their upcoming move. Jon assigned one of his planners, Richard, to work with the Facilities team on the layout and move plan for the group. Things seemed to be going fine—Jon saw Richard sitting down with the move coordinator, and they seemed to be on track.

The day before the move, Jon hung up the phone from a particularly tense tele-conference with a Canadian subcontractor. Production was not going well, and product availability would be tight for the rest of the quarter. Clustered around his desk were Richard, Cindy, and a person he hadn't met yet, Susan. After hur-ried introductions, Susan told Jon that his filing cabinets could not be moved. The cabinets are large lateral files, five feet wide and two feet deep, a combination of both filing cabinets and bookshelves. Jon brought them with him from Corporate because he thought they looked nice with their dark grey steel sides and wood ve-neer tops. Susan told him that he would have to replace them with new corporate standard cabinets, virtually the same size. Jon said, "You mean you want me to throw away perfectly good filing cabinets and spend another $2,000 on new ones, just so they match? I won't do it!"

Susan replied, "Then I won't authorize the movement of the old cabinets."

Jon said, "You're joking—these cabinets are grey, the new ones are grey—the only difference is the wood top! You'd throw away $2,000 for nothing?"

Susan replied stiffly, "I'm sorry, that's the policy."

Jon said, "I don't care what the policy is. If I have to move them myself, those cabinets are not going to the dump. My division is losing money and I'm not go-ing to throw money away. If you don't like it, you're going to have to get your gen-eral manager to convince my general manager to make me do it. Now would you please leave so I can get some work done."

1. If you were Susan, what would you do?
2. What, if anything, could Susan have done differently to avoid this problem?
3. What could the management of Cerberus do to more effectively manage situa-tions like this?

Managing Project Teams

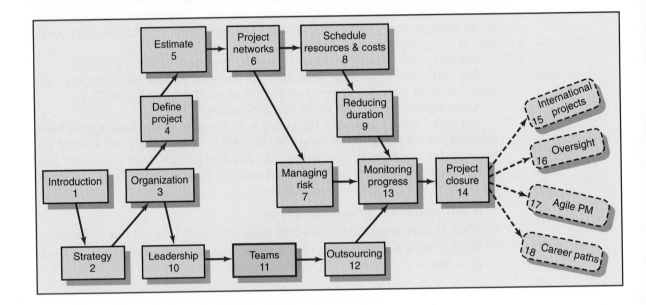

The difference in productivity between an average team and a turned-on, high-performing team is not 10 percent, 20 percent, or 30 percent, but 100 percent, 200 percent, even 500 percent!

—Tom Peters, management consultant and writer

The magic and power of teams is captured in the term "synergy," which is derived from the Greek word *sunergos:* "working together." There is positive and negative synergy. The essence of positive **synergy** can be found in the phrase "The whole is greater than the sum of the parts." Conversely, negative synergy occurs when the whole is less than the sum of the parts. Mathematically, these two states can be symbolized by the following equations:

$$\text{Positive Synergy } 1 + 1 + 1 + 1 + 1 = 10$$
$$\text{Negative Synergy } 1 + 1 + 1 + 1 + 1 = 2 \text{ (or even } -2)$$

Synergy perhaps can best be seen on a basketball court, a soccer pitch, or a football field where teammates play as one to defeat a superior foe (see Snapshot from Practice: The 2008 Olympic Redeem Team). Although less visible than in team sports, positive and negative synergy can also be observed and felt in the daily operations of project teams. Here is a description from one team member we interviewed:

> Instead of operating as one big team we fractionalized into a series of subgroups. The marketing people stuck together as well as the systems guys. A lot of time was wasted gossiping and complaining about each other. When the project started slipping behind schedule, everyone started covering their tracks and trying to pass the blame on to others. After a while we avoided direct conversation and resorted to e-mail. Management finally pulled the plug and brought in another team to salvage the project. It was one of the worst project management experiences in my life.

This same individual fortunately was also able to recount a more positive experience:

> There was a contagious excitement within the team. Sure we had our share of problems and setbacks, but we dealt with them straight on and, at times, were able to do the impossible. We all cared about the project and looked out for each other. At the same time we challenged each other to do better. It was one of the most exciting times in my life.

The following is a set of characteristics commonly associated with high-performing teams that exhibit **positive synergy:**

1. The team shares a sense of common purpose, and each member is willing to work toward achieving project objectives.
2. The team identifies individual talents and expertise and uses them, depending on the project's needs at any given time. At these times, the team willingly accepts

SNAPSHOT FROM PRACTICE
The 2008 Olympic Redeem Team*

In the 2004 Olympics in Athens, twelve years after Magic Johnson and Michael Jordon led the U.S. Dream Team to Olympic gold in Barcelona, the U.S. Basketball Team composed of NBA stars lost not once but three times to international competition. For the first time in Olympic history the U.S. settled for a bronze medal in men's basketball. Basketball was no longer America's game.

An autopsy of the debacle in Athens turned up a severe case of negative synergy. The causes were many. The team featured only three holdovers from the group that had qualified the previous summer. Seven of the original invitees withdrew. In the end some 14 players turned down Uncle Sam, invoking excuses from family obligations to nagging injuries to the security situation in Greece. As a result, coach Larry Brown took charge of a team with an average age of 23 years, and it showed. Behind the scenes, problems of dress and punctuality festered and on the eve of the games Brown wanted to send several players home. The million dollar players were overconfident, and assumed that their individual brilliance would prevail. An over reliance on one-on-one basketball and poor team defense doomed them as they lost games to Puerto Rico, Lithuania, and Argentina.

Enter Jerry Colangelo, 68, former coach, player, and president of the Phoenix Suns. "The way they conducted themselves left a lot to be desired," he says of the 2004 team. "Watching and listening to how people reacted to our players, I knew we'd hit bottom." Colangelo told NBA commissioner David Stern that he would only assume duties as managing director if he was given complete control. As a measure of how abysmal the situation was, he immediately got what he asked for.

In 2005 Colangelo met face-to-face with every prospective national player, to hear in their own words why they wanted to represent their country. The few good men to set things right wouldn't be paid or guaranteed playing time, much less a starting spot. A key recruit was superstar LeBron James who had been tagged "LeBronze" after his performance on the disappointing 2004 team. Colangelo says, "I got buy-in. Halfway through my talk with him, LeBron said, I'm in." Kobe Bryant soon followed and all but two of the 30 top NBA stars turned Colangelo down.

Mike Kryzewski, the college coach at Duke, was hired with one project objective in mind—win the gold medal. To do so he had to change the attitude of team USA. They had to subordinate their superstar egos and buy-in to the concept of team ball. A blessing in disguise was being knocked out of the 2006 world championship by a Greek team. The players came away

© AP Photo/Dusan Vranic

from that disappointment committed to team ball as extra passes became the staple in practices. The change in attitude was evident in more subtle ways. The USA on the uniforms was bright red, while the players' names were muted blue. The players no longer referred to hoops as "our game" and spoke about how it had become the world's game. Even the team's official slogan (United we rise) and unofficial nickname (the Redeem Team) implied room for improvement.

The team bought into a common objective. Team USA marched to the final gold medal game by beating opponents by an average margin of 30+ points. Experts marveled not so much by the victory margin, but by how well they played as a team. "Our goal is to win a gold medal and be humble about it," says Jason Kidd, six time all-pro point guard, "and if we do it by 50, to make sure it's because we're playing the right way." Nothing exemplified the right way more than a moment in the final, in which flawless ball movement from the Redeemers for 16 seconds, without a dribble being taken, culminated with Dwight Howard receiving a perfect pass for an uncontested dunk.

In the end, they didn't dominate the gold medal game. Spain proved to be inspired opponents. They simply closed the game out and for the first time since NBA players have come to the Olympics the USA played as a team rather than showboating individuals.

* Wolff, Alexander. "The Redeem Team: New nickname, new outlook for U.S. at Olympics," http://sportsillustrated.cnn.com/2008/writers/alexander_wolff/07/22/redeem.team0728/index.html

Varkonyi, Greg. "The Redeem Team played like a dream in the Olympic basketball final," http://www.sportingo.com/olympic-games/basketball/a10072_redeem-team-played-like-dream-olympic-basketball-final

the influence and leadership of the members whose skills are relevant to the immediate task.

3. Roles are balanced and shared to facilitate both the accomplishment of tasks and feelings of group cohesion and morale.

4. The team exerts energy toward problem solving rather than allowing itself to be drained by interpersonal issues or competitive struggles.
5. Differences of opinion are encouraged and freely expressed.
6. To encourage risk taking and creativity, mistakes are treated as opportunities for learning rather than reasons for punishment.
7. Members set high personal standards of performance and encourage each other to realize the objectives of the project.
8. Members identify with the team and consider it an important source of both professional and personal growth.

High-performing teams become champions, create breakthrough products, exceed customer expectations, and get projects done ahead of schedule and under budget. They are bonded together by mutual interdependency and a common goal or vision. They trust each other and exhibit a high level of collaboration.

The Five-Stage Team Development Model

Just as infants develop in certain ways during their first months of life, many experts argue that groups develop in a predictable manner. One of the most popular models identifies five stages (see Figure 11.1) through which groups develop into effective teams:

1. **Forming.** During this initial stage the members get acquainted with each other and understand the scope of the project. They begin to establish ground rules by trying to find out what behaviors are acceptable with respect to both the project (what role they will play, what performance expectations are) and interpersonal relations (who's really in charge). This stage is completed once members begin to think of themselves as part of a group.
2. **Storming.** As the name suggests, this stage is marked by a high degree of internal conflict. Members accept that they are part of a project group but resist the

FIGURE 11.1
The Five-Stage Team Development Model

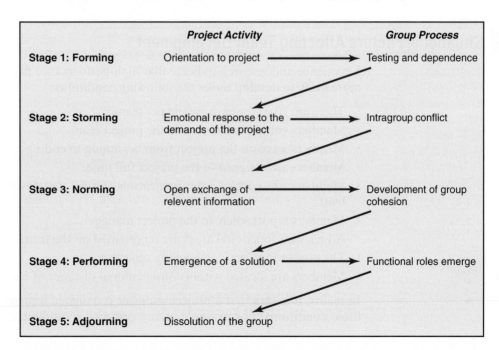

	Project Activity	Group Process
Stage 1: Forming	Orientation to project	Testing and dependence
Stage 2: Storming	Emotional response to the demands of the project	Intragroup conflict
Stage 3: Norming	Open exchange of relevent information	Development of group cohesion
Stage 4: Performing	Emergence of a solution	Functional roles emerge
Stage 5: Adjourning	Dissolution of the group	

constraints that the project and group put on their individuality. There is conflict over who will control the group and how decisions will be made. As these conflicts are resolved, the project manager's leadership becomes accepted, and the group moves to the next stage.

3. **Norming.** The third stage is one in which close relationships develop and the group demonstrates cohesiveness. Feelings of camaraderie and shared responsibility for the project are heightened. The norming phase is complete when the group structure solidifies and the group establishes a common set of expectations about how members should work together.

4. **Performing.** The team operating structure at this point is fully functional and accepted. Group energy has moved from getting to know each other and how the group will work together to accomplishing the project goals.

5. **Adjourning.** For conventional work groups, performing is the last stage of their development. However, for project teams, there is a completion phase. During this stage, the team prepares for its own disbandment. High performance is no longer a top priority. Instead attention is devoted to wrapping up the project. Responses of members vary in this stage. Some members are upbeat, basking in the project team's accomplishments. Others may be depressed over loss of camaraderie and friendships gained during the project's life.

This model has several implications for those working on project teams. The first is that the model provides a framework for the group to understand its own development. Project managers have found it useful to share the model with their teams. It helps members accept the tensions of the storming phase, and it directs their focus to moving toward the more productive phases. Another implication is that it stresses the importance of the norming phase, which contributes significantly to the level of productivity experienced during the performing phase. Project managers, as we shall see, have to take an active role in shaping group norms that will contribute to ultimate project success. For an alternative model of group development see the Punctuated Equilibrium Research Highlight.

Situational Factors Affecting Team Development

Experience and research indicate that high-performance project teams are much more likely to develop under the following conditions:

- There are 10 or fewer members per team.
- Members volunteer to serve on the project team.
- Members serve on the project from beginning to end.
- Members are assigned to the project full time.
- Members are part of an organization culture that fosters cooperation and trust.
- Members report solely to the project manager.
- All relevant functional areas are represented on the team.
- The project involves a compelling objective.
- Members are located within conversational distance of each other.

In reality, it is rare that a project manager is assigned a project that meets all of these conditions. For example, many projects' requirements dictate the active

Gersick's research suggests that groups don't develop in a universal sequence of stages as suggested by the five-phase model. Her research, which is based on the systems concept of *punctuated equilibrium,* found that the *timing* of when groups form and actually change the way they work is highly consistent. What makes this research appealing is that it is based on studies of more than a dozen field and laboratory task forces assigned to complete a specific project. This research reveals that each group begins with a unique approach to accomplishing its project that is set in its first meeting and includes the behavior and roles that dominate phase I. Phase I continues until one-half of the allotted time for project completion has expired (regardless of actual amount of time). At this midpoint, a major transition occurs that includes the dropping of the group's old norms and behavior patterns and the emergence of new behavior and working relationships that contribute to increased progress toward completing the project. The last meeting is marked by accelerated activity to complete the project. These findings are summarized in Figure 11.2.

The remarkable discovery in these studies was that each group experienced its transition at the same point in its calendar—precisely halfway between the first meeting and the completion deadline—despite the fact that some groups spent as little as an hour on their project while others spent six months. It was as if the groups universally experienced a midlife crisis at this point. The midpoint appeared to work like an alarm clock, heightening members' awareness that time was limited and they needed to get moving. Within the context

of the five-stage model, it suggests that groups begin by combining the forming and norming stages, then go through a period of low performing, followed by storming, then a period of high performing, and finally adjourning.

Gersick's findings suggest that there are natural transition points during the life of teams in which the group is receptive to change and that such a moment naturally occurs at the scheduled midpoint of a project. However, a manager does not want to have to wait 6 months on a complicated 12-month project for a team to get its act together! Here it is important to note that Gersick's groups were working on relatively small-scale projects, i.e., a 4-person bank task force in charge of designing a new bank account in one month and a 12-person medical task force in charge of reorganizing two units of a treatment facility. In most cases no formal project plan was established. If anything, the results point to the importance of good project management and the need to establish deadlines and milestones. By imposing a series of deadlines associated with important milestones, it is possible to create multiple transition points for natural group development. For example, a 12-month construction project can be broken down into six to eight significant milestones with the challenge of meeting each deadline producing the prerequisite tension for elevating team performance.

* Connie J. Gersick, "Time and Transition in Work Teams: Toward a New Model of Group Development," *Academy of Management Journal,* Vol. 31, No. 1 (March 1988), pp. 9–41; and Connie J. Gersick, "Making Time Predictable Transitions in Task Groups," *Academy of Management Journal,* Vol. 32, No. 2 (June 1989), pp. 274–309.

FIGURE 11.2
The Punctuated Equilibrium Model of Group Development

SNAPSHOT FROM PRACTICE Managing Martians*

Donna Shirley's 35-year career as aerospace engineer reached a pinnacle in July 1997 when Sojourner—the solar-powered, self-guided, microwave-oven-sized rover—was seen exploring the Martian landscape in Pathfinder's spectacular images from the surface of the red planet. The event marked a milestone in space exploration: No vehicle had ever before roamed the surface of another planet. Shirley, a manager at the Jet Propulsion Laboratory's Mars Exploration Program, headed the mostly male team that designed and built Sojourner. In her insightful memoir, *Managing Martians*, written with Danelle Morton, she makes the following observation about managing creative teams:

Courtesy of NASA.

When you are managing really brilliant, creative people, at some point you find it's impossible to command or control them because you can't understand what they are doing. Once they have gone beyond your ability to understand them, you have a choice to make as a manager. You can limit them and the project by your intelligence, which I think is the wrong way to do it. Or you can trust them and use your management skills to keep them focused on the goal.

A lot of bad managers get threatened when their "subordinates" know more than they do. They either hire people who are inferior to them so they can always feel in control or they bottleneck people who know something they don't so they can maintain control. The whole project suffers from the manager's insecurities.

* Donna Shirley and Danelle Morton, *Managing Martians* (New York: Broadway Books, 1998), pp. 88–89.

See the Managing Martians snapshot for further advice on recruiting team members.

After reviewing needed skills, the manager should try and find out through the corporate grapevine who is good, who is available, and who might want to work on the project. Some organizations may allow direct interviews. Often a manager will have to expend political capital to get highly prized people assigned to the project.

In matrix environments, the project manager will have to request appointments with functional managers to discuss project requirements for staffing. The following documents should be available at these discussions: an overall project scope statement, endorsements of top management, and a description of the tasks and general schedule that pertain to the people from their departments. Managers need to be precise as to what attributes they are seeking and why they are important.

Functional managers should be encouraged to suggest names of people within their departments as candidates. If the project manager is asked to suggest names, it might be wise to say, "Well, I would really like Pegi Young, but I know how critical her work is. How about Billy Talbot?" If the conversation goes this way, the project manager may be able to cut a deal then and there and will want to be sure to put the agreement in writing immediately after the meeting as a memorandum of understanding.

If, on the other hand, the functional manager balks at the suggestions and the meeting is not progressing, the project manager should adroitly terminate the conversation with an understanding that the matter will be discussed again in a few days. This technique demonstrates persistence and a desire to do what it takes to resolve the issue. Ultimately, of course, the project manager will have to settle on the best offer. Managers should exercise care not to reveal how different members of the team were selected. The project might be crippled at the start if reluctantly assigned members are identified and the team perceives differences in attitude and commitment.

Conducting Project Meetings

The First Project Team Meeting

Research on team development confirms what we have heard from project managers: The first **project kick-off meeting** is critical to the early functioning of the project team. According to one veteran project manager:

> The first team meeting sets the tone for how the team will work together. If it is disorganized, or becomes bogged down with little sense of closure, then this can often become a self-fulfilling prophecy for subsequent group work. On the other hand, if it is crisply run, focusing on real issues and concerns in an honest and straightforward manner, members come away excited about being part of the project team.

There are typically three objectives project managers try to achieve during the first meeting of the project team. The first is to provide an overview of the project, including the scope and objectives, the general schedule, method, and procedures. The second is to begin to address some of the interpersonal concerns captured in the team development model: Who are the other team members? How will I fit in? Will I be able to work with these people? The third and most important objective is to begin to model how the team is going to work together to complete the project. The project manager must recognize that first impressions are important; her behavior will be carefully monitored and interpreted by team members. This meeting should serve as an exemplary role model for subsequent meetings and reflect the leader's style.

The meeting itself comes in a variety of shapes and forms. It is not uncommon in major projects for the kick-off meeting to involve one or two days, often at a remote site away from interruptions. This retreat provides sufficient time for preliminary introduction, to begin to establish ground rules, and to define the structure of the project. One advantage of off-site kick-off meetings is that they provide ample opportunity for informal interaction among members during breaks, meals, and evening activities; such informal interactions are critical to forming relationships.

However, many organizations do not have the luxury of holding elaborate retreats. In other cases the scope of project and level of involvement of different participants does not warrant such an investment of time. In these cases, the key operating principle should be KISS (keep it simple stupid!). Too often when constrained by time, project managers try to accomplish too much during the first meeting; in doing so, issues do not get fully resolved, and members come away with an information headache.

The primary goal is to run a productive meeting, and objectives should be realistic given the time available. If the meeting is only one hour, then the project manager should simply review the scope of the project, discuss how the team was formed, and provide an opportunity for members to introduce themselves to the team.

Establishing Ground Rules

Whether as part of an elaborate first meeting or during follow-up meetings, the project manager must quickly begin to establish operational ground rules for how the team will work together. These ground rules involve not only organizational and procedural issues but also normative issues on how the team will interact with each other. Although specific procedures will vary across organizations and projects, some of the major issues that need to be addressed include the following:

Planning Decisions

- How will the project plan be developed?
- What tools will be used to support the project?
- Will a specific project management software package be used? If so, which one?
- Who will enter the planning information?
- What are the specific roles and responsibilities of all the participants?
- Who needs to be informed of decisions? How will they be kept informed?
- What are the relative importance of cost, time, and performance?
- What are the deliverables of the project planning process?
- What format is appropriate for each deliverable?
- Who will approve and sign off at the completion of each deliverable?
- Who receives each deliverable?

Tracking Decisions

- How will progress be assessed?
- At what level of detail will the project be tracked?
- How will team members get data from each other?
- How often will they get this data?
- Who will generate and distribute reports?
- Who needs to be kept informed about project progress, and how will they be informed?
- What content/format is appropriate for each audience?
- Meetings
  - Where will meetings be located?
  - What kind of meetings will be held?
  - Who will "run" these meetings?
  - How will agendas be produced?
  - How will information be recorded?

Managing Change Decisions

- How will changes be instituted?
- Who will have change approval authority?
- How will plan changes be documented and evaluated?

Relationship Decisions

- What department or organizations will the team need to interact with during the project?
- What are the roles and responsibilities of each organization (reviewer, approver, creator, user)?
- How will all involved parties be kept informed of deliverables, schedule dates, expectations, etc.?

- How will the team members communicate among themselves?
- What information will and won't be exchanged?

Checklists like these are only a guide; items should be added or deleted as needed. Many of these procedures will have already been established by precedent and will only have to be briefly reviewed. For example, *Microsoft Project* or *Primavera* may be the standard software tool for planning and tracking. Likewise, a specific firm is likely to have an established format for reporting status information. How to deal with other issues will have to be determined by the project team. When appropriate, the project manager should actively solicit input from the project team members and draw upon their experience and preferred work habits. This process also contributes to their buying into the operational decisions. Decisions should be recorded and circulated to all members.

During the course of establishing these operational procedures, the project manager, through word and deed, should begin working with members to establish the norms for team interaction. Below are examples of some of the norms researchers have found associated with high-performance teams.

- Confidentiality is maintained; no information is shared outside the team unless all agree to it.
- It is acceptable to be in trouble, but it is not acceptable to surprise others. Tell others immediately when deadlines or milestones will not be reached.
- There is zero tolerance for bulling a way through a problem or an issue.
- Agree to disagree, but when a decision has been made, regardless of personal feelings, move forward.
- Respect outsiders, and do not flaunt one's position on the project team.
- Hard work does not get in the way of having fun.

One way of making these norms more tangible is by creating a team charter that goes beyond the scope statement of the project and states in explicit terms the norms and values of the team. This charter should be a collaborative effort on the part of the core team. Project managers can lead by proposing certain tenets, but they need to be open to suggestions from the team. Once there is general agreement to the rules of conduct, each member signs the final document to symbolize commitment to the principles it contains.

Unfortunately, in some cases charters become a meaningless ritual because the charter is signed and filed away, never to be discussed again. To have a lasting effect, the charter has to be a legitimate part of the project monitoring system. Just as the team reviews progress toward project objectives, the team assesses the extent to which members are adhering to the principles in the charter.

Project managers play a major role in establishing team norms through personal example. If they freely admit mistakes and share what they have learned from them, other team members will begin to do the same. At the same time, project managers need to intervene when they believe such norms are being violated. They should talk to offenders privately and clearly state their expectations. The amazing thing about groups is that once a group is cohesive, with well-established norms, the members will police themselves so that the manager doesn't have to be the heavy. For example, one project manager confided that his team had a practice of having a small bean bag present at every meeting. If any one member felt that a colleague was shooting hot air or shading the truth, he or she was obligated to toss the bean bag at the speaker. See the snapshot: Mattel's Project Platypus for examples of norms that encourage innovation.

SNAPSHOT FROM PRACTICE Mattel's Project Platypus*

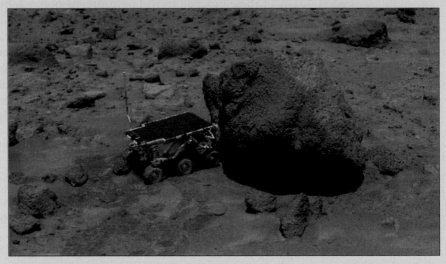

AP/Wide World.

Mattel is the largest toy manufacturing company in the world with product lines that include Barbie dolls, Fisher-Price toys, and Hot Wheels. Mattel stumbled when it missed out on the girl empowerment trend in the late 1990s. Vowing never to have this happen again, Mattel re-engineered its product development processes by instituting Project Platypus.

Project Platypus consists of people from a variety of functional areas who leave their regular jobs for three months and move out of Mattel headquarters to a separate location where they work collaboratively on new product ideas. Team members in Mattel's Project Platypus sometimes spend their days dropping eggs from a 14-foot ladder or throwing stuffed animals at each other. It is all part of team-building activities designed to get people to think differently and come up with creative ideas for new toys.

According to Ivy Ross, head of Mattel's girl design division, exercises such as devising a method to prevent an egg from breaking when dropped from 14 feet or throwing stuffed bunnies at a teammate to release inhibitions are ways to get people to think outside the box and discover consumer trends and marketplace changes. "Other companies have skunk works," Ross says, "we have platypus. I looked up the definition and it said, 'an uncommon mix of different species.'"

The strength of the Platypus lies in its members' ability to build on one another's creative ideas. A key group norm is no one owns an idea. Everything belongs to the group, which helps eliminate competitiveness.

Project Platypus is also designed to encourage team bonding, so that people will continue to share ideas and collaborate once the creative ideas move further into product development and production. Previously, product development at Mattel involved a lot of "baton passing," as Ross puts it. Mattel now wants everyone to collaborate in a design and development process where there's a shared sense of ownership and achievement. Participants in the project work in a huge open space with no walls or cubicles. Desks are on wheels to encourage spontaneous sharing and collaboration. Project members can post their sketched ideas on the walls and invite others for suggestions.

The first Project Platypus effort is a new toy called Ello, a hybrid between a construction set and activity kit. Ello sets consist of interconnected pieces that allow children to explore their imagination to build anything from jewelry to buildings. Platypus project teams are continuing to work to develop two to three new product ideas a year.

* Chuck Salter, "Ivy Ross Is Not Playing Around," *Fast Company,* Issue 64, November 2002, p. 104.

Managing Subsequent Project Meetings

The project kick-off meeting is one of several kinds of meetings required to complete a project. Other meetings include status report meetings, problem-solving meetings, and audit meetings. Issues unique to these meetings will be discussed in subsequent chapters. For now, here are some general guidelines for running effective meetings. They speak directly to the person chairing the meeting:

- Start meetings on time regardless of whether everyone is present.
- Prepare and distribute an agenda prior to the meeting.
- Identify an adjournment time.
- Periodically take time to review how effective previous meetings have been.
- Solicit recommendations and implement changes.
- Assign good recordkeeping.
- Review the agenda before beginning, and tentatively allocate time for each item.
- Prioritize issues so that adjustments can be made given time constraints.
- Encourage active participation of all members by asking questions instead of making statements.
- Summarize decisions, and review assignments for the next meeting.
- Prepare and distribute a summary of the meeting to appropriate people.
- Recognize accomplishments and positive behavior.

Meetings are often considered an anathema to productivity, but this does not have to be the case. The most common complaint is that meetings last too long. Establishing an agenda and adjournment time helps participants budget discussion time and provides a basis for expediting the proceedings. Recordkeeping can be an unwelcome, tedious task. Utilizing laptop computers to record decisions and information in real time can facilitate the communication process. Careful preparation and consistent application of these guidelines can make meetings a vital part of projects.

Establishing a Team Identity

One of the challenges project managers often face in building a team is the lack of full-time involvement of team members. Specialists work on different phases of the project and spend the majority of their time and energy elsewhere. They are often members of multiple teams, each competing for their time and allegiance. Project expert David Frame points out that for many of these specialists a specific project is an abstraction; as a consequence their level of motivation suffers. Project managers need to try to make the project team as tangible as possible to the participants by developing a unique team identity to which participants can become emotionally attached. Team meetings, co-location of team members, team names, and team rituals are common vehicles for doing so.

- *Effective use of meetings.* Periodic project team meetings provide an important forum for communicating project information. A less obvious function of project meetings is to help establish a concrete team identity. During project meetings, members see that they are not working alone. They are part of a larger project team, and project success depends on the collective efforts of all the team members. Timely gatherings of all the project participants help define team membership and reinforce a collective identity.

SNAPSHOT FROM PRACTICE "Rat Fax" Galvanizes ELITE Team at Newspaper*

Knight-Ridder's *Tallahassee Democrat,* like many American newspapers in the late 1980s, was struggling to survive in the face of declining revenues. Fred Mott, the general manager of the *Democrat,* was convinced that the key to the newspaper's future was becoming more customer-focused. Despite his best efforts, little progress was being made toward becoming a customer-driven newspaper. One area that was particularly problematic was advertising, where lost revenues due to errors could be as high as $10,000 a month.

Fred Mott decided to create a team of 12 of his best workers from all parts of the newspaper. They became known as the ELITE team because their mission was to "ELIminate The Errors." At first the team spent a lot of time pointing fingers at each other rather than coming to grips with the error problems at the newspaper. A key turning point came when one member produced what became known as "the rat tracks fax" and told the story behind it. It turns out a sloppily prepared ad arrived through a fax machine looking like "a rat had run across the page." Yet the ad passed through the hands of seven employees and probably would have been printed if it had not been totally unreadable. The introduction of this fax broke the ice, and the team started to admit that everyone—not everyone else—

was at fault. Then, recalls one member, "We had some pretty hard discussions. And there were tears at those meetings."

The emotional responses galvanized the group to the task at hand and bonded them to one another. The ELITE team looked carefully at the entire process by which an ad was sold, created, printed, and billed. When the process was examined, the team discovered patterns of errors, most of which could be attributed to bad communication, time pressures, and poor attitude. They made a series of recommendations that completely transformed the ad process at the *Democrat.* Under ELITE's leadership, advertising accuracy rose sharply and stayed above 99 percent. Lost revenues from errors dropped to near zero. Surveys showed a huge positive swing in advertiser satisfaction.

The impact of ELITE, however, went beyond numbers. The ELITE team's own brand of responsiveness to customer satisfaction spread to other parts of the newspaper. In effect this team of mostly frontline workers spearheaded a cultural transformation at the newspaper that emphasized a premium on customer service.

* Jon R. Katzenbach and Douglas K. Smith, *The Wisdom of Teams* (Boston: Harvard Business School Press, 1993), pp. 67–72. Copyright McKinsey & Co., Inc.

- *Co-location of team members.* The most obvious way to make the project team tangible is to have members work together in a common space. This is not always possible in matrix environments where involvement is part time and members are working on other projects and activities. A worthwhile substitute for co-location is the creation of a project office, sometimes referred to as the project war room or clubhouse. Such rooms are the common meeting place and contain the most significant project documentation. Frequently, their walls are covered with Gantt charts, cost graphs, and other output associated with project planning and control. These rooms serve as a tangible sign of project effort.

- *Creation of project team name.* The development of a team name such as the "A-Team" or "Casey's Crusaders" is a common device for making a team more tangible. Frequently an associated team logo is also created. Again the project manager should rely on the collective ingenuity of the team to come up with the appropriate name and logo. Such symbols then can be affixed to stationery, T-shirts, coffee mugs, etc., to help signify team membership.

- *Get the team to build or do something together early on.* Nothing reinforces a sense of a team more than working on something together. In the case of one international project, the manager simply hosted a potluck dinner where each member brought a dish his or her country was famous for.

- **Team rituals.** Just as corporate rituals help establish the unique identity of a firm, similar symbolic actions at the project level can contribute to a unique team subculture. For example, on one project members were given ties with stripes that corresponded to the number of milestones on the project. After reaching each milestone, members would gather and cut the next stripe off their ties to signify progress. Ralph Katz reports it was common practice for Digital Equipment's alpha chip design team to recognize people who found a bug in the design by giving them a phosphorescent toy roach. The bigger the bug that was discovered, the bigger the toy roach received. Such rituals help set project work apart from mainstream operations and reinforce a special status.

Creating a Shared Vision

Unlike project scope statements, which include specific cost, completion dates, and performance requirements, a **vision** involves the less tangible aspects of project performance. It refers to an image a project team holds in common about how the project will look upon completion, how they will work together, and/or how customers will accept the project. At its simplest level, a shared vision is the answer to the question, "What do we want to create?" Not everyone will have the same vision, but the images should be similar. Visions come in a variety of shapes and forms; they can be captured in a slogan or a symbol or can be written as a formal vision statement.

What a vision is, is not as important as what it does. A vision inspires members to give their best effort. (See A Good Man in a Storm Snapshot.) Moreover, a shared vision unites professionals with different backgrounds and agendas to a common aspiration. It helps motivate members to subordinate their individual agendas and do what is best for the project. As psychologist Robert Fritz puts it, "In the presence of greatness, pettiness disappears." Visions also provide focus and help communicate less tangible priorities, helping members make appropriate judgment calls. Finally, a shared vision for a project fosters commitment to the long term and discourages expedient responses that collectively dilute the quality of the project.

Visions can be surprisingly simple. For example, the vision for a new car could be expressed as a "pocket rocket." Compare this vision with the more traditional product description—"a sports car in the midprice range." The "pocket rocket" vision provides a much clearer picture of what the final product should be. Design engineers would immediately understand that the car will be both small and fast and that the car should be quick at the getaway, nimble in the turns, and very fast in the straightaways. Obviously, many details would have to be worked out, but the vision would help establish a common framework for making decisions.

There appear to be four essential qualities of an effective vision (see Figure 11.4): First, its essential qualities must be able to be communicated. A vision is worthless if it only resides in someone's head. Second, visions have to be challenging but also realistic. For example, a task force directed at overhauling the curriculum at the college of business at a state university is likely to roll its eyes if the dean announces that their vision is to compete against the Harvard Business School. Conversely, developing the best undergraduate business program in that state may be a realistic vision for that task force. Third, the project manager has to believe in the vision. Passion for the vision is an essential element of an effective vision. Finally, it should be a source of inspiration to others.

Once a project manager accepts the importance of building a shared vision, the next question is how to get a vision for a particular project. First, project managers don't get visions. They act as catalysts and midwives for the formation of a shared vision of a project team. In many cases visions are inherent in the scope

SNAPSHOT FROM PRACTICE A Good Man in a Storm*

 Once upon a time, back in 1976, Data General Corporation needed to come up quickly with a fast, reasonably priced 32-bit mini-computer to compete with Digital Equipment Corporation's VAX. Data General CEO Edson de Castro launched the Fountainhead Project and gave it the best people and ample resources to complete the 32-bit initiative. As a back-up to the Fountainhead project, Data General created the Eagle project within the Eclipse group under the leadership of Tom West. Work on both projects began in 1978.

In 1980 Data General announced its new computer, featuring simplicity, power, and low cost. This computer was not the Fountainhead from the well-funded "best" DG group but the Eagle from Tom West's under-funded Eclipse team. Tracy Kidder saw all this happen and told the story in *The Soul of a New Machine,* which won a Pulitzer Prize in 1982. This book, which Kidder thought might be of interest to a handful of computer scientists, has become a project management classic.

In the beginning of his book, Kidder introduces the readers to the book's protagonist Tom West by telling the story of him sailing a yacht across rough seas off the coast of New England. Kidder's title for the prologue was "A Good Man in a Storm."

Twenty years after Kidder's book was published Tom West was interviewed by Lawrence Peters for the *Academy of Management Executive.* Below are some excerpts that capture Tom's views on managing innovative projects:

On selecting team members:

You explain to a guy what the challenge was, and then see if his eyes light up.

On motivating team members:

. . . Challenge was everything. People, especially creative technical people who really want to make a difference, will do whatever is possible or whatever is necessary. I've done this more than once, and I've repeated it over and over. It seems to work.

On the importance of having a vision:

. . . you've got to find a rallying cry. You need to have something that can be described very simply and has that sort of ring of truth to an engineer that says "yes that's the thing to be doing right now." Otherwise you're going to be rolling rocks up hill all the time.

On the role of being a project manager:

You have to act as a cheerleader. You have to act as the instructor. You have to constantly bring to mind what the purpose is and what's moving the ball towards the goal post, and what's running sideways, and you have to take up a lot of battles for them. I mean you really don't want your design engineer arguing with the guy in the drafting shop about why he ought to do it the designer's way. I can do that, and I can pull rank too, and sometimes I did just that.

* Tracy Kidder, *The Soul of a New Machine* (New York: Avon Books, 1981); Lawrence H. Peters, "'A Good Man in a Storm': An Interview with Tom West," *Academy of Management Executive,* Vol. 16, No. 4, 2002, pp. 53–60.

FIGURE 11.4
Requirements for an Effective Project Vision

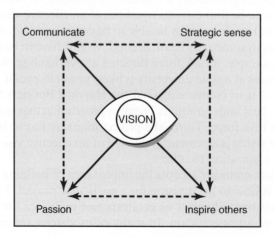

and objectives of the project. People get naturally excited about being the first ones to bring a new technology to the market or solving a problem that is threatening their organization. Even with mundane projects, there are often ample opportunities for establishing a compelling vision. One way is to talk to various people involved in the project and find out early on what gets them excited about the project. For some it may be doing a better job than on the last project or the satisfaction in the eyes of the customers when the project is over. Many visions evolve reactively in response to competition. For example, the Kodak team responsible for developing the single-use FunSaver camera was driven by the vision of beating a similar effort by Fuji to the market.

Some experts advocate engaging in formal vision-building meetings. These meetings generally involve several steps, beginning with members identifying different aspects of the project and generating ideal scenarios for each aspect. For example, on a construction project the scenarios may include "no accidents," "no lawsuits," "winning a prize," or "how we are going to spend our bonus for completing the project ahead of schedule." The group reviews and chooses the scenarios that are most appealing and translates them into vision statements for the project. The next step is to identify strategies for achieving the vision statements. For example, if one of the vision statements is that there will be no lawsuits, members will identify how they will have to work with the owner and subcontractors to avoid litigation. Next, members volunteer to be the keeper of the flame for each statement. The vision, strategies, and the name of the responsible team member are published and distributed to relevant stakeholders.

In more cases than not, shared visions emerge informally. Project managers collect information about what excites participants about the project. They test bits of their working vision in their conversations with team members to gauge the level of excitement the early ideas elicit in others. To some extent they engage in basic market research. They seize opportunities to galvanize the team, such as a disparaging remark by an executive that the project will never get done on time or the threat of a competing firm launching a similar project. Consensus in the beginning is not essential. What is essential is a core group of at least one-third of the project team that is genuinely committed to the vision. They will provide the critical mass to draw others aboard. Once the language has been formulated to communicate the vision, then the statement needs to be a staple part of every working agenda, and the project manager should be prepared to deliver a "stump" speech at a moment's notice. When problems or disagreements emerge, all responses should be consistent with the vision.

Much has been written about visions and leadership. Critics argue that vision is a glorified substitute for shared goals. Others argue that it is one of the things that separates leaders from managers. The key is discovering what excites people about a project, being able to articulate this source of excitement in an appealing manner, and finally protecting and nurturing this source of excitement throughout the duration of the project.

Managing Project Reward Systems

Project managers are responsible for managing the reward system that encourages team performance and extra effort. One advantage they have is that often project work is inherently satisfying, whether it is manifested in an inspiring vision or simple sense of accomplishment. Projects provide participants with a change in scenery, a chance to learn new skills, and an opportunity to break out of their departmental cocoon. Another inherent reward is what was referred to in *The Soul of a New Machine* as "pinball"—project success typically gives team members an option to play another exciting game.

Still, many projects are underappreciated, boring, interfere with other more significant priorities, and are considered an extra burden. In some of these cases, the biggest reward is finishing the project so that team members can go back to what they really enjoy doing and what will yield the biggest personal payoffs. Unfortunately, when this attitude is the primary incentive, project quality is likely to suffer. In these circumstances, external rewards play a more important role in motivating team performance.

Most project managers we talk to advocate the use of group rewards. Because most project work is a collaborative effort, it only makes sense that the reward system would encourage teamwork. Recognizing individual members regardless of their accomplishments can distract from team unity. Project work is highly interdependent, so it can become problematic to distinguish who truly deserves additional credit. Cash bonuses and incentives need to be linked to project priorities. It makes no sense to reward a team for completing their work early if controlling cost was the number one priority.

One of the limitations of lump-sum cash bonuses is that all too often they are consumed by the household budget to pay the dentist or mechanic. To have more value, rewards need to have lasting significance. Many companies convert cash into vacation rewards, sometimes with corresponding time off. For example, there is one firm that rewarded a project team for getting the job done ahead of schedule with a four-day, all-expenses-paid trip to Walt Disney World for the members' entire families. That vacation not only will be remembered for years, but it also recognizes spouses and children who, in a sense, also contributed to the project's success. Similarly, other firms have been known to give members home computers and entertainment centers. Wise project managers negotiate a discretionary budget so that they can reward teams surpassing milestones with gift certificates to popular restaurants or tickets to sporting events. Impromptu pizza parties and barbecues are also used to celebrate key accomplishments.

Sometimes project managers have to use negative reinforcement to motivate project performance. For example, Ritti recounts the story of one project manager who was in charge of the construction of a new, state-of-the-art manufacturing plant. His project team was working with a number of different contracting firms. The project was slipping behind schedule, mostly because of a lack of cooperation among the different players. The project manager did not have direct authority over many key people, especially the contractors from the other companies. He did, however, have the freedom to convene meetings at his convenience. So the project manager instituted daily "coordination meetings," which were required of all the principals involved, at 6:30 A.M. The meetings continued for about two weeks until the project got back on schedule. At that time the project manager announced that the next meeting was canceled, and no further sunrise meetings were ever scheduled.

While project managers tend to focus on group rewards, there are times when they need to reward individual performance. This is done not only to compensate extraordinary effort but also to signal to the others what exemplary behavior is. More specifically, among the rewards they use to motivate and recognize individual contributions are the following:

- **Letters of commendation.** While project managers may not have responsibility for their team members' performance appraisals, they can write letters commending their project performance. These letters can be sent to the workers' supervisors to be placed in their personnel files.
- **Public recognition for outstanding work.** Superlative workers should be publicly recognized for their efforts. Some project managers begin each status review meeting with a brief mention of project workers who have exceeded their project goals.
- **Job assignments.** Good project managers recognize that, while they may not have much budgetary authority, they do have substantial control over who does what, with whom, when, and where. Good work should be rewarded with desirable job assignments. Managers should be aware of member preferences and, when appropriate, accommodate them.
- **Flexibility.** Being willing to make exceptions to rules, if done judiciously, can be a powerful reward. Allowing members to work at home when a child is sick or excusing a minor discretion can engender long-lasting loyalty.

We reiterate that individual rewards should be used judiciously, and the primary emphasis should be on group incentives. Nothing can undermine the cohesiveness of a team more than members beginning to feel that others are getting special treatment or that they are being treated unfairly. Camaraderie and collaboration can quickly vanish only to be replaced by bickering and obsessive preoccupation with group politics. Such distractions can absorb a tremendous amount of energy that otherwise would be directed toward completing the project. Individual rewards typically should be used only when everyone in the team recognizes that a member is deserving of special recognition.

Orchestrating the Decision-Making Process

Most decisions on a project do not require a formal meeting to discuss alternatives and determine solutions. Instead decisions are made in real time as part of the daily interaction patterns between project managers, stakeholders, and team members. For example, as a result of a routine "how's it going?" question, a project manager discovers that a mechanical engineer is stuck trying to meet the performance criteria for a prototype he is responsible for building. The project manager and engineer go down the hallway to talk to the designers, explain the problem, and ask what, if anything, can be done. The designers distinguish which criteria are essential and which ones they think can be compromised. The project manager then checks with the marketing group to make sure the modifications are acceptable. They agree with all but two of the modifications. The project manager goes back to the mechanical engineer and asks whether the proposed changes would help solve the problem. The engineer agrees. Before authorizing the changes he calls the project sponsor, reviews the events, and gets the sponsor to sign off on the changes. This is an example of how, by practicing MBWA (management by wandering around), project managers consult team members, solicit ideas, determine optimum solutions, and create a sense of involvement that builds trust and commitment to decisions.

Still, projects encounter problems and decisions that require the collective wisdom of team members as well as relevant stakeholders. Group decision making should be used when it will improve the quality of important decisions. This is often the case with complex problems that require the input of a variety of different specialists. Group decision making should also be used when strong commitment to the decision is needed and there is a low probability of acceptance if only one person makes the decision. Participation is used to reduce resistance and secure support for the decision. Group decision making would be called for with controversial problems which have a major impact on project activities or when trust is low within the project team. Guidelines for managing group decision making are provided below.

Facilitating Group Decision Making

Project managers play a pivotal role in guiding the group decision-making process. They must remind themselves that their job is not to make a decision but to facilitate the discussion within the group so that the team reaches a consensus on the best possible solution. Consensus within this context does not mean that everyone supports the decision 100 percent, but that they all agree what the best solution is under the circumstances. Facilitating group decision making essentially involves four major steps. Each step is briefly described next with suggestions for how to manage the process.

1. **Problem identification.** The project manager needs to be careful not to state the problem in terms of choices (e.g., should we do X or Y?). Rather the project manager should identify the underlying problem to which these alternatives and probably others are potential solutions. This allows group members to generate alternatives, not just choose among them. One useful way of defining problems is to consider the gap between where a project is (i.e., the present state) and where it should be (desired state). For example, the project may be four days behind schedule or the prototype weighs two pounds more than the specifications. Whether the gap is small or large, the purpose is to eliminate it. The group must find one or more courses of action that will change the existing state into the desired one.

    If one detects defensive posturing during the problem identification discussion, then it may be wise to postpone the problem-solving step if possible. This allows for emotions to subside and members to gain a fresh perspective on the issues involved.

2. **Generating alternatives.** Once there is general agreement as to the nature of the problem(s), then the next step is to generate alternative solutions. If the problem requires creativity, then **brainstorming** is commonly recommended. Here the team generates a list of possible solutions on a flipchart or blackboard. During that time the project manager establishes a moratorium on criticizing or evaluating ideas. Members are encouraged to "piggyback" on other's ideas by extending them or combining ideas into a new idea. The object is to create as many alternatives as possible no matter how outlandish they may appear to be. Some project managers report that for really tough problems they have found it beneficial to conduct such sessions away from the normal work environment; the change in scenery stimulates creativity.

3. **Reaching a decision.** The next step is to evaluate and assess the merits of alternative solutions. During this phase it is useful to have a set of criteria for evaluating the merits of different solutions. In many cases the project manager can draw upon the priorities for the project and have the group assess each alternative in terms of its impact on cost, schedule, and performance as well as reducing the problem gap. For example, if time is critical, then the solution that solves the problem as quickly as possible would be chosen.

    During the course of the discussion the project manager attempts to build consensus among the group. This can be a complicated process. Project managers

SNAPSHOT FROM PRACTICE   Managing Low-Priority Projects

So far the discussion of team building has been directed primarily to significant projects that command the attention and involvement of assigned members. But what about projects that have low priority for team members: The perfunctory task forces that members begrudgingly join? The committee work people get assigned to do? The part-time projects that pull members away from the critical work they would rather be doing? Projects that cause members to privately question why they are doing this?

There is no magic wand available that transforms mildly interested, part-time project teams into high-performance teams. We interviewed several project managers about such project scenarios. They all agreed that these can be very difficult and frustrating assignments and that there are limits to what is possible. Still, they offered tips and advice for making the best of the situation. Most of these tips focus on building commitment to the project when it does not naturally exist.

One project manager advocated orchestrating a large "time" investment upfront on such projects—either in the form of a lengthy meeting or a significant early assignment. He viewed this as a form of down payment that members would forfeit if they didn't carry the project to completion.

Others emphasize interjecting as much fun into activities as possible. Here rituals discussed under building team identity come into play. People become committed because they enjoy working together on the project. One project manager

even confided that the perfect attendance at her project meetings was due primarily to the quality of the doughnuts she provided.

Another strategy is to make the benefits of the project as real to the team members as possible. One project manager escalated commitment to a mandated accidents prevention task force by bringing accident victims to a project meeting. Another project manager brought the high-ranking project sponsor to recharge the team by reinforcing the importance of the project to the company.

Most project managers emphasized the importance of building a strong personal relationship with each of the team members. When this connection occurs, members work hard not so much because they really care about the project but because they don't want to let the project manager down. Although not couched in influence currency terms, these managers talked about getting to know each member, sharing contacts, offering encouragement, and extending a helping hand when needed.

Finally, all project managers cautioned that nothing should be taken for granted on low-priority projects. They recommend reminding people about meetings and bringing extra copies of materials to meetings for those who have forgotten them or can't find them. Project managers should remain in frequent contact with team members and remind them of their assignments. One manager summed it up best when he said, "Sometimes it all boils down to just being a good nag."

need to provide periodic summaries to help the group keep track of its progress. They must protect those members who represent the minority view and ensure that such views get a fair hearing. They need to guarantee that everyone has an opportunity to share opinions and no one individual or group dominates the conversation. It may be useful to bring a two-minute timer to regulate the use of air time. When conflicts occur, managers need to apply some of the ideas and techniques discussed in the next section.

Project managers need to engage in consensus testing to determine what points the group agrees on and what are still sources of contention. They are careful not to interpret silence as agreement; they confirm agreement by asking questions. Ultimately, through thoughtful interaction, the team reaches a "meeting of the minds" as to what solution is best for the project.

4. **Follow-up.** Once the decision has been made and implemented, it is important for the team to find the time to evaluate the effectiveness of the decision. If the decision failed to provide the anticipated solution, then the reasons should be explored and the lessons learned added to the collective memory bank of the project team.

avoid acting defensively and instead encourage critical debate. They should exhibit effective listening skills and summarize the key issues before responding. They should check to see if others agree with the opposing point of view. Finally, project managers should value and protect dissenters. Organizations have a tendency to create too many yes-men, and the emperor needs to be told when he doesn't have any clothes on.

Managing Dysfunctional Conflict

Managing dysfunctional conflict is a much more challenging task than encouraging functional conflict. First, dysfunctional conflict is hard to identify. A manager might have two highly talented professionals who hate each other's guts, but in the heat of competition they produce meritorious results. Is this a pleasant situation? No. Is it functional? Yes, as long as it contributes to project performance. Conversely, sometimes functional conflict degenerates into dysfunctional conflict. This change occurs when technical disagreements evolve into irrational personality clashes or when failure to resolve an issue causes unnecessary delays in critical project work.

The second major difficulty managers face is that there is often no easy solution to dysfunctional conflict. Project managers have to decide among a number of different strategies to manage it; here are five possibilities:

1. **Mediate the conflict.** The manager intervenes and tries to negotiate a resolution by using reasoning and persuasion, suggesting alternatives and the like. One of the keys is trying to find common ground. In some cases the project manager can make the argument that the win/lose interchange has escalated to the point that it has become lose/lose for everyone and now is the time to make concessions.

2. **Arbitrate the conflict.** The manager imposes a solution to the conflict after listening to each party. The goal is not to decide who wins but to have the project win. In doing so, it is important to seek a solution that allows each party to save face; otherwise the decision may provide only momentary relief. One project manager admits that she has had great success using a King Solomon approach to resolving conflict. She confided she announces a solution that neither party will like and gives the opponents two hours to come up with a better solution they can both agree on.

3. **Control the conflict.** Reducing the intensity of the conflict by smoothing over differences or interjecting humor is an effective strategy. If feelings are escalating, the manager can adjourn the interaction and hope cooler heads prevail the next day. If the conflict continues to escalate, project assignments may need to be rearranged if possible so that two parties don't have to work together.

4. **Accept it.** In some cases the conflict will outlive the life of the project and, though a distraction, it is one the manager has to live with.

5. **Eliminate the conflict.** Sometimes the conflict has escalated to the point that it is no longer tolerable. In this case the manager removes the members involved from the project. If there is a clear villain then only he or she should be removed. If, as is often the case, both parties are at fault, then it would be wise if possible to eliminate both individuals. Their removal would give a clear signal to the others on the team that this kind of behavior is unacceptable.

In summary, project managers establish the foundation for functional conflict by establishing clear roles and responsibilities, developing common goals or a shared vision, and using group incentives that reward collaboration. Project managers have to be adroit at reading body language to identify unspoken disagreement. They also have to keep in touch with what is going on in a project to identify small problems that might escalate into big conflicts. Well-timed humor and redirecting the focus to what is best for the project can alleviate the interpersonal tensions that are likely to flare up on a project team.

Rejuvenating the Project Team

Over the course of a long project, a team sometimes drifts off course and loses momentum. The project manager needs to swing into action to realign the team with the project objectives and step on the pedal. There are both formal and informal ways of doing this. Informally, the project manager can institute new rituals like the "toy roaches" to reenergize a team. On one project that was experiencing rough going, the project manager stopped work and took the team bowling to relieve frustrations. On another project, a manager showed her team the movie *The Shawshank Redemption* to rekindle hope and commitment to success.

Another option is to have the project sponsor give a pep talk to the "troops." In other cases, a friendly challenge can reinvigorate a team. For example, one project sponsor offered to cook a five-course meal if the project got back on track and hit the next milestone.

Sometimes more formal action needs to be taken. The project manager may recognize the need for a team-building session devoted to improving the work processes of the team. This meeting is particularly appropriate if she senses that the team is approaching a transition point in its development. The goal of such a session is to improve the project team's effectiveness through better management of project demands and group processes. It is an inward look by the team at its own performance, behavior, and culture for the purpose of eliminating dysfunctional behaviors and strengthening functional ones. The project team critiques its performance, analyzes its way of doing things, and attempts to develop strategies to improve its operation.

Oftentimes an external consultant is hired, or an internal staff specialist is assigned to facilitate the session. This process brings a more objective, outside perspective to the table, frees the project manager to be part of the process, and provides a specialist trained in group dynamics. Furthermore, if preliminary information is to be collected, team members may be more candid and open to an outsider.

One caveat about using outside consultants is that too often managers resort to this as a method for dealing with a problem that they have been unable or unwilling to deal with. The marching order to the consultant is "fix my team for me." What the managers fail to recognize is that one of the keys to fixing the team is improving the working relationship between themselves and the remainder of the team. For such sessions to be effective, project managers have to be willing to have their own role scrutinized and be receptive to changing their own behavior and work habits based on the comments and suggestions of the project team.

Consultants use a wide variety of **team-building** techniques to elevate team performance. Here is a brief description of one of the more common approaches. The first step is to gather information and make a preliminary diagnosis of team performance. Whether through individual interviews or in a group forum, the consultant asks general questions about the project team performance, that is, what obstacles are getting in the way of the team being able to perform better? This information is summarized in terms of themes. When everyone has understood the themes, the group ranks them in terms of both their importance and the extent the team has ownership over them. This last dimension is critical. *Ownership* refers to whether the team has direct influence over the issue. For example, a team probably has little influence over delivery of contracted supplies, but team members do control how quickly they inform each other of sudden changes in plans.

If the group becomes preoccupied with issues outside its control, the meeting can quickly evolve into a demoralizing gripe session. Therefore, the most important issues they have direct control over become the subjects of the agenda. During the course of the meeting, much interpersonal and group process information will be generated, and that is examined too. Thus, the group works on two sets of items: the agenda items and the items that emerge from the interaction of the participants. This is where the expertise of the external facilitator becomes critical for identifying interaction patterns and their implications for team performance.

As important problems are discussed, alternatives for action are developed. The team-building session concludes by deciding on specific action steps for remedying problems and setting target dates for who will do what, when. These assignments can be reviewed at project status meetings or at a special follow-up session.

It has become fashionable to link team-building activities with outdoor experiences. The outdoor experience—whether it is whitewater rafting down the Rogue River in Oregon or rock climbing in Colorado—places group members in a variety of physically challenging situations that must be mastered through teamwork, not individual effort. By having to work together to overcome difficult obstacles, team members are supposed to experience increased self-confidence, more respect for another's capabilities, and a greater commitment to teamwork. No empirical data are available to support such exotic endeavors other than the enthusiastic support of the participants. Such activities are likely to provide an intense common experience that may accelerate the social development of the team. Such an investment of time and money communicates the importance of teamwork and is considered by some a perk for being on the project. At the same time, unless the lessons from these experiences can be immediately transferred to actual project work, their significance is likely to vanish.

Managing Virtual Project Teams

Building a high-performance project team among a mixture of part-time and full-time members is a challenging task. Consider how much more challenging it is to build a team when members cannot engage in face-to-face interactions. Such would be the case for a **virtual project team** in which the team members are geographically situated so that they may seldom, if ever, meet face-to-face as a team. For example, Hewlett-Packard's integrated circuit business headquarters and a portion of the R&D facilities are located in Palo Alto, California; the two wafer fabrication operations are located in Corvallis, Oregon, and Fort Collins, Colorado; and the packaging assembly process is primarily in Singapore and Korea. It is not uncommon for professionals at each of these locations to be involved in the same project. When team members are spread across different time zones and continents, the opportunity for direct communication is severely limited. Electronic communication such as the Internet, e-mail, and teleconferencing takes on much more importance in virtual projects because this is the primary means of communication. See Snapshot from Practice: Managing Virtual Global Teams for an example of how this works.

Two of the biggest challenges involved in managing a virtual project team are developing trust and effective patterns of communication. Trust is difficult to establish in virtual project management. Unlike working as a traditional team, where members can see whether someone has done what they say they have done, virtual team members depend on the word of distant members. At the same time, it can be difficult to trust someone whom you may have met only one or two times or not at all. Geographical separation also prohibits the informal social interactions that are often essential to building camaraderie among team members. As one virtual team member put it, "You can't have a beer together over the Internet."

So how can a project manager facilitate the development of trust within a virtual team? First, if it is impossible to hold a face-to-face meeting in the beginning, managers need to orchestrate the exchange of social information—who everyone is and some personal background information during the initial electronic interchange. Second, they need to set clear roles for each team member. Ideally, specific tasks should be assigned to each member so that they can make an immediate contribution to the project. Trust in virtual projects grows through team member reliability, consistency, and responsiveness. Finally, the project manager must consistently display enthusiasm and an action orientation in all messages; this spirit will hopefully spread to other team members.

The second major challenge for managing a virtual project team is to establish effective patterns of communication. E-mail and faxes are great for communicating facts—but not the feelings behind the facts; nor do they allow for real-time communication. Conference calls and project chat rooms can help, but they also have their limitations. Videoconferencing is a significant improvement over nonvisual electronic forms of communication. Still, it is a very expensive medium, and real-time interaction is available on only the most advanced and expensive systems. The maxim is match technology to the communication need. Here are some guidelines developed by 3M for use on their distributed projects:

- *When to e-mail.* To distribute important information and news in a one-to-one or one-to-many frame of reference.
- *When to use electronic bulletin boards.* To encourage discussion and flush out diversity of opinion on issues.
- *When to videoconference.* Videoconference when you need to see each other's face and expressions. This is important during the early phases of a project, when you are building relationships and developing a common understanding of what needs to be done. Use, again, when working on critical decisions and/or contentious issues.
- *When to use conference calls.* When people in different locations are working with common documents, presentations, sketches, and models. Use for status report meetings and to sustain social camaraderie.
- *When to fly.* Fly to build or repair trust. Use travel budget to get all key players together early on to instill commitment to the goals of the project and engage in team-building activities.

Even with the best communication system, managers have to overcome the problem of time zone differences, cultural nuances, and finding a convenient time for people to conference.

SNAPSHOT FROM PRACTICE Managing Virtual Global Teams*

 Carl A. Singer, a senior program manager at IBM Global Services, described how global time zones were used to complete a time intensive project. The project required subject matter experts (SMEs) to document existing best practices in maintenance domain and to port these into a knowledge management tool. The most proficient SMEs available were on opposite sides of the globe—Australia and Scotland. Review and control of the project was from the United States.

Management realized that just working harder and smarter was not going to meet the time and quality targets. For this project they used the dimension of time to their benefit. Applying sound management principles as well as taking advantage of electronic communication systems, the team was able to create a virtual 24-hour workday for quick responses and accelerated reviews.

Each team consisted of veteran professionals familiar with the rigors of time-pressured consulting projects. A local point person was identified for each team and mutually agreed-upon targets, terminology, and processes were established.

An all-hands kick-off meeting was organized in which participants were able to socialize, understand local and project-wide constraints, and finalize an agreed-upon plan. The meeting was held at a corporate hotel with dining accommodations. The facility was considered an "assisted living community for IBM consultants." This hastened recovery from jet lag and provided an interruption-free work environment.

Upon returning to their home bases, each team created the majority of their deliverables independently with periodic three-way conference calls to maintain coordination. A project control book was established electronically so that all participants had access to the latest project documents.

The final phase of the project required intense interfacing and reviews between the teams. These reviews necessitated changes to deal with concerns, differences among subprojects, and other issues. It was here that the worldwide nature of the project was leveraged. Using a "dry cleaning approach" (in by 5 P.M. out by 9 A.M.) team members in Australia and Scotland were able to address issues generated during the U.S.-based external reviews and provide concrete responses by the beginning of the next business day. Conference calls at 6:00 A.M. (U.S. EST) were used to coordinate responses and resolve issues. Conference calls at the end of the U.S. workday were used to finalize issues and assignments. Figure 11.6 (page 403) depicts the 24-hour clock used to align communication schedules.

Telephone conferencing was used instead of videoconferencing due to the setup lead time and because it would force participants to leave their offices. E-mail was used extensively for general communication. An electronic repository of project work was used to coordinate global involvement. In practice, a participant could draft a document and deposit it electronically only to wake up the next day to find the document annotated with suggested revisions. Likewise, one could start the day by checking an in-basket populated with documents to review and issues to address. Over time, "G'day" and "Cheers" crept into the U.S. speech—a clear indicator of team cohesion.

Singer identified a number of lessons learned from the project. These included:

- The all-hands kick-off meeting was critical for establishing goals and procedures as well as "rules of courtesy."
- Loosen the reins—establish clear deliverables and then step out of the way and let the professionals do their work.
- Establish and enforce agreed-upon quality standards and deliverable templates.
- Maintain a regular schedule of conference calls, even if only to say "Hello, we have nothing to talk about today." Conference calls should be guided by pre-established agendas, note-taking procedures, and reviews.

* Carl A. Singer, "Leveraging a Worldwide Project Team," *PM Network,* April 2001, pp. 36–40.

Below are some additional tips for alleviating communication problems and enhancing the performance of virtual teams:

1. **Keep team members informed on how the overall project is going.** Use shareware or develop a central access point such as either a Web site or LAN account to provide members with updated project schedules. Team members need to know where they fit in the big picture.
2. **Don't let team members vanish.** Virtual teams often experience problems getting in touch with each other. Use an Internet scheduling software to store members' calendars.
3. **Establish a code of conduct to avoid delays.** Team members need to agree not only on what, when, and how information will be shared but also on how and

FIGURE 11.6
24-Hour Global Clock

United States (East Coast)	Australia	Scotland	Comments
12 midnight	2 PM	5 AM	
1 AM	3 PM	6 AM	
2 AM	4 PM	7 AM	
3 AM	5 PM	8 AM	
4 AM	6 PM	9 AM	Australia handoff for off-shift review
5 AM	7 PM	10 AM	
6 AM	8 PM	11 AM	3-way conferencing window (primary)
7 AM	9 PM	12 noon	3-way conferencing window (primary)
8 AM	10 PM	1 PM	3-way conferencing window (primary)
9 AM	11 PM	2 PM	
10 AM	12 midnight	3 PM	
11AM	1 AM	4 PM	
12 noon	2 AM	5 PM	Scotland handoff for off-shift review
1 PM	3 AM	6 PM	
2 PM	4 AM	7 PM	
3 PM	5 AM	8 PM	
4 PM	6 AM	9 PM	3-way conferencing window (secondary)
5 PM	7 AM	10 PM	3-way conferencing window (secondary)
6 PM	8 AM	11 PM	U.S. handoff for off-shift review
7 PM	9 AM	12 midnight	
8 PM	10 AM	1 AM	
9 PM	11 AM	2 AM	
10 PM	12 noon	3 AM	
11 PM	1 PM	4 AM	
12 midnight	2PM	5 AM	

☐ Prime time   ▨ Secondary time   ▨ Downtime

when they will respond to it. Develop a priority system to distinguish messages that require immediate response from those with longer time frames.

4. **Establish clear norms and protocols for surfacing assumptions and conflicts.** Because most communication is nonvisual, project managers cannot watch body language and facial expressions to develop a sense of what is going on. They need to probe deeper when communicating to force members to explain their viewpoints, actions, and concerns more clearly; they must double-check comprehension.

5. **Share the pain.** Do not require everyone to conform to your time zone and preferences. Rotate meeting times so that all team members have a turn working according to their clock.

To some extent managing a virtual project team is no different from managing a regular project team. The key is working within the constraints of the situation to develop effective ways for team members to interact and combine their talents to complete the project.

Project Team Pitfalls

High-performance project teams can produce dramatic results. However, like any good thing, there is a dark side to project teams that managers need to be aware of. We referred to this phenomenon as *projectitis* in Chapter 3. In this section we examine in more detail some of the pathologies that high-performance project teams can succumb to and highlight what project managers can do to reduce the likelihood of these problems occurring.

Groupthink

Janis first identified *groupthink* as a factor that influenced the misguided 1961 Bay of Pigs invasion of Cuba. His term refers to the tendency of members in highly cohesive groups to lose their critical evaluative capabilities. This malady appears when pressures for conformity are combined with an illusion of invincibility to suspend critical discussion of decisions. As a result decisions are made quickly with little consideration of alternatives; often the practice leads to fiascoes that, after the fact, appear totally improbable. Some of the symptoms of groupthink include the following:

- *Illusion of invulnerability.* The team feels invincible. It is marked by a high degree of esprit de corps, an implicit faith in its own wisdom, and an inordinate optimism that allows group members to feel complacent about the quality of their decisions.
- *Whitewash of critical thinking.* The group members discuss only a few solutions, ignoring alternatives; they fail to examine the adverse consequences that could follow their preferred course of action; and they too quickly dismiss any alternatives that, on the surface, appear to be unsatisfactory.
- *Negative stereotypes of outsiders.* "Good guy/bad guy" stereotypes emerge in which the group considers any outsiders who oppose their decisions as the bad guys, who are perceived as incompetent and malicious and whose points are unworthy of serious consideration.
- *Direct pressure.* When a team member does speak out or question the direction in which the team is headed, direct pressure is applied to the dissenter. He or she is reminded that speed is important and that the aim is agreement, not argument.

Bureaucratic Bypass Syndrome

Project teams are often licensed to get things done without having to go through normal protocols of the parent organization. Bypassing bureaucratic channels is appealing and invigorating. However, if bypassing becomes a way of life, it results in the rejection of bureaucratic policies and procedures, which provide the glue for the overall organization. A team that operates outside the organization may alienate other workers who are constrained by the norms and procedures of the organization; eventually, these outside bureaucrats will find ways to put up roadblocks and thwart the project team.

SNAPSHOT FROM PRACTICE Nominal Group Technique*

GE Appliances, U.S. West, Marriott Corp., and Hewlett-Packard are among the many firms that use **nominal group technique (NGT)** to guide decisions on projects. The NGT begins by gathering project team members and/or stakeholders around a table and identifying the project problem at hand. Each member then writes his or her solutions. Next, each member presents his or her solution to the group, and the leader writes these solutions on a chart. No criticism is allowed. This process continues until all of the ideas have been expressed. Each solution then is discussed and clarified by the group. After all the ideas have been discussed, the group members privately rank-order their preferred solutions. The balloting is tallied to create a rank-ordering of each solution.

These steps are repeated if necessary to refine the list further in order to get the most preferred solution.

NGT provides an orderly process for dealing with potentially inflammatory problems. It also prevents groupthink from occurring. NGT discourages any pressure to conform to the wishes of a high-status, powerful group member since all ideas are discussed and all preferences are expressed privately. Creativity should be enhanced since members are able to offer a solution based on their expertise and viewpoint. Finally, important decisions can be made in a relatively timely manner. NGT works best when there is a well-defined problem.

* Andrew Delbeeq, Andrew H. Van de Ven, and D. H. Gustafson, *Group Techniques for Program Planning* (Glenview, II: Scott Foresman, 1975).

Team Spirit Becomes Team Infatuation

High-performance project teams can be a tremendous source of personal satisfaction. The excitement, chaos, and joy generated by working on a challenging project can be an invigorating experience. Leavitt and Lipman-Blumen even go so far as to say that team members behave like people in love. They become infatuated with the challenge of the project and the talent around them. This total preoccupation with the project and the project team, while contributing greatly to the remarkable success of the project, can leave in its wake a string of broken professional and personal relationships that contribute to burnout and dis-orientation upon completion of the project.

Going Native

Going native is a phrase first used by the British Foreign Service during colonial times to describe agents who assumed the customs, values, and prerogatives of their foreign country assignment. They did so to the point that they were no longer representing the best interests of the British government but rather those of the natives. This same phenomenon can occur within project teams working abroad or in those who become closely identified with their customers. In essence, the customer's interests take precedence over the parent organization's interests. This change in viewpoint can lead to excessive scope creep and open defiance of corporate policy and interests.

Dealing with these maladies is problematic because, in most cases, they are a distortion of a good thing, rather than a simple evil. Awareness is the first step for prevention. The next step is to take preemptive action to reduce the likelihood of these pitfalls occurring. For example, managers can reduce the isolation of the project team by creating work-related connections outside the project team. These interactions naturally occur in a matrix environment where members work on multiple projects and maintain ties to their home department. Likewise, the isolation of dedicated project teams can be reduced by the timely involvement of external specialists. In either case, the active involvement of relevant members of the parent organization at project status meetings can help maintain the link between the project and the rest of the organization. If the team appears to be suffering from groupthink, then the project manager can encourage functional conflict by playing a devil's advocate role to encourage dissent or using a structured problem-solving approach like the nominal group technique (see Snapshot). Finally, formal team-building sessions may reveal dysfunctional norms and refocus the attention of the team on project objectives.

Summary

Project managers often work under less-than-ideal conditions to develop a cohesive team committed to working together and completing the project to the best of their abilities. They have to recruit personnel from other departments and manage the temporary involvement of team members. They have to bring strangers together and quickly establish a set of operational procedures that unite their efforts and contributions. They have to be skilled at managing meetings so that they do not become a burden but rather a vehicle for progress. Project managers need to forge a team identity and a shared vision, that command the attention and allegiance of participants. They need to use group incentives to encourage teamwork while recognizing when it is appropriate to single out individuals for special recognition. Project managers have to encourage functional conflict that contributes to superior solutions while being on guard against dysfunctional conflict that can break a team apart. In doing these things, they have to be careful not to do too good a job and avoid the pitfalls of excessive group cohesion.

While agendas, charters, visions, rewards, and so forth are important tools and techniques, it has been emphasized both in this chapter and in Chapter 10 that the most important tool a project manager has to build an effective project team is his or her own behavior. Just as the founding members of an organization shape the culture of the organization, the project manager shapes and influences the internal culture of the project team. A positive example can define how team members respond to changes, how they handle new tasks, and how they relate to one another and the rest of the organization. There is no easy way to lead by example. It requires personal conviction, discipline, sensitivity to team dynamics, and a constant awareness of how personal actions are perceived by others.

Key Terms

Brainstorming, *394*
Dysfunctional conflict, *397*
Functional conflict, *397*
Groupthink, *404*

Nominal group technique (NGT), *405*
Positive synergy, *375*
Project kick-off meeting, *383*

Project vision, *390*
Team building, *399*
Team rituals, *388*
Virtual project team, *400*

Review Questions

1. What are the differences between the five-stage model of team development and the punctuated equilibrium model?
2. What are the elements of an effective project vision? Why are they important?
3. Why should a project manager emphasize group rewards over individual rewards?
4. What is the difference between functional and dysfunctional conflict on a project?
5. When would it be appropriate to hold a formal team-building session on a project?
6. What are the unique challenges to managing a virtual project team?
7. What can a project manager do to avoid some of the pitfalls of a highly cohesive project team?

Exercises

1. The following activities are based on a recently completed group project that you have been involved in. This project may have been a student project, a work project, or an extracurricular project.

   a. Analyze the development of the team in terms of the five-phase model and the punctuated equilibrium model. Which model does the best job of describing how the team evolved?

   b. Analyze the group in terms of the nine situational factors that influence team development. What factors positively contributed to group performance? What factors negatively contributed to group performance? How did the group try to overcome the negative factors? What could you have done differently to overcome these negative factors?

   c. Analyze how effectively the group managed meetings. What did the group do well? What didn't the group do well? If the group were formed again, what specific recommendations would you make about how the group should manage meetings?

2. Assume that you have the following decision-making options: (1) make the decision on your own with available information, (2) consult others before making a decision, and (3) call a meeting and reach a consensus, seeking to arrive at a final decision everyone can agree on. Which approach would you use to make each of the following decisions and why?

   a. You are the project leader for Casino Night on campus, a charitable event organized by your group to raise money for the homeless. The event was a big success, garnering a net profit of $3,500. Before the event your team researched nearby organizations that support the homeless and to whom the money could be given. You narrowed the choices to the "Chunk of Coal House" and "St. Mary's Soup Kitchen." Eventually your group decided that the funds be given to Chunk of Coal. You are about to write a check to its director when you read in the local newspaper that the Chunk of Coal House has terminated operations. What should you do with the money?

   b. You are a golf course designer hired by Trysting Tree Golf Club to renovate their golf course. You have worked closely with the board of directors of the club to develop a new layout that is both challenging and aesthetically pleasing. Everyone is excited about the changes. The project is nearly 75 percent complete when you encounter problems on the 13th hole. The 13th hole at Trysting Tree is a 125-yard par three in which golfers have to hit their tee shots over a lake to a modulated green. During the construction of the new tee box, workers discovered that an underground spring runs beneath the box to the lake. You inspected the site and agreed with the construction supervisor that this could create serious problems, especially during the rainy winter months. After surveying the area, you believe the only viable option would be to extend the hole to 170 yards and create elevated tees on the adjacent hillside.

   c. You are the leader of a new product development project. Your team has worked hard on developing a third-generation product that incorporates new technology and meets customer demands. The project is roughly 50 percent complete. You have just received a report from the marketing department detailing a similar product that is about to be released by a competitor. The product appears to utilize radical new design principles that expand the functionality of the product. This poses a serious threat to the success of organizing Kerzner's 10th anniversary celebration. She was excited about the project because she would report directly to top management.

CEO Tubbs briefed her as to the purpose and objectives of the celebration. Tubbs stressed that this should be a memorable event and that it was important to celebrate Kerzner's success since the dark days of the layoffs. Moreover, he confided that he had just read a book on corporate cultures and believed that such events were important for conveying the values at Kerzner. He went on to say that he wanted this to be an employee celebration—not a celebration conjured up by top management. As such, she would be assigned a task force of 14 employees from each of the major departments to organize and plan the event. Her team was to present a preliminary plan and budget for the event to top management within three months. When discussing budgets, Tubbs revealed that he felt the total cost should be somewhere in the $150,000 range. He concluded the meeting by offering to help Briggs in any way he could to make the event a success.

Soon thereafter Briggs received the list of the names of the task force members, and she contacted them either by phone or e-mail to arrange today's meeting. She had to scramble to find a meeting place. Her cubicle in human resources was too small to accommodate such a group, and all the meeting rooms at Kerzner were booked or being refurbished. She settled on the cafeteria because it was usually deserted in the late afternoon. Prior to the meeting she posted the agenda on a flipchart (see Figure C11.1) adjacent to the table. Given everyone's busy schedules, the meeting was limited to just one hour.

FIGURE C11.1
Celebration Task Force

Agenda

3:00	Introductions
3:15	Project overview
3:30	Ground rules
3:45	Meeting times
4:00	Adjourn

THE FIRST MEETING

Briggs began the meeting by saying, "Greetings. For those who don't know me, I'm Amber Briggs from human resources and I've been assigned to manage the 10th anniversary celebration at Kerzner. Top management wants this to be a special event—at the same time they want it to be our event. This is why you are here. Each of you represents one of the major departments, and together our job is to plan and organize the celebration." She then reviewed the agenda and asked each member to introduce him/herself. The tall, red-haired woman to the right of Briggs broke the momentary silence by saying, "Hi, I'm Cara Miller from Plastics. I guess my boss picked me for this task force because I have a reputation for throwing great parties."

In turn each member followed suit. Below is a sampling of their introductions:

"Hi, I'm Mike Wales from maintenance. I'm not sure why I'm here. Things have been a little slow in our department, so my boss told me to come to this meeting."

"I'm Megan Plinski from domestic sales. I actually volunteered for this assignment. I think it will be a lot of fun to plan a big party."

"Yo, my name is Nick Psias from accounting. My boss said one of us had to join this task force, and I guess it was my turn."

"Hi, I'm Rick Fennah. I'm the only one from purchasing who has been here since the beginning. We've been through some rough times, and I think it is important to take time and celebrate what we've accomplished."

"Hi, I'm Ingrid Hedstrom from international sales. I think this is a great idea, but I should warn you that I will be out of the country for most of the next month."

"I'm Abby Bell from engineering. Sorry for being late, but things are a bit crazy in my department."

Briggs circled the names of the two people who were absent and circulated a roster so that everyone could check to see if their phone numbers and e-mail addresses were correct. She then summarized her meeting with Tubbs and told the group that he expected them to make a formal presentation to top management within 10 weeks. She acknowledged that they were all busy people and that it was her job to manage the project as efficiently as possible. At the same time, she reiterated the importance of the project and that this would be a very public event: "If we screw up, everyone will know about it."

Briggs went over the ground rules and emphasized that from now on meetings would start on time and that she expected to be notified in advance if someone was going to be absent. She summarized the first part of the project as centering on five key questions: when, where, what, who, and how much? She created a stir in the group when she responded to a question about cost by informing them that top management was willing to pay up to $150,000 for the event. Megan quipped, "This is going to be one hell of a party."

Briggs then turned the group's attention to identifying a common meeting time. After jousting for 15 minutes, she terminated the discussion by requesting that each member submit a schedule of free time over the next month by Friday. She would use this information and a new planning software to identify optimal times. She ended the meeting by thanking the members for coming and asking them to begin soliciting ideas from co-workers about how this event should be celebrated. She announced that she would meet individually with each of them to discuss their role on the project. The meeting was adjourned at 4:00 P.M.

1. Critique Briggs's management of the first meeting. What, if anything, should she have done differently?
2. What barriers is she likely to encounter in completing this project?
3. What can she do to overcome these barriers?
4. What should she do between now and the next meeting?

Case

Ajax Project

Tran was taking his dog Callie on her evening walk as the sun began to set over the coastal range. He looked forward to this time of the day. It was an opportunity to enjoy some peace and quiet. It was also a time to review events on the Ajax project and plot his next moves.

Ajax is the code name given by CEBEX for a high-tech security system project funded by the U.S. Department of Defense (DOD). Tran is the project manager and his core team consisted of 30 full-time hardware and software engineers.

Tran and his family fled Cambodia when he was four years old. He joined the U.S. Air Force when he was 18 and used the education stipend to attend Washington State University. He joined CEBEX upon graduating with a dual degree in mechanical and electrical engineering. After working on a variety of projects for 10 years Tran decided he wanted to enter management. He went to night school at the University of Washington to earn an MBA.

Tran became a project manager for the money. He also thought he was good at it. He enjoyed working with people and making the right things happen. This was his fifth project and up to now he was batting .500, with half of his projects coming ahead of schedule. Tran was proud that he could now afford to send his oldest child to Stanford University.

Ajax was one of many defense projects the CEBEX Corporation had under contract with DOD. CEBEX is a huge defense company with annual sales in excess of $30 billion and more than 120,000 employees worldwide. CEBEX's five major business areas are Aeronautics, Electronic Systems, Information & Technology Services, Integrated Systems & Solutions, and Space Systems. Ajax was one of several new projects sponsored by the Integrated Systems & Solutions division aimed at the homeland security business. CEBEX was confident that it could leverage its technical expertise and political connections to become a major player in this growing market. Ajax was one of several projects directed at designing, developing, and installing a security system at an important government installation.

Tran had two major concerns when he started the Ajax project. The first was the technical risks inherent in the project. In theory the design principles made sense and the project used proven technology. Still the technology had never been applied in the field in this matter. From past experience, Tran knew there was a big difference between the laboratory and the real world. He also knew that integrating the audio, optical, tactile, and laser subsystems would test the patience and ingenuity of his team.

The second concern involved his team. The team was pretty much split down the middle between hardware and electrical engineers. Not only did these engineers have different skill sets and tend to look at problems differently, but generational differences between the two groups were evident as well. The hardware engineers were almost all former military, family men with conservative attire and beliefs. The electrical engineers were a much motlier crew. They tended to be young, single, and at times very cocky. While the hardware engineers talked about the Seattle Mariners, raising teenagers, and going to Palm Desert to play golf, the software engineers talked about Vapor, the latest concert at the Gorge amphitheater, and going mountain biking in Peru.

To make matters worse, tension between these two groups within CEBEX festered around salary issues. Electrical engineers were at a premium, and the hardware engineers resented the new hires' salary packages, which were comparable to what they were earning after 20 years of working for CEBEX. Still the real money was to be made from the incentives associated with project performance. These were all contingent on meeting project milestones and the final completion date.

Before actual work started on the project, Tran arranged a two-day team-building retreat at a lodge on the Olympic peninsula for his entire team as well as key staff from the government installation. He used this time to go over the major objectives of the project and unveil the basic project plan. An internal consultant facilitated several team-building activities that made light of cross-generational issues. Tran felt a real sense of camaraderie within the team.

The good feelings generated from the retreat carried over to the beginning of the project. The entire team bought into the mission of the project and technical challenges it represented. Hardware and electrical engineers worked side by side to solve problems and build subsystems.

The project plan was built around a series of five tests, with each test being a more rigorous verification of total system performance. Passing each test represented a key milestone for the project. The team was excited about conducting the first Alpha test one week early—only to be disappointed by a series of minor technical glitches that took two weeks of problem solving to resolve. The team worked extra hard to make up for the lost time. Tran was proud of the team and how hard members had worked together.

The Alpha II test was conducted on schedule, but once again the system failed to perform. This time three weeks of debugging was needed before the team received the green light to move to the next phase of the project. By this time, team goodwill had been tested, and emotions were a bit frayed. A cloud of disappointment descended over the team as hopes of bonuses disappeared with the project falling further behind schedule. This was augmented by cynics who felt that the original schedule was unfair and the deadlines were impossible to begin with.

Tran responded by starting each day with a status meeting where the team reviewed what they accomplished the previous day and set new objectives for that day. He believed these meetings were helpful in establishing positive momentum and reinforcing a team identity among the engineers. He also went out of his way to spend more time with the "troops," helping them solve problems, offering encouragement, and a sincere pat on the back when one was deserved.

He was cautiously optimistic when the time came to conduct the Alpha III test. It was the end of the day when the switch was turned on, but nothing happened. Within minutes the entire team heard the news. Screams could be heard down the hallway. Perhaps the most telling moment was when Tran looked down at the company's parking lot and saw most of his project team walking by themselves to their cars.

As Callie chased some wild bunnies, Tran pondered what he should do next.

1. How effective has Tran been as a project manager? Explain.
2. What problem(s) does Tran face?
3. How would you go about solving them? Why?

Case

Franklin Equipment, Ltd.*

Franklin Equipment, Ltd. (FEL), with headquarters and main fabrication facilities in Saint John, New Brunswick, was founded 75 years ago to fabricate custom-designed large machines for construction businesses in the Maritime Provinces. Over the years its product lines became strategically focused on creating rock-crushing equipment for dam and highway construction and for a few other markets that require the processing of aggregate. FEL now designs, fabricates, and assembles stationary and portable rock-crushing plants and services its own products and those of its competitors.

In the 1970s, FEL began to expand its market from the Maritime Provinces to the rest of Canada. FEL currently has several offices and fabrication facilities throughout the country. More recently, FEL has made a concerted effort to market its products internationally.

Last month, FEL signed a contract to design and fabricate a rock-crushing plant for a Middle East construction project, called Project Abu Dhabi. Charles Gatenby secured this contract and has been assigned as project manager. This

* Courtesy of John A. Drexler Jr., Oregon State University.

project is viewed as a coup because FEL has wanted to open up markets in this area for a long time and has had difficulty getting prospective customers to realize that FEL is a Canadian firm and not from the United States. Somehow these customers view all North American vendors as the same and are reluctant to employ any of them because of international political considerations.

A project of this scope typically starts with the selection of a team of managers responsible for various aspects of the design, fabrication, delivery, and installation of the product. Manager selection is important because the product design and fabrication vary with the unique needs of each customer. For example, the terrain, rock characteristics, weather conditions, and logistical concerns create special problems for all phases of plant design and operations. In addition, environmental concerns and labor conditions vary from customer to customer and from region to region.

In addition to the project manager, all projects include a design engineer; an operations manager, who oversees fabrication and on-site assembly; and a cost accountant, who oversees all project financial and cost reporting matters. Each of these people must work closely together if a well-running plant is to be delivered on time and within cost constraints. Because international contracts often require FEL to employ host nationals for plant assembly and to train them for operations, a human resource manager is also assigned to the project team. In such cases, the human resource manager needs to understand the particulars of the plant specifications and then use this knowledge to design selection procedures and assess particular training needs. The human resource manager also needs to learn the relevant labor laws of the customer's country.

FEL assigns managers to project teams based on their expertise and their availability to work on a particular project given their other commitments. This typically means that managers without heavy current project commitments will be assigned to new projects. For instance, a manager finishing one project will likely be assigned a management position on a new project team. The project manager typically has little to say about who is assigned to his or her team.

Because he secured Project Abu Dhabi and has established positive working relationships with the Abu Dhabi customer, Gatenby was assigned to be project manager. Gatenby has successfully managed similar projects. The other managers assigned to Project Abu Dhabi are Bill Rankins, a brilliant design engineer, Rob Perry, operations manager with responsibility for fabrication and installation, Elaine Bruder, finance and cost accounting manager, and Sam Stonebreaker, human resource manager. Each of these managers has worked together on numerous past projects.

A few years ago, FEL began contracting for team facilitator services from several consulting firms to help new project teams operate effectively. Last month, FEL recruited Carl Jobe from one of these consulting firms to be a full-time internal consultant. A number of managers, including Gatenby, were so impressed with Jobe's skills that they convinced FEL top management of the need to hire a permanent internal facilitator; Jobe was the obvious choice.

Because Gatenby was instrumental in hiring Jobe at FEL, he was excited at the prospect of using Jobe to facilitate team building among Project Abu Dhabi team members. Gatenby was very proud of having secured this project and had expected to be appointed project manager. He knew that this project's success would be instrumental in advancing his own career.

Gatenby told Jobe, "This project is really important to FEL and to me personally. I really need for you to help us develop into a team that works well together to achieve the project's goals within budget. I've observed your success in developing teams on other projects, and I expect you'll do the same for Project Abu Dhabi. I'll take care of you if you help me make this work."

Jobe outlined for Gatenby how he would proceed. Jobe would begin by interviewing team members individually to learn their perceptions of each other and of the promises and pitfalls of being involved in this project. Meetings of the entire team would follow these interviews using the information he collected to help establish a team identity and a shared vision.

Jobe interviewed Bruder first. She expressed skepticism about whether the project could succeed. During the interview, Bruder appeared to be distant, and Jobe could not figure out why he had not established good rapport with her. Bruder intimated that she expected a lot of cost overruns and a lot of missed production deadlines. But not knowing Jobe well, Bruder was reluctant to identify any specific barriers to the project's success. While she would not directly say so, it was clear to Jobe that Bruder did not want to be a part of Project Abu Dhabi. Jobe left this interview confused and wondering what was going on.

Jobe's next interview was with Perry, the operations manager. Perry has worked at FEL for 15 years, and he immediately came to the point: "This project is not going to work. I cannot understand why upper management keeps assigning me to work on projects with Rankins. We simply cannot work together, and we don't get along. I've disliked him from day one. He keeps dropping the fact that he has earned all these advanced degrees from Purdue. And he keeps telling us how things are done there. I know he's better educated than I am, and he's really smart. But I'm smart too and am good at what I do. There's no need for Rankins to make me feel like an idiot because I don't have a degree. Jobe, I'll be honest with you. Rankins has only been here for five years, but I hold him personally responsible for my problem with alcohol, and for its resulting effect on my marriage. I got divorced last year, and it's Rankins's fault."

Jobe next talked with Rankins, who said, "I don't care what you do. Perry and I simply can't work closely together for the nine months it will take to get it done. One of us will kill the other. Ever since I arrived at FEL, Perry has hated my guts and does everything he can to sabotage my designs. We usually worry about customers creating change orders; here it's the fabrication and operations manager who is responsible for them. Perry second-guesses everything I do and makes design changes on his own, and these are always bad decisions. He is out of control. I swear he stays awake at nights thinking up ways to ruin my designs. I don't have this problem with any other manager."

Jobe left these interviews thoroughly discouraged and could not imagine what would come up in his interview with Stonebreaker. But Stonebreaker was quite positive: "I enjoy these international projects where I get to travel abroad and learn about different cultures. I can't wait to get started on this."

Jobe asked Stonebreaker about the ability of various team members to work together. Stonebreaker replied, "No problem! We've all worked together before and have had no problems. Sure, there have been ruffled feathers and hurt feelings between Rankins and Perry. Rankins can be arrogant and Perry stubborn, but it's never been anything that we can't work around. Besides, both of them are good at what they do—both professionals. They'll keep their heads on straight."

Jobe was even more bewildered. Gatenby says this project's success rides on Jobe's facilitation skills. The finance manager appears to want off this project team. The design engineer and operations manager admit they detest each other and cannot work together. And the human resources manager, having worked on projects with Perry and Rankins before, expects a rosy working relationship and anticipates no problems.

Jobe had a second meeting with Gatenby. Before discussing the design of the team-building sessions, he asked questions to learn what Gatenby thought about the ability of team members to work together. Gatenby admitted that there has been very bad blood between Perry and Rankins, but added, "That's why we hired you. It's your job to make sure that the history between those two doesn't interfere with Project Abu Dhabi's success. It's your job to get them to work well together. Get it done."

Their dialogue toward the end of this meeting progressed as follows:

> **Jobe:** "Why do you expect Rankins and Perry to work well together, given their history? What incentives do they have to do so?"
>
> **Gatenby:** "As you should know, FEL requires formal goal setting between project managers and functional managers at the beginning of each project. I've already done this with Bruder, Stonebreaker, Perry, and Rankins. Perry and Rankins have explicit goals stating they must work well together and cooperate with each other."
>
> **Jobe:** "What happens if they do not meet these goals?"
>
> **Gatenby:** "I've already discussed this with top management. If it appears to me after two months that things are not working out between Perry and Rankins, FEL will fire Rankins."
>
> **Jobe:** "Does Perry know this?"
>
> **Gatenby:** "Yes."

1. Evaluate the criteria FEL uses to assign managers to project teams. What efficiencies do these criteria create? What are the resulting problems?

2. Why is it even more important that project team members work well together on international projects such as Project Abu Dhabi?

3. Discuss the dilemma that Jobe now faces.

4. What should Jobe recommend to Gatenby?

Outsourcing: Managing Interorganizational Relations

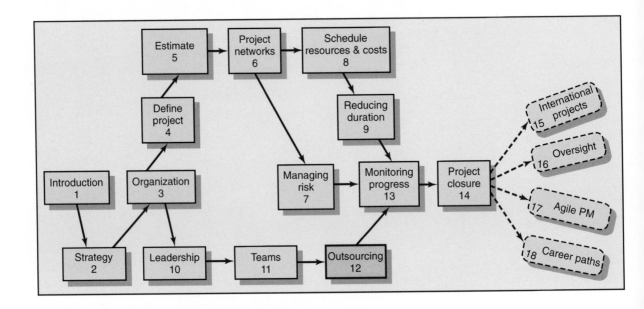

Outsourcing: Managing Interorganizational Relations

Outsourcing Project Work

Best Practices in Outsourcing Project Work

The Art of Negotiating

A Note on Managing Customer Relations

Summary

Appendix 12.1: Contract Management

. . . being a good partner has become a key corporate asset. I call it a company's collaborative advantage. In the global economy, a well-developed ability to create and sustain fruitful collaborations gives companies a significant competitive leg up.

—*Rosabeth Moss Kanter, Harvard Business School professor*

It is rare in today's flat world to find important projects that are being completed totally in-house. Outsourcing or contracting significant segments of project work to other companies is commonplace. For example, nine states attempting to unify the accounting of all their state agencies did not have the internal resources to implement such a large project. Hence, project teams were formed consisting of personnel from software, hardware, and accounting firms to implement the projects. Small high-tech firms outsource research to determine what features customers value in new products they are developing. Even industry giants such as Microsoft and Intel commonly hire independent firms to test new products they are developing.

Contracting project work has long been the norm in the construction industry, where firms hire general contractors who, in turn, hire and manage cadres of subcontractors to create new buildings and structures. For example, the Chunnel project, which created a transportation tunnel between France and England, involved more than 250 organizations. Contracting is not limited to large projects. For example, an insurance company worked with an outside contractor to develop an answering service that directs customers to specific departments and employees. The trend for the future suggests that more and more projects will involve working with people from different organizations.

This chapter extends the previous two chapters' discussion of building and managing relations by focusing specifically on issues surrounding working with people from other organizations to complete a project. First, the advantages and disadvantages of outsourcing project work are introduced. This is followed by a discussion of *best practices* used by firms to outsource and collaborate with each other on projects. The focus then shifts to the art of negotiating, which is at the heart of effective collaboration. Negotiating skills and techniques for resolving disagreements and reaching optimal solutions are then presented. The chapter closes with a brief note on managing customer relations. In addition, an appendix on contract management is included to augment our discussion of how organizations work together on projects.

Outsourcing Project Work

The term **outsourcing** has traditionally been applied to the transferring of business functions or processes (e.g., customer support, IT, accounting) to other, often foreign companies. For example, when you call your Internet provider to solve a technical problem you are likely to talk to a technician in Bangalore, India, or Bucharest, Romania. Outsourcing is now being applied to contracting significant

FIGURE 12.1
Reclining Chair
Project

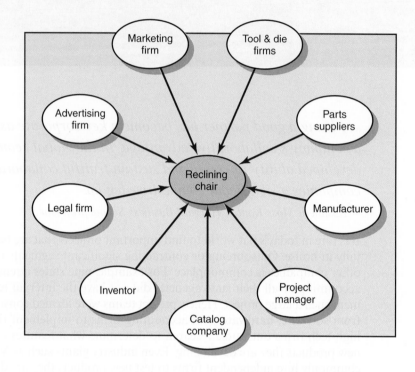

chunks of project work. For example, HP and Dell work closely with hard drive manufacturers to develop next-generation laptops. Toyota and DaimlerChrysler collaborate with suppliers to develop new automobile platforms.

The shift toward outsourcing is readily apparent in the film industry. During the golden era of Hollywood, huge, vertically integrated corporations made movies. Studios such as MGM, Warner Brothers, and 20th Century–Fox owned large movie lots and employed thousands of full-time specialists—set designers, camera people, film editors, and directors. Star actors like Humphrey Bogart and Marilyn Monroe were signed to exclusive studio contracts for a set number of films (e.g., six films over three years). Today, most movies are made by a collection of individuals and small companies who come together to make films project-by-project. This structure allows each project to be staffed with the talent most suited to its demands rather than choosing from only those people the studio employs. This same approach is being applied to the creation of new products and services. For example, see Figure 12.1.

Figure 12.1 depicts a situation in which a zero-gravity reclining chair is being developed. The genesis for the chair comes from a mechanical engineer who developed the idea in her garage. The inventor negotiates a contract with a catalog firm to develop and manufacture the chair. The catalog company in turn creates a project team of manufacturers, suppliers, and marketing firms to create the new chair. Each participant adds requisite expertise to the project. The catalog firm brings its brand name and distribution channels to the project. Tool and die firms provide customized parts which are delivered to a manufacturing firm that will produce the chair. Marketing firms refine the design, develop packaging, and test market potential names. A project manager is assigned by the catalog firm to work with the inventor and the other parties to complete the project.

Many outsourced projects operate in a virtual environment in which people are linked by computers, faxes, computer-aided design systems, and video teleconferencing. They rarely, if ever, see one another face-to-face. See the Snapshot from

(In August 2004) Intel software manager Connie Martin arrived for work and received a new identity. She was handed some fake rupees and a nametag that read "Rekha Gupta," and was told that from now she hailed from a northern Indian trading family. For the next eight hours, she hit books, studying subtle dietary differences between Jainism and Hinduism, Indian political history and Bollywood movies. At the end of the day, she was given a test on it all, which she aced.

A North Carolina native, Martin is a graduate of "Working with India," a training class that Intel began offering to employees in 2002. With so much work being outsourced to India, other high-tech companies like Adaptec, AMD, Intuit, and Rockwell Automation have instituted similar training courses. According to Ashok Mathur, an associate at Charis Intercultural (which runs Intel's Indian cultural training program), the biggest problems addressed by the classes are communications breakdowns around conflict. Sometimes Indian workers "make promises they can't keep to maintain harmony, but then they'll run into problems at the end of a project," Mathur says.

That's what happened at Adaptec, a Milpitas, Calif., maker of memory hardware, where managers requested Indian cultural training after a major chip manufacturing project ran more than a month late. "My gut feeling was that our Indian engineers didn't understand the sense of urgency," says David Sommers, Adaptec's vice president of engineering. After employees received training—which included everything from lessons on communications styles ("yes" doesn't always mean yes) to tips on how to distinguish first and last names in various clans—Adaptec's project got back on schedule. "Things became more predictable, with fewer problems that I could attribute to cultural differences," Sommers says.

* R. Rosmarin, "Mountain View Masala: High-Tech Firms Are Turning to Indian Cultural Training to Boost Performance," *Business 2.0,* March 1, 2005.

Practice: Silicon Valley Tandoori for an example of how companies train their people to work with contractors in India. On other projects, participants from different organizations work closely together, for example, at a construction site or in shared office space. In either case, people come and go as services are needed, much as in a matrix structure, but they are not formal members of one organization, just technical experts who form a temporary alliance with an organization, fulfill their contractual obligations, and then move on to the next project.

The advantages of outsourcing project work are many:

1. *Cost reduction.* Companies can secure competitive prices for contracted services, especially if the work can be outsourced offshore. Furthermore, overhead costs are dramatically cut since the company no longer has to internally maintain the contracted services.

2. *Faster project completion.* Not only can work be done more cheaply, but it can also be done faster. Competitive pricing means more resources for the dollar. For example, you can hire three Indian software engineers for the price of one American software engineer. Furthermore, outsourcing can provide access to equipment that can accelerate completion of project tasks. For example, by contracting a backhoe operater you are able to accomplish in four hours what it would take a landscaping crew four days to complete.

3. *High level of expertise.* A high level of expertise and technology can be brought to bear on the project. A company no longer has to keep up with technological advances. Instead, it can focus on developing its core competencies and hire firms with the know-how to work on relevant segments of the project.

4. *Flexibility.* Organizations are no longer constrained by their own resources but can pursue a wide range of projects by combining their resources with talents of other companies. Small companies can instantly go global by working with foreign partners.

SNAPSHOT FROM PRACTICE   Competing Against the Giants*

SATT Control (SC) is a Swedish electronics firm that sells electronic products and control systems worldwide. It has 550 employees in Sweden and about the same number abroad. So how does SC successfully bid against such electronic giants as ABB, Siemens, and Hewlett-Packard on major contracts for equipment that the company has never sold before? In the words of Hedberg and his coauthors, SC does so by acting as system integrator. In this role SC recruits a contracting syndicate by preparing a system description and dividing the system into various subsystems with each potential partner bidding for a part of the system. SC's ability to describe the system and divide it into subsystems that can be outsourced are two of its core competencies.

Another core competence at SC is project management. After the company has received an order for a project, one of the first actions taken is to work with the customer to develop clear specification of functions. While time consuming, this process is critical to be successful. The first step is to specify what the system is supposed to do, before deciding how it is to be done. This is commonly referred to as designing system architecture. It is crucial that the specifications are correct at the outset otherwise errors reappear all down the line. SC works hard at developing a common agreement among all the partners as to what the basic concept of the project is.

SC is also adroit at establishing a collaborative atmosphere among all the partners. The key is instilling a sense of "what is good for you is good for me." This comes from a history of treating each other with mutual respect and drafting contracts that share risks not isolate risks.

* B. Hedberg, G. Dahlgren, J. Hansson, and N-G. Olve, *Virtual Organizations and Beyond* (New York: Wiley, 1997), pp. 82–84.

The disadvantages of outsourcing project work are less well documented:

1. *Coordination breakdowns.* Coordination of professionals from different organizations can be challenging, especially if the project work requires close collaboration and mutual adjustment. Breakdowns are exacerbated by physical separation with people working in different buildings, different cities, if not different countries.

2. *Loss of control.* There is potential loss of control over the project. The core team depends on other organizations that they have no direct authority over. While long-term survival of participating organizations depends on performance, a project may falter when one partner fails to deliver.

3. *Conflict.* Projects are more prone to interpersonal conflict since the different participants do not share the same values, priorities, and culture. Trust, which is essential to project success, can be difficult to forge when interactions are limited and people come from different organizations.

4. *Security issues.* Depending on the nature of the project, trade and business secrets may be revealed. This can be problematic if the contractor also works for your competitor. Confidentiality is another concern and companies have to be very careful when outsourcing processes like payroll, medical transcriptions, and insurance information.

Few people disagree that reducing costs is the primary motive behind outsourcing project work. However, recent industry polls indicate a shift away from simply nailing the best low-cost deal to securing services from companies that provide the best value in terms of both cost and performance. Performance is not limited to simply the quality of specific work but also ability to collaborate and work together. Companies are doing their homework to determine "Can we work with these people?"

Best Practices in Outsourcing Project Work

This section describes some of the best practices we have observed being used by firms that excel in project management (see Figure 12.2). Although the list is by no means comprehensive, it reflects strategies used by organizations with extensive outsourcing experience. These practices reveal an underlying theme in how firms approach contracted work on projects. Instead of the traditional master–slave relationship between owner and provider or buyer and seller, all parties work together as partners sharing the ultimate goal of a successful project. See the Snapshot from Practice: Competing Against the Giants for an example of how a small firm leverages this approach to succeed in a very competitive industry.

Differences between the traditional approach and the partnering approach to managing contracted relationships are summarized in Table 12.1. Partnering requires more than a simple hand-shake. It typically entails a significant commitment of time and energy to forge and sustain collaborative relations among all parties. This commitment is reflected in the seven best practices which will be discussed next.

Well-Defined Requirements and Procedures

Convincing people from different professions, organizations, and cultures to work together is difficult. If expectations and requirements are fuzzy or open to debate, this is even harder. Successful firms are very careful in selecting the work to be outsourced. They often choose to contract only work with clearly defined deliverables with measurable outcomes. For example, contractors hire electric firms to install heating and air-conditioning systems, electronic firms use design firms to fabricate enclosures for their products, and software development teams outsource the testing of versions of their programs. In all of these cases, the technical requirements are spelled out in detail. Even so, communicating requirements can be troublesome, especially with foreign providers (see the Snapshot from Practice: Four Strategies for Communicating with Outsourcers), and extra care has to be taken to ensure that expectations are understood.

Not only do requirements have to be spelled out, but the different firms' project management systems need to be integrated. Common procedures and terminology need to be established so that different parties can work together. This can be problematic when you have firms with more advanced project management systems working with less developed organizations. Surprisingly, this often is the case when U.S. firms outsource software work to India. We have heard reports that Indian providers are shocked at how unsystematic their U.S. counterparts are in their approach to managing software projects.

FIGURE 12.2

Best Practices in Outsourcing Project Work

- Well-defined requirements and procedures.
- Extensive training and team-building activities.
- Well-established conflict management processes in place.
- Frequent review and status updates.
- Co-location when needed.
- Fair and incentive-laden contracts.
- Long-term outsourcing relationships.

TABLE 12.1
Key Differences Between Partnering and Traditional Approaches to Managing Contracted Relationships

Partnering Approach	Traditional Approach
Mutual trust forms the basis for strong working relationships.	Suspicion and distrust; each party is wary of the motives for actions by the other.
Shared goals and objectives ensure common direction.	Each party's goals and objectives, while similar, are geared to what is best for them.
Joint project team exists with high level of interaction.	Independent project teams; teams are spatially separated with managed interactions.
Open communications avoid misdirection and bolster effective working relationships.	Communications are structured and guarded.
Long-term commitment provides the opportunity to attain continuous improvement.	Single project contracting is normal.
Objective critique is geared to candid assessment of performance.	Objectivity is limited due to fear of reprisal and lack of continuous improvement opportunity.
Access to each other's organization resources is available.	Access is limited with structured procedures and self-preservation taking priority over total optimization.
Total company involvement requires commitment from CEO to team members.	Involvement is normally limited to project-level personnel.
Integration of administrative systems equipment takes place.	Duplication and/or translation takes place with attendant costs and delays.
Risk is shared jointly among the partners, which encourages innovation and continuous improvement.	Risk is transferred to the other party.

The best companies address this issue up front instead of waiting for problems to emerge. First they assess "fit" between providers' project management methods and their own project management system. This is a prime consideration in choosing vendors. Work requirements and deliverables are spelled out in detail in the procurement process. They invest significant time and energy to establishing project communication systems to support effective collaboration.

Finally, whenever you work with other organizations on projects, security is an important issue. Security extends beyond competitive secrets and technology to include access to information systems. Firms have to establish robust safeguards to prevent information access and the introduction of viruses due to less secure provider systems. Information technology security is an additional cost and risk that needs to be addressed up front before outsourcing project work.

Extensive Training and Team-Building Activities

Too often managers become preoccupied with the plans and technical challenges of the project and assume that people issues will work themselves out over time. Smart firms recognize that people issues are as important, if not more important than technical issues. They train their personnel to work effectively with people from other organizations and countries. This training is pervasive. It is not limited to management but involves all the people, at all levels, who interact with and are dependent upon outsourcers. Whether in a general class on negotiation or a specific one on working with Chinese programmers, team members are provided with

SNAPSHOT FROM PRACTICE   Four Strategies for Communicating with Outsourcers*

Dr. Adam Kolawa offers four strategies for overcoming poor communication with offshore project partners.

STRATEGY 1: RECOGNIZE CULTURAL DIFFERENCES

Realize that not everyone you communicate with shares your assumptions. What is obvious to you is not necessarily obvious to your partner. This is especially true with foreign outsourcers. As an American, you likely assume that laws are generally obeyed. Believe it or not, that's generally not true in most of the world, where laws are guidelines that are not necessarily followed. This can lead to major communication problems! You think if you write a contract, everybody is going to adhere to it. For many people, a contract is merely a suggestion.

STRATEGY 2: CHOOSE THE RIGHT WORDS

When you explain your requirements to an outsourcer, word choice is critical. For many outsourcers, English is still a foreign language—even in India, where both outsourcing and the English language are common. No matter how prevalent English has become, your outsourcer might have a basic understanding of each word you utter yet be not completely clear on the exact meaning of the message you're trying to convey. This is why you should speak in a direct manner using short sentences made of basic, simple words.

STRATEGY 3: CONFIRM YOUR REQUIREMENTS

You should take the following steps to confirm that the outsourcer thoroughly understands your requirements:

1. *Document your requirements.* Follow up your conversations in writing. Commit your requirements to paper for the outsourcer. Many people understand written language better than spoken language, probably because they have more time to process the message.

2. *Insist your outsourcer re-document your requirements.* Leave nothing to chance. Require outsourcers to write the requirements in their own words. If outsourcers cannot relay to you what you explained to them, then they didn't understand.

3. *Request a prototype.* After the requirements are written, ask the outsourcer to create a prototype for you. This is a safety net to ensure that your wants and needs are positively understood. Ask the provider to sketch what you want your final product to look like or build a quick, simple program that reflects how the final product will look.

STRATEGY 4: SET DEADLINES

Another important cultural difference relates to schedules and deadlines. To most Americans, a deadline is a set completion date. In many other cultures, a deadline is a suggestion that maybe something will be finished by that indicated date. To ensure that outsourced work is completed on time it is imperative to add a penalty clause to your contract or enforce late fees.

Although these strategies were directed toward working with foreign outsourcers, you would be surprised to find how many project managers use them when working with their American counterparts!

* Adam Kolawa, "Four Strategies for Communicating with Outsourcers," *Enterprise Systems Journal* at www.esj.com, accessed September 13, 2005.

a theoretical understanding of the barriers to collaboration as well as the skills and procedures to be successful.

The training is augmented by interorganizational team-building sessions designed to forge healthy relationships before the project begins. Team-building workshops involve the key players from the different firms, for example, engineers, architects, lawyers, specialists, and other staff. In many cases, firms find it useful to hire an outside consultant to design and facilitate the sessions. Such a consultant is typically well-versed in interorganizational team building and can provide an impartial perspective to the workshop.

The length and design of the team-building sessions will depend on the experience, commitment, and skill level of the participants. For example, one project, in which the owner and the contractors were relatively inexperienced at working together, utilized a two-day workshop. The first day was devoted to ice-breaking activities and establishing the rationale behind partnering. The conceptual foundation was supported by exercises and minilectures on teamwork, synergy, win/win, and constructive feedback. The second day began by examining the problems and barriers that prevented collaboration in the past. Representatives from the different organizations were separated and each asked the following:

- What actions do the other groups engage in that create problems for us?
- What actions do we engage in that we think create problems for them?
- What recommendations would we make to improve the situation?

The groups shared their responses and asked questions on points needing clarification. Agreements and disparities in the lists were noted and specific problems were identified. Once problem areas were noted, each group was assigned the task of identifying its specific interests and goals for the project. Goals were shared across groups, and special attention was devoted to establishing what goals they had in common. Recognition of shared goals is critical for transforming the different groups into a cohesive team.

The team-building sessions often culminate with the creation of a **partnering charter** signed by all of the participants. This charter states their common goals for the project as well as the procedures that will be used to achieve these goals (see Figure 12.3 for an example of the first page of a project charter).

Well-Established Conflict Management Processes in Place

Conflict is inevitable on a project and, as pointed out in the previous chapter, disagreements handled effectively can elevate performance. Dysfunctional conflict, however, can catch fire and severely undermine project success. Outsourced projects are susceptible to conflicts since people are unaccustomed to working together and have different values and perspectives. Successful firms invest significant time and energy up front in establishing the "rules of engagement" so that disagreements are handled constructively.

Escalation is the primary control mechanism for dealing with and resolving problems. The basic principle is that problems should be resolved at the lowest level within a set time limit (say, 24 hours), or they are "escalated" to the next level of management. If so, the principals have the same time limit to resolve the problem, or it gets passed on to the next higher level. No action is not an option. Nor can one participant force concessions from the other by simply delaying the decision. There is no shame in pushing significant problems up the hierarchy; at the same time, managers should be quick to point out to subordinates those problems or questions that they should have been able to resolve on their own.

If possible, key personnel from the respective organizations are brought together to discuss potential problems and responses. This is usually part of a coordinated series of team-building activities discussed earlier. Particular attention is devoted to establishing the change management control system where problems often erupt. People who are dependent on each other try to identify potential problems that may occur and agree in advance how they should be resolved. See the Snapshot from Practice: "Partnering" a Flu Shot for Projects for the benefits of doing this.

Finally, principled negotiation is the norm for resolving problems and reaching agreements. This approach, which emphasizes collaborative problem solving, is discussed in detail later in this chapter.

Frequent Review and Status Updates

Project managers and other key personnel from all involved organizations meet on a regular basis to review and assess project performance. Collaborating as

FIGURE 12.3 Project Partnering Charter

Partnering Charter

Edwards AFB — F-22 Fighter Building 1870

**U.S. Air Force F-22 CTF, 411 FLTS • Edwards AFB Civil Engineers
Computer Science Corporation • Lockheed Martin • Telecom Solutions
U.S. Army Corps of Engineers • Valenzuela Engineering, Inc • VRR & Associates**

We, the partners of the F-22 design and construction team, recognizing the unique nature of this project, commit to creating an environment of trust and communication to design and build a quality project which meets or exceeds the customer's requirements. We commit to maintaining a positive and optimistic work environment in which all partners goals can be achieved.

- **Quality Project**
  - Meet program requirements for F-22 Support Systems.
  - Complete on schedule and within cost constraints.
  - Incorporate lessons learned from other F-22 projects.
  - Create an environment for a fair and reasonable profit.
  - Create an enjoyable work environment.

- **Safe Project**
  - Provide a safe environment.
  - With no lost-time accidents.

- **Maintain positive, cooperative relationships**
  - Clear and open communications through appropriate channels.
  - No surprises.
  - No hidden agendas.
  - Minimum delays of paperwork.
  - Resolve problems quickly at the lowest level.

The Partnering concept is a team relationship that promotes the achievement of mutually beneficial goals. This Partnering Charter does not create any legally enforceable rights or duties. Any changes to the contracts must be made by the contracting officers under the terms of the written contracts.

U.S. Department of Defense's Value Engineering Awards*

As part of an effort to cut costs the United States Department of Defense (DoD) issues annual Value Engineering Awards. Value engineering is a systematic process to analyze functions to identify actions to reduce cost, increase quality, and improve mission capabilities across the entire spectrum of DoD systems, processes, and organizations. The Value Engineering Awards Program is an acknowledgment of outstanding achievements and encourages additional projects to improve in-house and contractor productivity.

In 2005 a team of contractors led by Northrop Grumman Corporation received a value-engineering achievement award from the U.S. Air Force for implementing innovative changes to the 1.6 billion intercontinental ballistic missile (ICBM) guidance replacement program that will result in a projected five-year savings of $32.9 million.

"The Air Force's desire to keep costs low on the guidance replacement program contract and Northrop Grumman's desire to enhance contract incentive performance dovetail into a mutually beneficial effort to decrease production costs," said John Clay, vice president and general manager of the ICBM prime integration project at Northrop Grumman's Mission Systems sector. "The changes we've made in partnership with the Air Force and our subcontractor, The Boeing Company, realize the goals of all parties."

To achieve the high level of savings, Northrop Grumman eliminated the need for expensive external shields to protect critical guidance system parts from nuclear environments. The

Photo by Sgt. Ken Hammond, U.S. Air Force.

critical material used in the shields was difficult to work with and cost approximately $90,000 per unit.

Instead the Northrop Grumman project team chose to improve the chassis construction of two components—the missile-guidance set control and the missile-guidance computer—with a rugged coating, thus eliminating the need for external shields, which reduces production costs and eliminates the need for multiple shield inspections.

The total cost savings is projected at $32.9 for 348 systems. The changes will save the Air Force two hours per system Inspection and two hours per system deployment over the remaining life of Minuteman III.

* http://www.irconnect.com/noc/press/pages/news_releases. html?d=86128.

information about different types of contracts is presented in this chapter's appendix on contract management.

Companies recognize that contracts can discourage continuous improvement and innovation. Instead of trying some new, promising technique that may reduce costs, contractors will avoid the risks and apply tried and true methods to meet contracted requirements. Companies that treat contractors as partners consider continuous improvement as a joint effort to eliminate waste and pursue opportunities for cost savings. Risks as well as benefits are typically shared 50/50 between the principals, with the owner adhering to a fast-track review of proposed changes.

How the U.S. Department of Defense reaps the benefits of continuous improvement through value engineering is highlighted in the Snapshot from Practice: Value Engineering Awards.

Long-Term Outsourcing Relationships

Many companies recognize that major benefits can be enjoyed when outsourcing arrangements extend across multiple projects and are long term. For example, Corning and Toyota are among the many firms that have forged a network of long-term strategic partnerships with their suppliers. A recent study indicates that the average large corporation is involved in around 30 alliances today versus fewer than 3 in the early 1990s. Among the many advantages for establishing a long-term partnership are the following:

- **Reduced administrative costs**—The costs associated with bidding and selecting a contractor are eliminated. Contract administration costs are reduced as partners become knowledgeable of their counterpart's legal concerns.
- **More efficient utilization of resources**—Contractors have a known forecast of work while owners are able to concentrate their workforce on core businesses and avoid the demanding swings of project support.
- **Improved communication**—As partners gain experience with each other, they develop a common language and perspective, which reduces misunderstanding and enhances collaboration.
- **Improved innovation**—The partners are able to discuss innovation and associated risks in a more open manner and share risks and rewards fairly.
- **Improved performance**—Over time partners become more familiar with each other's standards and expectations and are able to apply lessons learned from previous projects to current projects.

Working as partners is a conscious effort on the part of management to form collaborative relationships with personnel from different organizations to complete a project. For outsourcing to work, the individuals involved need to be effective negotiators capable of merging interests and discovering solutions to problems that contribute to the project. The next section addresses some of the key skills and techniques associated with effective negotiation.

The Art of Negotiating

Effective negotiating is critical to successful collaboration. All it takes is one key problem to explode to convert a sense of "we" into "us versus them." At the same time, negotiating is pervasive through all aspects of project management work. Project managers must negotiate support and funding from top management. They must negotiate staff and technical input from functional managers. They must coordinate with other project managers and negotiate project priorities and commitments. They must negotiate within their project team to determine assignments, deadlines, standards, and priorities. Project managers must negotiate prices and standards with vendors and suppliers. A firm understanding of the negotiating process, skills, and tactics is essential to project success.

Many people approach negotiating as if it is a competitive contest. Each negotiator is out to win as much as he or she can for his or her side. Success is measured by how much is gained compared with the other party. While this may be applicable when negotiating the sale of a house, it is not true for project management. *Project management is not a contest!* First, the people working on the project, whether they represent different companies or departments within the same organization, are not enemies or competitors but rather allies or partners. They have formed a temporary alliance to complete a project. For this alliance to work requires a certain degree of trust, cooperation, and honesty. Second, although the parties within this alliance may have different priorities and standards, they are bound by the success of the project. If conflicts escalate to the point where negotiations break down and the project comes to a halt, then everyone loses. Third, unlike bartering with a street vendor, the people involved on project work have to continue to work together.

Therefore, it behooves them to resolve disagreements in a way that contributes to the long-term effectiveness of their working relationship. Finally, as pointed out in the previous chapter, conflict on a project can be good. When dealt with effectively it can lead to innovation, better decisions, and more creative problem solving.

Project managers accept this noncompetitive view of negotiation and realize that negotiation is essentially a two-part process: The first part deals with reaching an agreement; the second part is the implementation of that agreement. It is the implementation phase, not the agreement itself, that determines the success of negotiations. All too often, managers reach an agreement with someone only to find out later that they failed to do what they agreed to do or that their actual response fell far short of expectations. Experienced project managers recognize that implementation is based on satisfaction not only with the outcome but also with the process by which the agreement was reached. If someone feels bullied or tricked into doing something, this feeling will invariably be reflected by half-hearted performance.

Veteran project managers do the best they can to merge individual interests with what is best for the project and come up with effective solutions to problems. Fisher and Ury from the Harvard Negotiation Project champion an approach to negotiating that embodies these goals. It emphasizes developing win/win solutions while protecting yourself against those who would take advantage of your forthrightness. Their approach is called **principled negotiation** and is based on four key points listed in Table 12.2 and discussed in the following sections.

TABLE 12.2
Principled
Negotiation

1. Separate the people from the problem
2. Focus on interests, not positions
3. Invent options for mutual gain
4. When possible, use objective criteria

1. Separate the People from the Problem

Too often personal relations become entangled with the substantive issues under consideration. Instead of attacking the problem(s), people attack each other. Once people feel attacked or threatened their energy naturally goes to defending themselves, and not to solving the problem. The key, then, is to focus on the problem—not the other person—during the negotiation. Avoid personalizing the negotiation and framing the negotiation as a contest. Instead, try to keep the focus on the problem to be resolved. In Fisher and Ury's words: *Be hard on the problem, soft on the people.*

By keeping the focus on the issues and not the personalities, negotiators are better able to let the other person blow off steam. On important problems it is not uncommon for people to become upset, frustrated, and angry. However, one angry attack produces an angry counterattack, and the discussion quickly escalates into a heated argument, an emotional chain reaction.

In some cases people use anger as a means of intimidating and forcing concessions because the other person wishes to preserve the relationship. When people become emotional, negotiators should keep a cool head and remember the old German proverb, "Let anger fly out the window." In other words, in the face of an emotional outburst, imagine opening a window and letting the heat of the anger out the window. Avoid taking things personally, and redirect personal attacks back to the question at hand. Don't react to the emotional outburst, but try to find the issues that triggered it. Skilled negotiators keep their cool under stressful times and, at the same time, build a bond with others by empathizing and acknowledging common sources of frustration and anger.

While it is important to separate the people from the problem during actual negotiations, it is beneficial to have a friendly rapport with the other person prior to negotiating. Friendly rapport is consistent with the social network tenet introduced in Chapter 10 of building a relationship before you need it. Reduce the likelihood of misunderstandings and getting off on the wrong foot by having a history of interacting in a friendly, responsive manner with the other person. If, in the past, the relationship has been marked by healthy give-and-take, in which both parties have demonstrated a willingness to accommodate the interests of the other, then neither individual is likely to adopt an immediate win/lose perspective. Furthermore, a positive relationship adds a common interest beyond the specific points of contention. Not only do both parties want to reach an agreement that suits their individual interests, but they also want to do so in a manner that preserves their relationship. Each is therefore more likely to seek solutions that are mutually beneficial.

2. Focus on Interests, Not Positions

Negotiations often stall when people focus on positions:

> I'm willing to pay $10,000. No, it will cost $15,000.
>
> I need it done by Monday. That's impossible, we can't have it ready until Wednesday.

While such interchanges are common during preliminary discussions, managers must prevent this initial posturing from becoming polarized. When such positions are stated, attacked, and then defended, each party figuratively begins to draw a line he or she will not cross. This line creates a win/lose scenario in which someone has to lose by crossing the line in order to reach an agreement. As such, the negotiations can become a war of wills, with concessions being seen as a loss of face.

The key is to focus on the interests behind your positions (what you are trying to achieve) and separate these goals from your ego as best you can. Not only should you be driven by your interests, but you should try to identify the interests of the other party. Ask why it will cost so much or why it can't be done by Monday. At the same time, make your own interests come alive. Don't just say that it is critical that it be done by Monday; explain what will happen if it isn't done by Monday.

Sometimes when the true interests of both parties are revealed, there is no basis for conflict. Take, for example, the Monday versus Wednesday argument. This argument could apply to a scenario involving a project manager and the production manager of a small, local firm that was contracted to produce prototypes of a new generation of computer mouse. The project manager needs the prototypes on Monday to demonstrate to a users' focus group. The production manager said it would be impossible. The project manager said this would be embarrassing because marketing had spent a lot of time and effort setting up this demonstration. The production manager again denied the request and added that he already had to schedule overtime to meet the Wednesday delivery date. However, when the project manager revealed that the purpose of the focus group was to gauge consumers' reactions to the color and shape of the new devices, not the finished product, the conflict disappeared. The production manager told the project manager that she could pick up the samples today if she wanted because production had an excess supply of shells.

When focusing on interests, it is important to practice the communication habit: *Seek first to understand, then to be understood.* This involves what Stephen Covey calls empathetic listening, which allows a person to fully understand another person's frame of reference—not only what that person is saying but also how he or she feels. Covey asserts that people have an inherent need to be understood. He goes on to observe that satisfied needs do not motivate human behavior, only unsatisfied needs do. People try to go to sleep when they are tired, not when they are rested. The key point is that until people believe they are being understood, they will repeat their points and reformulate their arguments. If, on the other hand, you satisfy this need by seeking first to understand, then the other party is free to understand your interests and focus directly on the issues at hand. Seeking to understand requires discipline and compassion. Instead of responding to the other person by asserting your agenda, respond by summarizing both the facts and feelings behind what the other person has said and checking the accuracy of comprehension.

3. Invent Options for Mutual Gain

Once the individuals involved have identified their interests, then they can explore options for mutual gain. This is not easy. Stressful negotiations inhibit creativity and free exchange. What is required is collaborative brainstorming in which people work together to solve the problem in a way that will lead to a win/win scenario. The key to brainstorming is separating the inventing from the deciding. Begin by taking 15 minutes to generate as many options as possible. No matter how outlandish any option is, it should not be subject to criticism or immediate rejection. People should feed off the ideas of others to generate new ideas. When all the possible options are exhausted, then sort through the ideas that were generated to focus on those with the greatest possibilities.

Clarifying interests and exploring mutual options create the opportunity for dovetailing interests. Dovetailing means one person identifies options that are of low cost to them but of high interest to the other party. This is only possible if each party knows what the other's needs are. For example, in negotiating price with a parts supplier, a project manager learned from the discussion that the supplier was in a cash flow squeeze after purchasing a very expensive fabrication machine. Needed cash was the primary reason the supplier had taken such a rigid position on price. During the brainstorming session, one of the options presented was to prepay for the order instead of the usual payment on delivery arrangement. Both parties seized on this option and reached an amicable agreement in which the project manager would pay the supplier for the entire job in advance in exchange for a faster turnaround time and a significant price reduction. Such opportunities for win/win agreements are often overlooked because the negotiators become fixated on solving their problems and not on opportunities to solve the other person's problems.

4. When Possible, Use Objective Criteria

Most established industries and professions have developed standards and rules to help deal with common areas of dispute. Both buyers and sellers rely on the blue book to establish price parameters for a used car. The construction industry has building codes and fair practice policies to resolve proof of quality and safe work procedures. The legal profession uses precedents to adjudicate claims of wrongdoing.

Whenever possible, you should insist on using external, objective criteria to settle disagreements. For example, a disagreement arose between a regional airlines firm and the independent accounting team entrusted with preparing the annual financial statement. The airline firm had made a significant investment by leasing several used airplanes from a larger airline. The dispute involved whether this lease should be classified as an operating or capital lease. This was important to the airline because if the purchase was classified as an operating lease, then the associated debt would not have to be recorded in the financial statement. However, if the purchase was classified as a capital lease, then the debt would be factored into the financial statement and the debt/equity ratio would be much less attractive to stockholders and would-be investors. The two parties resolved this dispute by deferring to formulas established by the Financial Accounting Standards Board. As it turns out the accounting team was correct, but, by deferring to objective standards, they were able to deflect the disappointment of the airline managers away from the accounting team and preserve a professional relationship with that firm.

Dealing with Unreasonable People

Most people working on projects realize that in the long run it is beneficial to work toward mutually satisfying solutions. Still, occasionally you encounter someone who has a dominant win/lose attitude about life and will be difficult to deal with. Fisher and Ury recommend that you use negotiation jujitsu when dealing with such a person. That is, when the other person begins to push, don't push back. As in the martial arts, avoid pitting your strengths against another's directly; instead use your skill to step aside and turn that person's strength to your ends. When someone adamantly sets forth a position, neither reject it nor accept it. Treat it as a possible option and then look for the interests behind it. Instead of defending your ideas, invite criticism and advice. Ask why it's a bad idea and discover the other's underlying interest.

Those who use negotiation jujitsu rely on two primary weapons. They ask questions instead of making statements. Questions allow for interests to surface and do not provide the opponent with something to attack. The second weapon is silence. If the other person makes an unreasonable proposal or attacks you personally, just sit there and don't say a word. Wait for the other party to break the stalemate by answering your question or coming up with a new suggestion.

The best defense against unreasonable, win/lose negotiators is having what Fisher and Ury call a strong **BATNA (best alternative to a negotiated agreement).** They point out that people try to reach an agreement to produce something better than the result of not negotiating with that person. What those results would be the true benchmark for determining whether you should accept an agreement. A strong BATNA gives you the power to walk away and say, "No deal unless we work toward a win/win scenario."

Your BATNA reflects how dependent you are on the other party. If you are negotiating price and delivery dates and can choose from a number of reputable suppliers, then you have a strong BATNA. If on the other hand there is only one vendor who can supply you with specific, critical material on time, then you have a weak BATNA. Under these circumstances you may be forced to concede to the vendor's demands. At the same time, you should begin to explore ways of increasing your BATNA for future negotiations. This can be done by reducing your dependency on that supplier. Begin to find substitutable material or negotiate better lead times with other vendors.

Negotiating is an art. There are many intangibles involved. This section has reviewed some time-tested principles of effective negotiating based on the groundbreaking work of Fisher and Ury. Given the significance of negotiating, you are encouraged to read their book as well as others on negotiating. In addition, attending training workshops can provide an opportunity to practice these skills. You should also take advantage of day-to-day interactions to sharpen negotiating acumen.

A Note on Managing Customer Relations

In Chapter 4 it was emphasized that ultimate success is not determined by whether the project was completed on time, within budget, or according to specifications, but whether the customer is satisfied with what has been accomplished. Customer satisfaction is the bottom line. Bad news travels faster and farther than good news. For every happy customer who shares his satisfaction regarding a particular product or service with another person, a dissatisfied customer is likely to share her dissatisfaction with eight other people. Project managers need to cultivate positive working relations with clients to preserve their reputations.

Customer satisfaction is a complex phenomenon. One simple but useful way of viewing customer satisfaction is in terms of **met expectations.** According to this model, customer satisfaction is a function of the extent to which perceived performance (or outcome) exceeds expectations. Mathematically, this relationship can be represented as the ratio between perceived performance and expected performance (see Figure 12.5). When performance falls short of expectations (ratio < 1), the customer is dissatisfied. If the performance matches expectations (ratio = 1), the customer is satisfied. If the performance exceeds expectations (ratio > 1), the customer is very satisfied or even delighted.

High customer satisfaction is the goal of most projects. However, profitability is another major concern. Exceeding expectations typically entails additional costs. For example, completing a construction project two weeks ahead of schedule may involve significant overtime expenses. Similarly, exceeding reliability requirements for a new electronic component may involve considerably more design and debugging effort. Under most circumstances, the most profitable arrangement occurs when the customer's expectations are only slightly exceeded. Returning to the mathematical model, with all other things being equal, one should strive for a satisfaction ratio of 1.05, not 1.5!

The met-expectations model of customer satisfaction highlights the point that whether a client is dissatisfied or delighted with a project is not based on hard facts and objective data but on perceptions and expectations. For example, a customer may be dissatisfied with a project that was completed ahead of schedule and under budget if he thought the work was poor quality and that his fears and concerns were not adequately addressed. Conversely, a customer may be very satisfied with a project that was over budget and behind schedule if she felt the project team protected her interests and did the best job possible under adverse circumstances.

Project managers must be skilled at managing customer expectations and perceptions. Too often they deal with these expectations after the fact when they try to alleviate a client's dissatisfaction by carefully explaining why the project cost more or took longer than planned. A more proactive approach is to begin to shape the proper expectations up front and accept that this is an ongoing process throughout the life of a project. Project managers need to direct their attention both to the customer's base expectations, the standard by which perceived performance will be evaluated, and to the customer's perceptions of actual performance. The ultimate goal is to educate clients so that they can make a valid judgment as to project performance.

FIGURE 12.5
The Met-Expectations Model of Customer Satisfaction

$$0.90 \quad = \quad \frac{\text{Perceived performance}}{\text{Expected performance}} \quad = \quad 1.10$$

Dissatisfied   Very satisfied

Managing customer expectations begins during the preliminary project approval phase of negotiations. It is important to avoid the temptation to oversell the virtues of a project to win approval because this may create unrealistic expectations that may be too difficult, if not impossible, to achieve. At the same time, project proponents have been known to lower customer expectations by underselling projects. If the estimated completion time is 10 to 12 weeks, they will promise to have the project completed within 12 to 14 weeks, therefore increasing the chances of exceeding customer expectations by getting the project completed early.

Once the project is authorized, the project manager and team need to work closely with the client organization to develop a well-defined project scope statement that clearly states the objectives, parameters, and limits of the project work. The project scope statement is essential to establishing customer expectations regarding the project. It is critical that all parties are in agreement as to what is to be accomplished and that people are reading as best they can from the same page. It is also important to share significant risks that might disrupt project execution. Customers do not like surprises, and if they are aware in advance of potential problems they are much more likely to be accepting of the consequences.

Once the project is initiated it is important to keep customers abreast of project progress. The days when you would simply take orders from customers and tell them to return when the project is done are over. More and more organizations and their project managers are treating their customers as de facto members of the project team and are actively involving them in key aspects of project work. In the case of consulting assignments project managers sometimes *morph* into a member of the client organization (see Research Highlight: IT Project Managers).

Project managers need to keep customers informed of project developments so that customers can make adjustments in their own plans. When circumstances dictate changing the scope or priorities of the project, project managers need to be quick to spell out as best they can the implications of these changes to the customers so that they can make an informed choice. Active customer involvement allows customers to naturally adjust their expectations in accordance with the decisions and events that transpire on a project, while at the same time, the customer's presence keeps the project team focused on the customer's objectives for the project.

Active customer involvement also provides a firmer basis for assessing project performance. The customer not only sees the results of the project but also acquires glimpses of the effort and actions that produced those results. Naturally project managers want to make sure these glimpses reflect favorably on their project teams, so they exercise extra care that customer interactions are handled in a competent and professional manner. In some respects, customer perceptions of performance are shaped more by how well the project team deals with adversity than by actual performance. Project managers can impress customers with how diligently they deal with unexpected problems and setbacks. Likewise, industry analysts have noted that customer dissatisfaction can be transformed into customer satisfaction by quickly correcting mistakes and being extremely responsive to customer concerns.

Managing customer relations on a project is a broad topic; we have only highlighted some of the central issues involved. This brief segment concludes with two words of advice passed on by veteran project managers:

Speak with one voice. Nothing erodes confidence in a project more than for a customer to receive conflicting messages from different project members. The project manager should remind team members of this fact and work with them to ensure that appropriate information is shared with customers.

Webber and Torti studied the multiple roles project managers play on IT projects. Based on a comprehensive set of interviews with project managers and clients in three different information-technology service organizations, they identified five key roles critical to successfully implement IT projects in client organizations: entrepreneur, politician, friend, marketer, and coach. They are described in part in Table 12.3.

Webber and Torti observed that instead of maintaining a clearly defined relationship with the client, project managers become part of the client organization. They report that project managers attempt to "dress like the client, act like the client, and participate in the client organization's activities (i.e., social gatherings, blood drives, etc.)." They become such an integral part of their existence that many client employees, over the course of time, forget that the project manager is not an employee of the client organization. This helps establish a degree of trust essential to effective collaboration.

* S. S. Webber, and M. T. Torti, "Project Managers Doubling as Client Account Executives," *Academy of Management Executive,* Vol. 18, No. 1, pp. 60–71, 2004.

TABLE 12.3
Project Roles, Challenges, and Strategies

Project Manager Roles	Challenges	Strategies
Entrepreneur	Navigate unfamiliar surroundings	Use persuasion to influence others
Politician	Understand two diverse cultures (parent and client organization)	Align with the powerful individuals
Friend	Determine the important relationships to build and sustain outside the team itself	Identify common interests and experiences to bridge a friendship with the client
Marketer	Understand the strategic objectives of the client organization	Align new ideas/proposals with the strategic objectives of the client organization
Coach	Motivate client team members without formal authority	Provide challenging tasks to build the skills of the team members

Speak the language of the customer. Too often project members respond to customer inquiries with technical jargon that exceeds the customer's vocabulary. Project managers and members need to describe problems, trade-offs, and solutions in ways that the customer can understand.

Summary

Outsourcing has become an integral part of project management. More and more companies are collaborating with each other on projects to compete in today's business world. The advantages of outsourcing include cost reduction, quicker completion times, greater flexibility, and higher level of expertise. Disadvantages include coordination problems, loss of control, conflicts, and security issues.

A number of proactive best practices have emerged among firms that have mastered the outsourcing process. These practices include establishing well-defined requirements and procedures and utilizing fair and incentive-laden contracts. Team-building sessions are held before the project begins to forge relationships between personnel from different organizations. Escalation guidelines for resolving conflicts are established, as are provisions for process improvement and risk sharing. On highly critical work, arrangements are made so that key personnel work together, face to face. Joint assessments of how well people are collaborating is the norm during status report briefings. Finally, many companies are realizing the benefits of forming long-term alliances with each other on projects. The ultimate goal is to work together as partners.

Effective negotiating skills are essential to working on projects as partners. People need to resolve differences at the lowest level possible in order to keep the project on track. Veteran project managers realize that negotiating is not a competitive game and work toward collaborative solutions to problems. They accomplish this by separating people from the problem, focusing on interests and not positions, inventing options for mutual gain, and relying on objective criteria whenever possible to resolve disagreements. They also recognize the importance of developing a strong BATNA, which provides them with the leverage necessary to seek collaborative solutions.

Customer satisfaction is the litmus test for project success. Project managers need to take a proactive approach to managing customer expectations and perceptions. They need to actively involve customers in key decisions and keep them abreast of important developments. Active customer involvement keeps the project team focused on the objectives of the project and reduces misunderstandings and dissatisfaction.

Key Terms

Best alternative to a negotiated agreement (BATNA), *435*
Co-location, *428*
Escalation, *426*
Met-expectations model, *436*
Outsourcing, *419*
Partnering charter, *426*
Principled negotiation, *432*

Review Questions

1. Why do firms outsource project work?
2. What are the best practices used by firms to outsource project work?
3. What does the term "escalate" refer to, and why is it essential to project success?
4. Why is the principled negotiation approach recommended for negotiating agreements on projects?
5. What does the acronym BATNA refer to, and why is it important to being a successful negotiator?
6. How can a project manager influence customer expectations and perceptions?

Exercises

1. Break into groups of four to five students. Assign half of the groups the role of Owner and the other half the role of Contractor.

   Owners: After saving for many years you are about to hire a contractor to build your "dream home." What are your objectives for this project? What concerns or issues do you have about working with a general contractor to build your home?

   Contractors: You specialize in building customized homes. You are about to meet with prospective owners to begin to negotiate a contract for building their "dream home." What are your objectives for this project? What concerns or issues do you have about working with the owners to build their home?

   Each Owner group meets with another Contractor group and shares their objectives, concerns, and issues.

   Identify what objectives, issues, and concerns you have in common and which ones are unique. Discuss how you could work together to realize your objectives. What would be the keys to working as partners on this project?

FOUR MONTHS LATER

The project seemed to be falling apart. What happened to the positive attitude fostered at the team-building workshop? One contractor wrote a formal letter complaining that another contractor was sitting on a coding decision that was delaying their work. The letter went on: "We cannot be held responsible or liable for delays caused by others." The project was already two months behind, so problems were becoming very real and serious. Karin finally decided to call a meeting of all parties to the project and partnering agreement.

She began by asking for problems people were encountering while working on the project. Although participants were reluctant to be first for fear of being perceived as a complainer, it was not long before accusations and tempers flared out of control. It was always some group complaining about another group. Several participants complained that others were sitting on decisions that resulted in their work being held up. One consultant said, "It is impossible to tell who's in charge of what." Another participant complained that although the group met separately on small problems, it never met as a total group to assess new risk situations that developed.

Karin felt the meeting had degenerated into an unrecoverable situation. Commitment to the project and partnering appeared to be waning. She quickly decided to stop the meeting and cool things down. She spoke to the project stakeholders: "It is clear that we have some serious problems, and the project is in jeopardy. The project must get back on track, and the backbiting must stop. I want each of us to come to a meeting Friday morning with concrete suggestions of what it will take to get the project back on track and specific actions of how we can make it happen. We need to recognize our mutual interdependence and bring our relationships with each other back to a win/win environment. When we do get things back on track, we need to figure out how to stay on track."

1. Why does this attempt at project partnering appear to be failing?
2. If you were Karin, what would you do to get this project back on track?
3. What action would you take to keep the project on track?

Case

Buxton Hall

Chad Cromwell, head of university housing, gazed up at the tower at Buxton Hall and smiled as he walked toward the landmark building.

Buxton Hall was built in 1927 as a residential complex for over 350 students at Pacifica State University. At the time Buxton was the tallest building on campus, and its tower had a panoramic view of the athletic fields and coastal range. Buxton quickly became a focal point at Pacifica State. Students perched on the tower dominated the campus during the annual spring water fight with their huge slingshots and catapults. The first intranet on the Pacific coast was created at Buxton that linked students' computers and allowed them to share printers. Around the 1970s, some student artists began the tradition of painting their room doors. Whether a Rolling Stones logo or Bugs Bunny on a skateboard, these colorful doors were an artistic legacy that caught the attention of students and faculty.

Buxton Hall served as a residence hall for the university for many years, but time was not kind to the stately building. Leaks destroyed plaster in the interior. Wiring and plumbing became outdated and so dangerous that the building was deemed unsafe. Buxton Hall's doors were closed to students and windows boarded up at the end of the 1996 spring quarter. For 10 years Buxton sat silent and over time became a symbol of the general decline of Pacifica State. Now thanks to state bonds and generous contributions, Buxton Hall was about to be reopened after a $20 million renovation.

18 MONTHS AGO

Chad and key representatives from university facilities were engaged in the second of a two-day partnering workshop. Also in attendance were managers from Crawford Construction, the chief contractor for the Buxton renovation project, as well as several key subcontractors and architects from the firm of Legacy West. During the first day a consultant ran them through a series of team-building and communication exercises that accentuated the importance of open communication, principle negotiation, and win/win thinking. Today's session began with the "project from hell" exercise, with each group describing the worst project they had ever worked on. Chad was surprised that the people from Crawford and Legacy West descriptions were very similar to his own. For example, each group talked about how frustrating it was when changes were made without proper consultation or costs were hidden until it was too late to do anything about them. This was followed by a discussion of the best project they had ever worked on. The consultant then asked the groups which of the two they wanted the Buxton project to be. A genuine sense of common purpose emerged, and everyone became actively engaged in spelling out in specific terms how they wanted to work together. The session concluded with all of the participants signing a partnering charter followed by a picnic and a friendly softball game.

12 MONTHS AGO

Chad was on his way, with Nick Bolas, to meet Dat Nguyen, the Crawford Project Manager, on the third floor at Buxton tower. Dat had contacted him to discuss a problem with the tile work in one of the communal bathrooms. Dat's people had completed the work, but Nick, who was a Pacifica facilities manager, refused to sign off on it claiming that it was not up to spec. After a 24-hour impasse, the Crawford foreman exercised the escalation clause in partnering agreement and passed the issue up to management's level to be resolved. Dat and Chad inspected the work. While both agreed that the job could have been prettier, it did meet specification and Chad told Nick to sign off on it.

Chad met Dat again later in the day at the weekly Buxton status report meeting. The meeting kicked off with a brief review of what had been accomplished during the past week. Discussion centered on the removal of elm trees. Alternative strategies for dealing with the city inspector, who had a reputation of being a stickler for details, were considered. The project was two weeks behind schedule, which is an important issue since it was imperative that the building be ready for students to move in at the 2008 fall term. The project was also on a very tight budget, and the management reserve had to be carefully administered.

Renovation of existing buildings was always a bit of a gamble, since you never knew what you would find once you began tearing down walls. Fortunately, only small amounts of asbestos were found, but rot was much more severe than anticipated.

The meeting included a partnering assessment. The results of a Web survey filled out by all the principals were distributed. The results revealed a dip in the ratings between the Crawford foremen and university officials regarding timely collaboration and effective problem solving. One of Chad's people said that the primary source of frustration was Crawford foremen failing to respond to e-mail and telephone messages. Dat asked for the names of his people and said he would talk to each of them. The Crawford foremen complained that the university officials were being too nit-picky. "We don't have the time or money to do A+ work on everything," argued a foreman. Chad told Dat and his people that he would talk to facilities guys and ask them to focus on what is really important.

6 MONTHS AGO

The project status report meeting started on time. Crawford had been able to make up for lost time, and it now looked like the building would open on time. Chad was glad to see that the partnering assessment had been positive and steady over the past month. The big issue was the surge in costs consuming all but $50,000 of management reserve. With six months to go everyone knew that this would not cover all the change orders needed to have the building ready. After all, there was already $24,000 worth of change orders pending.

Chad looked across the table and saw nothing but grim faces. Then one of the Crawford foremen proposed postponing treating all of the exterior walls. "Instead of cleaning and preserving the entire brick building, let's only do the front entrance and the North and South walls that the public sees. We can just refurbish the interior court walls as well as the West side. This would be adequate for at least eight years, in which time money should be available to complete the job."

At first Chad didn't like this idea, but eventually he realized that this was the only way they could have the building ready for the students. Friendly arguments broke out over which exterior segments needed the full treatment and which ones didn't. The whole team ended up touring the outside of the building identifying what kind of work needed to be done. In the end, only 70 percent of exterior brick walls were reconditioned according to plan with a savings of over $250,000. While this boost to the reserve would still make things tight everyone felt that they now had a fighting chance to complete the project on time.

TODAY

As Chad mingled with a glass of champagne, no one talked about the walls that still needed to be refurbished—tonight was a night to celebrate. All of the major participants and their spouses were at the party, and the university was hosting a five-course meal at the top of the tower. During the toasts, jokes were exchanged and stories told about the ghosts in the west wing and the discovery of a dead skunk in the south basement. Everyone talked about how proud they felt about bringing back to life the grand old building. More than one person mentioned that this was much more satisfying than tearing down an old relic and constructing a new building. The president of the university concluded the festivities by thanking everyone for their hard work and proclaiming that Buxton would become a bright, shining icon for Pacifica State.

1. How successful was this project?
2. What best practices were evident in the case? How did they contribute to project objectives?

Case

Goldrush Electronics Negotiation Exercise

OBJECTIVE

The purpose of this case is to provide you with an opportunity to practice negotiations.

PROCEDURE

STEP 1

The class is divided into four groups, each comprising the project management group for one of four projects at Goldrush Electronics.

STEP 2

Read the Goldrush Electronics "Background Information" section given below. Then read the instructions for the project you represent. Soon you will meet with the management of the other projects to exchange personnel. Plan how you want to conduct those meetings.

BACKGROUND INFORMATION

Goldrush Electronics (GE) produces a range of electronic products. GE has a strong commitment to project management. GE operates as a projectized organization with each project organized as a fully dedicated team. The compensation system is based on a 40 + 30 + 30 formula. Forty percent is based on your base salary, 30 percent on your project performance, and 30 percent on overall performance of the firm.

Four new product development projects have been authorized. They are code named: Alpha, Beta, Theta, and Zeta. The preliminary assignment of personnel is listed below. You are assigned to represent the management of one of these projects.

The policy at GE is that once preliminary assignments are made project managers are free to exchange personnel as long as both parties agree to the transaction. You will have the opportunity to adjust your team by negotiating with other project managers.

Alpha Project		
Software Engineer	**Hardware Engineer**	**Design Engineer**
Jill	Cameron	Mitch
John	Chandra	Marsha

Beta Project		
Software Engineer	**Hardware Engineer**	**Design Engineer**
Jake	Casey	Mike
Jennifer	Craig	Maria

Theta Project		
Software Engineer	**Hardware Engineer**	**Design Engineer**
Jack	Chuck	Monika
Johan	Cheryl	Mark

Zeta Project		
Software Engineer	**Hardware Engineer**	**Design Engineer**
Jeff	Carlos	Max
Juwoo	Chad	Maile

Personnel may be traded for one or more other personnel.

STEP 3

Meet and negotiate with the other project managers.

STEP 4

Individual project scores are totaled and posted.

STEP 5

DISCUSSION QUESTIONS

1. What was your initial strategy before starting the actual negotiations? How did you view the other groups?
2. Did your initial strategy change once negotiations began? If so, how and why?
3. What could top management at GE have done to make it easier to reach agreement with the other groups?

Appendix 12.1

Contract Management

Since most outsourced work on projects is contractual in nature, this appendix discusses the different kinds of contracts that are used, their strengths and weaknesses, and how contracts shape the motives and expectations of different participants. Contract management is a key element of any project procurement management system. It is beyond the scope of this book to describe this system. However, the basic processes are listed here to put contract management and related topics like Request for Proposal (RFP) (see Appendix 2.1) in perspective. Six main steps comprise procurement management:

- **Planning purchases and acquisitions** involves determining what to procure, when, and how. This entails the classic build-versus-buy analysis as well as determination of the type of contract to use.
- **Planning contracting** involves describing the requirements for products or services desired from outsourcing and identifying potential suppliers or sellers. Outputs include procurement documents such as a (RFP) as well as selection criteria.
- **Requesting seller responses** involves obtaining information, quotes, bids, or proposals from sellers and providers. The main outputs of this process include a qualified sellers list and specific proposals.
- **Selecting sellers** involves choosing from potential suppliers through a process of evaluating potential providers and negotiating a contract.
- **Administering the contract** involves managing the relationship with the selected seller or provider.
- **Closing the contract** involves completion and settlement of the contract.

Most companies have purchasing departments that specialize in procurement. Often purchasing agents will be assigned to project teams and they work with other team members to come up with optimum solutions for the project. Even if project teams are not directly involved in contract negotiations and the decision to outsource project work, it is important that the team understand the procurement process and the nature of different kinds of contracts.

CONTRACTS

A contract is a formal agreement between two parties wherein one party (the contractor) obligates itself to perform a service and the other party (the client) obligates itself to do something in return, usually in the form of a payment to the contractor. For example, an insurance firm contracted with a consulting firm to reprogram segments of their information system to conform to MS Seven.

A contract is more than just an agreement between parties. A contract is a codification of the private law, which governs the relationship between the parties to it. It defines the responsibilities, spells out the conditions of its operations, defines the rights of the parties in relationship to each other, and grants remedies to a party if the other party breaches its obligations. A contract attempts to spell out in specific terms the transactional obligations of the parties involved as well as contingencies associated with the execution of the contract. An ambiguous or inconsistent contract is difficult to understand and enforce.

There are essentially two different kinds of contracts. The first is the "fixed-price" contract in which a price is agreed upon in advance and remains fixed as long as there are no changes to scope or provisions of the agreement. The second is a "cost-plus" contract in which the contractor is reimbursed for all or some of the expenses incurred during the performance of the contract. Unlike the fixed-price contract, the final price is not known until the project is completed. Within these two types of contracts, several variations exist.

FIXED-PRICE CONTRACTS

Under a fixed-price (FP) or lump-sum agreement, the contractor agrees to perform all work specified in the contract at a fixed price. Clients are able to get a minimum price by putting out the contract to competitive bid. Advertising an invitation for bid (IFB) that lists customer requirements usually results in low bids. Prospective contractors can obtain IFB notices through various channels. In the case of large business organizations and government agencies, potential contractors can request to be included on the bidder's list in the area of interest. In other cases, IFBs can be found by scanning appropriate industry media such as newspapers, trade journals, and Web sites. In many cases, the owner can put restrictions on potential bidders, such as requiring that they be ISO 9000 certified.

With fixed-price contract bids, the contractor has to be very careful in estimating target cost and completion schedule because once agreed upon, the price cannot be adjusted. If contractors overestimate the target cost in the bidding stage, they may lose the contract to a lower-priced competitor; if the estimate is too low, they may win the job but make little or no profit.

Fixed-price contracts are preferred by both owners and contractors when the scope of the project is well defined with predictable costs and low implementation risks. Such might be the case for producing parts or components to specifications, executing training programs, or orchestrating a banquet. With fixed-price contracts, clients do not have to be concerned with project costs and can focus on monitoring work progress and performance specifications. Likewise, contractors prefer fixed-price contracts because the client is less likely to request changes or additions to the contract. Fewer potential changes reduce project uncertainty and allow the contractors to more efficiently manage their resources across multiple projects.

The disadvantage of a fixed-price contract for owners is that it is more difficult and more costly to prepare. To be effective, design specifications need to be spelled out in sufficient detail to leave little doubt as to what is to be achieved. Because the contractor's profit is determined by the difference between the bid and the actual costs, there is some incentive for contractors to use cheaper quality materials, perform marginal workmanship, or extend the completion date to reduce costs. The client can counteract these by stipulating rigid end-item specifications and completion date and by supervising work. In many cases, the client will hire a consultant who is an expert in the field to oversee the contractor's work and protect the client's interest.

The primary disadvantage of a fixed-price contract for contractors is that they run the risk of underestimating. If the project gets into serious trouble, cost overruns may make the project unprofitable, and, in some cases, may lead to bankruptcy. To avoid this, contractors have to invest significant time and money to ensure that their estimates are accurate.

Contracts with long lead times such as construction and production projects may include escalation provisions that protect the contractor against external cost increases in materials, labor rates, or overhead expenses. For example, the price may be tied to an inflation index, so it can be adjusted to sudden increases in labor and material prices, or it may be redetermined as costs become known. A variety of redetermination contracts are used. Some establish a ceiling price for a contract and permit only downward adjustments, others permit upward and downward adjustments; some establish one readjustment period at the end of the project, others use more than one period. Redetermination contracts are appropriate where engineering and design efforts are difficult to estimate or when final price cannot be estimated for lack of accurate cost data.

While, in principle, redetermination contracts are used to make appropriate adjustments in cost uncertainties, they are prone to abuse. A contractor may win an initial low bid contract, initiate the contracted work, and then "discover" that the costs are much higher than expected. The contractor can take advantage of redetermination provisions and a client's ignorance to justify increasing the actual cost of the contract. The contract evolves into a cost-plus contract.

To alleviate some of the disadvantages of a fixed-price contract while maintaining some certainty as to final cost, many fixed-price contracts contain incentive clauses designed to motivate contractors to reduce costs and improve efficiency. For example, a contractor negotiates to perform the work for a target price based on a target cost and a target profit. A maximum price and maximum profit are also established. If the total cost ends up being less than the target cost, the contractor makes a higher profit up to the profit maximum. If there is a cost overrun, the contractor absorbs some of the overrun until a profit floor is reached.

Profit is determined according to a formula based on a cost-sharing ratio (CSR). A CSR of 75/25, for example, indicates that for every dollar spent above target costs, the client pays 75 cents and the contractor pays 25 cents. This provision motivates contractors to keep costs low since they pay 25 cents on every dollar spent above the expected cost and earn 25 cents more on every dollar saved below the expected cost. Fixed-price incentive contracts tend to be used for long-duration projects with fairly predictable cost estimates. The key is being able to negotiate a reasonable target cost estimate. Unscrupulous contractors have been known to take advantage of the ignorance of the client to negotiate an unrealistically high target cost and use performance incentives to achieve excessive profits.

COST-PLUS CONTRACTS

Under a cost-plus contract the contractor is reimbursed for all direct allowable costs (materials, labor, travel) plus an additional fee to cover overhead and profit. This fee is negotiated in advance and usually involves a percentage of the total costs. On small projects this kind of contract comes under the rubric "time and materials contract" in which the client agrees to reimburse the contractor for labor cost and materials. Labor costs are based on an hourly or daily rate, which includes direct and indirect costs as well as profit. The contractor is responsible for documenting labor and materials costs.

Unlike fixed-price contracts, cost-plus contracts put the burden of risk on the client. The contract does not indicate what the project is going to cost until the end of the project. Contractors are supposed to make the best effort to fulfill the specific technical requirements of the contract but cannot be held liable, in spite of their best efforts, if the work is not produced within the estimated cost and time frame. These contracts are often criticized because there is little formal incentive for the contractors to control costs or finish on time because they get paid regardless of the final cost. The major factor motivating contractors to control costs and schedule is the effect overruns have on their reputation and their ability to secure future business.

The inherent weakness of cost-plus contracts has been compensated for by a variety of incentive clauses directed at providing incentives to contractors to control costs, maintain performance, and avoid schedule overruns. Contractors are reimbursed for costs, but instead of the fee being fixed, it is based on an incentive formula and subject to additional provisions. This is very similar to fixed-price incentive contracts, but instead of being based on a target cost, the fee is based on actual cost, using a cost-sharing formula.

Progress and Performance Measurement and Evaluation

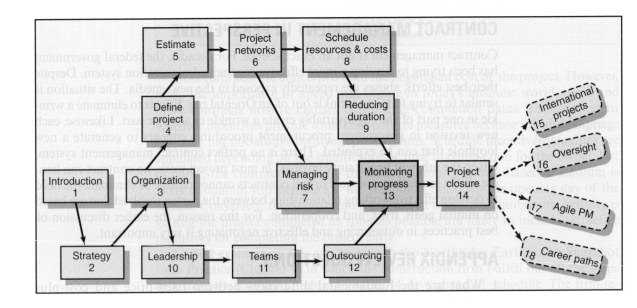

Box	Label
5	Estimate
6	Project networks
8	Schedule resources & costs
4	Define project
9	Reducing duration
1	Introduction
3	Organization
7	Managing risk
13	Monitoring progress
14	Project closure
15	International projects
16	Oversight
17	Agile PM
18	Career paths
2	Strategy
10	Leadership
11	Teams
12	Outsourcing

Progress and Performance Measurement and Evaluation

Structure of a Project Monitoring Information System

The Project Control Process

Monitoring Time Performance

Development of an Earned Value Cost/Schedule System

Developing a Status Report: A Hypothetical Example

Indexes to Monitor Progress

Forecasting Final Project Cost

Other Control Issues

Summary

Appendix 13.1: The Application of Additional Earned Value Rules

Appendix 13.2: Obtaining Project Performance Information from MS Project

How does a project get one year late?

. . . One day at a time.

—Frederick P. Brooks, *The Mythical Man Month, p. 153*

Evaluation and control are part of every project manager's job. Control by "wandering around" and/or "involvement" can overcome most problems in small projects. But large projects need some form of formal control. Control holds people accountable, prevents small problems from mushrooming into large problems, and keeps focus. Except for accounting controls, project control is not performed well in most organizations. Control is one of the most neglected areas of project management. Unfortunately, it is not uncommon to find resistance to control processes. In essence, those who minimize the importance of control are passing up a great opportunity to be effective managers and, perhaps, allow the organization to gain a competitive edge. Neglecting control in organizations with multiple projects is even more serious. For effective control, the project manager needs a single information system to collect data and report progress on cost, schedule, and specifications. The general structure of such a system is discussed next.

Structure of a Project Monitoring Information System

A project monitoring system involves *determining what* data to collect; *how, when,* and *who* will collect the data; *analysis* of the data; and *reporting* current progress.

What Data Are Collected? Data collected are determined by *which* metrics will be used for project control. Typical key data collected are actual activity duration times, resource usage and rates, and actual costs, which are compared against planned times, resources, and budgets. Since a major portion of the monitoring system focuses on cost/schedule concerns, it is crucial to provide the project manager and stakeholders with data to answer questions such as:

- What is the current status of the project in terms of schedule and cost?
- How much will it cost to complete the project?
- When will the project be completed?
- Are there potential problems that need to be addressed now?
- What, who, and where are the causes for cost or schedule overruns?
- What did we get for the dollars spent?
- If there is a cost overrun midway in the project, can we forecast the overrun at completion?

The performance metrics you need to collect should support answering these questions. Examples of specific metrics and tools for collecting data will be discussed in detail later in this chapter.

453

Gantt charts (bar charts) and control charts are the typical tools used for communicating project schedule status. As suggested in Chapter 6, the Gantt chart is the most favored, used, and understandable. This kind of chart is commonly referred to as a tracking Gantt chart. Gantt and control charts serve well as a means for tracking and trending schedule performance. Their easy-to-understand visual formats make them favorite tools for communicating project schedule status—especially to top management, who do not usually have time for details. Adding actual and revised time estimates to the Gantt chart gives a quick overview of project status on the report date.

Tracking Gantt Chart

Figure 13.1 presents a baseline Gantt chart and a tracking Gantt chart for a project at the end of period 6. The solid bar below the original schedule bar represents the actual start and finish times for completed activities or any portion of an activity completed (see activities A, B, C, D, and E). For example, the actual start time for activity C is period 2; the actual finish time is period 5; the actual duration is three time units, rather than four scheduled time periods. Activities in process show the actual start time; the extended bar represents the expected remaining duration (see activities D and E). The remaining duration for activities D and E are shown with the hatched bar. Activity F, which has not started, shows a revised estimated actual start (9) and finish time (13).

Note how activities can have durations that differ from the original schedule, as in activities C, D, and E. Either the activity is complete and the actual is known, or new information suggests the estimate of time be revised and reflected

FIGURE 13.1
Baseline Gantt Chart

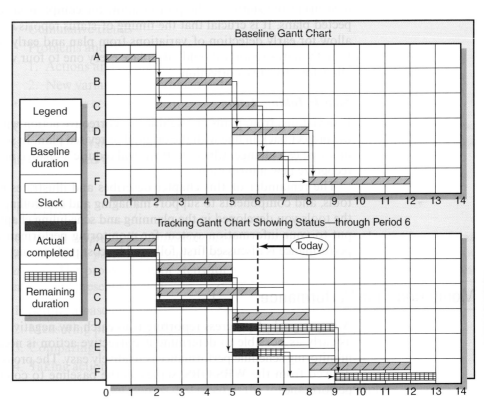

in the status report. Activity D's revised duration results in an expected delay in the start of activity F. The project is now estimated to be completed one period later than planned. Although sometimes the Gantt chart does not show dependencies, when it is used with a network, the dependencies are easily identified if tracing is needed.

Control Chart

This chart is another tool used to monitor past project schedule performance and current performance and to estimate future schedule trends. Figure 13.2 depicts a project control chart. The chart is used to plot the difference between the scheduled time on the critical path at the report date with the actual point on the critical path. Although Figure 13.2 shows the project was behind early in the project, the plot suggests corrective action brought the project back on track. If the trend is sustained, the project will come in ahead of schedule. Because the activity scheduled times represent average durations, four observations trending in one direction indicate there is a very high probability that there is an identifiable cause. The cause should be located and action taken if necessary. Control chart trends are very useful for giving warning of potential problems so appropriate action can be taken if necessary.

Control charts are also frequently used to monitor progress toward milestones, which mark events and as such have zero duration. Milestones are significant project events that mark major accomplishments. To be effective, milestones need to be concrete, specific, measurable events. Milestones must be easily identifiable by all project stakeholders—for example, product testing complete. Critical merge activities are good candidates for milestones. Control charts very similar to the example shown in Figure 13.2 are often used to record and communicate project progress toward a milestone.

Schedule slippage of one day seldom receives a great deal of attention. However, one day here and another there soon add up to large delay problems. It is well

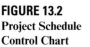

FIGURE 13.2
Project Schedule Control Chart

SNAPSHOT FROM PRACTICE Status Reports at Microsoft*

When Bill Gates was in charge of Microsoft, project teams sent reports each month to top executives, as well as to the managers of all related projects. The status reports were brief and had a standard format. Gates read most of them quickly, and spotted potential delays, or changes he did not want. He especially looked for schedule slips, cutting too many product features, or the need to change a specification. Gates usually responded to the relevant managers or developers directly by electronic mail. Status reports are an important mechanism for communicating between top management and projects. As Gates explained:

"I get all the status reports. Right now there might be a hundred active projects. . . . [The status reports] contain the schedule, including milestones dates, and any change in spec, and any comments about 'Hey, we can't hire enough people,' or 'Jeez, if this OLE (Object Linking and Embedding) 2 Mac release isn't done, we're just going to have to totally slip.' . . . They know [their report] goes up to all the people who manage all

the other groups that they have dependencies with. So if they don't raise it in the status report and then two months later they say something, that's a breakdown in communication. . . . The internal group is totally copied on those things, so it's sort of the consensus of the group."

* From *Microsoft Secrets: The World's Most Powerful Software Company Creates Technology.* Copyright © 1995 by Michael A. Cusumano and Richard W. Selby.

© AP Photo/Keystone, Alessandro della Valle

known that once work gets behind, it has a tendency to stay behind because it is difficult to make up. Examples of causes of schedule slippage are unreliable time estimates, minor redesign, scope creep, and unavailable resources. Using slack early in a path may create a problem for someone responsible for a later activity; flexibility and potential opportunities are reduced. For these reasons, having frequent and clearly defined monitoring points for work packages can significantly improve the chances of catching schedule slippage early. Early detection reduces the chance of small delays growing to large ones and thereby reducing opportunities for corrective action to get back on schedule. See Snapshot from Practice: Status Reports at Microsoft.

Development of an Earned Value Cost/Schedule System

Earned value is not new; although its initial use was in military contracts, in recent years the private sector has come to depend on the system for managing multiple and large projects.

The original earned value cost/schedule system was pioneered by the U.S. Department of Defense (DOD) in the 1960s. It is probably safe to say project managers in every major country are using some form of the system. The system is being used on internal projects in the manufacturing, pharmaceutical, and high-tech industries. For example, organizations such as EDS, NCR, Levi Strauss, Tektronics, and Disney have used earned value systems to track projects. The basic framework of the earned value system is withstanding the test of time. Most project management software includes the original framework; many systems have added industry-specific variations

TABLE 13.1
Glossary of Terms

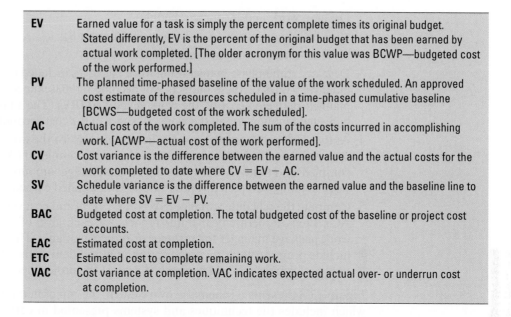

EV	Earned value for a task is simply the percent complete times its original budget. Stated differently, EV is the percent of the original budget that has been earned by actual work completed. [The older acronym for this value was BCWP—budgeted cost of the work performed.]
PV	The planned time-phased baseline of the value of the work scheduled. An approved cost estimate of the resources scheduled in a time-phased cumulative baseline [BCWS—budgeted cost of the work scheduled].
AC	Actual cost of the work completed. The sum of the costs incurred in accomplishing work. [ACWP—actual cost of the work performed].
CV	Cost variance is the difference between the earned value and the actual costs for the work completed to date where CV = EV − AC.
SV	Schedule variance is the difference between the earned value and the baseline line to date where SV = EV − PV.
BAC	Budgeted cost at completion. The total budgeted cost of the baseline or project cost accounts.
EAC	Estimated cost at completion.
ETC	Estimated cost to complete remaining work.
VAC	Cost variance at completion. VAC indicates expected actual over- or underrun cost at completion.

to more precisely track progress and costs. This chapter presents the "generic" core of an integrated cost/schedule information system.

The earned value system starts with the time-phased costs that provide the project budget *baseline,* which is called the planned budgeted value of the work scheduled (PV). Given this time-phased baseline, comparisons are made with actual and planned schedule and costs using earned value. The earned value approach provides the missing links not found in conventional cost-budget systems. At any point in time, a status report can be developed for the project.

The earned value cost/schedule system uses several acronyms and equations for analysis. Table 13.1 presents a glossary of these acronyms. You will need this glossary as a reference. In recent years acronyms have been shortened to be more phonetically friendly. This movement is reflected in material from the Project Management Institute, in project management software, and by most practitioners. This text edition follows the recent trend. The acronyms found in brackets represent the older acronyms, which are often found in software programs. To the uninitiated, the terms used in practice appear horrendous and intimidating. However, once a few basic terms are understood, the intimidation index will evaporate.

Following five careful steps ensures that the cost/schedule system is integrated. These steps are outlined here. Steps 1, 2, and 3 are accomplished in the planning stage. Steps 4 and 5 are sequentially accomplished during the execution stage of the project.

1. Define the work using a WBS. This step involves developing documents that include the following information (see Chapters 4 and 5):
   a. Scope.
   b. Work packages.
   c. Deliverables.
   d. Organization units.
   e. Resources.
   f. Budgets for each work package.

2. Develop work and resource schedule.

   a. Schedule resources to activities (see Chapter 8).

   b. Time-phase work packages into a network.

3. Develop a time-phase budget using work packages included in an activity. The cumulative values of these budgets will become the baseline and will be called the planned budgeted cost of the work scheduled (PV). The sum should equal the budgeted amounts for all the work packages in the cost accounts (see Chapter 8).

4. At the work package level, collect the actual costs for the work performed. These costs will be called the actual cost of the work completed (AC). Collect percent complete and multiply this times the original budget amount for the value of the work actually completed. These values will be called earned value (EV).

5. Compute the schedule variance (SV = EV − PV) and cost variance (CV = EV − AC). Prepare hierarchical status reports for each level of management—from work package manager to customer or project manager. The reports should also include project rollups by organization unit and deliverables. In addition, actual time performance should be checked against the project network schedule.

Figure 13.3 presents a schematic overview of the integrated information system, which includes the techniques and systems presented in earlier chapters. Those who have tenaciously labored through the early chapters can smile! Steps 1 and 2 are already carefully developed. Observe that control data can be traced backward to specific deliverables and organization unit responsible.

The major reasons for creating a baseline are to monitor and report progress and to estimate cash flow. Therefore, it is crucial to integrate the baseline with the performance measurement system. Costs are placed (time-phased) in the baseline exactly as managers expect them to be "earned." This approach facilitates tracking costs to their point of origin. In practice, the integration is accomplished by using the same rules in assigning costs to the baseline as those used to measure progress

FIGURE 13.3
**Project Management
Information System
Overview**

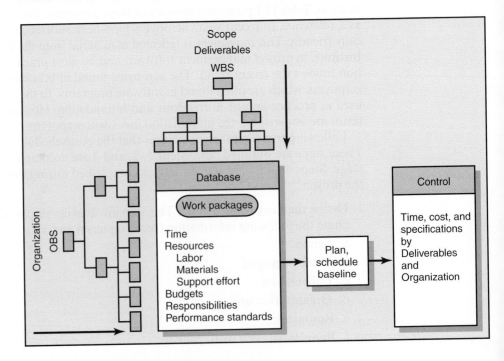

using earned value. You may find several rules in practice, but percent complete is the workhorse most commonly used. Someone familiar with each task estimates what percent of the task has been completed or how much of the task remains.

Percent Complete Rule

This rule is the heart of any earned value system. The best method for assigning costs to the baseline under this rule is to establish frequent checkpoints over the duration of the work package and assign completion percentages in dollar terms. For example, units completed could be used to assign baseline costs and later to measure progress. Units might be lines of code, hours, drawings completed, cubic yards of concrete in place, workdays, prototypes complete, etc. This approach to percent complete adds "objectivity" to the subjective observation approaches often used. When measuring percent complete in the monitoring phase of the project, it is common to limit the amount earned to 80 or 90 percent until the work package is 100 percent complete.

What Costs Are Included in Baselines?

The baseline (PV) is the sum of the cost accounts, and each cost account is the sum of the work packages in the cost account. Three direct costs are typically included in baselines—labor, equipment, and materials. The reason: these are direct costs the project manager can control. Overhead costs and profit are typically added later by accounting processes. Most work packages should be discrete, of short time span, and have measurable outputs. If materials and/or equipment are a significant portion of the cost of work packages, they can be budgeted in separate work packages and cost accounts.

Methods of Variance Analysis

Generally the method for measuring accomplishments centers on two key computations:

1. Comparing earned value with the expected schedule value.
2. Comparing earned value with the actual costs.

These comparisons can be made at the project level or down to the cost account level. Project status can be determined for the latest period, all periods to date, and estimated to the end of the project.

Assessing the current status of a project using the earned value cost/schedule system requires three data elements—planned cost of the work scheduled (PV), budgeted cost of the work completed (EV), and actual cost of the work completed (AC). From these data the schedule variance (SV) and cost variance (CV) are computed each reporting period. *A positive variance indicates a desirable condition, while a negative variance suggests problems or changes that have taken place.*

Cost variance tells us if the work accomplished costs more or less than was planned at any point over the life of the project. If labor and materials have not been separated, cost variance should be reviewed carefully to isolate the cause to either labor or materials—or to both.

Schedule variance presents an overall assessment of *all* work packages in the project scheduled to date. It is important to note schedule variance contains *no* critical path information. Schedule variance measures progress in dollars rather than time units. Therefore, it is unlikely that any translation of dollars to time will yield accurate information telling if any milestone or critical path is early, on time,

FIGURE 13.6 **Work Breakdown Structure with Cost Accounts**

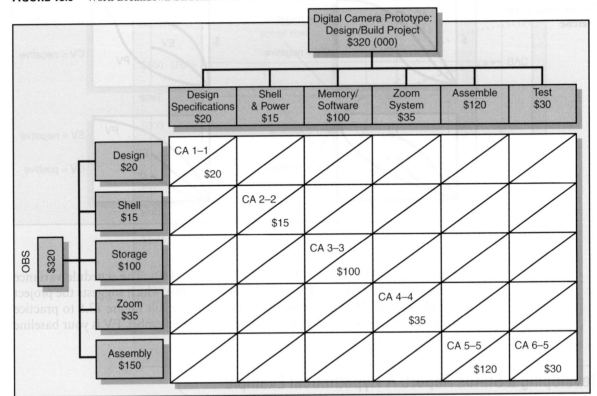

FIGURE 13.7
Digital Camera Prototype Project Baseline Gantt Chart

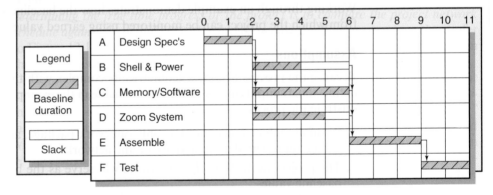

budget baseline. Figure 13.8 **(Project Baseline Budget)** presents a worksheet with an early start baseline developed with costs assigned. They are assigned "exactly" as managers plan to monitor and measure schedule and cost performance.

Development of the Status Report

A status report is analogous to a camera snapshot of a project at a specific point in time. The status report uses earned value to measure schedule and cost performance. Measuring earned value begins at the work package level. Work packages are in one of three conditions on a report date:

1. Not yet started.
2. Finished.
3. In-process or partially complete.

FIGURE 13.8
Digital Camera
Prototype Project
Baseline Budget
($000)

ACT/WP	DUR	ES	LF	SL	Total PV	0	1	2	3	4	5	6	7	8	9	10	11
	Schedule information					Baseline budget needs — Time period											
A	2	0	2	0	20	10	10										
B	2	2	6	2	15			5	10								
C	4	2	6	0	100			20	30	30	20						
D	3	2	6	1	35			15	10	10							
E	3	6	9	0	120							30	40	50			
F	2	9	11	0	30										10	20	
Total PV by period						10	10	40	50	40	20	30	40	50	10	20	
Cumulative PV by period						10	20	60	110	150	170	200	240	290	300	320	

Earned values for the first two conditions present no difficulties. Work packages that are not yet started earn zero percent of the PV (budget). Packages that are completed earn 100 percent of their PV. In-process packages apply the percent complete rule to the PV baseline to measure earned value (EV). In our camera example we will only use the percent complete rule to measure progress.

Table 13.2 presents the completed, separate status reports of the Digital Camera Prototype project for periods 1 through 7. Each period percent complete and actual cost were gathered for each task from staff in the field. The schedule and cost variance are computed for each task and the project to date. For example, the status in period 1 shows only Task A (Design Specifications) is in process and it is 50 percent complete and actual cost for the task is 10. The planned value at the end of period 1 for Task A is 10 (see Figure 13.8). The cost and schedule variance are both zero, which indicates the project is on budget and schedule. By the end of period 3, Task A is finished. Task B (Shell & Power) is 33 percent complete and AC is 10; Task C is 20 percent complete and AC is 30; and D is 60 percent complete and AC is 20. Again, from Figure 13.8 *at the end of period 3,* we can see that the PV for Task A is 20 (10 + 10 = 20), for Task B is 5, for Task C is 20, and for Task D is 15. At the end of period 3 it is becoming clear the actual cost (AC) is exceeding the value of the work completed (EV). The cost variance (see Table 13.2) for the project at the end of period 3 is negative 24. Schedule variance is positive 6, which suggests the project may be ahead of schedule.

It is important to note that since earned values are computed from costs (or sometimes labor hours or other metrics), the relationship of costs to time is not one-for-one. For example, it is possible to have a negative SV variance when the project is actually ahead on the critical path. Therefore, it is important to remember, SV is in dollars and is not an accurate measure of time; however, it is a fairly good indicator of the status of the whole project in terms of being ahead or behind schedule after the project is over 20 percent complete. Only the project network, or Tracking Gantt chart, and actual work completed can give an accurate assessment of schedule performance down to the work package level.

By studying the separate status reports for periods 5 through 7, you can see the project will be over budget and behind schedule. By period 7 Tasks A, B, and D are finished, but all are over budget—negative 10, 5, and 25. Task C (Memory/Software) is 90 percent complete. Task E is late and hasn't started because Task C is not yet completed. The result is that, at the end of period 7, the digital camera project is over budget $70,000, with a schedule budget over $40,000.

TABLE 13.2
Digital Camera
Prototype Status
Reports: Periods 1–7

Cost Variance		CV = EV − AC				
Schedule Variance		SV = EV − PV				

Status Report: Ending Period 1

Task	%Complete	EV	AC	PV	CV	SV
A	50%	10	10	10	0	0
Cumulative Totals		**10**	**10**	**10**	**0**	**0**

Status Report: Ending Period 2

Task	%Complete	EV	AC	PV	CV	SV
A	Finished	20	30	20	−10	0
Cumulative Totals		**20**	**30**	**20**	**−10**	**0**

Status Report: Ending Period 3

Task	%Complete	EV	AC	PV	CV	SV
A	Finished	20	30	20	−10	0
B	33%	5	10	5	−5	0
C	20%	20	30	20	−10	0
D	60%	21	20	15	+1	+6
Cumulative Totals		**66**	**90**	**60**	**−24**	**+6**

Status Report: Ending Period 4

Task	%Complete	EV	AC	PV	CV	SV
A	Finished	20	30	20	−10	0
B	Finished	15	20	15	−5	0
C	50%	50	70	50	−20	0
D	80%	28	30	25	−2	+3
Comulative Totals		**113**	**150**	**110**	**−37**	**+3**

Status Report: Ending Period 5

Task	%Complete	EV	AC	PV	CV	SV
A	Finished	20	30	20	−10	0
B	Finished	15	20	15	−5	0
C	60%	60	100	80	−40	−20
D	80%	28	50	35	−22	−7
Cumulative Totals		**123**	**200**	**150**	**−77**	**−27**

Status Report: Ending Period 6

Task	%Complete	EV	AC	PV	CV	SV
A	Finished	20	30	20	−10	0
B	Finished	15	20	15	−5	0
C	80%	80	110	100	−30	−20
D	Finished	35	60	35	−25	0
Cumulative Totals		**150**	**220**	**170**	**−70**	**−20**

Status Report: Ending Period 7

Task	%Complete	EV	AC	PV	CV	SV
A	Finished	20	30	20	−10	0
B	Finished	15	20	15	−5	0
C	90%	90	120	100	−30	−10
D	Finished	35	60	35	−25	0
E	0%	0	0	30	0	−30
F	0%	0	0	0	0	0
Cumulative Totals		**160**	**230**	**200**	**−70**	**−40**

FIGURE 13.9
Digital Camera
Prototype Summary
Graph ($000)

Figure 13.9 shows the graphed results of all the status reports through period 7. This graph represents the data from Table 13.2. The cumulative actual costs (AC) to date and the earned value budgeted costs to date (EV) are plotted against the original project baseline (PV). The cumulative AC to date is $230; the cumulative EV to date is $160. Given these cumulative values, the cost variance (CV = EV − AC) is negative $70 (160 − 230 = −70). The schedule variance (SV = EV − PV) is negative $40 (160 − 200 = −40). Again, recall that only the project network or Tracking Gantt chart can give an accurate assessment of schedule performance down to the work package level.

A Tracking Gantt bar chart for the Digital Camera Prototype is shown in Figure 13.10. From this figure you can see Task C (Memory/Software), which had an original duration of 4 time units, now is expected to require 6 time units. This delay of 2 time units for Task C will also delay Tasks E and F two time units and result in the project being late 2 time periods.

FIGURE 13.10
Digital Camera
Project-Tracking
Gantt Chart Showing
Status—Through
Period 7

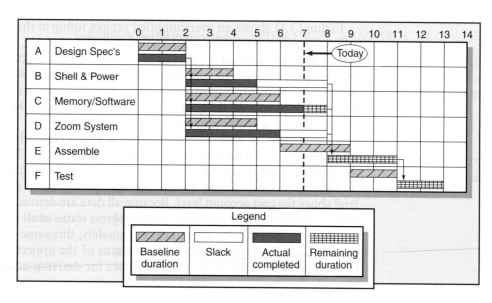

FIGURE 13.12

Indexes Periods 1–7

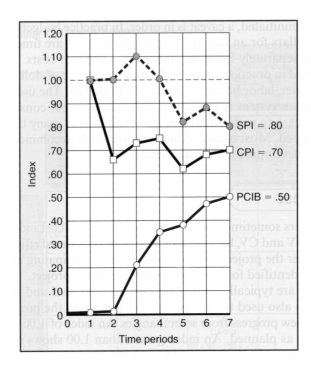

budget of work complete is the most reliable information to measure project percent complete. The second index assumes the actual costs-to-date and expected cost at completion are the most reliable for measuring project percent complete. These indexes compare the to-date progress to the end of the project. The implications underlying use of these indexes are that conditions will not change, no improvement or action will be taken, and the information in the database is accurate. The first index looks at percent complete in terms of *budget* amounts:

$$\text{Percent complete index PCIB} = \text{EV/BAC} = 160/320 = .50 \ (50\%)$$

This PCIB indicates the work accomplished represents 50 percent of the total budgeted (BAC) dollars to date. Observe that this calculation does not include actual costs incurred. Because actual dollars spent do not guarantee project progress, this index is favored by many project managers when there is a high level of confidence in the original budget estimates.

The second index views percent complete in terms of *actual* dollars spent to accomplish the work to date and the actual expected dollars for the completed project (EAC). For example, at the end of period 7 the staff re-estimates that the EAC will be 575 instead of 320. The application of this view is written as

$$\text{Percent complete index PCIC} = \text{AC/EAC} = 230/575 = .40 \ (40\%)$$

Some managers favor this index because it contains actual and revised estimates that include newer, more complete information.

These two views of percent complete present alternative views of the "real" percent complete. These percents may be quite different as shown above. (Note: The PCIC index was not plotted in Figure 13.12. The new figures for EAC would be derived each period by estimators in the field.)

Technical Performance Measurement

Measuring technical performance is as important as measuring schedule and cost performance. Although technical performance is often assumed, the opposite can be true. The ramifications of poor technical performance frequently are more profound—something works or it doesn't if technical specifications are not adhered to.

Assessing technical performance of a system, facility, or product is often accomplished by examining the documents found in the scope statement and/or work package documentation. These documents should specify criteria and tolerance limits against which performance can be measured. For example, the technical performance of a software project suffered because the feature of "drag and drop" was deleted in the final product. Conversely, the prototype of an experimental car exceeded the miles per gallon technical specification and, thus, its technical performance. Frequently tests are conducted on different performance dimensions. These tests become an integral part of the project schedule.

It is very difficult to specify how to measure technical performance because it depends on the nature of the project. Suffice it to say, measuring technical performance must be done. Technical performance is frequently where quality control processes are needed and used. Project managers must be creative in finding ways to control this very important area.

Software for Project Cost/Schedule Systems

Software developers have created sophisticated schedule/cost systems for projects that track and report budget, actual, earned, committed, and index values. These values can be labor hours, materials, and/or dollars. This information supports cost and schedule progress, performance measurements, and cash flow management. Recall from Chapter 5 that budget, actual, and committed dollars usually run in different time frames (see Figure 5.6). A typical computer-generated status report includes the following information outputs:

1. Schedule variance (EV − PV) by cost account and WBS and OBS.
2. Cost variance (EV − AC) by cost account and WBS and OBS.
3. Indexes—total percent complete and performance index.
4. Cumulative actual total cost to date (AC).
5. Expected costs at completion (EAC).
6. Paid and unpaid commitments.

The variety of software packages, with their features and constant updating, is too extensive for inclusion in this text. Software developers and vendors have done a superb job of providing software to meet the information needs of most project managers. Differences among software in the last decade have centered on improving "friendliness" and output that is clear and easy to understand. Anyone who understands the concepts and tools presented in Chapters 4, 5, 6, 8, and 13 should have little trouble understanding the output of any of the popular project management software packages.

Additional Earned Value Rules

Although the percent complete rule is the most-used method of assigning budgets to baselines and for cost control, there are additional rules that are very

The index of 1.78 indicates that each remaining dollar in the budget must earn $1.78 in value. There is more work to be done than there is budget left. Clearly, it would be tough to increase productivity that much to make budget. The work to be done will have to be reduced or you will have to accept running over budget. If the TCPI is less than 1.00, you should be able to complete the project without using all of the remaining budget. A ratio of less than 1.00 opens the possibility of other opportunities such as improving quality, increasing profit, or expanding scope.

Research data indicate that on large projects that are more than 15 percent complete, the model performs well with an error of less than 10 percent. This model can also be used for WBS and OBS cost accounts that have been used to forecast remaining and total costs. It is important to note that this model assumes conditions will not change, the cost database is reliable, EV and AC are cumulative, and past project progress is representative of future progress. This objective forecast represents a good starting point or benchmark that management can use to compare other forecasts that include other conditions and subjective judgments.

Exhibit 13.1 presents an abridged monthly status report similar to one used by a project organization. The form is used for all projects in their project portfolio. (Note that the schedule variance of −$22,176 does not translate directly to days. The 25 days were derived from the network schedule.)

EXHIBIT 13.1
Monthly Status
Report 2010

Project number: 163   **Project manager:** Connor Gage
Project priority now: 4
Status as of: April 1, 2010
Earned value figures:

PV	EV	AC	SV	CV	BAC
588,240	566,064	596,800	−22,176	−30,736	1,051,200
EAC	**VAC**	**EAC$_f$**	**CPI**	**PCIB**	**PCIC**
1,090,640	−39,440	1,107,469	.95	.538	.547

Project description: A computer-controlled conveyor belt that will move and position items on the belt with accuracy of less than one millimeter.
Status summary: The project is approximately 25 days behind schedule. The project has a cost variance of ($30,736).
Explanations: The schedule variance has moved from noncritical activities to those on the critical path. Integration first phase, scheduled to start 3/26, is now expected to start 4/19, which means it is approximately 25 days behind schedule. This delay is traced to the loss of the second design team which made it impossible to start utilities documentation on 2/27 as planned. This loss illustrates the effect of losing valuable resources on the project. The cost variance to date is largely due to a design change that cost $21,000.
Major changes since last report: The major change was loss of one design team to the project.
Total cost of approved design changes: $21,000. Most of this amount is attributed to the improved design of the serial I/O drivers.
Projected cost at completion: EAC$_f$ is estimated to be $1,107,469. This represents an overrun of $56,269, given a CPI of .95. The CPI of .95 causes the forecast to be greater than the VAC −$39,440.
Risk watch: Nothing suggests the risk level of any segments has changed.

Portland General Electric Company has been charged with decommissioning the Trojan Nuclear Plant. This is a long and complex project extending over two decades. The first segment of the project of moving the used reactors to a storage location is complete and was awarded the Project of the Year, 2000, by the Project Management Institute (PMI). The remainder of the project—decontamination of the remaining structures and waste—is ongoing.

The Exhibit 13.2 on page 476 shows their earned value status report through December 2000. This report measures schedule and cost performance for monitoring the project. The report also serves as a basis for funding for rate filings with the Public Utilities Commission.

The SPI (0.94) suggests the project schedule is falling behind. Resolving issues with a major vendor and solutions for technical problems should solve these delay problems. The CPI (1.14) for the project is positive. Some of this good cost

Brendan McDermid/EPA/Landov.

performance is attributed to partnering and incentive arrangements with vendors and labor unions.

Interview with Michael B. Lackey, general manager, Trojan, PGE (September 2001).

Another summary report is shown in the Snapshot from Practice: Trojan Decommissioning Project. Compare the differences in format.

Other Control Issues

Scope Creep

Large changes in scope are easily identified. It is the "minor refinements" that eventually build to be major scope changes that can cause problems. These small refinements are known in the field as **scope creep.** For example, the customer of a software developer requested small changes in the development of a custom accounting software package. After several minor refinements, it became apparent the changes represented a significant enlargement of the original project scope. The result was an unhappy customer and a development firm that lost money and reputation.

Although scope changes are usually viewed negatively, there are situations when scope changes result in positive rewards. Scope changes can represent significant opportunities. In product development environments, adding a small feature to a product can result in a huge competitive advantage. A small change in the production process may get the product to market one month early or reduce product cost.

Scope creep is common early in projects—especially in new-product development projects. Customer requirements for additional features, new technology, poor design assumptions, etc., all manifest pressures for scope changes. Frequently these changes are small and go unnoticed until time delays or cost overruns are observed. Scope creep affects the organization, project team, and project suppliers. Scope changes alter the organization's cash flow requirements in the form of

FIGURE 13.13

**Scope Changes
to a Baseline**

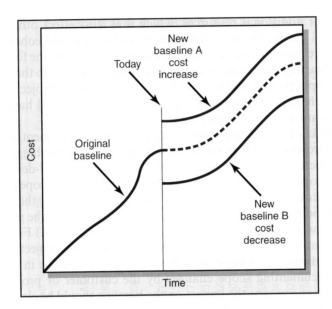

should be accepted and signed off by the project customer. Figure 13.13 depicts the cost impact of a scope change on the baseline at a point in time—"today." Line A represents a scope change that results in an increase in cost. Line B represents a scope change that decreases cost. Quickly recording scope changes to the baseline keeps the computed earned values valid. Failure to do so results in misleading cost and schedule variances.

Care should be taken to not use baseline changes to disguise poor performance on past or current work. A common signal of this type of baseline change is a constantly revised baseline that seems to match results. Practitioners call this a "rubber baseline" because it stretches to match results. Most changes will not result in serious scope changes and should be absorbed as positive or negative variances. Retroactive changes for work already accomplished should not be allowed. Transfer of money among cost accounts should not be allowed after the work is complete. Unforeseen changes can be handled through the contingency reserve. The project manager typically makes this decision. In some large projects, a partnering "change review team," made up of members of the project and customer teams, makes all decisions on project changes.

The Costs and Problems of Data Acquisition

Data acquisition is time consuming and costly. The Snapshot from Practice: A Pseudo-Earned Value Percent Complete Approach captures some of the frequent issues surrounding resistance to data collection of percent complete for earned value systems. Similar pseudo-percent complete systems have been used by others. Such pseudo-percent complete approaches appear to work well in multiproject environments that include several small and medium-sized projects. Assuming a one-week reporting period, care needs to be taken to develop work packages with a duration of about one week long so problems are identified quickly. For large projects, there is no substitute for using a percent complete system that depends on data collected through observation at clearly defined monitoring points.

In some cases data exist but are not sent to the stakeholders who need information relating to project progress. Clearly, if the information does not reach the right people in a timely manner, you can expect serious problems. Your communication

SNAPSHOT FROM PRACTICE

A Pseudo-Earned Value Percent Complete Approach

A consultant for the U.S. Forest Service suggested the use of earned value to monitor the 50-plus timber sale projects taking place concurrently in the district. As projects were completed, new ones were started. Earned value was tried for approximately nine months. After a nine-month trial, the process was to be reviewed by a task force. The task force concluded the earned value system provided good information for monitoring and forecasting project progress; however, the costs and problems of collecting timely percent complete data were unacceptable because there were no funds available to collect such data.

The level of detail dilemma was discussed, but no suggestions satisfied the problem. The discussion recognized that too little data fail to offer good control, while excessive reporting requires paperwork and people, which are costly. The task force concluded progress and performance could be measured using a pseudo-version of percent complete while

not giving up much accuracy for the total project. This modified approach to percent complete required that very large work packages (about 3 to 5 percent of all work packages in a project) be divided into smaller work packages for closer control and identification of problems sooner. It was decided work packages of about a week's duration would be ideal. The pseudo-version required only a telephone call and "yes/no" answers to one of the following questions to assign percent complete:

Has work on the work package started?	No = 0%
Working on the package?	Yes = 50%
Is the work package completed?	Yes = 100%

Data for the pseudo-earned value percent complete system was collected for all 50-plus projects by an intern working fewer than eight hours each week.

plan developed in the project planning stage can greatly mitigate this problem by mapping out the flow of information and keeping stakeholders informed on all aspects of project progress and issues. See Figure 13.14 for an internal communication plan for a WiFi Project. The information developed in this chapter contributes significant data to support your communication plan and ensures correct dissemination of the data.

FIGURE 13.14
Conference Center WiFi Project Communication Plan

What Information	When?	Mode?	Responsible?	Recipient?
Milestone report	Bimonthly	E-mail	Project office	Senior management
Time/cost report	Weekly	E-mail	Project office	Staff and customer
Risk report	Weekly	E-mail	Project office	Staff and customer
Issues	Weekly	E-mail	Anyone	Staff and customer
Team meeting times	Weekly	Meeting	Project manager	Staff and customer
Outsourcing performance	Bimonthly	Meeting	Project manager	Project office, staff, and customer
Change requests	Anytime	Document	Project manager, customer, design	Project office, staff, and customer
Stage gate decisions	Monthly	Meeting	Project office	Senior management

Summary

The best information system does not result in good control. Control requires the project manager to *use* information to steer the project through rough waters. Control and Gantt charts are useful vehicles for monitoring time performance. The cost/schedule system allows the manager to have a positive influence on cost and schedule in a timely manner. The ability to influence cost decreases with time; therefore, timely reports identifying adverse cost trends can greatly assist the project manager in getting back on budget and schedule. The integrated cost/schedule model provides the project manager and other stakeholders with a snapshot of the current and future status of the project. The benefits of the cost/schedule model are as follows:

1. Measures accomplishments against plan and deliverables.
2. Provides a method for tracking directly to a problem work package and organization unit responsible.
3. Alerts all stakeholders to early identification of problems, and allows for quick, proactive corrective action.
4. Improves communication because all stakeholders are using the same database.
5. Keeps customer informed of progress, and encourages customer confidence that the money spent is resulting in the expected progress.
6. Provides for accountability over individual portions of the overall budget for each organizational unit.

With your information system in place, you need to use your communication plan to keep stakeholders informed so timely decisions can be made to ensure the project is managed effectively.

Key Terms

Baseline budget, *464*
Budget at completion (BAC), *459*
Control chart, *457*
Cost performance index (CPI), *469*
Cost variance (CV), *459*
Earned value (EV), *455*
Estimated cost at completion—Forecasted (EAC$_f$), *473*

Estimated cost at completion—Revised estimates (EAC$_{re}$), *472*
Percent complete index—budget costs (PCIB), *470*
Percent complete index—actual costs (PCIC), *470*
Schedule performance index (SPI), *469*

Schedule variance (SV), *459*
Scope creep, *475*
To complete performace index (TCPI), *473*
Tracking Gantt chart, *456*
Variance at completion (VAC), *459*

Review Questions

1. How does a Tracking Gantt chart help communicate project progress?
2. How does earned value give a clearer picture of project schedule and cost status than a simple plan versus actual system?
3. Schedule variance (SV) is in dollars and does not directly represent time. Why is it still useful?
4. How would a project manager use the CPI?
5. What are the differences between BAC and EAC?
6. Why is it important for project managers to resist changes to the project baseline? Under what conditions would a project manager make changes to a baseline? When would a project manager not allow changes to a baseline?

Exercises

1. In month 9 the following project information is available: actual cost is $2,000, earned value is $2,100, and planned cost is $2,400. Compute the SV and CV for the project.
2. On day 51 a project has an earned value of $600, an actual cost of $650, and a planned cost of $560. Compute the SV, CV, and CPI for the project. What is your assessment of the project on day 51?

3. Given the project network and baseline information below, complete the form to develop a status report for the project at the end of period 4 and the end of period 8. From the data you have collected and computed for periods 4 and 8, what information are you prepared to tell the customer about the status of the project at the end of period 8?

Task	DUR	ES	LF	SL	Budget (PV)	0	1	2	3	4	5	6	7	8	9	10	11	12	13	14	15
A	2	0	2	0	400	200	200														
B	6	2	8	0	2400			200	600	200	600	200	600								
C	5	2	9	2	1500			200	400	500	100	300									
D	4	8	12	0	1600									400	400	400	400				
E	3	7	12	2	900								300	400	200						
F	3	12	15	0	600													200	100	300	
Period PV total						200	200	400	1000	700	700	500	900	800	600	400	400	200	100	300	
Cumulative PV total						200	400	800	1800	2500	3200	3700	4600	5400	6000	6400	6800	7000	7100	7400	

Project baseline (PV) (in $)

End of Period 4

Task	Actual % Complete	EV	AC	PV	CV	SV
A	Finished	——	300	400	——	——
B	50%	——	1000	800	——	——
C	33%	——	500	600	——	——
D	0%	——	0	——	——	——
E	0%	——	——	——	——	——
Cumulative Totals		——	——	——	——	——

5. Given the following project network, baseline, and status information, develop status reports for periods 1–4 and complete the project summary graph (or a similar one). Report the final SV, CV, CPI, and PCIB. Based on your data, what is your assessment of the current status of the project? At completion?

	Schedule information					Baseline budget needs ($ 000)						
ACT/ WP	DUR	ES	LF	SL	Total PV	Time period						
						0	1	2	3	4	5	6
1	2	0	3	1	12	4	8					
2	3	0	3	0	15	3	7	5				
3	2	0	2	0	8	4	4					
4	2	2	5	1	6			3	3			
5	2	3	5	0	10				6	4		
6	3	2	5	0	9			3	3	3		
7	1	5	6	0	5							5
Total PV by period						11	19	11	12	7	5	
Cumulative PV by period						11	30	41	53	60	65	

Status Report: Ending Period 1   **($000)**

Task	%Complete	EV	AC	PV	CV	SV
1	50%	——	6	4	——	——
2	40%	——	8	3	——	——
3	25%	——	3	——	——	——
Cumulative Totals		——	**17**	——	——	——

Status Report: Ending Period 2   **($000)**

Task	%Complete	EV	AC	PV	CV	SV
1	Finished	——	13	——	——	——
2	80%	——	14	——	——	——
3	75%	——	8	——	——	——
Cumulative Totals		——	**35**	——	——	——

Status Report: Ending Period 3   **($000)**

Task	%Complete	EV	AC	PV	CV	SV
1	Finished	12	13	——	——	——
2	80%	——	15	——	——	——
3	Finished	——	10	——	——	——
4	50%	——	4	——	——	——
5	0%	——	0	——	——	——
6	33.3%	——	4	——	——	——
Cumulative Totals		——	——	——	——	——

Status Report: Ending Period 4   **($000)**

Task	%Complete	EV	AC	PV	CV	SV
1	Finished	12	13	——	——	——
2	Finished	15	18	——	——	——
3	Finished	——	10	——	——	——
4	Finished	——	8	——	——	——
5	30%	——	3	——	——	——
6	66.7%	——	8	——	——	——
7	0%	——	0	——	——	——
Cumulative Totals		——	——	——	——	——

Summary Graph

6. The following labor hours data have been collected for a nanotechnology project for periods 1 through 6. Compute the SV, CV, SPI, and CPI for each period. Plot the EV and the AC on the summary graph provided (or a similar one). Plot the SPI, CPI, and PCIB on the index graph provided (or a similar one). What is your assessment of the project at the end of period 6?

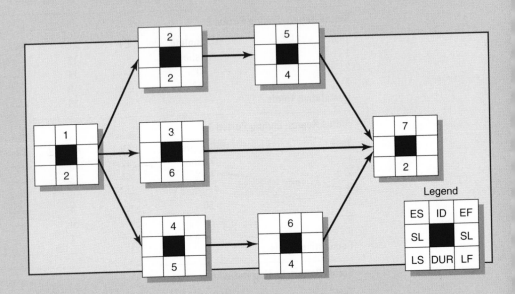

Schedule information						Baseline budget needs–labor hours (00)														
						Time period														
ACT/WP	DUR	ES	LF	SL	Total PV	0	1	2	3	4	5	6	7	8	9	10	11	12	13	14
1	2	0	2	0	20	10	10													
2	2	2	7	3	24			16	8											
3	6	2	11	3	30			5	5	10	3	2	5							
4	5	2	7	0	25			10	10	2	2	1								
5	4	4	11	3	16					4	4	4	4							
6	4	7	11	0	20								5	5	6	4				
7	2	11	13	0	10													5	5	
				Total PV by period		10	10	31	23	16	9	7	14	5	6	4	5	5		
				Cumulative PV by period		10	20	51	74	90	99	106	120	125	131	135	140	145		

Status Report: Ending Period 1

Task	%Complete	EV	AC	PV	CV	SV
1	50%	——	500	1000	——	——
Cumulative Totals		——	**500**	**1000**	——	——

Status Report: Ending Period 2

Task	%Complete	EV	AC	PV	CV	SV
1	Finished	——	1500	2000	——	——
Cumulative Totals		——	**1500**	**2000**	——	——

Status Report: Ending Period 3

Task	%Complete	EV	AC	PV	CV	SV
1	Finished	2000	1500	2000	——	——
2	0%	——	0	——	——	——
3	10%	——	200	——	——	——
4	20%	——	500	——	——	——
Cumulative Totals		——	**2200**	——	——	——

Status Report: Ending Period 4

Task	%Complete	EV	AC	PV	CV	SV
1	Finished	2000	1500	2000	——	——
2	50%	——	1000	——	——	——
3	30%	——	800	——	——	——
4	40%	——	1500	——	——	——
Cumulative Totals		——	**4800**	——	——	——

Status Report: Ending Period 5

Task	%Complete	EV	AC	PV	CV	SV
1	Finished	2000	1500	2000	——	——
2	Finished	——	2000	——	——	——
3	50%	——	800	——	——	——
4	60%	——	1500	——	——	——
5	25%	——	400	——	——	——
Cumulative Totals		——	**6200**	——	——	——

Status Report: Ending Period 6

Task	%Complete	EV	AC	PV	CV	SV
1	Finished	2000	1500	2000	——	——
2	Finished	——	2000	——	——	——
3	80%	——	2100	——	——	——
4	80%	——	1800	——	——	——
5	50%	——	600	——	——	——
Cumulative Totals		——	**8000**	——	——	——

Period	SPI	CPI	PCIB
1	——	——	——
2	——	——	——
3	——	——	——
4	——	——	——
5	——	——	——
6	——	——	——

$SPI = EV/PV$
$CPI = EV/AC$
$PCIB = EV/BAC$

Summary Graph

Indexes Periods 1–6

7. The following data have been collected for a British health care IT project for two-week reporting periods 2 through 12. Compute the SV, CV, SPI, and CPI for each period. Plot the EV and the AC on the summary graph provided. Plot the SPI, CPI, and PCIB on the index graph provided. (You may use your own graphs.) What is your assessment of the project at the end of period 12?

		Baseline (PV) ($00)														
Task	DUR	ES	LF	SL	PV ($00)	0	2	4	6	8	10	12	14	16	18	20	22
1	4	0	4	0	8	4	4										
2	8	4	14	2	40			10	10	10	10						
3	6	4	10	0	30			10	15	5							
4	4	4	10	2	20			10	10								
5	4	10	14	0	40							20	20				
6	8	8	18	2	60						20	20	10	10			
7	4	14	18	0	20									10	10		
8	4	18	22	0	30											20	10
Period PV total						4	4	30	35	35	50	30	20	10	20	10
Cumulative PV total						4	8	38	73	108	158	188	208	218	238	248

Status Report: Ending Period 2 ($00)

Task	%Complete	EV	AC	PV	CV	SV
1	50%	—	4	—	—	—
Cumulative Totals		—	4	—	—	—

Status Report: Ending Period 4 ($00)

Task	%Complete	EV	AC	PV	CV	SV
1	Finished	——	10	——	——	——
Cumulative Totals		——	**10**	——	——	——

Status Report: Ending Period 6 ($00)

Task	%Complete	EV	AC	PV	CV	SV
1	Finished	——	10	——	——	——
2	25%	——	15	——	——	——
3	33%	——	12	——	——	——
4	0%	——	0	——	——	——
Cumulative Totals		——	**37**	——	——	——

Status Report: Ending Period 8 ($00)

Task	%Complete	EV	AC	PV	CV	SV
1	Finished	——	10	——	——	——
2	30%	——	20	——	——	——
3	60%	——	25	——	——	——
4	0%	——	0	——	——	——
Cumulative Totals		——	**55**	——	——	——

Status Report: Ending Period 10 ($00)

Task	%Complete	EV	AC	PV	CV	SV
1	Finished	——	10	——	——	——
2	60%	——	30	——	——	——
3	Finished	——	40	——	——	——
4	50%	——	20	——	——	——
5	0%	——	0	——	——	——
6	30%	——	24	——	——	——
Cumulative Totals		——	**124**	——	——	——

Status Report: Ending Period 12 ($00)

Task	%Complete	EV	AC	PV	CV	SV
1	Finished	——	10	——	——	——
2	Finished	——	50	——	——	——
3	Finished	——	40	——	——	——
4	Finished	——	40	——	——	——
5	50%	——	30	——	——	——
6	50%	——	40	——	——	——
Cumulative Totals		——	**210**	——	——	——

Period	SPI	CPI	PCIB
2	——	——	——
4	——	——	——
6	——	——	——
8	——	——	——
10	——	——	——
12	——	——	——

$SPI = EV/PV$
$CPI = EV/AC$
$PCIB = EV/BAC$

8.*Part A. You are in charge of the Aurora Project. Given the following project network, baseline, and status information, develop status reports for periods 1–8 and complete the performance indexes table. Calculate the EAC_f and VAC_f. Based on your data, what is the current status of the project? At completion?

* The solution to this exercise can be found in Appendix 1.

ID	Budget ($000)	1	2	3	4	5	6	7	8	9	10	11	12	13
A	100	50	50											
B	250			100	50	100								
C	450			150	150	150								
D	200						100	100						
E	300								200	100				
F	300								100	50	150			
G	200										150	50		
H	200												100	100
Total	2000	50	50	250	200	250	100	100	300	150	300	50	100	100
Cumulative		50	100	350	550	800	900	1000	1300	1450	1750	1800	1900	2000

Status Report: Ending Period 1 ($000)

Task	% Complete	EV	AC	PV	CV	SV
A	25%	——	50	——	——	——
Cumulative Totals		——	**50**	——	——	——

Status Report: Ending Period 2 ($000)

Task	% Complete	EV	AC	PV	CV	SV
A	50%	——	100	——	——	——
Cumulative Totals		——	——	——	——	——

Status Report: Ending Period 3 ($000)

Task	% Complete	EV	AC	PV	CV	SV
A	100%	——	200	——	——	——
B	0%	——	0	——	——	——
C	0%	——	0	——	——	——
Cumulative Totals		——	——	——	——	——

Status Report: Ending Period 4 ($000)

Task	% Complete	EV	AC	PV	CV	SV
A	100%	——	200	——	——	——
B	60%	——	100	——	——	——
C	50%	——	200	——	——	——
Cumulative Totals		——	**500**	——	——	——

Status Report: Ending Period 5 ($000)

Task	% Complete	EV	AC	PV	CV	SV
A	100%	——	200	——	——	——
B	100%	——	200	——	——	——
C	100%	——	400	——	——	——
Cumulative Totals		——	**800**	——	——	——

Status Report: Ending Period 6 ($000)

Task	% Complete	EV	AC	PV	CV	SV
A	100%	——	200	——	——	——
B	100%	——	200	——	——	——
C	100%	——	400	——	——	——
D	75%	——	100	——	——	——
Cumulative Totals		——	**900**	——	——	——

Status Report: Ending Period 7 ($000)

Task	% Complete	EV	AC	PV	CV	SV
A	100%	——	200	——	——	——
B	100%	——	200	——	——	——
C	100%	——	400	——	——	——
D	100%	——	150	——	——	——
E	20%	——	100	——	——	——
F	5%	——	50	——	——	——
Cumulative Totals		——	**1100**	——	——	——

Status Report: Ending Period 8 ($000)

Task	% Complete	EV	AC	PV	CV	SV
A	100%	——	200	——	——	——
B	100%	——	200	——	——	——
C	100%	——	400	——	——	——
D	100%	——	150	——	——	——
E	100%	——	350	——	——	——
F	10%	——	100	——	——	——
Cumulative Totals		——	**1400**	——	——	——

Performance Indexes Summary

Period	EV	AC	PV	SPI	CPI	PCI-B
1	——	——	——	——	——	——
2	——	——	——	——	——	——
3	——	——	——	——	——	——
4	——	——	——	——	——	——
5	——	——	——	——	——	——
6	——	——	——	——	——	——
7	——	——	——	——	——	——
8	——	——	——	——	——	——

$EAC_f =$ _____ $VAC_f =$ _____

Part B. You have met with your Aurora project team and they have provided you with the following revised estimates for the remainder of the project:

- Activity F will be completed at the end of period 12 at a total cost of 500.
- Activity G will be completed at the end of period 10 at a total cost of 150.
- Activity H will be completed at the end of period 14 at a total cost of 200.

Calculate the EAC_{re} and VAC_{re}. Based on the revised estimates, what is the expected status of the project in terms of cost and schedule? Between the VAC_f and the VAC_{re}, which one would you have the greatest confidence in?

$EAC_{re} =$ _____ $VAC_{re} =$ _____

References

Abramovici, A., "Controlling Scope Creep," *PM Network,* Vol. 14, No. 1, January 2000, pp. 44–48.

Anbari, F. T., "Earned Value Project Management Method and Extensions," *Project Management Journal,* Vol. 34, No. 4, December 2003, pp. 12–22.

Brandon, D. M. Jr., "Implementing Earned Value Easily and Effectively," *Project Management Journal,* Vol. 29, No. 3, June 1998, pp. 11–17.

Fleming, Q., and Joel M. Koppelman, *Earned Value Project Management,* 3rd ed. Newton Square, PA: (Project Management Institute, 2006).

Kerzner, H., "Strategic Planning for a Project Office," *Project Management Journal,* Vol. 34, No. 2, June 2003, pp. 13–25.

Webb, A., *Using Earned Value: A Project Manager's Guide,* (Aldershot, UK: Gower Publishing Co., 2003).

Case

Scanner Project

You have been serving as Electroscan's project manager and are now well along in the project. Develop a narrative status report for the board of directors of the chain store that discusses the status of the project to date and at completion. Be as specific as you can using numbers given and those you might develop. Remember, your audience is not familiar with the jargon used by project managers and computer software personnel; therefore, some explanation may be necessary. Your report will be evaluated on your detailed use of the data, your total perspective of the current status and future status of the project, and your recommended changes (if any).

Electroscan, Inc. 555 Acorn Street, Suite 5 Boston, Massachusetts				29 In-store Scanner Project (thousands of dollars) Actual Progress as of January 1				
Name	PV	EV	AC	SV	CV	BAC	EAC$_f$	
Scanner project	420	395	476	−25	−81	915	1103	
H 1.0 Hardware	92	88	72	−4	16	260	213	
H 1.1 Hardware specifications (DS)	20	20	15	0	5	20	15	
H 1.2 Hardware design (DS)	30	30	25	0	5	30	25	
H 1.3 Hardware documentation (DOC)	10	6	5	−4	1	10	8	
H 1.4 Prototypes (PD)	2	2	2	0	0	40	40	
H 1.5 Test prototypes (T)	0	0	0	0	0	30	30	
H 1.6 Order circuit boards (PD)	30	30	25	0	5	30	25	
H 1.7 Preproduction models (PD)	0	0	0	0	0	100	100	
OP 1.0 Operating system	195	150	196	−45	−46	330	431	
OP 1.1 Kernel specifications (DS)	20	20	15	0	5	20	15	
OP 1.2 Drivers	45	55	76	10	−21	70	97	
OP 1.2.1 Disk drivers (DEV)	25	30	45	5	−15	40	60	
OP 1.2.2 I/O drivers (DEV)	20	25	31	5	−6	30	37	
OP 1.3 Code software	130	75	105	−55	−30	240	336	
OP 1.3.1 Code software (C)	30	20	40	−10	−20	100	200	
OP 1.3.2 Document software (DOC)	45	30	25	−15	5	50	42	
OP 1.3.3 Code interfaces (C)	55	25	40	−30	−15	60	96	
OP 1.3.4 Beta test software (T)	0	0	0	0	0	30	30	
U 1.0 Utilities	87	108	148	21	−40	200	274	
U 1.1 Utilities specifications (DS)	20	20	15	0	5	20	15	
U 1.2 Routine utilities (DEV)	20	20	35	0	−15	20	35	
U 1.3 Complex utilities (DEV)	30	60	90	30	−30	100	150	
U 1.4 Utilities documentation (DOC)	17	8	8	−9	0	20	20	
U 1.5 Beta test utilities (T)	0	0	0	0	0	40	40	
S 1.0 System integration	46	49	60	3	−11	125	153	
S 1.1 Architecture decisions (DS)	9	9	7	0	2	10	8	
S 1.2 Integration hard/soft (DEV)	25	30	45	5	−15	50	75	
S 1.3 System hard/software test (T)	0	0	0	0	0	20	20	
S 1.4 Project documentation (DOC)	12	10	8	−2	2	15	12	
S 1.5 Integration acceptance testing (T)	0	0	0	0	0	30	30	

Appendix 13.1

The Application of Additional Earned Value Rules

The following example and exercises are designed to provide practice in applying the following three earned value rules:

- Percent complete rule
- 0/100 rule
- 50/50 rule

See the chapter for an explanation of each of these rules.

SIMPLIFYING ASSUMPTIONS

The same simplifying assumptions used for the chapter example and exercises will also be used here.

1. Assume each cost account has only one work package, and each cost account will be represented as an activity on the network.

2. The project network early start times will serve as the basis for assigning the baseline values.

3. Except when the 0/100 rule or 50/50 rule is used, baseline values will be assigned linearly, unless stated differently. (Note: In practice estimated costs should be applied "exactly" as they are expected to occur so measures of schedule and cost performance are useful and reliable.)

4. For purposes of demonstrating the examples, from the moment work on an activity begins, some actual costs will be incurred each period until the activity is completed.

5. When the 0/100 rule is used, the total cost for the activity is placed in the baseline on the early finish date.

6. When the 50/50 rule is used, 50 percent of the total cost is placed in the baseline on the early start date and 50 percent on the early finish date.

APPENDIX EXERCISES

1. Given the information provided for development of a product warranty project for periods 1 through 7, compute the SV, CV, SPI, and CPI for each period. Plot the EV and the AC on the PV graph provided. Explain to the owner your assessment of the project at the end of period 7 and the future expected status of the project at completion. Figure A13.1A presents the project network. Figure A13.1B presents the project baseline noting those activities using the 0/100 (rule 3) and 50/50 (rule 2) rules. For example, activity 1 uses rule 3, the 0/100 rule. Although the early start time is period 0, the budget is not placed in the time-phased baseline until period 2 when the activity is planned to be finished (EF). This same procedure has been used to assign costs for activities 2 and 7. Activities 2 and 7 use the 50/50 rule. Thus, 50 percent of the budget for each activity is assigned on its respective early start date (time period 2 for activity 2 and period 11 for activity 7) and 50 percent for their respective finish dates. Remember, when assigning earned value as the project is being implemented, if an activity actually starts early or late, the earned values must shift with the actual times. For example, if activity 7 actually starts in period 12 rather than 11, the 50 percent is not earned until period 12.

FIGURE A13.1A

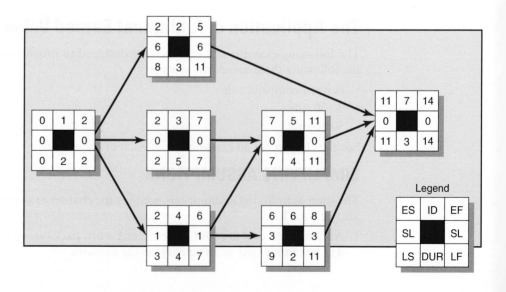

FIGURE A13.1B

EV Rule	ACT/WP	DUR	ES	LF	SL	Total PV	0	1	2	3	4	5	6	7	8	9	10	11	12	13	14
3	1	2	0	2	0	6		6														
2	2	3	2	11	6	20			10		10											
1	3	5	2	7	0	30			9	6	6	6	3									
1	4	4	2	7	1	20			8	2	5	5										
1	5	4	7	11	0	16									4	4	4	4				
1	6	2	6	11	3	18								9	9							
2	7	3	11	14	0	8													4		4
					Total PV by period		0	6	27	8	21	11	12	13	4	4	4	4	0		4
					Cumulative PV by period		0	6	33	41	62	73	85	98	102	106	110	114	114		118

Schedule information | Baseline budget needs / Time period

Rule
1 = %complete
2 = 50/50
3 = 0/100

Status Report: Ending Period 1

Task	%Complete	EV	AC	PV	CV	SV
1	0%	—	3	0	—	—
Cumulative Totals		—	**3**	**0**	—	—

Status Report: Ending Period 2

Task	%Complete	EV	AC	PV	CV	SV
1	Finished	6	5	—	—	—
Cumulative Totals		**6**	**5**	—	—	—

Status Report: Ending Period 3

Task	%Complete	EV	AC	PV	CV	SV
1	Finished	6	5	—	—	—
2	0%	—	5	—	—	—
3	30%	—	7	—	—	—
4	25%	—	5	—	—	—
Cumulative Totals		—	**22**	—	—	—

Status Report: Ending Period 4

Task	%Complete	EV	AC	PV	CV	SV
1	Finished	6	5	—	—	—
2	0%	—	7	—	—	—
3	50%	—	10	—	—	—
4	50%	—	8	—	—	—
Cumulative Totals		—	**30**	—	—	—

Status Report: Ending Period 5

Task	%Complete	EV	AC	PV	CV	SV
1	Finished	6	5	—	—	—
2	50%	—	8	—	—	—
3	60%	—	12	—	—	—
4	70%	—	10	—	—	—
Cumulative Totals		—	**35**	—	—	—

Status Report: Ending Period 6

Task	%Complete	EV	AC	PV	CV	SV
1	Finished	6	5	——	——	——
2	50%	——	10	——	——	——
3	80%	——	16	——	——	——
4	Finished	——	15	——	——	——
Cumulative Totals		——	**46**	——	——	——

Status Report: Ending Period 7

Task	%Complete	EV	AC	PV	CV	SV
1	Finished	6	5	——	——	——
2	Finished	——	14	——	——	——
3	Finished	——	20	——	——	——
4	Finished	——	15	——	——	——
5	0%	——	0	——	——	——
6	50%	——	9	——	——	——
Cumulative Totals		——	**63**	——	——	——

Period	SPI	CPI	PCIB
1	——	——	——
2	——	——	——
3	——	——	——
4	——	——	——
5	——	——	——
6	——	——	——
7	——	——	——

$$SPI = EV/PV$$
$$CPI = EV/AC$$
$$PCIB = EV/BAC$$

FIGURE A13.1C

FIGURE A13.1D

CPI =

SPI =

PCIB =

2. Given the information provided for development of a catalog product return process for periods 1 through 5, assign the PV values (using the rules) to develop a baseline for the project. Compute the SV, CV, SPI, and CPI for each period. Explain to the owner your assessment of the project at the end of period 5 and the future expected status of the project at the completion.

FIGURE A13.2A

FIGURE A13.2B

Status Report: Ending Period 1

Task	%Complete	EV	AC	PV	CV	SV
1	40%	——	8	——	——	——
2	0%	——	12	——	——	——
3	30%	——	10	——	——	——
Cumulative Totals		——	**30**	——	——	——

Status Report: Ending Period 2

Task	%Complete	EV	AC	PV	CV	SV
1	80%	——	20	——	——	——
2	Finished	——	18	——	——	——
3	50%	——	12	——	——	——
Cumulative Totals		——	**50**	——	——	——

Status Report: Ending Period 3

Task	%Complete	EV	AC	PV	CV	SV
1	Finished	——	27	——	——	——
2	Finished	——	18	——	——	——
3	70%	——	15	——	——	——
4	0%	——	5	——	——	——
5	30%	——	8	——	——	——
Cumulative Totals		——	**73**	——	——	——

Status Report: Ending Period 4

Task	%Complete	EV	AC	PV	CV	SV
1	Finished	——	27	——	——	——
2	Finished	——	18	——	——	——
3	Finished	——	22	——	——	——
4	0%	——	7	——	——	——
5	60%	——	22	——	——	——
Cumulative Totals		——	**96**	——	——	——

Status Report: Ending Period 5

Task	%Complete	EV	AC	PV	CV	SV
1	Finished	——	27	——	——	——
2	Finished	——	18	——	——	——
3	Finished	——	22	——	——	——
4	Finished	——	8	——	——	——
5	70%	——	24	——	——	——
6	30%	——	10	——	——	——
Cumulative Totals		——	**109**	——	——	——

FIGURE A13.2C

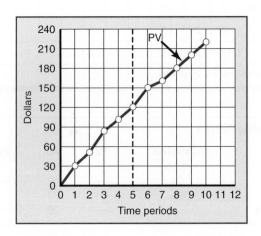

Period	SPI	CPI	PCIB	
1	——	——	——	
2	——	——	——	SPI = EV/PV
3	——	——	——	CPI = EV/AC
4	——	——	——	PCIB = EV/BAC
5	——	——	——	

Appendix 13.2

Obtaining Project Performance Information from MS Project

The objective of this appendix is to illustrate how one can obtain the performance information discussed in Chapter 13 from MS Project 2007. One of the great strengths of MS Project is its flexibility. The software provides numerous options for entering, calculating, and presenting project information. Flexibility is also the software's greatest weakness in that there are so many options that working with the software can be frustrating and confusing. The intent here is to keep it simple and present basic steps for obtaining performance information. Students with more ambitious agendas are advised to work with the software tutorial or consult one of many instructional books on the market.

For purposes of this exercise we will use the Digital Camera project, which was introduced in Chapter 13. In this scenario the project started as planned on March 1 and today's date is March 7. We have received the following information on the work completed to date:

Design Spec.s took 2 days to complete at a total cost of $20.

Shell & Power took 3 days to complete at a total cost of $25.

Memory/Software is in progress with 4 days completed and two days remaining. Cost to date is $100.

Zoom System took 2 days to complete at a cost of $25.

All tasks started on time.

STEP 1 ENTERING PROGRESS INFORMATION

We enter this progress information in the TRACKING TABLE from the GANTT CHART VIEW ▶ TABLE ▶ TRACKING:

TABLE A13.2A Tracking Table

ID	Task Name	Act. Start	Act. Finish	% Comp.	Act. Dur.	Rem. Dur.	Act. Cost	Act. Work
1	**Digital Camera Prototype**	3/1	NA	61%	6.72 days	4.28 days	$170.00	272 hrs
2	Design Spec.s	3/1	3/2	100%	2 days	0 days	$20.00	32 hrs
3	Shell & Power	3/3	3/7	100%	3 days	0 days	$25.00	40 hrs
4	Memory/Software	3/3	NA	67%	4 days	2 days	$100.00	160 hrs
5	Zoom System	3/3	3/4	100%	2 days	0 days	$25.00	40 hrs
6	Assemble	NA	NA	0%	0 days	3 days	$0.00	0 hrs
7	Test	NA	NA	0%	0 days	2 days	$0.00	0 hrs

Project Closure

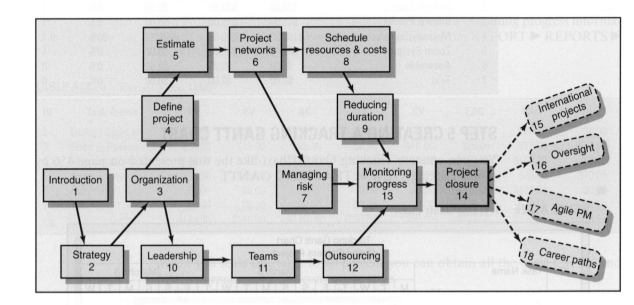

Those who cannot remember the past are condemned to relive it.

—George Santayana, 1863–1952

Every project comes to an end eventually. But how many project participants get excited about closing out a project? The deliverables are complete. Ownership is ready to be transferred. Everyone's focus is what's next—hopefully a new, exciting project. Carefully managing the closure phase is as important as any other phase of the project. Observation tells us that organizations that manage closure and review well prosper. Those who don't tend to have projects that drag on forever and repeat the same mistakes over and over.

Closing out a project includes a daunting number of tasks. In the past and on small projects the project manager was responsible for seeing all tasks and loose ends were completed and signed off. This is no longer true. In today's project-driven organizations that have many projects occurring simultaneously, the responsibility for completing closure tasks has been parsed among the project manager, project teams, project office, an oversight "review committee," and an independent retrospective facilitator. Many tasks overlap, occur simultaneously, and require coordination and cooperation among these stakeholders.

The three major deliverables for **project closure** are described below (see Figure 14.1):

1. *Wrapping up the project.* The major wrap-up task is to ensure the project is approved and accepted by the customer. Other wrap-up activities include closing accounts, paying bills, reassigning equipment and personnel, finding new opportunities for project staff, closing facilities, and the final report. Checklists are used extensively to ensure tasks are not overlooked. In many organizations, the lion's share of closure tasks are largely done by the project office in coordination with the project manager. The final report writing is usually assigned to one project office staff member, who assembles input from all

FIGURE 14.1
Project Closure and Review Deliverables

stakeholders. In smaller organizations and projects, these closure activities are left to the project manager and team.

2. *Evaluation of performance and management of the project.* Evaluation includes team, individual team members, and project manager performance. Vendors and the customer may provide external input. Evaluation of the major players provides important information for the future.

3. *Retrospectives.* Retrospectives of lessons learned are designed to improve performance on current and future projects. Today, most retrospectives are the responsibility of an independent facilitator. The facilitator also provides major input to the closure report that will include lessons learned. These post-project reviews should be held with the team to catch any missing issues or gaps.

This chapter begins with the recognition that projects are shut down for many reasons. Not all projects end with a clear "Finished" and are turned over to a customer. Regardless of the conditions for ending a project, the general process of closure is similar, though the endings may differ significantly. Wrap-up closure tasks are noted first. These tasks represent all the tasks that must be "cleaned up" before the project is terminated. Evaluation of project performance is next. Finally, lessons learned or retrospective methods are examined in detail.

Types of Project Closure

On some projects the end may not be as clear as would be hoped. Although the scope statement may define a clear ending for a project, the actual ending may or may not correspond. Fortunately, a majority of projects are blessed with a well-defined ending. Regular project reviews will identify projects having endings different from plans. The different types of closure are identified here:

Normal The most common circumstance for project closure is simply a completed project. For many development projects, the end involves handing off the final design to production and the creation of a new product or service line. For other internal IT projects, such as system upgrades or creation of new inventory control systems, the end occurs when the output is incorporated into ongoing operations. Some modifications in scope, cost, and schedule probably occurred during implementation.

Premature For a few projects, the project may be completed early with some parts of the project eliminated. For example, in a new product development project, a marketing manager may insist on production models before testing:

> Give the new product to me now, the way it is. Early entry into the market will mean big profits! I know we can sell a bazzillion of these. If we don't do it now, the opportunity is lost!

The pressure is on to finish the project and send it to production. Before succumbing to this form of pressure, the implications and risks associated with this decision should be carefully reviewed and assessed by senior management and all stakeholders. Too frequently, the benefits are illusory, dangerous, and carry large risks.

Perpetual Some projects never seem to end. The major characteristic of this kind of project is constant "add-ons," suggesting a poorly conceived project scope. At some point the review group should recommend methods for bringing final closure to this type of project or the initiation of another project. For example, adding a new feature to an old project could replace a segment of a project that appears to be perpetual.

SNAPSHOT FROM PRACTICE   Project Canceled*

Germany is the major crossroad for Europe's international commercial trucks. The German government felt the need to have international trucks (over 12 tons) using their road infrastructure assist in paying for the road maintenance and additional new infrastructure. The project objectives were clear—a new electronic truck toll-collection system that ensures accurate charges and easy fee collection across German, Swiss, and Austrian highways by August 31, 2003. The technology relied on global positioning systems (GPS), telecommunications, and software to record miles and charges, without using toll booths along the highways.

Several problems sabotaged the project. Time-to-market deadlines were impossible to meet. Delayed launch dates were caused by technical problems with truck tracking units and software that failed to function as expected. Interface communication with public and private stakeholders failed. As a result,

the August 2003 deadline was never met. The revised November 2003 deadline was not met. Finally, in March 2004 the German government pulled the plug and canceled the project.

The cancellation of the project had serious impacts on other governmental programs. The shortfall of not receiving the revenue from the new toll system is estimated at $1.6 billion. Some of those revenues were destined for a high-speed maglev train in Munich and other infrastructure projects.

Lessons learned reveal that lack of project management knowledge was evident. More importantly, failure to identify and assess the impact of schedule and complex technology risks resulted in the death of the project. Perhaps a simpler, cheaper microwave system recommended by the Swiss and Austrians to be operational by 2005 would have sufficed. See http://www.toll-collect.de/frontend/HomepageVP.do: Jsessionid-F840E12142D.

* "Case Analysis: Taking a Toll," *PM Network,* Vol. 18, No. 3, March, 2004, p. 1.

Failed Project   Failed projects are usually easy to identify and easy for a review group to close down. However, every effort should be made to communicate the technical (or other) reasons for termination of the project; in any event project participants should not be left with an embarrassing stigma of working on a project that failed. Many projects will fail because of circumstances beyond the control of the project team. See Snapshot from Practice: Project Canceled.

Changed Priority   Organizations' priorities often change and strategy shifts directions. For example, during the 2008–10 financial crisis organizations shifted their focus from money-making projects to cost savings projects. The oversight group continually revises project selection priorities to reflect changes in organizational direction. Projects in process may need to be altered or canceled. Thus, a project may start with a high priority but see its rank erode or crash during its project life cycle as conditions change. When priorities change, projects in process may need to be altered or canceled.

Different types of project termination present unique issues. Some adjustments to generic closure processes may be necessary to accommodate the type of project termination you face.

Wrap-up Closure Activities

The major challenges for the project manager and team members are over. Getting the project manager and project participants to wrap up the odds and ends necessary to fully complete a project is often difficult. It's like the party is over—now who wants to help clean up? Much of work is mundane and tedious. Motivation can be the chief challenge. For example, accounting for equipment and completing final reports are perceived as dull administrative tasks by project professionals who are action-oriented individuals. The project manager's challenge is to keep the project team focused on the remaining project activities and delivery to the customer until the project is complete. Communicating a closure and review plan and schedule early allows the project team to (1) accept the psychological fact the project will end and (2) prepare to move on. The ideal scenario is to have the team member's next assignment ready when project completion is announced. Project managers need to be careful to maintain their enthusiasm for completing the project and hold people accountable to deadlines, which are prone to slip during the waning stages of the project.

Implementing the closure process includes several wrap-up activities. Many organizations develop lengthy lists for closing projects as they gain experience. These are very helpful and ensure nothing is overlooked. Implementing closedown includes the following six major activities:

1. Getting delivery acceptance from the customer.
2. Shutting down resources and releasing to new uses.
3. Reassigning project team members.
4. Closing accounts and seeing all bills are paid.
5. Delivering the project to the customer.
6. Creating a final report.

Administering the details of closing out a project can be intimidating. Some organizations have checklists of over 100 wrap-up tasks! These checklists deal with closure details such as facilities, teams, staff, customer, vendors, and the project itself. A partial administrative closure checklist is shown below in Table 14.1.

Getting delivery acceptance by the customer is a major and critical closure activity. Delivery of some projects to the customer is straight forward. Others are

TABLE 14.1
Wrap-up Closure Checklist

	Task	Completed? Yes/No
	Team	
1	Has a schedule for reducing project staff been developed and accepted?	
2	Has staff been released or notified of new assignments?	
3	Have performance reviews for team members been conducted?	
4	Has staff been offered outplacement services and career counseling activities?	
	Vendors/contractors	
5	Have performance reviews for all vendors been conducted?	
6	Have project accounts been finalized and all billing closed?	
	Customer/Users	
7	Has the customer signed-off on the delivered product?	
8	Has an in-depth project review and evaluation interview with the customer been conducted?	
9	Have the users been interviewed to assess their satisfaction with the deliverables? With the project team? With vendors? With training? With support? With maintenance?	
	Equipment and facilities	
10	Have project resources been transferred to other projects?	
11	Have rental or lease equipment agreements been closed out?	
12	Has the date for the closure review been set and stakeholders notified?	
	Attach comments or links on any tasks you feel need explanation.	

SNAPSHOT FROM PRACTICE   New Ball Goes Flat in the NBA*

On October 31, 2006, the National Basketball Association (NBA) opened its 57th season with new official game balls. The new ball, manufactured by Spalding, featured a new design and a new material that together was believed to offer better grip, feel, and consistency than the previous leather ball. The material is microfiber composite with moisture management that provides superior grip and feel throughout the course of a game. Additionally, the new composite material eliminates the need for a break-in period, which is necessary for the current leather ball, and achieves consistency from ball to ball.

The NBA and Spalding subjected the ball to a rigorous evaluation process that included laboratory and on-court testing process. Every NBA team received the new ball and had the opportunity to use it in practice. The ball was also tested in the NBA summer development league.

At the press conference announcing the shift from leather to microfiber balls, NBA commissioner David Stern pronounced "The advancement that Spalding has made to the new game ball ensures that the best basketball players in the world will be playing with the best basketball in the world."

Animal rights advocates applauded the shift from leather to microfiber. Such was not the case for the players who would actually use the new ball. Grumblings emerged immediately when training camps opened in October. Washington Wizards guard Gilbert Arenas said the new basketball gets slippery when it comes in contact even with small amounts of sweat. Then Miami Heat center Shaquille O'Neil said "it feels like one of those cheap balls that you buy at a toy store."

Some players, including league MVP Steve Nash, began complaining that the new ball was producing small cuts on their hands, "It's awful, (the friction burns) its like an irritant . . . sometimes I even have to tape my fingers in practice." Perhaps LeBron James from the Cleveland Cavaliers best summed up the players attitudes toward the NBA's introduction of the new ball when he said "You can change the dress code, you can make our shorts shorter, but when you take our basketball away from us, that not a transition we handle."

On December 1, 2006, four weeks into the season the NBA players union filed an unfair labor practice suit because the league management switched to the new ball without consulting the players. Ten days later, the NBA announced that they would revert back to the old leather ball beginning January 1st 2007. In a terse statement, Commissioner David Stern said "Our player's response to this particular composite ball has been overwhelmingly negative and we are acting accordingly."

The failure to check with the players (the end-users) and get buy-in for the new basketball was loudly criticized by the press. "How they could actually even get it that far and not have run it by the players is just an amazing, amazing exercise in ineptitude." Rob Frankel, a Los Angeles–based branding expert told Bloomberg News.

* "NBA Introduces New Game Ball", www.nba.com/news, posted 6-28-2006; Howard Bloom, "The NBA- uneventful 2006 II," *Sports Business News*, www.sportsbixnews.blogspot.com. 12-30-2006.

more complex and difficult. Ideally there should be no surprises. This requires a well-defined scope and an effective change management system with active customer involvement. User involvement is critical to acceptance (See Snapshot from Practice: New Ball Goes Flat in the NBA).

The conditions for completing and transferring the project should be set before the project begins. A completed software program is a good example of the need to work out the details in advance. If the user has problems using the software, will the customer withhold final payments? Who is responsible for supporting and training the user? If these conditions are not clearly defined up front, getting delivery acceptance can be troublesome.

Another delivery tactic (briefly mentioned in Chapter 7) for a project that has been outsourced is known as build, own, operate, and transfer (BOOT). In this type of project the contractor builds, owns, and operates the project deliverable for a set period of time. For example, Haliburton will operate a hydroelectric plant for six months before turning over operations to their Indian counterparts. During this time all the bugs are worked out and conditions for delivery are satisfied. Again, note the delivery conditions need to be carefully set up before the project begins; if not, wrap-up activities can develop a life of their own.

Releasing the project team typically occurs gradually during the closure phase. For some people, termination of their responsible activities ends before the project is delivered to the customer or user. Reassignment for these participants needs to take place well before the final finish date. For the remaining team members (full or part time), termination may result in a new project or returning to their functional job. Sometimes, on product development efforts, team members will be assigned to operations positions and play an activity role in the production of the new product. For contract people it may mean the end of their assignment to this project; in some cases there may be follow-up work or user support possiblities. A small number of part-time participants may be recommended to the user organization to train or operate new equipment or systems.

Since many work invoices are not submitted until after the project is officially over, closing out contracts is often messy and filled with untied ends. For example, it is improbable all invoices have been finalized, billed, and paid. Further, when contractors are used, there is a need to verify that all the contracted work has been done. Keeping contract records, such as progress reports, invoices, change records, and payment records, is important should a compliance or lawsuit occur. Too often in the haste to meet deadlines, paperwork and record keeping gets short changed, only to create major headaches when it comes time for final documentation.

There are many more wrap-up activities; it is important to complete all of them. Experience has proved time and again that not doing all the little cleanup tasks well will create problems later. Two other examples of closure checklists are shown in this chapter: Appendix 14.1 presents an example used by the state of Virgina and Appendix 14.2 presents an abridged closure checklist for the Euro Conversion project. The final wrap-up activity of closure that provides a clear signal that the project is truly over is submission of the final project report.

Creating the Final Report

The final project report summarizes project performance and provides useful information for continuous improvement. Although the final report will be customized to your project and organization, the content of the final report typically includes the following topics: executive summary, review and analysis, recommendations, lessons learned, and appendix.

Executive Summary   This summary simply highlights the key findings and facts relating to the project implementation. For example, the project goals for the customer were met, or not. Are stakeholders satisfied that their strategic intents have been met? What has been user reaction to quality of the deliverables? Are the project deliverables being used as intended and providing the expected benefits? Final time, cost, and scope performances are listed. Any major problems encountered and addressed are noted. Key lessons learned are identified.

Review and Analysis   Data are collected to record the project history, management performance, and lessons learned to improve future projects. Analysis examines in detail the underlying causes of problems, issues, and successes. The analysis section includes succinct, factual review statements of the project—for example, project mission and objectives, procedures and systems used, and organizational resources used. It is common to collect data from the organizational view and from the team view. The project office or closure facilitators often use questionnaires and surveys to pick up on issues and events that need to be examined further. For example, "Was the organizational culture supportive and correct for this type of project? Why? Why not?" Or, "Did the team have adequate access to organizational resources—people, budget, support groups, equipment?" The project office also provides project schedules, cost comparisons, scope data, and other needed data to tell the story of performance. This information is used to create a final project report.

Recommendations   Usually, review recommendations represent major improvement actions that should take place. They are often technical in nature and focus on solutions to problems that surfaced. For example, to avoid rework, the report for a construction project recommended shifting to more resilient building material. In other cases, they may include terminating or sustaining vendor or contractor relationships.

Lessons Learned   Perhaps lessons learned are the most valuable contribution of the closure process. Given the process evaluation and input from the stakeholder meetings, lessons learned should be succinctly and clearly set out. Stress the need to help others in future projects. In practice, new project teams studying past project reports similar to the project they are about to start have found past review reports very useful. Team members will frequently remark later, "The recommendations were good, but the 'lessons learned' section really helped us avoid many pitfalls and made our project implementation smoother." It is for precisely this reason that lessons learned in the form of project retrospectives have taken on greater prominence in the field and warrant an extended discussion at the end of this chapter. See Snapshot from Practice: Lessons Learned from Katrina.

Appendix   The appendix may include backup data or details of analysis that would allow others to follow up if they wished. It should not be a dumping ground used for filler; only critical pertinent information should be attached.

Post-Implementation Evaluation

The purpose of **project evaluation** is to assess how well the project team, team members, and project manager performed.

Team Evaluation

Evaluation of performance is essential to encourage changes in behavior and to support individual career development and continuous improvement through organizational learning. Evaluation implies measurement against specific criteria. Experience corroborates that before commencement of a project, the stage must be set so expectations, standards, supportive organizational culture, and constraints are in place; if not, the effectiveness of the evaluation process will suffer.

In a macro sense, the evidence today suggests that performance evaluation is not done well. See Research Highlight: Measures of Team Performance. The major reasons cited by practitioners are twofold:

1. Evaluations of individuals are still left to supervisors of the team member's home department.
2. Typical measures of team performance center on time, cost, and specifications.

SNAPSHOT FROM PRACTICE   Lessons Learned from Katrina*

On August 25, 2005, winds of 145 miles per hours and rains covered 80 percent of New Orleans with some areas under 20 feet of water. Hurricane Katrina dispersed havoc on every corner of New Orleans. In its trail it left over 1,300 people dead in Louisiana and Mississippi. Katrina will long be remembered as the costliest and most deadly hurricane ever recorded in the United States.

Response came from many different groups from within the country and from other countries. Katrina also drew the largest response of The National Guard to a national emergency in history. Governors from every state sent National Guard troops to support and assist the state of Mississippi. By September 8, 51,000 troops were responding to the emergency. Many other nonprofit groups offered help in a variety of ways—food, shelter, financial, health care, and transportation. Groups that contributed support have reviewed their efforts to see what lessons learned can be used to improve future emergency efforts. The results of the review of The National Guard efforts follow here:

Three of the key lessons from The National Guard retrospective are described.

- *Lack of equipment was one of the biggest problems—especially communication equipment. Ability to communicate among the many different support groups (e.g., civilian and military) was thwarted by incompatible systems or simple lack of availablity.*

    Action Item: $1.3 billion has been authorized for new equipment that is compatible across major emergency groups.

- *Lack of protocols and standardization of reports, graphics, and communication caused delays and poor coordination among the many support groups.*

Action Item: A single standard protocol for all states is now being applied.

- *The National Guard is under state control. Guard troops integrated quickly into the host-state command structures and cooperation ensued.*

    Action Item: Maintain status quo

Because Guard soldiers are controlled by the states, they were empowered to enforce civil laws, something federal troops are prohibited from doing, except under the provisions of the insurrection laws. Fortunately, coordination and cooperation among state and federal troop command work reasonably well. However, the federal agencies (e.g., Homeland Security) need to incorporate the Guard into planning and preparation for the federal response to catastrophic disasters.

Lessons learned from the Katrina disaster are not limited to the military. Almost every agency and support group, such as individuals, communities, churches, and other groups, have developed lessons learned from their project response experience. For example, the Red Cross and state guard have better plans for handling thousands of people problems involving shelter, evacuation, and medical assistance. These lessons learned from Katrina are ready to go and should be enormously helpful in future hurricane situations.

* Les A. Melnyk, "Katrina Lessons Learned," *Soldiers Magazine,* June 20, 2006 and "Lessons Learned from Katrina: Preparing Your Institution for a Catastrophic Event." Federal Deposit Insurance Corporation is the source of this information. 1/20/08

Most organizations do not go beyond these measures, although they are important and critical. Organizations should consider evaluating the team-building process, effectiveness of group decision and problem-solving processes, group cohesion, trust among team members, and quality of information exchanged. Measurement of customer and user satisfaction with project deliverables (i.e., the project results) is often missed completely. Yet, project success depends significantly on satisfying these two very important groups. The quality of the deliverables is the responsibility of the team.

Before an evaluation of the project team can be effective and useful, a minimum core of conditions needs to be in place before the project begins (see Chapter 11). Some typical conditions are listed here in the form of questions:

1. Do standards for measuring performance exist? (You can't manage what you can't measure.) Are the goals clear for the team and individuals? Challenging? Attainable? Lead to positive consequences?

2. Are individual and team responsibilities and performance standards known by all team members?

If team evaluation is not done well in practice, how bad is it? Joseph Fusco surveyed 1,667 project managers representing 134 different projects. Fifty-two percent of the respondents indicated their team received no collective evaluation of their team performance. Of the 22 percent who indicated their team was evaluated, further probing found their evaluation was informal, lasting little more than 20 minutes. This apparent lack of team evaluation practices may be sending the wrong signal. Individual team members can slough off poor team performance by relying on the old saying, "I did my job." Strong team evaluation practices need to emphasize team members are "in this together," while minimizing individual performance. Nearly every company in Fusco's survey lacked an effective project management reward system.

* Joseph Fusco, "Better Policies Provide the Key to Implementing Project Management," *Project Management Journal,* Vol. 28, No. 3, September 1997, p. 38.

3. Are team rewards adequate? Do they send a clear signal that senior management believes that the synergy of teams is important?

4. Is a clear career path for successful project managers in place?

5. Is the team empowered to manage short-term difficulties?

6. Is there a relatively high level of trust emanating from the organizational culture?

7. Team evaluation should go beyond time, cost, and specifications. Are there criteria beyond the constraint criteria? Creation of project deliverables would be a good place to start. The "characteristics of highly effective teams" from Chapter 11 can easily be adapted as measurements of team performance.

The "in-place conditions" will support any evaluation approach for teams and their members.

In practice, the actual team evaluation process takes many forms—especially when evaluation goes beyond time, budget, and specifications. The typical mechanism for evaluation of teams is a survey administered by a consultant, a staff member from the human resources department, or through computer e-mail. The survey is normally restricted to team members, but in some cases, other project stakeholders interacting with the team may be included in the survey. An example of a partial survey is found in Table 14.2. After the results are tabulated, the team meets with the facilitator and/or senior management, and the results are reviewed.

This session is comparable to the team-building sessions described in Chapter 11, except that the focus is on using the survey results to assess the development of the team, its strengths and weaknesses, and the lessons that can be applied to future

TABLE 14.2
Sample Team Evaluation and Feedback Survey

Using the scale below, assess each statement.	Disagree				Agree
1. The team shared a sense of common purpose, and each member was willing to work toward achieving project objectives.	1	2	3	4	5
2. Respect was shown for other points of view. Differences of opinion were encouraged and freely expressed.	1	2	3	4	5
3. All interaction among team members occurred in a comfortable, supportive atmosphere.	1	2	3	4	5

SNAPSHOT FROM PRACTICE The 360-Degree Feedback*

More and more companies are discarding the traditional superior-subordinate performance feedback process and replacing it with 360-degree feedback systems. The 360-degree feedback approach gathers behavioral observations from many sources within the organization and includes employee self-assessment. The individual completes the same structured evaluation process that superiors, project team members, peers and, in many cases, external customers use to evaluate a performance. Survey questionnaires, augmented by a few open-ended questions, are typically used to gather information.

Summary results are compared against organizational strategies, values, and business objectives. The feedback is communicated to the individual with the assistance of the company's human resource department or an outside consultant. The technique is used by a growing number of firms including General Electric, AT&T, Mobil Oil, Nabisco, Hewlett-Packard, and Warner-Lambert.

The objective of the 360-degree process is to identify areas for individual improvement. When anonymous feedback solicited from others is compared with the individual's self-evaluations, the individual may form a more realistic picture of her strengths and weaknesses. This may prompt behavioral change if the weaknesses identified were previously unknown to the individual. Such appears to be the case for Jerry Wallace,

an up-and-coming manager at General Motors. "The strongest message I got was that I need to delegate more," he says, "I thought I'd been doing it. But I need to do it more and sooner. My people are saying, 'Turn me loose.'"

Many firms obtain feedback from internal and external project customers. For example, a client may evaluate a project manager or member of the project team according to, "How effectively does the individual get things done without creating unnecessary adversarial relationships?" Incorporating customer feedback in the evaluation process underscores collaboration and the importance of client expectations in determining project success.

William J. Miller, a program director at Du Pont, helped install a 360-degree feedback system for 80 scientists and support people. "A high or low score didn't predict a scientist's ability to invent Teflon," says Miller. "But what feedback did was really improve the ability of people to work in teams. Their regard for others and behaviors that were damaging and self-centered are what changed."

* Brian O'Reilly, "360 Feedback Can Change Your Life," *Fortune*, October, 17, 1994, pp. 93–100; Robert Hoffman, "Ten Reasons You Should Be Using 360 Degree Feedback," *HR Magazine*, April 1995, pp. 82–85; Dick Cochran, "Finally, a Way to Completely Measure Project Manager Performance," *PM Network*, September 2000, pp. 75–80.

project work. The results of team evaluation surveys are helpful in changing behavior to better support team communication, the team approach, and continuous improvement of team performance.

Individual, Team Member, and Project Manager Performance Reviews

Organizations vary in the extent to which their project managers are actively involved in the appraisal process of team members. In organizations where projects are managed within a functional organization, the team member's area manager, not the project manager, is responsible for assessing performance. The area manager may solicit the project manager's opinion of the individual's performance on a specific project; this will be factored into the individual's overall performance. In a balanced matrix, the project manager and the area manager jointly evaluate an individual's performance. In project matrix and project organizations in which the lion's share of the individual's work is project related, the project manager is responsible for appraising individual performance. One process that appears to be gaining wider acceptance is the multirater appraisal or "360-degree feedback," which involves soliciting feedback concerning team members' performance from all the people their work affects. This would include not only project and area managers, but also peers, subordinates, and even customers. See Snapshot from Practice: The 360-Degree Feedback.

Performance appraisals generally fulfill two important functions. The first is developmental in nature: the focus is on identifying individual strengths and weaknesses and developing action plans for improving performance. The second is evaluative and involves assessing how well the person has performed in order to determine salary or merit adjustments. These two functions are not compatible. Employees, in their eagerness to find out how much pay they will receive, tend to tune out constructive feedback on how they can improve their performance. Likewise, managers tend to be more concerned with justifying their decision than engaging in a meaningful discussion on how the employee can improve his or her performance. It is difficult to be both a coach and a judge. As a result, several experts on performance appraisal systems recommend that organizations separate performance reviews, which focus on individual improvement, and pay reviews, which allocate the distribution of rewards.

In some matrix organizations, project managers conduct the performance reviews, while area managers are responsible for pay reviews. In other cases, performance reviews are part of the project closure process, and pay reviews are the primary objective of the annual performance appraisal. Other organizations avoid this dilemma by allocating only group rewards for project work and providing annual awards for individual performance. The remaining discussion is directed at reviews designed to improve performance because pay reviews are often outside the jurisdiction of the project manager.

Individual Reviews

Organizations employ a wide range of methods to review individual performance on a project. In general, review methods of individual performance center on the technical and social skills brought to the project and team. Some organizations rely simply on an informal discussion between the project manager and the project member. Other organizations require project managers to submit written evaluations that describe and assess an individual's performance on a project. Many organizations use rating scales similar to the team evaluation survey in which the project manager rates the individual according to a certain scale (i.e., from 1 to 5) on a number of relevant performance dimensions (i.e., teamwork, customer relations). Some organizations augment these rating schemes with behaviorally anchored descriptions of what constitutes a 1 rating, a 2 rating, and so forth. Each method has its strengths and weaknesses, and, unfortunately, in many organizations the appraisal systems were designed to support mainstream operations and not unique project work. The bottom line is that project managers have to use as best they can the performance review system mandated by their organization.

Regardless of the method, the project manager needs to sit down with each team member and discuss his or her performance. Here are some general tips for conducting performance reviews:

- Always begin the process by asking the individual to evaluate his or her contributions to the project. First, this approach may yield valuable information that you were not aware of. Second, the approach may provide an early warning for situations in which there is disparity in assessments. Finally, this method reduces the judgmental nature of the discussion.
- Avoid, when possible, drawing comparisons with other team members; rather, assess the individual in terms of established standards and expectations. Comparisons tend to undermine cohesion and divert attention away from what the individual needs to do to improve performance.
- When you have to be critical, focus the criticism on specific examples of behavior rather than on the individual personally. Describe in specific terms how the behavior affected the project.

- Be consistent and fair in your treatment of all team members. Nothing breeds resentment more than if, through the grapevine, individuals feel they are being held to a different standard than are other project members.
- Treat the review as only one point in an ongoing process. Use it to reach an agreement as to how the individual can improve his or her performance.

Both managers and subordinates may dread a formal performance review. Neither side feels comfortable with the evaluative nature of the discussion and the potential for misunderstanding and hurt feelings. Much of this anxiety can be alleviated if the project manager is doing her job well. Project managers should be constantly giving team members feedback throughout the project so that individual team members can have a pretty good idea how well they have performed and how the manager feels before the formal meeting. Post-project angst can be avoided if pre-project expectations are discussed before the project and regularly reenforced during project performance.

While in many cases the same process that is applied to reviewing the performance of team members is applied to evaluating the project manager, many organizations augment this process, given the importance of the position to their organization. This is where conducting the **360-degree review** is becoming more popular. In project-driven organizations, the project office typically will be responsible for collecting information on a specific project manager from customers, vendors, team members, peers, and other managers. This approach has tremendous promise for developing more effective project managers.

In addition to performance reviews, data are collected for project retrospectives, which can present situations that may influence performance. In these situations performance evaluations should recognize and note the unusual situation.

Retrospectives

Why Retrospectives?

Lessons learned represent *an analysis carried out during and shortly after the project life cycle; they attempt to capture positive and negative project learning.* That is, "what worked and what didn't?" Lessons learned (postmortems, post-project review, or whatever name you choose to use) have long been part of project management. Peter Senge's *The Fifth Discipline: The Art and Practice of the Learning Organization* drew attention to institutionalizing organizational learning.

Although the past processes have been useful for closure and lessons learned, sadly their real value has not been exploited. Large, multinational companies with projects spread across the globe have been disappointed in their failure to effectively mine lessons learned. Smaller organizations observed, they too were not reaping the golden rewards of lessons learned. The same mistakes continue year after year. In the words of one executive: "Lessons learned are worth their weight in gold. I do not understand why we don't do a better job nurturing, dispersing, and implementing lessons learned." The processes for capturing lessons learned continue to evolve, but there are still many barriers to effectively mining the lessons learned that have been identified by practitioners. A few of the most ubiquitous barriers are noted here.

- The most common reason given for not creating lessons learned is lack of time.
- Most lessons learned are captured when the project is complete; teams get little direction or support after the lessons are reported.

- Lessons learned often degenerate into blame sessions that became emotionally damaging.
- Lessons learned are not being used across different locations.
- Lessons learned while implementing the project are seldom used to improve the remaining work in the project.
- Too often the lessons learned are not used in future projects because the organizational culture fails to recognize the value of learning.

What is needed to overcome these barriers is a methodology and management philosophy to ensure lessons learned are identified, utilized, and become a significant part of the project management organizational culture. The keys are to turn lessons learned into actions taken and to have someone own the lesson. One effort that appears to address the barriers and offer a solution is **retrospectives.** The military has long used retrospectives to improve their operations (e.g., after each maneuver). Retrospectives have emerged as a strong process and management philosophy used by project-driven organizations around the world to mine the gold that lessons learned can provide. Retrospectives are championed by Norman Kerth in his text *Project Retrospectives. A retrospective is a methodology that analyzes a past project event to determine what worked and what didn't, develops lessons learned, and creates an action plan that ensures lessons learned are used to improve management of future projects.* The major goals of retrospectives are to reuse solutions and stop repetitive mistakes across the organization.

Retrospectives methodology has several embedded, distinguishing characteristics to ensure its effectiveness and value:

- Uses an independent facilitator.
- Includes a minimum of three in-process learning gates during the project life cycle.
- Has an owner.
- Develops a repository that is easy to use.
- Mandates a discipline that ensures retrospectives are used.

Initiating the Retrospective Review

The review process depends primarily on organization size and project size. Every effort should be made to make the project review a normal process rather than a surprise notice. In small organizations and projects where face-to-face contact at all levels is prevalent, the closure may be informal and only represent another staff meeting. But even in these environments the content of a formal project review should be examined and covered with notes made of the lessons learned. In some organizations, review initiation comes from a formal project review group or can be automatic. For example, in the latter case, all projects are reviewed at specific stages in the project life cycle—perhaps when a project is 10 to 20 percent complete in time or money, 50 percent complete, and after completion. In most other multiproject organizations, reviews (called stage gates) are planned for the completion of major milestones. The review is not linked to percent complete. Milestones are binary; either you have reached requirements completion or you have not. Regardless of how reviews are set up, they should be set up in the project planning stage—before the project begins.

Use of an Independent Facilitator

The retrospective methodology uses an independent **facilitator** to collect and implement lessons learned to improve management of current and future projects. *A* **project facilitator** *is a guide who leads the project team through an analysis of project activities that went well, what needs improvement, and development of a follow-up action plan with goals and accountability.*

Selection of a Facilitator

Characteristics of a Facilitator

Any project review starts with staffing. That is, who will facilitate the review and be accountable for conducting it? Perhaps nothing influences the success of project review more than the selection of the closure facilitator. Selection of the facilitator should not be a random selection from the project office! The key requirement in selection of the facilitator is *independence*. It is imperative that the closure facilitator possess the following characteristics, at a minimum:

1. No direct involvement or direct interest in the project.
2. Perceived as impartial and fair.
3. Respect of senior management and other project stakeholders.
4. Willingness to listen.
5. Independence and authority to report review results without fear of recriminations from special interests.
6. Perceived as having the best interests of the organization in making decisions.
7. Broad-based experience in the organization or industry.

Other review participants should have similar characteristics even if they are selected for their special expertise.

Roles of a Facilitator

There are good reasons for using an independent facilitator. Lessons learned exercises can have negative consequences. The exercise can degenerate into a griping session that places blame. Word of the negative consequences travels fast and results in poor, guarded participation. The focus fails to stay on causes and improving future performance. The facilitator needs to be careful to avoid blame and allow stakeholders to feel safe to provide input.

A trained independent facilitator is often capable of gleaning information that would not be forthcoming to the project manager. Project participants report they are far more willing to attend and contribute to a lessons learned session run by an *independent* facilitator who can eliminate most political aspects in gathering lessons learned. The facilitator can deliver bad news to the project sponsor or senior management without recriminations. For example, since it is never pleasant for the project manager to deliver bad or potentially bad news to senior management or the project owner, many people wait until it is too late. In one project the facilitator received information and was able to give senior management a heads-up that there was a better than 60 percent risk of a delay of new, self-controlled, diesel railcars from a vendor having financial difficulties. Action was taken and money was loaned to the railcar company to avoid delay.

In the words of one project manager, "The facilitator takes the monkey off my back." For this and other reasons, many organizations use an independent retrospective facilitator to manage the retrospective process. Team members may be intimidated when the project manager or senior management attends team meetings. A recognized facilitator can elicit a 360-degree view/input from all stakeholders to create a richer, fuller picture of project issues and successes. The key criterion for selecting a project facilitator is that the facilitator has an independent and unbiased relationship to the project. Nike, Intel, Portland General Electric, Conway trucking, and various state governments use trained independent facilitators for lessons learned on large projects.

Managing a Retrospective

Having a facilitator available at the start of a project is preferred. The retrospective approach stresses gathering lessons learned during project execution and using them to change remaining work. Experience tells us memories fade as time passes; people leave the project. If lessons learned are not captured early, they may be lost. Catching lessons midway in the project life cycle allows for changing the way the remaining work is performed. (Some practitioners call this process "correcting course while the project is in flight.") Most retrospective methods use a minimum of three gates during the project life cycle to collect lessons learned that can be used to self correct the remainder of project execution. See Figure 14.2 for a flow chart of the collection of lessons learned.

It is critical to have a separate repository or library where reports and lessons learned are accessible and easy to retrieve. Your authors have encountered more than one organization that does a nice job of creating a closure report, but the report is placed in someone's bottom drawer or file cabinet, never to be seen again. This is truly a big mistake! The lessons learned are often the single best information a project manager or team can use in planning a future project. Repeatedly, project managers tell stories of how lessons learned "saved their lives" by allowing them to avoid a pitfall. Presentations at organization meetings or conferences encourage others to use and develop lessons learned. It also provides a chance to shine. The responsibility for maintaining a repository for lessons learned and

FIGURE 14.2   Retrospectives Process

The Standish Group International is a market research and advisory firm specializing in mission-critical software and electronic commerce. They have conducted and published extensive research on the success and failure of software development/application projects. Their research, code name "CHAOS," shows that a staggering 31 percent of software projects will be canceled before they are ever completed. In addition, 53 percent of projects will cost 189 percent of their original estimates. In terms of success, on the average only 16 percent of software projects are completed on time and within budget. In larger companies, the success rate is much worse—9 percent. The Standish Group estimated that in 1995 American companies and government agencies spent $81 billion for canceled software projects.

The CHAOS research is based on "key findings" from research surveys and personal interviews. The respondents were information technology (IT) executive managers. The sample included large, medium, and small companies across major industry segments, for example, banking; securities; manufacturing; retail; wholesale; health care; insurance service; and local, state, and federal organizations. The total sample size was 365 respondents and represented 8,380 projects.

Based on an in-depth comparison of successful versus unsuccessful software projects, the Standish Group created a success potential chart that identifies key factors associated with project success. The success criteria were weighted based on the input from the surveyed IT managers. The most important criterion, "user involvement," was given 19 success points, while the least important, "hard-working, focused staff," was given 3 success points. The following chart lists the criteria in order of importance:

* Used by permission of the Standish Group International, Inc., 196 Old Town House Rd., West Yarmouth, MA 02673. The CHAOS report was updated in 2001 and 2009. Although improvement was noted (e.g., cost overruns were reduced to 145 percent), the magnitude of the core problems remains the same.

Success Criteria	Points
1. User involvement	19
2. Executive management support	16
3. Clear statement of requirements	15
4. Proper planning	11
5. Realistic expectations	10
6. Smaller project milestones	9
7. Competent staff	8
8. Project team ownership	6
9. Clear vision and objectives	3
10. Hard-working, focused staff	3
Total	100

encouraging its use is normally the responsibility of the project office or oversight committee. See Research Highlight: CHAOS: Software Projects.

Overseeing a Post-Project Retrospective

In the past, lessons learned were primarily collected from a post-project survey. Someone reviewed the answers, summarized the results, and filed the document. In retrospective methodology, the facilitator uses several questionnaires as a starting point to conduct the post-project retrospective. These surveys often offer clues to unrecognized deeper problems. A facilitator relates that clues to areas needing improvement are often found by checking the changes running through the project's change management system. These hard data can point directly to areas that hold potential for improvement. In some cases the data direct the facilitator to the area where a problem was solved.

TABLE 14.3
Project Process
Review Questionnaire

	Item	Comments
1.	Were the project objectives and strategic intent of the project clearly and explicitly communicated?	
2.	Were the objectives and strategy in alignment?	
3.	Were the stakeholders identified and included in the planning?	
4.	Were project resources adequate for this project?	
5.	Were people with the right skill sets assigned to this project?	
6.	Were time estimates reasonable and achievable?	
7.	Were the risks for the project appropriately identified and assessed before the project started?	
8.	Were the processes and practices appropriate for this type of project? Should projects of similar size and type use these systems? Why/why not?	
9.	Did outside contractors perform as expected? Explain.	
10.	Were communication methods appropriate and adequate among all stakeholders? Explain.	
11.	Is the customer satisfied with the project product?	
12.	Are the customers using the project deliverables as intended? Are they satisfied?	
13.	Were the project objectives met?	
14.	Are the stakeholders satisfied their strategic intents have been met?	
15.	Has the customer or sponsor accepted a formal statement that the terms of the project charter and scope have been met?	
16.	Were schedule, budget, and scope standards met?	
17.	Is there any one important area that needs to be reviewed and improved upon? Can you identify the cause?	

Process and Methods Review

Process review begins with a review of the strategic intent of the project, selection criteria, project charter, project objectives, project scope, and acceptance criteria. This starting point reinforces and clarifies the business case for the project and the final project deliverables. Additional data gathering for process review is initiated through a questionnaire that is distributed to all major project stakeholders for responses. Some typical questions used are shown in Table 14.3. Although this questionnaire has some areas of omission, it can be used to initiate developing a questionnaire for your project.

Organizational Review

One of the themes of this text is that project performance is strongly influenced by organizational culture. It is therefore important to assess what fundamental organizational culture properties affect project successes and failures or become a hindrance to project teams. Again, survey questionnaires are easy, quick, and inexpensive to develop and collect data. Table 14.4, Organizational Culture Review, shows a partial organizational survey found in practice.

It is rare that important problems or successes will not show up in answers to a well-developed questionnaire.

TABLE 14.4
Organizational
Culture Review
Questionnaire

	Item	Comments
1.	Was the organizational culture supportive for this type of project?	
2.	Was senior management support adequate?	
3.	Were people with the right skills assigned to this project?	
4.	Did the project office help or hinder management of the project? Explain.	
5.	Did the team have access to organizational resources (people, funds, equipment)?	
6.	Was training for this project adequate? Explain.	
7.	Were lessons learned from earlier projects useful? Why? Where?	
8.	Did the project have a clear link to organizational objectives? Explain.	
9.	Was project staff properly reassigned?	
10.	Was the Human Resources Office helpful in finding new assignments? Comment.	

With survey information in hand, the facilitator then visits one-on-one with project team members, the project manager, and other stakeholders to dive deeper into cause-effect impacts. Fundamentally, the attempt is to isolate "the lack of x resulted in y." It is important to stay with the big lessons. For example, the facilitator might ask team members, "What was the biggest pain point in the project?" From these discussions the facilitator synthesizes collective wisdom.

Armed with the information gleaned from one-on-one sessions and other sources, the facilitator leads a team retrospective session. This session first reviews the facilitator's report and attempts to add key information. In fact, one of the roles of the facilitator is to lead the team in exploring new ways for solving a problem. Once the team reaches consensus of the key retrospective(s), the team develops and documents an action plan for improving future projects. Each retrospective should have at least one lesson that will improve current or future projects. One person needs to be assigned "owner" of the lesson learned and serve as the go-to person for more information. If possible, the facilitator should get senior management's commitment to implement the lesson.

An additional task of a facilitator is a review of the archived lessons to identify any trends across similar projects. For example, are there affinities between problems and successes among many projects? Have resources been inadequate? Has senior management visibly supported mining lessons learned? What fundamental organizational culture dimensions affect project successes and failures or become a hindrance to project teams?

In a conversation with one project office manager, she related that a facilitator found that the same problem across most multicountry projects had been occurring for over four years! It is difficult to believe no one picked up on such an obvious problem on so many projects. In this organization, U.S. managers were too focused on schedules, performance, and the bottom line; they neglected to establish a personal relationship with their foreign counterparts—e.g., the counterpart's key interests, family, holiday celebrations, and many other cultural aspects. Relationships were often strained and performance suffered. The result was that the project participants in each country are now required to attend a culture awareness class of the country of their counterparts to learn of customs, culture, and mores. Results improved dramatically.

Utilization of Retrospectives

Each retrospective is assigned an owner, typically a team member who is very interested in and familiar with the retrospective. This team member/owner will serve as the contact point for anyone needing information (expertise, contacts, templates, etc.) relating to the retrospective.

Another task of the retrospective facilitator is to guarantee there is a clear process to ensure retrospectives are used to improve management of future projects. Where retrospective methodology is used, some organizations mandate that the team of a new project review the retrospectives of similar projects. This mandate is one tactic that ensures that the most significant lessons are institutionalized. There is no excuse for not using past best practices and avoiding past mistakes. If the project managers before your project had completed retrospectives more effectively, your project might have avoided many mistakes. Of course, a requirement is archiving the lessons in a repository/library. But beyond a retrospective lessons learned library, a simple, easy to use, consistent format is necessary to ensure that information is easily found, used, and updated over time. A blog can be used to receive user comments on how helpful the retrospective is in improving a process or product.

Archiving Retrospectives

If retrospectives are to be used, it is critical to have a repository where reports and retrospective/lessons learned are accessible and easily retrieved. This is usually done using a Web site or other electronic means. For example, a round table of project office directors estimated that among their group of companies, 60–70 percent of their projects are global and virtual; all use some version of a Web-based system to collaborate and archive learning (e.g., Basecamp, SharePoint, Net Meeting, Voice Over IP). The responsibility for maintaining a repository for retrospectives and encouraging their use is normally the responsibility of the project office or oversight committee. Encouraging use of the repository depends on the ease of searching for information that is relevant to your project. Utilizing the information is defeated if information is difficult to find. For example, one project manager reported to your authors, "There are so many lessons learned items in the retrospectives library, I can't find information that applies to my project." This manager either wasn't interested in learning from others or the archive was poorly arranged.

At a minimum the repository should classify projects by type or characteristics. Each project review is categorized because there are differences in the way projects with different characteristics are managed and handled in an organization. A prospective project manager of a software coding project will have little interest in the construction of a clean room or recycling of inkjet reservoirs for printers. A prospective project manager of a small project will not be as interested in a computer project planning and control system as a project manager who is going to manage a very large project. The classification of projects by characteristics allows prospective readers, teams, and project managers to be selective in the search and use of report content.

One repository search engine uses the following classification scheme to allow prospective project stakeholders to start their search for information related to their prospective project:

- Project type—e.g., development, marketing, systems, construction.
- Size—monetary.
- Number of staff.
- Technology level—low, medium, high, new.
- Strategic or support.

Other classifications relevant to the organization could be included to drill further in search of projects that match the features of the prospective project. For example, another classification system indexes retrospectives by issues and problems.

Celebration A final wrap-up activity for the facilitator is the project closure celebration. An upbeat, festive celebration brings closure to the enjoyable experiences everyone has had and the need to say good-bye. Celebration is an opportunity to recognize the effort project stakeholders contributed. Even if the project did not reach its objectives, recognize the effort and goals that were achieved. If the project was a success, invite everyone who in some way contributed to project success. Thank the team and each one individually. The spirit of the celebration should be one in which the stakeholders are thanked for a job well done and leave with a good feeling of accomplishment and success.

Concluding Retrospective Notes

The retrospective methodology is more inclusive and disciplined than past lessons learned approaches. The impetus for its success has been accompanied by greater recognition of the real value of lessons learned in improving the management of projects. For example, Intel, which has project teams dispersed over 290 locations in 45 countries, has found using trained facilitators to be highly effective in mining and using retrospectives. Intel continues to train 15 new facilitators each year. Retrospective methodology is now standard operating procedure in many project-driven organizations. The lessons learned are often the single best source of information a project manager or team can use in planning their next project. Retrospectives are a main change agent for developing best project-management practices across the organization. Retrospective methodology is one positive step toward ensuring lessons learned are developed and implemented.

Summary

The goals of project closure are to complete the project and to improve performance of future projects. Implementing closure and review has three major closure deliverables: wrap-up, evaluation, and retrospectives. Wrap-up closure activities include delivering the final project deliverable, closing accounts, finding new opportunities for project staff, closing facilities, and creating the final report. Project evaluation verifies and documents project performance. The retrospectives methodology promises lessons learned are identified and used. Too often we spend massive dollars planning a project and little to nothing learning from the experience of completing the project. Failure to review, assess, and record successes and failures has consistently proven to be a costly waste. Retrospective methodology addresses this waste.

Key Terms

Lessons learned, *516*   Project evaluation, *511*   Team evaluation, *511*
Performance review, *514*   Project facilitator, *518*   360-degree review, *516*
Project closure, *505*   Retrospective, *517*

Review Questions

1. How does the project closure review differ from the performance measurement control system discussed in Chapter 13?
2. What major information would you expect to find in a project review?
3. Why is it difficult to perform a truly independent, objective review?
4. Comment on the following statement: "We cannot afford to terminate the project now. We have already spent more than 50 percent of the project budget."
5. Why should you separate performance reviews from pay reviews? How do you do this?
6. Advocates of retrospective methodology claim there are distinguishing characteristics that increase its value over past lessons learned methods. What are they? How does each characteristic enhance project closure and review?

Exercises

1. Consider a course that you recently completed. Perform a review of the course (the course represents a project and the course syllabus represents the project plan).
2. Imagine you are conducting a review of the International Space Station project. Research press coverage and the Internet to collect information on the current status of the project. What are the successes and failures to date? What forecasts would you make about the completion of the project, and why? What recommendations would you make to top management of the program, and why?
3. Interview a project manager who works for an organization that implements multiple projects. Ask the manager what kind of closure procedures are used to complete a project and whether lessons learned are used.
4. What are some of the lessons learned from a recent project in your organization? Was a retrospective done? What action plans were generated to improve processes as a result of the project?

References

Anonymous, "Annual Survey of Business Improvement Architects," Toronto, Canada, in *PM Network,* "Deliverables," Vol. 21, No. 4, April, 2007, p. 18.

Cochran, D., "Finally, a Way to Completely Measure Project Manager Performance," *PM Network,* September 2000, pp. 75–80.

Cooke-Davies, T., "Project Management Closeout Management: More than Simply Saying Good Bye and Moving On," in J. Knutson (Ed.), *Project Management for Business Processionals,* John Wiley and Sons, Indianapolis, IN 2001, pp. 200–14.

Fretty, P., "Why Do Projects Really Fail?" *PM Network,* March 2006, pp. 45–48.

Gobeli, D., and E. W. Larson, "Barriers Affecting Project Success," in *1986 Proceedings Project Management Institute: Measuring Success* (Upper Darby, PA: Project Management Institute, 1986), pp. 22–29.

Hoffman, R., "Ten Reasons You Should Be Using 360 Degree Feedback," *HR Magazine,* April, 1995, pp. 82–85.

	Item	Status	Comments/Plan to Resolve
6	Has operations management formally accepted responsibility for operating and maintaining the product(s) or service(s) delivered by the project?		
6.1	Has the documentation relating to operation and maintenance of the product(s) or service(s) been delivered to, and accepted by, operations management?		
6.2	Has training and knowledge transfer of the operations organization been completed?		
6.3	Does the projected annual cost to operate and maintain the product(s) or service(s) differ from the estimate provided in the project proposal? If so, note and explain the difference in the Comments column.		
7	Have the resources used by the project been transferred to other units within the organization?		
8	Has the project documentation been archived or otherwise disposed as described in the project plan?		
9	Have the lessons learned been documented in accordance with the Commonwealth Project Management guideline?		
10	Has the date for the post-implementation review been set?		
10.1	Has the person or unit responsible for conducting the post-implementation review been identified?		

Signatures

The signatures of the people below relay an understanding that the key elements within the Closeout Phase section are complete and the project has been formally closed.

Position/Title	Name	Date	Phone Number

Source: http://www.vita.virginia.gov/projects/cpm/cpmDocs/CPMG-SEC5-Final.pdf

Appendix 14.2

Euro Conversion—Project Closure Checklist

Project _____ *Euro Conversion* _____   Customer _____ *Finance Department* _____

Project manager _____ *Hans Kramer* _____   Completion date _____ *12 December XX* _____

	Due date	Person responsible	Notes
1. Document finance department acceptance	16/12	Hans	
2. Customer training in Euro software	28/12	Joan	Train all departments before conversion
3. Archive all			
Schedules/actuals	31/12	Maeyke	
Budgets/actual costs	31/12	Maeyke	
Changes	31/12	Maeyke	
4. Close out all accounts with vendors	31/12	Guido	
5. Close out all work orders	31/12	Mayo	
6. Close out partner accounts	31/12	Guido	
7. Reassign project staff	16/12	Sophie	
8. Evaluation of			
Vendors	31/12	Mayo	Use standard questionnaire for vendors
Staff members	31/12	Sophie	Have HR department develop and administer
9. Final report and lessons learned meeting	4/1	Hans	Send notice to all stakeholders
10. Lessons learned archive to database	10/1	Maeyke	Contact IS department
...tribute awards		Sophie	Notify all stakeholders

Case

Maximum Megahertz Project

Olaf Gundersen, the CEO of Wireless Telecom Company, is in a quandary. Last year he accepted the Maximum Megahertz Project suggested by six up-and-coming young R&D corporate stars. Although Olaf did not truly understand the technical importance of the project, the creators of the project needed only $600,000, so it seemed like a good risk. Now the group is asking for $800,000 more and a six-month extension on a project that is already four months behind. However, the team feels confident they can turn things around. The project manager and project team feel that if they hang in there a little longer they will be able to overcome the roadblocks they are encountering—especially those that reduce power, increase speed, and use a new technology battery. Other managers familiar with the project hint that the power pack problem might be solved, but "the battery problem will never be solved." Olaf believes he is locked into this project; his gut feeling tells him the project will never materialize, and he should get out. John, his human resource manager, suggested bringing in a consultant to axe the project.

Olaf decided to call his friend Dawn O'Connor, the CEO of an accounting software company. He asked her, "What do you do when project costs and deadlines escalate drastically? How do you handle doubtful projects?" Her response was, "Let another project manager look at the project. Ask: 'If you took over this project tomorrow, could you achieve the required results, given the extended time and additional money?' If the answer is no, I call my top management team together and have them review the doubtful project in relation to other projects in our project portfolio." Olaf feels this is good advice.

Unfortunately, the Maximum Megahertz Project is not an isolated example. Over the last five years there have been three projects that were never completed. "We just seemed to pour more money into them, even though we had a pretty good idea the projects were dying. The cost of those projects was high; those resources could have been better used on other projects." Olaf wonders, "Do we ever learn from our mistakes? How can we develop a process that catches errant projects early? More importantly, how do we ease a project manager and team off an errant project without embarrassment?" Olaf certainly does not want to lose the six bright stars on the Maximum Megahertz Project.

Olaf is contemplating how his growing telecommunications company should deal with the problem of identifying projects that should be terminated early, how to allow good managers to make mistakes without public embarrassment, and how they all can learn from their mistakes.

Give Olaf a plan of action for the future that attacks the problem. Be specific and provide examples that relate to Wireless Telecom Company.

Epilogue

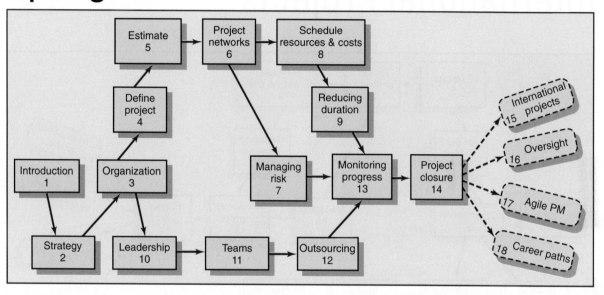

With Chapter 14 the project life cycle is complete. You have been exposed to the core elements of project management. We have consciously tried to incorporate a blend of socialcultural and process practices required to successfully manage any project. These best practices are transferable across industries. Your understanding of these chapters should enhance your ability to make a positive contribution in any project environment.

The supplemental chapters that follow expand on the core by covering international project management, oversight, and Agile methods.

- Chapter 15. Explores different international environments in which you may have to manage a project. In large high technology firms we estimate that 60–90 percent of their projects are virtual and across many cultures. If you find yourself new in this environment, the international chapter is an excellent primer on the types of conditions and issues you may encounter in an international project.
- Chapter 16. Oversight of managing projects is growing and evolving. Depending on the degree of oversight, oversight will set the operating environment in which you manage your project.
- Chapter 17. Agile methodology is used in complex projects (e.g., software and new innovation products) where the final design requirements are not known and evolve as the project is implemented. The methodology breaks requirements into small functional pieces that allow rapid response to change. Agile embraces flexibility, change, small teams, and owner involvement.

Familiarity and understanding these different operating environments should give you confidence to enter and manage your project. We encourage you to read these chapters to increase your overall understanding of project management.

Chapter 18 presents thoughts on career paths. You may find them useful as you consider your future.

International Projects

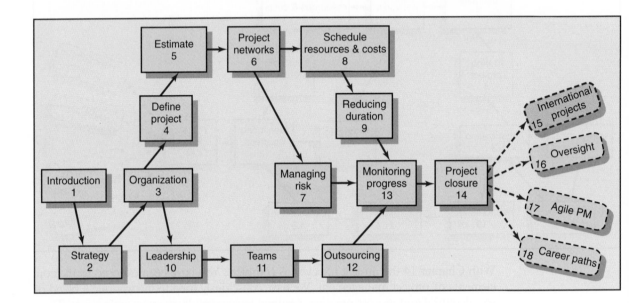

International Projects

Environmental Factors

Project Site Selection

Cross-Cultural Considerations: A Closer Look

Selection and Training for International Projects

Summary

The principal benefit of living abroad is that it enables us to get glimpses of ourselves as others see us and to realize that others' views are more accurate than ours. Progress begins with grasping the truth about ourselves, however unpleasant it may be.

—*Russel Ackoff, The Wharton School, University of Pennsylvania*

Projects are frequently classified as domestic, overseas, foreign, or global. A domestic project is one performed in its native country for a resident firm (a construction firm building a bridge in its state). An overseas project is one executed in a foreign country for a native firm (a Swedish company building a truck factory in the United States for their native company). A foreign project is executed in a foreign country for a foreign firm (a U.S. firm developing an information system in Malaysia for Malaysian banks). A global project consists of teams formed from professionals spanning multiple countries, continents, and cultures with their work integrated for the entire enterprise (e.g., multinational enterprise developing a global distribution system). Global teams are a crisscross of functions, work locale, markets, culture, and products. Today, these distinctions become blurred as the world economy and organizations become more integrated.

This chapter targets the international project manager who must resettle in a foreign environment to manage the project. The chapter also includes useful information for project professionals working overseas as well as those working on virtual projects involving colleagues from different countries.

There is no generally accepted framework or road map for project managers given international assignments. These project managers typically face a difficult set of problems—for example, absence from home, friends, and sometimes family; personal risks; missed career opportunities; foreign language, culture, and laws; adverse conditions. Of course there are positives—for example, increased income, increased responsibilities, career opportunities, foreign travel, new lifetime friends. How the international project manager adapts and approaches problems encountered in the host country often determines the success or failure of a project.

This chapter focuses on four major issues surrounding the management of international projects. First, major environmental factors that impact project selection and implementation are briefly highlighted. Second, an example of how organizations decide where to expand globally is provided. Third, the challenge of working in a strange and foreign culture is addressed. Finally, how companies select and train professionals for international projects is discussed. Although by no means comprehensive, this chapter attempts to provide a solid understanding of the major issues and challenges confronting the international project manager.

you included possible terrorist targets (facilities and personnel) in your hazard and vulnerability analysis? Have you conducted a counterterrorism exercise complete with law enforcement, fire, medical, and emergency management participation? What should your organization's policy be on negotiating with a person threatening a terrorist act?

Managing projects in a dangerous world is a tough assignment. Security precautions are major cost considerations not only in dollars and cents, but also in the psychological well-being of personnel sent abroad. Effective risk management is critical to success.

Geography

One factor that is often underestimated until project personnel actually arrive at a foreign destination is the geography of the country. Imagine what it is like to deplane from a modern aircraft and encounter the 105-degree heat and 90 percent humidity of Jakarta, Indonesia, or three feet of fresh snow and −22 degree temperatures in Kokkla, Finland. Whether it is the wind, the rain, the heat, the jungle, or the desert, more than one project manager has asserted that their greatest challenge was overcoming the "elements." Mother Nature cannot be ignored.

The planning and implementation of a project must take into account the impact the country's geography will have on the project. For example, a salvage operation off the coast of Greenland can only be scheduled one month out of the year because the waterway is frozen over during the remainder of the year. Construction projects in Southeast Asia have to accommodate the monsoon season when rainfall can be as high as 50 inches per month. Geography does not just affect outdoor projects. It can have an indirect effect on "indoor" projects. For example, one information systems specialist reported that his performance on a project in northern Sweden declined due to sleep deprivation. He attributed his problems to the 20 hours of daylight this part of the world experiences during summer months. Finally, extreme weather conditions can make extraordinary demands on equipment. Projects can grind to a halt because of equipment breakdown under the brunt of the elements. Working under extreme conditions typically requires special equipment, which increases the costs and complexity of the project.

Before beginning a project in a foreign land, project planners and managers need to study carefully the unique characteristics of the geography of that country. They need to factor into project plans and schedules such items as climate, seasons, altitude, and natural geographical obstacles. See the Snapshot from Practice: The Filming of *Apocalypse Now* for an example of a poorly planned endeavor in the Philippines.

Economic

How business is conducted in the host country can influence project success. Basic economic factors in foreign countries and regions influence choices of site selection and how business will be conducted for potential projects. The gross domestic product (GDP) of a country suggests the level of development of a country. A faltering economy may indicate fewer sources of capital funding. For example,

SNAPSHOT FROM PRACTICE The Filming of *Apocalypse Now**

In February 1976, Francis Ford Coppola took his Hollywood film crew to the Philippines to shoot *Apocalypse Now,* a film adaptation of Joseph Conrad's *Heart of Darkness* within the context of the Vietnam conflict. The Philippines was chosen because the terrain was similar to Vietnam's, and the government was willing to rent its helicopter force for the movie. At the time, the U.S. military was unwilling to cooperate on a film about Vietnam. An additional advantage was cheap labor. Coppola was able to hire more than 300 laborers at $1 to $3 per day to construct elaborate production sets, including an impressive Cambodian temple. *Apocalypse Now* was scheduled for 16 weeks of shooting at a budget of $12 to $14 million.

Months earlier, George Lucas, of *Star Wars* fame, warned Coppola against filming the movie in the Philippines. He said, "It's one thing to go over there for three weeks with five people and scrounge some footage with the Filipino Army, but if you go over there with a big Hollywood production, the longer you stay the more in danger you are of getting sucked into the swamp." His words turned out to be prophetic.

A civil war was going on between government forces and communist rebels. Shooting was repeatedly interrupted because the Philippine military ordered their helicopter pilots to leave the set and fly to the mountains to fight the rebels.

In May 1976, a typhoon struck the Philippine Islands, destroying most of the movie sets. The film team was forced to shut down production and returned to the United States for two months.

The lead character was played by Martin Sheen, who suffered a serious heart attack under the stress and heat of the filming and had to return to the United States. Coppola scrambled to film the scenes that did not require Sheen, but eventually production came to a standstill until Sheen's return nine weeks later.

The entire project proved to be a traumatic experience for Coppola, who had enjoyed Academy Award success with his previous *Godfather* movies. "There were times when I thought I was going to die, literally, from the inability to move the problems I had. I would go to bed at four in the morning in a cold sweat."

Film production ended in May 1977 after more than 200 days of shooting. The final cost was about $30 million. To date, *Apocalypse Now* has earned more than $150 million throughout the world.

* *Hearts of Darkness: A Filmmaker's Apocalypse* (Paramount Pictures, 1991).

---

changes in protectionist strategies of a host country, such as import quotas and tariffs, can quickly alter the viability of projects. Other factors such as balance of payments, currency fluctuations, hyperinflation, population growth, education level of workforce, and market size can influence project choices and operations. For example, the economic downturn in Southeast Asia during the late 1990s saw local economies in Thailand, Malaysia, and Indonesia being devastated by inflation rates in excess of 60 percent. A company can protect against currency fluctuations by hedging or tying costs to a strong currency such as the U.S. dollar, British pound, or Euro. Still, the social upheaval caused by such dramatic economic events cannot be underestimated.

Bartering is a form of compensation that is still used by some countries and organizations. For example, one project in Africa was paid in goat skins. The goat skins were eventually sold to an Italian manufacturer of gloves. Another project along the Caspian Sea was paid for in oil. There is a small group of firms that specialize in bartering for project contractors. These intermediaries charge a commission to sell the bartered goods (e.g., oil) for the contractor. However, dealing with commodities can be a risky enterprise.

Skills, educational level, and labor supply prevalent in a host country can determine the choice of a project site. Is project selection driven by low wage levels or availability of technically skilled talent? For example, you can hire three computer programmers in Ukraine for the price of one programmer in the United States. Conversely, many high-tech companies are willing to endure the additional expense of setting up joint projects in Switzerland and Germany to take advantage of their engineering prowess.

Infrastructure

Infrastructure refers to a country or community's ability to provide the services required for a project. Infrastructure needs for a project could be communication, transportation, power, technology, and education systems. For example, developing an electric steel plant to be near a major market requires a reliable supply of electric power. If reliable power is not sufficient, other alternatives need to be considered. Software projects across borders are common today; however, they depend on reliable telecommunication networks. These networks simplify and facilitate project coordination and management among project stakeholders in different locations. If the project depends on a high ratio of vendor suppliers, good roads, and other transportation modes such as air and seaports, a good infrastructure will be imperative.

An example of a project that failed to take into account the needs and infrastructure of the host nation involved a U.S. company that was awarded the contract for building a hospital in an African nation. The local African officials wanted a "low-tech" health care facility that would take local traditions into consideration. Because their relatives generally accompanied patients, space had to be provided for them, too. Electricity was not reliably supplied, and it was doubtful whether well-educated doctors would want to spend careers away from the city. Therefore, the locals wanted a hospital for basic care with minimum technology. The construction company doing the building, on the other hand, had a preconceived notion of what a hospital should be and was not going to be accused of building a second-rate facility. It built a modern hospital that could have stood in any U.S. city. The building was completed; however, even after several years it was not used because the electricity was not sufficient, the air-conditioning could not be used, and doctors refused to live in the rural area.

Organizations need to consider the needs of the families of personnel they send overseas. Will the facilities and living conditions for the expatriate families place an undue hardship on families? Will schooling for children be available? The welfare and comfort of expatriate families play an important role in retaining good project managers and promoting their peak performance.

Culture

Visiting project managers must accept and respect the customs, values, philosophies, and social standards of their host country. Global managers recognize that if the customs and social cultural dimensions of the host country are not accommodated, projects will not succeed. Too many project audits and final reports of international projects reflect challenges and problems linked to cultural differences.

For most project managers, the biggest difference in managing an international project is operating in a national culture where things are done differently. For example, most developed nations use the same project management techniques (CPM, risk analysis, trade-off analysis). However, how activity work is performed can be very different in the host country.

SNAPSHOT FROM PRACTICE   River of Doubt*

After his crushing election defeat in 1912 as a third-party candidate, former president Theodore ("Teddy") Roosevelt set his sights on a grand adventure, the first descent of an unmapped rapids-choked tributary of the Amazon aptly titled the "River of Doubt." Together with Brazil's most famous explorer, Candido Mariano da Silva Rondon, Roosevelt accomplished a feat that belongs in the annals of great expeditions.

Along the way, Roosevelt and his men faced an unbelievable series of hardships, losing their canoes and supplies to crushing whitewater rapids, and enduring starvation, Indian attacks, disease, drowning, and even murder within their ranks. Candice Millard brings alive these extraordinary events in her nonfiction thriller *The River of Doubt*. While her account details the ill-fated journey it also reveals insights into international project management as it describes the collaboration between the American and Brazilian cohorts. While each party ultimately earned the respect and admiration of the other, friction between the two parties simmered from the outset.

One source of consternation was the amount of supplies and luggage that the Americans required for the journey. Warned that the luggage requirements of the former president and his party would be extensive, the Brazilian commodore Rondon ordered 110 mules and 17 pack oxen to be used for the expedition's overland journey across the Brazilian highland to the great river. Surely, he felt, this would be more than necessary for such a trip.

The Brazilians were astounded by the sheer volume of baggage that was unloaded from Roosevelt's ship, the *Vandycks*. There were mountains of crates: guns and ammunition, chairs and tables, tents and cots, equipment for collecting and preserving specimens, surveying the river, and cooking meals. An exhausted stevedore elicited a roar of laughter from the onlooking crowd when he announced, "Nothing lacking but the piano!"

Rather than risk embarrassment by telling Roosevelt that they were not prepared to take so much luggage, Rondon scrambled to find additional animals. Extra oxen and mules

© Fotomas/Topham/The Image Works

were located, but they were far from tame. Loaded with supplies, the oxen would buck and throw off the packs. The expedition was delayed as gauchos (South American cowboys) endeavored to "break" the animals as quickly as possible.

Within days of finally setting off across the vast highlands, Roosevelt and his men began to experience the harsh realities that were to plague the expedition. After crossing a bone-strewn graveyard of oxen and mules that had starved to death or been eaten during previous expeditions, they were stunned by the sight of unopened supply crates, all clearly marked "Roosevelt South American Expedition." The pack animals, still making their weary away across the plateau ahead of the them, had begun bucking off their heavy loads!

As the officers rode slowly past the boxes, they wondered what they were leaving behind and how precious it might become in the months ahead. Little did they know how true those fears would be.

* Candice Millard, *The River of Doubt* (New York: Doubleday), 2005.

Will English be the operating language, or will the project manager need to be fluent in the foreign language? Will translation services be available and sufficient? Communication problems—because of language differences—often become a major problem in carrying out even simple tasks. Although the use of translators can help tremendously, their use does not solve the communication problem completely because something is lost in translation. For example, consider the disastrous consequences of differences in interpretations and expectations between the Brazilians and Americans highlighted in the Snapshot from Practice: River of Doubt.

Will religious factors influence the project? For example, religious factors touched the spouse of a Scandinavian project manager responsible for building a water desalination plant from sea water in a Middle East country. She was restricted to the living compound for families of foreign guest workers. Going outside the compound to a nearby city meant covering her head, arms, and legs and being accompanied by another woman or, preferably, a man. A physical altercation in the city concerning her clothing was traumatic for her. She left the country and returned home. Her husband requested a transfer back home three months later. The loss of the original project manager from the project required the assigned project manager to establish relationships with the project team and host country's nationals to get the project moving smoothly again.

Not only do project managers have to adapt to the culture of the host country, but often-times overseas projects require working with people from different countries. For example, on a light rail project in the Philippines, an American firm was hired to oversee the interests of local real estate companies who were funding the project. The American project manager had to work with Czech representatives who were providing the rail equipment, Japanese engineers responsible for building the rail, Australian bankers who were providing additional financing, an Indian firm that were the principal architects, as well as the native Filipinos.

Of all the factors, working within a multicultural environment is most often the greatest challenge for project managers. It will be dealt with in detail later in this chapter.

Project Site Selection

As the project manager studies the factors contributing to site selection, he will see that inherent in all of these factors is the risk level senior management and directors are willing to accept for the potential rewards of a successful international project. One approach for the project manager to digest, clarify, and understand the factors leading to the selection of a specific project is to use a risk matrix similar to those found in Chapter 7. The major difference lies in the selection of the risk factors for different project sites.

Figure 15.2 presents a truncated matrix for project site selection of the construction of a laser printer factory in Singapore, India, or Ireland. In this example,

FIGURE 15.2
Assessment Matrix
Project Site Selection

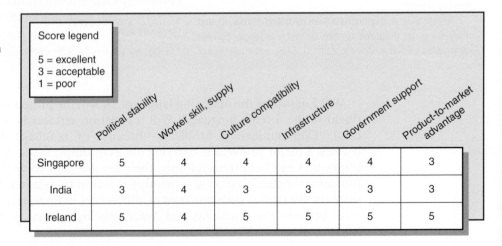

Score legend

5 = excellent
3 = acceptable
1 = poor

	Political stability	Worker skill, supply	Culture compatibility	Infrastructure	Government support	Product-to-market advantage
Singapore	5	4	4	4	4	3
India	3	4	3	3	3	3
Ireland	5	4	5	5	5	5

FIGURE 15.3
Evaluation Matrix
Breakdown for
Infrastructure

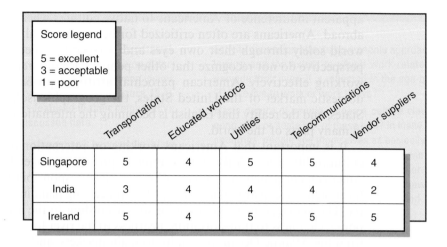

	Transportation	Educated workforce	Utilities	Telecommunications	Vendor suppliers
Singapore	5	4	5	5	4
India	3	4	4	4	2
Ireland	5	4	5	5	5

Score legend

5 = excellent
3 = acceptable
1 = poor

political stability, worker skill and supply, culture compatibility, infrastructure, government support, and product-to-market advantage were the major assessment factors. Each project site is compared against each factor. Figure 15.3 depicts a further breakdown of the infrastructure evaluation factor. In this example, transportation, educated workforce, utilities, telecommunications, and vendor suppliers are considered important to evaluating the infrastructure for each site. The scores given in Figure 15.3 are used to assign values to the infrastructure factor of the assessment matrix, Figure 15.2. In this project, Ireland was the choice. Clearly, Singapore and Ireland were very close in terms of infrastructure and several other factors. However, the major assessment factor of using Ireland to access the EEC (product-to-market advantage) turned the decision.

Given the macro economic factors, the firm's strategic posture toward global projects, and the major considerations for selecting this project, it is imperative the project manager quickly become sensitized to the foreign cultural factors that can spell project success or failure.

Cross-Cultural Considerations: A Closer Look

The concept of culture was introduced in Chapter 3 as referring to the unique personality of a particular firm. More specifically, culture was defined as a system of shared norms, beliefs, values, and customs that bind people together, creating shared meaning and a unique identity. *Culture* is a concept created for descriptive purposes and depends on the group that is the focus of attention. For example, within a global context culture can refer to certain regions (i.e., Europeans, Arabs), to specific nations (i.e., French, Thai), or to certain ethnic or religious groups (i.e., Kurds, African-Americans). This chapter looks at national cultures; we freely recognize that many cultural characteristics are borderless and that there is considerable variation within any one country. Still, national cultures provide a useful anchor for understanding different habits, customs, and values around the world.

Right or wrong, Americans have a reputation for not being able to work effectively in foreign cultures. (When we use the term "American," we are referring to people from the United States; we apologize to our friends in Canada and Central and South America.) In the 1960s, the term "Ugly American" encapsulated the

The Hofstede framework grew from a study of 88,000 people working in IBM subsidiaries in 50 countries and 3 multicountry regions. Based on responses to a 32-item questionnaire, Dutch social scientist Geert Hofstede developed different dimensions for examining cultures:

1. Individualism versus collectivism. Identifies whether a culture holds individuals or the group responsible for each member's welfare.

2. Power distance. Describes the degree to which a culture accepts status and power differences among its members.

3. Uncertainty avoidance. Identifies a culture's willingness to accept uncertainty and ambiguity about the future.

4. Masculinity-femininity. Describes the degree to which the culture emphasizes competitive and achievement-oriented behavior or displays concerns for relationships.

Figure 15.5 shows how he ranked selected countries according to collectivism-individualism and power distance. Wealth appears to influence both factors. Power distance is correlated with income inequality in a country while individualism is correlated with national wealth (Per Capita Gross National Product). As a result high power distance and collectivism are often found together, as are low power distance and individualism. This can affect decision making on project teams. For example, while the high collectivism may lead a project team in Thailand to operate consensually, the high power distance may cause decisions to be heavily influenced by the desires of the project manager. Conversely, a similar team operating in more individualistic and low power distance such as Great Britain or America might make decisions with more open debate including challenging the preferences of the project manager.

* G. Hofstede, *Culture's Consequences: Comparing Values, Behaviors, Institutions and Organizations Across Nations,* 2nd Edition (Thousand Oaks, CA: Sage Publications, 2001). http://www.geerthofstede.nl

FIGURE 15.5
Sample Country Clusters on Hofstede's Dimensions of Individualism-Collectivism and Power Distance

Collectivism		Columbia, Peru, Thailand, Singapore, Mexico, Turkey, Indonesia
Individualism	Israel, Finland, Germany, Ireland, New Zealand, Canada, Great Britain, United States	Spain, South Africa, France, Italy, Belgium
	Low power distance	High power distance

America "time is money," and a premium is placed on working quickly. Other cultures do not share Americans' sense of urgency and are accustomed to a much slower pace of life. They can't understand why Americans are always in such a hurry. Punctuality varies across cultures. For example, Americans will generally tolerate someone being 5 to 10 minutes late. In contrast, among Peruvians, the period before an apology or explanation for being late is expected might be 45 minutes to an hour!

While working on multicultural projects, managers sometimes encounter ethical dilemmas that are culturally bound. For example, the 1999 Olympic site selection scandal featured the sordid details of committee members peddling their votes for a wide range of gifts (i.e., university scholarships for their children, extravagant trips). In many societies such "bribes" or "tributes" are expected and the only way to conduct meaningful business. Moreover, many cultures will not grant a female project manager the same respect they will a male project manager. Should U.S. management increase project risk or violate its own sex-discrimination policy?

These cultural differences are just the tip of the iceberg. There are numerous "How to Do Business in . . ." books written by people who have traveled and worked abroad. Although these books may lack rigor, they typically do a good job of identifying local customs and common mistakes made by outsiders. On the other hand, anthropologists have made significant contributions to our understanding of why and how the cultures of societies are different (see the accompanying Research Highlights). Students of international project management are encouraged to study these works to gain a deeper understanding of the root causes of cultural diversity.

So what can be said to prepare people to work on international projects? The world is too diverse to do justice in one chapter to all the cultural variations managers are likely to encounter when working on international projects. Instead, a sample of some of these differences will be highlighted by discussing working on projects in four different countries: Mexico, France, Saudi Arabia, and China. We apologize to our readers outside the United States because briefings are presented from the viewpoint of a U.S. project manager working in these countries. Still, in an effort not to be too ethnocentric, we present a fifth scenario for foreign project managers assigned to working in the United States. Although by no means exhaustive, these briefings provide a taste of what it is like to work in and with people from these countries.

Working in Mexico

America developed historically in an environment where it was important for strangers to be able to get along, interact, and do business. On the American frontier almost everyone was a stranger, and people had to both cooperate and keep their distance. The New England Yankee sentiment that "Good fences make good neighbors" expresses this American cultural value well. Conversely, Mexico developed historically in an environment where the only people to trust were family and close friends—and by extension, people who were known to those whom you knew well. As a consequence, personal relationships dominate all aspects of Mexican business. While Americans are generally taught not to do business with friends, Mexicans and other Latin Americans are taught to do business with no one but friends.

The significance of personal relationships has created a *compadre* system in which Mexicans are obligated to give preference to relatives and friends when hiring, contracting, procuring, and sharing business opportunities. North Americans often complain that such practices contribute to inefficiency in Mexican firms. While this may or may not be the case, efficiency is prized by Americans, while Mexicans place a higher value on friendship.

Mexicans tend to perceive Americans as being "cold." They also believe that most Americans look down on them. Among the most effective things an American can do to prevent being seen as a typical *Gringo* is to take the time and effort in the beginning of a working relationship to really get to know Mexican counterparts. Because family is all-important to Mexicans, a good way for developing a personal relationship is exchanging information about each other's family. Mexicans will often gauge people's trustworthiness by the loyalty and attention they devote to their family.

The *mañana* syndrome reflects another cultural difference between Americans and Mexicans. Mexicans have a different concept of time than Americans do. Mexicans feel confined and pressured when given deadlines; they prefer open-ended schedules.

They generally consider individuals to be more important than sticking to a schedule. If a friend drops in at work, most Mexicans will stop and talk, regardless of how long it takes, and even if chatting makes their work late. This sometimes contributes to the erroneous perception that Mexicans lack a work ethic. Quite the contrary; given a minimal incentive, Mexicans can be quite industrious and ambitious.

Finally, as in many other cultures, Mexicans do not share Americans' confidence that they control their own destiny. While Americans are taught, "When the going gets tough, the tough get going," Mexicans are taught, "Taking action without knowing what is expected or wanted can have dangerous consequences." Mexicans tend to be more cautious and want to spend more time discussing risks and potential problems that Americans might dismiss as improbable or irrelevant.

Other useful guidelines for working with Mexicans on projects include the following:

1. Americans tend to be impersonal and practical when making arguments; Mexicans can be very passionate and emotional when arguing. They enjoy a lively debate.

2. Where Americans tend to use meetings as the place to work things out publicly, Mexicans tend to see meetings as the place where persons with authority ratify what has been decided during informal private discussions.

3. While Mexicans can be emotional, they tend to shy away from any sort of direct confrontation or criticism. A long silence often indicates displeasure or disagreement.

4. Speech in Mexico is often indirect. People rarely say no directly but are more likely to respond by saying maybe *(quizas)*, or by saying "I will think about it" or changing the subject. Yes *(si)* is more likely to mean "I understand you" than "yes."

5. Titles are extremely important in Mexico and are always used when a person is introducing him- or herself or being introduced. Pay as much attention to remembering a person's title as to remembering his or her name.

Today, with NAFTA and increased international business activity in Mexico, old traditions are disappearing. American managers report that cultural differences are less evident in northern Mexico where many multinational firms operate. Here *hora americana* (American time) rather than *hora mexicana* tends to be used when dealing with foreigners. Project managers should devote up-front effort to understanding how much older mores of Mexican culture apply to their project.

Working in France

Some Americans consider the French the most difficult to work with among Europeans. This feeling probably stems from a reflection of the French culture, which is quite different from that in the United States.

In France, one's social class is very important. Social interactions are constrained by class standing, and during their lifetimes most French people do not encounter much change in social status. Unlike an American, who through hard work and success can move from the lowest economic stratum to the highest, a successful French person might, at best, climb one or two rungs up the social ladder. Additionally, the French are very status conscious and like to provide signs of this status, such as knowledge of literature and arts; a well-designed, tastefully decorated house; and a high level of education.

The French tend to admire or be fascinated with people who disagree with them; in contrast, Americans are more attracted to those who agree with them. As a result, the French are accustomed to conflict and, during negotiations, accept the fact that some positions are irreconcilable and must be accepted as such. Americans, on the other hand, tend to believe that conflicts can be resolved if both parties make an extra effort and are willing to compromise. Also, the French often determine a person's trustworthiness based on their first-hand, personal evaluation of the individual's character. Americans, in contrast, tend to evaluate a person's trustworthiness on the basis of past achievements and other people's evaluations.

The French are often accused of lacking an intense work ethic. For example, many French workers frown on overtime and on average they have one of the longest vacations in the world (four to five weeks annually). On the other hand, the French enjoy a reputation for productive work, a result of the French tradition of craftsmanship. This tradition places a greater premium on quality rather than on getting things accomplished quickly.

Most French organizations tend to be highly centralized with rigid structures. As a result, it usually takes longer to carry out decisions. Because this arrangement is quite different from the more decentralized organizations in the United States, many U.S. project managers find the bureaucratic red tape a source of considerable frustration.

In countries like the United States, a great deal of motivation is derived from professional accomplishments. The French do not tend to share this same view of work. While they admire American industriousness, they believe that quality of life is what really matters. As a result they attach much greater importance to leisure time, and many are unwilling to sacrifice the enjoyment of life for a dedication to project work.

Cautions to remember with the French include these:

1. The French value punctuality. It is very important to be on time for meetings and social occasions.
2. Great importance is placed on neatness and taste. When interacting with French businesspeople, pay close attention to your own professional appearance and appear cultured and sophisticated.
3. The French can be very difficult to negotiate with. Often, they ignore facts, no matter how convincing they may be. They can be quite secretive about their position. It is difficult to obtain information from them, even in support for their position. Patience is essential for negotiating with them.
4. French managers tend to see their work as an intellectual exercise. They do not share the American view of management as an interpersonally demanding exercise, where plans have to be constantly "sold" upward and downward using personal skills.
5. The French generally consider managers to be experts. They expect managers to give precise answers to work-related questions. To preserve their reputation, some French managers act as if they know the answers to questions even when they don't.

Working in Saudi Arabia

Project management has a long tradition in Saudi Arabia and other Arab countries. Financed by oil money, European and American firms have contributed greatly to the modernization of Arab countries. Despite this tradition, foreigners often find it very hard to work on projects in Saudi Arabia. A number of cultural differences can be cited for this difficulty.

One is the Arabian view of time. In North America, it is common to use the cliché, "The early bird gets the worm." In Saudi Arabia, a favorite expression is, "Bukra insha Allah," which means, "Tomorrow if God wills," an expression that reflects the Saudis' approach to time. Unlike Westerners, who believe they control their own time, Arabs believe that Allah controls time. As a result, when Saudis commit themselves to a date in the future and fail to show up, there is no guilt or concern on their part because they have no control over time in the first place. In planning future events with Arabs, it pays to hold lead time to a week or less, because other factors may intervene or take precedence.

An associated cultural belief is that destiny depends more on the will of a supreme being than on the behavior of individuals. A higher power dictates the outcome of important events, so individual action is of little consequence. As a result, progress or the lack of progress on a project is considered more a question of fate than effort. This leads Saudis to rely less on detailed plans and schedules to complete projects than Americans do.

Another important cultural contrast between Saudi Arabians and Americans is emotion and logic. Saudis often act on the basis of emotion; in contrast, those in an Anglo culture are taught to act on logic. During negotiations, it is important not only to share the facts but also to make emotional appeals that demonstrate your suggestion is the right thing to do.

Saudis also make use of elaborate and ritualized forms of greetings and leave-takings. A businessperson may wait far past the assigned meeting time before being admitted to a Saudi office. Once there, the individual may find a host of others present; one-on-one meetings are rare. Moreover, during the meeting there may be continuous interruptions. Visitors arrive and begin talking to the host, and messengers may come in and go out on a regular basis. The business-person is expected to take all this activity as perfectly normal and to remain composed and ready to continue discussions as soon as the host is prepared to do so.

Initial meetings are typically used to get to know the other party. Business-related discussions may not occur until the third or fourth meeting. Business meetings typically conclude with an offer of coffee or tea. This is a sign that the meeting is over and that future meetings, if there are to be any, should now be arranged.

Saudis attach a great deal of importance to status and rank. When meeting with them, defer to the senior person. It is also important never to criticize or berate anyone publicly. This causes the individual to lose face; the same is true for the person who makes these comments. Mutual respect is expected at all times.

Other useful guidelines for working in an Arab culture such as Saudi Arabia include the following:

1. It is important never to display feelings of superiority because this makes the other party feel inferior. No matter how well someone does something, the individual should let the action speak for itself and not brag or draw attention to himself.

2. A lot of what gets done is a result of going through administrative channels in the country. It is often difficult to sidestep a lot of this red tape, and efforts to do so can be regarded as disrespect for legal and governmental institutions.

3. Connections are extremely important in conducting business. More important people get fast service from less important people. Close relatives take absolute priority; non-relatives are kept waiting.

4. Patience is critical to the success of business negotiations. Time for deliberations should be built into all negotiations to prevent a person from giving away too much in an effort to reach a quick settlement.

5. Important decisions are usually made in person and not by correspondence or telephone. While Saudis seek counsel from many people, the ultimate power to make a decision rests with the person at the top, and this individual relies heavily on personal impressions, trust, and rapport.

Working in China

In recent years the People's Republic of China (PRC, or China, for short) has moved away from isolation to encourage more business with the rest of the world. While China holds tremendous promise, many Western firms have found working on projects in China to be a long, grueling process that often results in failure. One of the primary reasons for problems is the failure to appreciate Chinese culture.

Chinese society, like those of Japan and Korea, is influenced by the teachings of Confucius (551–478 B.C.). Unlike America, which relies on legal institutions to regulate behavior, in Confucian societies the primary deterrent against improper or illegal behavior is shame or loss of face. Face is more than simply reputation. There is a Chinese saying that, "Face is like the bark of a tree; without its bark, the tree dies." Loss of face not only brings shame to individuals but also to family members. A member's actions can cause shame for the entire family, hampering that family from working effectively in Chinese society.

In China, "whom you know is more important than what you know." The term *guanxi* refers to personal connections with appropriate authorities or individuals. China observers argue that *guanxi* is critical for working with the Chinese. Chinese are raised to distrust strangers, especially foreigners. Trust is transmitted via *guanxi*. That is, a trusted business associate of yours must pass you along to his trusted business associates. Many outsiders criticize *guanxi,* considering it to be like nepotism where decisions are made regarding contracts or problems based on family ties or connections instead of an objective assessment of ability.

Many believe that the quickest way to build *guanxi* relationships is through tendering favors. Gift-giving, entertainment at lavish banquets, questionable payments, and overseas trips are common. While Westerners see this as nothing short of bribery, the Chinese consider it essential for good business. Another common method for outsiders to acquire *guanxi* is by hiring local intermediaries, who use their connections to create contacts with Chinese officials and businesspeople.

In dealing with the Chinese, you must realize they are a collective society in which people pride themselves on being a member of a group. For this reason, you should never single out a Chinese for specific praise because this is likely to embarrass the individual in front of his peers. At the same time, you should avoid the use of "I" because it conveys that the speaker is drawing attention to himself or herself.

Chinese do not appreciate loud, boisterous behavior, and when speaking to each other they maintain a greater physical distance than is typical in America. Other cautions include the following:

1. Once the Chinese decide who and what is best, they tend to stick to their decisions. So while they may be slow in formulating a plan, once they get started they make good progress.
2. Reciprocity is important in negotiations. If Chinese give concessions, they expect some in return.
3. The Chinese tend to be less animated than Americans. They avoid open displays of affection and physical contact; they are more reticent and reserved than Americans.
4. The Chinese place less value on the significance of time and often get Americans to concede concessions by stalling.
5. In Confucian societies those in position of power and authority are obligated to assist the disadvantaged. In return they gain face and a good reputation.

For more insights on Chinese culture see the Snapshot from Practice: Project Management X-Files.

Working in the United States

In the world of international projects, professionals from other countries will come to the United States to manage projects. To them, the United States is a foreign assignment. They will have to adapt their management style to the new environment they find in the States.

Immigration has made the United States a melting pot of diverse cultures. While many are quick to point out the differences between North and South, Silicon Valley and Wall Street, social anthropologists have identified certain cultural characteristics that shape how many Americans conduct business and manage projects.

Mainstream Americans are motivated by achievement and accomplishment. Their identity and, to a certain extent, their self-worth are measured by what they have achieved. Foreigners are often astounded by the material wealth accumulated by Americans and the modern conveniences most Americans enjoy. They are also quick to point out that Americans appear too busy to truly enjoy what they have achieved.

Americans tend to idolize the self-made person who rises from poverty and adversity to become rich and successful. Most Americans have a strong belief that they can influence and create their future, that with hard work and initiative, they can achieve whatever they set out to do. Self-determination and pragmatism dominate their approach to business.

Although Americans like to set precise objectives, they view planning as a means and not an end. They value flexibility and are willing to deviate from plans and improvise if they believe change will lead to accomplishment. Obstacles on a project are to be overcome, not worked around. Americans think they can accomplish just about anything, given time, money, and technology.

Americans fought a revolution and subsequent wars to preserve their concept of democracy, so they resent too much control or interference, especially by governments. While more an ideal than practice, there is deep-rooted belief in American management philosophy that those people who will be affected by decisions should be involved in making decisions. Many foreign businesspeople

SNAPSHOT FROM PRACTICE   Project Management X-Files

Americans tend to discount the significance of luck and believe that good fortune is generally a result of hard work. In other cultures, luck takes on greater significance and has supernatural ramifications. For example, in many Asian cultures certain numbers are considered lucky, while others are unlucky. In Hong Kong the numbers 7, 3, and especially 8 (which sounds like the word for prosperity) are considered lucky, while the number 4 is considered unlucky (because it is pronounced like the word "death"). Hong Kong businesspeople go to great lengths to avoid the number 4. For example, there is no fourth floor in office and hotel buildings. Business executives have been known to reject ideal sites in heavily congested Hong Kong because the address would contain the number 4. They pay premium prices for suitable sites containing addresses with the lucky numbers. Likewise, Hong Kong business managers avoid scheduling important events on the fourth day of each month and prefer to arrange critical meetings on the eighth day.

Hong Kong is also a place where the ancient art of *Feng shui* (literally "wind water") is practiced. This involves making sure a site and buildings are aligned in harmony with the earth's energy forces so that the location will be propitious. Feng shui practitioners are often called in on construction projects to make sure that the building is aligned correctly on the site. In some cases, the technical design of the building is changed to conform to the recommendations of such experts. Similarly, Feng shui experts have been known to be called in when projects are experiencing problems. Their recommendations may include repositioning the project manager's desk or hanging up mirrors to deflect the flow of unharmonious influences away from the building or site of the project.

© Rob Brimson/Taxi/Getty Images

In cultures where luck is believed to play a role in business, people who discount luck may not only insult the luck seekers, they may risk being thought negligent in not paying enough attention to what is viewed as a legitimate business concern.

are surprised at the amount of autonomy and decision-making authority granted to subordinates. Foreign personnel have to learn to interact with American professionals below their rank in their own organizations.

Businesspeople from different African, Asian, and Latin American countries are amazed and often somewhat distressed at the rapid pace of America. "Getting things done" is an American characteristic. Americans are very time-conscious and efficient. They expect meetings to start on time. They tinker with gadgets and technological systems, always searching for easier, better, more efficient ways of accomplishing things. American professionals are often relentless in pursuing project objectives and expect that behavior of others also.

Americans in play or business generally are quite competitive, reflecting their desire to achieve and succeed. Although the American culture contains contradictory messages about the importance of success (i.e., "It's not whether you win or lose but how you play the game" versus "nice guys finish last"), winning and being number one are clearly valued in American society. Foreigners are often surprised at how aggressively Americans approach business with adversarial attitudes toward competitors and a desire to not just meet but to exceed project goals and objectives.

Other guidelines and cautions for working with Americans on projects include:

1. More than half of U.S. women work outside the home; females have considerable opportunity for personal and professional growth, guaranteed by law. It is not uncommon to find women in key project positions. Female professionals expect to be treated as equals. Behavior tolerated in other countries would be subject to harassment laws in the States.

2. In the United States, gifts are rarely brought by visitors in a business situation.

3. Americans tend to be quite friendly and open when first meeting someone. Foreigners often mistake this strong "come-on" for the beginning of a strong reciprocal friendship. This is in contrast to many other cultures where there is more initial reserve in interpersonal relations, especially with strangers. For many foreigners, the American comes on too strong, too soon, and then fails to follow up with the implicitly promised friendship.

4. Although in comparison to the rest of the world Americans tend to be informal in greeting and dress, they are a noncontact culture (e.g., they avoid embracing in public usually) and Americans maintain certain physical/psychological distance with others (e.g., about two feet) in conversations.

5. American decision making is results oriented. Decisions tend to be based on facts and expected outcomes, not social impact.

Summary Comments about Working in Different Cultures

These briefings underscore the complexity of working on international projects. It is common practice to rely on intermediaries—often natives who are foreign educated—to bridge the gap between cultures. These intermediaries perform a variety of functions. They act as translators. They use their social connections to expedite transactions and protect the project against undue interference. They are used to sidestep the touchy bribery/gift dilemma (see the Dealing with Customs Snapshot from Practice). They serve as cultural guides, helping outsiders understand and interpret the foreign culture. In today's world, there are a growing number of consulting firms that perform these functions by helping foreign clients work on projects in their country.

The international briefings also highlight the importance of project managers doing their homework and becoming familiar with the customs and habits of the host country they are going to be working in. As far as possible, the project should be managed in such a way that local-country norms and customs are honored. However, there are limits to the extent to which you should accommodate foreign cultures. *Going native* is generally not an alternative. After all, it took a Russian his entire life to learn how to be a Russian. It would be foolish to think an outsider could learn to be one in six months, two years, or perhaps ever.

The remainder of this chapter focuses on the selection and training of project personnel for international projects. But before these issues are discussed, this section concludes with a discussion of the phenomenon of culture shock, which can have a profound effect on a foreigner's performance on a project in a strange culture.

SNAPSHOT FROM PRACTICE Dealing with Customs

Will corruption influence the project? Bribes are illegal in the United States, but in some countries they are the usual way to do business. For example, one American project manager in a foreign country requested that a shipment of critical project equipment be sent "overnight rush." Two days later, inquiries to the sender confirmed the materials had been delivered to the nearby airport. Further inquiries to the port found the shipment "waiting to pass customs." Locals quickly informed the American that money paid to the chief customs inspector would expedite clearance. The American project manager's response was, "I will not be held hostage. Bribes are illegal!" Two more days of calling government officials did not move the shipment from customs. The manager related his problem to a friendly businessman of the host nation at a social affair. The local businessman said he would see if he could help. The shipment arrived the next morning at 10:00 A.M. The American called his local business friend and thanked him profusely. "I owe you one." "No," replied the local. "You owe me a $50 dinner when I visit you in the States." The use of an intermediary in such situations may be the only avenue available to a manager to reduce the stress and personal conflict with the U.S. value system.

Culture Shock

> My first few weeks in Chiang Mai [Thailand] were filled with excitement. I was excited about the challenge of building a waste treatment plant in a foreign country. I was fascinated with Thai customs and traditions, the smells and sights of the night market. Soon I noticed a distinct change in my attitude and behavior. I started having problems sleeping and lacked energy. I became irritable at work, frustrated by how long things took to accomplish, and how I couldn't seem to get anything accomplished. I started staying up late at night watching CNN in my hotel room.

This engineer is experiencing what many would call "culture shock." *Culture shock* is a natural psychological disorientation that most people suffer when they move into a culture different from their own. The culture shock cycle has four stages (see Figure 15.6):

1. *Honeymoon*—You start your overseas assignment with a sense of excitement. The new and the unusual are welcomed. At first it is amusing not to understand or be understood. Soon a sense of frustration begins to set in.

FIGURE 15.6
Culture Shock Cycle

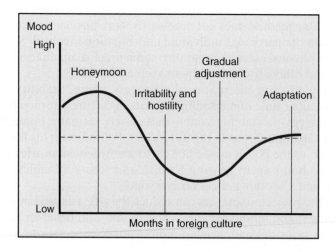

2. *Irritability and hostility*—Your initial enthusiasm is exhausted, and you begin to notice that differences are greater than you first imagined. You become frustrated by your inability to get things done as you are accustomed to. You begin to lose confidence in your abilities to communicate and work effectively in the different culture.

3. *Gradual adjustment*—You begin to overcome your sense of isolation and figure out how to get things done in the new culture. You acquire a new perspective of what is possible and regain confidence in your ability to work in the culture.

4. *Adaptation*—You recover from your sense of psychological disorientation and begin to function and communicate in the new culture.

Culture shock is not a disease but a natural response to immersing yourself in a new environment. Culture shock results from a breakdown in your selective perception and effective interpretation system. At a subliminal level, your senses are being bombarded by a wide variety of strange sounds, sights, and smells. At the same time, the normal assumptions you are accustomed to using in your home culture to interpret perceptions and to communicate intentions no longer apply. When this happens, whether in a business context or in normal attempts to socialize, confusion and frustration set in. The natives' behavior does not seem to make sense, and, even more importantly, your behavior does not produce expected results. Frustration occurs because you are used to being competent in such situations and now find you are unable to operate effectively.

Culture shock is generally considered a positive sign that the professional is becoming involved in the new culture instead of remaining isolated in an expatriate ghetto. The significant question is how best to manage culture shock, not how to avoid it. The key appears to be managing the stress associated with culture shock.

Stress-related culture shock takes many forms: disappointment, frustration, withdrawal, anxiety, and physiological responses such as fatigue, sleeplessness, and headaches. Stress is induced by the senses being overwhelmed by foreign stimuli and the inability to function effectively in a strange land. Stress is exacerbated when one encounters disturbing situations that, as a foreigner, are neither understood nor condoned. For example, many North Americans are appalled by the poverty and hunger in many underdeveloped countries.

Coping with Culture Shock

There are a wide range of stress management techniques for coping with culture shock. One method does not necessarily work any better than another; success depends on the particular individual and situation involved. Some people engage in regular physical exercise programs, some practice meditation and relaxation exercises, and others find it healthy to keep a journal.

Many effective international managers create "stability zones." They spend most of their time immersed in the foreign culture but then briefly retreat into an environment—a stability zone—that closely recreates home. For example, when one of the authors was living in Kraków, Poland, with his family, they would routinely go to the Polish movie houses to see American movies with Polish subtitles. The two hours spent hearing English and seeing a familiar environment on the screen had a soothing effect on everyone.

On the project, managers can reduce the stress caused by culture shock by recognizing it and modifying their expectations and behavior accordingly. They can redefine priorities and develop more realistic expectations as to what is possible.

They can focus their limited energy on only the most important tasks and relish small accomplishments.

After three to six months, depending on the individual and assignment, most people come up from their culture shock "low" and begin living a more normal life in the foreign country. They talk to acquaintances from the host country and experienced outsiders from their own culture to find out how to behave and what to expect. Little by little they learn how to make sense of the new environment. They figure out when "yes" means "yes" and when it means "maybe" and when it means "no." They begin to master the language so that they can make themselves understood in day-to-day conversations.

The vast majority of people eventually make the adjustment, although for some people it can take much longer than three to six months. A smaller number never recover, and their international experience turns into a nightmare. Some exhibit severe stress symptoms (e.g., alcoholism, drug abuse, nervous breakdown) and must return home before finishing their assignment.

Professionals can use project work as a bridge until they adjust to their new environment. Unfortunately, spouses who do not work do not have this advantage. When spouses are left to cope with the strange environment on their own, they often have a much more difficult time overcoming culture shock. The effect on spouses cannot be underestimated. The number one reason expatriate managers return home is that their spouses failed to adjust to the new environment.

Project professionals working overseas accept that they are in a difficult situation and that they will not act as effectively as they did at home, especially in the initial stages. They recognize the need for good stress management techniques, including stability zones. They also recognize that it is not an individual problem and invest extra time and energy to help their spouses and families manage the transition. At the same time, they appreciate that their colleagues are experiencing similar problems and are sensitive to their needs. They work together to manage the stress and pull out of a culture shock low as quickly as possible.

It is somewhat ironic, but people who work on projects overseas experience culture shock twice. Many professionals experience the same kind of disorientation and stress when they return home, although it is usually less severe. For some, their current job has less responsibility and is boring compared with the challenge of their overseas assignment. For others, they have problems adjusting to changes made in the home organization while they were gone. This can be compounded by financial shock when the salary and fringe benefits they became accustomed to in the foreign assignment are now lost, and adjusting to a lower standard of living is difficult. It typically takes six months to a year before managers operate again at full effectiveness after a lengthy foreign assignment.

Selection and Training for International Projects

When professionals are selected for overseas projects and they do not work out, the overall costs can be staggering. Not only does the project experience a serious setback, but the reputation of the firm is damaged in the region. This is why many firms have developed formal screening procedures to help ensure the careful selection of personnel for international projects. Organizations examine a number of characteristics to determine whether an individual is suitable for overseas work. They may look for work experience with cultures other than one's own, previous overseas travel, good physical and emotional health, a knowledge of a host nation's language, and even recent immigration background or heritage. Prospective candidates and their family members are often interviewed by trained psychologists, who assess their ability to adapt and function in the new culture.

While there is growing appreciation for screening people for foreign assignments, the number one reason for selection is that the personnel assigned are the best people available for the technical challenges of the project. Technical know-how takes precedence over cross-cultural sensitivity or experience. As a consequence, training is critical to fill in the cultural gaps and prepare individuals to work in a foreign land.

Training varies widely, depending on the individual, company, nature of the project, and cultures to work with. Project professionals assigned to foreign countries should have a minimal understanding of the following areas:

- Religion.
- Dress codes.
- Education system.
- Holidays—national and religious.
- Daily eating patterns.
- Family life.
- Business protocols.
- Social etiquette.
- Equal opportunity.

An example of a short-term training program is the one developed by Underwriter Laboratories, Inc., to train staff who travel to Japan to work with clients on projects. The program is designed around a series of mini-lectures that cover topics ranging from how to handle introductions to the proper way to exchange gifts to the correct way of interpreting Japanese social and business behavior. The two-day program consists of lectures, case studies, role plays, language practice, and a short test on cultural terminology; it concludes with a 90-minute question-and-answer period. At the end of the program, participants have a fundamental understanding of how to communicate with the Japanese. More importantly, they know the types of information they lack and how to go about learning more to become effective intercultural communicators.

Other training programs are more extensive. For example, Peace Corps volunteers undergo an intense two- to four-month training program in their country of service. The training includes classes on the history and traditions of the country, intensive language instruction, and cross-cultural training as well as home-stays with local families. Many companies outsource training to one of the many firms specializing in overseas and intercultural training.

Figure 15.7 attempts to link the length and type of training with the cultural fluency required to successfully complete the project. Three different learning approaches are highlighted:

1. The "information-giving" approach—the learning of information or skills from a lecture-type orientation.
2. The "affective" approach—the learning of information/skills that raise the affective responses on the part of the trainee and result in cultural insights.
3. The "behavioral/experiential" approach—variant of the affective approach technique that provides the trainee with realistic simulations or scenarios.

FIGURE 15.7
Relationship between Length and Rigor of Training and Cultural Fluency Required

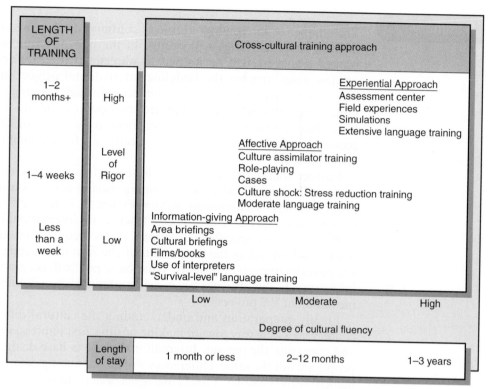

According to this framework, the length and level of training would depend on the degree of cultural fluency required to be successful. In general, the longer the person is expected to work in the foreign country, the more intensive the training should be. Length of stay should not be the only consideration; high levels of cultural fluency, and therefore more extensive training, may be required to perform short-term, intense projects. In addition, location is important. Working in Australia will likely require less cultural fluency than working on a project in Pakistan.

While English is rapidly becoming the international language for business in many parts of the world, you should not underestimate the value of being able to speak the language of the host country. At a minimum you should be able to exchange basic pleasantries in the native tongue. Most foreigners consider this a sign of respect, and even if you stumble they appreciate the effort.

In many situations translators are used to facilitate communication. While time-consuming, this is the only way to communicate with non-English-speaking personnel. Be careful in the selection of translators, and do not just assume they are competent. For example, one of the authors enlisted the help of a Polish translator to conduct a meeting with some Polish managers. After the meeting the translator, who taught English at a local university, asked if the author "had good time." I responded that I felt things went well. The translator repeated her question. Puzzled, I reaffirmed that I felt things went well. After the interchange was repeated several times, the translator finally grabbed my wrist, pointed at my watch, and asked again if I "had good time?" Doubts arose concerning the accuracy of the meeting translation!

Summary

The number of international projects continues to increase, and nothing on the horizon suggests things will change in the new millennium. More and more project managers will be needed to implement international projects. There are few guidelines for the fledgling international project manager. Preparing for international projects can be enhanced through training. As a general background, potential international project managers can benefit from a basic international business course that sensitizes them to the forces of change in the global economy and to cultural differences. Learning a foreign language is also strongly recommended.

Further training specific to the host country is a very useful preproject endeavor. The length and type of training usually depend on the duration of the project manager's assignment. Review Figure 15.7. Still, self-learning, on-the-job training, and experience are the best teachers for international project managers.

Preparing for a specific international project requires serious preproject homework. Understanding the motivation of the firm in selecting the project and its site provides important insights. What basic political, geographic, economic, and infrastructure factors were key considerations? How will they impact the implementation of the project?

Finally, preparation and understanding the cultural differences of the host country go a long way toward making positive first impressions with the nationals and managing the project. International projects have distinct personalities. All people are not the same. Differences within and among countries and cultures are numerous and complex. Project managers need to accept these differences and treat them as real—or live with the consequences. What works at home may not work in the foreign country. Americans are regarded as friendly by our neighbors in the global village, but Americans are also noted to be insensitive to differences in local cultures and customs and awkward in our use of languages other than English. Although most attention in foreign projects is focused on technical efforts and their cost, the project must be carried out within the environment of the country's social customs, work practices, government controls, and religious beliefs. In most cultures, sincerity and flexibility will pay off.

Key Terms

Cross-cultural
  orientations *543*
Culture *538*

Culture shock *554*
Infrastructure *538*

Review Questions

1. How do environmental factors affect project implementation?
2. What role do local intermediaries play in helping an outsider complete a project?
3. Why is it important to honor the customs and traditions of a country when working on an international project?
4. What is culture shock? What can you do to reduce the negative effects of culture shock?
5. How should you go about preparing yourself for an international project?

Exercises

1. Interview someone who has worked or lived in a foreign country for more than six months.

   a. What was his experience with culture shock?

   b. What did he learn about the culture of the country he lived in?

   c. What advice would he give to someone who would be working on a project in that country?

2. Try as best you can to apply the Kluckhohn-Strodtbeck cross-cultural framework to the four countries discussed in this chapter: Mexico, France, Saudi Arabia, and China. Where do you think these countries lie on each of the cultural issues?

3. Place in order the following countries in terms of what you would think would be the least to most corrupt:

   United States, Denmark, Saudi Arabia, Russia, Australia, Hong Kong, Nepal, China, Kenya, Indonesia, Botswana, Greece, Chile.

   Use an Internet search engine to find the most recent International Corruptions Perceptions Index (CPI) released by the Berlin-based organization Transparency International.

   a. Check your predictions with the Index.

   b. How well did you do? What countries surprised you? Why?

References

Ackoff, R. L., *Ackoff's Fables: Irreverent Reflections on Business and Bureaucracy* (New York: Wiley, 1991), p. 221.

Alder, N., *International Dimensions of Organizational Behavior,* 2nd ed. (Boston: PWS-Kent Publishing, 1991).

Borsuk, R., "In Indonesia, a Twist on Spreading the Wealth: Decentralization of Power Multiplies Opportunities for Bribery, Corruption," *The Wall Street Journal,* January 29, 2003, p. A16.

Contingency Planning and Management.com, "Strohl Systems Offers Terrorism Readiness Questionnaire," September 24, 2001.

Deneire, M., and M. Segalla, "Mr. Christian Pierret, Secretary of State for Industry (1997–2002), on French Perspectives on Organizational Leadership and Management," *Academy of Management Executive,* 16 (4) November 2002, pp. 25–30.

Doh, J. P., P. Rodriguez, K. Uhlenbruck, J. Collins, and L. Eden, "Coping with Corruption in Foreign Markets," *Academy of Management Executive,* 17 (3) August 2003, pp. 114–27.

Graham, J. L., and N. M. Lam, "The Chinese Negotiation," *Harvard Business Review,* October 1, 2003, pp. 82–91.

Graham, S., "Relief Agency Suspends Afghan Operations," *www.guardian.co.uk,* June 3, 2004.

Hallowell, R., D. Bowen, and C. I. Knoop, "Four Seasons Goes to Paris," *Academy of Management Executive,* 16 (4) November 2002, pp. 7–24.

Henry, W. L., and J. J. DiStefano, *International Project Management,* 2nd ed. (Boston: PWS-Kent Publishing, 1992).

Hodgetts, R. M., and F. Luthans, *International Management: Culture, Strategy, and Behavior,* 5th ed. (Boston: McGraw-Hill/Irwin, 2003).

Hofstede, G., *Cultures Consequences: International Difference in Work-Related Values* (Beverly Hills, CA: Sage Publishing, 1980).

Hooker, J., *Working across Cultures* (Stanford, CA: Stanford Business Books, 2003).

Kluckhohn, F., and F. L. Strodtbeck, *Variations in Value Orientations* (Evanston, IL: Row, Peterson, 1961).

Krane, J., "Intelligence Companies Help Overseas Business Travelers," *The Cincinnati Enquirer,* April 2, 2002, website.

Kras, E., *Management in Two Cultures: Bridging the Gap between U.S. and Mexican Managers,* rev. ed. (Yarmouth, ME: Intercultural Press, 1995).

Lieberthal, K., and G. Lieberthal, "The Great Transition," *Harvard Business Review,* October 1, 2003, pp. 71–81.

Mendenhall, M. E., E. Dunbar, and G. R. Oddou, "Expatriate Selection, Training, and Career-Pathing: A Review and Critique," *Human Resource Management,* 26 (3) Fall 1987, pp. 331–45.

Milosevic, D. Z., "Echoes of the Silent Language of Project Management," *Project Management Journal,* 30 (1) March 1999, pp. 27–39.

Ricks, D. A., *Blunders in International Business* (London: Blackwell, 2000).

Saunders, C., C. Van Slyke, and D. R. Vogel "My Time or Yours? Managing Time Visions in Global Virtual Teams," *Academy of Management Executive,* 18 (1) 2004, pp. 19–31.

Scown, M. J., "Managers Journal: Barstool Advice for the Vietnam Investor," *Asian Wall Street Journal,* July 15, 1993.

Tung, R. L., "Expatriate Assignments: Enhancing Success and Minimizing Failure," *Academy of Management Executive,* 1 (2) 1987, pp. 117–26.

Yeung I., and R. L. Tung, "Achieving Business Success in Confucian Societies: The Importance of Guanxi (Connections)," *Organizational Dynamics,* 25 (2) Autumn 1996, pp. 54–65.

Case

AMEX, Hungary

Michael Thomas shouted, "Sasha, Tor-Tor, we've got to go! Our driver is waiting for us." Thomas's two daughters were fighting over who would get the last orange for lunch that day. Victoria ("Tor-Tor") prevailed as she grabbed the orange and ran out the door to the Mercedes Benz waiting for them. The fighting continued in the back seat as they drove toward the city of Budapest, Hungary. Thomas finally turned around and grabbed the orange and proclaimed that he would have it for lunch. The back seat became deadly silent as they made their way to the American International School of Budapest.

After dropping the girls off at the school, Thomas was driven to his office in the Belvéros area of Budapest. Thomas worked for AMEX Petroleum and had been sent to Budapest four months earlier to set up business operations in central Hungary. His job was to establish 10 to 14 gas stations in the region by purchasing existing stations, building new ones, or negotiating franchise arrangements with existing owners of stations. Thomas jumped at this project. He realized that his career at AMEX was going nowhere in the United States, and if he were going to realize his ambitions, it would be in the "wild, wild east" of the former Soviet empire. Besides, Thomas's mother was Hungarian, and he could speak the language. At least he thought he could until he arrived in Budapest and realized that he had greatly exaggerated his competence.

As he entered the partially refurbished offices of AMEX, he noticed that only three of his staff were present. No one knew where Miklos was, while Margit reported that she would not be at work today because she had to stay at home to take care of her sick mother. Thomas asked Béla why the workmen weren't present to work on finishing the office. Béla informed him that the work had to be halted until they received approval from the city historian. Budapest, anxious to preserve its historical heritage, required that all building renovations be approved by the city historian. When Thomas asked Béla how long it would take, Béla responded, "Who knows—days, weeks, maybe even months." Thomas muttered "great" to himself and turned his attention to the morning business. He was scheduled to interview prospective employees who would act as station managers and staff personnel.

The interview with Ferenc Erkel was typical of the many interviews he held that morning. Erkel was a neatly dressed, 42-year-old, unemployed professional who could speak limited English. He had a masters degree in international economics and had worked for 12 years in the state-owned Institute for Foreign Trade. Since being laid off two years ago, he has been working as a taxicab driver. When asked about his work at the Institute, Erkel smiled sheepishly and said that he pushed paper and spent most of the time playing cards with his colleagues.

To date Thomas had hired 16 employees. Four quit within three days on the job, and six were let go after a trial period for being absent from work, failing to perform duties, or showing a lack of initiative. Thomas thought that at this rate it would take him over a year just to hire his staff.

Thomas took a break from the interview schedule to scan the *Budapest Business Journal,* an English newspaper that covered business news in Hungary. Two items caught his eye. One article was on the growing threat of the Ukrainian Mafia in Hungary, which detailed extortion attempts in Budapest. The second story was that inflation had risen to 32 percent. This last item disturbed Thomas because at the time only one out of every five Hungarian families owned a car. AMEX's strategy in Hungary depended on a boom in first-time car owners.

Thomas collected his things and popped a few aspirin for the headache he was developing. He walked several blocks to the Kispipa restaurant where he had a supper meeting with Hungarian businessman Zoltán Kodaly. He had met Kodaly briefly at a reception sponsored by the U.S. consulate for American and Hungarian businesspeople. Kodaly reportedly owned three gas stations that Thomas was interested in.

Thomas waited, sipping bottled water for 25 minutes. Kodaly appeared with a young lady who could not have been older than 19. As it turned out Kodaly had brought his daughter Annia, who was a university student, to act as translator. While Thomas made an attempt to speak in Hungarian at first, Kodaly insisted that they use Annia to translate.

After ordering the house specialty, *szekelygulas,* Thomas immediately got down to business. He told Kodaly that AMEX was willing to make two offers to him. They would like to either purchase two of his stations at a price of $150,000 each, or they could work out a franchise agreement. Thomas said AMEX was not interested in the third station located near Klinikak because it would be too expensive to modernize the equipment. Annia translated, and as far as Thomas could tell she was doing a pretty good job. At first Kodaly did not respond and simply engaged in side conversations with Annia and exchanged pleasantries with people who came by. Thomas became frustrated and reiterated his offer. Eventually Kodaly asked what he meant by franchising, and Thomas tried to use the local McDonald's as an example of how it worked. He mentioned that Kodaly would still own the stations, but he would have to pay a franchisee fee, share profits with AMEX, and adhere to AMEX procedures and practices. In exchange, AMEX would provide petroleum and funds to renovate the stations to meet AMEX standards.

Toward the end of the meal Kodaly asked what would happen to the people who worked at the stations. Thomas asserted that according to his calculation the stations were over-staffed by 70 percent and that to make a profit, at least 15 workers would have to be let go. This statement was greeted with silence. Kodaly then turned the conversation to soccer and asked Thomas if it was true that in America girls play "football." Thomas said that both of his daughters played AYSO soccer in America and hoped to play in Hungary. Kodaly said girls don't play football in Hungary and that Annia was an accomplished volleyball player. Thomas pressed Kodaly for a response to his offer, but Kodaly rose and thanked Thomas for the meal. He said he would think about his offer and get back in touch with him.

Thomas left the Kispipa wondering if he would ever see Kodaly again. He returned to his office where an urgent message was waiting from Tibor. Tibor was responsible for retrofitting the first station Thomas had purchased for AMEX. The new tanks had not arrived from Vienna, and the construction crew had spent the day doing nothing. After several phone calls he found out that the tanks were being held at the border by customs. This irritated him because he had been assured by local officials that everything had been taken care of. He asked his secretary to schedule an appointment with the Hungarian trade office as soon as possible.

At the end of the day he checked his e-mail from the States. There was a message from headquarters asking about the status of the project. By this time he had hoped to have his office staffed and up and running and at least three stations secured. So far he had only one-third of his staff, his office was in shambles, and only one station was being retrofitted. Thomas decided to wait until tomorrow to respond to the e-mail.

Before returning home Thomas stopped off at the English Pub, a favorite hangout for expats in Budapest. There he met Jan Krovert, who worked for a Dutch company that was building a large discount retail store on the outskirts of Badapest. Thomas and Krovert often talked about being "strangers in a strange land" at the pub. Thomas talked about the interviews and how he could just see in their eyes that they didn't have the drive or initiative to be successful. Krovert responded that Hungary has high unemployment but a shortage of motivated workers. Krovert confided that he no longer interviewed anyone over the age of 30, claiming that what fire they had in their bellies was burned out after years of working in state-run companies.

1. What are the issues confronting Thomas in this case?
2. How well is Thomas dealing with these issues?
3. What suggestions would you have for Thomas in managing this project?

Case

Ghost Stories

On December 26, 2004, an earthquake reaching 9.1 on the Richter scale triggered a series of devastating tsunamis off the coast of Indonesia. They spread throughout the Indian Ocean, killing large numbers of people and inundating coastal communities across South and Southeast Asia, including parts of Indonesia, Sri Lanka, India, and Thailand. The 2004 Asian tsunami was one of the deadliest catastrophes in modern history, with more than 220,000 lives lost.

Nils Lofgrin, who had managed several construction projects in Australia and New Guinea, was sent by his construction firm to restore a five-star resort along the Andaman coast in southern Thailand that had been ravaged by this tsunami. Casualties at the resort included 12 staff and 37 guests. This was Nils's first assignment in Thailand.

Nils flew down and toured the site. His assessment of the damage was that it was not as severe as feared. The basic infrastructure was intact but debris needed to be cleared and the resort refurbished. He reported back to headquarters that with a bit of luck he should have the resort up and running in a matter of months. Little did he realize how soon he would regret making such a promise.

The problems began immediately when he was unable to recruit workers to help clean up the mess at the resort. The Burmese migrant workers who comprised a significant portion of the workforce in this region had fled into the hills out of growing fears of being arrested and deported. Even when he offered double wages he was not able to recruit many Thais. At first he attributed their reluctance to the shock caused by the devastation of the tsunami. Everyone he met seemed to know someone who had died or even worse had just disappeared. But he soon realized there was more going on than just shock.

Nils was at a restaurant having a lunch with a Thai friend when an animated discussion broke out among some Thai patrons nearby. He asked his friend what was going on. The friend said someone was telling the story of a local taxi driver who had picked up three foreign tourists and was driving them to Kata Beach when he looked around and found his cab empty. Another told the story of a local family whose telephone rings constantly through the day and night. When answered, the voices of missing friends and relatives cry out for help.

Nils sank in his chair when he began to realize that no one wanted to work for him because prospective workers believed that the region and his resort are haunted by ghosts.

1. What options are available to Nils?
2. What would you do and why?

Oversight

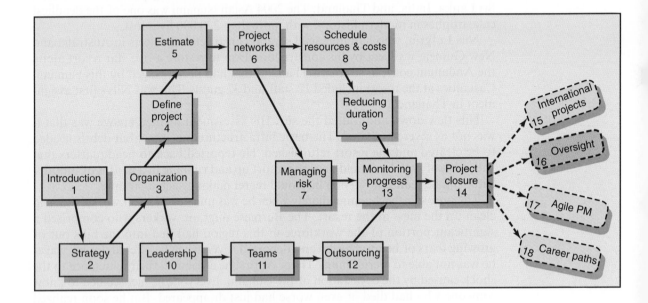

Oversight

Project Oversight

Organization Project Management in the Long Run

Summary

Without continual growth and progress, such words as achievement and success have no meaning.

—*Benjamin Franklin*

Project Oversight

In the last few years the paradigm shift to project oversight/governance has been profound. **Project oversight** can be defined as *a set of principles and processes to guide and improve the management of projects.* The intent is to ensure projects meet the needs of the *organization* through standards, procedures, accountability, efficient allocation of resources, and continuous improvement in the management of projects. A second purpose is to support the project manager. We estimate over 95 percent of project-driven organizations have been implementing some form of oversight for several years. Progress has been rapid and steady. The typical activities of project oversight cover two dimensions: organization and project. Here are some of the major oversight activities used in practice:

At the Organization Level

- Project selection.
- Portfolio management.
- Improving the way all projects are managed over time.
- Assessing and elevating the maturity level of the organization's project management system.
- Using the balanced scorecard approach to review progress on strategic priorities.

At the Project Level

- Review projects' objectives.
- Decide on issues raised by the project manager such as resource needs and escalation.
- Track and assist the project to resolve bottlenecks.
- Review status reports from the project manager.
- Audit and review lessons learned.
- Authorize any major deviations from the original scope.
- Cancel the project.

All of these activities are designed to bring consistency, structure, accountability, and improvement to the management of projects. Today, project oversight, through an executive committee, oversight group, or a project office, covers every aspect of managing projects in the organization.

Importance of Oversight to the Project Manager

What does this solid paradigm shift mean to a project manager who is normally in charge of only one or two projects? Four things. First, in almost all cases oversight is interested in supporting and helping the project manager where needed. This is an improvement over the past. Second, the oversight function determines the environment in which the project manager will implement his or her project. This can affect the management of a project in a positive or negative manner. Third, depending on the size and complexity of the project, methods used to hold the project manager responsible and accountable will influence how performance is measured. Finally, the project manager, who is responsible for day-to-day management, will probably be reporting to this oversight group at predetermined phases in the project. In short, project oversight supports project management at the organization and project levels.

As a project manager you need to be aware of how these oversight activities can and will influence management of your projects. A short description of each of these oversight activities follows.

Portfolio Project Management

When project effort moves from tactical to strategic, project selection, project processes, and resources are brought under one system known as portfolio project management. Remember from Chapter 2 that portfolio management integrates projects with current priorities, strategic thrust, and overall allocation of scarce organization resources. Here is a typical definition:

> *Portfolio project management* is the centralized management of projects to ensure that the allocation of resources to projects is directed toward projects that contribute the greatest value to organization goals.

Project portfolio management supports management of multiple projects in a coordinated way to obtain the benefits not available from managing them individually. The development of portfolio project management is complemented by the movement to use project management offices.

Project Office

Most project-driven organizations have set up project offices. The appearance of a project office frequently follows the implementation of project portfolio management efforts. The project office is now used as the vehicle to support and manage oversight activities. Here is one definition:

> The *project office (PO)* is the unit responsible for the continued support of consistent application of selection criteria, standards, and processes; training of and general assistance to project managers; and continued improvement and use of best practices.

The project office frequently includes project portfolio management. Project portfolios and project offices both result in an integration function for planning and control. The PO also supports the integration of the processes of managing projects within the social/cultural environment of the organization. High-tech firms such as Hewlett-Packard (HP), International Business Machines (IBM), and Dell all use project offices to coordinate projects and to ensure best practices are being used to manage projects. For example, HP has project offices in Europe/Middle

SNAPSHOT FROM PRACTICE The Project Office*

As more and more companies embrace project management as a critical vehicle for realizing corporate objectives, they are creating centralized project offices (POs) to oversee and improve the management of projects. PO functions vary widely by organization and need. In some cases, they serve as a simple clearinghouse for project management information. In other cases, they recruit, train, and assign managers to specific projects. As POs mature and evolve over time, they become full-service providers of project management expertise within a firm. The different services POs may provide include the following:

- Creating and maintaining the internal project management information system.

- Recruiting and selecting project managers both within and outside the organization.

- Establishing standardized project planning and reporting methodologies.

- Training personnel in project management techniques and tools.

- Auditing ongoing and recently completed projects.

- Developing comprehensive risk management programs.

- Providing in-house project management consulting and mentoring services.

- Maintaining an internal project management library containing critical documents, including project plans, funding papers, test plans, audit reports, and so forth.

- Establishing and benchmarking best practices in project management.

- Maintaining and tracking the portfolio of projects within an organization.

A good example of how project offices evolve is the global project office (GPO) at Citibank's Global Corporate Bank. GPO originated at the grassroots level within the small world of Operations and Technology for Global Cash Management. Committed to bringing order to the chaos of managing projects, GPO instituted training programs and professional project management practices on a very small scale. Soon the success of GPO-supported projects caught the eye of upper management. Within three years the department was expanded to offer a full range of PO services across Citibank's entire banking operation. GPO's mission is to establish project management as a core competency throughout the entire Citibank organization.

* T. R. Block and J. D. Frame, "Today's Project Office: Gauging Attitudes," *PM Network,* August 2001; W. Gradante and D. Gardner, "Managing Projects from the Future, Not from the Past," *Proceedings of the 29th Annual Project Management Institute 1998 Seminars and Symposium* (Newtown Square, PA: Project Management Institute, 1998), pp. 289–94.

East, Americas, Asia Pacific, and Japan with several others planned. Because projects are used to implement strategy, HP has created a new position—vice president of project offices. Project offices ensure a consistent approach to all projects in all locations. See Snapshot from Practice: The Project Office.

Figures 16.1 and 16.2 provide an example of a report the project office provides senior management of an international organization. Note that such a report requires a standard format for all projects. Figure 16.1 depicts a project portfolio cost summary report developed for top management. Figure 16.2 presents the same summary for project schedules. Additional detailed information for any specific highlighted project—such as the project schedule, cost status report, project team—is only a double click away. For example, the Smart Card project in the European Economic Community (EEC) appears to be behind schedule. The cause

FIGURE 16.1　**Project Portfolio Cost Summary Report for Top Management**

Location	Project ID	Description	PV	EV	AC	CPI	SPI	PCIB	BAC	EAC	VAC
Summary / All		Portfolio							$18,120		
United States									$10,500		
○	01-003	Digitize Fingerprints-FBI	3,000	3,500	3,230	1.08	1.17	97.2%	3,600	3,322	278
○	01-011	Encryption	270	250	250	1.00	0.93	71.4%	350	350	0
○	01-002	Internet Protocol--CIA						0.0%	950		
○	01-009	Supply Chain Partners	90	90	90	1.00	1.00	16.7%	540	540	0
	01-012	Bonus Mileage Awards						0.0%	630		
●	01-005	E-sales Claims	150	140	150	0.93	0.93	35.0%	400	429	-29
●	01-011	Procurement Net	400	340	380	0.89	0.85	27.6%	1,230	1,375	-145
○	01-008	Smart Tag Tracking	850	900	900	1.00	1.06	32.1%	2,800	2,800	0
Asia/Pacific									$2,800		
○	02-007	Currency Conversion	125	120	120	1.00	0.96	80.0%	150	150	0
○	02-002	Billing System	280	280	280	1.00	1.00	70.0%	400	400	0
○	02-005	Web-Based Cash Flow	210	220	200	1.10	1.05	73.3%	300	273	27
	02-004	Olympic Simulation						0.0%	1,950		
EEC									$4,820		
●	03-008	Smart Card	145	110	140	0.79	0.76	18.3%	600	764	-164
	03-003	Warranty						0.0%	70		
	03-004	Simulation--ESA						0.0%	800		
●	03-005	Air Reservation Net	510	490	520	0.94	0.96	35.0%	1,400	1,486	-86
●	03-007	Pilot Internet Log Syst.	540	490	550	0.89	0.91	57.6%	850	954	-104
○	03-006	Internet Telephone Syst.	850	850	860	0.99	1.00	77.3%	1,100	1,113	-13

Net Services, Inc. — View: Cost — Project Portfolio Cost Summary ($ 000) — Date:

Sidebar icons: Gantt, Network, Resource, Status, WBS, Sponsor, Team, Priority, Issues

LEGEND
○ Under Budget
◐ On Budget
● Over Budget

can be identified by "drilling down" to the project schedule, WBS, resources, or issues. Standard project formats such as these provide a wealth of information in multiproject organizations.

Project offices are known to result in positive benefits such as the following:

- They serve as a bridge between senior management and project managers.
- They support integration of all project management processes from selection through project closure and lessons learned.
- Through training they support the movement of the organization to a higher level of project management maturity.

The growth in the application of portfolio project management and project offices will continue. Portfolio management and project offices strongly influence how a project manager will manage his or her respective project. A more recent oversight activity has been the quick implementation of phase gate reviews.

Phase Gate Methodology

Phase gates provide an in-depth review of individual projects at *specific phases* in the project life cycle. These reviews cover assessments to continue or kill the project, reassess resource allocation, reassess prioritization, and evaluate execution progress,

FIGURE 16.2   Project Portfolio Schedule Summary Report for Project Schedules

	Location	Project ID	Description	Project Manager	Start Date	Finish Date	SPI	A M J J A S O N D J F M
Summary	All		Portfolio					
United States								
○		01-003	Digitize Fingerprints-FBI	Beth Gage	11/15	8/15	1.17	
●		01-011	Encryption	Alfonso Buco	1/1	9/25	0.93	
○		01-002	Internet Protocol--CIA		10/1	6/1		
○		01-009	Supply chain partners	Mike Chow	6/5	11/16	1.00	
○		01-012	Bonus Mileage Awards	Sally Peters	8/1	2/12		
●		01-005	E-sales Claims	Kevin Lee	2/4	11/15	0.93	
●		01-011	Procurement Net	Tzvi Jafarri	5/5	12/30	0.85	
○		01-008	Smart Tag Tracking	Jan Snyder	3/1	12/4	1.06	
Asia/Pacific								
○		02-007	Currency Conversion	Jeff Bush	2/1	7/10	0.96	
○		02-002	Billing System	Kia Wong	10/7	10/5	1.00	
○		02-005	Web-Based Cash Flow	Naoki Oshima	2/15	9/15	1.05	
○		02-004	Olympic Simulation		7/12	2/10		
EEC								
●		03-008	Smart Card	Ido Alons	4/16	9/15	0.76	
○		03-003	Warranty	Connor Gage	8/11	12/12		
○		03-004	Simulation--ESA	Ib Ericson	9/15	2/13		
○		03-005	Air Reservation Net	Dragan Milosovik	3/22	1/12	0.96	
●		03-007	Pilot Internet Log Syst.	Ken Thompson	3/1	10/3	0.91	
○		03-006	Internet Telephone Syst	Ann McGraddy	8/10	9/29	1.00	

Net Services, Inc.   View   Schedule   Project Portfolio Schedule Summary   Date:

Gantt   Network   Resource   Status   WBS   Sponsor   Team   Priority   Issues

LEGEND
○ Ahead of schedule
○ On schedule
● Behind schedule

as well as strategic alignment decisions. The phase review process serves the organization by having gatekeepers (usually selected from several areas of the firm) perform the review. The phase gate process is also designed to support the project manager on decisions and other issues such as escalation and resource needs. The idea of phase gate methodology fits effortlessly into the oversight function of the project office. Phase gate methodology was originally developed for product development, but the application of the methodology has grown beyond new product development to include all projects in the portfolio. One study by Morris and Jamieson showed 85 percent of those surveyed use phase review gates, while 85 percent who did not thought they should.

The original *Stage-Gate*™ model was pioneered by Robert G. Cooper several decades ago to improve management of new product development. The original model incorporates five stages: preliminary investigation, detailed investigation, development, testing and validation, and full production and market launch. Stages precede gates and represent information developed to enable gatekeepers to make the right decision at the next gate. These decision points at each gate are known as go, kill, hold, or recycle decisions. Given the information developed for each stage, the gatekeepers (the oversight team) can decide to continue with the project, abort the project, or revise/recycle.

Today, variations of the original model are being used across all industries to help manage project portfolios. These variations are not limited to new product development. The number of stages and gates varies. But the idea of oversight review several times throughout the project life cycle appears in all models. Each gate check will always, at a minimum, check the project against alignment with current strategic goals.

Phase gate methodology has appeal because it provides a clean-cut, structured process that can be consistently applied across all projects in the portfolio. Distinct review stages and go/kill gates comprise this oversight function. The major goals for phase gating are to ensure oversight and support for the project manager and the project team, to direct organization resources toward strategic goals, and to reduce the number of projects that do not support the forward direction of the organization. A multiproject organization having employees spread across many time zones that does not use some form of phase review methodology is rare. For example, companies such as 3M, General Motors, Northern Telecom, DuPont, Intel, Hewlett-Packard, and Dell all use some form of phase gating to manage projects.

The **phase gate** review process can be defined as a *structured process to review, evaluate, and document outcomes in each project phase and to provide management with information to guide resource deployment toward strategic goals.* This oversight activity begins with project selection and tracking the project life cycle through closure and lessons learned. Phase gates need to occur at consistent points in the project life cycle so each project encounters similar gates at predefined authorization points.

The phase review process may appear similar to the project audit discussed in an earlier chapter. Some overlap does occur, but the focus here is more integrated and holistic. Individual projects are reviewed as part of a total portfolio. For example, have strategic priorities changed the importance of the project? If the priorities of the organization have changed, a project that is executing on time, on budget, and meeting the project goals may have to be "killed." Phase review takes place at each phase from project selection through lessons learned as opposed to the audit, which often takes place at the end of the project. Phase gating provides a larger perspective to managing multiple projects in a project portfolio. Gatekeepers first focus on organization needs, with individual project needs second.

Figure 16.3 is a flow diagram of an abridged, generic variation of phase gate methodology that has application across all types of projects. Another practice used during the implementation phase is to create gates at significant milestones.

The decision gates focus on go/kill decisions based on major questions such as those shown in Gates 1 and 2 below (see the "Pull the Plug" reference). At a minimum each gate should include three components:

1. Required deliverables (e.g., project goals, progress, variances).
2. Gate criteria and specific outputs (e.g., adjusting project scope, schedule).
3. A clear yes/no decision on whether to go ahead.

The criteria for all of the gates during the project are selected *before* the start of the project.

The value of phase gating methods rests firmly on having enough information to support the gate decision. Significant amounts of support data must be gathered to answer critical gate questions. Using the best practices shown in earlier chapters will prepare you to easily answer critical gate questions. Frequent questions from practice for each gate are presented here.

FIGURE 16.3
**Abridged Generic
Phase Gate Process
Diagram**

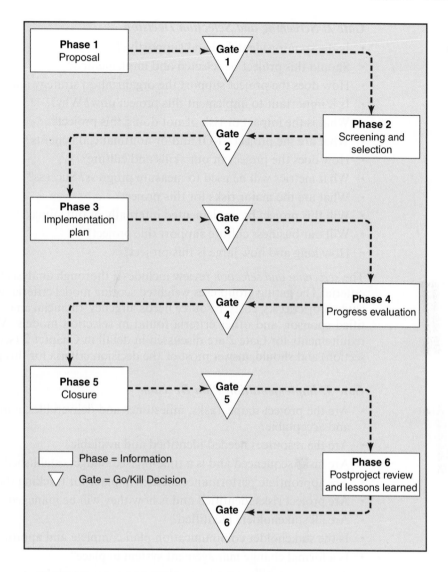

Gate 1: Proposal Decision

• What business problem does the proposed project solve?
• Does this project align with our strategic direction?
• What type of project is this? Strategic, organization maintenance, "must," etc.?
• Should the project be considered?

This *proposal* phase answers a fundamental question: Is the project a good idea and does it solve a business problem or issue? Basically, anyone can propose a project. However, the proposal should provide enough key information to allow an oversight team to decide if the proposal should be considered further. For example, the information might include the business problem the proposed project will solve, the urgency of the project, and clear, relevant project objectives. Gate 1 provides information at a minimal expenditure of cost and resources and in a short time, so the project can be reevaluated more thoroughly if it is perceived to have merits.

Gate 2: Screening and Selection Decision

- Is the sponsor identified and supportive?
- Should this project be selected and implemented?
- How does the project support the organization strategy and goals?
- Is it important to implement this project now? Why?
- What is the impact or risk of not doing this project?
- What are the project's ROI and/or nonfinancial benefits?
- How does the project fit our skills and culture?
- What metrics will be used to measure progress? Success?
- What are the major risks for this project?
- Will this project be implemented internally or outsourced?
- Will our business culture support this project?
- How long and how large is this project?

The *screening and selection* review includes a thorough analysis based on selection criteria. The gating group uses weighted scoring model criteria, which typically include project risks, costs, resource needs, urgency, financial analysis, benefits, identified sponsor, and other criteria found in selection models. Many information requirements for Gate 2 are discussed in detail in Chapter 2 (see project selection section) and should answer most of the decision criteria for this phase review.

Gate 3: Implementation Plan Decision

- Are the project scope, tasks, milestones and deliverables, and gates established and acceptable?
- Are the resources needed identified and available?
- Are tasks sequenced and is a time-phased budget established?
- Are appropriate performance metrics in place for tracking the project?
- Are project risks identified and is how they will be managed clearly stated?
- Are all stakeholders identified?
- Is the stakeholder communication plan complete and appropriate?
- Is a formal change management system in place?
- Are accountability metrics in place and is responsibility assigned?

The *implementation plan* review information should include the planning document developed in earlier chapters. For example, what are the specific goals for the project and what are the major deliverables (scope)? What tasks will be performed to complete the deliverables (WBS)? How are tasks sequenced (network)? When will the tasks be performed (schedule)? What resources are needed to complete the tasks (resource schedule)? What are the estimated costs for the tasks (time-phased budget)? What and how will performance be measured (variance metrics)? How will information be collected and distributed (communication plan)? What and how will project risks be identified and handled (risk plan)? What vendors will be used for procurement?

Gate 4: Progress Evaluation Decision

- Is the project still aligned with business requirements?
- Are activities completed according to the project plan?

- Are the technical requirements of the project being met?
- Are contractors meeting defined performance requirements?
- Are there urgent corrective actions that must be done quickly?
- Are time, costs, and scope performances within acceptable limits?
- Have the project objectives changed?
- What risks can be retired?

Your *progress evaluation* review covers the control activities of tracking progress, identifying variances from your plan, and taking corrective action. A major chunk of the data requirements for the phase review are simply measures against the project plan. Tracking progress and identifying variances against scope, time, budget, and control of changes and identified risks are easily accomplished using available software (see Chapters 7 and 13). For example, if the project is not going according to plan, your risk assessment plan may help you decide an action to be taken. Beyond these quantitative measures, there are always "issues" that deserve attention. Moreover, project priority must be checked against strategy to determine whether this measure is still valid. If not, a change in scope or killing the project may be necessary. Don Kingsberry, director of HP's Global Program Management Office, describes HP's progress phase review succinctly: "We have 42 health checks on current projects. We look at risks, issues, critical path analysis, resource analysis, sponsorship, alignment with strategy, earned value metrics, dependency, and other factors impacting the triple constraints of project management: time, cost, and scope." (See Boyer for more on HP's efforts.)

Gate 5: Closure

- Did the project deliver the business outcomes? Were the metrics and benefits used to justify the project met?
- Were project scope objectives met?
- Were project cost and schedule met?
- Are contracts closed out?
- Are the end users satisfied?
- Have staff been recognized and reassigned?
- Was the organization culture right for this type of project?
- Was senior management support adequate?
- Were the right people assigned to the project?
- Were project risks identified and assessed realistically?
- Did technology overextend our competencies?
- How will the project be delivered?

The *closure* and lessons learned activities closely follow the closure activities found in the audit chapter. Some organizations have wrapped phases 5 and 6—closure, post project review and lessons learned—into a single gate.

Gate 6: Lessons Learned

- Have we identified what went wrong and what contributed to success?
- Have changes to improve delivery of future projects been communicated and archived?
- Has an owner of each retrospective been identified?

- What hindered or contributed to delivering the expected ROI or business outcomes?
- Can others learn from this experience?
- What changes in scope or quality were made?
- Who will be responsible for archiving the lessons learned?

The questions shown above for each phase only touch the surface of those found in practice. Some are formalized, others very porous and less structured, but all phase review models are designed to check management of a project from selection to lessons learned. Key benefits of using phase gating are:

- Provides excellent training for functional staff who serve on oversight review groups.
- Encourages a larger perspective and role of projects within the organization.
- Is a clear-cut process, easily understood, and applicable to all projects in a portfolio.
- Provides a structured process for a project office to follow on all projects.
- Eliminates poor value projects.
- Supports faster decision making with predefined deliverables for each gate.

See Snapshot from Practice: Phase Gate Side Benefits for a project manager's opinion on the benefits of phase gating.

Another key oversight function is benchmarking your project management maturity against others in your industry.

Organization Project Management in the Long Run

Organization Project Management Maturity

Individual audits and phase gate reviews can yield valuable lessons that team members can apply to future project work. A more encompassing look, from an organizationwide point of view, uses a project maturity model that strives for a never-ending goal to continuously improve the management of projects. It is well established that project-driven companies with higher maturity levels are more successful in managing projects than those lacking project maturity programs. Project maturity has become a competitive edge. Companies are increasingly using outsourcing or external contractors and RFPs (Request for proposals) to look for contractors that have reached high maturity levels. Harold Kerzner, a project management consultant and professor, eloquently states why a company should pursue maturity:

> Given the fact that many executives today view their company as a stream of projects, project management permeates the entire organization, mandating that maturity is necessary. So only those companies that want to stay in business and remain competitive should pursue maturity. The alternative is rather unpleasant. (Quoted in Mueller)

The purposes of all maturity models, and many are available, are to enable organizations to assess their progress in implementing the best practices in their industry and continuously move to improvement. It is important to understand that the model does not ensure success; it serves only as a measuring stick and an indicator of progress.

The term *maturity model* was coined in the late 1980s from a research study by the United States government and the Software Engineering Institute (SEI) at Carnegie Mellon University. The government wanted a tool to predict successful software development by contractors. The outcome of this research was the Capability Maturity Model (CMM). The model focuses on guiding and assessing organizations in implementing concrete best practices of managing software development projects. Since its development, the model is used across all industries.

One newer model has received a great deal of publicity. In January 2004, after eight years of development, the Project Management Institute (PMI) rolled out its second version of the Organizational Project Management Maturity Model. The latest version is called OPM3 (See *www.pmi.org/opm3*). Typically, these models are divided into a continuum of growth levels: initial, repeatable, defined, managed, and optimized. Figure 16.4 presents our version, which borrows liberally from other models.

FIGURE 16.4
Project Management
Maturity Model

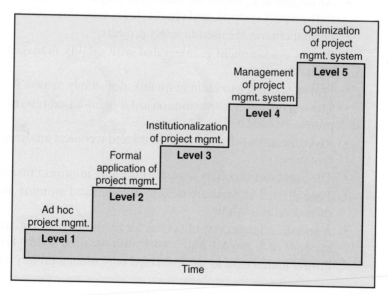

Level 1: Ad Hoc Project Management No consistent project management process is in place. How a project is managed depends upon the individuals involved. Characteristics of this level include:

- No formal project selection system exists—projects are done because people decide to use them or because a high-ranking manager orders them done.
- How any one project is managed varies by individual and thus is unpredictable.
- No investment is made in project management training.
- Working on projects is a struggle because it goes against the grain of established policies and procedures.

Level 2: Formal Application of Project Management The organization applies established project management procedures and techniques. This level is often marked by tension between project managers and line managers who need to redefine their roles. Features of this level include:

- Standard approaches to managing projects, including scope statements, WBS, and activity lists, are used.
- Quality emphasis is on the product or outcome of the project and is inspected instead of built in.
- The organization is moving in the direction of a stronger matrix with project managers and line managers working out their respective roles.
- Recognition of the need for cost control, not just scope and time management, is growing.
- No formal project priority selection system is established.
- Limited training in project management is provided.

Level 3: Institutionalization of Project Management An organizationwide project management system, tailored to specific needs of the organization with the flexibility to adapt the process to unique characteristics of the project, is established. Characteristics of this level include:

- An established process for managing projects is evident by planning templates, status report systems, and checklists for each stage of the project life cycle.
- Formal criteria are used to select projects.
- Project management is integrated with quality management and concurrent engineering.
- Project teams try to build in quality, not simply inspect it.
- The organization is moving toward a team-based reward system to recognize project execution.
- Risk assessment derived from WBS and technical analyses and customer input is in place.
- The organization offers expanded training in project management.
- Time-phased budgets are used to measure and monitor performance based on earned value analysis.
- A specific change control system for requirements, cost, and schedule is developed for each project, and a work authorization system is in place.
- Project audits tend to be performed only when a project fails.

SNAPSHOT FROM PRACTICE   Acer Attacks Costly Delays*

In today's rapidly changing world, the risk of failing to develop new products for the market on time is the difference between success and failure. The Mobile Systems Unit (MSU) of Taiwan computer maker Acer, which produces computer note-books, operates under extreme time-to-market pressures. By 1998 MSU development cycles had shrunk to eight months. Still, missing the market introduction window by only one month on any given model eliminated the unit's profit potential for that model.

MSU did a companywide analysis into the causes of costly delays in their projects. They discovered that schedule variance was a function of multiple causes. Vendors would occasionally not deliver sufficient volumes of a promised new component on time. Major customers such as IBM would change their requirements. Design problems with the mother-board would cause additional design loops. Negotiations among multiple parties might change internal specifications. Administrative pressure on engineers and insufficiently documented procedures led to shortcuts in testing, causing major rework at a more costly stage.

Acer attacked the multiple causes on multiple fronts. First, MSU management created resource buffers in the form of slack capacity by canceling two projects that were already delayed. This wasn't easy, because one was to be a show-piece, top-of-the-line model, and the decision to kill it was hotly contested. MSU then concentrated on improving

© Tom Wagner/Corbis

documentation of operating procedures in order to increase testing coverage and facilitate the training of young engineers. Those steps reduced the number of correction loops during product development and improved the quality of the compa-ny's manufacturing ramp-up. Acer also concentrated the re-sponsibility of product specifications in one group, thereby reducing negotiation loops and internally caused specification changes. Over the next two years, MSU more than doubled its sales and gained significant market share.

* B. Einhorn, "Acer's About Face," *BusinessWeek (International Edition),* April 23, 2000.

Level 4: *Management of Project Management System*   The organization develops a system for managing multiple projects that are aligned with strategic goals of the organization. Characteristics of this level include:

- Portfolio project management is practiced; projects are selected based on resource capacity and contribution to strategic goals.
- A project priority system is established.
- Project work is integrated with ongoing operations.
- Quality improvement initiatives are designed to improve both the quality of the project management process and the quality of specific products and services.
- Benchmarking is used to identify opportunities for improvement.
- The organization has established a Project Management Office or Center for Excellence.
- Project audits are performed on all significant projects and lessons learned are recorded and used on subsequent projects.
- An integrative information system is established for tracking resource usage and performance of all significant projects. See Snapshot from Practice: Acer Attacks Costly Delays.

Level 5: Optimization of Project Management System The focus is on continuous improvement through incremental advancements of existing practices and by innovations using new technologies and methods. Features include:

- A project management information system is fine-tuned; specific and aggregate information is provided to different stakeholders.
- An informal culture that values improvement drives the organization, not policies and procedures.
- There is greater flexibility in adapting the project management process to demands of a specific project.

Progress from one level to the next will not occur overnight. The Software Engineering Institute estimates the following median times for movement:

- Maturity level 1 to 2 is 22 months.
- Maturity level 2 to 3 is 29 months.
- Maturity level 3 to 4 is 25 months.
- Maturity level 4 to 5 is 13 months.

Why does it take so long? One reason is simply organizational inertia. It is difficult for social organizations to institute significant changes while at the same time maintaining business efficacy. "How do we find time to change when we are so busy just keeping our heads above water?"

A second significant reason is that one cannot leapfrog past any one level. Just as a child cannot avoid the trials and tribulations of being a teenager, people within an organization have to work through the unique challenges and problems of each level to get to the next level. Learning of this magnitude naturally takes time and cannot be avoided by using quick fixes or simple remedies.

Our best-guess estimates are that most companies are in the throes of moving from level 2 to level 3 and that fewer than 10 percent of those firms that actively practice project management are at either level 4 or 5. Remember, project maturity is not an end; project maturity is a never-ending process of continuous improvement. An additional view of the success of the projects you have selected over time is discussed next.

The Balanced Scorecard Model

Project priority selection models select which actions (projects) best support organizational strategy. The balanced scorecard model differs from selection models by reviewing projects over a longer horizon—5 to 10 years after the project is implemented. It is more "macro" in perspective than project selection models. This model measures the results of major activities taken to support the overall vision, mission, and goals of the organization. It helps answer two questions: Did we select the right projects? Did the projects contribute to long-range strategic direction of the firm? American Express, the U.S. Department of Transportation, ExxonMobil, Kaiser Permanente, National Semiconductor, and others are known to be using their own customized models of the balanced scorecard. (See Kaplan and Norton.)

The scorecard model limits measures of performance to goals in four main areas: *customer, internal, innovation and learning,* and *financial measures.* For example, a performance measure for a customer might be industry ranking for sales, quality, or on-time projects. Internal measures that influence employees' actions could mean time to market or reduction of design time to final product.

Innovation and learning measures frequently deal with process and product innovation and improvement. For example, the percentage of sales or profit from new products is often used as a performance goal and measure. Project improvement savings from partnering agreements are another example of an innovation and learning measure. Finally, financial measures such as ROI, cash flow, and projects on budget reflect improvement and actions that contribute value to the bottom line.

These four perspectives and performance measures keep vision and strategy at the forefront of employees' actions. The basic assumption underlying the balanced scorecard model is that people will take the necessary actions to improve the performance of the organization on the given measures and goals. The balanced scorecard model and priority selection models should never conflict with each other. If a conflict exists, both models should be reviewed and conflicts eliminated. When both models are used in project-driven organizations, focus on vision, strategy, and implementation are reinforced. Both models encourage employees to determine the actions needed to improve performance.

Summary

Oversight practices are directed to improving the way the organization manages all projects. Oversight or governance in multiproject organizations supports the trend of integration over the last three decades. Centralization of project management activities became imperative as projects became more numerous and became the means to implement organization strategy. Project portfolios and project offices serve to gain centralized control over all projects in the organization. The multiproject environment also assists as an impetus for phase gate checks at several points over the project life cycle. Benchmarking your project management maturity quickly surfaced as large organizations realized the amount of organization resources devoted to projects and the importance of projects to meeting competition. The need for assessing the long-run value of selected projects over several years continues to increase each year. The balance score card methodology appears to be meeting this need. Succinctly, the major goals of project oversight are to ensure the effective allocation of organization resources and to improve the management of projects. Oversight activities continue to be adopted by most organizations participating in the global economy. Oversight activities are not limited to only large organizations; oversight activities continue to move down the size ladder to smaller organizations where successful project management can be a significant competitive edge.

How projects are managed in your organization will depend heavily on the level of project oversight and maturity. As oversight continues to evolve, you will need to view your job as a project manager from a broader, top-down view of project management in your organization and even in the total field of project management.

Key Terms

Balanced scorecard, *578*

Oversight, *565*

Phase gating, *570*

Portfolio management, *566*

Project management maturity, *574*

Project office (PO), *566*

An Introduction to Agile Project Management

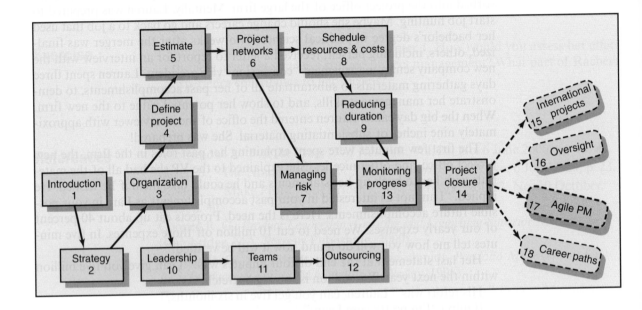

An Introduction to Agile Project Management

Traditional versus Agile Methods

Agile PM

Agile PM in Action: Scrum

Applying Agile PM to Large Projects

Limitations and Concerns

Summary

We know less about the project today than at any time in the future.
—*Chet Hendrickson*

As project management entered the new millennium, many professionals recognized that one-size fits all project management methods did not meet their needs. This recognition was especially true for those working on software and product development projects in which the end product is not well defined and evolves over time. This project environment requires flexibility and the ability to manage changes as more information and learning take place. Enter **Agile Project Management** (Agile PM). Instead of attempting to plan the entire project up front, Agile PM relies on incremental, iterative development cycles to complete projects.

Ken Schwaber uses the analogy of building a house to explain the difference between incremental, iterative development and traditional project management. The traditional approach would be that the buyers could not move into the house until the entire house is completed. The iterative approach would build the house room by room. The plumbing, electrical, and infrastructure would be built for the most important room (i.e., kitchen) first and then extended to each room as it was constructed. Each time a room is completed, the builders and the buyers would assess progress and make adjustments. In some cases, the buyers would realize that they didn't need that extra room they felt they had to have. In other cases, they would add features they didn't realize they needed to have. Ultimately the house is built to fit the customer's wishes.

Agile PM is ideal for exploratory projects in which requirements need to be discovered and new technology tested. It focuses on active collaboration between the project team and customer representatives, breaking projects into small functional pieces, and adapting to changing requirements. While iterative development principles have been around for some time, it is only recently that agile methodologies have taken root within the project management profession.

In this chapter the core principles of Agile PM are discussed and compared with traditional project management methods. A specific agile methodology called Scrum is used to describe these principles in action. The chapter concludes with a discussion of limitations and concerns. The goal is not to provide a comprehensive account of all the methods associated with Agile PM but to provide a primer on how agile works.

Traditional versus Agile Methods

Traditional approaches to project management concentrate firmly on thorough planning up front. The rationale is that if you plan, execute your plan, and take corrective action on deviations from plan, you have a high probability of success. Once the project scope has been firmly established, every detail of the project is defined through the WBS. Most problems and risks are identified and assessed before the project begins. Estimates are made, resources assigned,

FIGURE 17.1
Project Uncertainty

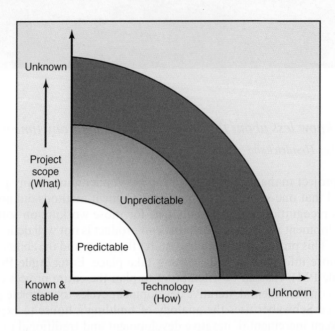

adjustments made, and ultimately a baseline schedule and budget are created. Control of the project is a comparison of plan versus actual and corrective action to get back on plan.

Traditional project management requires a fairly high degree of predictability to be effective. For plans to be useful managers have to have a firm idea on what is to be accomplished and how to do it. For example, when it comes to building a bridge across a river, engineers can draw upon proven technology and design principles to plan and execute the project. Not all projects enjoy such certainty. Figure 17.1 speaks to this issue and is often used to support the use of Agile PM.

Project uncertainty varies according to the extent the project scope is known and stable and the technology to be used is known and proven. Many projects, like the bridge example, as well as other construction projects, events, product extensions, marketing campaigns, and so forth have well-established scopes and use proven technology that provides a degree of predictability for effective planning. However, when the project scope and/or technology are not fully known, things become much less predictable. For example, software development projects, which are notorious for coming in late and over budget, typically involve many different customers with different needs. These needs frequently change and are often difficult to articulate. In many cases, customers only begin to understand what they actually desire when they are provided with someone's impression of what they want. Under these conditions it would be difficult if not futile to develop a detailed list of scope requirements at project launch.

Technology can be another source of unpredictability. For example, a development team charged with designing the next generation electric car may know they are to build a car that seats four adults comfortably and travels over 200 miles before being charged, but they may not know if the battery technology exists to power such a vehicle. Again it would be very difficult to develop a reliable schedule when such questions exist.

The key point is that traditional PM techniques were developed to operate in the predictable zone where the scope of the project is fairly well defined and

TABLE 17.1
Traditional Project Management versus Agile Project Management

Traditional	Agile
Design up front	Continuous design
Fixed scope	Flexible scope
Deliverables	Features/requirements
Freeze design as early as possible	Freeze design as late as possible
Low uncertainty	High uncertainty
Avoid change	Embrace change
Low customer interaction	High customer interaction
Conventional project teams	Self-organized project teams

technology to be used is established. Agile lives in the unpredictable zone. Agile PM represents a fundamental shift away from the traditional plan-driven project management approach by adopting a more experimental and adaptive approach to managing projects. Projects evolve rather than are executed. Some of the differences between Agile PM and traditional project management are displayed in Table 17.1.

Agile PM

Fundamentally, Agile PM is related to the rolling wave planning and scheduling project methodology (see Chapter 5). That is, the final project design is not known in great detail and is continuously developed through a series of incremental iterations over time. Iterations are short time frames ("time boxes") that typically last from one to four weeks. The goal of each iteration is to develop a workable product that satisfies one or more desired product features to demonstrate to the customer and other key stakeholders. At the end of each iteration, stakeholders and customers review progress and re-evaluate priorities to ensure alignment with customer needs and company goals. Adjustments are made and a different iterative cycle begins. Each new iteration subsumes the work of the previous iterations and adds new capabilities to the evolving product (see Figure 17.2) to produce a next,

FIGURE 17.2   Iterative, Incremental Product Development

SNAPSHOT FROM PRACTICE   IDEO: Masters of Design*

IDEO, headquartered in Palo Alto, California, is one of the premier design firms in the world. They are responsible for a wide range of product innovations including the first Apple mouse, Head's Airflow Tennis Racket, Zyliss Salad Spinner, and Nokia N-Gage Smart phones. IDEO's many clients include Pepsi-Cola, 3M, Logitech, Nike, and HBO. IDEO has won more of the *BusinessWeek/IDSA Industrial Design Excellence Awards* than any other firm.

IDEO's approach to product design relies heavily on an iterative development process in which product prototypes are used to explore and further refine product ideas. CEO Tim Brown states that the goal of prototyping "is to learn about the strengths and weaknesses of the idea and identify new directions that the prototype might take."

For example, IDEO worked with Procter and Gamble to develop a new Crest toothpaste tube. The challenge was to improve the traditional screw-on cap, which always gets gunked up with toothpaste. IDEO's first solution was a pop-on, pop-off cap. However, when designers created rough prototypes and watched people use them, they quickly noticed that users kept trying to unscrew the cap even though they were told how it worked. The designers concluded that the action was a well, ingrained habit that would probably be impossible to break. So they came up with a hybrid: a twist-off cap that had a short thread but would still be easy to clean.

Focused prototyping resolves critical problems one by one. Brown recommends that prototypes should only take as much time and effort needed to generate useful feedback and evolve an idea.

For example, IDEO was working on a chair for Vecta, a high-end office furniture manufacturer. The project had

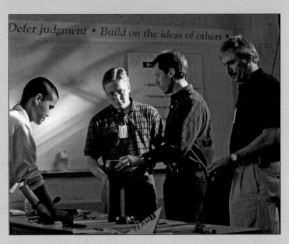

© Mark Richards/PhotoEdit

evolved to the point where the height adjustment lever that tilted with the chair became critical. The team didn't build the whole chair or even the tilt mechanism. They just built the little lever and its interface with the tilt mechanism. It took only a couple of hours. When finished the prototype quickly demonstrated that the principle would work.

"It doesn't matter how clever you are, your first idea about something is never right" Brown says, "so the great value of prototyping—and prototyping quickly and inexpensively—is that you learn about the idea and make it better."

* J. M. Pethokoukis, "The Deans of Design: From the Computer Mouse to the Newest Swiffer, IDEO is the Firm behind the Scenes," *U.S. News & World Report,* Posted 9-24-2008; Brown, T. "Design Thinking," *Harvard Business Review,* June 2008, pp. 84–95.

expanded version of the product See the Snapshot from Practice: IDEO for an example of iterative development in action.

Iterative development processes provide the following important advantages:

- Continuous integration, verification, and validation of the evolving product.
- Frequent demonstration of progress to increase the likelihood that the end product will satisfy customer needs.
- Early detection of defects and problems.

There is growing evidence that iterative and evolutionary development is superior to traditional plan-driven project management when it comes to creating new products (See Research Highlight: Product Development Practices that Work.)

Alan MacCormack and his colleagues at Harvard Business School conducted a two-year in-depth study of 29 software projects to answer the question: "Does evolutionary development, rather than the waterfall model, result in better success?" The waterfall model is the name used in the software industry for the traditional approach to project management in which a process breakdown structure (PBS) is used to first define all the requirements up front and then initiate a design, build, integrate, test, deploy sequence. Conversely, evolutionary development is an iterative approach in which customers test early versions of the software and requirements emerge and are refined after each demonstration. The study concluded:

> ... our research suggests a clear agenda for managers: Get a low-functionality version of the product into customer's hands at the earliest possible stage and thereafter adopt an iterative approach to adding functionality.

The study identified several practices that were statistically correlated with the most successful projects:

1. An iterative life cycle with early release of the evolving product to stakeholders for review and feedback.
2. Daily incorporation of new software and rapid feedback on design changes.
3. A team with a broad-based experience in shipping multiple projects.

MacCormack asserts that uncertainty on software projects dictates short "microprojects"—down to level of features. This is not limited to just software projects but to any new product endeavor where uncertainty is high and the need for customer feedback and refinement is critical to success.

* A. MacCormack, "Product-Development Practices that Work: How Internet Companies Build Software," *MIT Sloan Management Review*, 42(2), 2001, pp. 75–84.

It should be noted that Agile PM is not one set method, but a family of methods designed to respond to the challenges of unpredictable projects. A few of the more popular ones are listed here:

Scrum	RUP (Rational Unified Process)
Extreme Programming (XP)	Crystal Clear
Agile Modeling	Dynamic Systems Development Method (DSDM)
Lean Development	Rapid Product Development (RPD)

While each of these methods has unique elements and applications, most are based on the following Agile principles:

- Focus on customer value—Employ business-driven prioritizations of requirements and features.
- Iterative and incremental delivery—Create a flow of value to customers by "chunking" project delivery into small, functioning increments.
- Experimentation and adaptation—Test assumptions early and build working prototypes to solicit customer feedback and refine product requirements.
- Self-organization—Team members decide amongst themselves who and what should be done.
- Continuous improvement—Teams reflect, learn, and adapt to change; work informs the plan.

The Agile methodology known as "Scrum" will be used to illustrate how these core principles are put into action.

Agile PM in Action: Scrum

Scrum can be traced back to the work of Hirotaka Takeuchi and Ikujiro Nonaka who in 1986 described a new holistic approach in new commercial product development efforts. They compare this approach of a cross-functional team collaborating to develop a new product to rugby, where the whole team "tries to go the distance as a unit, passing the ball back and forth." The scrum metaphor has been expanded and refined into a fairly prescriptive framework that has enjoyed success on high-tech and software development projects (see Snapshot from Practice Soul Searching).

Scrum, like other Agile methods, begins with a high-level scope definition and ballpark time and cost estimates for the project. The scope and cost estimates should be complete enough that management is comfortable with the estimates. The theory is that since requirements evolve over time, detailed up-front planning will be wasted. In place of a product WBS, Scrum uses product *features* as deliverables. *A* **feature** *is defined as a piece of a product that delivers some useful functionality to a customer*. In the case of a software project, a feature may be a bank customer being able to change her PIN. In the case of a high-tech product, it may be 3G wireless access. Features are prioritized by their perceived highest value. The project team tackles the highest, feasible priority features first. Priorities are re-evaluated after each iteration. Iterations are called sprints and should last no longer than four weeks. The goal of each sprint is to produce fully functional features. This forces the team to tackle tough decisions early in order to create a workable demo.

Specific features are created according to four distinct phases: analysis, design, build, and test (see Figure 17.3). Each feature can be thought of as a mini-project. The first phase is analysis and review of functional requirements that will be needed to complete the feature. The team commits to meet these requirements. The second phase is the development of a design that meets the requirements of the feature. The third phase is to build the feature so that it is functional. Finally, the feature is tested and documented. At the end of each sprint, features are demonstrated. Within this sprint framework, Scrum relies on specific roles, meetings, and documents/logs to manage the project.

FIGURE 17.3 **Scrum Development Process**

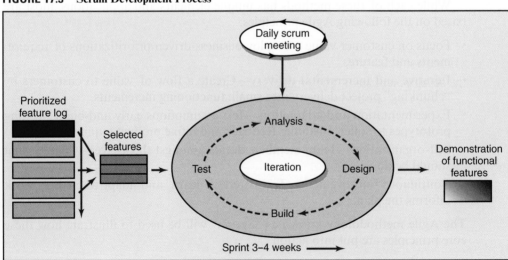

SNAPSHOT FROM PRACTICE   Soul Searching after 9/11*

Over 2,792 lives were lost in the collapse of the World Trade Center (WTC) on September 11, 2001. While rescuers labored night and day to recover the bodies, a small team of Michigan software engineers set about salvaging their identities.

New York City hired Gene Codes, the Ann Arbor, Michigan, bioinformatics company, to reinvent the science of DNA mass identification by creating software that would inventory and match the victims' remains and reunite them with their families. They were to do so as soon as possible with no errors. Experts predicted that the violence of the collapse and the intense heat of the fires meant that at best 25 percent of the victims would be identified.

Gene Codes hired William Wake, an independent software coach, to work with their team of eight software engineers on the project. Wake introduced the team to Agile PM. Under Wake's guidance an environment of intense interaction and communication was created within the programming team by scheduling frequent releases, tempered by constant testing, and feedback from its users. Testing was done, before, during, and after the code was written to ensure the same bugs (errors) didn't surface twice.

At the end of each week's iteration, the staff held a retrospective. They listed things that worked well and what needed improvement on fluorescent pink, green, and yellow Post-It notes, transforming the entire wall into a case of art imitating life. Under "Worked Well," a note said, "Figured out how to use debug form on a wrapped test class." One square under the "Needs Improvement" category merely read, "I'm tired."

Whether out of patriotism or professionalism, the team routinely arrived each day at 7:00 A.M. and worked till midnight. Engineers like Dave Relyea just wanted to help. "We thought about the victims, the families, and the people at the Office of the Chief Medical Examiner working around the clock. What they were going through made us feel like we could never work hard enough."

The product of their labor was the Mass Fatality Identification System (M-FISys) that contained more than 164,000 lines of code. M-FISys linked all the information in the identification project: 11,641 swab samples from 7,166 family members; 7,681 personal effects (i.e., toothbrushes, hair brushes) and the results of the three types of DNA tests; and nearly 20,000 human remains. The chance of false match was less than 1 in 3.58 million.

In the end, with the help of M-FISys, the New York Medical examiner was able to identify 1,521 of the 2,792 people who perished in the WTC disaster.

* Melissa Krause, "Soul Searching" *Bio-ITworld.* Accessed on 3/10/2008 at http://www.bio-itworld.com/archive/091103/soul.html.

Roles and Responsibilities

There are three key roles to the scrum process: Product owner, development team, and scrum master.

Product Owner   This person acts on behalf of customers to represent their interests. They are responsible for ensuring that the development team focuses their efforts on developing a product that will fulfill the business objective of the project. The product owner establishes the initial list of product features and prioritizes them in the product backlog. The product owner negotiates sprint goals and backlog items with the development team. The product owner has the option to change features and priorities at the end of each sprint if desired. *However, no changes should be made once a sprint has started.* The product owner is the final arbiter on requirements questions and is empowered to accept or reject each product increment. The product owner ultimately decides whether the project is completed. Product owners are the keeper of the product vision and watch dog on the return on investment.

Development Team   The team is responsible for delivering the product. A team is typically made up of five to nine people with cross-functional skill sets. There are no designated roles or titles; people take on different responsibilities depending on the nature of the work. The team is **self organizing** in the sense they decide both who and how the work is to be accomplished. Team members should be co-located so that intense face-to-face collaboration occurs. They are responsible for the achieving commitments they make at the sprint planning and sprint review meetings.

Scrum Master (aka Project Manager) The Scrum master facilitates the scrum process and resolves impediments at the team and organization level. The Scrum master is not the leader of the team (the team leads itself!) but acts as a buffer between the team and outside interference. They have no formal authority. Instead, they are responsible for making sure that the Scrum process is adhered to. They help the product owner with planning and try to keep the team energized. The Scrum master serves more as a coach than a manager.

Scrum Meetings

Scrum uses a series of coordinated meetings to manage the development process (see Figure 17.4).

Sprint Planning At the start of each sprint, the product owner and development team negotiate which product backlog items the team will attempt this sprint. The product owner is responsible for identifying which features are most important, and the team is responsible for determining what is possible within the sprint. If it is impossible to complete a certain key item within four weeks, the team works with the product owner to break the feature down into doable pieces. All committed items are recorded in a product backlog. The team uses this backlog to prioritize specific work to be done and assign initial responsibilities. These tasks are recorded in the sprint backlog. Once the meeting has adjourned the goals for the Sprint cannot be changed.

Daily Scrum The heartbeat of an Agile project is the daily meetings which are commonly referred to as the "Scrum." Each work day at the same time and place, team members stand in a circle and take turns answering the following key questions:

1. What have you done since the last Scrum?
2. What will you do between now and the next Scrum?
3. What is getting in the way (blocks) you from performing your work as effectively as possible?

The Scrum, which typically lasts 15 minutes, is held next to a whiteboard, at which time all tasks and blocks are recorded. The Scrum master erases blocks once they have been removed.

The meetings must start on time. A late fine (i.e., $1) collected by the Scrum master and donated to charity, is a popular rule. The meeting is limited to just those three core questions. Members stand to create a sense of urgency. Immediately afterwards, specific members may meet to resolve issues that surfaced.

FIGURE 17.4 **Scrum Meetings**

The value of the Scrum is that it creates a daily mechanism to quickly inform the team about the state of the project. It sustains a sense of team identity that encourages openness and resolution of problems in real time. Having everyone report what they plan to do for that day generates a social promise to the group, thereby building accountability.

Notice again that the team is self-managed. The Scrum master does not assign daily tasks to team members; the team decides amongst themselves. The Scrum master role is to see that the Scrum is running correctly. They are not "master" of the team but rather "master" of the process.

Sprint Review At the end of each sprint, the team demonstrates the actual work product increments they have built to the product owner and other relevant stakeholders. Feedback is solicited from the product owner and other relevant stakeholders. The product owner declares which items are "done" and which items need further work and are returned to the product backlog. The team can take this opportunity to suggest improvements and new features for the product owner to accept or reject. The sprint review meeting is an opportunity to examine and adapt the product as it emerges and iteratively refine key requirements. Such refinements will be the subject of the next sprint planning meeting.

Sprint Retrospective The purpose of the retrospective meeting is to reflect on how well the previous sprint went and identify specific actions that can improve future sprints. The Scrum master typically facilitates this meeting and the team decides which changes will be made in how they work together for the next sprint. The retrospective reflects Scrum's commitment to continuous improvement and the value it places on improving not only products but team interactions.

Product and Sprint Backlogs

Each project has a product backlog and a sprint backlog. The product owner controls the product backlog and the team controls the sprint backlog. The **product backlog** is the customer's prioritized list of key features desired when the project is completed. Only the product owner can change the product backlog and its priorities. The product backlog usually defines each feature and estimates of time, cost, and work remaining. By observing the feature completion rate (called the "burn rate"); the product owner can estimate the finish date and consider the trade-off of adding or reducing features. See Figure 17.5 for a partial product backlog for a software project.

FIGURE 17.5
Partial Product Backlog

	A	B	C	D	E	F	G
1		**Phone-In Prescription Software Project**					
2		**Product Backlog**					
3							
4	**ID**	**Product**	**Priority**	**Status**	**Estimate**	**Actual**	
5					**Hours**	**Hours**	
6							
7	1	Customer Information	2	Complete	100	90	
8	2	Insurance Information	1	Complete	160	180	
9	3	Drug Information	3	Started	80		
10	4	Doctor Information	5	Not started	40		
11	5	Inventory status	4	Started	120		
12							

FIGURE 17.6
Partial Sprint Backlog

	A	B	C	D	E	F	G	H	I
1	Phone-In Prescription Drug Project								
2	Sprint Backlog								
3									
4	Sprint Description	Responsible	Actual Hours	Remaining Hours	Defined	In Progress	Tested	Accepted	
5									
6									
7	Drug categories	RT	16	0	X	X	X	✔	
8	Generics	CG	32	0	X	X	X	✔	
9	Branded	AL	24	8	X	X	X		
10									
11									
12	Design drug inventory system	EL	40	0	X	X	X	✔	
13	Code inventory availability	CE		32					
14	Code manufacture order	MC		32					
15	Integrate all inventory systems	LE	4	16	X				
16									

The **sprint backlog** is developed and controlled by the team. It represents the amount of work the team commits to complete during the next sprint. The sprint backlog lists the tasks (activities) that must be completed to deliver a functional feature or segment of a feature. The sprint backlog also serves as a status document by listing the person responsible for each task, remaining hours of work, and recording the task as *finished, in process*, or *not yet started*. See Figure 17.6 for a partial example of a sprint backlog.

Scrum does not use any of the conventional project management tools like Gantt charts or network diagrams. Instead it relies on the daily scrums and the active involvement of the product owner to manage work flow. Risk is mitigated by short developmental cycles and rigorous testing.

Applying Agile PM to Large Projects

Scrum and most other Agile methods are ideally suited for distinct projects that can be completed by a small, five to nine person team. Agile methods can be used on larger scale projects in which several teams are working on different features at the same time. In practice this condition is called "**scaling.**" The chief challenge with scaling is integration—making sure that the different features being created work in harmony with each other.

There are no easy solutions to the integration challenge. Significant up-front planning is required to manage the interdependences of different features that will be developed. This is called "staging" and often is the subject of the first development iteration. Here protocols and roles for coordinating efforts and assuring compatibility are established. This is supported by establishing a clear product vision so that trade-off decisions are consistent at the local team level.

Agile advocates recommend creating a hub structure (see Figure 17.7) with overlapping roles and responsibilities to manage large projects. There are several feature development teams. A separate integration and build team is formed consisting of part-time members of each feature team. This team tackles the sticky integration issue through testing and establishing requirements for the feature teams. To coordinate the multiteam structure a central project team is created consisting of a higher level project manager, a product manager (who represents the interests of the customer), and the leads ("project managers") from the feature development teams. The project management team provides coordination and facilitates project decision making. Their role is to steer rather than command the

FIGURE 17.7
Hub Project
Management
Structure

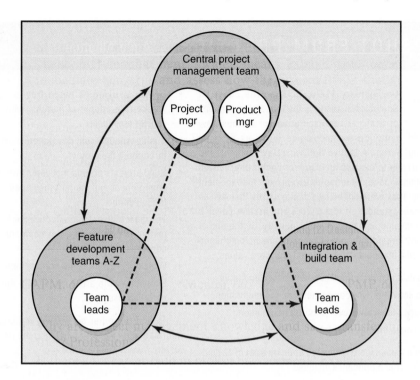

other teams. Teams may be real, virtual, or a combination. The entire system requires a spirit of collaboration to work.

Limitations and Concerns

Agile methods in the software industry grew at a grass roots level. Many engineers
saw traditional plan-driven project management as stifling effective development with
too much emphasis on processes and documentation and not enough on creativity
and experimentation. Early on there was a rebellious tone to the Agile movement, so
much so, that several of the key founders published an *Agile Manifesto* (see Snapshot
from Practice on Agile Alliance). The manifesto affirmed a different set of values
than those currently being applied by management to projects they were working on.

The revolutionary nature of Agile is reflected in the story one IT manager told
the authors about her efforts at using Agile PM. She worked for a large, multinational high-tech firm that had spent five years rigidly institutionalizing a set of
traditional project management policies and procedures. Despite their best efforts,
her department consistently completed projects behind schedule with several can-
cellations. Out of desperation she started secretly using Agile methods to complete
software projects. By using Agile PM her project teams were able to not only meet
but beat project schedules—a rarity within her company. When top management
confronted her for not conforming to procedure, she pointed to her recent success
rate to defend being left alone. Ultimately management couldn't argue with success, and she was allowed to expand her efforts.

Agile PM does not satisfy top management's need for budget, scope, and schedule control. Remember the new house analogy. The buyers got exactly what they
wanted but did not know how much it would cost. Nor did they know how long it
would take or even what it would look like when it was done. While ballpark
estimates are provided, Agile methods by their very nature do not provide the

On February 11–13, 2001, at The Lodge at Snowbird ski resort in the Wasatch mountains of Utah, 17 representatives of various new software methodologies (such as Extreme Programming, Scrum, Adaptive Software Development, and Crystal Clear) met to discuss the need for lighter alternatives to the traditional, documentation-driven project management methodology. They were united by a desire to free themselves of Dilbert manifestations of make-work and arcane policies and spark a revolution in the software industry. By the end of two days they formed the Agile Alliance to champion change and published a manifesto that declared four core values:

- Individuals and interactions over processes and tools.
- Working software over comprehensive documentation.
- Customer collaboration over contract negotiation.
- Responding to change over following a plan.

These four values were expanded upon by a set of 12 guiding principles. These principles included:

- Deliver working software frequently, from a couple of weeks to a couple of months, with a preference to the shorter timescale.
- Businesspeople and developers must work together daily throughout the project.
- Build projects around motivated individuals. Give them the environment and support they need, and trust them to get the job done.
- The most efficient and effective method of conveying information to and within a development team is face-to-face conversation.
- Working software is the primary measure of progress.
- Simplicity—the art of maximizing the amount of work not done—is essential.

To find the other six guiding principles and a wealth of information on Agile PM, log onto the Agile Alliance Web site at: http://www.agilealliance.org/

detail estimates of time and costs that management likes. No matter how realistic "it depends" is, management as well as customers are accustomed to working with a greater level of certainty than Agile provides. In response to the financial concerns, many organizations establish "ceilings," which is the maximum budget that should not be exceeded in the development of a given product or service.

Even if management totally buys into the value of Agile PM, one cannot simply install it into an organization over night, it needs to evolve over time. Many of the Agile principles, including self-organizing teams and intense collaboration, are incompatible with corporate cultures. For example, the principle of self-organizing teams, in which members decide who should do what, regardless of rank or title, contradicts command and control structures. Likewise, intense collaboration is not for everyone. One Agile manager confessed that she had to let several of her top engineers go because their lone-wolf personalities were not compatible with collaboration. Most companies report gradual introduction of Agile project management. For example, Siemens Medical Systems started with one Scrum team in 2004, then 10 Scrum teams in 2005, 70 teams in 2006, and over 97 teams in 2007.

As noted earlier, Agile methods appear to work best on small projects that require only five to nine dedicated team members to complete the work. Here face-to-face communication replaces time-consuming documentation and informal coordination supplants top-down control. Although some companies have successfully applied Agile PM to large projects, others have struggled with the scaling challenge. Too often coordination requirements undermine the adaptability of small teams, which is a chief strength of Agile PM.

Companies that enjoy success on large projects tend to have had a strong history of using Agile on smaller projects, and Agile principles are part of their product development culture.

Agile requires active customer involvement. Involvement comes in different shapes and forms. Designating an internal person to act as a product owner to represent the interests of customers is relatively easy. Soliciting the active participation of external customers can be more problematic. Even though there is consistent evidence that customer participation enhances project success, not all customers want to be that actively involved. Many are simply too busy. Others believe that they hired the project team so they would not have to be involved. Securing the cooperation of customers to devote the requisite time to support Agile PM is a common source of frustration in the field.

Agile PM frameworks, like Scrum, are used exclusively to complete software development projects from beginning to end. Other companies are using Agile PM only during the early exploratory phase of a project. Agile PM is used to develop critical breakthrough technology or define essential features. Once the features and technology are known then traditional project management is applied to complete the project.

Summary

Agile project management has emerged as a response to the challenges of managing projects with loosely defined scopes and high levels of uncertainty. Agile relies on an iterative development process in which the scope of the project evolves over time. Development teams create feature; driven working products at the end of each development cycle. Active customer involvement is used to guide this process. Here are some of the key advantages of Agile methods:

- Work is divided into smaller and smaller chunks that are more easily scheduled and controlled.
- Collaboration between the customer and designers is increased leading to solid change control.
- Methods demand that features be tested and functional when completed.

Agile PM is still evolving. While much of the attention in this chapter has been devoted to software development, Agile PM is being successfully applied to a wide range of unpredictable projects. New methods and approaches will continue to be developed and adapted to meet the specific needs of projects. Stay tuned.

Key Terms

Agile PM 583	Product backlog 591	Scrum meeting 590
Feature 588	Product owner 589	Self-organizing
Iterative incremental	Scaling 592	team 589
development (IID) 585	Scrum master 590	Sprint backlog 592

Review Questions

1. Why is the traditional project management approach less effective when project scope and technology are not well known?
2. What is iterative incremental development? Why is it useful for developing new products?
3. What are the advantages of Agile PM? What are the disadvantages of Agile PM?
4. What similarities and differences exist between a traditional project manager and a Scrum master?

Schwaber, K., *Agile Project Management with Scrum* (Redmond, WA: Microsoft Press, 2004).

Takeuchi, H., and I. Nonaka, "The New Product Development Game," *Harvard Business Review,* January–February 1986.

Worthen, B., "Try Software on Workers First, Fix It Later," *The Wall Street Journal,* September 25, 2007, pp. B1 and B4.

Case

Introducing Scrum at P2P

PART A

Kendra Hua had worked for six years as a software engineer in the IT department at Point 2 Point (P2P), a large freight moving company. She liked her job and the people she worked with. While she did some maintenance work, she worked primarily on projects, usually full time. Her work covered a wide range of projects including system upgrades, inventory control, GPS tracking, billing, and customer databases. These projects were typically able to meet project requirements but were consistently late. Within the IT department it was common practice for a betting pool to emerge regarding completion dates. The rule of thumb was to take the original schedule and multiply it by 1.5 and start guessing from then on.

Management decided to try to turn things around by changing the way P2P completed IT projects. Instead of the traditional waterfall approach in which all the requirements were defined up front, the IT department was to start using Agile project management, and more specifically Scrum, to complete their projects.

Kendra had just been assigned to the Big Foot project, which involved developing a system for monitoring P2P's carbon footprint. To prepare for this project, Kendra and her entire team of software engineers would attend a two-day Scrum workshop.

Everyone was given a book on Scrum to prepare themselves for the workshop. At first Kendra was overwhelmed by terminology—Scrum master, sprints, product manager, sprint logs, and so forth. She questioned the rugby metaphor, since the only thing she knew about the sport was that one of her ex-boyfriends in college would come back to the dorm inebriated and bloodied after a match. And why was the project manager called a master? It seemed demeaning to her. Still, she had heard some good things about Scrum from a friend who was using it in another company. He claimed it gave programmers more freedom to do their work, and work at a faster pace. So she approached the two-day workshop with an open mind.

The workshop was facilitated by a trainer who was well versed in the world of software development. Participants included her other five team members as well as Prem Gupta, a veteran project manager who would now assume the role of Scrum master, and Isaac Smith, who would act as the product manager representing the interests of the customers. At first everyone gave Prem a hard time, by bowing to him, pleading "master, master, master . . ." The facilitator quickly corrected them by saying he was not their master but rather master of the Scrum process. The facilitator went on to emphasize that they would work as a self-organizing team. Kendra wasn't exactly sure what that meant, but she felt it had something to do with the team managing itself, not Prem.

The workshop covered all the basic Scrum tools, concepts, and roles. Everyone got to practice the process by completing a simulated project involving the creation of a new board game. Kendra liked the idea of the standing Scrum meeting, since most of her meetings at P2P took way too long. She also liked having the product manager who was the ultimate decider on features and when work was completed. Everyone laughed at the "only one neck to wring" analogy that the facilitator used to describe this role. Overall she thought the process had promise and she was excited about trying it out on the Big Foot project. The Big Foot project was estimated to be completed after five sprints with each sprint lasting four weeks.

THE FIRST SPRINT

The first sprint planning meeting went pretty much by the book. Isaac had done his homework and came to the meeting with a comprehensive list of features the software needed to provide. There was healthy discussion, and Isaac amended the list to include some features that the team felt was necessary. The afternoon session featured Isaac, the product owner, prioritizing the features in the product backlog with feedback from the team. The final segment was devoted to the team deciding among themselves which high priority features they would commit to build within the four-week sprint. Prem did a good job of reminding the team that they were expected to build a fully functional feature. This tempered the team's enthusiasm, and in the end a challenging but doable set of features was assigned to the sprint backlog for the first sprint.

The first couple of daily Scrum meetings were a bit awkward as members were careful not to step on each others' toes. One of the first impediments identified was not having a shared understanding of how a self-organizing team worked. Prem kept emphasizing that it was up to the team to decide who does what and when. Then one morning it just suddenly clicked and members came forward claiming work they felt needed to be done. After that the daily scrums took on a life of their own, interrupted only when a member had to do five push-ups for every minute late. The pace of work picked up, and there was a shared enthusiasm as tasks and ultimately functional features were completed in rapid fashion. Kendra worked side by side with the other software engineers to solve problems and share what they had learned. Occasionally Isaac would be called into the project room to answer questions about specific features and be shown work in progress.

By the time of the first sprint review meeting, the team was able to demonstrate all but one of the designated features to Isaac and even three more that were not on the initial hit list. The team got some useful feedback not only from Isaac but also from a couple of the end users he brought with him. Eighty percent of the features were proclaimed done by Isaac while the others needed only slight modifications. Everyone agreed that the next Sprint review would even be more successful.

The sprint retrospective meeting was refreshing as members spoke candidly about both the good and the bad. Everyone agreed that the team needed to do a better job at documentation. Issues regarding fairness and spreading both the fun work and the tough work among the entire team was brought to the surface. Kendra was impressed by how everyone focused on what was best for the project not just themselves.

THE SECOND SPRINT

The second sprint meeting went well. The features that needed rework after the first sprint review meeting were at the top of the backlog and Isaac made appropriate adjustments in priorities and a couple of new features that were discovered during the sprint review meeting were added. The meeting convened with the team confident that they would be able to complete the work they had committed to.

Project work progressed quickly over the next week. Kendra felt pressure to accomplish what she said she would at the daily Scrum. At the same time, she felt a tremendous amount of satisfaction reporting work done. The entire team seemed energized. Then one day everything came to a standstill over a sticky integration problem. The team struggled over the next three days trying to solve the problem until at the next Scrum. Prem stepped forward saying "I think you should do this . . ." He then proceeded to outline a specific method for solving the problem, even assigning specific tasks to each team member. During the next two days Prem went back and forth between team members coordinating their work and solving problems. While there was some grumbling within the team, his solution worked, and Kendra was grateful to get back on track.

From then on Prem took a more active role in daily Scrum meetings, often having the final say as to the work agenda for that day. The meetings took on a different tone as members waited for Prem to speak first. Isaac was absent from the project room during this time as he was visiting sites that would be using the new software. Still features were being completed and Kendra was happy with its progress. Then one day Isaac showed up at the morning Scrum meeting. He had just gotten back and had fresh information he wanted to introduce into the project. He had rewritten the product log and added several new, high priority features and eliminated a few of the features that the team had been working on. He wanted the team to shift their efforts and complete the new features by the end of the sprint.

The team was shocked because one of the principles they had been taught is that you don't change course midway through a sprint. Prem did his best to explain this to Isaac, but he was insistent. He kept saying that these changes had to be made, otherwise much of the sprint output would be a waste of time. He kept repeating that the team needed to be flexible, "After all isn't that what the Agile approach is all about." The meeting came to an impasse until Prem came forward with a compromise. The team would agree to do the new work, but the sprint needed to be extended by two weeks. Everyone agreed and Kendra went back to work.

Up till the end of the second sprint, Prem continued to direct project work. When it came for the sprint review meeting four of the five new features were completed as well as most of the original features. However, the feature demonstrations did not go well. Isaac and several of the end users that were present were critical of the user friendliness of several of the completed features. Kendra and other team members defended their work by saying, "Why didn't you tell us you wanted it to perform that way?" Prem did his best to keep the meeting under control, but the team had little to say when an important feature simply did not work. In the end, only half of the features were accepted as being done.

Kendra walked out of the sprint review discouraged. Tomorrow morning was the sprint retrospective meeting. She had a lot on her mind, but wasn't sure what she should say or how to say it at the meeting.

1. How well is Scrum working?
2. What are the issues confronting the Big Foot project?

3. Assume you are Kendra. What would you want to say at the retrospective? How would you say it?

4. What improvements or changes need to be made?

PART B

Prem opened the retrospective by saying he had gotten a call from his boss and she was not happy with the progress. Prem said that he and the team were under the gun to get back on track. The list of things that went well during the second sprint was short and when it came time to discuss improvements there was an awkward silence. Kendra spoke up and began by saying she had gone back and reviewed the Scrum book. She went on to say that she thought the whole idea behind Scrum was that the team was to work to solve their own problems and it wasn't Prem's role to play task master. A couple of other team members murmured agreement. Prem became defensive and said if he had not intervened it would have taken days for the team to solve the problem.

Another member said he thought it was a mistake allowing Isaac to change the sprint commitments. Prem agreed that in principle that was true, but said sometimes you have to bend the rules to do what is right. He admonished the team by saying that they had to practice being more agile. The retrospective ended with few specific recommendations other than that in order to get back on track, Prem felt he would have to get even more involved in the execution of the project.

The subsequent sprint 3 planning meeting was more of a formality. Isaac updated the product backlog with revised priorities and Prem signed off for the team as to what they would commit to. There was little interaction between the team and Isaac except seeking clarification on performance requirements for specific features.

The team met under Prem's leadership for their daily Scrums. Sometimes the Scrums went beyond the normal 15 minutes as Prem reviewed progress and described in detail what needed to be done that day. Isaac would occasionally show up, change priorities, review work and answer questions. Kendra worked hard on her assignments and often received praise from Prem for work well done.

One evening when the team got together for a few beers and sushi, one of the team members pulled out a spreadsheet and asked who wanted to make the first bet on when they thought the project would be done.

After several sprints, Isaac finally signed off on the last feature and declared the project completed. A collective "yahoo" sprang from the team. After the meeting Kendra went around collecting money from each of her teammates—she had predicted that the project would take 12 weeks longer than planned.

1. How would you assess P2P effort at introducing Scrum?

2. What challenges does an organization face when adopting an Agile approach like Scrum?

3. What could P2P have done to enhance success?

Project Management Career Paths

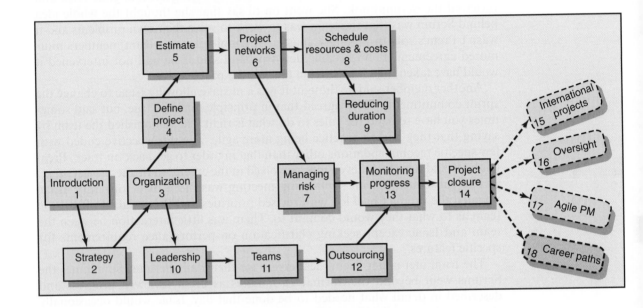

Eighty percent of success is showing up.

—*Woody Allen*

This chapter discusses basic issues regarding a career in project management. One point to remember is that pursuing a career in project management does not necessarily mean you will ever have the title of project manager. Yes, there are growing numbers of fields in which project manager is a career path, but there are many more jobs in which project management is not a title but a job requirement. This underscores a major advantage to being good at managing projects; and that is the basic project management methodology you have been exposed to in this text is transferable across most businesses and professions. Think back to the Snapshots from Practice contained in the different chapters. They were not limited to one or two industries or professions, but rather entailed a smorgasboard of industries and professions! So, whether you are interested in a formal career in project management or just see managing projects as being important for your aspirations, this chapter provides advice for further developing your project management skills and know-how.

Career Paths

There is no set career path for becoming a project manager. Career avenues vary from industry to industry, organization to organization, and from profession to profession. What can be said is that advancement occurs incrementally. You don't simply graduate and become a project manager. As in other careers, you have to work your way up to the position. For example, in project-based organizations such as construction firms, you may begin by working on several projects as an assistant engineer, then take an assignment as a project analyst. From there you are promoted to principal engineer, advance to assistant project manager, assume the role of project manager over a small project, and then continue to bigger, riskier projects. In other organizations, project management careers run parallel with functional advancement with many crossovers. For example, at Intel a management information systems (MIS) specialist might start his career as a designer, then take an assignment as a project specialist, later work as a project manager, and then return to a functional position as head of a department or as a product manager. See the Rod Gwinn Snapshot from Practice for an example of how a former student launched a career in project management.

Other people find that their project management responsibilities expand as they move up the organization's hierarchy. For example, a former marketing student began her career as an assistant buyer for a large retail company. She then became area sales manager at a specific store and became involved on a part-time basis in a series of projects, acting as a facilitator of focus groups. She was promoted to buyer and eventually became a store manager. In her current position, she coordinates a variety of projects ranging from improving the sales acumen of

SNAPSHOT FROM PRACTICE   Rod Gwinn

1988–2002	Information Technology Professional
2002–2006	B.S. Business Administration–Oregon State University
2005–2006	Project Management Intern–Symantec Inc.
2006–2008	IT Manager–ECOS Consulting
2008–Pres	IT Project Manager–State of Oregon

Over the years I have worked on, and managed, many technology projects. Some of these went well, others did not. In retrospect, I see that the projects that went smoothly were the ones that were well organized and had some sort of a plan to follow. I did not realize at the time how much project management played a role in even the smallest IT project.

After working in the IT field for almost 20 years, I decided it was time to head back to college to finish my elusive degree. In my junior year, our MIS class took on a project to assist Symantec Corporation with a small development project. This allowed me to directly utilize the skills I had acquired during my early career, plus my learning experiences from the College of Business. One of the outcomes of this project was that the representative from Symantec mentioned an intern program that may be of interest to us.

As we were nearing our summer break, I pursued the opportunity at Symantec. I started as an intern shortly before the end of my junior year, and worked with them through the end of 2005. This proved to be a tremendous opportunity. I was directly working on IT projects for one of the largest software organizations in the world. I was exposed to their very formal process for project management and had the chance to apply my recent classroom experience in a meaningful way.

After graduation, I accepted a position at ECOS, a small environmental consulting company, where I applied my newly developed skills to help shape their technology strategic plan. I continued to explore opportunities in project management and was made aware of a position with the state of Oregon that seemed to be a very good fit for my experience and education. In April 2008, I accepted the position of enhancement project manager. My primary responsibility was to oversee the enhancement phase (Version 1.5) of the new MMIS (Medicaid Management Information System). I am very satisfied to have a new career path, as an IT project manager, which allows me to utilize both my past experiences and my recent education. One of the things I enjoy most about this type of work is the sense of accomplishment in delivering a project that is useful, usable, and meets, or even exceeds, expectations.

her salesforce to altering the physical layout of the store. Although the title of project manager does not appear in her job description, more than 50 percent of her work involves managing projects.

Temporary Assignments

One aspect of project managing that is unique is the temporary nature of assignments. With line appointments, promotions are for the most part permanent and there is a natural, hierarchical progression to positions with greater authority and responsibility. In the example of the former marketing student, she progressed from assistant buyer to sales manager to buyer to store manager. Only under very unusual circumstances would she regress to being a buyer. Conversely, tenure is rarely granted to project managers. Once the project is completed, the manager may return to his previous department, even to a lesser position. Or, depending on the projects available, he may be assigned to manage a more or less significant project. Future work depends on what projects are available at the time the individual is available and how well the last project went. A promising career can be derailed by one unsuccessful project.

Pursuing a Career

If you are considering pursuing a career in project management, you should first find out what specific project job opportunities exist in your company. You should talk to people in project management positions and find out how they got to where they are and what advice they can give you. Because career paths, as noted earlier, vary from organization to organization, you need to be attuned to the unique pathways within your company. For example, retail companies naturally assign marketing managers to projects. Electronics firms, on the other hand, typically assign engineers to be project leads.

Once you have concluded that you wish to pursue a career in project management, or see project management as an avenue for advancement, you need to share your aspirations with your immediate superior. Your superior can champion your ambitions, sanction additional training in project management, and assign immediate work that will contribute to your project skill base.

Professional Training and Certification

Most project managers have never received formal training in project management. They mastered the job through on-the-job training, buttressed by occasional workshops on specific project topics such as project scheduling or negotiating contracts. It wasn't until recently that universities started offering courses on project management outside of schools of engineering; to date there are only a handful of degree programs in project management. Regardless of your level of training you will likely need to supplement your education. Many large companies have in-house training programs on project management. For example, at one time, Hewlett-Packard had more than 32 training modules in its project management curriculum, which is organized around five levels of experience: project team, new project manager, project manager, experienced project manager, and manager of project managers. Take advantage of professional workshops, which can cover a range of specific project management tools and topics. Continued education should not be restricted to project management. Many technical professionals return to universities to complete an MBA or take night classes in management to expand their general business background.

Many professionals find it beneficial to join the Project Management Institute (PMI). Membership entitles you to subscriptions to PMI publications including the academic *Project Management Journal* and the *PM Network,* a trade magazine. PMI sponsors workshops and national forums on project management. When you join PMI you also become a member of one of the more than 300 local chapters across North America. PMI also has local chapters in over 60 countries across the globe. These chapters meet on a monthly basis and provide project professionals with opportunities to network and learn from each other.

In addition, PMI, as part of its effort to advance the profession, certifies mastery of project manager competencies through a formal examination that covers the entire body of knowledge of project management. Two of the most popular certifications are Certified Associate in Project Management **(CAPM)** and Project Management Professional **(PMP).** The CAPM is designed for young

TABLE 18.1
PMI Certification
Requirements

	CAPM	**PMP**
Full Name:	Certified Associate in Project Management	Project Management Professional
Project Role:	Contributes to project team	Leads and directs project teams
Eligibility Requirements:	High school diploma/global equivalent **AND** 1,500 hours experience **OR** 23 hours project management education	High school diploma/global equivalent **5** years project management experience **35** hours project management education **OR** Bachelor's degree/global equivalent **3** years project management experience **35** hours project management education
Exam Information:	3 hours; 150 multiple-choice questions	4 hours; 200 multiple-choice questions

professionals getting started in the field while PMP is restricted to seasoned veterans with significant project management experience (see Table 18.1).

Most students, by taking a formal class in project management at the university level, qualify to sit for the CAPM exam. Both the CAPM and PMP exams are based on the official Project Management Body of Knowledge (PMBOK) published by PMI. There are several "prep" books available to assist students in taking the examinations. These books provide useful tips as well as practice exams.

Passing the exam and being certified as either a CAPM or PMP is a clearly visible way to signal your competence and interest. See the Ginger Butler Snapshot from Practice for an example of how one former student used the CAPM to launch a career in project management.

Gaining Visibility

As you accumulate knowledge and techniques, you need to apply them to your immediate job situation. Most people's jobs entail some form of project work, whether realizing a mandated objective or simply figuring out ways to improve the quality of performance. Gantt charts, responsibility matrixes, CPM networks, and other project management tools can be used to plan and implement these endeavors. It may also be wise to look outside the workplace for opportunities to develop project management skills. Active involvement in your local community can provide numerous opportunities to manage projects. Organizing a local soccer tournament, managing a charitable fund-raising event, or coordinating the renovation of the neighborhood park can allow you to practice project management. Furthermore, given the volunteer nature of most of these projects, they can provide you with an excellent training ground to sharpen your ability to exercise influence without formal authority.

Regardless of how competent and worthy you are, your project management skills must be visible to others for them to be recognized. Many project managers' careers began by volunteering for task forces and small projects. Ideally you should select task forces and projects that allow you access to higher-ups and other departments within your organization, providing you with opportunities to develop contacts.

This was certainly true for a former student of ours named Bob who escaped the trenches of a large corporation by volunteering to lead the organization's annual United Way campaign. While an important cause, directing the United Way campaign was generally given to someone who was expendable. This was true for

SNAPSHOT FROM PRACTICE   Ginger Butler

2000	B.S. Business Administration
2000-07	Software Analyst
2007	Master Business Administration (MBA) CAPM PMI Project Management Certification
2007	Project Manager
2008	Director Project Management Office
2009	Vice President, Products & Operations

After 10 years of bookkeeping, I decided to return to college to complete a bachelor's degree in business administration—management information systems. It was in my junior year that I took a project management (PM) course. I was impressed with how PM methods can break down the most complicated projects into steps that could then be turned into processes that would likely result in successful projects. The next seven years were spent as a software analyst. Time and time again, I could see the need for effective PM in our software development shop. Slowly, I started to apply what I had learned and began to realize how useful project management tools and techniques were to getting things done.

I knew that I needed to learn more. I was contemplating whether to take a project management course to acquire PM certification or make a bolder move and earn an MBA. I made the decision to earn the MBA and, once again, had the opportunity to take an advanced course in PM. Before I graduated, I orchestrated a PM certification prep course in which I and 11 other graduate students ultimately earned their certification.

One week after graduation, I took a project management position at Avant Assessment. PM certification was a requirement for the job. Avant Assessment (founded in 2001) designs, develops, and delivers four-skill language proficiency assessments that are standards-based, validated, and delivered in a Web environment. The company embraced the science of PM and provided an amazing opportunity for me to make a significant impact as a project manager. Within two years, I was promoted to director of our PM office. From there I was able to create cohesive and effective processes in our production department and have repeated the process development successes in our products department.

Recently, I was promoted to director of operations. This is a direct result of what I have been able to accomplish with the education and continued learning about project management. By coupling the MBA with PM, I was prepared to take on significant challenges and produce tactical, operational, and strategic improvements within and across departments. Granted, I was in the right place at the right time to get such a great opportunity at Avant Assessment. This company is an innovative thinking, action-oriented company that has been very rewarding to work for. Avant recognizes and encourages personal and professional growth and development. Thanks to the spark of interest found years ago in project management, and to Avant Assessment for igniting a passion for improvement, my career has skyrocketed.

Bob whose career had bottomed out. Bob took advantage of the United Way task force to show off his project management skills. Through recruiting key participants, establishing a shared vision, managing milestones, and contagious enthusiasm the campaign was a resounding success shattering previous records. Bob's efforts caught the attention of top management, and he was rewarded with more project work.

Mentors

In pursuing your ambition you should continually be on the lookout for a mentor. Most fast-track managers acknowledge that mentors played a significant role in their advancement. **Mentors** are typically superiors who take a special interest in you and your career. They use their clout to champion your ambitions and act as a personal coach, teaching you "the ropes to skip and the ropes to know." This special treatment does not come without a price. Mentors typically require fervent loyalty and superior performance; after all, the mentor's reputation rests on your performance. How do you find a mentor? Most people say it just happens. But it doesn't happen to everyone. Mentors typically seek A+ workers, not C workers, and you must make your abilities known to others.

Many organizations have instituted formal mentoring programs in which experienced project managers are assigned to promising young managers. Although the relationship may not evolve to the personal level experienced with an informal mentor, designated mentors play a very similar role in coaching and championing one's professional progress. You should take advantage of this opportunity to learn as much as you can from these seasoned veterans.

Since much project work is temporary and contractual in nature, it is important to develop professional contacts that may lead to future work. Attending conferences, trade fairs, and workshops provides good opportunities to "network" and develop social connections that might precipitate project assignments. These social/professional networks can provide a safety net for project work during times of downsizing and layoffs.

Success in Key Projects

Ultimately your goal is to accumulate a portfolio of project management experiences that broaden your skill base and reputation. Early on you should choose, when possible, projects with the greatest learning opportunities. Pick projects more for the quality of the people working on them than for the scope of the projects. There is no better way to learn how to be an effective project manager than by watching one at work. Keep a diary of your observations and review and refine lessons learned. Later, as your confidence and competency grow, you should try to get involved in projects that will enhance your reputation within the firm. Remember the comments about customer satisfaction. You want to exceed your superior's expectations. Avoid run-of-the-mill projects or assignments. Seek high-profile projects that have some risks and tangible payoffs. At the same time, be careful to be involved in projects commensurate with your abilities.

Finally, despite your efforts you may find that you are not making satisfactory progress toward your career goals. If this is your appraisal, you may wish to seriously consider moving to a different company or even a different industry that might provide more project management opportunities. Hopefully, you have managed to accumulate sufficient project management experience to aid in your job search. One advantage of project work over general management is that it is typically easier to highlight and "sell" your accomplishments.

Summary

It is rare to find a job or a career path that would not benefit from being good at managing projects. Students starting their careers should take advantage of every opportunity to continue to develop and expand their project management skills. They should volunteer to work on task forces, take advantage of training opportunities, and apply project management tools and techniques to their work. They should signal to their superiors their interest in project management and garner project assignments. Over time they should accumulate a portfolio of project management experiences that establishes their skill base and reputation as someone who gets things done quickly and done right.

As you pursue your career we leave you two suggestions as a project manager:

1. Maintain a sense of the big picture. Engage regularly in what some have called "helicopter management," which means expand your perspective beyond immediate concerns and assess how the project fits in the larger scheme of things. Project managers need to constantly assess how the project fulfills the mission and strategy of the firm, how the project is affecting the rest of the organization, whether the expectations of stakeholders are changing, and what key project interfaces have to be managed.

2. Remember that successful project management is essentially a balancing act. Project managers need to balance the soft (people) side of project management with the hard (technical) side, the demands of top management with the needs of team members, short-term gain with long-term need, and so forth.

Key Terms	CAPM, *605*	Mentor, *607*	PMP, *605*

Review Questions

1. Why are project management knowledge and skills transferable across industries? Professions?
2. Is there a set career path in project management? Explain.
3. How can a mentor help someone pursue a career in project management?

Exercises

1. Interview someone who has worked as a project manager or project management professional.
   a. How did they get started in the field?
   b. How has their career progressed?
   c. What advice would they give someone wishing to pursue a career in project management?
2. Interview someone who works in a field you are interested in pursuing.
   a. How did they get started in the field?
   b. How important is project management in the field? In their current job?
   c. What advice would they give someone wishing to pursue a career in their field?
3. Use an Internet job search engine (e.g., Monster.com) and search for jobs in the field of project management. What did this search reveal about
   a. the demand for project managers?
   b. the importance of certification?
   c. different industries looking for project managers?

References

Ferrazzi, K., and T. Rhaz, *Never Eat Alone: And Other Secrets to Success, One Relationship at a Time* (New York: Broadway Business, 2005).

Lientz, B. P., and K. P. Rea, *Project Management for the 21st Century* (San Diego: Academic Press, 1995).

Martin, P., and K. Tate, *Getting Started in Project Management* (New York: Wiley, 2004).

Solutions to Selected Exercises

Chapter 2

2-2. Payback = Investment/Annual Savings
Project Alpha: $150,000/$40,000 = 3.75 years
Project Beta: $200,000/$50,000 = 4.0 years
Project Alpha is the better payback.

2-5. The only project SIMSOX should consider is **Voyagers.** Each of the other two projects would not satisfy the high rate of return SIMSOX expects from its projects.

Project: **Dust Devils**

Year	Inflows	Outflows	Net flow	Discount Factor	NPV
0		500,000	(500,000)	1.00	(500,000)
1	50,000		50,000	0.81	40,500
2	250,000		250,000	0.66	165,000
3	350,000		350,000	0.54	189,000

Total: $(105,500)

If calculated in EXCEL: $(106,020)

Project: **Ospry**

Year	Inflows	Outflows	Net flow	Discount Factor	NPV
0		250,000	(250,000)	1.00	(250,000)
1	75,000		75,000	0.81	60,750
2	75,000		75,000	0.66	49,500
3	75,000		75,000	0.54	40,500
4	50,000		50,000	0.44	22,000

Total: $(77,250)

If calculated in EXCEL: $(77,302)

Project: **Yoyagers**

Year	Inflows	Outflows	Net flow	Discount Factor	NPV
0		75,000	(75,000)	1.00	(75,000)
1	15,000		15,000	0.81	12,150
2	25,000		25,000	0.66	16,500
3	50,000		50,000	0.54	27,000
4	50,000		50,000	0.44	22,000
5	150,000		150,000	0.36	54,000

Total: $(56,650)

If calculated in EXCEL: $(55,714)

Chapter 6

6-3. Activity C is a burst activity. Activity G is a merge activity.

6-11.

CP = A, C, E, G, J

PARK AND RIDE DESIGN

6-13.

Group Term Paper

6-20.

The only activities that have the start or finish on the critical path are E and K

Chapter 8

8-4.

Legend

ES	ID	EF
SL		SL
LS	DUR	LF

Resource

PLAN

Use the following heuristics:
Minimum slack
Smallest duration
Lowest identification number

RESOURCE SCHEDULE

ID	RES	DUR	ES	LF	SL	0	1	2	3	4	5	6	7	8	9	10	11	12	13	14	15
A	1	4	0	5	1	1	1	1	1												
B	2	5	0	5	0	2	2	2	2	2											
C	2	4	5	9	0						X	2	2	2	2						
D	1	5	5	12	2						1	1	1	1	1						
E	2	3	9	12	0						X	X	X	X	2	2	2				
F	2	2	12	14	0												X	X	2	2	
Resources scheduled						3	3	3	3	2	3	3	3	3	3	2	2	2	2		
Resources available						3	3	3	3	3	3	3	3	3	3	3	3	3	3		

8-7. You should not spend time planning how you are going to spend your bonus. The schedule will take 16 days.

8-10.

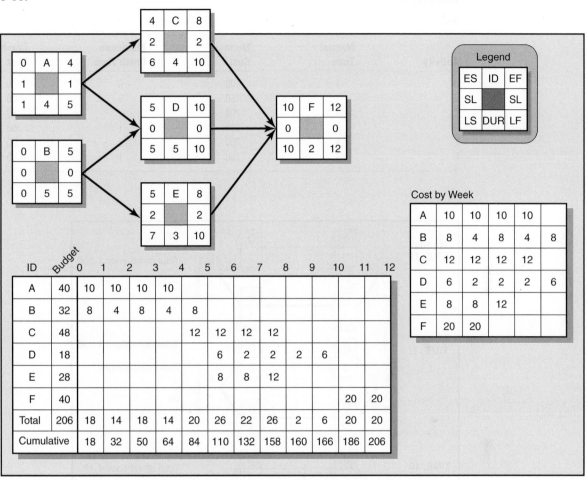

ID	Budget	0	1	2	3	4	5	6	7	8	9	10	11	12
A	40	10	10	10	10									
B	32	8	4	8	4	8								
C	48					12	12	12	12					
D	18					6	2	2	2	6				
E	28					8	8	12						
F	40											20	20	
Total	206	18	14	18	14	20	26	22	26	2	6	20	20	
Cumulative		18	32	50	64	84	110	132	158	160	166	186	206	

Cost by Week

A	10	10	10	10	
B	8	4	8	4	8
C	12	12	12	12	
D	6	2	2	2	6
E	8	8	12		
F	20	20			

Chapter 9

9-2.

Activity	Normal Time	Normal Cost	Maximum Crash Time	Crash Cost
A	1	100	0	0
B	3	150	2	100
C	4	200	1	50
D	3	200	1	60
E	4	200	2	70
F	3	150	1	90

9-8.

Activity	Normal Time	Normal Cost	Maximum Crash Time	Crash Cost
A	3	150	0	0
B	4	200	2	100
C	3	250	1	60
D	4	200	1	40
E	2	250	0	0
F	3	200	2	30
G	2	250	1	20
H	4	300	2	60
I	2	200	1	200

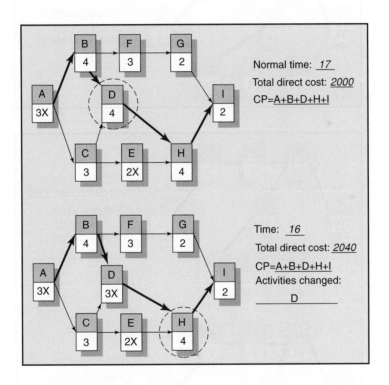

Normal time: _17_
Total direct cost: _2000_
CP=_A+B+D+H+I_

Time: _16_
Total direct cost: _2040_
CP=_A+B+D+H+I_
Activities changed:
_____D_____

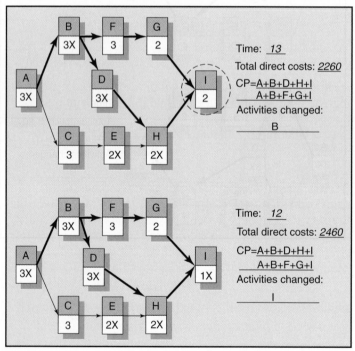

Duration	Direct Cost	Indirect Cost	Total Cost
17	2000	1500	3500
16	2040	1450	3490
15	2100	1400	3500
14	2160	1350	3560
13	2260	1300	3660
12	2460	1250	3860

The optimum time cost schedule would be 16 weeks at a cost of $3490.

Chapter 13

13-4.

Status Report: Ending Period 2   ($000)

Task	% Complete	EV	AC	PV	CV	SV
A	75%	30	25	20	5	10
B	50%	16	12	12	4	4
Cumulative Totals		46	37	32	9	14

Status Report: Ending Period 4   ($000)

Task	% Complete	EV	AC	PV	CV	SV
A	100%	40	35	40	5	0
B	100%	32	24	24	8	8
Cumulative Totals		72	59	64	13	8

Status Report: Ending Period 6   ($000)

Task	% Complete	EV	AC	PV	CV	SV
A	100%	40	35	40	5	0
B	100%	32	24	32	8	0
C	75%	36	24	24	12	12
D	0%	0	0	6	0	−6
E	50%	14	10	8	4	6
Cumulative Totals		122	93	110	29	12

Status Report: Ending Period 8   ($000)

Task	% Complete	EV	AC	PV	CV	SV
A	100%	40	35	40	5	0
B	100%	32	24	32	8	0
C	100%	48	32	48	16	0
D	33%	6	20	10	−14	−4
E	100%	28	20	28	8	0
Cumulative Totals		154	131	158	23	−4

Performance Indexes Summary ($000)

Period	EV	AC	PV	SPI	CPI	PCIB
2	46	37	32	1.44	1.24	22%
4	72	59	64	1.13	1.22	35%
6	122	93	110	1.11	1.31	59%
8	154	131	158	.97	1.18	75%

Forecast Costs at Completion

$$EAC_f = \frac{(BAC - EV)}{(EV/AC)} + AC$$

$$= \frac{(206 - 154)}{(154/131)} + 131$$

$$= 175$$

$$VAC_f = BAC - EAC_f$$

$$VAC_f = 206 - 175$$

$$VAC_f = 31$$

At the end of the 8th period three-quarters of the project has been completed at a savings of \$23,000. If the project continues to get \$1.18 worth of work for each dollar spent the project will be \$31,000 under budget at completion. The project appears to be slightly behind of schedule.

13-8. Part A

Status Report: **Ending Period 1** ($000)

Task	% Complete	EV	AC	PV	CV	SV
A	25%	25	50	50	−25	−25
Cumulative Totals		25	50	50	−25	−25

Status Report: **Ending Period 2** ($000)

Task	% Complete	EV	AC	PV	CV	SV
A	50%	50	100	100	−50	−50
Cumulative Totals		50	100	100	−50	−50

Status Report: **Ending Period 3** ($000)

Task	% Complete	EV	AC	PV	CV	SV
A	100%	100	200	100	−100	0
B	0%	0	0	100	0	−100
C	0%	0	0	150	0	−150
Cumulative Totals		100	200	350	−100	−250

Status Report: **Ending Period 4** ($000)

Task	% Complete	EV	AC	PV	CV	SV
A	100%	100	200	100	−100	0
B	60%	150	100	150	50	0
C	50%	225	200	300	25	−75
Cumulative Totals		475	500	550	−25	−75

Status Report: **Ending Period 5** ($000)

Task	% Complete	EV	AC	PV	CV	SV
A	100%	100	200	100	−100	0
B	100%	250	200	250	50	0
C	100%	450	400	450	50	0
Cumulative Totals		800	800	800	0	0

Status Report: **Ending Period 6** ($000)

Task	% Complete	EV	AC	PV	CV	SV
A	100%	100	200	100	−100	0
B	100%	250	200	250	50	0
C	100%	450	400	450	50	0
D	75%	150	100	100	50	50
Cumulative Totals		950	900	900	50	50

Status Report: **Ending Period 7** ($000)

Task	% Complete	EV	AC	PV	CV	SV
A	100%	100	200	100	−100	0
B	100%	250	200	250	50	0
C	100%	450	400	450	50	0
D	100%	200	150	200	50	0
E	20%	60	100	0	40	60
F	5%	15	50	0	−35	15
Cumulative Totals		1075	1100	1000	−25	75

Status Report: **Ending Period 8** ($000)

Task	% Complete	EV	AC	PV	CV	SV
A	100%	100	200	100	−100	0
B	100%	250	200	250	50	0
C	100%	450	400	450	50	0
D	100%	200	150	200	50	0
E	100%	300	350	200	−50	100
F	10%	30	100	100	−70	−70
Cumulative Totals		1330	1400	1300	−70	30

Performance Indixes Summary ($000)

Period	EV	AC	PV	SPI	CPI	PCIB
1	25	50	50	.50	.50	2%
2	50	100	100	.50	.50	3%
3	100	200	350	.29	.50	5%
4	475	500	550	.86	.95	24%
5	800	800	800	1.00	1.00	40%
6	950	900	900	1.06	1.06	48%
7	1075	1100	1000	1.08	.98	54%
8	1330	1400	1300	1.02	.95	67%

$$EAC_f = \frac{(BAC - EV)}{(EV/AC)} + AC$$

$$VAC_f = BAC - EAC_f$$

$$2105 = \frac{(2000 - 1330)}{(1330/1400)} + 1400$$

$$-105 = 2000 - 2105$$

With two-thirds of the project completed the forecast is that the project will be $105,000 over budget at completion.

13-8 Part B.

Revised Estimates: **Ending Period 14**

Task	% Complete	EV	AC	PV	CV	SV
A	100%	100	200	100	−100	0
B	100%	250	200	250	50	0
C	100%	450	400	450	50	0
D	100%	200	150	200	50	0
E	100%	300	350	300	−50	0
F	100%	300	500	300	−200	0
G	100%	200	150	200	50	0
H	100%	200	200	200	0	0
Cumulative Totals		2000	2150	2000	−150	0

$$EAC_{re} = AC + ETC_{re} \qquad 2150 = 1400 + 750$$
$$VAC_{re} = BAC - EAC_{re} \qquad -150 = 2000 - 2150$$

Revised Estimates indicate that the project will be one period behind schedule and $150,000 over budget.

Computer Project Exercises

In developing the exercises, trade-offs had to be made to enrich the learning experience. One of the major problems students initially encounter is data and detail overload. This reduces their ability to identify project and data problems and to compare alternatives. Although the project found in the exercises is real, it has been reduced and detail has been eliminated many times to concentrate on applying project management principles and understanding linkages. In addition, other simplifying assumptions have been made so that students and instructors can trace problems and discuss outcomes. These assumptions detract from reality, but they keep the focus on the objectives of the exercises and reduce student frustration with software intricacies. Moving from these exercises to real projects is primarily one of increasing detail. The simplifying assumptions are given below (make sure they are included in "default," "preferences," and/or "options" sections of the software used):

The POM+ Project*

Big Kola Company has been concerned that specialized fruit drinks have been eroding their cola market. The CEO mandates that "If you can't beat them, join them." Grape juice was the first product that was successful after an advertising blitz claiming the antitoxin benefits. Lately, competition is compressing grape juice margins and profits. Months of additional market surveys and focus groups have resulted in three potential high-margin drinks: cranberry, blueberry, and pomegranate. All these choices represent antitoxins. The decision is to produce the pomegranate drink that has many health claims. For example, the relative ability of these juices to eliminate harmful free radicals (antitoxins) is 71 percent for pomegranate, 33 percent for blueberry, and 20 percent for cranberry (Technion Institute of Technology). The market potential appears very attractive and should have a higher profit margin than the other potential juice products. Another appeal for pomegranate juice is its familiarity in the Middle East and Asia.

The Priority Matrix for the POM+ Project is:

	Time	Scope	Cost
Constrain			X
Enhance		X	
Accept	X		

* Cliff Gray, Erik Larson, & Pinyarat Sirisomboonsuk, doctoral candidate at Rawls College of Business, Texas Tech University.

Connor Gage, the project manager, has formed his project team and the members have come up with the following work breakdown structure.

1.0 POM+Project

1.1 R&D product development
      1.1.1 Need survey
      1.1.2 Set product specs
      1.1.3 Shelf life report
      1.1.4 Nutrition report

1.2 Secure fruit suppliers

1.3 Initial Production
      1.3.1 Equipment rehab
      1.3.2 Production trials
      1.3.3 Quality trials
      1.3.4 Quality metrics
      1.3.5 Quality training

1.4 Distribution
      1.4.1 Market testing
      1.4.2 Package design
      1.4.3 Select distributors

1.5 Legal
      1.5.1 Complete FDA certification
      1.5.2 Register trademark

1.6 Prepare product launch

Part 1

1. Develop the WBS outline using the software available (save your file).
2. Use this file and the information provided below to create a project schedule.
3. The following holidays are observed: January 1, Martin Luther King Day (third Monday in January), Memorial Day (last Monday in May), July 4th, Labor Day (first Monday in September), Thanksgiving Day (4th Thursday in November), December 25 and 26.
4. If a holiday falls on a Saturday then Friday will be given as an extra day off, and if it falls on a Sunday then Monday will be given off.
5. The project team works eight-hour days, Monday through Friday.
6. The project will begin on January 3, 2012.
7. Based on this schedule, submit a memo that answers the following questions:
    a. When is the project estimated to be completed? How many working days will it take?
    b. What is the critical path?
    c. Which activity has the most total slack?
    d. How sensitive is this network?
    e. Identify two sensible milestones and explain your choice.

Include the following (one page) printouts:

- A Gantt chart.
- A network diagram highlighting the critical path.
- A schedule table reporting ES, LS, EF, LF, and slack for each activity.

Hints: Change the timescale to months and weeks. The estimated duration of the project is 135 days.

Remember: Save your files for future exercises!

The following information has been derived from the WBS. *Note* that the activity number is what appears in the software with the complete WBS entered.

#*	Activity	Duration	Predecessor(s)
3	Need survey	20	None
4	Set product specs	15	3
5	Shelf life report	10	4
6	Nutrition report	5	4
7	Select fruit suppliers	20	5, 6
9	Equipment rehab	30	4
10	Production trials	15	7, 9
11	Quality trials	20	10
12	Quality metrics	5	11
13	Quality training	15	12
15	Market testing	30	5, 6
16	Package design	15	15
17	Select distributors	25	5, 6
19	Complete FDA certification	15	7, 15
20	Register trademark	5	7, 15
21	Prepare product launch	15	13, 16, 17, 19FS + 25 days, 20FS + 15 days

FS = Finish to Start lag

Part 2

Remember the old saying, "A project plan is not a schedule until resources are committed." This exercise illustrates this sometime subtle, but important point.

Using your files from Part 1, input resources and their costs if you have not already done so. All information is found in Tables A2.1 and A2.2.

Prepare a memo that addresses the following questions:

1. Which if any of the resources are overallocated?
2. Assume that the project is time constrained and try to resolve any overallocation problems by leveling within slack. What happens?
3. What is the impact of leveling within slack on the sensitivity of the network?

Include a Gantt chart with the schedule table after leveling within slack.

4. Assume the project is resource constrained and resolve any overallocation problems by leveling outside of slack. What happens?

TABLE A2.1
Resource Assignments

Activity	Resources
Need survey	MRKT (500%)
Set product specs	R&D (400%), MRKT (200%)
Shelf life report	R&D (300%)
Nutrition report	R&D (300%)
Select fruit suppliers	PURCH (100%)
Equipment rehab	ENG (1,000%), PROD (2,000%)
Production trials	PROD (1,500%), PURCH (100%), ENG (1,000%)
Quality trials	QUAL (300%), PROD (500%)
Quality metrics	QUAL (300%), PROD (100%)
Quality training	QUAL (300%), PROD (1,500%)
Market testing	MRKT (500%)
Package design	DESIGN (300%), MRKT (100%)
Select distributors	MRKT (500%)
Complete FDA certification	LEGAL (300%)
Register trademark	LEGAL (300%)
Prepare product launch	QUAL (300%), PURCH (200%), PROD (1,500%), MRKT (500%), ENG (500%), R&D (100%)

TABLE A2.2
Resources Availability and Pay Rates

Resource	Abbrev	Available	Hourly rate
Marketing staff	MRKT	5	$ 80/hr
R&D	R&D	5	$ 80/hr
Engineering	ENG	10	$100/hr
Purchasing	PURCH	2	$ 60/hr
Quality engineers	QUAL	3	$ 80/hr
Designers	DESIGN	3	$ 60/hr
Legal staff	LEGAL	3	$120/hr
Production	PROD	20	$ 60/hr

Include a Gantt chart with the schedule table after leveling outside of slack.

Note: No splitting of activities is allowed.

Note: No partial assignments (i.e., 50 percent). All resources must be assigned 100 percent.

Part 3

Top management has accepted the July 19th completion schedule created at the end of Part 2. Prepare a brief memo that addresses the following questions:

1. How much will the project cost? What is the most expensive activity?
2. What does the cash flow statement tell you about how costs are distributed over the life span of the project?

Include a monthly cash flow for the project.

Once you are confident that you have the final schedule, save the file as a baseline. **Hint:** Save a backup file just in case without baseline!

TABLE A2.3
Status Report
March 31, 2012

Activity	Actual Start	Actual Finish	Actual Duration	Remaining Duration
Need survey	1/3/12	2/2/12	22	0
Set product specs	2/3/12	2/28/12	18	0
Shelf life report	2/29/12	3/13/12	10	0
Nutrition report	3/14/12	3/19/12	4	0
Equipment rehab	2/29/12		23	12

Part 4 A

Assume that today is March 31, 2012, and Table A2.3 contains the tracking information for the project up till now. Enter this information into your saved baseline file and prepare a status report for the first three months of the POM+ project.

Your status report should also address the following questions:

1. How is the project progressing in terms of cost and schedule?
2. What activities have gone well? What activities have not gone well?
3. What do the PCIB and PCIC indicate in terms of how much of the project has been accomplished to date?
4. What is the forecasted cost at completion (EAC_f)? What is the predicted VAC_f?
5. Report and interpret the TCPI for the project at this point in time.
6. What is the estimated date of completion?
7. How well is the project doing in terms of its priorities?

Try to present the above information in a form worthy of consideration by top management.

Include an Earned Value table and a Tracking Gantt Chart.

Note: Insert March 31, 2012, as the status date in the Project Information box.

Part 4 B

Assume that today is May 31, 2012, and Table A2.4 contains the tracking information for the project up till now. Enter this information into your saved baseline file and prepare a status report for the POM+ project.

Your status report should address the following questions:

1. How is the project progressing in terms of cost and schedule?
2. What activities have gone well? What activities have not gone well?
3. What do the PCIB and PCIC indicate in terms of how much of the project has been accomplished to date?
4. What is the forecasted cost at completion (EAC_f)? What is the predicted VAC_f?
5. Report and interpret the TCPI for the project at this point in time.
6. What is the estimated date of completion?
7. How well is the project doing in terms of its priorities?

Try to present the above information in a form worthy of consideration by top management.

Include an Earned Value table and a Tracking Gantt Chart.

Note: Insert May 31, 2012, as the status date in the Project Information box.

TABLE A2.4
Status Report
May 31, 2012

Activity	Actual Start	Actual Finish	Actual Duration	Remaining Duration
Need survey	1/3/12	2/2/12	22	0
Set product specs	2/3/12	2/28/12	18	0
Shelf life report	2/29/12	3/13/12	10	0
Nutrition report	3/14/12	3/19/12	4	0
Select fruit suppliers	4/3/12	4/30/12	20	0
Equipment rehab	2/29/12	4/11/12	31	0
Production trials	4/17/12	5/4/12	14	0
Quality trials	5/7/12	5/31/12	18	0
Market testing	4/4/12	5/9/12	26	0
Package design	5/10/12	5/25/12	12	0
Select distributors	5/28/12		4	18
Complete FDA certification	5/11/12	5/31/12	14	0

Blue Zuma Project

The ARC Company specializes in developing and selling a wide range of high-quality scooters. Sales representatives report that there is a growing demand for racing scooters. ARC's president, Robin Lane, is excited about the possibilities and predicts that one day these kinds of razor scooters will be featured in X-Game events. ARC is a small company and uses a strong matrix to optimally utilize limited manpower.

The Project Priority Matrix for the Blue Zuma Project is:

	Time	Scope	Cost
Constrain		X	
Enhance	X		
Accept			X

Part 1

You are a member of a project team assigned to develop the new razor scooter code named "Blue Zuma." Table A2.5 contains the information necessary to create a project schedule. For the purpose of this case assume the following:

1. The project begins January 2, 2008.
2. The following holidays are observed: January 1, Memorial Day (last Monday in May), July 4th, Labor Day (first Monday in September), Thanksgiving Day (4th Thursday in November), December 25 and 26.
3. If a holiday falls on a Saturday, then Friday will be given as an extra day off, and if it falls on a Sunday, then Monday will be given as a day off.
4. The project team works eight-hour days, Monday through Friday.

Construct a network schedule for this project and prepare a memo that answers the following questions:

1. When is the project estimated to be completed? How long will the project take?
2. What is the critical path for the project?

TABLE A2.5   **Blue Zuma Project**

ID	Task Name	Duration	Predecessors	Resources
1	Product development project			
2	Market analysis	25 days		Marketing (4)
3	Product design	40 days	2	Marketing (1) Design (4) Development (2) Industrial (1) Purchasing (1)
4	Manufacturing study	20 days	2	Industrial (4) Development (2)
5	Product design selection	10 days	3,4	Marketing (2) Design (3) Development (2) Industrial (2) Purchasing (.25)
6	Detailed marketing plan	15 days	5	Marketing (4)
7	Manufacturing process	30 days	5	Design (1) Development (2) Industrial (4)
8	Detailed product design	50 days	5	Marketing (2) Design (4) Development (2) Industrial (2) Purchasing (.25)
9	Test prototype	10 days	8	Design (3) Development (2)
10	Finalized product design	25 days	7,9	Marketing (2) Design (3) Development (3) Industrial (2)
11	Order components	7 days	10	Purchasing (1)
12	Order production equipment	14 days	10	Purchasing (1)
13	Install production equipment	35 days	11F-S + 20 days, 12F-S + 40 days	Development (3) Industrial (4) Design (1)
14	Celebrate	1 day	6,13	Development (4) Industrial (4) Design (4) Marketing (4) Purchasing (1)

3. Which activity has the greatest amount of slack?
4. How sensitive is this network?
5. Identify two sensible milestones and explain your choices.
6. Compare the advantages/disadvantages of displaying the schedule as a network versus a Gantt chart.

Include the following printouts:

- A Gantt chart.
- A network diagram highlighting the critical path.
- A schedule table reporting ES, LS, EF, LF, and slack for each activity.

Part 2

The following personnel have been assigned to the Blue Zuma project team:

- 4 marketing specialists
- 4 design engineers
- 4 development engineers
- 4 industrial engineers
- 1 purchasing agent

Use the file from Part 1 and the information contained in Tables A2.5 and A2.6 to assign resources to the project schedule.

TABLE A2.6
Blue Zuma Project
Resources

Resource	$/hour	Number Available
Marketing specialist	$60	4
Design engineer	$90	4
Development engineer	$80	4
Industrial engineer	$70	4
Purchasing agent	$50	1

Part A

Prepare a memo that addresses the following questions:

1. Which if any of the resources are overallocated?
2. Which activities involve overallocated resources?
3. Assume that the project is time constrained and try to resolve any overallocation problems by leveling within slack. What happens?
4. What is the impact of leveling within slack on the sensitivity of the network?

Include a Gantt chart with the schedule table after leveling within slack.

Part B

Prepare a memo that addresses the following questions:

1. Assume that the project is resource constrained and no additional personnel are available. How long will the project take given the resources assigned? (Hint: Undo leveling performed in Part A before answering this question.)

Note: No splitting of activities is allowed.

2. How does the new duration compare with the estimated completion date generated from Part 1? What does this tell you about the impact resources can have on a schedule?

Include a Gantt chart with a schedule table depicting the resource-constrained schedule.

Part 3

Top management is not happy with the resource-constrained schedule generated at the end of Part 2. Robin Lane, the president, has promised retailers that production of the new scooters would start on February 1, 2009.

1. What options are available to meet this new deadline if the project is not resource constrained?
2. What options are available to meet this deadline if the project is resource constrained?

Dewey Martin, director of product development, has managed to make the following personnel available to work on specific activities on the project. Since there is an acute shortage of personnel at ARC he requests that you only use additional manpower that will help meet the new deadline. Your objective is to develop a schedule which will satisfy the deadline with minimum additional resource usage. The available personnel and impact on activity duration are presented in Table A2.7.

TABLE A2.7
Blue Zuma Project
Crashing Options

Activity	Additional Resources	Revised Duration Estimates
Detailed marketing plan	Marketing (2)	10 days
Detailed product design	Design (1) Development (1)	42 days
Install production equipment	Industrial (1) Development (1)	27 days

Pay rates for additional personnel: Marketing, $70/hour; Design, $100/hour; Development, $90/hour; and Industrial, $80/hour.

Prepare a memo that addresses the following questions:

1. Which additional personnel assignments would you choose to complete the project before the February 1st deadline? Explain your choices as well as the reasons for not choosing other options.
2. How have these changes affected the sensitivity of the network?

Include a Gantt chart with a schedule table presenting the new schedule.

Note: You cannot go back and relevel resources. These new resources are only available for the stated specific tasks according to the schedule created at the end of Part 2.

Part 4

Robin Lane and top management have approved the schedule generated at the end of Part 3. Save the file containing this schedule as a baseline schedule.

Prepare a memo that addresses the following questions:

1. How much is the project estimated to cost?
2. What activity is estimated to cost the most to complete?
3. What resource commands the greatest total cost?
4. During which month of the project are the highest and lowest costs expected to occur? What are those costs?
5. What likely costs are not contained in this budget?

Include a table containing the estimated costs for each activity and a cash flow schedule for each month of the project.

Part 5

Today's date is August 16, 2008. Table A2.8 summarizes the information regarding activities accomplished to date.

Robin Lane has requested a written status report for the Blue Zuma project.

1. Your status report should include a table containing the PV, EV, AC, BAC, EAC, SV, CV, and CPI for each activity and the whole project. The report should also address the following questions:

TABLE A2.8
Blue Zuma Project
Update

Activity	Start Date	Finish Date	Actual Duration	Remaining Duration
Market analysis	1/2/08	2/1/08	23	
Product design	2/4/08	3/20/08	34	
Manufacturing study	3/21/08	4/22/08	23	
Product design selection	4/23/08	5/13/08	15	
Manufacturing process	8/1/08		11	25
Detailed product design	5/14/08	7/31/08	55	
Test prototype	8/1/08	8/15/08	11	

Part 2

Use your file from Part 1 and the information provided below to complete this exercise. (See Table A2.11.)

1. Each work package will represent an activity.
2. The project begins January 4, 2010.
3. The following holidays are observed: January 1, Memorial Day (last Monday in May), July 4th, Labor Day (first Monday in September), Thanksgiving Day (4th Thursday in November), December 25 and 26.
4. If a holiday falls on a Saturday then Friday will be given as an extra day off, and if it falls on a Sunday, then Monday will be given as a day off.
5. The project teams work eight-hour days, Monday through Friday.

Warning: Experience has taught students to frequently make separate backup files for each exercise. The software is never as friendly as users expect!

Construct a network schedule for the conveyor belt project and prepare a memo that addresses the following questions:

1. When is the project estimated to be completed? How long will the project take?
2. What is the critical path(s) for the project?
3. Which activity has the greatest amount of slack?
4. How sensitive is this network?
5. Identify two sensible milestones and explain your choices.
6. Compare the advantages/disadvantages of displaying the schedule as a network versus a Gantt chart.

TABLE A2.11 **Conveyor Belt Project; Schedule**

Activity	Description	Resource	Duration (days)	Preceding Activity
1	Architectural decisions	Design	25	—
2	Hardware specifications	Development, design	50	1
3	Kernel specifications	Design	20	1
4	Utilities specifications	Development, design	15	1
5	Hardware design	Design, development	70	2
6	Disk drivers	Assembly, development	100	3
7	Memory management	Development	90	3
8	Operating system documentation	Design, documentation	25	3
9	Routine utilities	Development	60	4
10	Complex utilities	Development	80	4
11	Utilities documentation	Documentation, design	20	4
12	Hardware documentation	Documentation, design	30	5
13	Integration first phase	Assembly, development	50	6,7,8,9,10,11,12
14	Prototypes	Assembly, development	80	13
15	Serial I/O drivers	Development	130	13
16	System hard/software test	Assembly	25	14,15
17	Order circuit boards	Purchasing	5	16
18	Network interface	Development	90	16
19	Shell	Development	60	16
20	Project documentation	Documentation, development	50	16
21	Assemble preproduction models	Assembly, development	30	17F-S, lag 50 days
22	Integrated acceptance testing	Assembly, development	60	18,19,20,21

Include the following printouts:

- A Gantt chart.
- A network diagram highlighting the critical path.
- A schedule table reporting. ES, LS, EF, LF, and slack for each activity.

Hint: the project should be completed in 530 days.
Remember: Save your file for future exercises!

Part 3

Remember the old saying, "A project plan is not a schedule until resources are committed." This exercise illustrates this subtle, but very important, difference.

Part A

Using your files from Part 2 input resources and their costs if you have not already done so. All information is found in Tables A2.11 and A2.12.

Prepare a memo that addresses the following questions:

1. Which if any of the resources are overallocated?
2. Assume that the project is time constrained and try to resolve any overallocation problems by leveling within slack. What happens?
3. What is the impact of leveling within slack on the sensitivity of the network?

Include a Gantt chart with the schedule table after leveling within slack.

4. Assume the project is resource constrained and resolve any overallocation problems by leveling outside of slack. What happens? What are the managerial implications?
5. What options are available at this point in time?

Include a Gantt chart with the schedule table after leveling outside of slack.

Note: No splitting of activities is allowed.
Note: No partial assignments (i.e., 50 percent). All resources must be assigned 100 percent.

Part B

When you show the resource-constrained network to top management, they are visibly shaken. After some explanation and negotiation they make the following compromise with you:

- The project must be completed no later than February 2, 2012 (530 days).
- You may assign two additional development teams.

TABLE A2.12
Organization
Resources

Name	Group	Cost ($/hr)
Design	R&D (2 teams)	$100
Development	R&D (2 teams)	70
Documentation	R&D (1 team)	60
Assembly/test	R&D (1 team)	70
Purchasing	Procurement (1 team)	40

- If this does not suffice, you may hire other development teams from the outside. Hire as few external teams as possible because they cost $50 more per hour than your inside development people.

Internal Development

Add as many development units (teams) as needed to stay within the 530 days. If you need more than two internal development units, then hire as few external teams as necessary. Select the cheapest possibility! Change as few activities as possible. It is recommended you keep work packages which require cooperation of several organizational units inside your company. You decide how best to do this. **Hint:** Undo leveling prior to adding new resources.

Once you have obtained a schedule that meets the time and resource constraints, prepare a memo that addresses the following questions:

1. What changes did you make and why?
2. How long will the project take?
3. How did these changes affect the sensitivity of the network?

Include a Gantt chart with a schedule table presenting the new schedule.

Part 4

Based on the file created at the end of Part 3, prepare a memo that addresses the following questions:

1. How much will the project cost?
2. What does the cash flow statement tell you about how costs are distributed over the life span of the project?

Include a monthly cash flow and a cost table for the project.

Once you are confident that you have the final schedule, save the file as a baseline.
Hint: Save a backup file just in case without baseline!

Part 5

Prepare status reports for each of the first four quarters of the project given the information provided here. This requires saving your resource schedule as a baseline and inserting the appropriate status report date in the program. Assume that no work has been completed on the day of the status report.

Your status report should include a table containing the PV, EV, AC, BAC, EAC, SV, CV, and CPI for each activity and the whole project. The report should also address the following questions:

1. How is the project progressing in terms of cost and schedule?
2. What activities have gone well? What activities have not gone well?
3. What do the PCIB and PCIC indicate in terms of how much of the project has been accomplished to date?
4. What is the forecasted cost at completion (EAC_f)? What is the predicted VAC_f?
5. Report and interpret the TCPI for the project at this point in time.
6. What is the estimated date of completion?
7. How well is the project doing in terms of its priorities?

TABLE A2.13
April 1, 2010

Activity	Start Date	Finish Date	Actual Duration	Remaining Duration
Hardware specifications	2/9/10		37	8
Kernel specifications	2/8/10	3/12/10	25	0
Disk drivers	3/15/10		13	87
Memory management	3/15/10		13	77
Op. systems documentation	3/15/10		13	7
Utilities specifications	3/8/10	3/29/10	16	0
Complex utilities	3/30/10		2	85
Architectural decisions	1/4/10	2/5/10	25	0

Try to present the above information in a form worthy of consideration by top management.

Include a Tracking Gantt chart with each report.

First Quarter, April 1, 2010

Table A2.13 summarizes the information regarding activities accomplished to date.

Be sure to save your file after each quarterly report and use it to build the next report!

Second Quarter, July 1, 2010

Table A2.14 summarizes the information regarding activities accomplished since the last report.

Third Quarter, October 1, 2010

Table A2.15 summarizes the information regarding activities accomplished since the last report.

Fourth Quarter, January 1, 2011

Table A2.12 summarizes the information regarding activities accomplished since the last report.

TABLE A2.14
July 1, 2010

Activity	Start Date	Finish Date	Actual Duration	Remaining Duration
Hardware specifications	2/9/10	4/12/10	45	0
Hardware design	4/13/10		56	11
Kernel specifications	2/8/10	3/12/10	25	0
Disk drivers	3/15/10		77	33
Memory management	3/15/10		77	19
Op. systems documentation	3/15/10	4/16/10	25	0
Utilities specifications	3/8/10	3/29/10	16	0
Routine utilities*	4/26/10		47	18
Complex utilities	3/30/10		66	25
Utilities documentation	5/3/10	6/2/10	22	0
Architectural decisions	1/4/10	2/5/10	25	0

* The project manager for the external development team that was hired to perform routine utilities reported that due to commitments to other clients they would be able to start on that activity 4/26/10.

TABLE A2.15
October 1, 2010

Activity	Start Date	Finish Date	Actual Duration	Remaining Duration
Hardware specifications	2/9/10	4/12/10	45	0
Hardware design	4/13/10	7/16/10	67	0
Hardware documentation	7/19/10	8/24/10	27	0
Kernel specifications	2/8/10	3/12/10	25	0
Disk drivers	3/15/10	8/17/10	110	0
Memory management	3/15/10	7/30/10	98	0
Op. systems documentation	3/15/10	4/16/10	25	0
Utilities specifications	3/8/10	3/29/10	16	0
Routine utilities	4/26/10	7/27/10	65	0
Complex utilities	3/30/10	8/11/10	95	0
Utilities documentation	5/3/10	6/2/10	22	0
Architectural decisions	1/4/10	2/5/10	25	0
Integration 1st phase	8/25/10		26	24

TABLE A2.16
January 1, 2011

Activity	Start Date	Finish Date	Actual Duration	Remaining Duration
Hardware specifications	2/9/10	4/12/10	45	0
Hardware design	4/13/10	7/16/10	67	0
Hardware documentation	7/19/10	8/24/10	27	0
Prototypes	11/11/10		34	44
Kernel specifications	2/8/10	3/12/10	25	0
Disk drivers	3/15/10	8/17/10	110	0
Serial I/O drivers	11/11/10		34	119
Memory management	3/15/10	7/30/10	98	0
Op. systems documentation	3/15/10	4/16/10	25	0
Utilities specifications	3/8/10	3/29/10	16	0
Routine utilities	4/26/10	7/27/10	65	0
Complex utilities	3/30/10	8/11/10	95	0
Utilities documentation	5/3/10	6/2/10	22	0
Architectural decisions	1/4/10	2/5/10	25	0
Integration 1st phase	8/25/10	11/10/10	55	0

Part 6

You have received revised estimates for the remaining activities at the end of the fourth quarter:

- Prototypes will be completed on 3/8/11.
- Serial I/O drivers will be completed on 6/30/11.
- System hardware/software test will start on 7/1/11 and take 25 days.
- Order circuit boards will start on 8/8/11 and take 5 days.
- Assemble preproduction model will begin on 10/14/11 and take 18 days.
- Project documentation is expected to start on 8/8/11 and will take 55 days.
- Network interface is expected to start on 8/8/11 and will take 99 days.
- Shell is expected to start on 8/8/11 and will take 55 days.
- Integrated acceptance testing is expected to start on 12/29/11 and will take 54 days.

Prepare a memo that addresses the following questions:

1. What is the new EAC for the project? How long should the project take given these revised estimates?
2. How happy will top management be with these forecasts given the priorities of the project?
3. What recommendations would you make?

Include a revised schedule, a Tracking Gantt chart, and cost table with your memo.

GLOSSARY

A

activity   Task(s) of the project that consumes time while people/equipment either work or wait.

activity duration   Estimate of time (hours, days, weeks, months, etc.) necessary to complete a project task.

actual cost of the work completed (AC)   The sum of the cost incurred in accomplishing work. Previously this was called the actual cost of the work performed (ACWP).

actual cost of the work performed (ACWP)   Actual cost of the work performed in a given time period. The sum of the costs incurred in accomplishing work.

Agile Project Management (Agile PM)   A family of incremental, iterative development methods for completing projects.

analysis   Data are collected to record the project history, management performance, and lessons learned to improve future projects. Analysis examines in detail the underlying causes of problems, issues, and successes.

AOA   Activity-on-arrow method for drawing project networks. The activity is shown as an arrow.

AON   Activity-on-node method for drawing project networks. The activity is on the node (rectangle).

apportionment method   Costs allocated to a specific segment of a project by using a percentage of planned total cost—for example, framing a house might use 25 percent of the total cost, or coding a teaching module 40 percent of total cost.

avoiding risk   Elimination of the risk cause before the project begins.

B

backward pass   The method used to compute the late start and finish times for each activity in the project network.

balanced matrix   A matrix structure in which the project manager and functional managers share roughly equal authority over the project. The project manager decides what needs to be done; functional managers are concerned with how it will be accomplished.

balanced scorecard method   Model that measures the long-run results of major program activities in four areas—customer, internal, innovation and learning, and financial.

bar chart   A graphic presentation of project activities depicted as a time-scaled bar line (also called a Gantt chart).

baseline   A concrete document and commitment; it represents the first real plan with cost, schedule, and resource allocation. The planned cost and schedule performance are used to measure actual cost and schedule performance. Serves as an anchor point for measuring performance.

BATNA   Best alternative to a negotiated agreement. Strong or weak BATNA indicates your power to negotiate with the other party.

bottom-up estimates   Detailed estimates of work packages usually made by those who are most familiar with the task (also called micro estimates).

brainstorming   Generating as many ideas/solutions as possible without critical judgment.

budget at completion (BAC)   Budgeted cost at completion. The total budgeted cost of the baseline or project cost accounts.

budget reserve   Reserve setup to cover identified risks that may occur and influence baseline tasks or costs. These reserves are typically controlled by the project manager and the project team. See management reserve.

budgeted cost of the work performed (BCWP)   The value for completed work measured in terms of the planned budget for the work. The earned value or original budgeted cost for work actually completed.

build-own-operate-transfer (BOOT)   A risk management provision in which the prime contractor not only builds the facility, but also takes over ownership until its operation capacity has been proven before final transfer of ownership to the client.

burst activity   An activity that has more than one activity immediately following it.

C

capability maturity model (CMM)   A framework which describes the evolutionary stages of project management systems.

change control   The process of documenting, reviewing, accepting or rejecting change, and documenting any change to the project baseline.

change management system   A defined process for authorizing and documenting changes in the scope of a project.

chart of accounts   A hierarchical numbering system used to identify tasks, deliverables, and organizational responsibility in the work breakdown structure.

co-location   A situation in which project members including those from different organizations work together in the same location.

communication plan   A plan that defines information to be collected and distributed to stakeholders based on their requirements.

concurrent engineering or simultaneous engineering   Cross-functional teamwork in new-product development projects that provides product design, quality engineering, and manufacturing process engineering all at the same time.

consensus decision making   Reaching a decision that all involved parties basically agree with and support.

contingency fund   See contingency reserve.

contingency plan   A plan that covers possible identified project risks that may materialize over the life of the project.

contingency reserve   Usually an amount of money or time set aside to cover identified and unforeseen project risks.

contract   A formal agreement between two parties wherein one party (the contractor) obligates itself to perform a service and the other party (the client) obligates itself to do something in return, usually in the form of a payment to the contractor.

cost account   A control point of one or more work packages used to plan, schedule, and control the project. The sum of all the project cost accounts represents the total cost of the project.

cost performance index (CPI)   The ratio of work performed to actual costs (EV/AC).

cost-plus contract   A contract in which the contractor is reimbursed for all direct allowable costs (materials, labor, travel) plus an additional fee to cover overhead and profit.

cost variance (CV)   The difference between EV and AC (CV = EV − AC). Tells if the work accomplished cost more or less than was planned at any point over the life of the project.

crash cost   The direct cost of completing an activity in its crash time.

crash point   The most a project activity time can realistically be compressed with the resources available to the organization.

crashing   Shortening an activity or project.

crash time   The shortest time an activity can be completed (assuming a reasonable level of resources).

critical path   The longest activity path(s) through the network. The critical path can be distinguished by identifying the collection of activities that all have the same minimum slack.

critical path method (CPM)   A scheduling method based on the estimates of time required to complete activities on the critical path. The method computes early, late, and slack times for each activity in the network. It establishes a planned project duration, if one is not imposed on the project.

culture   The totality of socially transmitted behavior patterns, beliefs, institutions, and all other products of human work and thought characteristic of a community or country.

culture shock   A natural psychological disorientation that most people suffer when they move to a culture different from their own.

D

daily Scrum meeting   A short status meeting held daily by each team during which the team members synchronize their work and progress as well as report any impediments for removal by the Scrum master.

dedicated project team   An organizational structure in which all of the resources needed to accomplish a project are assigned full time to the project.

deliverable   A major product or result that must be finished to complete the project.

Delphi Technique   A group method to predict future events—e.g., time, cost.

direct costs   Costs that are clearly charged to a specific work package—usually labor, materials, or equipment.

dummy activity   An activity that does not consume time; it is represented on the AOA network as a dashed line. A dummy activity is used to ensure a unique identification number for parallel activities and used to maintain dependencies among activities on the project network.

duration (DUR)   The time needed to complete an activity, a path, or a project.

dysfunctional conflict   Disagreement that does not improve project performance.

E

early finish (EF)   The earliest an activity can finish if all its preceding activities are finished by their early finish times (EF = ES + DUR).

early start (ES) The earliest an activity can start. It is the largest early finish of all its immediate predecessors (ES = EF − DUR).

earned value (EV) The physical work accomplished plus the authorized budget for this work. Previously this was called the budgeted cost of work performed (BCWP).

emotional intelligence (EQ) The ability or skill to perceive, assess, and manage the emotions of one's self and others.

escalation A control mechanism for resolving problems in which people at the lowest appropriate level attempt to resolve a problem within a set time limit or the problem is "escalated" to the next level of management.

estimated cost at completion (EAC) The sum of actual costs to date plus revised estimated costs for the work remaining in the WBS. The text uses EAC_{re} to represent revisions made by experts and practitioners associated with the project. A second method is used in large projects where the original budget is less reliable. This method uses the actual costs to date plus an efficiency index (CPI = EV/AC) applied to the remaining project work. When the estimate for completion uses the CPI as the basis for forecasting cost at completion, we use the acronym EAC_f, where EAC_f = estimated costs at completion. Includes costs to date plus revised estimated costs for the work remaining. (Uses formula to compute EAC.)

ETC_f Estimated cost to complete (uses formula to compute estimates).

ETC_{re} Estimated cost to complete (uses expert estimates).

event A point in time when an activity(s) is started or completed. It does not consume time.

F

failure mode and effects analysis (FMEA) Each potential risk is assessed in terms of severity of impact, probability of the event occurring, and ease of detection.

fast-tracking Accelerating project completion typically by rearranging the network schedule and using start-to-start lags.

feature A piece of a product that delivers some useful functionality to a customer.

fixed-price or "lump sum" contract A contract in which the contractor agrees to perform all the work specified in the contract at a predetermined, fixed price.

float See slack.

forecasted estimated cost to complete (ETC_f) Estimated total cost of a project based on CPI. Uses formula to compute estimates.

forward pass The method for determining the early start and finish times for each activity in the project network.

free slack The maximum amount of time an activity can be delayed from its early start (ES) without affecting the early start (ES) of any activity immediately following it.

function points Points derived from past software projects to estimate project time and cost, given specific features of the project.

functional conflict Disagreement that contributes to the objectives of the project.

functional manager A manager responsible for activities in a specialized department or function (e.g., engineering, marketing, finance).

functional organization A hierarchical organizational structure in which departments represent individual disciplines such as engineering, marketing, purchasing.

G

Gantt chart See bar chart.

going native Adopting the customs, values, and prerogatives of a foreign culture.

Golden Rule Do unto others as you would wish them to do unto you.

groupthink A tendency of members in highly cohesive groups to lose their critical evaluative capabilities.

H

hammock activity A special-purpose, aggregate activity that identifies the use of fixed resources or costs over a segment of the project—e.g., a consultant. Derives its duration from the time span between other activities.

heuristic A rule of thumb used to make decisions. Frequently found in scheduling projects. For example, schedule critical activities first, then schedule activities with the shortest duration.

I

implementation gap The lack of consensus between the goals set by top management and those independently set by lower levels of management. This lack of consensus leads to confusion and poor allocation of organization resources.

incremental, iterative development (IID) A cyclical development process in which a project gradually evolves over time.

indirect costs Costs that cannot be traced to a particular project or work package.

infrastructure Basic services (i.e., communication, transportation, power) needed to support project completion.

in-process project audit Project audits early in projects that allow for corrective changes if they are needed on the audited project or others in progress.

insensitive network A network in which the critical path is likely to remain stable during the life of the project.

inspiration-related currencies Influence based on inspiration (opportunity to do good, be the best, etc.).

international project A project that includes tasks that will be completed in different countries.

ISO 9000 A set of standards governing the requirements for documentation of a quality program.

J

joint evaluation A process in which different parties involved in a project evaluate how well they work together.

L

lag The amount of time between the end of one activity and the start of another. A duration assigned to the activity dependency. The minimum amount of time a dependent activity must be delayed to begin or end.

lag relationship The relationship between the start and/or finish of a project activity and the start and/or finish of another activity. The most common lag relationships are (1) finish-to-start, (2) finish-to-finish, (3) start-to-start, and (4) start-to-finish.

late finish (LF) The latest an activity can finish and not delay a following activity (LF = LS + DUR).

late start (LS) The latest an activity can start and not delay a following activity. It is the largest late finish (LF) of all activities immediately preceding it (LS = LF − DUR).

law of reciprocity People are obligated to grant a favor comparable to the one they received.

leading by example Exhibiting the behaviors you want to see in others.

learning curves A mathematical curve used to predict a pattern of time reduction as a task is performed over and over.

leveling Techniques used to examine a project for an unbalanced use of resources, and for resolving resource over-allocations.

M

management by wandering around (MBWA) A management style in which managers spend the majority of their time outside their offices interacting with key people.

management reserve A percentage of the total project budget reserved for contingencies. The fund exists to cover unforeseen, new problems—not unnecessary overruns. The reserve is designed to reduce the risk of project delays. Management reserves are typically controlled by the project owner or project manager. See budget reserve.

matrix Any organizational structure in which the project manager shares responsibility with the functional managers for assigning priorities and for directing the work of individuals assigned to the project.

maturity model A model used to assess project management practices against others in the same industry and to guide and continuously strive to improve the management of projects. Most maturity models recognize levels of maturity so organizations can gauge their relative maturity against others in their industry.

mentor Typically a more experienced manager who acts as a personal coach and champions a person's ambitions.

merge activity An activity that has more than one activity immediately preceding it.

met-expectations model Customer satisfaction is a function of the extent to which perceived performance exceeds expectations.

milestone An event that represents significant, identifiable accomplishment toward the project's completion.

mitigating risk Action taken to either reduce the likelihood that a risk will occur and/or the impact the risk will have on the project.

Monte Carlo simulation A method of simulating project activity durations using probabilities. The method identifies the percentage of times, activities, and paths that are critical over thousands of simulations.

N

negative reinforcement A motivational technique in which negative stimuli are removed once desired behavior is exhibited.

net present value (NPV)   A minimum desired rate of return discount (e.g., 15 percent) is used to compute present value of all future cash inflows and outflows.

network   A logic diagram arranged in a prescribed format (e.g., AOA or AON) consisting of activities, sequences, interrelationships, and dependencies.

network organization   An alliance of several organizations created for the purpose of creating products and services for customers.

network sensitivity   The likelihood that the critical path will change on a project.

nominal group technique (NGT)   A structured problem-solving process in which members privately rank-order preferred solutions.

O

objective   An end you seek to create or acquire. Should be specific, measurable, realistic, assignable, and include a time frame for accomplishment.

organization breakdown structure (OBS)   A structure used to assign responsibility for work packages.

organizational culture   A system of shared norms, beliefs, values, and assumptions held by an organization's members.

organizational currencies   A set of currencies used as a medium of exchange within organizations to influence behavior.

organizational politics   Actions by individuals or groups of individuals to acquire, develop, and use power and other resources to obtain preferred outcomes when there is uncertainty or disagreement over choices.

outsourcing   Contracting for the use of external sources (skills) to assist in implementing a project.

overhead costs   Typically organization costs that are not directly linked to a specific project. These costs cover general expenses such as upper management, legal, market promotion, and accounting. Overhead costs are usually charged per unit of time or as a percentage of labor or material costs.

oversight   A set of principles and processes to guide and improve the management of projects. The intent is to ensure projects meet the needs of the organization through standards, procedures, accountability, efficient allocation of resources, and continuous improvement in the management of projects.

P

padding estimates   Adding a safety factor to a time or cost estimate to ensure the estimate is met when the project is executed.

parallel activity   One or more activities that can be carried on concurrently or simultaneously.

partnering   See project partnering.

partnering charter   A formal document that states common goals as well as cooperative procedures used to achieved these goals which is signed by all parties working on a project.

path   A sequence of connected activities.

payback method   The time it takes to pay back the project investment (investment/net annual savings). The method does not consider the time value of money or the life of the investment.

performance review   In general, all review methods of individual performance center on the technical and social skills brought to the project and team. These reviews stress personal improvement and are frequently used for salary and promotion decisions.

personal-related currencies   Influence based on enhancing another person's self-esteem.

phase estimating   This estimating method begins with a macro estimate for the project and then refines estimates for phases of the project as it is implemented.

phase gating   A structured process to review, evaluate, and document outcomes at each project phase and to provide management with information to guide resource deployment toward strategic goals.

phase project delivery   Delivering useful parts of a project in phases instead of when the project is entirely completed.

planned value (PV)   The planned time-phased baseline of the value of the work scheduled. Previously this was called budgeted cost of work scheduled (BCWS).

plan of record   The current official plan for the project in terms of scope, budget, and schedule.

portfolio management   Centralized selection and management of a portfolio of projects to ensure that allocation of resources is directed and balanced toward the strategic focus of the organization.

position-related currencies   Influence based on the ability to enhance someone else's position within an organization.

positive synergy A characteristic of high-performance teams in which group performance is greater than the sum of individual contributions.

precedence diagram method A method used to construct a project network that uses nodes (e.g., a rectangle) to represent activities and connecting arrows to indicate dependencies.

principled negotiation A process of negotiation that aims to achieve win/win results.

priority matrix A matrix that is set up before the project begins that establishes which criterion among cost, time, and scope will be enhanced, constrained, or accepted.

priority system The process used to select projects. The system uses selected criteria for evaluating and selecting projects that are strongly linked to higher-level strategies and objectives.

priority team The group (sometimes the project office) responsible for selecting, overseeing, and updating project priority selection criteria.

proactive Working within your sphere of influence to accomplish something.

process breakdown structure (PBS) A phase-oriented grouping of project activities that defines the total scope of the project. Each descending level represents an increasingly detailed description of project work.

product backlog A prioritized list of project requirements with estimated time to turn them into complete product functionality.

product owner The person responsible for managing the product backlog in Scrum so as to maximize the value of the project. The product owner represents all stakeholders.

project A temporary endeavor undertaken to create a unique product, service, or result.

project audit report A report that includes classification of the project, analysis of information gathered, recommendations, lessons learned, and an appendix of backup information.

project charter A document that authorizes the project manager to initiate and lead a project.

project closure All of the activities of shutting down a project. The major activities are evaluation of project goals and performance, developing lessons learned, releasing resources, and preparing a final report.

project cost—duration graph A graph that plots project cost against time; it includes direct, indirect, and total cost for a project over a relevant range of time.

project evaluation The process of assessing, verifying, and documenting project results.

project facilitator A guide who leads the project team through an analysis of project activities that went well, what needs improvement, and development of a follow-up action plan with goals and accountability.

project interfaces The intersections between a project and other groups of people both within and outside the organization.

projectitis A social phenomenon in which project members exhibit inappropriately intense loyalty to the project.

projectized organization A multi-project organization in which project managers have full authority to assign priorities and direct the work of persons assigned to their project.

project kick off meeting Typically the first meeting of the project team.

project life cycle The stages found in all projects—definition, planning, execution, and delivery.

project management The application of knowledge, skills, tools, and techniques to project activities to meet the project requirements.

Project Management Professional (PMP) An individual who has met specific education and experience requirements set forth by the Project Management Institute, has agreed to adhere to a code of professional conduct, and has passed an examination designed to objectively assess and measure project management knowledge. In addition, a PMP must satisfy continuing certification requirements or lose the certification.

project office (PO) A centralized unit within an organization or department that oversees and improves the management of projects.

project oversight See oversight.

project manager The individual responsible for managing a project.

project organization An organizational structure in which core work is accomplished by project teams.

project partnering A nonbinding method of transforming contractual relationships into a cohesive, cooperative project team with a single set of goals and established procedures for resolving disputes in a timely manner.

project portfolio Group of projects that have been selected for implementation balanced by project type, risk, and ranking by selected criteria.

project screening matrix   A matrix used to assess and compare the relative value of projects being considered for implementation.

project sponsor   Typically a high-ranking manager who champions and supports a project.

project vision   An image of what the project will accomplish.

R

ratio (parametric) methods   Uses the ratio of past actual costs for similar work to estimate the cost for a potential project. This macro method of forecasting cost does not provide a sound basis for project cost control since it does not recognize differences among projects.

relationship-related currencies   Influence based on friendship.

resource   Any person, groups, skill, equipment or material used to accomplish a task, work package, or activity.

resource-constrained project   A project that assumes resources are limited (fixed) and therefore time is variable.

resource profile   A chart showing the usage of a resource in a project over time. It is common to try to reduce the peak of the resource usage by leveling or smoothing, thereby improving the utilization of the resource.

responsibility matrix   A matrix whose intersection point shows the relationship between an activity (work package) and the person/group responsible for its completion.

retrospective   A methodology that analyzes a past project event to determine what worked and what didn't, develops lessons learned, and creates an action plan that ensures lessons learned are used to improve management of future projects.

revised estimated cost to complete (ETC$_{re}$)   Estimated total cost based on revised estimates made by experts and actual costs to date.

risk   The chance that an undesirable project event will occur and the consequences of all its possible outcomes.

risk breakdown structure (RBS)   A hierarchical depiction of the identified project risks arranged by risk category and subcategory that identifies the various areas and causes of potential risks.

risk profile   A list of questions that addresses traditional areas of uncertainty on a project.

risk severity matrix   A tool used to assess the impact of risks on a project.

S

"sacred cow"   A project that is a favorite of a powerful management figure who is usually the champion for the project.

scaling   Adapting Agile PM to large, multi-team projects.

scenario planning   A structured process of thinking about future possible environments that would have potential high impact to disrupt the way you do business, and then developing potential strategies to compete in these altered environments.

schedule performance index (SPI)   The ratio of work performed to work scheduled (EV/PV).

schedule variance (SV)   The difference between the planned dollar value of the work actually completed and the value of the work scheduled to be completed at a given point in time (SV = EV − PV). Schedule variance contains no critical path information.

scope creep   The tendency for the scope of a project to expand once it has started.

scope statement   A definition of the end result or mission of a project. Scope statements typically include project objectives, deliverables, milestones, specifications, and limits and exclusions.

Scrum   An incremental, iterative development approach to managing projects with a well-defined set of roles and processes.

Scrum master   The person responsible for the Scrum process and its correct application.

self-organizing team   A semi-autonomous team that manages itself.

sensitivity of a network   The likelihood that the critical path(s) will change once the project begins to be implemented.

sharing risk   Allocating proportions of risk to different parties.

slack (SL)   Time an activity can be delayed before it becomes critical.

social network building   The process of identifying and building cooperative relationships with key people.

sociotechnical perspective   A focus on the interaction between tools/methods and people.

splitting   A scheduling technique in which work is interrupted on one activity and the resource is assigned to another activity for a period of time, then reassigned to work on the original activity.

sprint   A fixed period of time during which a Scrum teams works to turn the product backlog it has selected into an increment of product functionality.

sprint backlog   A list of tasks that defines a Scrum team's work for a sprint. Each task identifies those responsible for doing the work and the estimated amount of work remaining on the task on any given day during the sprint.

sprint planning meeting   A Scrum meeting divided into two segments. During the first segment the product owner presents the highest priority product backlog to the team. The team and product owner collaborate to determine how much of the product backlog it can turn into functionality during the upcoming sprint. During the second segment, the team plans how it will meet his commitment by detailing its work as a plan in the sprint backlog.

sprint retrospective meeting   A Scrum meeting in which the team discusses the just concluded sprint and determines what could be changed that might make the next sprint more enjoyable and productive.

sprint review meeting   A Scrum meeting in which the team demonstrates to the product owner and any other interested parties what it was able to accomplish during the sprint.

stakeholders   Individuals and organizations that are actively involved in the project, or whose interests may be positively or negatively affected as a result of project execution or completion. They may also exert influence over the project and its results.

strong matrix   A matrix structure in which the project manager has primary control over project activities and functional managers support project work.

systems thinking   A holistic approach to viewing problems that emphasizes understanding the interactions among different problem factors.

T

task   See activity.

task-related currencies   Influence based, helping someone else do their work.

team-building   A process designed to improve the performance of a team.

team evaluation   Evaluating the performance of the project team using a minimum core of conditions in place before the project began. Evaluation practices should emphasize the team as a whole, while minimizing individual performance.

team rituals   Ceremonial actions that reinforce team identity and values.

template method   Use of a prepared form to develop project networks, costs, and time estimates.

360-degree feedback   A multirater appraisal system based on performance information that is gathered from multiple sources (superiors, peers, subordinates, customers).

time and cost databases   Collection of actual versus estimated times and costs of work packages over many projects that are used for estimating new project tasks and their expected possible error.

time buffer   A contingency amount of time for an activity to cover uncertainty—for example, availability of a key resource or merge event.

time-constrained project   A project that assumes time is fixed and, if resources are needed, they will be added.

time-phased baseline   A cost baseline that is derived from the WBS and project schedule. The budgeted costs are distributed to mirror the project schedule.

time-phased budgets   Planned costs that are broken down by distinct time periods (e.g., $5,000 per week) for a work package, as opposed to a budget for a whole job/project (6 months for a total of $130,000). Time phasing allows better cost control by measuring the actual rate of expenditure versus the planned expenditure rate over small pieces of the project.

total slack (TS)   The amount of time an activity can be delayed and not affect the project duration ($TS = LS - ES$ or $LF - EF$).

Tracking Gantt   A Gantt chart that compares planned versus actual schedule information.

transferring risk   Shifting responsibility for a risk to another party.

triple constraint   The competing demands of time, cost, and scope. These constraints frequently represent trade-off decisions to be dealt with by the project manager and/or sponsor.

top-down estimates   Rough estimates that use surrogates to estimate project time and cost (also called macro estimates).

V

variance at completion (VAC)   Indicates expected actual cost over- or underrun at completion ($VAC = BAC - EAC$).

virtual project team   Spatially separated project team whose members are unable to communicate face to face. Communication is usually by electronic means.

W

weak matrix   A matrix structure in which functional managers have primary control over project activities and the project manager coordinates project work.

work breakdown structure (WBS)   A hierarchical method that successively subdivides the work of the project into smaller detail.

work package   A task at the lowest level of the WBS. Responsibility for the package should be assigned to one person and, if possible, limited to 80 hours of work.

AC	Actual cost of work completed		**IFB**	Invitation for bid
ACWP	Actual cost of work performed		**KISS**	Keep it simple, stupid
AOA	Activity-on-arrow		**LF**	Late finish
AON	Activity-on-node		**LS**	Late start
BAC	Budget at completion		**MBWA**	Management by wandering around
BATNA	Best alternative to a negotiated agreement		**NIH**	Not invented here
BCWP	Budgeted cost of work performed		**NPV**	Net present value
BCWS	Budgeted cost of work scheduled		**OBS**	Organization breakdown structure
BOOT	Build-own-operate-transfer		**PCI**	Percent complete index
CAPM	Certified Associate in Project Management		**PCIB**	Percent complete index—budget costs
CCPM	Critical-chain approach to project planning and management		**PCIC**	Percent complete index—actual costs
			PDM	Precedence diagramming method
CPI	Cost performance index		**PERT**	Project evaluation review technique
CPM	Critical path method		**PO**	Project office
CV	Cost variance		**PMP**	Project Management Professional
DUR	Duration		**PV**	Planned value of work scheduled
EAC	Estimate at completion (with revised cost estimates)		**RBS**	Risk breakdown structure
EF	Early finish		**RM**	Responsibility matrix
EQ	Emotional intelligence		**SL**	Slack
ES	Early start		**SPI**	Schedule performance index
ETC	Estimate to complete		**SV**	Schedule variance
EV	Earned value		**TCPI**	To complete performance index
FAC	Forecast at completion		**VAC**	Variance at completion
FF	Free float		**WBS**	Work breakdown structure